D1548312

THE

PUBLICATIONS

OF THE

SURTEES SOCIETY

VOL. CXCIX

At a COUNCIL MEETING of the SURTEES SOCIETY, held on 13 December 1990, it was ORDERED —

'That the edition and calendar of the early Durham Quarter Sessions rolls prepared by Dr C. M. Fraser should be printed as the volume of the Society's publications for 1987 and 1988.'

A.J.Piper, *Secretary*
The Prior's Kitchen
The College
Durham

THE

PUBLICATIONS

OF THE

SURTEES SOCIETY

ESTABLISHED IN THE YEAR
M.DCCC.XXXIV

VOL. CXCIX
FOR THE YEARS M.CM.LXXXVII & M.CM.LXXXVIII

IN MEMORIAM

HILARY SETON OFFLER

3.ii.1913 – 24.i.1991

Secretary of the Society

1950 – 1966

President

1980 – 1987

DURHAM QUARTER SESSIONS ROLLS

1471 – 1625

EDITED AND CALENDARED
BY

C. M. FRASER

WITH AN INTRODUCTION
BY

KENNETH EMSLEY

TYPESET FROM DISC BY
ROGER BOOTH ASSOCIATES, NEWCASTLE UPON TYNE

PRINTED FOR THE SOCIETY BY
ATHENÆUM PRESS LIMITED, NEWCASTLE UPON TYNE
1991

CONTENTS

ACKNOWLEDGEMENTS

The origin of this work was a research project undertaken by Kenneth Emsley into the workings of the courts of the palatinate of Durham which came to fruition in a degree of LL.M. awarded in 1970 by Newcastle University and subsequently a book, *The Courts of the County Palatine of Durham*, published by the Durham County Local History Society in 1984. Mr Emsley kindly agreed to write the general introduction to this calendar of the first Durham quarter sessions records to ensure that the legal background was firmly sketched behind the social and economic implications. I wish also to thank Mr Emsley for his advice on various points in my own account of business in the sessions and elsewhere in the text.

Permission to transcribe and publish these records in the Public Record Office, London, Durham County Record Office and Durham University Library (Special Collections and Archives) has been generously given by all the appropriate bodies. I wish also to thank Miss J. Gill, Durham County Archivist, for her courtesy in depositing at the Northumberland Record Office some of the material in her custody to facilitate my work, and Mrs A. Burton, the Northumberland County Archivist, for receiving it. My thanks are also due to Mr A. J. Piper for his help in identifying many obscure places in county Durham and general advice about presentation.

Finally, I should like to remember the late Professor W. L. Burn, sometime deputy chairman of the Durham quarter sessions (1953–58) and chairman (1958), who must be pleased that I have at last seen the light.

C. M. Fraser

ABBREVIATIONS

1) bibliographical:

AA XVIII	*Archaeologia Aeliana*, 4th ser. (1940). C. H. H. Blair, "Mayors and Lord Mayors of Newcastle, 1216–1940"
AA XXI	–, (1943), 1–68, Id., "The Sheriffs of Northumberland, 1603–1942"
AA XXII	–, (1944), 22–82, Id., "The Sheriffs of the county of Durham"
AA XLIX	–. (1971), 139–51, C. M. Fraser & K. Emsley, "Some early Recorders of Newcastle upon Tyne"
Baker	J. H. Baker, *The Order of Serjeants at Law* (Selden Soc., Supplementary series 5, 1984)
Cal. Border Papers	J. Bain (ed.), *Calendar of Letters and Papers relating to the Borders of England and Scotland* 2 vols, 1894, 1896
Clarke	A. Clarke, *Register of the University of Oxford*, vol. 2, 4 parts, 1887–89
CJ	C. M. Fraser & K. Emsley, "The clerical justices of the peace in the North East, 1626–30" (AA 5 II [1974])
Courts	K. Emsley & C. M. Fraser, *The Courts of the County Palatine of Durham* (Durham County Local History Soc., 1984)
DK *Report*	*Report* of the Deputy Keeper [of the Public Records]
DNB	*Dictionary of National Biography*
Dur. Vis.	J. Foster, *Durham Visitation Pedigrees*, 1887
Fasti	D.S. Boutflower (ed.), *Fasti Dunelmenses*, (Surtees Soc., 139, 1926)
Foss	E. Foss, *A Biographical Dictionary of the Judges of England, 1066–1870*, 1870
Hutchinson	W. Hutchinson, *History of Durham* 3 vols., Newcastle, 1785–94
Metcalfe	W. C. Metcalfe, *Book of Knights Banneret, Knights of the Bath, and Knights Bachelor*, 1885
Mickleton MS	Durham University Library Special Collections
Reg.	*Register* of Gray's Inn (1889), Lincoln's Inn (1896), and Middle Temple (1937), as appropriate
Reg. Cath. D.	G. J. Armytage & E. A. White (eds), *The Registers of the Cathedral Church of Durham, 1609–1896*, (Harleian Soc., Register Section, 1897)
Surtees	R. Surtees, *History of Durham*, 4 vols, 1816–40
VCH	*Victoria County History: Durham*, 3 vols, 1905–28
	Yorkshire, N. Riding, 2 vols, 1914–23

Venn	J. & J. A. Venn, *Alumni Cantabrigienses*, 4 vols. Cambridge, 1922–27
Welford *H*	R. Welford, *History of Newcastle and Gateshead* 3 vols., 1884–87
Welford *M*	idem, *Men of Mark 'twixt Tyne and Tweed*, 3 vols, 1895
W & I,	*Wills & Inventories*, 4 vols (Surtees Soc., 2 [1835], 38 [1860], 112 [1906], 142 [1929])
York. Vis.	J. Foster, *The Visitation of Yorkshire, 1584/5* (1875)

2) in text

CRO	County Record Office
esq.	esquire
gen.	gentleman
JP	justice of the peace
knt/kt	knight
lab.	labourer
LL.B.	Bachelor of Law
LL.D.	Doctor of Law
M.A.	Master of Arts
PRO	Public Record Office, Chancery Lane, London
STB	*Sacrae Theologiae Baccalaureus*
STP	*Sacrae Theologiae Professor*
yeo.	yeoman

GLOSSARY

branded	mixture of red and black
gavelock	crowbar
hogg(aster)	young sheep of two years age
leap	fish basket
leister	fish spear
litster	dyer
lock	barrier in river
quey	heifer
stag colt	male colt
tinkler	tinker or itinerant vendor
wether	castrated male sheep

INTRODUCTION TO THE DURHAM QUARTER SESSIONS
by Kenneth Emsley

The bishops of Durham had ecclesiastical jurisdiction between the River Tees and the Scottish borders and over the lordship of Alston in Cumberland. Their temporal power, however, was concentrated on County Durham and its enclaves of Norhamshire, Islandshire and Bedlingtonshire in Northumberland and Crayke in North Yorkshire. Only there did they wield total power in the Middle Ages, and then subject to the good will of the king. If they crossed swords with a strong king such as Henry II or Edward I the result would not favour the bishop.[1]

The *Quo Warranto* proceedings of 1293 listed the comprehensive temporal powers of the bishops of Durham, and the theory of their palatinate status was first mooted the previous year in a suit against the archbishop of York brought by Edward I. Sir Thomas Duffus Hardy in the introduction to his edition of Bishop Kellawe's register stated that the existence of chancery rolls from the time of Bishop Bury (1333–45) proved that the bishop rigorously upheld his court of chancery and court of pleas in addition to the other rights of his office. There is no doubt that a chancery (writing) office existed in the twelfth century, but the court itself did not issue judicial decrees until the fifteenth century, about the same time as the royal chancery. Bishop Hatfield (1345–81) and Bishop Langley (1406–37) during their long occupations of the see of Durham continued to advance the powers of their office.[2]

The monarchs of England appear in early history as first of all franchise-holders in point of greatness. Under the king there existed a most important group of franchise-holders exercising "regalian" or palatine powers. They included the bishop of Durham, the earl of Chester and the duke of Lancaster, together with the Marcher lords of Wales and the holders of the liberties of Ely, Hexham and Pembroke. Chester had its own medieval register of original writs before it passed to the crown in the 1230s, and Lancaster was in private hands for 50 years before it became part of the crown lands in 1399. Durham's position, without royal connection, varied according to the relative strengths of the bishop and the king. Durham, with a bishop for its ruler, was recognised like Chester through prescription, whereas Lancaster was an artificial creation

---

[1] A general account of the bishop's authority may be found in G. T. Lapsley, *The County Palatine of Durham* (1900); K. Emsley & C. M. Fraser, *The Courts of the County Palatine of Durham* (1984); and K. Emsley, "The Yorkshire Enclaves of the Bishops of Durham", *Yorkshire Archaeological Journal* 47 (1975), 103–8.

[2] *Registrum Palatinum Dunelmense I* (Rolls Series, 1873), lxxxii–iv; G. V. Scammell, *Hugh du Puiset* (1956), 219–22; C. M. Fraser, *Antony Bek* (1957), 79–99; R. L. Storey, *Thomas Langley* (1961), 57–67.

which could not compare with Durham or Chester in antiquity. The prerogative of pardons was confined to king and lords palatine, the Durham bishops enjoying the privilege without interference from the king. According to Sir William Holdsworth in his *History of the English Law* all three palatinates had judicial systems almost identical during the period of their greatness. The bishops of Durham claimed to exercise all the rights of the kings of England. They commissioned their own justices, who followed the forms of English common law with the appropriate local modifications, and English statute law operated within the palatinate. This was regarded as an unique privilege, not a downgrading of their autonomy.[3] They appointed their own sheriffs and coroners and even claimed immunity from national taxation. The symbolic aura of St Cuthbert was an ever-powerful argument in favour of Durham's antiquity and uniqueness, and probably assisted with the idea of its special status, as when the bishop was given a special role in the coronation ceremony of the English monarch (as he has to this day).

It was during Bishop Tunstall's tenure in Durham (1530–59) that the bishop lost part of his judicial rights: the prerogative of pardoning treasons and felonies and the full recognition of himself as fount of justice, whereby all writs were issued in the bishop's name. Under the statute abolishing all special private jurisdictions, passed in 1536, all writs relating to Durham and its courts were to be issued still by the bishop's chancery but in the king's name – it became the king's peace and not the bishop's. The bishop's palatine status was finally absorbed into the crown by an act of 1836.[4]

AREA

The temporal jurisdiction of the bishop of Durham covered County Durham and the wapentake of Sadberge immediately north of the Tees. North Durham, comprising Norhamshire, Islandshire and Bedlingtonshire, and Craykeshire, north of the city of York, small areas owned by St Cuthbert from before the Norman Conquest, were within the jurisdiction of the Durham courts until the nineteenth century. The lands of Northallertonshire and Howdenshire in Yorkshire were within Durham's ecclesiastical (peculiar) jurisdiction but otherwise were normal lordships.

For the purposes of local government County Durham was divided into four wards – Chester-le-Street, Easington, Darlington and Stockton. The status of the wapentake of Sadberge, sometimes referred to as a county in its own right and at other times merged in the Stockton ward, was ambiguous. North Durham was deemed to be part of the Chester ward. By a statute of 1234 the local administrative courts of the hundred, ward or wapentake were to meet every three weeks, instead of the previous fortnightly court. No

---

[3] *Courts*, 28–30.   [4] *Ibid.*, 32, 46–4.

evidence has survived to show that the individual Durham wards possessed separate courts but a fortnightly court continued to be held at Durham and Norham under the auspices of the respective local sheriff. By the mid-fourteenth century, however, a new system of local government under the commission of the peace had been established.

QUARTER SESSIONS

While other courts of the bishop of Durham such as the courts of pleas and of gaol delivery and later the court of chancery were established on the precedent of royal jurisdiction adapted to the county palatine's special needs, the quarter sessions court was the only one within the county palatine to be based on parliamentary enactment. Conservators of the peace were first appointed in Durham in January 1312, when Ralph fitz William was appointed by Edward II. The following June Bishop Kellawe appointed Robert Hylton, a local baron, as *custos pacis* for the county "on account of the great number of vagabonds and disturbers of the peace". He was authorised to act in accordance with the customs of the kingdom and of the royal liberty of Durham. Further keepers of the peace were appointed until 1362, when all justices of the peace throughout England were ordered to hold their sessions four times a year, one session within a week of the feast of the Epiphany (6 January), the second within the week of Mid Lent (March), the third betwixt the feasts of Pentecost and of St John Baptist (June) and the fourth within eight days of Michaelmas (29 September). Thus began the system of quarter sessions which continued for over 600 years (until 1971), except for a short break during the civil wars of the seventeenth century.[5]

Usually the Durham sessions were held in Durham castle, although on occasion they were held at Bishop Auckland, Stanhope or elsewhere. The first recorded commission in Durham consisted of John Mowbray, Thomas Ingleby, Alan Skirlington, Roger Fulthorpe, Robert Umfraville, Richard of Barnard Castle, Robert Lumley, William Embleton and Walter Hawick, men who were a mixture of lawyers and local landowners. Mowbray, Ingleby and Fulthorpe all served the king as justices. Embleton was chancellor of Durham. Sometimes the Midsummer session was adjusted to coincide with the August assizes and a court of gaol delivery, to allow the king's justices to attend. This practice ceased some time after 1557. Otherwise the chancellor of Durham often presided. From the time of Toby Matthew (1595–1606) the bishop began increasingly to attend, as did the dean of Durham.

With a staff of law officers at hand to manage the Durham chancery court and court of pleas there was an abundance of legally

---

[5] *Ibid.* 46–47 and n. S.

trained personnel available for the bishop to nominate to the magistracy, as he was entitled to do in accordance with the act of 27 Henry VIII c. 24. His attorney-general and his solicitor-general sat as JPs, although the former was also the prosecutor in cases brought to the sessions. There was also on the bench a substantial number of senior clergy, graduates in theology and law. They would not, however, have a monopoly of legal training, as many gentlemen went to the Inns of Court as part of their education. A glance through the printed register of admissions to Gray's Inn notes Talbot Bowes in 1579, George Frevill in 1580, Ralph Fetherstonhaugh of Stanhope in 1591 and John Richardson of Durham in 1598. Lincoln's Inn admitted Thomas Calverley in 1552 and his son John in 1589/90, and William and Thomas Riddell of Gateshead in 1615 and 1619 respectively, with Linley and Charles Wren of Binchester in 1620. The Middle Temple admitted Timothy Whittingham of Holmside in 1576.[6] All appeared on the bench, although only John Richardson had a legal career, being solicitor-general to Bishop Matthew and Bishop James. He was "a principal officer in the Durham court of chancery, court of pleas, a solicitor and remembrancer, and had keeping of the records, rolls and coucher books and other writings ... and did take collections and abstracts for his Lordship's use and was steward of his Lordship's borough courts of the city of Durham and other places ... and was for divers years before his death escheator and feodary ... and had divers books, alphabets and calenders of the rolls, and was also a justice of the peace and gaol delivery in the county and much trusted in country affairs". His grandson, another John, was Durham clerk of the peace in 1640.[7]

OFFICERS OF THE COURT

By the early seventeenth century a large amount of criminal and administrative work had been given to the justices of the peace. From earliest times they had been responsible for regulating wages and prices. They had to ensure free trading by imposition of fines on those forestalling and engrossing grain and wool and retailing cattle. They had to enforce the laws against recusants, sturdy beggars and unlicenced alehouse-keepers. They had to prevent poaching in its forms of taking salmon out of season and tracing hares in the snow with greyhounds, and restrict the use of guns for sporting purposes. They relied on the clerk of the peace, appointed by the bishop, to keep them informed of their powers. On him lay the responsibility for ensuring that court procedure was in accordance with law and statute, to reduce the possibility of appeals to a higher court. The writ of *certiorari* could be used to remove proceedings from the

---

[6] For details see biographies below, Appendix 2, pp. 337–49.

[7] P[ublic] R[ecord] O[ffice], London, Durham 4/1, p. 653.

quarter sessions to the Durham court of pleas or court of gaol delivery or into the royal courts at Westminster, which had concurrent jurisdiction. To execute their decisions they relied on the sheriff and his bailiffs, to whom were directed the various judicial writs of *capias* to arrest for debt, *fieri facias* to enforce compliance, and writs to empanel juries. Although the writs may not have originated from the quarter sessions any defiance was likely to be a quarter-sessions matter, involving breach of the peace. Through such cases in quarter sessions one can trace business arising in the bishop's forest court at Stanhope, his halmote courts at Chester and elsewhere, the county court, the Durham court of pleas, the court of Durham gaol delivery and the assizes. Their other executive officers were the coroners, and the high and petty constables.

The sheriff of Durham was appointed by the bishop and served for many consecutive years.[8] Instead of accounting for the revenue of his office at the king's exchequer the sheriff had to account to the bishop at Durham. Following the appointment of the new sheriff a mandate was issued to the officers and people of Durham and Sadberge enjoining obedience to him. The sheriff presided over the ordinary and special meetings of the county court. The full county court was used for the public pronouncement of outlawries and pardons and the proclamation by the bishop of royal statutes. The sheriff was responsible for enquiries, the selection of jurors, the arrest of accused persons, and the transfer of persons between Durham and neighbouring counties. There was a separate sheriff for the liberty of Norham in North Durham, which being some sixty miles north of the Tyne required its own administrative and legal establishment based on the bishop's castle at Norham. This latter office became hereditary during the fifteenth century.

Coroners appeared in the English counties towards the end of the twelfth century. The earliest reference to a Durham coroner is dated 1279, and from then onwards coroners were appointed in each of the wards of the palatinate. Each newly-appointed coroner took his oath before the temporal chancellor of Durham in the exchequer, following which he undertook to serve the bishop loyally and to account for the business of his office. Elsewhere in England his duties were to keep a check on the power of the sheriff and assist in safeguarding the king's financial interests as well as to assist in keeping the peace in the country districts. Their national duties included inquisitions into the deaths of persons where the cause of death was unknown, inquests about wreck, royal fish and the discovery of treasure trove. In Durham the coroners also served as bailiffs for the county court and for the bishop's halmote (manorial) courts. There is reason to believe that in Durham and

---

[8] AA XXII, passim.

Northumberland the coroners' duties evolved from earlier and hereditary ward-bailiffships. The Durham coroners undertook the custody of vacant estates and compulsory purchases of provisions for the bishop. They were frequently included in the bishop's commissions of array for military service, where men were mustered by the ward, and they might serve on the grand jury for the quarter sessions. The coroners' fees by a Durham custom were paid in corn from the bishop's manors.[9]

Bailiffs were the sheriff's officers, responsible for serving all summonses and executing writs, precepts and warrants. It was an appointment fraught with danger. The rolls record over and over the names of bailiffs who were assaulted whilst executing distraint warrants. The office also provided opportunities for extortion, as in 1617 when Robert Maltby, bailiff at Gateshead and a frequent victim of assault, was presented for demanding a fee for serving the grand jury.

There were two military constables during the feudal period, in charge of the castles of Durham and Norham. In addition there were high constables who were officers of the peace under the supervision of the full quarter-sessions court. The precise manner of their selection is unclear, but in July 1624 the bench issued warrants to all the gentlemen "whose names the High Constables doe give in to be chosen for the new High Constable for to appear the next Sessions". The following January 1625 the duty of a high constable to recommend a short list of names from which the bench might appoint his successor is suggested by such a warrant to John Shipperdson of Wearmouth, high constable since July 1621 in the Easington ward. Similarly on 13 July 1625 Mr Peter Carter, one of the three high constables of the Darlington ward, was to be discharged from his office "upon finishing of his accompt with the Clerk of the Peace and giving in 4 sufficient Gentlemen's names" to undertake that service. At the sessions on 11 January 1626 Reginald Faucett and Guy Bainbrige were required to appear a fortnight later "to take upon them, or which of them the justice shall make choice of, to be High Constable of that division of Darnton ward". This latter order indicates sessions of the magistrates apart from the main quarter sessions and also explains why there were three high constables in the extensive Chester and Darlington wards and only two in the more compact Easington and Stockton wards.[10]

On 1 October 1617 the JPs approved the following high constables, who then took their oath:[11]

---

[9] Lapsley, *op. cit.* 86–88; R. F. Hunnisett, *The Medieval Coroner* (1961), 94, 150–1; *Courts*, 14–15, 33, 38, 67, 76; C. M. Fraser & K. Emsley, "Justice in North East England, 1256–1356", *The American Journal of Legal History xv* (1971), 165–67.

[10] Durham C[ounty] R[ecord] O[ffice], Q/S/O 1, pp. 208, 215, 221, 229, 249.

[11] Ibid., p.33.

Easington Ward: John Baynbrigg of Wheatley Hill, gen.
                   John Kinge[12] of Durham, gen.
Chester Ward: William Porter of Shield Row, gen.
                   Thomas Chambers of Cleadon, gen.
                   Peter Denton of Stobbilee, gen.
Stockton Ward: Thomas Tunstall of Coatham, gen.
                   Anthony Dodsworth of Stranton, gen.
Darlington Ward: Francis Wrenn of Henknoll, gen.
                   Richard Heighington of Greystones, gen.
                   John Burden of Langley, gen.

The oath taken by a high constable was recorded on 11 January 1626 before Richard Hunt, dean of Durham, and seven other JPs and sworn before the grand jury, when Mr John Garth took his oath as high constable for the Darlington ward in place of Mr Peter Carter. The terms of the oath were:

> You shall well and trulye exercise the office of a high Constable within the ward of ... and duly and truely shall kepe your pettie sessions and receive and take all informacioun and presentment to you made and presented, and retorne and certifie the same accordinglie: all maner of bloodsheds, assalts and affrays and outtries done and committed within the same wapentake [*sic*] according to your best knowledge ye shall present: all maner of writts, warrants and precepts to you lawfullie directed ye shall duely and truely execute: you shall diligently endeavour your selfe to take fellows and vagabondes, and doe your office upon them according to the law and statute made and provided in that behalf: yow shall also enquire of the defaultes in all under-constables within the said wapentake and the same with their names certifie at the Sessions of peace next following after the same inquerie had. The King Majesties peace in your owne person you shall as much as in you lies conserve and keepe, and in all other things that appertaine to your office you shall well and truely behave your selfe, soe helpe youe god.[13]

At each quarter sessions the high constables gave an account of their activities and received orders about general or specific policing duties. They also received their expenses and an honorarium from the county treasurer. No actual sum of money is mentioned until 1721.[14]

The petty or parish constables served under the high constables and were responsible for the local execution of summonses and warrants of the JPs. Their traditional place of appointment was the

---

[12] Kinge was a public notary (*Wills and Inventories* iv [Surtees Soc. 142, 1929], 174).

[13] Durham CRO, Q/S/O 1 p. 250.

[14] Ibid. passim.

court leet. This might have presented difficulties in County Durham, where there is little evidence of such an organisation, but at the July sessions in 1626 "it is ordered that Mr Sheriff shall provide a constable within Chopwell Lordship at his next Sheriff turn for the better execution of service in that part of the country".[15]

Durham was a palatinate with a multiplicity of courts, and its officers by general custom had a multiplicity of duties. The high constables were no exception. Several served as grand jurors or petty jurors, and sometimes in both capacities. Between 1614 and 1625 Peter Denton of Stobbilee, high constable in the Chester ward, served as petty juror at least three times. Richard Heighington of Greystones, high constable in the Darlington ward, served as grand juror five times and at least twice as a petty juror. Robert Farrow of Fishburn, high constable in the Stockton ward, served as a grand juror at least 14 times, mostly the first to be named on the panel, whilst William Pearson of Sherburn in the Easington ward served as a grand juror five times and at least once as a petty juror. These examples might well be multiplied greatly but for the fact that the high constables were listed only in the quarter-sessions order books, which do not appear to have survived before 1616.

JURIES

Under the Assize of Clarendon of 1166 a jury of presentment was to present to the king's justices for trial those in the neighbourhood suspected of crime. At what date these presentments ceased to be made from personal knowledge and the grand jury became a formal group representative of county opinion is unknown. The grand jurors at the assizes, courts of gaol delivery and quarter sessions met to decide whether the bills of indictment collected by the high constable at his "petty sessions" were true bills, i.e. whether a *prima facie* case had been made, whilst the petty jurors decided whether the presented person or persons were guilty or not guilty on the facts of the case as known to themselves. Testimony was, however, required where an indictment was brought by a private person.[16] As late as 1346 a majority decision by the petty jury was sufficient, just as it is to-day, but from the fifteenth century it had been settled that the jury must be unanimous in its decision. As the petty jurors could not separate until a decision had been taken it might seem remarkable that the same petty jury should pronounce a verdict on several cases the same day.[17] The local knowledge of the constables and jurors while working towards a firm verdict may have been detrimental to an unpopular suspected person.

---

[15] Ibid., p. 257.   [16] Ibid., p. 246.

[17] J. H. Baker, *An Introduction to English Legal History*, (1st ed. 1971), 89–90; F. Pollock & F. W. Maitland, *History of English Law* (2nd ed., reprinted, 1968) ii, 625–26.

The numbers of persons comprising the grand jury appear to differ in the legal textbooks between 12 and 23, and certainly in the palatinate they were variable until the mid-sixteenth century. Occasionally an esquire appears but both the grand jurors from 1471 and the few named petty jurors later were a mixture of gentlemen, normally with a lower social status to the justices, and yeomen. The first to be named were invariably gentlemen. Some of both status served fairly regularly. In the early rolls for the Durham quarter sessions numbers varied between 12 and 14 grand jurors, with a majority being of 13. Once at a gaol delivery in 1473 forty grand jurors were present, suggesting a general meeting of local notabilities. Again, on 26 March 1511, 26 grand jurors were present. Usually, however, it was still thirteen. By 1556 the number had grown to fifteen, and this remained the norm during the first quarter of the seventeenth century. The panels continued to have regular members. Composition by status was from two to eight gentlemen and the rest yeomen.

Further analysis of the panels reveals the persistence of several surnames. While it is virtually impossible to identify grand jurors on the 1471/3 rolls some were of obvious contemporary importance. John Redmayn served on 6 occasions. Benjamen Worsley and Thomas Fery served on 5 occasions, as did John Hewetson, James Typpyng and William Blithman. John Rakwood served on 4 occasions, as also did William Swalwell. Sixteen served at least twice, so they were not without experience of what was required of them. It would be interesting to know if they served the bishop's administration in other capacities, such as John Raket, who was a Durham chancery clerk.

Between 1510 and 1512 about another 70 served, including the 26 who attended the special session at Stanhope on 26 March 1511. Again there were multiple appearances, including John Porter (4), Thomas Kirkman (4), Robert Hagthorp (3), and John Ferrour (3). Again there were representatives of families who had been present in 1471/3, such as John Porter, William Hewetson, John Fossor and Nicholas Crosier. Looking forward, the same names would be found on the 1545/6 panels. In 1510/12 there was Alexander Blacket, and in 1545/6 Nicholas Blacket. In 1510/12 there was Matthew Bainbridge and in 1545/6 Philip Bainbridge. The Porters were represented by Robert, who made three appearances. Robert Bothe was succeeded by Roger Bothe, and John Ayton was succeeded by Robert. Robert Hagthorp figured on both, as did Nicholas Crosier.

With such earlier continuity it can be no surprise to find between 1545/6 and 1555/7 the same people recurring. Such include Christopher Ledall, Simon Welburie, German Pawle, Philip Bainbridge, Robert Porter, John Byllyngham and John Rakett. This continuity in families is shown by the presence in 1555/7 of John Blakiston, John Swalwell, John Hagthorp, John Claxton, Robert

Blenkinsopp and Robert Ayton. The Marian sessions, however, have their own peculiarities. There were 11 sessions recorded, which with panels varying between 13 and 15, could have seen 150 individuals serving. In fact there were only 54, with 22 serving only once. Leading attender was John Rakket with 9 appearances, closely followed by John Claxton, John Cragge, Christopher Ledall and Ralph Pratt with 8 each. John Blakiston, John Swalwell, John Hagthropp, Ralph Mayson and Nicholas Blackett each made 6 attendances. And to anticipate, there were still grand jurors in the early Stuart period who were Blacketts, Cragges, Crosiers, Farrowes and Swalwells.

Because the grand jurors at their time of service were mainly of the yeoman class they are hard to identify, except where their descendants rose in the world. The Blacketts flowered in the seventeenth century, when William left Weardale to become a Newcastle hostman and subsequently a baronet. The Hagthropps of Nettlesworth, Baynbriges of Wheatley Hill, Porters of Shield Row and Blenkensopps of Birtley all registered their coats of arms either at the heraldic visitation of 1575 or of 1615.[18] The Fetherstanhaughs, JPs by 1596, had been grand jurors in 1510/12, albeit styled as esquires. Another grand juror to be grandsire of an eminent family was John Eden, who married Elizabeth Lambton of Bellasis and whose descendants through further marriages with co-heiresses were ultimately raised to the peerage as Lord Auckland.

With the Visitation returns as a guide, supplemented by the first surviving quarter sessions order book, it is possible to locate many of the grand jurors between 1596 and 1626. Only in this way can it be seen how far there was any geographical distribution of service among the four wards of the county. An analysis of seven panels between these dates is inconclusive, except to the extent that the Stockton ward was notably under-represented. Probably the smallness of the county redressed the balance.

Again in this period some jurors were frequently called upon to serve. Among the most frequent were Robert Farrowe of Fishburn, gentleman, and John Swalwell of Ludworth, yeoman, who appeared on no less than 15 occasions, Farrowe generally heading the panel. Thomas Middleton of Seaton by Seaham (and later of Durham), regularly headed the panel from July 1622 to January 1625, followed by Christopher Hutchinson of Durham, gentleman, on 5 occasions. In all Hutchinson served on at least 8 occasions, as did William Trotter of Embleton, gentleman, John Shadforth of Murton and Richard Trotter of Auckland, both the latter being yeomen. Thomas Trotter "of the Ashes" put in 7 appearances and George Trotter four. Other multi-service families were the Emersons, Brian (4), Edward (2), and Thomas (4); the Middletons, Thomas (7), George and

---

[18] J. Foster, *Durham Visitation Pedigrees* (1887) passim.

William; the Pearsons, Robert, Roger and William (6); and the Robinsons, John (5), Richard (2) and Thomas (5). The Shacklocks of Murton, John, Richard and William, yeoman all, provided similar multiple service, and this repetition gives rise to speculation as to how the jurors were chosen. In January, May and October 1622 Christopher Hutchinson was a grand juror while simultaneously high constable in the Chester ward, and may still be found in this double capacity in January and April 1624. In July 1624 we find William Pearson a grand juror while serving as high constable of the Easington ward. In January 1625 Christopher Hutchinson was back again as a grand juror but at his last sessions as a high constable, having served since 1621. The panel again had William Pearson, who also stood down as part of a grand change in personnel apparently to remedy inefficiency in the collection of county dues.[19] The overlap in duties may indicate that grand jurors and high constables were drawn from the same social pool rather than sinister collusion. It would be an interesting hypothesis that the Durham quarter sessions represented the feudal power of the bishops of Durham as magnates, with the grand jurors owing suit of court. Certainly the frequency with which offences occurring at Whickham and Gateshead or Darlington and Weardale were presented would support the equation of quarter sessions as the court leet for the bishop's estates: but at least one third of the grand jurors seem to have been drawn from cathedral tenants, and South Shields does occur on occasion as the location of offences. A rare item of information about procedure concerning the grand jury occurs in the record of the sessions on 3 October 1626, when Thomas Fayerlee, Thomas Cragg and Leonard Somerside were each fined 20s "for departing from the rest of the grand jurors before they were licenced by the Court".[20]

Petty jurors were usually twelve in number, but occasionally eleven or thirteen. Like the grand jurors they were empanelled by the sheriff, who had a list of freeholders eligible for jury service. They are normally recorded only in the Order Books.

PROCEDURE

The approximate date for quarter sessions was fixed by statute. The clerk of the peace drew up a precept for holding the sessions, which was signed and sealed by the JPs, directing the sheriff to return panels of grand and petty jurors. On its return the clerk called and swore in a grand jury of 13, 15 or 17. This was followed by a "proclamation against vice and immorality" and the chairman delivered an address enumerating the offences currently of concern to the county. The justices then reviewed recognizances for

---

[19] Durham CRO, Q/S/O 1, pp. 221–22.
[20] Ibid., p. 269.

appearance in court and for good behaviour. At the sessions on 11 January 1626 "it is ordered that all such persons as proffer any indictments to the grand jurors for any offence against any person shall enter recognisances to prosecute and give evidence for the king at the next sessions after against such persons as by the said indictment shall be so found guilty by the grand jurors".[21]

Following presentation of indictments by the grand jury it was necessary to bring the parties into court. Sometimes they came voluntarily to the same sessions. Generally the case would be deferred to a subsequent session and the sheriff would bring them under arrest. Once the defendant(s) appeared it was necessary to secure agreement to have a jury, i.e. to stand on the verdict of the country. This consent was required from both defendant and accuser, as under common law a jury was optional to trial by battle. Occasionally the defendant admitted guilt and no jury was necessary. Where the sheriff was unable to arrest a defendant his default was published in the county court and after five such contempts the county coroners pronounced his outlawry.[22] The range of penalties available to the justices included fines, public whipping or setting in the stocks, but normally stopped short of capital punishment, as such felonies were transferred for consideration at the assizes.

Where the offence was established by statute punishment might include imprisonment, which otherwise was reserved as a means of detaining prisoners before trial or until such time as they were able to find sureties for their good behaviour or payment of fines. Durham gaol was situated in the outer gatehouse of Durham castle. The house of correction as rebuilt in 1632 was situated on the north end of Elvet Bridge. It was certainly in existence by April 1616, when the justices discussed the master's salary and allowed Roger Wall a yearly stipend of £4. This had increased by 1619 to £20, paid quarterly, but may have included the running costs. It was used as a place of confinement for those expiating social offences.[23]

Frequently offences under statute were brought to court not by the grand jury but by private informers. Their reward was to receive a fixed proportion of the fine.[24] Sometimes the information was successfully rebutted and the question of damages and costs for the defendant was ventilated. Fines in the sense of a pecuniary satisfaction for offences were normally paid to the bishop, except during vacancies. These become increasingly recorded from 1615. Assault cost 6s. 8d. unless aggravated. John Litster, possibly acting in

[21] Ibid., p. 246.
[22] See below, pp. 97, 99, 105–6, 108, 138, 140–1, 150, 178.
[23] Surtees, IV ii, 56; *Courts* 53–4.
[24] M. W. Beresford, "The Common Informer, the Penal Statutes and Economic Regulation", *Economic History Review* 2nd series x (1957), 221–22, 230–37.

self-defence, got off with a fine of 3s. 4d., which was then remitted on account of his poverty. John Smith was less fortunate when indicted for ambush. He was fined £3 6s. 8d. and committed to gaol until the fine was paid. Drunkenness attracted a fine of 3s. 4d., paid to the poor of the relevant parish through the churchwardens. These penalties seem very modest when compared with the statutory fines for engrossment, retailing, conversion to tillage, etc., calculated by value or by the duration of the offence. Petty thieves where found guilty were sentenced to be whipped in open market, normally at Durham, and discharged.

Richard Hutton whilst chancellor of Durham was interested in improving legal services and his reform of fees chargeable, agreed in 1616, has survived. Copies of indictments, informations or presentments cost 8d. a sheet of 12 lines each containing from 10 to 12 words. An indictment for felony cost 1s., for burglary 1s. 6d., and for riot etc. 3s. 4d. A return of *certiorari* for removing an indictment or other record cost 6s. 8d. Admittance of any person to his traverse (pleading not guilty) cost 6s. 8d. for the first named and 2s. for any named subsequently. Entering a verdict where no jury was involved cost 4s. 4d., but 6s. 8d. otherwise. It cost 2s. for a badger's or drover's licence with 4d. to the clerk that wrote it, and 1s. 4d. for an ale-house licence. For consulting the record within three years of entry a fee of 4d. was charged, but where it was older the fee (formerly 3s. 4d.) was to be 1s.[25] Recourse to the law was costly.

---

[25] Ushaw College Library, Durham, MS VII A 1 17, ff. 8–9.

DURHAM COMMISSIONS OF THE PEACE
AND BUSINESS IN QUARTER SESSIONS

The earliest quarter-sessions rolls for Durham known to survive date from 1471. That year Bishop Laurence Booth (1457–76) issued his commission of the peace to Ralph Neville, earl of Westmorland, and Ralph Neville his nephew, Guy Fairfax, Richard Pygot, Henry Gillowe, clerk, chancellor of Durham, Christopher Conyers, knight, Thomas Middleton, William Raket, Richard Bainbridge and John Raket.[1] These men represented the leading figures in county Durham, headed by the principal noble, Ralph Neville, earl of Westmorland and lord of Raby, and his nephew, who at this date was both heir to the earl and nephew by marriage to the bishop of Durham.[2] Guy Fairfax, who at this date was a king's serjeant, was almost certainly a royal assize judge on the northern circuit, as was probably true of Richard Pygot, also a king's serjeant.[3] Their associates were officials of the Durham palatinate. Henry Gillowe had been chancellor of Durham and the bishop's receiver-general since 1464,[4] and William Raket had been commissioned as a justice of assize by Bishop Neville (1438–57) in 1439, 1446 and 1455. John Raket was probably a relative, possibly his son, and in 1476 was appointed by the bishop clerk of the peace.[5] County families were represented by Sir Christopher Conyers, who was descended from the ancient Durham baronial family at Sockburn, Thomas Middleton, a younger son of the Middletons of Belsay in Northumberland, whose father had married the heiress of Silksworth, and Richard Bainbridge, who had married the heiress to Wheatley Hill and held lands at Darlington, Butterwick and Thorpe Bulmer.[6]

So much for the formal commission. The surviving rolls for 1471–3 indicate that whereas the earl, the two royal serjeants and the landowners Conyers and Middleton never actually sat on the Durham bench two other laymen and one chancery clerk certainly did. These were Thomas Moreslawe, John Catrik and Richard Raket. Moreslawe was described as skilled in the law in 1473 and Catrik had served in 1468 as arbiter in a suit of dower brought by Matilda, widow of Sir William Bowes.[7] Richard Raket, who sat only once, was

---

[1] DK *Report* xxxv (1874), 102.
[2] G. E. Cokayne (ed. V. Gibbs, H. A. Doubleday, etc.), *The Complete Peerage of England, Scotland, Ireland, Great Britain and the United Kingdom* (13 vols, 1910–40: reprinted 1982) xii, 551.
[3] J. H. Baker, *The Order of Sergeants at Law* (Selden Soc., Supplementary Series, 1984), 510, 533.
[4] *Fasti Dunelmenses* (Surtees Soc. 139, 1926), 51.
[5] PRO, Durham 3/36 m. 3: 3/46 m. 3d.: 13/227; DK *Report* xxxiv (1872) 176, 210: xxxv (1874) 99, 103.
[6] DK *Report* xxxv, 99, 102, 123; Surtees, I, 101, 245: III, 50.
[7] DK *Report* xxxv, 98, 106, 123.

probably the founder of the local family of chancery clerks of that name, being recorded by the later Durham attorney and antiquary, Christopher Mickleton (d. 1669), as clerk of the crown, of assize, of the peace and of halmotes and protonotary all in the time of Bishop Neville (1433–57).[8]

They sat in troubled times. Bishop Laurence Booth was by birth a Lancastrian and closely associated with Queen Margaret of Anjou, wife of Henry VI, serving as her chancellor before his appointment as keeper of the king's privy seal about 1456 and a tutor and guardian of the young Prince of Wales in 1457. His matching ecclesiastical career included the provostship of Beverley, 1453, archdeaconry of Richmond, 1454, and deanery of St Paul's, London, before consecration as bishop of Durham on 15 September 1457. With the overthrowal of his patroness his temporalities at Durham were seized between December 1462 and April 1464, when he succeeded in making his peace with Edward IV. He does not appear to have enjoyed full control of Durham again before 1471, although by 1473 he was acting-chancellor of England and in September 1476 was translated to the archbishopric of York.[9]

Despite the national disquiet the Durham bench was concerned in 1471–3 mainly with what was to be its staple business, theft of horses, cattle and sheep, with engrossing of grain and illegal hare-coursing. In January 1472 there was a bloody case of murder in Stanhope park in Weardale, where eight labourers armed with Carlisle-axes, clubstaff, spearstaff, pikestaff and broad arrow attacked a Richard Warde and killed him. At the following sessions on 20 April 1472 five gentleman, ten yeomen, a labourer and a husbandman were charged with assembly, armed as for war, with swords, sticks, staves, bows and arrows, to attack the bailiff of Sir John Athirton, then sheriff of Durham, thereby preventing execution of a warrant at Wolsingham. In January 1473 two men were presented as vagabonds "contrary to statute", and at the same sessions seven Durham workmen were charged with forcible entry of three empty burgages in Durham in South Street contrary to 5 Richard II. Durham justices of the peace enforced national statute law, even if the peace nominally belonged to the bishop.

Forty years on, in 1510, the chancellor of Durham still sat on the bench. The full commission of the peace of Bishop Thomas Ruthall (1509–23) as issued on 10 August 1509 consisted of Hugh Ashton as chancellor, the prior of Durham (Thomas Castell), Humphrey Conyngesby, a justice of King's Bench, Richard, Lord Lumley, Sir Ralph Eure, Sir Ralph Bowes, William Bulmer, esq., Thomas Tempest, John Batemanson, John Raket and John Bentley. They were empowered jointly and singly as justices to keep the peace, the

---

[8] PRO, Durham 4/2; Durham University Library, Special Collections, Mickleton/Spearman MS 2 ff. 66–67v.; Surtees IV ii, 140.
[9] DNB II, 849–50.

statutes of Winchester, Northampton and Westminster, the statutes
and ordinances of Cambridge touching traders, labourers, artificers,
inn-servants, beggars, vagabonds and travelling-men, the statutes of
Westminster of Henry I and Henry II, and statutes against liveries,
and to maintain public order in the counties of Durham and
Sadberge. To this end they were authorised to castigate offenders and
punish offences committed against the person or house-burning,
and take surety for keeping the peace and being of good behaviour,
failing which the offenders should be committed to gaol until they
complied. They were to enquire by oath of acceptable lawworthy
men of those counties into all felonies, trespasses, nuisances,
forestalling, regrating and extortions by whomsoever committed,
and punish offenders who by unlawful assembly or riding, maiming
or death, suits or maintenance, injured the *king's* people. They were
to prevent abuse of measures and weights and of regulations
touching the sale of victuals, breaches of the statutes relating to inn-
servants, mendicants and beggars, and were to correct any
negligence by sheriffs, mayors, bailiffs, stewards, constables and
gaolers in the execution of their offices. As this was the new
commission on the accession of Bishop Ruthall they were
empowered to continue and complete any unfinished business from
the time of his predecessor or *sede vacante*. In cases of difficulty,
however, judgment must be rendered only in the presence of a
justice of assize. The bishop's right to fines was safeguarded. The
sheriffs were to be ready to empanel juries as required. Finally, John
Raket was to ensure that all documentation was to hand, i.e. act as
clerk of the peace.[10] Confusingly, the justices as recorded on the
sessions roll also included William Hilton of Hylton, high forester of
Weardale and a Durham justice of gaol delivery, and Thomas Kay,
LLB, keeper of the bishop's great seal at Durham.[11]

While the details of a charge should not always be taken at face
value, it certainly appears that organised violence was a feature of
the county in 1510/11. Anthony Brakenbury brought at least 22
peace-breakers from Hornby near Bedale to Burn Hall by Durham as
part of a feud over inheritance from the Claxtons. In another charge
Thomas Berkhouse of Hedleywood, Northumberland, and eight
others drove off a flock of 86 sheep to Prudhoe castle. Meanwhile
John, Lord Lumley, and 60 others did battle with William Hilton and
his retinue of 80 on 29 September 1510 at Eastgate by Stanhope.
This can be related to rival claims to the office of master forester,
which had valuable perquisites as the master forester was responsible
for all leases in Weardale, including not only grazing but licences for
mining lead and iron. For over a century the office had been in the
Lumley family until the death of Richard, Lord Lumley, in 1510.
Thereupon the new bishop, Thomas Ruthall, had appointed William

---

[10] PRO, Durham 3/70 m. 2.
[11] For biographical references see Appendix 2, pp. 337–49.

Hilton (a "baron" of the bishopric but not of England) to the office. Hilton actually was John Lumley's uncle, but had no qualms about his nephew's expectations of inheriting the forestership, for which John even had the patent of appointment.[12] A further fracas was presented at the sessions in January 1511, with William Hilton in the chair, when Robert Harbottle of Prudhoe, gentleman, alias Sudden Robert, and 7 others with a minstrel attacked and wounded Thomas Hilton and John Greenwood, a servant of William Hilton. On the return affray 19 days later George Hilton and seven others attacked Nicholas Turpyn, a Harbottle retainer. A special sessions of the peace was then held at Stanhope on 26 March 1511, where to judge by their surnames the bulk of the grand jurors seem to have been drawn from upper Weardale; but the only offences were livestock rustling.

While the full commission of the peace regularly included such royal justices as were on Northern Circuit, even when in theory the bishop could select his own nominees, their actual appearance at the quarter sessions was unlikely unless these were made to coincide with their August assizes. Such an event took place on 4 August 1545, when the business included three disseisins, two breaches of close, a murder, an assault and a seizure of sheep. On the bench were two serjeants at law, John Hynde and Edmund Molyneux, both to become royal judges of Common Pleas, Robert Hyndmer, chancellor of Durham, Sir Ralph Hedworth of Harraton and Robert Meynell, who had been called to the bar at Lincoln's Inn and would become a serjeant at law in 1547. Hyndmer, who was a cleric, served as temporal chancellor of Durham between 1530 and his death in 1558. Meynell was already the attorney-general of the bishop of Durham and steward between 1541 and 1561. Fellow justices were the local landowners Ralph Claxton, Thomas Blakiston and Robert Tempest, nephew and heir of Sir Thomas Tempest, sometime steward of Durham.

A hint of what might lie behind disseisin and breach of close is offered by the presentment in August 1545 that William Allan, William Elstob and Robert Dukk "broke the close of Thomas Coundon at Egglescliffe, depastured his grass and ploughed his land". This strongly suggests that the violence expressed opposition to enclosure.[13] This theme was repeated at the sessions on 16

---

[12] Cf. J. L. Drury, "More stout than wise: tenant right in Weardale in the Tudor period", *The Last Principality*, ed. D. Marcombe, (1987), 76–79.

[13] M. E. James, *Family, Lineage and Civil Society* (1974), 76–77. E. M. Leonard, in "The Inclosure of the Common Fields in the Seventeenth Century", *Transactions*, Royal Historical Soc. NS xix (1905), 111, refers to the excellent indexing system whereby it is possible to trace Durham chancery decrees relating to enclosures in the county after 1633, when the surviving run of decree books begins. An index to earlier decree books now lost is preserved as Durham University Library, Special Collections, Mickleton MS 38. This

January 1546, when four presentments were brought, two concerning thefts from closes, one of ejection and one of depasturing a close. At the sessions on 22 May 1546 Henry Holland, gentleman, was charged with blocking a common way in Beamish park with a fence and ditch. James Lawson had blocked two common ways in Gateshead. Two cases concerned an enclosure at Friarside made by Ralph Rawe. William Newton late of Ryton had ejected Robert Porter from his close there and ploughed the land.

Ten years later in 1555 the situation was much the same. At the sessions on 22 June 1555 the bench still included Robert Hyndmer, the chancellor, and Robert Meynell, the bishop's attorney-general. The remainder were lay members, local gentlemen. Four cases were presented of which one was forcible disseisin and the others hedge-breaking. Again there was an August sessions, complete with two royal judges, Edward Saunders and William Dallyson, serjeant at law, the former already and the latter soon to be justices of king's and queen's bench. Twelve presentments were made, including a second instalment of the ejection of Sir Robert Brandling and associates from the manor of Stodhoe, and a riotous assault by more than 100 persons on a close of Lord Lumley at the Isle by Bradbury. Four oxen had been stolen from a close at Offerton, a wainload of hay from a close at Darlington, three horses and two mares from a close at Wingate Grange. There were four assaults, one resulting in a death. At the sessions in October 1555 there were five presentments, including a riot at Scremerston in Norhamshire when more than 200 men, led by Thomas Clavering of Wark on Tweed, broke into the

---

has no entries under "enclosure", but under "division" refers to the separation of Heighington moor from Walworth moor, with a note that a writ of perambulation was issued to the sheriff authorising him to act in this matter (pp. 37, 66, 131). From a marginal note it is known that the contents of this book extended no later than 1584, hence this is the earliest example of Durham chancery concern in such matters. Subsequent decrees included a confirmation of division at Hetton-le-Hole in 1617, at Escomb before 1618, and of meadow at Dalton between 1609 and 1630 (Mickleton MS 38, p. 37). The first surviving decree book is now PRO, Durham 4/1. This records a division of the moor between Winlaton and Ryton in 1634, at Sedgefield in 1636, at Aldin Grange in 1636 and again at Ryton in 1638, at Herrington in 1640, and a piece of moor at Lanchester in 1640 (PRO, Durham 4/1 pp. 159, 306, 374, 426, 497, 507, 625, 631, 751, 758). Chancery decree index references lead one to further divisions post 1640 at Bishop and West Auckland, Holmeclose in Blackwell, Boldon, Cleatlam, Chester-le-Street, Grangefield by Darlington, Morton in Dalton, Greatham, Haughton-le-Skerne, Hett, Norton, Redworth, Shadforth, Sherburn, Stockton, and between Haughton-le-Skerne and Cockerton (Mickleton MS 38, ff. 255–56, 262, 273, 283–84, 287, 290, 296). From a different source Miss Leonard was able to date decrees for Great Lumley and Morton in Dalton to 1585, for Thornley to about 1606, for Cornforth to 1628 and for Middleton One Row to 1632 (Leonard, 111n.).

manor of Robert Lawson[14] and seized wheat in the sheaf worth £15. In another riot at West Boldon Thomas Lawson of Little Usworth, gentleman, led over 60 people onto land of Robert Rickaby and seized five wainloads of hay. Rickaby in turn led 40 people into a close belonging to three of his neighbours at West Boldon and seized six wainloads of hay. There was a third instalment of the Brandling feud, and a Stanhope ambush, apparently short of death.

The feud between Percival Lumley of Darlington and John, Lord Lumley, over lands in Bradbury continued into the January sessions. It would seem that Percival was a kinsman of Lord Lumley and indeed is described in Glover's Visitation of 1584–5 as third son to Lord Lumley (forename omitted), married to a daughter of Sir George Hussey.[15] The Hussey connection seems to be supported by the names of Percival's associates, Thomas and John Hussey of Kirby Sigston. Thomas Hussey was subsequently implicated in the Earls' Rebellion of 1569 and his lands forfeited. Bradbury and the Isle had come into possession of the Lumley family through marriage between Elizabeth Thornton of Netherwitton, heiress of Roger Thornton, the many-times mayor of Newcastle (d. 1430) and Sir George, second Lord Lumley, but had been acquired by the Neville earls of Westmorland before 1569.[16]

In April 1556 there were seven presentments of which four concerned attempts to expel Percival Lumley from his freeholding at Bradbury and another concerned Percival and 15 others seizing hay and grain worth together £50 from the farm of George and Robert Archer in Bradbury. In another case bailiffs sent to distrain for arrears of rent at Silksworth were assaulted and the animals recovered, the first of a series of such offences to be presented with monotonous regularity – except perhaps for the bailiffs concerned, who had to accept such violence as an occupational hazard.

---

[14] The Lawsons were a family of wide ramifications. One branch, founded by James (d. before 1547), had gone into business in Newcastle. His eldest son Edmund had married Margery Swinnoe, heiress to Rock, Northumberland, and Scremerston on the death of her brother before 1537. She subsequently married Robert Lawson of Usworth, whose relationship to Edmund cannot be ascertained. Meanwhile a George Lawson of Little Usworth had been appointed by Henry VIII in 1545 constable of Wark Castle, Northumberland. He seems to have been uncle of the Robert in the lawsuit, who may have been his heir. Thomas Lawson of Usworth was Robert's elder brother (Surtees II, 4647; *Northumberland County History* II, 125: XI, 64–65: XIII, 387, 392–93). Thomas Clavering of Wark cannot be identified in the pedigree of Clavering of Callaly, Northumberland, but was named as living there in the muster roll for 1538. W. P. Hedley suggested that he might have been guardian of the young heir, Robert (*Northumberland Families* I (1968), 181).

[15] J. Foster, *The Visitation of Yorkshire* (1875), 210.

[16] Surtees III, 39.

The August sessions saw the royal judges again on the bench. There were 19 presentments in all. The violence at Bradbury continued, although some presentments were a simple repetition of previous indictments. Lord Lumley was now being attacked at Butterby by a mob led by William Wrenn of Binchester. More spectacularly, John Harbottle of Tughall and Percival and Roland Harbottle of Glendale in Northumberland led a force of 104 named and an estimated further 200 unknown miscreants "in warlike fashion and manner of new insurrection" to expel Roger Harbottle from his manor of Beckley. Here, as in the case of Percival Lumley, we may have rivalry among cadet branches of a family which in the Harbottle case had left the lordship of Tanfield to be divided among sisters and their husbands. Beckley had been a Harbottle estate since 1486, although it passed to the Porter family of Shield Row during the sixteenth century.[17] On the dorse of one of the two rolls for this sessions is the copy of a title-deed for a burgage in Barnard Castle. Use of legal rolls to preserve such evidence had been recommended by statute of Henry VIII (27 Hen. VIII c. 10).

The bench at the October sessions heard six presentments including two breaches of the free fishery in the Tyne at Blaydon belonging to the earl of Westmorland, who was actually present on the bench, two thefts from a close, an assault and a disseisin.

The January sessions of 1557 saw a continuation of the dispute over Beckley and illustrates a wide geographical sweep of offenders. The party of about 30 which Roger Harbottle of Beckley organised against Robert Porter of Shield Row on 18 October 1556 and 7 January 1557 included from Northumberland a Hubbocke from Haydon Bridge, and Rutherfords from Prudhoe and Rudchester, and from North Yorkshire a Harbottle from Danby Wiske. Men from Tanfield in Yorkshire and Chipchase in Northumberland were involved in an organised raid near Lanchester on Roger and Christabel Hilton, and similarly diverse origins were shown for the 17 who assaulted Marmaduke Baytmanson of Little Smeaton at Darlington "with intent to kill". This latter case clearly indicates the grounds for the jurisdiction of the Durham magistrates. A Yorkshireman was assaulted by his Yorkshire neighbours among others, but the offence took place within county Durham. In addition, six fishermen were presented for forestalling fish being brought to market; and nine men, all but one being yeomen, were presented for keeping greyhounds without proper property qualifications.

The five presentments in May 1557 included three assaults, a theft and a disseisin at Eastgate in Weardale. The ten presentments in August 1557 included a further incident in the Harbottle/Porter feud, when an attempt was made to waylay and murder Nicholas

---

[17] Ibid. II, 235.

Porter of Shield Row following a similar attempt by the Porters to ambush Ralph Harbottle a month earlier. The Porters had also tried to waylay one of Ralph's supporters, Edward Rutherford of Prudhoe, who himself had been charged and acquitted of highway robbery at Strothergate. There was a charge of murder at Barnard Castle and another at Wolsingham. In the latter case the widow was charged with "comforting" the principal assassin. The following sessions in November 1557 included another brutal murder of a husband with the wife as accomplice, and three cases of horse-stealing all on the same day, involving raiders from North and South Tynedale.

The lay magistrates who sat on the Durham bench in 1545/6 and 1555/7 were drawn from local landed families such as the Blakistons, Conyers, Claxtons, Hebburns, Salvins and Trollopps, who all were recorded in the heraldic visitations of Durham in 1575 or 1615. Perhaps because they were staunch supporters of the Catholic revival under Mary Tudor their next generation was conspicuously absent from the bench following the Rising of the North of 1569. Although Marmaduke Blakiston was able as an Anglican cleric to claw his way back, as was Ralph Conyers of a cadet branch of that family, the remainder figure prominently among the Catholic gentry suffering for their recusancy in 1607, 1615 and later.[18]

No quarter sessions rolls appear to survive between 1557 and 1596. For this reason no date can be given for the start of a striking feature of the later sessions, the presence of the bishop of Durham on the bench. Both Bishop Toby Matthew (1595–1606) and his immediate successor William James (1606–17) are known to have acted as agents for the privy council, sending up reports on local conditions.[19] James, as dean of Durham before his elevation, was particularly assiduous. Indictment rolls for Matthew's episcopate show him present on the bench for three sessions in 1596, three sessions in 1598, the April sessions and a special May sessions in 1599, and two sessions in 1600, 1601, 1602 and 1605 each and once in 1603, before his translation to York in 1606. During this same period William James as dean sat at the sessions with him in May 1599, January and April 1600, July 1601, April and July 1602, and January 1603, but more frequently attended when Bishop Matthew was absent. The chancellor of Durham continued normally to be present. The custom of holding an August session to enable the royal judges on circuit to attend had fallen into abeyance.

Outside this sequence of indictment rolls but deserving of record, there has survived a "brewsters session" held on 9 April 1589 before Thomas Calverley, esq., chancellor, John Conyers, esq., John Hedworth, esq., Ralph Talboys, John Heath, Christopher Chater, esq., Clement Colmore, LL.D., and Anthony Hutton, esq. The grand

---

[18] Surtees III, 34; James, 138–42; see below esp. 163–7, 169, 245–9, 265–7, 330–6.
[19] James, 76–77, 155, 157–58.

jury consisted of Ralph Blakiston, George Crosier, Robert Robson, William Williamson, William Claxton, John Lilborne, Leonard Porter, John Wadley and John Hedworth, gentlemen, and Thomas Younge, John Grexon, William Wilson, John Dobson, Edward Hall and Robert Brandson, yeomen. Presentments included 36 alehouse keepers in Gateshead, 5 in Lintzford, 3 in Ebchester, 2 each in Crook, Eddys Bridge and Chopwell, and one each in Shotley Bridge and Derwentcote, the latter being described as a miller to trade. Another man was charged with forestalling corn at Gateshead. On a bill dated to 1595 charges were brought against 34 people for failure to attend their parish church for three weeks.[20]

When the Durham quarter-sessions rolls resume in January 1596 the only business noted was the sheriff's return that he had outlawed certain accused persons. As the parchment has survived simply as the cover for later sessions it is virtually illegible. The bench was occupied solely by the bishop and his chancellor, as was the situation in April 1596, when again the record is probably incomplete. Business consisted of an assault, breach of close, a theft and a long warrant addressed to the sheriff to arrest felons located not only in Durham but also in Northumberland and Cumberland. In June 1596 the two heard an assault, two thefts and two prosecutions against sturdy beggars, and the sheriff returned the outlawry of various felons whom he had been ordered to arrest. No record survives for Michaelmas 1596.

In January 1597 the Durham chancellor presided, joined on the bench by the dean, 7 local gentlemen and the clerk of the peace. Twenty-six presentments were heard. These were geographically clustered, with nine relating to two cattle-thieves operating near Bishop Auckland on 6 September 1596. Seven concerned poachers. Three related to a series of riots at Chopwell involving Robert Dudley senior and junior and John and Peter Ward. Two concerned forcible resistance offered to law officers. The Dudley case sheds light on the descent of the Chopwell estate from Sir Robert Constable of Flamborough, who was granted the estate by Queen Elizabeth following its confiscation through the participation by its earlier owner, John Swinburne, in the Earls' Rebellion of 1569. Surtees thought that the Dudley interest began about 1608 with Ambrose Dudley, alderman of Newcastle, but it obviously went earlier with Ambrose's father, Robert, one of the customers of Newcastle, sheriff in 1586 and mayor in 1602.[21]

---

[20] Broken sessions files ranging in date between 1582 and 1618, with further files from 1674 to 1720, are boxed as PRO, Durham 17/1. They consist of original indictments marked "vera billa", recognizances, informations and a coroner's inquest for 1617 on a man found dead near Stockton, bludgeoned and with his throat cut.

[21] Surtees II, 277.

The record of three sessions has survived for 1598, namely, a full hearing of 17 charges in January, nothing for April, then 5 charges in July and a double hearing on 20 September, with 17 charges and an adjournment to 4 October. The January indictments included two murders, both of women, three assaults on law officers, two evictions from land, the stopping of a church-way, two assaults involving theft, three cases of cattle-stealing, and a general charge of brawling. The July cases all concerned execution of writs by bailiffs of the sheriff of Durham, some involving assaults on them, and others involving the outlawry of persistant defaulters. Cases at the Michaelmas sessions ranged from illegal shooting to assault, from taking salmon out of season to obstructing a road, from theft to gaol-breaking. Although only four magistrates sat in January there were twelve in July and fifteen in September.

Again in 1599 there was an extra sessions in May, held between the normal dates in April and June. Cases in April included arson, escape from arrest, hunting with a mastiff, and ejection of a tenant at Nesbit by members of the Trollopp family of Thornley. The special sessions in May heard only two indictments, but one was disseisin of a tenant of the dean and chapter of Durham. The dean was on the bench.

All four sessions survive for 1600, with an especially busy calendar in January. In addition to thefts of cattle and horses there were two presentments (one successfully rebutted) of trading without having served a 7-years' apprenticeship. The Durham bridges of Elvet and Framwellgate were presented as ruinous. In April the occupation by Ambrose Dudley of the manor of Chopwell had resulted in a riot. Another disputed tenancy had resulted in resistance to an arbitration award previously authorised by the Council of the North. This involved William Brakenbury of Langton. William was possibly kin to the Brakenburys of Killerby, of which family Oliver Brakenbury was head. Oliver was a member of the grand jury at this sessions. Nine persons were charged with engrossing malt and oats. Thirteen were charged with trading as butchers without serving their proper apprenticeship. Four were charged with tracing hares in the snow with a greyhound. Thirty-one were charged with fishing illegally out of season in the Tyne, Derwent and Wear. In June we find references to an informer reporting a case of engrossment of barley and rye for resale and claiming his reward of half the value of the penalty. Such informations were to increase in volume, the offences including engrossing of grain and butter, forestalling, cattle-dealing and, most importantly, conversions from tillage to pasturage. A foretaste of this latter problem, and resort to self-help, also appears in the October sessions, with two indictments for uprooting hedges, one at Lamesley and one at Gainford, in the north and south of the county.

In January 1601 there were further indictments concerning destruction of hedges and ditches, where Peter Denton of Farrington

Hall by Silksworth had fenced the High Close and where Lionel Martyne of Durham and Thomas Foster of Shincliffe had fenced the Low Field. Here the close had been sown with maslin, which local workers had ruined by turning in their livestock before ploughing up the land themselves. Eight enterprising yeomen of East Boldon themselves enclosed land on East Boldon moor, and by so doing blocked the road between Whitburn and Wardley. Even the indictments for horse- and cattle-stealing from closes may indirectly indicate the increasing use of fences to enable individuals to maximise their use of land. Ill feeling over the Boldon enclosure developed into a riotous assembly, presented in April 1601. The Brakenbury dispute re-appeared in July, now as an indictment against William for organising 60 persons including at least 13 women to tear down 3000 feet of quickset hedge on Selaby moor belonging to Henry Brakenbury. Christopher Fuister late of Stockton and four others destroyed 20 feet of quickset hedge at Stockton. Thomas Easterby of Seaham, parson of Seaham, was indicted for renting divers closes at Cocken, contrary to the statute of 21 Henry VIII, as he already had sufficient glebe-land. A rather different offence was presented in October 1601, namely that Nicholas Westgarth was lending money at more than 10%, contrary to the statutes against usury.

While assault and theft tended to be the staple business of the sessions sometimes the bench concentrated on other offences. In July 1602 there was a crack-down on butchers believed to be trading without having served a proper apprenticeship. Twenty-five were so prosecuted, their true occupations being listed variously as tailor, whitesmith, husbandman, yeoman and labourer. There were 30 prosecutions for illegal fishing in the Derwent. In October the magistrates began a drive against unlicenced keepers of tippling-houses. In January 1603 they sought to curb a wave of rescues from the bishop's pound at Stanhope of livestock distrained for failure to pay fines imposed at the forest court. In January 1604 poachers of salmon and trout and keepers of greyhounds were again singled out for punishment.

At the sessions in April 1605 the magistrates were turning their attention to enforcement of laws against recusants. William Marshall of Elvet was charged with failure to attend divine service at his parish church. Equally objectionable, Robert Marley of Stockley was charged with use of slighting words in respect of the sacraments and serving out the bread and wine at Brancepeth church after consecration, while Henry Horsley, who had taken some away, said: "Why might wee not take it, for we paide for itt?". On 2 October 1605 John Joplyng was charged with refusal to confine himself to his house in Sedgefield although he was infected with the plague.

Superficially the target for January 1607 was keepers of unlicenced alehouses. No less than 101 were indicted from all parts of the county. In fact the great preoccupation was still with recusancy, following the disclosure of the Gunpowder Plot of 5 November 1605, but the record was kept separate from the general indictment roll and survives only as a list of estreats. More than 415 persons were presented, charged with being over 16 years of age yet absenting themselves from church from 1 May until 17 September 1606 without good reason, thereby each incurring a fine of £100. If the total of over £415,000 were actually collected, it would have made the sum of £5000 at £40 a head, imposed similarly on Durham recusants in 1616, pale into insignificance.[22]

In July 1607 eight persons were prosecuted for trading as mercers and grocers in Darlington without having served an apprenticeship. Another three were charged with engrossing grain variously at Washington, Cleatlam and Castle Eden. Two at Cornforth and Mainsforth respectively had converted arable land to tillage, and there had been riotous assemblies at Staindrop and Great Kelloe. In October the apparatus against recusants slipped into gear again, with the prosecution of Sir William Blakiston for preventing the distraint of a cow ordered on account of his failure to pay a fine of 8s. levied on himself and his wife for absenting themselves from their parish church. This had been followed by a comprehensive order to seize his livestock and a posse of sheriff's officers had rounded up 19 horses, mares, geldings and a colt, together with 77 oxen, cows, bullocks and stirks, to drive them to Durham. Inevitably they had been rescued and the sheriff's officers assaulted. (Earlier in October 1606 Blakiston had been prosecuted for giving his servant James Grene a blue livery.) At the same October sessions George Collingwood of Eppleton was charged with harbouring two women recusants, probably as servants. Francis Lawson of Thorpe Bulmer, James Lawson of Neasham and Sir John Claxton were charged similarly with harbouring recusants.

The squeeze against recusants continued in January 1608, when Sir John Claxton of West Hall in Lanchester was indicted for living away from home after his presentment as a recusant. Later in the same sessions four Catholics were indicted for their failure to bring their infant sons for baptism at their parish church. Otherwise it was the usual business of assaults, thefts and close-breaking, except that John Cradock, rector of Gainford, was presented for blockage of the main road from Barnard Castle to Darlington with a stone wall 20 yards long, forcing a diversion of the road "to the nuisance of the inhabitants". Cradock was one of Bishop James's legal advisers and a future JP.

---

[22] Durham CRO, Q/S/I 3 (printed below as Appendix 1, pp. 330–6); K. M. Longley, "An Alternative to Taxation: The Crown raises £5,000 from Durham Recusants, 1616" *Northern Catholic History* 19 (1984), 9.

The April sessions does not appear to have survived, but in June 1608 there is reference to a disturbance at South Shields involving Stephen Kitching and Richard Matthew which presents points of interest. Firstly, there is the reference to Matthew's home having glass windows. This must be one of the first references to domestic glass in the town, where subsequently there were certainly glass-works.[23] Secondly there is reference to the Court House in which Kitching beat Matthew about the head with a great stone, nearly killing him. Matthew's son, another Richard, was to be an attorney in the Durham court of pleas until his death in January 1683.[24]

In January 1609 the main problem was again public order, particularly unlicenced taverns and excessive drinking therein and common brawling. In April over half the indictments (9 out of 16) involved violence in connection with closes built by William and John Lynn and William Wilkinson at Layton. These were objectionable to John Machel and others, who from 24 March 1609 assaulted William Lynn and his associates, destroyed 100 feet of fence and ditch with mattocks and forks, and drove in their own livestock to depasture them. When the Lynns and Wilkinsons tried to impound the animals they were further assaulted. In July the problems included resale of cattle (3), felling trees belonging to the bishop (7), shooting hares (3), hunting partridges with setting-dogs and nets (2), fishing for kipper (i.e. out-of-season) salmon (5), blocking the road from Darlington to the coal pits at Wackerfield, and illegal tippling.

The April sessions saw on the bench not only Bishop James but his new temporal chancellor Richard Hutton, serjeant at law, later to be knighted and a judge of Common Pleas (1617–38). Because of Hutton's London commitments he was not as constant an attender as some of his predecessors. He appeared again on 10 January and 11 April 1610, and on 27 March 1611, but possibly did not return until 7 April 1613. His technical expertise in chancery matters may have been supplemented by Henry Dethick, LLB, later a master in chancery, who figured on the Durham bench from October 1598.

No indictments seem to have survived for 1614, although some of the business can be reconstructed from adjourned hearings.

Riotous assemblies involving breach of close with destruction of a watercourse were presented on 11 January 1615, the aggrieved party being William Blakiston of Broomfield by Axwell house. It is not clear whether this was related to the destruction of 80 yards of gutter taking water from a spring on Seamer Moss on Gateshead moor for the public water supply. The latter was done on the orders of Thomas Liddell of Ravensworth, who subsequently was fined £50. The Liddells had extensive coal interests in the area and the gutter

---

[23] G. B. Hodgson, *The Borough of South Shields* (1903), 358–66.
[24] *Courts*, 18–19, 68–69.

might have had industrial implications. There followed 11 indictments for harbouring recusants and three for non-baptism of infants. In one such case the accused was able to convince the bench that he was the wrong man.

At the April sessions in 1615 there was a hint of dearth in the indictment of Edward Ewbank of Old Durham, gentleman, with others unknown, for breaking into a barn belonging to John Booth of Gilesgate and taking barley and oats. Ewbank had declared he would rather give his beasts straw and grain from the barn than that they should perish. Although there was no indication of such proceedings on the January roll, at the April sessions it was recorded that 320 named persons, having been summoned by the sheriff to appear before the magistrates for failure to attend their parish church for the space of three months, failed to appear. William Porter of Shield Row was separately charged with harbouring three recusants. Thirty-two persons were charged with offences relating to taverns and five with being common drunkards.

The July sessions reverted to more agricultural concerns such as close-breaking, milldam-breaking, conversion from tillage to pasture, and resale of livestock. There was also a major enquiry into the county bridges and what people were responsible for their upkeep.

The next available sessions is for 10 April 1616. A new offence concerned butchers killing cattle, sheep and pigs "within the walls of Durham". Six were so charged. Further business is missing, together with the record for the Midsummer sessions and the start of the October proceedings. The second stage of proceedings which had begun on 10 July 1616 was heard on 2 October, when on default of appearance 124 recusants were convicted of contempt of court.

The following sessions of 8 January 1617 reverted to assaults and thefts. Less usual, James Robson of Carlton admitted a charge of horse-wounding and was sentenced to three days in the Durham house of correction. He was then to be put in the stocks at Norton for six hours. By special grace his fine of 40s. was remitted as he was a poor man and also because he was to receive corporal punishment. In a second case John Brigges of Preston in Lancashire had been found begging at Lambton by William Bellasis, a JP, who arrested him as a loiterer pretending to have suffered great harm at Preston by reason of a fire. Brigges was brought to the bar of the court by the sheriff and admitted he was a sturdy beggar. He was sentenced to be branded with the letter R on his left arm and be returned to Preston. At the April sessions 7 men were charged with fishing in the Tees and the Grant beck for kipper salmon. There was also an information laid on the same subject. A total of 11 informations were laid at this sessions on charges including usury (2), purchase of wool (2), resale of livestock (1), conversion to tillage (1), and decay of bridges and roads (4). Except for the "decays", which were presented by JPs, the informant expected to be paid a proportion of the statutory fine, carefully calculated in his notification to the bench.

Bishop James, that assiduous agent of government policy, had died on 12 May 1617, leaving a vacancy to be filled by Richard Neile, bishop of Lincoln, who took up office on the following 9 October. Neile had strong political instincts, and by 1622 clerical JPs were strongly entrenched.[25] Although Bishop Neile was only intermittent in attendance Richard Hunt, dean of Durham, appeared regularly on the bench with John Cradock, the diocesan chancellor, the two archdeacons and assorted graduates such as Daniel Birkhead, STP, and Ferdinando Moorecroft, MA. The bishop's attorney-general, Robert Cooper, despite acting as prosecutor, also sat on the bench. As it happens, no indictments survive between October 1618 and October 1621, although somewhat confusingly the wrapper encasing the sessions from April 1616 to July 1618 describes itself as the index to the sessions rolls between 13 January 1619 and 12 January 1620. Equally nothing survives for 1623, except through subsequent reference.

By 1624 Robert Cooper had been replaced as attorney-general by William Smyth. At the January sessions nine men were charged with working a coal pit at Lumley in such a fashion that two men underground were in danger of suffocation. The case was removed from quarter sessions by *certiorari*. The severity of penalties for shooting game was brought home by an information that Thomas Johnson, late of Crook, had shot 13 woodcocks at Brancepeth "for which he should forfeit £130 at £10 an offence and incur 39 months' imprisonment without bail at 3 months for each offence". Two cases arose from Bedlington, which raises the question of how they were brought to the attention of the Durham quarter sessions, which apparently lacked both grand jurors and JPs associated with that area, although technically within the Chester ward.

At the sessions in April 1624 Isabel Carr, widow, was charged with the theft of a turkey cock worth 2s. 6d. and other poultry at Whitwell House by Kelloe. Another woman stole 2 fleeces direct from the wethers. More seriously, Marmaduke Robinson of Norton appeared in answer to a charge of evading arrest following the attempted execution of a summons issued by the Council of the North to appear at York on 30 September 1622. He had been duly arrested at Norton on 20 September but rescued by family and neighbours. The case had been brought to quarter sessions in January 1623 and referred to this later date.

While nothing of particular note occurred at the July sessions, in September there were two cases of blocked water-courses. Richard Hixon had allowed the Skerne to become choked with mud causing

---

[25] C. M. Fraser & K. Emsley, "The clerical Justices of the Peace in the North East, 1626–30", *AA* 5th ser. II (1974), 189–99.

his neighbours' lands to flood. He secured an acquittal by producing a royal pardon, issued to mark the accession of Charles I. Lindley Wrenn of Binchester had deliberately diverted a mill-race, thereby flooding the road between Binchester and Bishop Auckland.

In January 1625 Roger Akerman, a Durham labourer, was charged with obtaining 2 lbs of tobacco at Gateshead by deception and offering it for sale. There were three informations concerning engrossment of butter at Darlington. Another information accused Thomas Nicholson of Witton-le-Wear of lending money at usury, for which he should forfeit triple the amount loaned with imprisonment until he made fine and redemption at the king's will.

For reasons of length a halt has been made in this edition of the Durham quarter-sessions indictment rolls with the death of James I on 27 March 1625. These earliest rolls provide a vivid picture of life in the county with their brief glimpses for the mid-fifteenth and sixteenth centuries and especially for the first quarter of the seventeenth century. They indicate the common run of offences of theft and close breaking, poaching, tippling, breach of pound, assaults on bailiffs and the enforcement of laws against recusants. They also, by analysis, indicate firstly the role of the county landowners as upholders of law and order, even if in Durham the stiffening came from the bishop, the dean, the legal officers of the palatinate (chancellor and attorney-general) and the cathedral clergy, and secondly the role of the "yeoman" who served on the grand jury generation after generation.

EDITORIAL METHOD

The sessions have been arranged here in chronological order, and each given a number. This has involved considerable departures from the actual order of filing, which tends to be in reverse as each new session was impaled on the earlier one. In some rolls earlier "pagination" can be identified. This can illustrate vividly the present gaps in the surviving record. For instance, on Durham CRO, Q/S/I 6 (April 1616–?July 1618) the ten missing "pages" between 30 April and 1 October 1617 would have contained possibly further cases heard in April 1617 as well as the whole of the Midsummer sessions for that year. Each sessions normally has one heading indicating the date and magistrates present. In two special cases, 69A and 72A, however, although there is such a heading the matter contained on the roll obviously represents a continuation of business at the same sessions but with fewer magistrates on the bench. In a third case, 90A, there is no heading but a strong possibility that it is such a continuation.

Whereas the order for the indictment roll for 1555–57 is basically in reverse, the order for the indictment rolls 1 and 2 in Durham CRO can best be described as stuttering. The chronological order for Durham CRO, Q/S/I 1 is as follows: mm. 31–33, 28–30, 24–25, 29, 27, 23, 22, 21, 19, 16–18, 15, 12–13, 11, 10, 9, 8, 7, 6, 5, 4, 3, 1–2; with membrane 20 a numbered fragment only. Durham CRO, Q/S/I 2 runs: mm. 65–66, 60–64, 59, 57–58, 56, 55, 54, 50–53, 47–49, 43–46, 40–42, 36–39, 34–35, 32–33, 28–31, 25B 27, 24–25, 23, 22, 20–21, 18–19, 15–17, 13–14, 8, 11–12, 9–10, 1–7. The precise dates of sessions are indicated in the heading to each document.

The early indictment rolls rarely indicate subsequent pleadings. Room for such insertions starts to be left from about 1607, although not necessarily used. For a time around 1615 no such gaps were left, but a strip of parchment recording subsequent hearings was sewn across the record. These strips have now been given lettering, so that Indictment Roll 4, membrane 1, carries five such strips identified by the letters A–E, etc. As the stitching decayed the strips became detached, subsequently to be secured by pins. They have now been sewn firmly to the left edge of their respective membrane.

The vicissitudes of preservation are illustrated by the present locations of the rolls. The first three are now in London in the Public Record Office, Chancery Lane, one catalogued as Durham Proceedings, (Durham 19/11); one as a Durham chancery patent roll (Durham 3/75); and one enmeshed among the proceedings of the Durham court of pleas (Durham 13/265 mm. 7–8). Others may still await discovery in boxes of miscellanea such as Durham 17/1. Whereas these sessions rolls were sent to London as part of the palatinate records another group came into the hands of the Ecclesiastical Commissioners, to be duly returned to Durham in

1956. They are housed at present within the Durham University Library (Archives and Special Collections) at 5 The College. The remainder are among the records of Durham County Council in their archive department at County Hall.

The earliest roll is here presented in its entirety, except where there is virtual repetition, as in a murder indictment involving numerous assailants. Here [etc.] has been inserted. Thereafter the rolls are calendared, each presentment being separately numbered by session. The date in the sessions heading is given its regnal/pontifical year, which thereafter is tacitly converted to the Christian millenium.

The name, status, and place of residence of each party is recorded, but the county should be understood as county Durham except where otherwise stated. Once another county, however, is identified, subsequent locations are assumed to be in that same county until a new county is named. Place names are in their modern form except when unidentifiable, when they are printed in italics. There is a possibility of confusion where there has been subsequent differentiation in spelling, as with Morton and Murton, and Bellasis and Belasis. Where they identify a grand juror the known residence of these (where given by Surtees in his *History*) has been used as guide. The spelling used by A. Mawer in *The Place-Names of Northumberland and Durham* (1920) has been adopted, except where there has been a change in usage recorded on Ordnance Survey maps. Where the location is in Norhamshire, Islandshire or Bedlingtonshire, then part of the palatinate but since 1845 part of Northumberland, the county Durham reference is prefixed by an asterisk. This mark has also been applied to Crayke in Yorkshire. As a matter of interest the doublet form of Gateside for Gateshead has been preserved, as has been the varying use of Chester and Chester-le-Street. For conciseness the earlier Middleton Row has been adopted for Middleton One Row.

Where a statute has been quoted in full on its first occurrence it is subsequently indicated by the opening phrase, then [etc]. Charges and court procedure similarly are condensed, although on their first appearance they are recorded in some detail. For instance, the full formula for a traverse by a defendant is "having heard the information and having understood it he complained he was seriously vexed and protested that the information was insufficient in law and he should not be required to answer and pleaded not guilty of the charge and put himself on his country". This has been shortened to "demurred" and/or "pleaded not guilty". The fact that both prosecutor and defendant had formally to agree to trial by jury is indicated by the names of these parties. Where details from case to case are virtually identical this is indicated by [etc.]. From 1596 charges of assault were usually coupled with affray and have been rendered here as "attacked".

Deletions are indicated by diamond brackets. Insertions and marginalia are indicated by round brackets. Where from 1616 it has been possible to supply the territorial designation of grand jurors from the Order Books (Durham CRO, Q/S/O 1 *passim*) these have been added within square brackets. Blanks in the MS are indicated either by a hyphen or by [*blank*]. Dialect words have been printed in italics as have most field names. Spaces of more than 5 cms. between cases are noted.

1471–1473

Public Record Office, London: Durham 19/1/1 This roll of 4 membranes records sessions of the peace on 4 November and 2 December 1471; and on 13 January, 10 February, 20 April, 24 September, 6 October and 17 December 1472. In addition there are the gaol deliveries held on 13 January 1472 and 20 and 30 January 1473.

[*Cover*] Rotulus Pacis tempore Laurencij Booth Episcopi

1

[*m.1.*] Placita et presentaciones capta apud Dunelm' die Lune quarto die Novembris anno pontificatus domini Laurencij episcopi Dunelmensis quintodecimo [*1471*], coram Radulfo Nevill' nepote Radulfi comitis Westmerland, Henrico Gyllowe clerico, cancellario Dunelmensi, Thoma Moreslawe, Ricardo Baynbrig et sociis suis, custodibus pacis et justiciariis dicti domini Episcopi ad diverses felonias, transgressiones et alia malefacta in comitatu Dunelmensi audiendum et terminandum assignatis.

(Dunolm') Jurata xij videlicet Johannes Redmayn, Thomas Lawys, Willelmus Lawys, Jacobus Oldom, Robertus Cuthbert, Johannes Rakwod, Thomas Fery, Willelmus Hall de Chester, Johannes Gamylsey, Johannes Watson, Willelmus Watson, Willelmus Swalwels et Johannes Lawes, juratores,

1) Qui dicunt super sacramentum suum quod Thomas Smyth de villa Novi Castri super Tynam, baxtor, xx^{mo} die Marcij anno pontificatus domini Laurencij episcopi Dunelmensis xiij^{mo} [*1470*] suum lucrum singulare maius cupiens quam commune proficuum decius populi domini regis apud Nethirheworth in comitatu Dunolmensi vi et armis unam celdram frumenti ingressam emebat de Willelmo Huntlie pro xl s., altioris precij quam commune precium in foro Dunelm' pro x s., sciens illud esse lucrum viciosum, ad grave dampnum tocius communis populi ibidem commorati et contra pacem dicti domini episcopi.

2) Item dicunt quod Willelmus Palyser de Freresyde juxta Wolsyngham in comitatu Dunolmensi laborer' xx^{mo} die Octobris anno pontificatus domini Laurencij episcopi Dunelmensis xiiij^{mo} [*1470*] apud Weysyll in comitatu Dunolmensi duas juvencas precij octo solidorum de bonis et catallis Willelmi Ferrour adtunc et ibidem inventas felonice furatus fuit etc.

ponit se. Et nec respondit.

3) Item dicunt quod Henricus Stokhall de Newburgh infra libertatem de Tyndale husbondman et Johannes Stokhall alias Godelad de eadem infra libertatem predictam husbandman in vigilia sancti Michaelis archangeli anno pontificatus domini Laurencij episcopi Dunelmensis secundo [*1458*] apud Essh in comitatu Dunolmensi unam equam nigri coloris precij xx s. de bonis et catallis Roberti Emreson nuper de Essh et adtunc et ibidem inventam felonice furati

fuerunt etc. Et quod Johannes Palasere de Caldrowley in comitatu Dunolmensi husbondman, sciens dictos Henricum et Johannem Stokehall alias Godelad feloniam predictam sic fecisse, dictis die et anno super moram juxta Aleynesford eos felonice receptavit et confortavit.

4) Item dicunt quod Thomas Dixson de Wolsyngham in comitatu Dunelmensi laborer, alias dictus Thomas Nixson de Wolsyngham in comitatu Dunolmensi vagabund, die Veneris sub nocte proximo ante festum Corporis Christi anno pontificatus domini Laurencij episcopi Dunolmensis xiiij° [7 June 1471] apud Spirleswode in comitatu Dunelmensi tres equas cum uno pullo precij xlvj s. viij d. de bonis et catallis Johannis Myres de Eglyston adtunc et ibidem inventas felonice furatus fuit etc.

5) Item dicunt quod Johannes Clogh de Dunelm' in comitatu Dunelmensi shomaker die Dominica xxvij^{mo} die Octobris anno pontificatus domini Laurencij episcopi Dunelmensis xv^{mo} [1471] ad horam decimam sub nocte vi et armis insultum fecit in Willelmum Mayson de Dunelm' fletcher et ipsum Willelmum adtunc et ibidem cum uno gestro precij quatuor denariorum in ventre sub latere sinistro felonice percussit et dedit ei plagam mortalem de qua plage idem Willelmus instanter obiit.

6) Item dicunt quod Robertus Laton de Brawath in comitatu Eboracensi armiger, Isabella Laton uxor eius de eadem in eodem comitatu husweyf, et Willelmus Wode de Wealworth in comitatu Dunelmensi husbondman aggregati sibi aliis quampluribus malefactoribus et pacis domini episcopi perturbatoribus die Veneris xxv^{to} die Octobris anno pontificatus domini Laurencij episcopi Dunelmensis xv [1471] apud Walworth predictam quatuor boves Johannis Robynson de Denton precij liij s. iiij d. adtunc et ibidem inventos vi et armis ac modo guerrino arraiati ceperunt et abduxerunt et usque Brawath predictam in comitatu Eboracensi fugaverunt et ibidem detinuerunt et sic regiam libertatem Dunelmensem fregerunt in magnum contemptum domini episcopi ac grave dampnum ipsius Johannis Robynson et contra pacem dicti domini episcopi etc.

2

Placita et presentaciones capta apud Dunelm' die Lune secundo die Decembris anno pontificatus domini Laurencij episcopi Dunelmensis quintodecimo [1471] coram Henrico Gyllowe clerico, cancellario Dunelmensi, Willelmo Raket, Ricardo Raket et sociis suis, custodibus pacis et justis [sic] dicti domini episcopi ad diverses felonias transgressiones et alia malefacta in comitatu Dunelmensi audiendum et terminandum assignatis.

(Dunelm') Jurata xij videlicet Johannes Fossour, Galfridus Boutfloure, Johannes Wylly, Nicholas Crosyer, Johannes Hunter de Aukelande sancte Elene, Willelmus Tebson, Nicholas Ferrour, Willelmus

Plomer, Johannes Fenwyk, Johannes Hewetson, Willelmus Swalwell, Johannes Walker de Middrig et Benjamin Worsley juratores,

1) Qui dicunt super sacramentum suum quod Willelmus Bolton nuper de Ile in comitatu Dunelmensi yoman, Thomas Grundy nuper de Cokyn in eadem comitatu yoman, Willelmus Shotton de Estraynton in eodem comitatu husbondman, Robertus Shotton de eadem in eodem comitatu husbondman, Johannes Grange de Hetton in the Hole in eodem comitatu husbondman et Johannes Bryce de eadem in eodem comitatu husbondman die Sabbati ultimo die Novembris anno pontificatus domini Laurencij episcopi Dunelmensis quintodecimo [1471] domum Matilde Breten apud Hawthorne in comitatu predicto felonice fregerunt et combusserunt et ipsam Matildam adtunc et ibidem felonice rapuerunt et abduxerunt contra pacem dicti domini episcopi.

2) Item dicunt quod Thomas Stevenson de Dunelm' in comitatu Dunelmensi flesshewer, Johannes Stevenson de Morehouse in eodem comitatu husbondman, Willelmus Stevenson de Evenwod in eodem comitatu husbondman et Radulfus Stevenson de eadem in eodem comitatu husbondman, laici homines non habentes nec aliquis eorum habens terras seu tenementa ad valenciam quadraginta solidorum per annum ultra reprisam, tenent leporarios et venati fuerunt et quilibet eorum venatus fuit et die Mercurij quinto die Novembris anno pontificatus domini Laurencij episcopi Dunelmensis quintodecimo [1471] in nive lepores investigaverunt et in campo de Evenwod quinque lepores interfecerunt contra formam statuti in huiusmodi casu proviso etc.

3) Item dicunt quod Willelmus Marshall de Cokerton in comitatu Dunolmensi husbondman et Johannes Marshall de eadem in eodem comitatu husbondman die Lune xxmo die Novembris anno pontificatus domini Laurencij episcopi Dunelmensis xvmo [1471] apud Derlyngton in foro ibidem quam ceteris festivitatibus emebant quatuor quarteria frumenti, ij quarteria siliginis et tria quarteria avene sic quolibet die mercati hoc contumand' et ingrossaverunt causa sui singularis lucri, pauperes opprimentes et diciores decipientes lucrum scienter viciosum, et dicta grana postea altioris precij redimerunt maius suum singularem lucrum affectantes quam commune proficuum sive lucrum communis populi, in magnum gravamen derogacionem et dispendium tocius communis populi domini regis ac contra formam statuti in huiusmodi casu editi etc.

4) Item dicunt quod Nicholas Roundthwaye de Dunelm' in comitatu Dunelmensi dyer primo die Decembris anno pontificatus domini Laurencij episcopi Dunelmensis xv [1471] apud Dunelm' vi et armis videlicet baculis et cultellis in Willelmum Smyth ballivum dicti domini episcopi juratum et cognitum insultum fecit et recussit ubi dictus Willelmus dictis die et anno et loco virtute cuiusdem warranti eiusdem domini episcopi eidem Willelmo directi predictum Nicholam secundum legem et consuetudinem regni Anglie ac regie

libertatis Dunelmensis arestare voluisset, in magnum contemptum dicti domini episcopi et contra pacem etc.

5) Item dicunt quod Thomas Shatour de Dunelm' in comitatu Dunelmensi waller furtive equitat et vigilat sub nocte jacens in incidiis in altis viis et locis furtive et in arte sua propria non laborat nec nullum magistrum habet de quo victum aut vestitum haberet nec ullam culturam circa quam se laborare aut occupare poterit et nullis mercandis utitur, et die Martis xxviiij^{mo} die Novembris anno pontificatus domini episcopi xv^{mo} [1471] ad horam ix^{em} sub nocte jacuit in incidiis apud Sunderland Brigges expectans adventum hominum ibidem venientum et pertranseuntum, et cotidie et noctanter equitat et felonice et ociose vagat contra formam statuti in huiusmodi casu proviso etc.

6) Item dicunt quod Thomas Saweter de Dunelm' in comitatu Dunelmensi capellanus, non promotus ad beneficium valoris x li. per annum, tenet leporarios et venatus fuit et lepores interfecit hoc continuando contra formam statuti in huiusmodi casu proviso etc.

3

Placita et presentaciones capta apud Dunelm' die Lune xiij^{mo} die Januarij anno pontificatus domini Laurencij episcopi Dunelmensis xv [1472] coram Radulfo Nevill armigero, Thoma Moreslawe, Johanne Catrik et sociis suis, custodibus pacis et justiciariis dicti domini episcopi ad diverses felonias, transgressiones et alia malefacta in comitatu Dunelmensi audiendum et determinandum assignatis.

(Dunelm') Jurata xij, videlicet Johannes Redmayn, Jacobus Typpyng, Jacobus Oldum, Willelmus Blithman, Johannes Torkyngton, Nicholas Crosyer, Thomas Barton, Johannes Rakwod, Thomas Fery, Johannes Hewetson, Ricardus More, Ricardus Moderby, Thomas Goldsmyth, juratores,

1) Qui dicunt super sacramentum suum quod Johannes Richardson nuper serviens Willelmi Marley de Wysyll in comitatu Dunolmensi laborer xx die Novembris anno pontificatus domini Laurencij episcopi Dunelmensis xv^{mo} [1471] apud Colynwod in comitatu Dunelmensi unum equum badij coloris de bonis et catallis Petri Colynwod precij xiij s. iiij d. ad tunc et ibidem inventum felonice furatus fuit etc.

2) Item dicunt quod predictus Johannes Rychardson de Woysyll in comitatu Dunelmensi laborer viij^{mo} die Januarij anno pontificatus domini Laurencij episcopi Dunelmensis xij^{mo} [1469] apud Shirburn juxta Dunelm' duas equas cum duobus pullis de bonis et catallis Johannis Lilford clerici precij xxvj s. viij d. adtunc et ibidem inventas felonice furatus fuit etc.

3) Item dicunt super sacramentum suum quod Johanna Richardson nuper de Bysshopton in comitatu Dunelmensi laborer ultimo die Decembris anno pontificatus domini Laurencij episcopi Dunelmensis xv^{mo} [1471] quindecim solidos in pecunia numerata, unum annulum

de argento et deaurato precij viginti denariorum, i kertyllum precij trium solidorum de bonis et catallis Johannis Henryson apud Bysshopton infra comitatu Dunelmensi inventos felonice furata fuit etc.

4) Item dicunt quod Edwardus Huntershels de Colleyrawe juxta Cokfeld in comitatu Dunolmensi laborer xx^{mo} die Novembris anno pontificatus domini Laurencij episcopi Dunelmensis quintodecimo [1471] apud Fylerawe juxta Cokfeld in comitatu predicto domum Christoferi Warde adtunc et ibidem vi et armis fregit et Isabellam uxorem dicti Christoferi insultum fecit et ipsam verberavit et male tractavit contra pacem dicti domini episcopi etc.

n.1d.] 5) Item dicunt quod [Adamarus Harperley de Brafferton] in comitatu Dunolmensi laborer x^{mo} die Septembris anno pontificatus domini Laurencij episcopi Dunelmensis quartodecimo [1471] unum equum coloris grey precij decem solidorum de bonis et catallis Johannis [...] apud Aclyff in comitatu Dunelmensi inventum felonice furatus fuit, [et ...] de Brafferton in comitatu Dunolmensi laborer sciens dictum Adamarum Harperley feloniam predictam fecisset predictum Adamarum dictis die et anno apud Brafferton predictam felonice confortavit et receptavit contra pacem dicti domini episcopi etc.

6) Item dicunt quod Johannes Henrison de Aclyff in comitatu Dunelmensi smyth et Ricardus Dyken de Hoghton in eodem comitatu husbondman xvj die mensis Augusti anno pontificatus domini Laurencij episcopi Dunelmensis xiiij° [1471] apud Midelham in comitatu Dunelmensi vi et armis videlicet arcubus sagittis et aliis armis defensivis parcum de Midelham fregerunt et viij equos diversis coloribus de bonis et catallis Laurencij Dunelmensis episcopi precij inter se xx li. adtunc et ibidem inventos felonice furati fuerunt etc.

7) Item dicunt quod Arundellus Jakson nuper de Whitle in comitatu Dunelmensi husbondman (suspend'), Johannes Blakehede nuper de Helmparke in eodem comitatu yoman (suspend'), Willelmus Stevenson nuper de Romond[by] lonyng in eodem comitatu husbondman (suspend'), Johannes Sawyer nuper de Bycheburn in eodem comitatu yoman (suspend'), Robertus Hogge nuper de Wotton in Werdale in eodem comitatu laborer die Jovis quarto die Septembris anno pontificatus domini Laurencij episcopi Dunelmensis quartodecimo [1471] sex boves precij inter se quattuor librarum de bonis et catallis Willelmi Johnson apud Hunwayk adtunc et ibidem inventos felonice furati fuerunt etc.

8) Item dicunt quod Arundellus Jakson nuper de Whitle in comitatu Dunelmensi husbondman, Johannes Blakeheued de Helmparke in eodem comitatu yoman, Willelmus Stevenson nuper de Romondby lonyng in eodem comitatu husbondman, Johannes Sawyer nuper de Bychburn in eodem comitatu yoman et Robertus Hogge nuper de Wotton in Werdall in eodem comitatu laborer xx^{mo} die Septembris anno pontificatus domini Laurencij episcopi Dunelmensis xiiij° [1471] unam equam cum i pullo precij inter se xiij s. iiij d. de bonis

et catallis Willelmi Dekeson apud Bycheburn adtunc et ibidem inventa felonice furati fuerunt etc.

9) Item dicunt quod Robertus Birden de Dunelm' in comitatu Dunelmensi husbondman xxiiij^to die Augusti anno pontificatus domini Laurencij episcopi Dunelmensis x^o [1467] vi et armis scilicet gestris et cultellis domum Sibille Blaykeston apud Dunolm' fregit et unam cosur' ipsius Sibille adtunc et ibidem inventam precij decem librarum cepit et asportavit contra pacem dicti domini episcopi etc.

10) Item dicunt quod Thomas Preston nuper de Aukeland sancte Elene in comitatu Dunelmensi gentylman apud Dunelm' die Martis xvij die Decembris anno pontificatus domini Laurencij episcopi Dunelmensis xv^mo [1471] unam murram precij xx s. de bonis et catallis Johannnis Palman adtunc et ibidem inventam felonice furatus fuit etc.

4

[m.2]   Deliberacio Gaole Castri Dunelmensis facta coram Radulfo Neville armigero, Thoma Moreslawe et Ricardo Baynbrig justiciariis domini episcopi Dunelmensis de prisonibus in eadem existentibus deliberandum assignatis apud Dunelm' die Lune xiij die Januarij anno pontificatus domini Laurencij episcopi Dunelmensis xv [1472].

1) Simon Wat de Tofthill in comitatu Dunelmensi potter alias captus per indictamentum factum coram justiciariis domini episcopi ad assisas in comitatu Dunelmensi conservandas assignatis de eo quod ipse iiij^to die Septembris anno pontificatus domini Laurencij episcopi Dunelmensis xiiij^mo [1471] apud Tofthill in comitatu Dunelmensi duas oves matricas precij duorum solidorum de bonis et catallis Johannis Danyell adtunc et ibidem inventas felonice furatus fuit, modo venit hic in custodia vicecomitis ductus. Et viso indictamento predicto per justiciarios hic idem Simon instanter allocutus qualiter de premissis se acquietare velit dicit quod ipse in nullo est inde colpabilis et inde de bono et malo ponit se super patriam etc. Ideo fiat inde jurata etc. Et super hoc jurata venit qui de consensu predicti Simonis electi triati et jurati ad veritatem in premissis dicendam; qui dicunt super sacramentum suum quod predictus Simon in nullo est culpabilis de felonia predicta pro domino episcopo superius sibi imposita nec unquam occacionis felonie illius aliqualiter se retraxit. Ideo ipse eat inde quietus etc.

2) Johannes Clemet de Ravensworth in comitatu Eboracensi trumper alias captus per indictamentum factum coram justiciariis domini ad assisas in comitatu Dunelmensi conservandas assignatis de eo quod ipse xx die Novembris anno pontificatus domini Laurencij episcopi Dunelmensis xv^mo [1471] apud Whessowe predictam i scotyon argentum precij iiij s. de bonis et catallis Johannis Trumper magistris sui adtunc et ibidem inventum felonice furatus fuit etc. Modo venit hic in custodia vicecomitis ductus, et viso indictamento predicto per justiciarios hic idem Johannes Clemet instanter allocutus qualiter de premissis se acquietare velit dicit quod ipse in nullo est inde

culpabilis et inde de bono et malo ponit se super patriam etc. Ideo fiat inde juratores etc. Et super hoc juratores venerunt qui de consensu predicti Johannis Clemet electi triati et jurati ad veritatem in premissis dicendam; qui dicunt super sacramentum suum quod predictus Johannes Clemet est culpabilis de felonia predicta pro domino episcopo sibi superius imposita. Ideo consideratur quod ipse suspendatur etc.

S[uspend'] Catalla eius nulla etc.

3) Thomas Preston nuper de Aukeland sancte Elene in comitatu Dunelmensi gentylman alias captus per indictamentum factum coram justiciariis domini episcopi ad pacem in comitatu Dunelmensi conservandam assignatis de eo quod ipse apud Dunelm' die Martis xvij die Decembris anno pontificatus domini Laurencij episcopi Dunelmensis xv^mo [1471] unam murram precij xx s. de bonis et catallis Johannis Palman adtunc et ibidem inventam felonice furatus fuit etc. Modo venit hic in custodia vicecomitis ductus et viso indictamento predicto [etc.] Thomas [etc.] ipse in nullo est inde culpabilis [etc.]. Qui dicunt super sacramentum suum quod predictus Thomas est culpabilis de felonia predicta pro domino episcopo sibi superius imposita. Ideo consideratur quod ipse suspendatur etc.

S[uspend'] Catalla eius nulla etc.

4) Johannes Richardson de Weysil in comitatu Dunelmensi laborer alias captus per indictamentum factum coram justiciariis domini episcopi ad pacem in comitatu Dunelmensi conservandam assignatis de eo quod ipse xx^mo die Novembris anno pontificatus domini Laurencij episcopi Dunelmensis xv^mo [1471] apud Colynwod in comitatu Dunelmensi unum equum badij coloris de bonis et catallis Petri Colynwod precij xiij s. iiij d. adtunc et ibidem inventum felonice furatus fuit; et de eo quod ipse octavo die Januarij anno pontificatus domini Laurencij episcopi Dunelmensis duodecimo [1469] apud Shirbourne in comitatu Dunelmensi juxta Dunelm' duas equas cum duobus pullis de bonis et catallis Johannis Lylford clerici precij xxvj s. viij d. adtunc et ibidem inventas felonice furatus fuit etc. Modo venit hic in custodia vicecomitis ductus et visis indictamentis predictis per justiciarios hic idem Johannes Richardson instanter allocutus qualiter de premissis se acquietare velit dicit quod ipse in nullo est inde culpabilis et inde de bono et malo ponit se super patriam etc. [etc.]. Qui dicunt super sacramentum suum quod predictus Johannes Richardson est culpabilis de feloniis predictis pro domino episcopo sibi superius impositis. Ideo consideratur quod ipse suspendatur etc.

S[uspend'] Catalla eius nulla etc.

5) Johanna Richardson nuper de Bysshopton in comitatu Dunelmensi laborar alias capta per indictamentum factum coram justiciariis domini episcopi ad pacem in comitatu Dunelmensi conservandam assignatis de eo quod ipsa ultimo die Decembris anno pontificatus domini Laurencij episcopi Dunelmensis xv [1471] quindecim solidos

in pecunia numerata, unum annulum argenteum et deauratum precij viginti denariorum, i kirtillam precij trium solidorum de bonis et catallis Johannis Henryson apud Bisshopton in comitatu Dunelmensi inventos felonice furata fuit etc. Modo venit hic [*etc.*] ipse in nulla est inde culpabilis [*etc.*]. Qui dicunt super sacramentum suum quod predicta Johanna est culpabilis de felonia predicta [*etc.*]. Ideo consideratur quod ipsa suspenderatur, cum executione judicij predicti respectuata quousque purificetur eo quod impregnata est. Et post purificacionem consideratur quod ipsa habeat execucionem judicij predicti scilicet suspendatur etc. Catalla eius nulla etc.

Cul[pabilis] Catalla nulla

5

Placita et presentaciones capta apud Dunelmum die Lune x^mo die Februarii anno pontificatus domini Laurencij episcopi Dunelmensis xv^mo [*1472*] coram Radulfo Nevylle armigero, Thoma Moreslaw, Ricardo Baynbrig et sociis suis custodibus pacis et justiciariis dicti domini episcopi ad diverses felonias transgressiones et alia malefacta in comitatu Dunelmensi audiendum et terminandum assignatis.

(Dunelm') Jurata xij videlicet Jacobus Tippyng, Willelmus Blythman, Willelmus Elstob, Johannes Walker de Middrige, Thomas Emreson, Thomas Folanceby, Johannes Rakwod, Ricardus Moderby, Johannes Fenwyk, Thomas Goldsmyth, Willelmus Wadley, Johannes Hewetson et Willelmus Swalwels, juratores,

1) Qui dicunt super sacramentum suum quod Robertus Richardson nuper de Derlyngton in comitatu Dunolmensi harpour in festo sancti Andrea anno pontificatus domini Laurencij episcopi Dunelmensis quintodecimo [*30 November 1471*] apud Haughton in comitatu predicto vi et armis videlicet baculis et cultellis et ex malicia precogitata jacuit in incidiis, expectans adventum Willelmi Spenser ad ipsum Willelmum adtunc et ibidem interficiendum et in ipsum Willelmum adtunc et ibidem insultum fecit et ipsum verberavit, vulneravit et maletractavit ita quod de vita eius desperabatur, contra pacem dicti domini episcopi etc.

6

[*m.2d.*] Placita et presentaciones capta apud Dunelm' die Lune xx die Aprilis anno pontificatus domini Laurencij episcopi Dunelmensis xv [*1472*] coram Henrico Gyllow clerico, cancellario Dunelmensi, Ricardo Baynbrig, Willelmo Raket et sociis suis, custodibus pacis et justiciariis dicti domini episcopi ad diverses felonias transgressiones et alia malefacta in comitatu Dunelmensi audiendum et terminandum assignatis.

(Dunelm') Jurata xij videlicet Jacobus Typpyng, Johannes Redmayn, Beniamin Worsley, Willelmus Whelden senior, Thomas Warrewyk, Thomas Hogeson, Willelmus Smyth de Whitehall, Thomas Fery, Thomas Hedlam, Willelmus Fossour, Johannes Fenwyk, Willelmus

Layng senior, Robertus Swalwell, juratores,

1) Qui dicunt super sacramentum suum quod Johannes Whaplowe nuper de Wolsingham in comitatu Dunelmensi laborer xx die Aprilis anno pontificatus domini Laurencij episcopi Dunelmensis terciodecimo [1470] unam equam coloris badij cum uno pullo precij xiij s. iiij d. de bonis et catallis Willelmi Hedryngton apud Whessowe in comitatu Dunelmensi inventam felonice furatus fuit; et quod Johannes Blakhede nuper de Holmparke in comitatu Dunelmensi yoman sciens predictus Johannes Whaplowe feloniam predictam in forma predicta fecisse predictum Johannem Whaplowe die et anno supradictis apud Helmparke in comitatu Dunelmensi felonice receptavit et confortavit contra pacem dicti domini episcopi etc.

2) Item dicunt quod Rogerus Rottour de Midelton in comitatu Sadberge yoman, Willelmus Rottour de eadem in eodem comitatu yoman et Christoforus Rottour de eadem in eodem comitatu yoman die Dominica xix die Aprilis anno pontificatus domini Laurencij episcopi Dunelmensis xv [1472] domum Ricardi Emreson apud parcum de Stanhop' in comitatu Dunelmensi fregerunt et unum leporarium ipsius Ricardi adtunc et ibidem inventum ceperunt et abduxerunt etc.

3) Item dicunt quod Johannes Sawr de Bycheburn in comitatu Dunelmensi yoman xxij die Julij anno pontificatus domini Laurencij episcopi Dunelmensis xiij [1470] apud Hopeland in comitatu predicto duas oves matrices precij trium solidorum de bonis et catallis Thome Ramshawe adtunc et ibidem inventas felonice furatus fuit etc.

4) Item dicunt quod dictus Johannes Sawr xxvj die Maij anno terciodecimo supradicto [1470] apud Retford in comitatu Dunelmensi unum multonem vocatum a rygald precij xvj d. adtunc et ibidem inventum de bonis et catallis Rollandi Rychardson felonice furatus fuit etc.

5) Item dicunt quod Henricus Vasy de Neweland in comitatu Dunelmensi gentylman, Willelmus Merlay de Weysill in eodem comitatu junior gentylman, Robertus Vasy de Newland in eodem comitatu gentylman, Johannes Vasy de Newland in eodem comitatu gentylman, Robertus Merley de Landewe in eodem comitatu gentylman, Willelmus Merley de Wysew in eodem comitatu yoman, Willelmus Merley de Harop in eodem comitatu yoman, Johannes Merley de parco de Wolsyngham in eodem comitatu yoman, Jacobus Herper nuper de Neweland in eodem comitatu yoman, Johannes Herper nuper de Wolsyngham in eodem comitatu laborer, Radulfus Vasy de Fawreleys in eodem comitatu yoman, Nicholas Merle de parco de Wolsyngham in eodem comitatu yoman, Robertus Chepman de Frosterley in eodem comitatu yoman, Willelmus Ferrour de Weysill in eodem comitatu husbondman, [...]asleys de Ladle in eodem comitatu yoman, et Thomas Merle de parco de Wolsyngham in eodem comitatu yoman die Dominica quintodecimo die Marcij anno pontificatus domini Laurencij episcopi Dunelmensis xv [1472]

apud Wolsyngham in eodem comitatu aggregatis illis quampluribus malefactoribus et pacis domini regis perturbat[oribus modo guerrino araiatis] vi et armis videlicet gladiis baculis fustibus arcubus et sagittis et aliis ad ar[... Ricardum Coke] ballivum Johannis Athirton armigeri, vicecomitis Dunelmensis, apud Wolsingham predictum insultum fecerunt [...]. Et ubi predictus Ricardus Coke predictis die et anno apud Wolsyngham predictum quoddam [breve ...] vicecomiti directum adtunc et ibidem ut ballivus et deputatus ipsius vicecomitis in hac parte nomine [secundum con]suetudinem regni Anglie et regie libertatis Dunelmensis exequi voluisset predicti Henricus [etc., etc.] predictum [Ricardum Co]ke apud Wolsyngham execucionem warranti predicti propter periculum mortis sue exequi non potuit, in magnum contemptum dicti domini episcopi et contra pacem etc.

6) Item dicunt quod Ricardus Whyte de Neufeld (ponit se quietus nec respondit) in comitatu Dunelmensi yoman, Jacobus Trotter (ponit se quietus nec respondit) de Byres juxta Brauncepath in eodem comitatu yoman, Robertus Merley de Stokley in eodem comitatu yoman, Willelmus Hakforth (mortuus) de Sunderland juxta Dunelm' in eodem comitatu junior yoman, et Willelmus Dalton de eadem in eodem comitatu yoman die Sabbati xviij die Aprilis anno pontificatus domini Laurencij episcopi Dunelmensis xv [1472] ex malicia precogitata ac modo guerrino arraiati vi et armis jacuerunt in incidiis in Sadlergate in Dunelm' expectantes adventum Roberti Batmanson de Langley ad ipsum Robertum adtunc et ibidem felonice interficiendum et murdrandum et in ipsum Robertum Batmanson adtunc et ibidem insultum fecerunt. Et quod predictus Ricardus Whyte adtunc et ibidem cum quodam baculo vocato a karlilaxe precij octo denariorum predictum Robertum Batmanson in pectore supra mamillam suam dexteram felonice percussit et dedit ei plagam mortalem de qua plaga idem Robertus Batmanson instanter obiit. Et quod predictus Jacobus adtunc et ibidem cum quodam baculo vocato bill' precij sex denariorum predictum Robertum Batmanson super posteriorem partem capitis sui felonice percussit et dedit ei plagam mortalem de qua plaga idem Robertus Batmanson instanter obiisset si predictus Ricardus Whyte eundem Robertum Batmanson non percussisset. Et quod predictus Robertus Merley cum quodam baculo vocato a axe precij quatuor denariorum predictum Robertum Batmanson adtunc et ibidem in dorso felonice percussit [etc.]. Et quod predictus Willelmus Hackforth adtunc et ibidem cum quodam baculo vocato a Walsshbill precij duodecim denariorum predictum Robertum Batmanson super anteriorem partem capitis sui felonice percussit [etc.]. Et quod predictus Willelmus Dalton cum quodam baculo vocato bill' precij decem denariorum dictum Robertum Batmanson super sinistram partem capitis sui felonice percussit [etc.]. etc.

7) Item dicunt super sacramentum suum quod Johannes Redhed de Wotton in comitatu Dunelmensi yoman, Willelmus Wylson de Newelandsyd in eodem comitatu yoman, Thomas Wylson de eadem

in eodem comitatu yoman, Petrus Wylson de eadem in eodem comitatu yoman et Robertus Wylson nuper de eadem in eodem comitatu yoman aggregatis illis quampluribus malefactoribus et pacis dicti domini episcopi perturbatoribus modo guerrino araiati vi et armis apud Stanehope in comitatu Dunelmensi xiij° die Decembris anno pontificatus domini Laurencij episcopi Dunelmensis xv^{mo} [1471] felonice jacuerunt in incidiis ad interficiendum Johannem Westwod et in eundem Johannem Westwod adtunc et ibidem insultum fecerunt et dederunt ei duas plagas mortales in capite et alias quamplurimas plagas in corpore de quibus plagis idem Johannes Westwod interiit et sic eum felonice interfecerunt.

(contra nec respond')

8) Item dicunt super sacramentum suum quod Laurencius Herper nuper de Stanhop in comitatu Dunelmensi yoman, Willelmus Shortrede de eadem in eodem comitatu laborer, Roulandus Shortrede de eadem in eodem comitatu laborer, Ricardus Shortrede de eadem [etc.] laborer, Johannes Gybson nuper [etc.] laborer, Willelmus Robynson nuper [etc.] laborer, Robertus Shortrede nuper [etc.] laborer, Johannes Westwod nuper [etc.] laborer die Martis vij die Januarij anno pontificatus domini Laurencij episcopi Dunelmensis xv° [1471] apud parcum de Stanhope in comitatu Dunelmensi vi et armis in Ricardum Warde insultum fecerunt, et predictus Willelmus Shortrede adtunc et ibidem cum quodam baculo vocato a karlilaxe precij duodecim denariorum predictum Ricardum Warde super capud felonice percussit unde idem Ricardus Warde obiit; et predictus Laurencius Harper cum quodam baculo vocato a karlilaxe precij viginti denariorum predictum Ricardum Warde super capud felonice percussit et dedit ei plagam mortalem de quo plaga predictus Ricardus Warde obiisset si per predictum Willelmum Shortrede non percussus fuerit; et predictus Rollandus Shortrede adtunc et ibidem cum quodam baculo vocato a karlilaxe precij sex denariorum predictum Ricardum Warde super caput felonice percussit et dedit ei plagam mortalem de qua plaga idem Ricardus interiisset si per predictum Willelmum Shortrede percussus non fuisset; et predictus Ricardus Shortreade adtunc et ibidem cum una sagitta vocata a brode arewe precij duorum denariorum predictum Ricardum Warde in ventrem felonice percussit et dedit ei plagam mortalem de qua plaga idem Ricardus Warde obiisset si per predictum Willelmum Shortrede non percussus fuisset; et predictus Johannes Gybson adtunc et ibidem cum quodam baculo vocato a spere staff precij quatuor denariorum predictum Ricardum Warde in pectorem felonice percussit et dedit ei plagam mortalem de qua [etc.]; et predictus Willelmus Robynson adtunc et ibidem cum quodam baculo vocato a clubstaff precij quatuor denariorum predictum Ricardum Warde super capud felonice percussit [etc.]; et predictus Robertus Shortrede adtunc et ibidem cum quodam gladio precij octo denariorum predictum Ricardum Warde in ventrem felonice percussit [etc.]; et

predictus Johannes Westwod adtunc et ibidem cum quodam baculo
vocato a pykestaff precij sex denariorum predictum Ricardum Warde
super capud felonice percussit [*etc.*]; et quod Margareta Gybson nuper
de Stanhope in comitatu Dunelmensi vidua et Agnes Gybson de
eadem in eodem comitatu servaunt dictis die et anno et loco adtunc
et ibidem fuerunt abbettantes, supportantes et auxiliantes predictos
Willelmum Laurencium Roulandum Ricardum Johannem Willelmum
Robertum et Johannem felonias predictas fecisse etc.
contra nec respond'

7

[*m.3*]   Placita et presentaciones capta apud Aukeland Episcopi die Jovis
xxiiij^to die Septembris anno pontificatus domini Laurencij episcopi
xv [*1472*] coram Henrico Gyllowe clerico, cancellario Dunelmensi,
Thoma Moreslawe, Ricardo Baynbrig' et sociis suis, custodibus pacis
et justiciarij domini episcopi ad diversas felonias, transgressiones et
alia malefacta in comitatu Dunelmensi audiendum et terminandum
assignatis etc.
Jurata xv videlicet Johannes Redmayn, Jacobus Tippyng, Thomas
Folanceby, Willelmus Nodder, Thomas Buk, Johannes Rakwod,
Johannes Walker de Midrig', Willelmus Blythman, Johannes
Huetson, Thomas Wyndleston, Jacobus Oldum, Johannes Dale,
Willelmus Walker, Willelmus Claxton et Biniamin Worsley juratores,

1) Qui dicunt super sacramentum suum quod Thomas Robynson
nuper de Swalwals in comitatu Dunelmensi yoman (ponit se quietus
nec respondit), Roulandus Robynson nuper de Swalwals in eodem
comitatu yoman (ponit se quietus nec respondit) et Johannes
Robynson nuper de Urpath in eodem comitatu husbondman (ponit
se quietus nec respondit) x die Marcij anno pontificatus domini
Laurencij episcopi Dunelmensis xv [*1472*] tres vaccas precij xxvj s.
viij d. et sex boviculos precij xl s. de bonis et catallis Willelmi Rethern
apud Wardon in comitatu Dunelmensi inventos felonice furati
fuerunt: et quod Willelmus Rawe nuper de Colyerley in comitatu
Dunelmensi husbondman et Willelmus Rawe nuper de eadem in
eodem comitatu junior laborer scientes predictos Thomam
Roulandum et Johannem feloniam predictam in forma predicta
fecisse, predictos Thomam Roulandum et Johannem die et anno
predictis apud Colyerley predictam felonice receptaverunt et
confortaverunt etc.

2) Item dicunt super sacramentum suum quod Johannes Robynson
nuper de Cokerton in comitatu Dunelmensi junior husbondman
xxviij die Augusti anno pontificatus domini Laurencij episcopi
Dunelmensis xv [*1472*] apud Cokerton predictam in Johannem
Neweham et Willelmum Neweham insultum fecit et ipsos Johannem
Newham et Willelmum Neweham adtunc et ibidem verberavit et
vulneravit et male tractavit contra pacem dicti domini episcopi etc.

3) Item dicunt super sacramentum suum quod Johannes Neweham

nuper de Cokerton in comitatu Dunelmensi husbondman et
Willelmus Newham nuper de eadem in eodem comitatu
husbondman octavo die Augusti anno pontificatus domini Laurencij
episcopi Dunelmensis xv [1472] apud Cokerton predictam in
Johannem Robynson insultum fecerunt et ipsum Johannem
Robynson adtunc et ibidem verberaverunt, vulneraverunt et male
tractaverunt contra pacem dicti domini episcopi etc.

4) Item dicunt super sacramentum suum quod Willelmus Milner de
Aclyff in comitatu Dunelmensi husbondman, Johannes Hurworth de
eadem in eodem comitatu husbondman et Ricardus Hurworth nuper
de eadem in eodem comitatu husbondman xx die Julij anno
pontificatus domini Laurencij episcopi Dunelmensis xv [1472] apud
Aclyff in comitatu predicto in Adamarum Tode, Jacobum Westwod et
Johannem Atkynson alias dictum Johannem Kerber insultum
fecerunt et ipsos Adamarum, Jacobum et Johannem Atkynson adtunc
et ibidem verberaverunt, vulneraverunt et male tractaverunt, contra
pacem dicti domini episcopi etc.

5) Item dicunt super sacramentum suum quod Adamarus Tode nuper
de Derlyngton in comitatu Dunelmensi husbondman, Jacobus
Westwod de eadem in eodem comitatu husbondman et Johannes
Atkynson alias dictus Johannes Kerber de eadem in eodem comitatu
husbondman xx die Julij anno pontificatus domini Laurencij episcopi
Dunelmensis xv [1472] apud Aclyff in comitatu predicto in
Willelmum Mylner, Johannem Hurworth et Ricardum Hurworth
insultum fecerunt et ipsos Willelmum, Johannem Hurworth et
Ricardum adtunc et ibidem verberaverunt, vulneraverunt et male
tractaverunt contra pacem dicti domini episcopi etc.

6) Item dicunt super sacramentum suum quod Christoforus Holm' de
Hilton in comitatu Dunelmensi yoman et Robertus Couper de eadem
in eodem comitatu yoman xviij die Septembris anno pontificatus
domini Laurencij episcopi Dunelmensis xv [1472] apud Gatesheued
in comitatu Dunelmensi in Thomam Walker ballivum domini
episcopi ville sue predicte insultum fecerunt et ad ipsum cum sagittis
sagittaverunt et male tractaverunt, contra pacem dicti domini
episcopi.

7) Item dicunt quod Johannes Raughton de Silkesworth in comitatu
Dunelmensi yoman viij die Maij anno pontificatus domini Laurencij
episcopi Dunelmensis xv [1472] apud les Cloudes juxta Houghton in
comitatu Dunelmensi in Willelmum Kave servientem Henrici
Gyllowe clerici insultum fecit et male tractavit, contra pacem dicti
domini episcopi.

8) Item dicunt quod Christoforus Holme de Hilton in comitatu
Dunelmensi yoman, Willelmus Slutheman de eadem in eodem
comitatu yoman et Robertus Smales de eadem in eodem comitatu
yoman quinto die Augusti anno pontificatus domini Laurencij
episcopi Dunelmensis xv [1472] apud Sunderland juxta mare in
comitatu Dunelmensi in Thomam Roye capellanum adtunc et ibidem

insultum fecerunt et ipsum Thomam adtunc et ibidem verberaverunt, vulneraverunt et male tractaverunt ita quod de vita eius disperabatur, contra pacem dicti domini episcopi etc.

9) Item dicunt super sacramentum suum quod Radulfus Wadley de Hamsterley in comitatu Dunelmensi yoman xxiiij die Julij anno pontificatus domini Laurencij episcopi Dunelmensis xv [1472] apud Hamsterley predictam in Rogerum Hogeson adtunc et ibidem insultum fecit et ipsum Rogerum verberavit, vulneravit et male tractavit, contra pacem dicti domini episcopi etc.

10) Item dicunt super sacramentum suum quod Christoforus Holm de Hilton in comitatu Dunelmensi yoman, Willelmus Slutheman de eadem in eodem comitatu yoman et Robertus Couper de eadem in eodem comitatu yoman xxij die Septembris anno pontificatus domini Laurencij episcopi Dunelmensis xv [1472] apud Westboldon in comitatu predicto in Robertum Patonson insultum fecerunt et ipsum Robertum Patonson adtunc et ibidem verberaverunt, vulneraverunt et male tractaverunt, contra pacem dicti domini episcopi etc.

11) Item dicunt quod Elena Hede nuper de Belshoue juxta Cornesowe in comitatu Dunelmensi laborer sexto die Decembris anno pontificatus domini Laurencij episcopi Dunelmensis xv [1471] unum quarterium seye coloris nigri precij quinque solidorum de bonis et catallis Henrici Gyllowe clerici apud Dunelm' inventum felonice furata fuit etc.

12) Item dicunt super sacramentum suum quod Rogerus Hogeson de Hamsterley in comitatu Dunelmensi yoman, Ricardus Gybon de Lynesake in comitatu Dunelmensi smyth xxiiij die Julij anno pontificatus domini Laurencij episcopi Dunelmensis xv [1472] apud Hamsterley predictam in Radulfum Wadley adtunc et ibidem insultum fecerunt et ipsum Radulfum verberaverunt, vulneraverunt et male tractaverunt, contra pacem dicti domini episcopi etc.

13) Item dicunt quod Christoforus Wadley de Hamsterley in comitatu Dunelmensi yoman xx die Augusti anno pontificatus domini Laurencij episcopi Dunelmensis xv [1472] apud Hamsterley predictam in Rogerum Hogeson adtunc et ibidem insultum fecit et ipsum Rogerum verberavit, vulneravit et male tractavit, contra pacem dicti domini episcopi etc.

8

Placita et presentaciones capta apud Cestre die Martis vj die Octobris anno pontificatus domini Laurencij episcopi Dunelmensis xvj [1472] coram Henrico Gyllowe clerico, cancellario Dunelmensis, Thoma Moreslawe et sociis suis, custodibus pacis et justiciariis domini episcopi ad diversas felonias transgressiones et alia malefacta in comitatu Dunelmensi audiendum et terminandum assignatis.

Jurata xv videlicet Willelmus Merley, Ricardus Scrutvyle, Willelmus Fossour, Robertus Hall senior, Robertus Blenkansop, Robertus Porter,

Jacobus Horner, Thomas Hogeson, Robertus Neuton, Robertus Waylde, Johannes Warde de Conset, Johannes Moreton, Johannes Broun, Johannes Hall et Johannes Gamylsby senior, juratores,

1) Qui dicunt super sacramentum suum quod Rogerus Vyncent de Smeton in comitatu Eboracensi gentylman (ponit se) die Martis proximo ante festum beate Marie Magdalene anno pontificatus domini Laurencij episcopi Dunelmensis xiiij [16 July 1471] apud Aclyff in comitatu Dunelmensi unum equum precij xl s. de bonis et catallis Willelmi Raynwyk adtunc et ibidem inventum felonice furatus fuit; et eundem equum usque Smeton in comitatu Eboracensi abduxit et sic regiam libertatem Dunelmensem fregit.

2) Item dicunt super sacramentum suum quod Johannes Atkynson de Rowleygilet in comitatu Dunelmensi husbondman secundo die Septembris anno pontificatus domini Laurencij episcopi Dunelmensis xiiijmo [1471] in Robertum Burdale apud Hedle in comitatu Dunelmensi insultum fecit et ipsum Robertum adtunc et ibidem verberavit, vulneravit et male tractavit, contra pacem dicti domini episcopi etc.

3) Item dicunt dicti juratores super sacramentum suum quod Willelmus Tyndale de Haydenbrigge in comitatu Northumbr' yoman et Willelmus Reghawe de Bewecastell infra libertatem de Tyndale laborer secundo die Novembris anno pontificatus domini Laurencij episcopi Dunelmensis xiiij [1470] sex boves precij iiij li. de bonis et catallis Willelmi White apud capellam de Hayrom juxta Dunelmum inventos felonice furati fuerunt, etc.

4) Item dicunt super sacramentum suum quod Johannes Whepdale de Plenmellour in comitatu Northumbr' laborer et Robertus Bernardstede de Neweburgh infra libertatem de Tyndale yoman vij die Octobris anno pontificatus domini Laurencij episcopi Dunelmensis xiiij [1470] decem bovettos precij vj li. de bonis et catallis Johannis Esshe armigeri apud Essh in comitatu Dunelmensi inventos felonice furati fuerunt; et quod Thomas Dyxson de Cowbyres in comitatu Northumbr' yoman sciens predictos Johannem et Robertum feloniam predictam in forma predicta fecisse predictos Johannnem et Robertum apud Cowbyres predictam felonice receptavit et confortavit etc.

5) Item dicunt super sacramentum suum quod Edwardus Shirwod de Aldyngryge in comitatu Dunelmensi yoman iiijto die Maij anno pontificatus domini Laurencij episcopi Dunelmensis xiiij [1471] in Gilbertum Johnson apud Aldyngrige predictam insultum fecit et ipsum Gilbertum adtunc et ibidem verberavit, vulneravit et male tractavit, contra pacem dicti domini episcopi etc.

6) Item dicunt quod Johannes Suthwyk de Silkesworth in comitatu Dunelmensi yoman iiijto die Maij anno pontificatus domini Laurencij episcopi Dunelmensis xv [1472] in quodam bosco domini episcopi vocato Cloudes juxta Hoghton in comitatu Dunelmensi quatuor sercinas virgarum de hesyll precij vj s. viij d. de bonis et catallis dicti

domini episcopi succidit, cepit et asportavit, contra pacem eiusdem domini episcopi etc.

7) Item dicunt dicti juratores super sacramentum suum quod Thomas Marshall nuper de Satley in comitatu Dunelmensi yoman iij die Septembris anno pontificatus domini Laurencij episcopi Dunelmensis xiiij [1471] in Willelmum Atkynson de Hallhlll apud Halhill in comitatu Dunelmensi insultum fecit et ipsum Willelmum adtunc et ibidem verberavit, vulneravit et male tractavit, contra pacem dicti domini episcopi.

8) Item dicunt quod Willelmus Atkynson de Roweleygilet in comitatu Dunelmensi laborer ijᵒ die Septembris anno pontificatus domini Laurencij episcopi Dunelmensis xiiijᵒ [1471] in Robertum Burdale apud Hedle in comitatu Dunelmensi insultum fecit et ipsum Robertum adtunc et ibidem verberavit, vulneravit et male tractavit, contra pacem dicti domini episcopi etc.

9

[m.3d.]   Placita et presentaciones capta apud Dunelm' die Jovis proximo post festum sancte Lucie virginis anno pontificatus domini Laurencij episcopi Dunelmensis xvjᵒ [17 December 1472] coram Henrico Gyllowe clerico, cancellario Dunelmensi, Thoma Moreslawe, Willelmo Raket et sociis suis, custodibus pacis et justiciariis domini episcopi ad diversas felonias, transgressiones et alia malefacta in comitatu Dunelmensi audiendum et terminandum assignatis.

Jurata xij videlicet Jacobus Oudom, Beniaminus Worsley, Johannes Torkyngton, Thomas Fery, Johannes Warde, Willelmus Milne, Willelmus Stayndrop, Willelmus Blithman, Johannes Wren, Willelmus Swalwell, Johannes Hewetson et Ricardus Moderby, juratores,

1) Qui dicunt super sacramentum suum quod Johannes Thomson nuper de Forde in comitatu Northumbr' laborer die Jovis proximo ante festum Omnium Sanctorum anno pontificatus domini Laurencij episcopi Dunelmensis xvjᵒ [29 October 1472] apud Wyndilston in comitatu Dunelmensi quandam bursam continentem sexdecim denarios in pecunia numerata, quoddam gestrum precij quatuordecim denariorum et quoddam capicium precij duodecim denariorum de bonis et catallis Willelmi Swaynston et quandam togam russeti coloris precij duorum solidorum de bonis et catallis Roberti Waweri adtunc et ibidem inventa felonice furatus fuit etc.

2) Item dicunt super sacramentum suum quod Johannes Thomson nuper de Ford in comitatu Northumbr' laborer x die Octobris anno pontificatus domini Laurencij episcopi Dunelmensis xv [1471] apud Wyndelston in comitatu Dunelmensi quandem camisiam precij decem denariorum, quandam anulum argenteum precij duodecim denariorum et viginti et duos denarios in pecunia numerata de bonis et catallis Willelmi Smyth adtunc et ibidem felonice furatus fuit etc.

3) Item dicunt super sacramentum suum quod Johannes Burn de

Northaukeland in comitatu Dunelmensi flesshewer xx⁰ die Novembris anno pontificatus domini Laurencij episcopi Dunelmensis xvj⁰ [1472] octo multones precij xvj s. de bonis et catallis Thome Laton armigeri apud Northaukeland inventos felonice furatus fuit etc.

4) Item dicunt super sacramentum suum quod Johannes Burn de Northaukeland in comitatu Dunelmensi flesshewer die Lune proximo post Dominicam in Ramis Palmarum anno pontificatus domini Laurencij episcopi Dunelmensis xv [23 March 1472] quatuor oves matrices precij inter se octo solidorum apud Aldburgh in comitatu Dunelmensi inventas de bonis et catallis Willelmi Parkynson felonice furatus fuit etc.

5) Item dicunt super sacramentum suum quod Johannes Milner nuper de Stokton in comitatu Dunelmensi laborer alias dictus Johannes Stokall nuper de Stokton in comitatu Dunelmensi servitor quintodecimo die Novembris anno pontificatus domini Laurencij episcopi Dunelmensis xvj [1472] viginti et quinque multones precij l s. de bonis et catallis Thome Smyth, Willelmi Lege et Henrici Carleton apud Stokton inventos felonice furatus fuit etc.

6) Item dicunt super sacramentum suum quod Adam Archer nuper de Hartley in comitatu Westmerland laborer xx die Octobris anno pontificatus domini Laurencij episcopi Dunelmensis xvj⁰ [1472] xl multones precij iiij li. de bonis et catallis Thome Langton apud Raby inventos felonice furatus fuit etc.

7) Item dicunt super sacramentum suum quod Thomas Mathewe nuper de Novo Castro super Tynam walker vj⁰ die Marcij anno pontificatus domini Laurencij episcopi Dunelmensis xv [1472] apud Crawecroke in comitatu Dunelmensi quandam equam coloris baye precij tresdecim solidorum et quatuor denariorum de bonis et catallis Willelmi Bell adtunc et ibidem inventam felonice furatus fuit, cepit et abduxit etc.

8) Item dicunt super sacramentum suum quod Robertus Croke nuper de Stanehope in comitatu Dunelmensi laborer et Alicia Gresward nuper de eadem in eodem comitatu husewyff xx⁰ die Maij anno pontificatus domini Laurencij episcopi Dunelmensis xv [1472] apud Stanehope in comitatu predicto quandam ollam eneam precij ij s., unam ulnam panni lanei vocatam karesaye precij ij s., unam parem linthiameni precij Cij s. iiij d., quatuor gallinas et unum gallum precij viij d., xxiiij cranas lini precij v s., v modios frumenti et siliginis precij v s. et unum maskyng tub precij xij d. de bonis et catallis Ade Gresward adtunc et ibidem inventa felonice furati fuerunt.

9) Item dicunt super sacramentum suum quod Robertus Claxton de Heworth in comitatu Dunelmensi gentylman, Johannes Henryson de Acley in eodem comitatu smyth, Johannes Lessebyry de eadem in eodem comitatu laborer, Johannes Forman de eadem in eodem comitatu milner, Georgius Wilkynson de eadem in eodem comitatu barker, Johannes Claxton de eadem in eodem comitatu milner, Ricardus Serill de Brafferton in eodem comitatu laborer, Willelmus

Serill de eadem in eodem comitatu laborer et Thomas Watson de Heworth predictam in eodem comitatu laborer sexto die Novembris anno pontificatus domini Laurencij episcopi Dunelmensis xvj [1472] vi et armis videlicet gladiis arcubus et sagittis apud Segefeld in comitatu predicto in Willelmum Helburn insultum fecerunt et ipsum adtunc et ibidem verberaverunt et male tractaverunt, contra pacem dicti domini episcopi etc.

10) Item dicunt super sacramentum suum quod Johannes Harlawe de Estbuttesfeld in comitatu Dunelmensi laborer die Veneris xx die Novembris anno pontificatus domini Laurencij episcopi Dunelmensis xvj [1472] ad horam terciam post merediem eiusdem die apud Westbuttesfeld in comitatu predicto vi et armis videlicet baculis et cultellis jaciit in incidiis expectans adventum Roberti Wollour ad ipsum Robertum adtunc et ibidem cum gestro suo quod tunc in manu sua tenuit in pectorem suum et ventrem trina vice percussit felonice et letalie vulneravit, de quibus ictibus idem Robertus incontinenti obiit et sic predictus Johannes dictum Robertum adtunc et ibidem felonice interfecit et murdravit etc.

11) Item dicunt super sacramentum suum quod Robertus Sotheron de Lofthouslintes in comitatu Dunelmensi husbondman aggregatus sibi aliis quampluribus malefactoribus et pacis domini episcopi perturbatoribus modo guerrino arraiatis videlicet gladiis parmis et cultellis contra formam statuti inde editi ad festum Pentecost' anno pontificatus domini Laurencij episcopi Dunelmensis xiij [10 June 1470] domos et clausum Thome Midelton, Johannis Katerik et Willelmi Bland apud Lofthouslyntes predictam vi et armis intravit et dictos Thomam Johannem et Willelmum vi et armis expulsit et adhuc vi et armis tenet, contra pacem dicti domini episcopi etc.

12) Item dicunt super sacramentum suum quod Thomas Richardson nuper de villa Novi Castri super Tynam shipman xx die Augusti anno pontificatus domini Laurencij episcopi Dunelmensis xv° [1472] unam pelvem eneam precij quatuor solidorum et unum pestrum precij trium solidorum de bonis et catallis Johannis Shirwod clerici et Johannis Goldesburch clerici apud Whitbern inventos felonice furatus fuit etc.

10

(Durham') Placita et presentaciones capta apud Dunelm' die Mercurii xx die Januarij anno pontificatus domini Laurencij episcopi Dunelmensis xvj° [1473] coram Radulfo domino de Neville, Thoma Moreslawe, Ricardo Baynbrig et sociis suis, justiciariis domini episcopi ad gaolam apud Dunelm' deliberandam assignatis etc.

Jurata xij videlicet Johannes Redmayn, Willelmus Milner, Jacobus Toppyng, Willelmus Wadle, Johannes Rakwod, Willelmus Blitheman, Henricus Masse, Johannes Hall, Willelmus Tebson, Johannes Moreton, Robertus Emreson, Robertus Hall, Nicholas Ferrour,

1) Qui dicunt super sacramentum suum quod ubi Johannes Sawerde

nuper de Bycheburn in comitatu Dunelmensi yoman, Johannes Blakheued nuper de Helmepark in eodem comitatu yoman et Willelmus Stevenson nuper de Romondby lonyng in eodem comitatu husbandman die Jovis quarto die Septembris anno pontificatus domini Laurencij episcopi Dunelmensis xiiij [1471] sex boves precij inter se quatuor librarum de bonis et catallis Willelmi Johnson apud Hunwyk adtunc et ibidem inventos felonice furati fuerunt et de felonia predicta arestati fuerunt et prisone dicti domini episcopi comissi fuerunt; postea tamen predicti Johannes Sawer, Johannes Blakheued et Willelmus Stevenson in prisona predicta existentes secundo die Septembris anno pontificatus domini Laurencij episcopi Dunelmensis xv [1472] prisonam dicti domini episcopi in Dunelmo felonice fregerunt etc.

2) Item dicunt super sacramentum suum quod Willelmus Chilton de Heghyngton in comitatu Dunelmensi yoman, Willelmus Serill de Brafferton in eodem comitatu yoman, Richardus Serill de eadem in eodem comitatu yoman, Willelmus Watson de Herdwyk in eodem comitatu junior yoman, Thomas Watson de eadem in eodem comitatu yoman, Johannes Smyrke de Hoton in eodem comitatu yoman, Johannes Thorp de Elwyk in eodem comitatu yoman, Johannes Robynson de Wetlawe in eodem comitatu yoman, Robertus Lambe de eadem in eodem comitatu yoman, Robertus Coucart de eadem in eodem comitatu yoman, Johannes Pycher de Thornlawe in eodem comitatu yoman, Willelmus Ayr de Tunstall in eodem comitatu yoman, Johannes Smyth de eadem in eodem comitatu yoman, Thomas Smyth de eadem in eodem comitatu yoman, Alanus Alanson de Thornton in eodem comitatu yoman, Willelmus Shotton de Raynton in eodem comitatu senior yoman, Jacobus Tod de Epplyngden in eodem comitatu yoman, Willelmus Tod de eadem in eodem comitatu yoman et Willelmus North de Esyngton in eodem comitatu yoman, laici homines non habentes nec aliqui eorum habens terras seu tenementa ad valorem quadraginta solidorum per annum, contra formam statuti inde editi, tenent leporarios et quolibet eorum tenet leporarios et leciscas et in nive lepores investigaverunt et xij die Januarij anno pontificatus domini Laurencij episcopi Dunelmensis xvj° [1473] in campo de Hoghton sex lepores interfecerunt etc.

3) Item dicunt super sacramentum suum quod Petrus Stayndrop de Heghyngton in comitatu Dunelmensi capellanus et Thomas Areke de Esyngton in comitatu Dunelmensi capellanus, non promoti ad beneficium valoris decem librarum per annum, tenent leporarios et leciscas, contra formam statuti inde editi, et in nive ultimo preterito lepores investigaverunt et in campo de Heghyngton tres lepores interfecerunt.

4) 4) Item dicunt super sacramentum suum quod Willelmus Sclater de Kirkemeryngton in comitatu Dunelmensi laborer in festo Apostolorum Petri et Pauli anno pontificatus domini Laurencij episcopi Dunelmensis xv° [29 June 1472] apud parcum de Aukeland

sex ussos de bonis et catallis dicti domini episcopi precij xl s. decortuavit exitus inde provenientes cepit et asportavit etc.

5) Item dicunt super sacramentum suum quod Ricardus Gybon (finis) de Lynesak in comitatu Dunelmensi smyth et Willelmus Gybon (finis) de eadem in eodem comitatu smyth xvij die Januarij anno pontificatus domini Laurencij episcopi Dunelmensis xvj [1473] apud Lynesak predictam in Ricardum Banes vi et armis insultum fecit et ipsum Ricardum Banes adtunc et ibidem verberaverunt et male tractaverunt, contra pacem dicti domini episcopi etc.

6) Item dicunt super sacramentum suum quod Christoforus Herpour de Stanehop in comitatu Dunelmensi yoman xx die Septembris anno pontificatus domini Laurencij episcopi Dunelmensis xvᵒ [1472] apud Billelawes in comitatu Dunelmensi x multones de bonis et catallis Thome Wren precij xvj s. viij d. et x multones de bonis et catallis Willelmi Wren precij xvj s. viij d. adtunc et ibidem inventos felonice furatus fuit.

7) Item dicunt super sacramentum suum quod Thomas Milnburn de Westbrandon in comitatu Dunelmensi laborer et Andreas Milnburn de eadem in eodem comitatu laborer in festo Circumcisionis domini anno pontificatus domini Laurencij episcopi Dunelmensis xvjᵒ [1 January 1473] vi et armis videlicet gladiis baculis et cultellis ex malicia precogitata apud Brauncepeth in comitatu predicto jacuerunt in incidiis expectantes adventum Roberti Hakforth nuper de Morley, ad ipsum Robertum adtunc et ibidem felonice interficiendum; et predictus Thomas cum quadam lancea precij duodecim denariorum quam in manibus suis tenuit in predictum Robertum adtunc et ibidem insultum fecit et ipsum Robertum super anteriorem partem capitis sui felonice percussit et dedit ei plagam mortalem unde idem Robertus obiit, et sic dictus Thomas dictum Robertum felonice interfecit. Et predictus Andreas cum uno baculo vocata clobe precij sex denariorum quod in manibus suis tenuit in predictum Robertum adtunc et ibidem insultum fecit et ipsum Robertum super posteriorem partem capitis sui felonice percussit et dedit ei plagam mortalem unde idem Robertus obiisset si a prefato Thoma idem Robertus minime percussus fuisset; et sic predictus Andreas ipsum Robertum adtunc et ibidem felonice interfecit.

8) Item dicunt super sacramentum suum quod Robertus Wharham de Farnetonhall in comitatu Dunelmensi yoman, Radulfus Ledale de Langley juxta Dunelm' in eodem comitatu yoman et Radulfus Bee de eadem in eodem comitatu yoman apud Langley juxta Dunelm' in comitatu predicto xxᵐᵒ die Julij anno pontificatus domini Laurencij episcopi Dunelmensis xv [1472] unam equam precij vj s. viij d. de bonis et catallis Roberti Batmanson senioris adtunc et ibidem inventam felonice furati fuerunt.

(ponit se quietus nec r[espondit])
(ponit se quietus nec r[esponit])

9) Item dicunt super sacramentum suum quod Radulfus Bee de

Langley juxta Dunelm' in comitatu predicto die Veneris proximo
ante festum Omnium Sanctorum anno pontificatus domini Laurencij
episcopi Dunelmensis quintodecimo [*30 October 1471*] duodecim
vaccas precij inter se vj li. xij s. et sex boves precij lxxij s. de bonis et
catallis Roberti Batmanson senioris adtunc et ibidem inventos
felonice furati fuerunt etc.
(ponit se quietus nec r[espondit])
(ponit se quietus nec r[espondit])
10) Item dicunt super sacramentum suum quod Radulfus Bee de
Langley juxta Dunelm' in comitatu Dunelmensi yoman die Martis
proximo ante festum Sancti Cuthberti in Septembri anno pontificatus
domini Laurencij episcopi Dunelmensis xv [*1 September 1472*] apud
Langley juxta Dunelm' in comitatu predicto unum equam precij liij s.
iiij d. de bonis et catallis Roberti Batmanson junioris adtunc et
ibidem inventum felonice furatus fuit etc.
11) Item dicti juratores dicunt super sacramentum suum quod
Ricardus Skerawe de Ivesley in comitatu Dunelmensi yoman, Thomas
Milnburn de Westbrandon in eodem comitatu laborer et Andreas
Milnburn de eadem in eodem comitatu laborer in festo Natalis
domini anno pontificatus domini Laurencij episcopi Dunelmensis xvj
[*25 December 1472*] vi et armis videlicet gladiis baculis et cultellis et
ex malicia precogitata apud Brauncepath in comitatu predicto
jacuerunt in incidiis expectantes adventum Johannis Hakforth de
Waterhous senioris, Johannis Hakforth junioris et Roberti Hakforth
adtunc et ibidem ipsos interficiendum et in ipsos Johannem,
Johannem et Robertum adtunc et ibidem insultum fecerunt contra
pacem; et predictus Ricardus Skerawe cum quodam gladio quem in
manibus suis tenuit predictum Johannem Hakforth seniorem adtunc
et ibidem in medio capitis percussit unde tam graviter vulneratus fuit
quod de vita sua disperabatur, contra pacem dicti domini episcopi
etc. Et predictus Thomas Milnburn cum quodam baculo vocato a
pykedstaf quem in manibus suis tenuit predictum Johannem
Hakforth juniorem adtunc et ibidem super humerum brachij sinistri
percussit unde tam graviter vulneratus fuit quod de vita sua
disperabatur. Et predictus Andreas prefatum Robertum cum quodam
baculo vocato a club quem in manibus suis tenuit adtunc et ibidem
super sinistram partem capitis percussit unde idem Robertus tam
grave et immane vulnus habuit quod de vita sua similiter disperatus
fuit, contra pacem domini episcopi etc.
12) Item dicunt super sacramentum suum quod Johannes Langton,
prior de Tynmouth, xxiiij^to die Januarii anno pontificatus domini
Laurencij episcopi Dunelmensis quinto [*1462*] arbores et subboscum
ipsius episcopi apud parcum de Wolsyngham crescentes ad valenciam
ducentarum librarum succidit, cepit et asportavit contra pacem dicti
domini episcopi etc.
13) Item dicunt super sacramentum suum quod Willelmus Horsley de
Fenton in comitatu Northumbr' gentylman et Ricardus Snawdon de

eadem in eodem comitatu yoman vicesimo die Junij anno
pontificatus domini Laurencij episcopi Dunelmensis quintodecimo
[1472] unum bovem precij decem solidorum de bonis et catallis
Willelmi Marche et unum equm baeij coloris precij viginti et sex
solidorum de bonis et catallis Johannis Grevay apud Crawcruk in
comitatu Dunelmensi inventos felonice furati fuerunt etc.

11

(Dunelm') Placita et presentaciones capta apud Dunelm' die Sabbati
xxxº die Januarij anno pontificatus domini Laurencij episcopi
Dunelmensis sextodecimo [1473] coram Radulfo Nevill domino de
Nevill, Thoma Moreslawe et sociis suis, justiciariis domini episcopi ad
gaolam apud Dunelm' deliberandam assignatis etc.

Jurata videlicet Robertus Claxton miles, Rogerus Conyers miles,
Willelmus Pudsay miles, Robertus Evers senior, Willelmus Claxton
de Halywell, Thomas Lomley, Willelmus Lambton, Thomas
Blaykeston, Robertus Tempest, Thomas Trollop, Thomas Midilton,
Thomas Popeley, Johannes Park, Willelmus Wilberfosse, Willelmus
Conyers, Thomas Surtes, Thomas Basworth, Robertus Eures,
Robertus Molet, Christoforus Baumford, Willelmus Mordon,
Willelmus Elstob, Johannes Dale, Willelmus Whelpdale senior,
Johannes Redmayn, Jacobus Tippyng, Willelmus Blythman, Jacobus
Horner, Willelmus Fossour, Robertus Emreson de Willyngton,
Robertus Porter, Robertus Hall, Willelmus Tebson, Beniamin
Worsley, Thomas Fery, Walterus Robson, Robertus Blenkensop,

1) Qui dicunt super sacramentum suum quod Johannes Dunsforth de
Plawesworth in comitatu Dunelmensi husbondman xxviij die
Januarij anno pontificatus domini Laurencij episcopi Dunelmensis
xvjº [1473] xxiij oves matrices precij inter se xl s. de bonis et catallis
Roberti Johnson apud Middrige Grange in comitatu Dunelmensi
adtunc et ibidem inventas felonice furatus fuit etc.
cul[pabilis] S[uspend']

2) Item dicunt super sacramentum suum quod Johannes Silvertop de
Lamesley in comitatu Dunelmensi husbandman et Mariona uxor eius
die Lune videlicet in festo Conversionis sancti Pauli anno
pontificatus domini Laurencij episcopi Dunelmensis xvj [25 January
1473] vi et armis videlicet gladiis baculis et fustibus liberum
tenementum Radulfi Herbotell apud Kyblesworth intraverunt et
quendam stipitem cum apibus et melle ipsius Radulfi adtunc et
ibidem inventum ad valenciam vj s. viij d. ceperunt et asportaverunt
ad grave dampnum ipsius Radulfi et contra pacem nostram etc.

3) Item dicunt super sacramentum suum quod Alexander Milburn
nuper de Westbrandon in comitatu Dunelmensi laborer primo die
Januarij anno pontificatus domini Laurencij episcopi Dunelmensis
xvjº [1473] apud Brauncepath in comitatu predicto in Robertum a
Hakforth vi et armis insultum fecit et ipsum Robertum cum quodam
baculo vocato a clubstaff precij quatuor denariorum super capud

felonice percussit et dedit ei plagam mortalem unde idem Robertus instanter obiit; et sic dicunt quod predictus Alexander eundem Robertum felonice interfecit etc.

4) Item dicunt super sacramentum suum quod Thomas Joys de Dunelm' in comitatu Dunelmensi vagabund et Alexander Swynburn de eadem in eodem comitatu vagabund, nullam artem nec ullum magistrum (aut liberum tenementum) habentes unde victam aut vestitos haberent nec ullam culturam circa quam se laborare poterint aut occupare, in civitati Dunelm' indies ociose vagant vestiti ut generosi et null' sic unde vivunt, contra formam statuti inde provisi; ideo capiantur ad respondendum etc., et ad inveniendum sufficientem securitatem de bono gestu scilicet etc.

5) Item dicunt super sacramentum suum quod Robertus Billy nuper de Chestre in comitatu Dunelmensi yoman primo die Februarij anno pontificatus domini Laurencij episcopi Dunelmensis xvj° [1473] apud Chestre in the strete in comitatu Dunelmensi in Willelmum Neuton adtunc et ibidem vi et armis insultum fecit et ipsum Willelmum cum quodem baculo vocato karlilaxe precij xij d. quem in manibus suis tenuit eundem Willelmum in cruram s[...] felonice percussit et dedit ei plagam mortalem de qua plaga idem Willelmus instanter obiit etc.

6) Item dicunt super sacramentum suum quod Johannes Heddon de Aclyff in comitatu Dunelmensi yoman, Nicholas Colson de eadem in eodem comitatu laborer, Willelmus Serll de Brafferton in eodem comitatu laborer, Thomas Tod de Langle juxta Berepark in eodem comitatu yoman, Willelmus Stevenson de Evenwod in eodem comitatu yoman, Radulfus Stevenson de eadem in eodem comitatu yoman, Christoforum Stevenson de eadem in eodem comitatu yoman, Willelmus Bland de Stayndrop in eodem comitatu yoman, Robertus Hall de Langley milne in eodem comitatu yoman et Johannes Redmayn de Langley in eodem comitatu yoman, laici homines non habentes terras nec tenementa aut annualia feoda pro termino vite valoris xl s. per annum, tenent leporarios et quolibet eorum tenet leporarios, et quarto die Januarij anno pontificatus domini Laurencij episcopi Dunelmensis xvj [1473] lepores investigaverunt in nive et in campo de Aclyff quatuor lepores interfecerunt contra formam statuti in huiusmodi casis provisi etc.

7) Item dicunt super sacramentum suum quod Willelmus Watkynson de Dunelm' in comitatu Dunelmensi w[...] penam de transgressione in parcis vivariis aut libera warenna non verens xij die Novembris anno pontificatus domini Laurencij episcopi Dunelmensis xvj° [1472] vi et armis liberam warennam Willelmi Raket et aliorum feoffatorum Ricardi Belyngham apud Crokehall juxta Dunelm' intravit et sex perdices adtunc et ibidem interfecit contra formam statuti inde editi etc.

8) Item dicunt super sacramentum suum quod Johannes Harlawe nuper de Estbuttesfeld in comitatu Dunelmensi laborer die Veneris proximo ante festum sancte Katerine anno pontificatus domini

Laurencij episcopi Dunelmensis xvjᵒ [*20 November 1472*] apud Westbuttesfeld in comitatu predicto vi et armis insultum fecit in Robertum Woller et cum quodam dagario precij vj d. quod in manibus suis tenuit predictum Robertum adtunc et ibidem in ventrem suum felonice percussit et dedit ei plagam mortalem unde idem Robertus incontinenter obiit. Et quod Robertus Harlawe de Estbuttesfeld predicta in comitatu predicto yoman, sciens prefatum Johannem feloniam predictam ut supradictum est fecisse eundem Johannem apud Estbuttesfeld predicta die et anno predictis felonice receptavit et confortavit et ind[...] receptat et confortat etc.

9) Item dicunt super sacramentum suum quod Johannes Thomson nuper de Swynhopburn in parco de Stanehop in comitatu Dunelmensi yoman xᵒ die Julij anno pontificatus domini Laurencij episcopi Dunelmensis ixᵒ [*1466*] apud Bolyhop in Werdale quinquaginta bovettos precij quinquaginta marcarum de bonis et catallis cuiusdem ignoti adtunc et ibidem inventos felonice furatus fuit etc.

Po[nit] se q[uietus] nec r[espondit]

Po[nit] se q[uietus] nec r[espondit]

[*m.4d.*]   10) [Item dicunt] super sacramentum suum quod Willelmus Fethirstaneha[ugh] de Stanehope in comitatu Dunelmensi [... anno pontificatus] domini Laurencij episcopi Dunelmensis [...*illegible*].

11) [Item dicunt...*illegible*]

12) Item dicunt super sacramentum suum quod Johannes [...*illegible*]

13) Item dicunt super sacramentum quod Thomas Colpottys de Midilton in Tesedale in comitatu Sadberge [...] unacum Stephanus Colpottys de eadem in eodem comitatu yoman, Johannes Maneley de eadem in eodem comitatu yoman et Robertus Natresse nuper de Stanehope in comitatu Dunelmensi yoman modo guerrino arraiati et ex malicia precognita vi et armis die Dominica proxima ante festum sancte Trinitatis anno pontificatus domini Laurencij episcopi Dunelmensis xvᵒ [*17 May 1472*] apud Midilton in comitatu Dunelmensi [...] Willelmum Rottour adtunc et ibidem insultum fecerunt [...] Thomas cum quodam baculo vocato a club precij quatuor denariorum prefatum Willelmum super anteriorem partem [...] felonice percussit et dedit ei plagam [mortalem unde] idem Willelmus instanter obiit, et predictus Stephanus cum quodam baculo vocato a pikestaffe precij [...] denariorum predictum Willelmum super sinistram partem capitis felonice percussit et dedit ei plagam mortalem unde idem Willelmus instanter obiisset [si] prefatus Thomas ipsum Willelmum non percussisset, et predictus Johannes cum quodam baculo vocato a castang predictum Willelmum Rottour super sinistram partem capitis felonice percussit et dedit ei plagam mortalem unde idem Willelmus instanter obiisset [*etc.*], et predictus Robertus cum quodam [baculo ...] precij [...] denariorum predictum Willelmum super posteriorem partem capitis sui felonice percussit et dedit ei plagam mortalem unde idem

Willelmus instanter obiisset si a prefatis Thoma et Stephano et Roberto immo percussus fuisset, et quilibet eorum interfecit etc.
S[uspend'] q[uiet']

14) Item dicunt super sacramentum suum quod cum in statuto in parliamento Ricardi secondi nuper Regis Anglie [anno regni] sui quinto [1381/2] tento edito auctoritate eiusdem parliamenti inter alia ordinatus fuerit et statutus quod nullus [...] ingressum in aliqua terras seu tenementa nisi in casu ubi ingressus datur per legem et in tale non vi nec multitudine gentium, et si aliquis contrarium inde fecit et indebit' commot' f[...] per imprisonem corporis sui et ad voluntatem domini regis redimatur prout in eodem statuto plenius [...] tamen Robertus Paterson de Dunelm' in comitatu Dunelmensi barker, Robertus Joplyn de eadem in eodem comitatu laborer, Willelmus Goldsmyth de eadem in eodem comitatu barker, Ricardus Rychardson de eadem in eodem comitatu barker, Georgius Richardson de eadem in eodem comitatu barker, Thomas Hall de eadem in eodem comitatu wever, et Georgius Da de eadem in eodem comitatu wever statutum predictum non verentes die Lune proxima post Dominicam in Ramis Palmarum anno pontificatus domini Laurencij episcopi Dunelmensis quintodecimo [23 March 1472] vi et armis videlicet gladiis baculis et fustibus apud Dunelm' tria burgagia vasta cum suis pertinentibus Willelmi Whelden senioris scituata in quodam vico vocato Southstrete adtunc et ibidem manuforti ingressi fuerunt contra formam statuti predicti ad grave dampnum dicti Willelmi Whelden et contra pacem dicti domini episcopi etc.

15) Item dicunt super sacramentum suum quod Stephanus Laybourne nuper de Consyd in comitatu Dunelmensi yoman, Nicholas Laybourne de eadem in eodem comitatu yoman, Willelmus Laybourne nuper de eadem in eodem comitatu yoman, et Johannes Gyllayn de eadem in eodem comitatu yoman vj^{to} die Julij anno pontificatus domini Laurencij episcopi Dunelmensis vj^{to} [1463] [...] precij quatuordecim solidorum, unam vaccam precij decem solidorum et unam juvencam precij sex solidorum de bonis et catallis Willelmi Wadley et Roberti Smyth apud Widyfeld in comitatu Dunelmensi adtunc et ibidem inventas felonice furati fuerunt; et quod Thomas Laybourne nuper de Consyd in comitatu Dunelmensi yoman sciens predictos Stephanum Nicholaum Willelmum et Johannem feloniam predictam in forma predicta fecisse predictos Stephanum Nicholaum Willelmum et Johannem predictis die et anno apud Consyd predictos felonice receptavit et confortavit etc.

16) Item dicunt super sacramentum suum quod Lionellus Ussher nuper de Prudhowe in comitatu Northumbr' yoman, Roulandus Ussher nuper de Morpeth in eodem comitatu yoman, Georgius Thirwall nuper de Prudhowe in eodem comitatu yoman, Georgius Chatour nuper de Whittamstall in eodem comitatu yoman et David Robson nuper de Prudhowe in eodem comitatu yoman xij die Decembris anno pontificatus domini Laurencij episcopi Dunelmensis

xvj° [1472] septem boves precij C s. de bonis et catallis Henrici
Gyllowe clerici, unum boviculum et unam juvencam precij inter se
xx s. de bonis et catallis Willelmi Lambton armigeri apud Bedyk in
comitatu Dunelmensi adtunc et ibidem inventos felonice furati
fuerunt etc.

17) Item dicunt super sacramentum suum quod Willelmus Paton
nuper de Hilton in comitatu Dunelmensi yoman et Henricus Ocke
nuper de eadem in eodem comitatu yoman xij die Decembris anno
pontificatus domini Laurencij episcopi Dunelmensis xvj° [1472] apud
Lamesley in comitatu Dunelmensi unam vaccam precij decem
solidorum de bonis et catallis Johannis Gamylsby senioris adtunc et
ibidem inventam felonice furati fuerunt etc.

18) Item dicunt super sacramentum suum quod Alanus Rottour nuper
de Midilton in comitatu Sadberg yoman xij die Septembris anno
pontificatus domini Laurencij episcopi Dunelmensis vj^{to} [1462]
centum oves matrices precij inter se x li. de bonis et catallis Rogeri
Baynbrig apud Midilton in comitatu Dunelmensi adtunc et ibidem
inventas felonice furatus fuit etc.

19) Item dicunt super sacramentum suum quod Ricardus
Fethirstanehalgh nuper de Stanehope in comitatu Dunelmensi
yoman xij die Marcij anno pontificatus domini Laurencij episcopi
Dunelmensis xiiij^{mo} [1471] quendam equum coloris albi precij iiij^{or}
marcarum de bonis et catallis Rollandi Hall apud Bromewham in
comitatu Dunolmensi adtunc et ibidem inventam felonice furatus
fuit etc.

20) Item dicunt super sacramentum suum quod idem Ricardus
Fethirstanehalgh et Johannes Fethirstanehalgh nuper de Stanhope in
comitatu Dunelmensi yoman, Robertus Crok nuper de eadem in
eodem comitatu yoman et Thomas Waynher de eadem in eodem
comitatu yoman x° die Junij anno pontificatus domini Laurencij
episcopi Dunelmensis xiiij^{mo} [1471] duos equos coloris albi precij
decem marcarum de bonis et catallis Ricardi Clervaw apud Derlyngton
in comitatu Dunelmensi inventos felonice furati fuerunt etc.

21) Item dicunt super sacramentum suum quod Edwardus Andrewe
(utlag') nuper de Satley in comitatu Dunelmensi laborer x die Junij
anno pontificatus domini Laurencij episcopi Dunelmensis x^{mo} [1468]
quendam bovem precij decem solidorum de bonis et catallis Thome
Marshall apud Satley predictam adtunc et ibidem inventum felonice
furatus fuit etc.

Culpat' S[uspend']

22) Item dicunt super sacramentum [suum] quod Johannes Redley de
Walltown infra libertatem de Tynedale gentylman, Thomas Ridley de
eadem yoman et Ricardus Heryngton de Coklawe infra libertatem de
Hexham yoman, aggregatis sibi aliis quampluribus malefactoribus et
pacis domini regis perturbatoribus, xv° die Novembris anno domini
Laurencij episcopi Dunelmensis ix° [1465] apud Witton in Werdall in
Radulfum Eure insultum fecerunt et ipsum Radulfum de xx li. in

pecunia numerata et de duobus equis precij quatuor librarum felonice depredati fuerunt; et ipsum Radulfum cum pecunia et equis predictis preter et contra voluntate sui usque Lynnelford infra libertatem de Hexham extra regiam libertatem Dunelmensem duxerunt in magnum contemptum domini episcopi ac enervacionem et derogacionem regie libertatis Dunelmensis etc.

23) Item dicunt super sacramentum suum quod Alexander Madyson de Unthank in Werdale in comitatu Dunelmensi gentylman, aggregatis sibi aliis quampluribus malefactoribus et pacis domini episcopi perturbatoribus, modo guerrino arraiti vi et armis videlicet baculis et cultellis in Thomam Kelynghall apud Coves in Werdall in comitatu predicto insultum fecit et ipsum Thomam preter et contra voluntatem suam usque domum Ricardi Doket chivaleri in Lonesdale extra regiam libertatem Dunelmensem duxit et eundem Thomam ibidem detinuit quousque idem Thomas corporale prestitit juramentum ad complendum et perficiendum voluntatem predicti Alexandri, ad grave dampnum ipsius Thome et contra pacem dicti domini episcopi ac enervacionem et derogacionem et gravem lesionem regie libertatis Dunelmensis etc.

24) Item dicunt super sacramentum suum quod Johannes Cramer nuper de Ogle in comitatu Northumbr' yoman in vigilia Natalis domini anno pontificatus domini Laurencij episcopi Dunelmensis xvjo [24 December 1472] cum aliis quampluribus malefactoribus et pacis domini regis perturbatoribus arraiti vi et armis videlicet baculis et gladiis domum Johannis Thomson apud Brereton in comitatu Dunelmensi felonice deburgavit et fregit et ipsum Johannem Thomson cepit et abduxit et eundem Johannem Thomson preter et contra voluntatem suam eidem Johanne Cramer sufficientem securitatem invenire coegit ad interessendum apud Novum Castrum extra libertatem, in enervacionem et derogacionem regie libertatis Dunelmensis dictique Johannis Thomson grave dampnum ac dicti domini episcopi magnum contemptum etc.

PRO, Durham 3/75 This consists of four membranes filed chronologically as 4, 2 (with insertion from membrane 3), and 1: being for sessions at Durham on 27 May, and 21 and 26 October 1510; 27 January, 26 March (at Stanhope) and 20 October 1511; and 18 February 1512. It has been wrongly classified among the Durham chancery patent rolls.

12

[*m.4*] (Durham) Pleas and presentments at Durham on 27 May 1 Thomas [Ruthall] [*1510*] before Hugh Asshton, clerk, chancellor of Durham, William Hylton, esq., William Bulmer senior, esq., John Rakett and fellow keepers and justices of the bishop's peace assigned to hear and terminate divers felonies, trespasses and other misdeeds in co. Durham.

Jury: John Hedworth, esq., William Esshe, esq., John Fetherstanehalghe, esq., Thomas Fyshburn, Adam Blaxton, John Swynburn, William Lawson, Richard Garmondisway, John Aston, Robert Bothe, John Porter, Henry Bayncrofte and William Warde, testify:

1) William Herryson (hanged by the neck) of Aycliffe, co. Durham, butcher, on 14 Feb. 1510 at Coundon drove off 19 sheep worth 26s. 8d. belonging to Thomas Laynge and Thomas Hopper, against the bishop's peace.
Void, see below <Antony Brakenbery late of Hornby, co. Richmond, gen., Charles Brakenbery late of the same, gen., Percival Madyson of the same, yeo., John Skone of the same, yeo., Christopher Hogeson of the same, yeo., John Crawfurthe of Raby, co. Durham, yeo., John Taillyour of Staindrop, husbandman, Henry Pygg of Summerhouse, husbandman, John Tayte of Selaby in co. Sadberge, lab., and David Hyne late of Hornby, co. Richmond, yeo., on Tues., 10 Sept. 1509, assembled with other malefactors and disturbers of the king's peace to the number of 22 and by force and arms with bows and arrows, swords and lances and other arms came from Hornby into the liberty of St Cuthbert to the manor of Burn Hall, co. Durham.>

2) John Watson (hanged by the neck) late of Warkworth, Northumberland, yeo., on 3 March 1510 at Darlington, co. Durham, about the twelfth hour after noon entered the parish church of Darlington and a house situated within the church called *le Tresourhouse*, and with sticks and knives broke and entered and stole 13 belts of silver and gilt called *oure lady jowell* worth £10, a golden horn set with a precious stone called *a saphir* worth 10 marks, a golden eagle worth 13s. 4d., a silver-gilt reliquary worth 13s. 4d., a jewel called *an agnus dei* with a silver-gilt brooch worth 6s. 8d., and a silver image worth 6s. 8d., being the goods and chattels of the church and in the custody of John Thomson and William Stapilton, against the bishop's peace.

3) Thomas Berkhous of Hedleywood, Northumberland, yeo., John Elryngton of the same, yeo., Robert Taillyour of the same, yeo., Richard Heworthe of the same, yeo., John Smythe of the same, yeo., Christopher Surtes of the same, yeo., Edward Slater of the same, yeo., Robert Sklater of the same, yeo., and William Hynmers of the same, yeo., on 8 April 1510 with force and arms with swords and lances, bows and arrows and other defensive arms assembled riotously at Chopwell moor in the bishopric of Durham and seized 86 sheep worth 100s. belonging to William Hedlee, Andrew Hedlee, George Joplyn, William Thomson and Robert Surtes and drove them to Prudhoe castle, Northumberland, beyond the liberty of Durham, in violation of that liberty and against the peace of the bishop.

4) Thomas Elrington of Espershields, co. Durham, gen., Thomas Watson of Edmundbyers, yeo., Edward Dennyng of Espershields, yeo., and John Dennyng of Newbiggin, lab., on 9 May 1510 assembled riotously with other malefactors and disturbers of the king's peace in warlike fashion to the number of 20 with swords, lances, bows and arrows, etc. at Burnmoor by Durham and assaulted Anthony Brakenbery and threatened him with malicious and opprobrious words and struck him, against the bishop's peace and the form of the statute.

5) Anthony Brakenbery late of Hornby, co. Richmond, gen., Charles Brakenbery late of the same, gen., Percival Madyson of the same, yeo., John Skeene of the same, yeo., Christopher Hogeson of the same, yeo., John Crawfurthe of Raby, co. Durham, yeo., John Taillour of Staindrop, husbandman, Henry Pigge of Summerhouse, husbandman, John Tayte of Selaby, co. Sadberge, lab., and David Hyne late of Hornby, co. Richmond, yeo., on Tues., 10 September 1509, assembled with other malefactors to the number of 20 with bows and arrows, swords and lances [etc.] and from Hornby entered the liberty of St Cuthbert at the manor of Burn Hall on the land of Joan Laburne, daughter and heiress of Eleanor, daughter and heiress of Henry Fethirstanehalgh, cousin and heir of William Claxton late of Burn Hall, and drove away 5 cows and heifers of Robert Tenaunte, bailiff of Durham, 12 cows of Elizabeth Iles, and other cattle found there to Selaby within the demesne of Barnard Castle, against the liberty and franchise of St Cuthbert and the king's peace.

6) William Herrison (hanged by the neck) of Aycliffe, lab., on 12 Feb. 1510 with force and arms, namely sticks and knives, broke and entered the close of Thomas Layng and Thomas Hopper at Coundon field and stole 19 sheep worth 26s. 8d. belonging to Thomas Layng and Thomas Hopper, against the bishop's peace.

13

(Durham) Pleas and presentments at Durham on 21 Oct. 1510 before John Rakett and John Bentley, keepers of the bishop's peace in co. Durham.

Jury: Richard Bothe, William Hewetson, Thomas Kirkman, Robert Hagthorp, John Porter, Roland White, Thomas Kyrstone, William Pykryng, John Ferrour, Robert Selby, Thomas Mosse, John Ayton, John Jakson, testify:

1) Henry Emerson late of Bradley, co. Durham, yeo., on 22 May 1507 with sticks and knives at Rookhope in Weardale stole a cow worth 10s. belonging to Thomas, prior of Hexham, against the bishop's peace.

14

(Durham) Pleas and presentments at Durham on 26 Oct. 1510 before John Rakett and John Bentley, keepers of the bishop's peace in co. Durham.

Jury: Robert Tenaunt, Robert Symson, Richard Buk, John Herryson, Richard Downes, Robert Whelpden, Robert Hedworthe, John Richerdson, Richard Aldwodd, John Robynson, Robert Bylle, Roger Richerdson, testify:

1) Henry Emerson late of Bradley, co. Durham, yeo., on 22 May 1507 with sticks and knives [etc. as above].

[endorsed] Second year of the pontificate of Thomas, bishop of Durham.

15

[m. 2]   Pleas and presentments at Durham held on Sat., 26 October 1510, before John Rakett and John Bentley, keepers of the bishop's peace in co. Durham.

Jury: Robert Tennante, Robert Symson, Richard Buk, Richard Downes, Robert Hedworthe, John Richerdson, Richard Aldwod, John Robynson, Robert Bylle, Nicholas Hunter, Nicholas Crosyer, Robert Richerdson, testify:

1) John Lomley, Lord Lomley, lately of the Isle, co. Durham, esq., Edward Harbottle of Prudhoe, Northumberland, esq., John Scrope of Bolton, co. Richmond, esq., and Roger Lomley of Lumley, co. Durham, esq., on Sunday the feast of St Michael [29 September] 1510 assembled with other malefactors and disturbers of the bishop's peace to the number of 60 and in warlike fashion armed with jacks, salets, brigandines, lances, bows and arrows, swords and bills at Wolsingham in the fashion of new uprising moved riotously onto Stanhope where they put themselves in array against William Hylton of Hylton, esq., and others associating with him at Eastgate to assault and kill William and his company, against the bishop's peace and setting a pernicious example to other delinquents.

2) William Hylton of Hylton, esq., John Musgrave of Bewcastle, Cumberland, knt, John Fethirstanehalgh of Stanhope Hall, co. Durham, esq., and Henry Walles of Knaresdale, Cumberland, gen., on Sunday the feast of St Michael [29 September] 1510 assembled with other malefactors and unknown disturbers of the peace to the

number of 80 in warlike fashion with jacks, salets, brigandines, lances, bows and arrows, swords and bills at Stanhope park by Eastgate in fashion of new uprising and riotously put themselves in array against John, lord Lomley of the Isle, esq., and others in his company at the rectory at Stanhope to assault, wound and kill John Lomley against the bishop's peace and set a pernicious example to other delinquents.

16

3] Pleas and presentments at Durham on Monday 27 Jan. 1511 before William Hylton, esq., Thomas Tempest and John Rakett, justices to keep the bishop's peace in co. Durham.

Jury: John Forsour, esq., John Ayton, Thomas Kirkman, George Blaxton, Ralph Gyllowe, Robert Richerdson, Robert Currey, Robert Hall, John Porter, William Warde, Nicholas Crosier, William Lawson, Robert Gray testify:

1) Robert Herbotell of Prudhoe, Northumberland, gen., alias Sodron Robert, William Skuttsfeld of the same, gen., Henry Percy of the same, gen., Edmund Hogeson of Fenham, yeo., Guy Hogeson of Prudhoe, yeo., Thomas Smythe of the same, yeo., Cuthbert Rogerley of the same, yeo., Henry Carlell of the same, gen., and [blank] Tawdry of the same, minstrel, on 21 Dec. 1510 riotously assembled at Gateshead in the house of William Cooke and there assaulted Thomas Hilton and John Grenwodd, servant of William Hilton, esq., and wounded Thomas Hilton so that his life was despaired of, against the bishop's peace.

2) George Hilton of Hylton, gen., and Thomas Lyle of the same, gen., Roger Merley of the same, gen., George Lawson of the same, gen., Roland Blenkynsopp of the same, gen., Simon Kirver of the same, lab., Gerard Nikson of the same, yeo., and Thomas Habraham of the same, yeo., on 9 Jan. 1511 at *Langacres* assembled riotously and assaulted Nicholas Turpyn, servant of Guygerd [*sic*] Herbotell and [*blank*] servant of Nicholas, and injured Nicholas so that his life was despaired of, against the bishop's peace.

3) Whereas it was ordained that no layman should have greyhounds, sleuthhounds (*ordorencetos*) or nets called *pursnett* or any other engines of chase unless they had lands worth 40s., Robert White of Newfield, co. Durham, yeo., Edward White of the same, yeo., John Etton of North Auckland, yeo., John Stevynson of the same, yeo., John Ledale of Sunderland by Croxdale [*blank*].

17

.2] Pleas and presentments at Stanhope on 26 March 1511 before Thomas Kay, clerk, LL.B., William Hylton, esq., Thomas Tempest, John Rakett and John Bentley, justices and keepers of the bishop's peace in co. Durham.

Jury: Thomas Nevyll, John Fethirstanhalgh, Alexander Blakett,

Robert Todd, Robert Emerson of Eastgate, Ralph Walker, Robert Braidley, Roland Herryson, William Emerson senior, Roland Gybson, William Herryson, Edward Emerson, Guy Fethirstanhalgh, Thomas Mallom, Edward Samson, Matthew Baynbrig, William Gybson, Thomas Todd, Robert Emerson of Ireshopeburn, Richard Emerson, John Yonger, Jenkin Natres, Robert Freres, Richard Berwyk, Anthony Herryson and William Bromyll testify:

1) Henry Emerson late of Stanhope, co. Durham, on Friday after St Michael 1 Henry VIII and 1 Thomas [5 Oct. 1509] with sticks and knives stole a mare worth 5s. belonging to Christopher Barburn at Stanhope, against the bishop's peace.

2) Roger Stapulton of Bewcastle, Cumberland, yeo., Nicholas Stapilton of the same, yeo., and John Bradley of the same, yeo., on 10 Sept. 1504 at night about the tenth hour stole at Wolsingham 40 rams (arietes) worth 60s. belonging to Thomas Berker and drove them off against the bishop's peace. Lionel Madyson of Unthank, co. Durham, yeo., knowing Roger, Nicholas and John to be common thieves and indicted of various felonies feloniously comforted them the same day at Stanhope in a shieling (shela) by Unthank lonyng and gave them a pasty (pastellam ferine), 4 wheaten loaves and a bottle of ale brought by William Madyson, son of the said Lionel, against the bishop's peace.

3) Thomas Madyson late of Stanhope, yeo., on 12 Sept. 1507 with force and arms, namely swords, sticks and knives, drove off 3 cows and 20 sheep worth 60s. of Richard Atkynson and Robert Whitfeld at Stanhope, against the bishop's peace.

4) William Ridlee, servant of Nicholas Rydlee of Willimontswick in the liberty of Hexham, yeo., Roland Tweddell of Gilsland, Cumberland, yeo., and Robert Tweddell of the same, yeo., on 10 May 1509 at Swinhope, co. Durham, drove off 8 horses of Roland Herryson worth 50 marks and 4 horses of Robert Blount of Durham, against the bishop's peace.

[m.2d.] 5) Nicholas Ledebeter son of William Ledebeter of Weardale, co. Durham, yeo., John Natres of Blakelough, yeo., Roger Baynbryge of Wearhead, yeo., William Natres of the same, yeo., Adam Watson of Holehouse, yeo., Ralph Nevell of Milnehouse, yeo., Richard Hyndeson of Dobes, yeo., John Hogeson of Turnmore, yeo., Christopher Richerdson of Weardale, yeo., Edward Wall of Horsley, yeo., Roland Hall of Stanhope, yeo., Robert Emerson of Stanhope, yeo., John Peirce of West Blackdene, yeo., Patrick Madewell of [blank], chaplain, Adam Watson of Ireshopeburn, yeo., Ralph Emerson son of Hugh Emerson of Weardale, yeo., [blank].

18

(Durham) Pleas and presentments at Durham on 20 Oct. 1511 before John Rakett and John Bentley, justices to keep the bishop's peace in co. Durham.

Jury: John Hebburn, Robert Tailboys, William Lawson, Robert Hagthorp, John Wadle, Thomas Morgane, William Stayndrop, John Ferrour, William Johnson, Robert Currey, Thomas Kirkman, William Thorp, Gilbert Claxton testify:

1) Edward Ridley of *Dryburnhalgh*, Northumberland, yeo., alias Edward Henhed of *Dryburnhalgh*, yeo., Ranulph Ridley of Yearhaugh, yeo., Hugh Ridle of *Aldshelis*, yeo., Thomas Ridlee of *Tiphaldwater* yeo., alias Thomas Ridlee son of Nicholas Ridle of Walltown, yeo., and William Herdman of Walltown, yeo., on 1 Sept. 1511 broke with force and arms, namely swords, bows and arrows, and entered the close and houses of Robert Bradley at Wolsingham, co. Durham, and drove away 3 cows and 3 calves worth 20s. 8d. belonging to the same, against the bishop's peace.

2) Robert Delavale of Prudhoe, Northumberland, gen., on 10 July 1511 at Lintzford, co. Durham, assaulted Gerard Garshopp late of Lintz with force and arms, namely swords, sticks and knives, and struck him on the head with a sword worth 2s. held in his hands, giving him a mortal wound from which he languished until 18 July when he died. They said that Robert feloniously killed and murdered Gerard and that Lancelot Hedlee of Prudhoe, Northumberland, yeo., Ralph Maxwell of the same, yeo., William Scrutfeld of the same, yeo., and John Besyn of *Shirwenthousez*, co. Durham, yeo., were present, aiding and abetting him, against the bishop's peace.

3) Robert Tenante, bailiff of Durham, allowed vagabonds and Scots to roam, lodge and overnight within the borough without punishment, against the statute [*19 Hen. VII, c. 12*] and the responsibility of his office.

4) John Robynson, deputy bailiff of Aukland, allowed vagabonds and Scots to roam and lodge overnight within the borough against the statute and the responsibility of his office.

5) John Richerdson, bailiff of Gateshead, allowed vagabonds and Scots to roam and lodge overnight within the borough against the statute and the responsibility of his office.

6) John Herrison, bailiff of Wolsingham, allowed vagabonds and Scots to roam and overnight within the town (*villam*) against the statute and the responsibility of his office.

19

.1] Pleas and presentments at Durham held on 18 Feb. 1512 before [*illegible*].

Jury: Richard Both, Anthony Brakenbery, John Ayton, William Hewetson, John Atkynson, Thomas Fishburn, Thomas Kyrkeman, Richard Aldwodd, Ralph Walker, John Ferrour, Robert Hagthorp, Robert Hall, John Portour and William Warde testify:

1) Robert Wynke late of Darlington, co. Durham, yeo., on 3 Jan. 1512 at Darlington stole a chalice worth 40s. from Thomas Paull, Henry Lasenby, Robert May and Nicholas Robynson, churchwardens of

Marton (*Mortonchurche*) in Cleveland, and John Thomson of Darlington, *berker*, alias Jenkyn Thomson of Darlington, yeo., and William Stapilton of the same, yeo., knowing that Robert Wynke had stolen the same, arrested Wynke with the chalice: and the same day the said John and William allowed Wynke to escape after his arrest and took the chalice to their own use, thereby receiving, aiding and abetting, against the bishop's peace.

2) William Marche of Darlington, yeo., John Fraunche of the same, yeo., and John Hindles of the same, yeo., on 9 Jan. 1512 at Darlington in a field called *Dodmerfeld* made riotous affray against Thomas Cowper of Darlington with sticks and knives and maliciously wounded him, against the bishop's peace.

3) Robert Wynke late of Darlington, yeo., on 3 Jan. 1512 at Darlington stole [*etc. as above, without the charge against Thomson and Stapilton*].

4) John Hogeson of Wingate, co. Durham, yeo., Robert Hogeson of the same, lab., and Richard Smythe of Shadforth on 5 Jan. 1512 riotously lay in wait with sticks and knives for William Robynson of Wingate, yeo., at *Pykstones* by Wingate, made affray and wounded him so that his life was despaired of, against the bishop's peace.

5) James Galile of Gateshead, co. Durham, butcher, on 28 Jan. 1512 at Gateshead assaulted with sticks and knives William Wright, servant of Thomas, prior of Durham, and carried off 2 quarters of barley worth 10s. belonging to the prior, against the bishop's peace.

6) John Whetely, servant of Roland Tempest, on 7 Dec. 1511 made affray on Thomas Kay, clerk, the bishop's surveyor, against the bishop's peace.

1545–1546

Public Record Office, London, Durham 13/265 These membranes are filed after the rolls of the Durham courts of gaol delivery and of pleas held on 3 August 1545. The dates of the sessions are 3 August and 10 October 1545 and 16 January and 22 May 1546.

20

7] Sessions of the peace at Durham on Mon., 3 Aug. 37 Henry VIII, king of England, France and Ireland, defender of the faith and supreme head on earth of the church in England and Ireland, and 16 Cuthbert [Tunstall], bishop of Durham, [1545] before John Hynde, king's serjeant at law, Edmund Molyneux, king's serjeant at law, Robert Hyndmer, clerk, chancellor of Durham, Ralph Hedworth, knt, Ralph Claxton, Thomas Blaxton, Robert Meynell and Robert Tempest, esqs.

Jury: William Blaxton, esq., Roland Maddison, gen., Nicholas Blakkett, gen., Roger Boythe, gen., Philip Baynbrygg, gen., Robert Portour, gen., Robert Ayton, gen., Simon Welburye, yeo., Robert Hagthropp, gen., Thomas Conyers, gen., Christopher Ledell, yeo., Henry Garnett, yeo., and Nicholas Crosyer, gen., testify:

1) Whereas by statute of 8 Henry VI [1429/30] at Westminster on disseisin it was stated that if any person were disseised from any tenement he be entitled to sue and if the aggrieved party recover by verdict or due action of law he should recover triple damages and redemption be paid to the king, Robert Laburn late of Muggleswick park, co. Durham, yeo., on 5 May 1545 forcibly ejected Stephen Marley, clerk, from his tenement at Muggleswick at Healeyfield and held it against the king's peace.

2) John Maytland late of High Friarside, co. Durham, lab., Gilbert Looge of the same, lab., and Robert Ladley of the same, lab., on 14 May 1545 assembled riotously at Low Friarside with swords, sticks and other defensive arms and assaulted and wounded Roger Battlyf so that his life was despaired of, against the king's peace.

3) William Alleyn late of Egglescliffe, co. Durham, yeo., William Elstob late of the same, lab., and Robert Dukk late of the same, lab., on 11 May 1545 riotously broke the close of Thomas Cundon at Egglescliffe and seized 5 oxen and 3 cows of the same, against the king's peace.

4) William Allan late of Egglescliffe, yeo., William Elstob late of the same, lab., and Robert Dukk late of the same, lab., on 8 June 1545 riotously broke the close of Thomas Cundon at Egglescliffe, depastured his grass with livestock and ploughed his land, against the king's peace.

5) Whereas by statute of 8 Henry VI on disseisin [etc.] John Darley late of Billingside, co. Durham, husbandman, and Robert Wilkynson late of Bushblades, husbandman, on 17 June 1545 on the orders of [illegible] Rawe late of High Friarside, spinster, and Ralph Rawe late of the same [illegible] riotously entered a messuage of Robert Claxton, clerk, at Low Friarside and ejected him from his house to his grave

damage and against the king's peace.

6) Ralph Hedworth late of Whickham, co. Durham, gen., on 7 May 1545 feloniously assaulted Anthony Eliner in the village of Whickham, struck him with a pikestaff worth 2d. on the forehead and inflicted a mortal wound from which he languished and died on 9 May at Newcastle upon Tyne, thereby killing him against the king's peace.

7) William Typpe late of Whitehall, co. Durham, yeo., on 6 Feb. 1545 riotously and feloniously with swords and knives took from the common pasture at Wolsingham 7 sheep worth 13s. 4d. belonging to Robert Tempest, esq., against the king's peace.

21

[m.7d.]   Pleas and presentments at Durham on Saturday, 10 Oct. 37 Henry VIII [1545], before Robert Hyndmer, clerk, chancellor of Durham, and Robert Meynell, esq.

Jury: Robert Melot, Roger With, Robert Portour, William Pykeryng, John Wadlee, Roland Maddyson, Thomas Dixson, Ralph Garrys, John Elstobb, John Byllyngham, Robert Ayton, Philip Baynbrigg and Robert Hall testify:

1) Edmund Hogeson late of Darlington alias Darneton, co. Durham, mercer, John Claxton late of the same, gen., Stephen Wylde late of the same, yeo., Edward Priorman late of the same, lab., William Spyser late of the same, lab., and Robert Hall late of Hurworth, husbandman, not regarding God nor fearing the king or the law and by diabolic instigation on 12 Aug. 1545 at Neasham attacked John Orton with sticks, swords and knives, and Edmund Hogeson feloniously struck Orton on the forehead with a stick worth 2d. from which blow he died instantly. The remainder aided and abetted Hogeson in his felony and thereby all feloniously killed John Orton against the king's peace. (pardon)

22

Pleas and presentments at Durham on Saturday, 16 Jan. 37 Henry VIII [1546], before Robert Hyndmer, clerk, chancellor of Durham, Ralph Hedworthe, knt, and Robert Meynell.

Jury: Roger Boithe, Robert Portour, William Pykeryng, John Wadlee, Ralph Garrys, Robert Ayton, John Hall, Thomas Forsour, Christopher Ledall, Richard Downes, John Rakkett senior, Robert Hall and John Rakket junior testify:

1) Thomas Elynour of Hutton, co. Durham, husbandman, on 20 Oct. 1544 feloniously broke the close of Thomas Gregson of Hutton at Hutton and took 15 hens together worth 5s. belonging to the same against the king's peace. (acquitted by verdict)

2) George Stevynson late of Durham, butcher, on 20 Oct. 1545 broke the close of Ralph Mallom at Stanley and feloniously took 11 rams worth 33s. belonging to the same against the king's peace, his crown and dignity.

3) Whereas by statute of 8 Henry VI against disseisin [etc.], John Burn of Little Usworth, yeo., William Burn late of the same, yeo., George Burn late of the same, yeo., John Burn of Gateshead, lab., Ralph Burn of Newcastle upon Tyne, merchant, and Richard Burn of Newcastle upon Tyne, merchant, on 11 Jan. 1546 riotously ejected Edmund Lawson, gen., and Margery his wife from their tenement at Little Usworth and dispossessed them from 11 until 16 Jan., to the king's contempt and against his peace.

4) Robert Claxton of Farnacres, co. Durham, chaplain, Richard Claxton of the same, gen., Roger Claxton of the same, gen., Roger Ratclyf of the same, lab., Alexander Brown of the same, miller, Thomas Knyght of the same, lab., John Cooke of Gateshead, lab., Richard Hynd of *Cokkeclose* in the parish of Lamesley, lab., Robert Andrewe of Blackburn Mill, lab., John Coltman of Hollingside, lab., and William Teesdayll of Whickham, lab., with others unknown on 25 Aug. 1545 at Low Friarside assembled riotously and broke the close of Ralph Rawe and depastured the same against the king's peace.

23

[f.8] Pleas and presentments at Durham on Sat., 22 May 1546, before Robert Hyndmer, clerk, chancellor of Durham, Ralph Hedworthe, knt, and Robert Meynell, esq.

Jury: John Trollopp, Thomas Forsour, George Blaxton, German Pawll, Roger Boyth, John Rakkett junior, Ralph Garrys, Roland Maddyson, John Waddley, John Hall, Lionel Fisheburn, Arthur Nevyll, William Pykeryng, John Warde and Robert Hall testify:

1) Henry Holland of Beamish, co. Durham, gen., on 19 April 1546 at Beamish Park blocked a common way or king's street on the south side of the park with a fence and a thorn-ditch, to the nuisance of the common people and against the king's peace [etc.]

2) Roland Fewster of Durham, saddler, (paid) on 7 Feb. 1546 in a main road *(communi vice)* at Durham obstructed a cart drawn by 3 horses belonging to Roger Boith using divers beams deliberately placed, against the king's peace [etc.].

3) Thomas Robynson late of Low Friarside, co. Durham, lab., and John Claxton of Farnacres, gen., on 24 March 1546 broke the close of Ralph Rawe at Friarside and damaged and overturned newly erected fences and ditches against the king's peace.

4) Richard Claxton late of Farnacres, co. Durham, gen., John Claxton of the same, gen., and George White of the same, yeo., on 4 Feb. 1546 broke the close of Ralph Rawe at Friarside and damaged and overturned newly-erected fences and ditches.

5) William Newton late of Ryton, co. Durham, husbandman, on 8 May 1545 broke the close of Robert Porter at Ryton, ejected Porter, and ploughed his land by which Porter lost the profit of his soil, against the form of the statute [etc.].

6) William Dixson late of Gateshead, co. Durham, butcher, on 4 Oct.

1545 with swords and knives broke the close at Whickham of Anthony Byrd late of Whickham, gen., and stole a bay mare worth 13s. 4d. belonging to the same, against the king's peace [*etc.*]

7) James Lawson of Newcastle upon Tyne, merchant, on 20 March 1546 blocked with divers fences and ditches two common highways at Gateshead, one called *le way* leading to the low road (*nether way*) from Gateshead to Durham and the other *le common churche way* from Gateshead to Saltwellside and Darncrook, against the king's peace [*etc.*]

[*m.8d., blank*]

Durham University Library, Archives & Special Collections, C.C. 220736A 1/3 The 11 membranes are filed in reverse order. Sessions were held on 22 June, 12 August and 5 October 1555; 18 January, 18 April, 3 August and 10 October 1556; and 23 January, 7 May, 9 August and 6 November 1557.

24

.11]   Sessions of the peace held at Durham on 22 June 1/2 Philip & Mary, king and queen of England, France, Naples, Jerusalem and Ireland, defender(s) of the faith, prince(s) of the Spains and Sicily, archduke(s) of Austria, duke(s) of Milan, Burgundy and Brabant, count(s) of Hapsburg, Flanders and Tyrol [1555] before Robert Hyndmer, clerk, chancellor of Durham, Robert Meynell, serjeant at law, Robert Tempest, esq., Thomas Blaxton, esq., Richard Hebburn, esq., Thomas Trolloppe, esq., and Gerard Salvayn, JPs.

Edward Telfurth, John Rakket, Ralph Garrye, John Blaxton, George Gudyer, John Swalwell, John Hagthroppe, John Claxton, Christopher Ledall, German Pawle, John Cusson, John Stellyng, John Cragge, jurors.

1) Anthony Androw late of Ebchester, co. Durham, yeo., on 16 June 1555 lay in wait for Richard Maltland late of Ebchester at Ebchester and assaulted him with a pikestaff worth 12d. held in both hands on the left side of the head to the brain, of which blow he died instantly, so murdering him.

2) William Selbey of Grindon Rigg in the liberty of Norham, gen., assembled with two others unknown on 1 June 1555 with force and arms at Twizell in the liberty of Norham and attacked Giles Storrye on the king's highway and put him in mortal fear so that his life was despaired of and feloniously took from his person 35s. in money in a purse, 4 ells of velvet, 100 ells of linen, 4 gross of silk points of divers colours, 4 pairs of women's stockings, 36 ells of canvas, 100 ells of ribbons of divers colours, 24 silver rings, 12 silver clasps and a tunic of white russet cloth worth in all £40, belonging to the same Giles Storye.

3) Whereas by statute of 8 Henry VI against forcible disseisin it was decreed that if anyone were forcibly disseised of his lands he should have the assize of novel disseisin or writ of trespass, and if he should recover by verdict or other due form of law he should receive triple damages and a fine and redemption be paid to the Crown, George Dooys of Whitehouse by Durham, yeo., and Ralph Wille of the same, yeo., on 14 May 1555 dispossessed Robert Brandlyng, knt, and Anne his wife, Thomas Blaxton, esq., and Elizabeth his wife (held as by right of the same Elizabeth and Anne) and Francis Wyclif of their capital messuage or manor at Stodhoe by force and arms and still hold the free tenement.

4) Henry Foster of Barton, Yorks., gen., John Wrangham senior of Bolam, co. Durham, husbandman, William Wrangham of the same,

husbandman, Humphrey Wrangham of the same, lab., John Wrangham junior of the same, lab., and Thomas Murton of Morton, husbandman, with 10 others unknown assembled riotously with force and arms on 23 March 1555 and broke and entered a close of Edmund Maburner, knt, Francis Wandisforth and John Fultroppe, esqs, at St Helen Auckland and broke and spoiled their hedges there and uprooted 300 thorn trees called *whickwodde* worth together 40s., against the peace.
[*m.11d., blank*]

25

[*m.10*] Sessions of the peace at Durham on 12 Aug 2/3 Philip & Mary [*1555*] before Edward Sanders, justice of Common Pleas, knt, William Dallyson, serjeant at law, Robert Hyndmer, clerk, chancellor of Durham, and Robert Meynell, serjeant at law, JPs.

George Blaxton, gen., John Rakket, John Blakston, John Byllyngham, John Hagthroppe, John Claxston, German Paull, Anthony Thomlyngson, Philip Baynbrige, Ralph Pratt, Simon Welburie, John Morgayn, Robert Porter, jurors.

1) William Smith of Esh, co. Durham, esq., Robert Emerson of the same, husbandman, John Short of the same, husbandman, Henry Richardson of the same, lab., Cuthbert Richeson of the same, lab., William Walshe of the same, lab., Robert Key of Great Chilton, husbandman, Thomas Meryman of the same, husbandman, Thomas Key of the same, husbandman, John Watter of the same, husbandman, Thomas Darneton of the same, husbandman, William Darneton of the same, lab., William Maltbey of the same, husbandman, Robert Darnton of the same, husbandman, George Key of the same, husbandman, Matthew Gray of the same, lab., Robert Maltbey of the same, lab., Robert Mayson of Little Chilton, husbandman, Richard Hucheson of Thrislington, husbandman, Henry Middilton of the same, husbandman, William Recheson of Ferryhill, husbandman, Robert Wilye of the same, husbandman, Thomas Richeson of the same, husbandman, William Kerkehowse of the same, husbandman, Martin Smithe of the same, husbandman, Christopher Wilye of the same, husbandman, William Person of the same, husbandman, John Harper of the same, husbandman, Cuthbert Widifeld of the same, husbandman, Robert Rose of the same, husbandman, John Graye of the same, husbandman, Cuthbert Robenson of the same, husbandman, Thomas Ferye of the same, husbandman, John Wodd of Kirk Merrington, husbandman, John Recheson of the same, husbandman, William Middleton of the same, husbandman, Thomas Wyet of the same, husbandman, Richard Lyndley of the same, lab., William Helmysley of the same, lab., with 100 others unknown on 12 July 1555 with force and arms, namely sticks, daggers, shields [*etc.*] riotously assembled at Isle, co. Durham, and broke and entered the close of John Lumley, knt, Lord Lumley, at

Isle called *Mylne Carr* and seized 28 wainloads of hay worth £7 belonging to the same.

2) Thomas Hilderton of Whitehouse by Durham, gen., George Doce of the same, lab., James Chepman of the same, lab., John Harbottell of the same, lab., and Anthony Doys of the same, lab., with 6 others unknown assembled riotously with force and arms, namely swords, sticks, lances, knives, bows, arrows and other arms in warlike fashion on 20 July 1555 and entered the free tenement of Robert Brandlyng, knt, and Anne his wife, Thomas Blaxton and Elizabeth his wife, and Francis Wyklyf at Stodhoe, co. Durham, and attacked Ralph Willey so that his life was despaired of.

3) Oswald Fenneke of Newcastle, merchant, Thomas Fenneke of the same, merchant, and Thomas Harreson of Northumberland, yeo., assembled riotously with others unknown at Offerton, co. Durham, on 9 Aug. 1555 and broke and entered a pasture called *le oxe pasture* and drove off 4 oxen belonging to Edmund Parkynson.

4) Hugh Sotheron of Darlington, co. Durham, yeo., Ralph Coteman of Walworth, yeo., Bartholomew Wilkyngson of Darlington, yeo., and Cuthbert Walker of the same, yeo., assembled riotously with 8 others armed in warlike fashion and with force and arms on 5 Aug. 1555 broke and entered the close of Robert Emerson and Cuthbert Nycholson at Darlington and carried off a wainload of hay worth 10s. belonging to Robert Emerson and Cuthbert Nycholson and committed other enormities.

5) Edmund Blacket of Stanhope, yeo., on 4 July 1555 at Brandon field lay in ambush on the highway to kill Nicholas Barrow of Woodcroft, lab., and assaulted the same.

.10d.] 6) Edmund Blacket of Stanhope, yeo., on 18 July 1555 with force and arms broke and entered the close of Nicholas Blacket of Woodcroft, gen., and lay in wait to kill and assaulted Nicholas Barrow.

7) Laurence Hayle late of Durham city, yeo., Edward Hudspath of the same, tanner, and Robert Bradshaw of the same, glover, on 24 May 1555 on Framwellgate bridge [Durham] assembled riotously and assaulted William Wright, merchant of Durham.

8) Anthony Mylburn late of *Bors* in Tynedale, Northumberland, husbandman, Ald' Suddle Anton late of the same, husbandman, and John Mylburn late of the same, husbandman, on 10 Oct. 1554 with force and arms at Rookhope in Weardale, co. Durham, stole 28 sheep worth £7 belonging to Richard Emerson and 8 sheep worth 40s. belonging to Thomas Emerson.

9) John Revyley late of Berrington, *co. Durham, yeo., on 8 July 1555 with force and arms at Berrington assaulted Thomas Thurbrand and struck him on his left side under the breast with a dagger worth 2s. held in his right hand, giving him a mortal wound from which he died instantly.

10) Cuthbert Forster of *Darmansteid* in Gilsland, Cumberland, yeo., and Matthew Tayler of Harperhill in Gilsland, yeo., on 9 Feb. 1555

with force and arms broke and entered a close of Christopher Hall of Wingate Grange, co. Durham, at Wingate Grange and stole 2 bay horses worth £10 and a bay mare worth £5 belonging to the same.

11) Cuthbert Forster of *Dormansteid* in Gilsland, yeo., and Matthew Tayler of Harperhill in Gilsland, yeo., on 9 Feb. 1555 with force and arms broke and entered a close of Christopher Hall of Wingate Grange, co. Durham, at Wingate Grange and stole a black mare worth £8 belonging to John Hall son of Christopher Hall.

12) Thomas Hedryngton late of *Edyssgill* in Gilsland, Cumberland, lab., John Blakburne late of *Lukkous* in Gilsland, lab., and Rinian Blakburne late of the same, lab., on 10 July 1555 with force and arms at West Thickley, co. Durham, stole a bay horse worth £10, a grey horse worth £4 and a grey mare worth £6 13s. 4d. belonging to George Tonge, gen.

26

[*m.9*]   Sessions of the peace at Durham on 5 Oct. 2/3 Philip & Mary [*1555*] before Robert Hyndmer, clerk, Robert Meynell, serjeant at law, Robert Tempest, Thomas Trolloppe, Richard Hebburn, William Claxton and Ralph Dalton.

John Hall, John Franklayn, Simon Welbury, George Gudyer, Ralph Pratt, John Cragg, John Claxton, Ralph Mayson, Ralph Elstobb, William Smythe, Ralph Garrye, John Rakkett, John Swalwall, Robert Blenkynsopp, jurors.

1) Thomas Claveryng of Wark [on Tweed], Northumberland, gen., Edward Chamerlen of the same, yeo., Nicholas Eberd of the same, yeo., John Pearth of the same, yeo., Christopher Ebord of the same, yeo., Edward More of the same, yeo., William Eborde of the same, yeo., Edward West of the same, yeo., William Charleton of the same, yeo., Alexander Ebarde senior of the same, yeo., William Robson of the same, yeo., Ralph Ebarde of the same, yeo., Robert Ebarde of the same, yeo., Richard Peersye of the same, yeo., William Grae of the same, yeo., Richard Ebarde of the same, yeo., William Goddye of the same, yeo., George Ebarde of the same, yeo., Alexander Ebarde junior of the same, yeo., Robert Butt of the same, yeo., David Huntour of the same, lab., Scot, William Hopkirk of the same, Scot, lab., Robert Chamerley of the same, lab., Thomas Johnson, Scot, lab., Thomas Pattenson of the same, lab., Scot, Thomas Huntley of Carham, yeo., William Errisdell of the same, yeo., John Dodd of the same, yeo., Cuthbert Ebarde of the same, yeo., Edward Wilson of Berwick-on-Tweed, Northumberland, yeo., Richard Carr of Ford, gen., Marmaduke Shaftowe of Felkington within the liberties of Norham, gen., John Selby junior of Twizell in the same liberties, gen., William Selbye of the same, gen., Oliver Selbye of Learmouth, gen., John Johnson of the same, yeo., Richard Persye of the same, yeo., Affton Lather of the same, yeo., William Lucke of the same, yeo., Alexander Swarlen of the same, yeo., John Swarlen of the same, yeo., Ralph

Thomson of the same, yeo., Nicholas Cuthbert of the same, yeo.,
Thomas Cuthbert of the same, yeo., Roger Frost of the same, yeo.,
Alexander Cuthbert of the same, yeo., Charles Haward of the same,
yeo., John Swan of the same, yeo., Thomas Johnson of the same,
yeo., William Salbye of Mindrum, yeo., Thomas Atchynson of the
same, yeo., Robert Tailyour of the same, yeo., John Tayte of the same,
yeo., Henry Whyte of the same, yeo., Odinel Selbye of the same, yeo.,
Alexander Dodd of the same, yeo., Thomas Tyndayll of the same,
yeo., Charles Tailyour of the same, yeo., John Chanlez of the same,
yeo., John Tailyour of the same, yeo., Henry Reveley of Duddoe in
the liberties of Norham, yeo., Robert Jakson of the same, yeo., John
Heslopp of the same, yeo., Edward Jakson of the same, yeo., Gilbert
Selbye of Tillmouth, Northumberland, yeo., William Selbye of the
same, yeo., John Fett of the same, yeo., and Christopher Saunders of
the same, yeo., with about 200 others unknown with force and arms,
namely bows, arrows, swords, lances, sticks, knives and other arms in
warlike fashion in manner of new insurrection on 21 Sept. 1555
assembled riotously and entered the manor of Robert Lawson, gen.,
and Margery his wife at Scremerston in the liberties of Norham
illegally and riotously and put John Nevyll and Thomas Thew in
mortal fear and seized 170 thraves of wheat worth £15 belonging to
Robert Lawson.
2) Thomas Lawson of Little Usworth, co. Durham, gen., Thomas
Sparrowe of the same, yeo., Thomas Richardson of the same, yeo.,
Henry Walton of the same, yeo., John Leremowthe of the same,
piper, William Lawson of Washington, gen., John Lawson of *Aldem'*,
gen., William Browne of the same, yeo., William Sparroo of the same,
yeo., Roland Lawson of Saltwellside, gen., John Nevyll of the same,
yeo., Lancelot Kirkley of the same, yeo., Thomas Heryson of the
same, yeo., Edmund Lawson of Great Usworth, yeo., Cuthbert Hylton
of the same, gen., John [Hedworth] of Harraton, gen., Richard
Harbattell of the same, yeo., Richard Hereson of the same, yeo.,
Gregory Baynbrige of the same, yeo., John Tailyour of Southwick,
husbandman, Edward Tailyour of the same, lab., Robert Atkynson of
Hedworth, husbandman, Cuthbert Atkynson of the same, lab.,
Anthony Brunton of the same, husbandman, Cuthbert Eden of the
same, lab., William Hynde of East Boldon, husbandman, Robert
Cragge of the same, husbandman, Richard Kechyng of Whitburn,
husbandman, John Kechyng senior of the same, husbandman, John
Kechyng junior of the same, lab., Robert Ayre of the same,
husbandman, Samson Hogeson of West Boldon, – , John Redewe of
the same, lab., William Chambre of the same, lab., Henry Robyson of
the same, lab., Richard Chambre of the same, lab., Thomas Robyson
senior of the same, lab., Thomas Robynson junior of the same, lab.,
John Robynson of the same, lab., George Archebaude of the same,
lab., William Smythe of the same, lab., Alan Bedlyngton of the same,
webster, John Walshe of the same, husbandman, Robert Walshe of

the same, lab., Thomas Wodde of the same, webster, John Newland of the same, butcher, John Sylvartop of the same, lab., Robert Bedlyngton of the same, lab., John Stevynson of the same, lab., Thomas Sotheron of the same, lab., Edward Johnson of the same, miller, Robert Stevynson of the same, lab., Thomas Leiyhe of Cleadon, husbandman, and William Mathewe of the same, husbandman, with 12 others unknown assembled riotously with force and arms, namely sticks, shields, lances and halberds in warlike fashion on 9 Aug. 1555 on the tenement of Robert Rikabye at West Boldon and seized 5 wainloads of hay worth 33s. 4d. belonging to Robert Rekabye.

[m.9d.]   3) Robert Rikarby of East Boldon, co. Durham, yeo., Conan Barton of Durham, gen., William Rickerbye of Stainton-in-the-Street, husbandman, John Tunstall of Bishop Auckland, yeo., Stephen Day of Bradbury, yeo., Charles Shawe of Durham, cutler, George Petarkyn of the same, walker, John Smythe of Stainton-in-the-Street, lab., Thomas Devande of East Boldon, lab., John Arrowe of the same, lab., Leonard Bolland of Follingsby, lab., John Clarke of the same, lab., Thomas Walles of East Boldon, lab., John Claxton of Stainton-in-the-Street, husbandman, and Ralph Trotter of Bishop Auckland, yeo., with 26 others unknown illegally and riotously assembled with force and arms on 15 July 1555 at West Boldon and broke and entered the close of Thomas Robynson, Robert Atcheson and John Walshe at West Boldon and seized 6 wainloads of hay worth £20 belonging to the same.

4) Thomas Hilderton of Whitehouse by Durham, gen., George Doose of the same, yeo., and James Chapman of the same, yeo., on 20 Sept. 1555 at Studhoe illegally and riotously assembled and broke and entered the close of Robert Brandlyng, knt, and Anne his wife, Thomas Blaxton and Elizabeth his wife and Francis Wiclyf and seized 40 ewes worth £4 belonging to Percival Shawe and drove them away.

5) Robert Emerson of Ludwell in the parish of Stanhope, co. Durham, yeo., Adam Emerson of Gatecastle in Stanhope parish, yeo., and Henry Wrenne of Westernhopeburn (*Wastnopburn*) in Stanhope parish, yeo., with 10 others unknown assembled riotously on 13 July 1555 at Great Burdon with force and arms and lay in wait to kill Robert Hudlei, assaulted him, and put him in mortal fear so that his life was despaired of.

27

[m.8]   Sessions of the peace at Durham on 18 Jan. 2/3 Philip & Mary [1556] before Robert Hyndmer, clerk, chancellor of Durham, Robert Meynell, serjeant at law, Robert Tempest, Richard Hebburn, William Claxton and Gerard Salwayn, esqs., JPs.

Thomas Lawson, John Hall, John Blenkynsopp, John Swalwell, Ralph Pratt, John Blakston, Christopher Ledyll, Robert Blenkynsop, Ralph Elstobb, Ralph Mayson, Robert Shotwell, Nicholas Blakkett,

John Cragg, Cuthbert Chapman, jurors.

1) Richard Nichall of Durham city, merchant, on 8 Oct. 1555 with force and arms broke and entered the close and house of John Harper at Durham city and stole 16 silver spoons worth £3 12s. 4d., 2 gold rings and 4 gold rials called *newe ryals* worth £3, a *george* worth 5s., a *yokendayll* worth 4s. 6d., and a half and a quarter *yokendayll* worth 3s. 3d.

2) Christopher Bowman late of Winston, co. Durham, yeo., on 6 Sept. 1555 with force and arms broke and entered the park of Bishop Tunstall at Evenwood and stole a black horse worth £5 belonging to Cuthbert Neville, esq.

3) Christopher Bowman late of Winston, yeo., on 6 Sept. 1555 with force and arms broke and entered the park of Bishop Tunstall at Evenwood and stole a white-grey horse worth £4 belonging to Stephen Duffeilde.

4) Christopher Bowman late of Winston, yeo., on 6 Sept. 1555 with force and arms broke and entered the park of Bishop Tunstall at Evenwood and stole a sorrel-bay horse worth 5 marks belonging to Francis Wiclyf, esq.

5) Richard Blakkett of *Sowandburn* in the parish of Stanhope, co. Durham, yeo., and Edmund Blakkett of the same, yeo., with 4 other unknown malefactors on 20 Sept. 1555 assembled riotously by the special order and procurement of William Blakkett of *Sowandburn* at *Ferrefeilde* in the parish of Stanhope and assaulted Alice Maddyson, widow, so that her life was despaired of.

6) Percival Lumley late of Darlington, esq., Richard Lumley late of Chester-le-Street, gen., Thomas Hussye of Sigston, Yorks., esq., John Hussye of the same, gen., Roland Mordyn of Grindon, co. Durham, gen., Stephen Kay late of Nunstainton, yeo., James Bullokke late of Darlington, yeo., Anthony Morres of Sigston, Yorks., yeo., William Bryan late of Aycliffe, co. Durham, lab., William Mylnar late of Darlington, lab., and Richard Adhee of Bradbury, lab., with 14 others unknown on 15 Nov. 1555 with force and arms, namely swords, shields, daggers, sticks and knives etc. in warlike fashion assembled riotously in a great illegal conventicle at Bradbury and dispossessed John Lumley, knt, Lord Lumley, of his free tenement there, which they still hold.

7) Whereas by statute against disseisin of 8 Henry VI [*etc.*], Percival Lumley late of Darlington, esq., Richard Lumley late of Chester-le-Street, gen., Thomas Hussye of Sigston, Yorks., esq., John Hussye of the same, gen., Roland Morden of Grindon, co. Durham, Stephen Kaye late of Nunstainton, yeo., James Bullokke late of Darlington, yeo., George Davye of Sigston, Yorks., yeo., Anthony Morres of the same, yeo., William Bryen of Aycliffe, co. Durham, lab., and George Thakerley of the same, yeo., on 12 Nov. 1555 forcibly disseised John Lumley, knt, Lord Lumley, of a free tenement at Bradbury and held it from 12 Nov. until 17 Jan. and until now.

[*m.8d.*]   8) Percival Lumley late of Darlington, esq., Richard Lumley of Chester-
le-Street, gen., Thomas Hussye of Sigston, Yorks., esq., John Hussye of
the same, gen., Roland Morden of Grindon, co. Durham, gen.,
Stephen Kay of Nunstainton, yeo., James Bullokke late of Darlington,
yeo., Anthony Morres of Sigston, Yorks., yeo., George Thakkerley of
the same, yeo., George Davy of Sigston, Yorks., William Bryan of
Aycliffe, co. Durham, lab., William Milner late of Darlington, lab.,
and Richard Adhe of Bradbury, lab., with 14 others unknown on 12
Nov. 1555 with force and arms, namely swords [*etc.*] at Bradbury
forcibly disseised John Lumley, knt, Lord Lumley, of his free
tenement.

9) Whereas by statute against disseisin of 8 Henry VI [*etc.*], Percival
Lumley late of Darlington, esq., Richard Lumley late of Chester-le-
Street, gen., Thomas Hussey of Sigston, Yorks., esq., John Hussey of
the same, gen., Roland Morden of Grindon, co. Durham, gen.,
Stephen Kaye late of Nunstainton, yeo., James Bullokke late of
Darlington, yeo., George Davye late of Sigston, Yorks., yeo., Anthony
Morres of the same, yeo., George Thakkrley of the same, yeo.,
William Bryan late of Aycliffe, co. Durham, lab., William Mylner of
Darlington, lab., and Richard Adhe of Bradbury, lab., with 14 others
unknown on 16 Nov. 1555 forcibly dispossessed John Lumley, knt,
Lord Lumley, of a messuage at Bradbury and held the same from 12
Nov. until 17 Jan. and until now.

28

[*m.7*]   Sessions of the peace held at Durham on 18 April 2/3 Philip & Mary
[*1556*] before Robert Hyndmer, clerk, chancellor of Durham, Robert
Meynell, serjeant at law, Robert Tempest, esq., and Gerard Salvayn,
esq., JPs.

John Hagthropp, John Blaxton, John Swalwell, Ralph Pratt, John
Claxton, Christopher Ledayll, Robert Blenkynsopp, Ralph Mayson,
Robert Shotwell, Nicholas Blakkett, German Pawle, John Cusson,
John Stelling, Robert Todde, jurors.

1) Whereas by statute against forcible disseisin of 8 Henry VI [*etc.*],
Robert Small of Berwick, Northumberland, yeo., George Selbye of the
same, gen., and Thomas Wallesse of the same, yeo., with other
malefactors assembled on 3 May 1554 at Ord and Horncliffe in the
liberties of Norhamshire and Islandshire illegally and riotously and
disseised Ralph Graye of Chillingham, Northumberland, esq., of his
free fishery in the River Tweed at Ord and Horncliffe and still hold it.

2) Whereas John Hall of Finchale, co. Durham, yeo., and Thomas
Harreson of the same, yeo., bailiffs and servants of Robert Lewen,
esq., on 11 April 1556 wished to distrain for the rent of £8 from the
township of Silksworth and took 6 oxen according to the law and
custom of England to impound them, Robert Wilson of Silksworth,
husbandman, William Wilson of the same, husbandman, Thomas
Burdon of the same, husbandman, John Burdon of the same,

husbandman, Robert Biddyke of the same, husbandman, John Burdon of the same, husbandman, Robert Biddyke of the same, husbandman, William Rutar of the same, husbandman, and John Wilkynson of the same, husbandman, with force and arms riotously recovered the same from Hall and Harreson at Silksworth to their damage and against the peace.

3) Edward Watson (fine) of Nunstainton, co. Durham, yeo., Henry Richardson of the same, lab., William Walshe of the same, lab., William Galaley of Bradbury, lab., John Chilton of the same, yeo., William Chilton of the same, yeo., Cuthbert Chilton of the same, yeo., *Thomas Chilton of the same, yeo., John Peerson of the same, Robert Archer of the same, yeo., *Ralph Atkynson of the same, Denis Mawer of the same, yeo., Edward Hykson of Preston-le-Skerne, yeo., Henry Browne of the same, yeo., Robert Hoope of Moorsholm, Yorks., yeo., Robert Thomson of Bradbury, co. Durham, yeo., Gerard Heawe of the same, lab., Thomas Skathelok of the same, yeo., John Peterall of the same, yeo., Robert Patereld of the same, yeo., and Thomas Newton of the same, yeo., on 13 Nov. 1555 with force and arms assembled illegally and riotously at Bradbury to disseise Percival Lumley, esq., of his free tenement at Bradbury.

4) [Similar charge as (3), omitting *Thomas Chilton, yeo., dated 12 Nov. 1555, cancelled.]

5) [Similar charge charge as (3), except that *Ralph Atkynson is called Robert, and dated 14 Nov. 1555, cancelled.]

7d.] 6) Whereas by statute against disseisin of 8 Henry VI [etc.], John Rowse late of Durham city, gen., Edward Watson of Nunstainton, yeo., Edward Hikson of Preston-le-Skerne, yeo., Henry Browne of the same, yeo., George Auderson of – , yeo., John Chilton of Bradbury, yeo., Richard Rawe of – , yeo., and John Peerson of Bradbury, yeo., on 17 Dec. 1555 with force and arms assembled riotously at Bradbury and expelled Percival Lumley from his free tenement there, which they still hold.

7) Percival Lumley late of Darlington, esq., Richard Lumley of Chester-le-Street, esq., Thomas Hussey late of Sigston, North Riding of Yorks., esq., Roland Mordon of Grindon, co. Durham, gen., Stephen Kaye of Heworth, yeo., and James Bullokke late of Darlington, yeo., with 10 other unknown malefactors on 12 Nov. 1555 with force and arms broke riotously into the house of George Archer and Robert Archer at Bradbury and found and carried away 20 wainloads of hay worth £10 and 100 quarters of threshed oats, beans and peas worth together £40, belonging to George and Robert Archer, and consumed the same with their livestock.

8) Christopher Chaytour of Durham city, gen., and Anthony Middylton of the same, gen., on 19 April this year before Robert Hyndmer, clerk, chancellor of Durham, in their own persons stood pledge for Laurence Haley of Durham city, yeo., to keep the peace until the next general sessions of the peace after Michaelmas next

and to appear etc. Each surety provided bail of £20 and Haley provided bail of £40.

9) John Todde of North Auckland, co. Durham, yeo., and Roland Emerson of Rookhope in Stanhope parish, yeo., on 18 April this year stood pledge for Richard Blakkett of *Sowandeburn* in the parish of Stanhope, yeo., William Blakkett of the same, yeo., Edward Blakkett of the same, yeo., and Richard Blakkett of the same, yeo., to keep the peace until the next general sessions in county Durham and to appear: each pledge under pain of £10 and the bound parties of £20.

29

[*m.5*]   Sessions of the peace at Durham on Mon. 3 Aug. 3/4 Philip & Mary [*1556*] before Edward Saunders, knt, William Dallison, justice of Common Pleas, Robert Meynell, serjeant at law and Gerard Salvein, JPs.

John Swynburn, John Byllyngham, Philip Bainbrege, Ralph Prat, Christopher Ledell, Nicholas Blakket, John Crage, John Rakket, John Blaxton, John Hagthroppe, German Paule, John Claxton, John Wadley, Arthur Nevyll, Henry Follancebye, jurors.

1) John Hudson late of Lumley, co. Durham, husbandman (insufficient), Robert Hableym late of Newcastle, yeo., Edward Hyxson late of Preston-le-Skerne, co. Durham, yeo., John Stoddart late of Bolam, yeo., Richard Dawson late of Durham city, yeo., (fine), Robert Person late of the same, yeo., (fine), Robert Hedley late of the same, yeo., (fine), Henry Blenkyngsoppe late of the same, (fine), yeo., and William Lokewodd late of the same, yeo., assembled with 40 other unknown malefactors on 3 May 1556 with force and arms and riotously entered a messuage, lands and tenements of Roland Mordon, gen., and William Wreen, gen., which they held for a term of years.

2) <John Rowse late of Durham city>, gen., Edward Watson late of Nunstainton, yeo. (fined), Edward Hykeson late of Preston-le-Skerne, yeo., Henry Browne of the same, yeo., <George Awderson> late of Durham city, yeo., John Chilton of Bradbury, yeo., Richard Rawe late of Harraton, yeo., and John Person of Bradbury, yeo., on 17 Dec. 1555 entered illegally into the tenement leased to Percival Lumley, esq., in Bradbury, in contempt of the Crown, to the damage of Percival Lumley and contrary to the form of the statute.

3) Edmund Watson late of Nunstainton, husbandman, John Hyxson late of Preston-le-Skerne, husbandman, John Person late of Bradbury, husbandman, Thomas Chylton late of the same, husbandman, Thomas Skaythloke late of the same, <yeo> husbandman, Robert Withfeild late of the same, husbandman, John Perye late of the same, husbandman, Robert Erle late of the same, husbandman, Robert Archare late of the same, husbandman, and John Chilton late of the same, husbandman, on 24 July 1556 with force and arms riotously assembled in Bradbury and broke and entered the closes of Ralph

Addye at Bradbury to his great damage.

4) <Ralph Vasye late of Lumley Park, yeo., Lancelot Cote late of the same, yeo.>, Christopher Heryson late of Lumley, husbandman, John Brase (fine 12d.) late of Trimdon, miller, and William Clerkson (dead) late of *Jarrowclyff*, yeo., on 10 July 1556 with force and arms riotously entered the messuage of Richard Lumley, esq., at Butterby and expelled him.

5) William Wren senior (fine) of Binchester, co. Durham, gen., Anthony Wren (fine) of the same, gen., Roland Morden of Mordon, gen., Thomas Blakett of Woodcroft, gen., George Mordon of Grindon, Robert Cooke of the same, yeo., Ralph Jaxson of Elstob, husbandman, William Bryan of Aycliffe, lab., Richard Farrallers of Brancepeth, tailor, Anthony Jenkenson (fine) of the same, yeo., Thomas Laffield (fine 20d.) of Butterby, yeo., and William Kendell (fine) of Brancepeth, yeo., with 30 unknown malefactors with force and arms, namely swords, sticks, knives, bows and arrows [*etc.*] in warlike fashion on 3 May 1556 assembled at the manor of John Lumley, knt, Lord Lumley, at Butterby, being a pernicious example to all such delinquents.

6) Percival Lumley late of Darlington, esq., Richard Lumley late of Chester-le-Street, gen., Thomas Hussye of Sigston, Yorks., esq., James Bulloke late of Darlington, co. Durham, yeo., Stephen Key late of Heworth, yeo., and William Bryan of Aycliffe, lab., on 12 Nov. 1555 with force and arms assembled riotously at Bradbury and broke and entered the close and house of Robert Archer at Bradbury and attacked him and Agnes his wife so that their lives were despaired of and carried off 40 thraves of oats worth £3, 4 wainloads of hay worth 40s., 4 wainloads of coal worth 26s. 8d., 4 hens worth 20d., a hatchet worth 7d. and 2 iron forks worth 20d. belonging to Robert Archer, esq.

5d.] 7) <Ralph Vasye late of Lumley Park, co. Durham, yeo.>, Lancelot Cottes late of the same, yeo., John Hudson (fine) late of Woodstonehouse, yeo., and Christopher Herryson late of Lumley, husbandman, on 9 July 1556 with force and arms at Butterby assembled riotously with many other malefactors with intent to enter the messuage at Butterby possessed by Richard Lumley, esq.

8) Ralph Byrtfeild (<pardon>) late of Gateside, co. Durham, tanner, on 23 June 1556, contrary to the statute, disseised Simon Swynburn of a messuage with appurtenances in Gateside and was still in possession.

9) Andrew Marchell late of Layton, co. Durham, lab., on 28 Sept. 1555 with force and arms broke and entered the close of William Kendall, yeo., at Thorpe Thewles and stole a black bull worth 40s. belonging to the same. Cuthbert Conyers of Layton, esq., knowing that Marshall had committed the deed received and comforted him at Layton and elsewhere on 28 Sept., against the peace.

10) Edward Robinson late of Newcastle, yeo., on 6 Sept. 1552 with force and arms broke and entered the close of Anthony Tomlyngson,

gen., at Gateside and stole a grey gelded horse and a bay mare worth together 20 marks.

11) John Haveloke late of Melkridge, Northumberland, yeo., Cuthbert Huchetson late of *Burn Tonges*, yeo., and John Eddryngton alias Harbatt John late of *Hattersgyll*, Cumberland, yeo., on 22 May 1556 with force and arms broke and entered the close of John Rakket at Quarrington, co. Durham, and stole 4 grey horses together worth £13 6s. 8d. and a grizzled mare worth £3 6s. 8d.

12) Edward Blakburn of Carlisle, Cumberland, yeo., on 7 Dec. 1555 at Harwood in the forest of Teesdale, co. Durham, stole a bay horse worth 20s. 8d. belonging to George Roise.

13) Edward Lawson late of Newcastle, lab., on 4 Dec. 1555 with force and arms broke and entered the close of Richard Collyng at Longnewton and stole a dun horse worth 40s. belonging to the same.

14) Edward Lawson late of Newcastle, lab., on 4 Dec. 1555 with force and arms broke and entered the close of Thomas Rogerson at Longnewton and stole a grizzled mare worth 20s. belonging to the same.

15) William Patynson late of Darlington, cutler, on 6 Jan. 1555 with force and arms broke and entered the house of John Robinson at Darlington about 8 p.m. and stole 11 yards of woollen cloth worth 20d. belonging to the same.

[m.6] 16) John Harbottell of Tughall Hall, Northumberland, gen., Percival Harbottle of Glendale, gen., Roland Harbottell of the same, gen., Edward Bell of Doxford, yeo., Henry Guttergill of Beadnell, yeo., Robert Grame of *Eske* in the same county, yeo., Robert Porter senior of Shield Row, co. Durham, yeo., Robert Porter junior of the same, yeo., William Porter of Tynemouth, Northumberland, yeo., Michael Porter of the same, yeo., Nicholas Porter of Shield Row, co. Durham, yeo., Leonard Porter of the same, yeo., John Porter junior of the same, yeo., Robert Porter of the same, yeo., James Porter of Bushblades, yeo., John Porter of the same, yeo., Edward Porter of Whickham, yeo., Peter Porter of the same, yeo., George Porter of the same, yeo., Edward Porter junior of the same, yeo., Lancelot Porter of the same, yeo., John Elleson of Shield Row, yeo., Robert Brake of Bushblades, yeo., Thomas Colson of Shield Row, yeo., John Herryson of Whickham, yeo., Richard Herryson of the same, yeo., – Herryson of the same, yeo., – Herryson of the same, yeo., – Herryson of the same, yeo., – Herryson of the same, yeo., James Arnold of the same, lab., John Sothurrone of Ravensworth, yeo., Alexander Sothorn of Hedley Hall, yeo., Thomas Sothorn of Ravensworth, yeo., Henry Whelpton of Kyo Lawes, yeo., Roland Whelpton of Shield Row, yeo., William Pekkerryng of Lintz, yeo., James Rawe of Friarside, yeo., John Mawtland of Lintzford mill, yeo., Thomas Mawtland of the same, yeo., Richard Golland of the same, yeo., Gilbert Luge of Friarside, yeo., Robert Mylburn of the same, yeo., Alexander Wilkyngson of the same, yeo., Roland Wilkynson of Lintz Green, yeo., John Haukesley

of Smalleys, yeo., Richard Kyrkeley of Knitsley, yeo., William
Kyrkeley of the same, yeo., Nicholas Kyrkeley of *Holmes,* yeo.,
Thomas Maddeson of Consett, yeo., Richard Wild of Spen, yeo.,
James Wild of the same, yeo., Matthew Wild of the same, yeo.,
George Scott senior of Medomsley, yeo., George Scott junior of the
same, yeo., George Pemmerton late of Stanhope in Weardale, yeo.,
Cuthbert Vayse of Wolsingham Park, yeo., Nicholas Gybson of
Wolsingham, yeo., Robert Gybson of the same, yeo., Percival Vayse of
Durham city, yeo., John Lowder of Wolsingham, yeo., Robert Gybson
of the same, yeo., Edward Cornforth of the same, yeo., Lionel
Thompson of the same, yeo., Lancelot Chapman of Frosterley, yeo.,
Richard Morgan of the same, yeo., Ralph Horne of Wolsingham, yeo.,
Ralph Dyxson of the same, yeo., Christopher Stobbes of the same,
yeo., William Kyrkkeley of Wolsingham Park, yeo., Thomas Kyrkeley
of the same, yeo., Robert Kyrkeley of the same, yeo., William
Keyrkeley of the same, yeo., Lancelot Yonger of the same, yeo., John
Colson of the same, yeo., Thomas Colson of the same, yeo., Lancelot
Colson of the same, yeo., James Dyxson of Wolsingham, yeo., Roger
Walle of the same, yeo., John Rawe of the same, yeo., William
Richardson of the same, yeo., John Graunge of the same, yeo.,
Christopher Graunge of the same, yeo., Lancelot Herryson of the
same, yeo., Nicholas Herryson of the same, yeo., Richard Vasye of
Newland, yeo., John Kyrkkeley of Wolsingham Park, yeo., Nicholas
Graunge of the same, yeo., Cuthbert Kyrkeley of the same, yeo.,
Robert Colson of the same, yeo., James Ledem of Wolsingham, yeo.,
William Marley of Wolsingham Park, yeo., Thomas Raynold of the
same, yeo., Robert Elleson of Durham city, yeo., Lancelot Chapman
of Frosterley, yeo., Edward Todd of the same, yeo., Ralph Carlell of
the same, yeo., Francis Nedem of Newcastle, yeo., Francis Comyng of
the same, yeo., Thomas Whelwright of the same, gunner,
Christopher Porter of the same, yeo., John Elleson of Chilton field,
Northumberland, yeo., Cuthbert Ward of the same, yeo., Ralph
Mettrike of Redholme, Yorks., yeo., Richard Mettrike of Little Danby,
Yorks., yeo., James Mettrik of the same, yeo., and Vincent Mettrike of
the same, yeo., with other unknown malefactors estimated at 200
with force and arms assembled riotously with bows, arrows, lances,
swords, sticks, scythes [*etc.*] in warlike fashion and manner of new
insurrection on 25 May 1556 at Tanfield with the intention to expel
Roger Harbotley of Beckley, gen., from his tenement of Beckley.
17) Thomas Hall of Stranton, co. Durham, lab., Richard Sharpp (made
fine) of the same, lab., John Patryke of the same, lab., James Wooppe
of the same, lab., William Sympson of the same, lab., Edmund
Martyn (made fine) of the same, lab., Thomas Thorrowby (made fine)
of the same, lab., John Day of the same, lab., Robert Broune of the
same, lab., Nicholas Wyld of the same, lab., John Dochson (made
fine) of the same, lab., and Richard Close (made fine) of the same,
lab., with 10 others unknown assembled on 8 May 1556 with force

and arms and broke and entered the close of Thomas Jackeson at Stranton and trampled down and depastured with livestock the oats and beans of the same Thomas Jackeson growing there.

18) Elizabeth Slayter late of Wylam, Northumberland, spinster, on 1 Aug. 1556 with force and arms broke and entered the close and house of John Cokden at Ryton, co. Durham, and stole a dress called *womans gown* worth 40s., 11s. in coins, a silver-gilt ring worth 3s. 4d. and 2 woollen sleeves worth 8s. belonging to the same John Cokeden.

19) John Sander (fine) of Lumley, co. Durham, lab., on 16 July 1556 with force and arms broke and entered the close of Christopher Herryson and Edward Pounchon at Lumley and carried off half a wain of hay worth 8s. belonging to the same Christopher and Edward.

[*m.6d.*]   20) MEMO that on 3 Aug. [1556] John Layton of West Layton, Yorks., gen., came before Robert Meynell, serjeant at law and keeper of the rolls of the peace in co. Durham, and John Taliffare, clerk of the peace in the same county, and proffered an indenture, acknowledged it as his own deed, and asked it to be enrolled as follows:

[*in English*] The indenture of 20 April 1556 between John Layton of West Layton, Yorks., gen., and William Highley of Whorlton, co. Durham, yeo., recognises that for the sum of £20 paid by William Hyghley John Layton has sold him a burgage in Barnard Castle, co. Durham, in a street called *Thorngate* lying between a burgage of John Laidman to the south and a burgage of Jennett Forrest, widow, to the north, together with all appurtenances and title deeds: to be delivered to William Hyghley, his heirs or assigns before Michaelmas next to hold in fee simple with warranty. These are to be free of all charges except such as be due to the chief lord and an annual rent-charge of 6s. payable to the sisters and bedeswoman and sisters [*sic*] of the hospital of St John the Baptist in Barnard Castle.

30

[*m.4*]   Sessions of the peace at Durham on 10 Oct. 3/4 Philip & Mary [*1556*] before Henry, earl of Westmorland, Robert Meynell, serjeant at law, Ralph Hedworth, knt, Robert Tempest, esq., Thomas Trollopp, Ralph Dalton and Gerard Salveyn.

John Hinton, John Hall, Anthony Scurfeild, George Gudyer, Thomas Whithedd, John Rakkett, John Crage, Robert Shutwell, John Claxton of Thickley, Ralph Pratt, John Vasey, Thomas Phillppe, Christopher Liddell, German Pawler, John Haggthropp, jurors.

1) Edward Denham (fine) of Aislaby, co. Durham, husbandman, Alexander Lylburn of the same, husbandman, John Carr of the same (fine 2s.), husbandman, Henry Purssyke (made fine) of the same, husbandman, <William Denham>, Thomas Prissyke (fine) of the same, husbandman, William Denham of the same, lab., Robert Watt of the same, lab., John Brewell of the same, lab., Roland Hedley of

the same, lab., and Thomas Pounchon (fine) of the same, yeo., with 16 other unknown malefactors on 29 Sept. 1556 unlawfully and riotously assembled at Aislaby and broke and entered the close of William Lambert and stole 3 cows of the same, grazing, and drove them to the village of Sadberge.

2) Alexander Lilburn of Aislaby, husbandman, Edward Denham of the same, husbandman, Matthew Pryssyke (fine) of the same, husbandman, and William Ryppon (fine 2s.) of the same, husbandman, with 6 other unknown malefactors on 27 Aug. 1556 with force and arms riotously assembled at Aislaby and broke and entered the close of James Garnett and drove away half a wainload of hay worth 10s. in a stack.

3) Robert Trotter of Smalleys <Ley>, husbandman, John Trotter of the same, currier, Lionel Trotter of the same, lab., Alice Trotter of the same, wife of Robert, and Joan Trotter of the same, spinster, on 2 Oct. 1556 forcibly entered the tenement of Arthur Trotter of Smalleys at Smalleys and disseised Arthur thereof, contrary to statute.

4) Christopher Smurthwayt of Durham city, miller, and George Johnson of Quarry House by Durham, lab., alias George Wainman of Quarry House, lab., on 16 Aug. 1556 with force and arms broke and entered the close and orchard of John Dukkett, chaplain, at Durham and assaulted Dukkett so that his life was despaired of.

5) Robert Hendrye of Walbottle, Northumberland, husbandman, William Hendrye of the same, lab., George Hendrie of Lemington, lab., William Hendrye of Berwick Hill, lab., and William Raw of Callerton, lab., on 5 Aug. 1556 with force and arms broke into the free fishery of Henry, earl of Westmorland, at Blaydon, co. Durham, and stole a boat and a net worth together 4 marks, belonging to John Reppeth at Blaydon.

6) Robert Hendrye of Walbottle, Northumberland, husbandman, William Hendrye of the same, lab., George Hendrye of Lemington, lab., William Hendrie of Berwick Hill, lab., and William Raw of Callerton, lab., on 5 Aug. 1556 with force and arms broke into the free fishery of Henry, earl of Westmorland, at Blaydon and stole a boat and net worth together 4 marks belonging to John Bell and John Moreman at Blaydon.

[m.4d., blank]

31

3d.] Sessions of the peace held at Durham on 23 Jan. 3/4 Philip & Mary [1557] before Robert Hyndmer, clerk, chancellor of Durham, Ralph Hedworth, knt, Robert Meynell, serjeant at law, Robert Tempest, William Claxton, Richard Hebburn and Thomas Trollopp, JPs.

William Smythe, John Hall of Greencroft, John Hagthrop, John Eden, Christopher Morland, John Blenkinsopp, Conan Barton, John Rakkett, Nicholas Blackkett, John Cragge, John Cusson, Henry Follanceby, Simon Welbury, jurors.

1) Whereas by statute against disseisin of 8 Henry VI [etc.], Roger

Harbottell of Beckley, co. Durham, gen., John Harbottell of the same, gen., Thomas Mawteman of the same, yeo., Roland Grounddye (fine) of Hedley, yeo., Edward West of the same, yeo., Simon Rodderfurthe late of Ryton, gen., Arthur Hommell late of the same, yeo., Anthony Dotchon of the same, yeo., Robert Hubbocke of Haydon Bridge, Northumberland, yeo., and Ralph Harbottell of Danby on Wiske, North Riding of Yorks., gen., with many other malefactors in warlike fashion assembled unlawfully and riotously on 7 Jan. 1557 at Beckley, co. Durham, and violently entered the house and close of Robert Porter of Shield Row, gen., at Beckley and expelled the same and continued in possession until the present and with their animals consumed his grass.

2) William Moode of Tanfield, Yorks., yeo., William Emerson of Esh, co. Durham, yeo., Matthew Smyth of the same, yeo., Anthony Smyth of Chipchase in Tynedale, Northumberland, yeo., George Grynwell of Heugh by Esh, yeo., and Nicholas Grynwell of the same, yeo., with 16 other malefactors assembled with swords, sticks, knives, bows and arrows and other arms in warlike fashion on 30 Nov. 1556 and forcibly entered the free tenement of Roger Hilton and Christabel his wife at Heugh in the parish of Lanchester and maltreated the same Roger and Christabel.

3) Simon Rodderforth late of Ryton, co. Durham, gen., Arthur Hommell late of the same, yeo., Anthony Dotchon of the same, yeo., John Harbottell junior of Beckley, gen., Ralph Harbottell of Danby on Wiske, North Riding of Yorks., gen., Robert Hubbucke of Haydon Bridge, Northumberland, yeo., – Dobyson of Langley, yeo., Edward Roderforth of Prudhoe, yeo., Ralph Rodderforth of Rudchester, gen., John Harbottell of Prudhoe, yeo., and Nicholas Grene of Dotland, yeo., assembled riotously with 18 other malefactors in warlike fashion on 18 Oct. 1556 at Team Bridge, co. Durham, by special order of Roger Harbottell of Beckley and attacked Robert Porter junior of Shield Row.

4) Anthony Coot of Durham city, slater, on 9 Jan. 1557 with force and arms broke and entered the close of Christopher Hochenson at Durham and stole a wainload of stones worth 2s.

5) Robert Spark of Greatham, co. Durham, clerk, John Snawball of Medomsley, yeo., Thomas Wilkinson (fine) of Rainton, yeo., John Jackson (process by chancellor) of the same, yeo., William Robinson (fine) of the same, yeo., Thomas Busby of Owton, yeo., Ralph Davyson of Bewley grange, yeo., Robert Sheraton of Stockton, yeo., and Richard Rawe of the same, yeo., having neither land nor tenements worth 40s. a year, on 20 Jan. 1557 kept greyhounds contrary to the statute.

6) John Crawe of Durham city, fisher, William Watson of the same, fisher, John Watson of the same, fisher, Richard Jakson of Sunderland, fisher, Richard Morey of the same, fisher, and Roland Ledebeater of the same, fisher, on 20 Jan. 1557 and some days earlier

forestalled fish coming to the lord's market, contrary to divers statutes.

7) John Burnett of Breakhouse by Eryholme in North Riding, Yorks., yeo., John Bukke of Sadberge, co. Durham, yeo., Marmaduke Bukke of the same, yeo., John Ranald of the same, lab., William Wormeley of Eryholme, Yorks., yeo., John Braunson of the same, yeo., Thomas Wrightson of the same, yeo., William Frear of the same, husbandman, James Frear of the same, lab., Thomas Neceham of the same, husbandman, Miles Barnes of the same, wright, Thomas Wrenne of the same, lab., Anthony Husband of Neasham, co. Durham, yeo., Ninian Brear of Usworth, husbandman, Thomas Braunson of Blackwell, husbandman, Henry Brauneson of the same, lab., and Robert Teysdell of Richmond, Yorks., yeo., on 21 Dec. 1556 illegally and riotously assembled at Darlington and assaulted Marmaduke Baytmanson of Little Smeaton, Yorks., gen., with intent to kill.

8) [*badly rubbed and virtually illegible, being the outer cover of roll*]

32

] Sessions of the peace held at Durham on Friday, 7 May 3/4 Philip & Mary [*1557*], before Robert Hindmer, clerk, chancellor of Durham, Robert Meynell, serjeant at law, and Thomas Trollopp, esq., JPs.

Robert Ayton, Conan Barton, Robert Blenkinsop, John Claxton, John Claxton [*sic*] , John Rakkett, John Blenkinsop, John Swalwell, Christopher Ledell, Robert Shotwell, Ralph Mayson, Nicholas Blakkett, John Cragge, jurors.

1) Christopher Burdon late of Darlington, co. Durham, lab., on 24 April 1557 with force and arms broke and entered the close of Richard Laxe at Ferryhill and stole a web of linen cloth worth 7s.

2) John Philip (fine) of Wath Cote, North Riding of Yorks., yeo., Christopher Johnson of the same, lab., John Naler of the same, lab., Thomas Gaole of the same, lab., Robert Warde (fine) of Darlington, co. Durham, yeo., Thomas Ward (fine) of the same, yeo., Richard Warde (fine) of the same, yeo., Thomas Waistell (fine) of Haughton field, yeo., Richard Segesweke (fine) of the same, yeo., John Johnson (fine) of the same, yeo., William Yonge of Darlington, yeo., and Robert Jefrason (fine) of the same, yeo., on 25 March 1557 with force and arms assembled unlawfully at Haughtonfield and riotously attacked Thomas Hereson so that his life was despaired of.

3) Simon Fulthropp (fine) of Silksworth, co. Durham, gen., on 6 May 1557 with force and arms at Houghton attacked Francis Tierman so that his life was despaired of.

4) Andrew Joplynge of Roughside in the parish of Edmundbyers, co. Durham, wheelwright, on 1 May 1557 with force and arms at Roughside attacked Lionel Snawe and Christopher Vasey so that their lives were despaired of, and stole an axe worth 12d. belonging to Christopher Vasey.

5) Whereas by the statute against disseisin of 8 Henry VI [*etc.*], William Phillipe of Hylton, co. Durham, yeo., Robert Wilson of Snowclose in the parish of Stanhope, yeo., George Gray of Blackhouse *Ele*, yeo., Alexander Blacklok of *Brademedowe*, yeo., and Roland Emerson of the same, yeo., on 4 May 1557 with force and arms entered the free tenement of Lancelot Trotter, yeo., at Eastgate in Weardale and expelled him.

33

[*m.2*]   Sessions of the peace at Durham held on Mon., 9 Aug. 4/5 Philip & Mary [*1557*], before William Rastell, serjeant at law, Robert Hyndmer, clerk, chancellor of Durham, and Robert Meynall, serjeant at law, JPs.
    John Hall of Greencroft, Anthony Middilton, John Rakkett, Peter Alwent, John Claxton, Nicholas Blakkett, John Eden, Ralph Pratt, Gilbert Mayson, Christopher Morland, Christopher Ledaile, Robert Lisle, Martin Brakenbury, gentlemen, jurors.
1) Cuthbert Vasie late of Wolsingham, co. Durham, gen., George Pemberton late of Wolsingham, yeo., and Richard Fetherstonhaughe of Wolsingham, yeo., on 23 April 1557 attacked Thomas Boune at Wolsingham Park. Vasie struck him with a lance-staff worth 10d. held in his hands to the right of his back, from which blow Boune died immediately. Pemberton struck him another blow on the face with a sword worth 5s. held in his right hand, which would have killed him, and Fetherstonhaughe struck him in the throat with a dagger worth 1s. held in his right hand, which would have killed him, and so the three murdered him. Margaret Boune, late wife of Thomas, late of Billingham, spinster, and Joan Braidley of Billingham, spinster, knowingly received, comforted and aided the said Cuthbert Vasie at Billingham on 26 April following.
2) Henry Richardson late of Barnard Castle, co. Durham, yeo., on 29 June 1557 with force and arms assaulted Thomas Runtheweit at Barnard Castle in *Peitpott Rayne*, striking Thomas on the crown of the head with a bill worth 10d. held in his hands, being a mortal blow. (outlawed)
3) Henry Corbet of Orchardhouse, Cumberland, lab., Thomas Noble of Bewcastle, lab., and Cuthbert Foster of Gilsland, lab., on 8 July 1557 with force and arms broke and entered the close of John Natrisse at Burtree ford, co. Durham, and stole a red-bay mare worth £3 6s. 8d. (outlawed)
4) Henry Corbet of Orchardhouse, Cumberland, lab., Cuthbert Foster of Gilsland, lab., and Thomas Noble of Bewcastle, lab., on 8 July 1557 with force and arms broke and entered the close of John Todd junior at Burtree ford, co. Durham, and stole a black-bay mare worth £4. (outlawed)
5) Edward Roderforth (acquitted) late of Prudhoe, Northumberland, gen., and Simon Roderforth late of Rudchester, gen., on 5 May 1555 with force and arms waylaid at Winlaton, co. Durham, at *Stroderyaite*

and attacked Peter Wylkinson of Lintzford, lab., on the king's highway and robbed him of 2s. in money and a purse worth 4d.

6) Henry Corbett of Orchardhouse, Cumberland, lab., Cuthbert Foster of Gilsland, lab., and Thomas Nobyll of Bewcastle, lab., on 8 July 1557 with force and arms broke and entered the close of John Todd of Burtree ford at Burtree ford and stole a white-grey horse worth 4 marks and a black-grey horse worth – marks.

7) Edward Roderfurth of Prudhoe, Northumberland, gen., Ralph Harbottle of the same, yeo., Alexander Blaklocke of the same, yeo., Michael Harbottell late of Tughall Hall, yeo., and Percival Tompson late of Newsham, yeo., on 24 July 1557 with many other malefactors assembled with scythes, lances and other weapons at Fawside in the parish of Lanchester, co. Durham, and laid in ambush on the king's highway to murder Nicholas Porter of Shield Row, gen., and Leonard Porter of the same, gen., and attacked the same.

8) Nicholas Porter late of Shield Row, co. Durham, gen., William Porter late of the same, gen., Leonard Porter late of the same, gen., and John Elyson late of the same, yeo., on 1 June 1557 with force and arms at Tanfield waylaid Edward Rotherforth and attacked the same so that his life was despaired of.

9) Robert Porter junior late of Shield Row, gen., William Porter late of the same, gen., Nicholas Porter late of the same, gen., Leonard Porter late of the same, gen., Robert Mylburn late of the same, yeo., Cuthbert Warde late of Waskerley, yeo., John Andrewe of Shotley Bridge, yeo., and John Bakworthe late of the same, yeo., with 4 others unknown in warlike fashion on 25 June 1557 with force and arms assembled riotously at Tanfield to ambush Ralph Harbottell, being a pernicious example to other malefactors and to the great terror of the lieges.

10) Whereas Thomas Johnson, itinerant bailiff of the sheriff of Durham in the Darlington ward, on 24 April 1557 distrained on Bartholomew Lylburn of Shildon by an ox for an amercement of 3s. 4d. imposed for various trespasses presented in the sheriff's tourn [*illegible*].

[*m.2d., blank*]

34

Sessions of the peace held at Durham on Sat., 6 Nov. 4/5 Philip & Mary [*1557*], before Robert Hyndmers, clerk, chancellor of Durham, Robert Meynell, serjeant at law, and Gerard Salvayn, esq., JPs.

Conan Barton, Ralph Pratt, John Claxton, John Rakket, John Swalwell, John Hall of Birtley, Robert Blenkynsopp, Ralph Claxton, Henry Follencebye, John Cragge, William Punchdon, Ralph Mayson, Christopher Ledell, gentlemen, jurors.

1) Griffith Rice late of North Auckland, co. Durham, esq., alias Sir Griffith Rice, esq., James Hall late of the same, tailor, and Agnes Walshe of the same, widow, alias Agnes wife of Matthew Walshe, on

30 Sept. 1557 with force and arms at North Auckland about 8 p.m. with malice aforethought laid in wait for Matthew Walshe and the said Griffith Rice struck Matthew on the back of his head with a sword worth 10s. held in his right hand, giving a mortal blow 7 inches in length and 3 inches deep down to the brain, from which Matthew died instantly. Rice then struck him on the right side of the head with his sword, inflicting another mortal wound 4 inches long and down to the brain which would have killed him; then another great blow on the face from right to left ear down to the brain; then another with his sword across his nose, mouth, chin and throat which would have killed him; another with his sword across nose and mouth from the right to left of his neck and 4 inches deep which would have killed him; and another across his chin to his throat which would have killed him; so murdering Matthew. James Hall and Agnes Walsh were present, so abetting, comforting and aiding Rice, and all subsequently fled the county.

2) William Charlton late of the Eales in the parish of Bellingham, Northumberland, alias William of the Eales, yeo., John Peirson late of Haydon Bridge, yeo., and Roland Read late of the same, yeo., on 12 Sept. 1557 with force and arms broke and entered the close of Thomas Herryson at Haughton field, co. Durham, and stole a white horse worth 40s., 2 grey fillies jointly worth 40s., a white filly worth 20s., and a grizzled mare worth 20s. belonging to Thomas Herryson.

3) Robert Blenkinsopp of Tanfield, co. Durham, tailor, on 5 Oct. 1557 with force and arms at Beckley assaulted and made affray with Robert Mylburn of Beckley, lab., striking him 3 blows on the shoulders and arms with a pikestaff worth 6d. and on the head with a dagger worth 12d. so that he languished from 5 Oct. until the present, affording a pernicious example of such delinquency.

4) William Charlton late of the Eales, Northumberland, alias William of the Eales, yeo., and John Peirson late of Haydon Bridge and Roland Reade late of the same, yeo., on 12 Sept. 1557 with force and arms broke and entered the close of Nicholas Sympson at Coatham, co. Durham, and stole a white mare worth 13s. 4d., a bay mare worth 26s. 8d., and a grey mare worth 13s. 4d. belonging to Nicholas Sympson.

5) Robert Brown late of Newfield in the parish of St Andrew Auckland, co. Durham, yeo., alias Robert Hangershawe late of Newfield, on 7 Oct. 1557 with force and arms broke and entered the close of William Wren, gen., at Binchester and stole a grey horse worth £5 belonging to Nicholas Croser.

6) William Charlton late of the Eales, Northumberland, alias William of the Eales, yeo., and John Peirson late of Haydon Bridge, yeo., and Roland Read late of the same, yeo., on 12 Sept. 1557 with force and arms broke and entered the close of Thomas Wastell of Haughton at Haughton field and stole a bay mare worth 53s. 4d. and a white mare worth 40s. belonging to the same.

[m.1d., blank]

1596–1608

Durham CRO Q/S/I 1 The 33 membranes are filed by session roughly in reverse order. The dates covered are 7 January, 21 April and 30 June 1596; 12 January 1597; 11 January, 5 July, 20 September and 4 October 1598; 18 April, 22 May and 27 June 1599; 10 January, 1 April, 25 June and 1 October 1600; 9 January, 22 April, 8 July and 7 October 1601; 13 January, 14 April, 7 July and 6 October 1602; 12 January and 8 June 1603; and 11 January 1604. The head of the roll for the sessions on 30 March 1608 has been attached in error..

35

31]   Pleas and presentments at the sessions of the peace at Durham on 7 Jan. 38 Elizabeth [*1596*] before Bp Matthew and Thomas Calverley, chancellor of Durham, and fellow JPs.
[*blank of 76 cms*]

31d.]   [*18 cms illegible, as reused as wrapper*]
1) Order that John Somerson and others appear before the queen's justices on 22 April to answer for felonies. On that day Robert Tailbois, attorney-general for Bp Matthew on behalf of the queen ... And John Conyers, esq., sheriff of Durham, returned that at the county court at Durham on Mon., 26 Jan. 1596, he pronounced the first exaction against John Somerson and others, and thereafter on Mon., 23 Feb., 22 March, 19 April, 17 May, after which their outlawry was pronounced by Michael Calverley and John Hawkins, coroners.
[*blank of 49 cms*]

36

32]   Pleas and presentments at the sessions of the peace at Durham on 21 April 38 Elizabeth [*1596*], before Bp Matthew, Thomas Calverley, chancellor of Durham, and fellow JPs.

Christopher Wharton	Cuthbert Hutcheson
John Garthorne	William Trotter
John Swalwell	Richard Kaie
George Crosier	Robert Wawghe
James Walton	William Scurfeild
Anthony Shaldforth	William Watson
William Punshon	Gerard Liddell
Edward Hall, jurors	

1) Robert Bullock of Durham city, yeo., on 20 April 1596 assaulted in Durham city Richard Spurner of Durham city, yeo., queens's constable in the borough of Elvet.
2) Anthony Homble of Daniel, co. Durham, yeo., George Homble of the same, yeo., and Robert Homble of the same, yeo., on 20 Jan. 1596 broke the close called *the Longlee* of John Hedworth of Ryton Woodside, gen., at Ryton Woodside and trampled and depastured it with wains and livestock, namely horses and cattle.
3) Gabriel Simpson late of Blackwell, co. Durham, lab., on 10 Dec.

1595 broke into the residence of John Middleton of Blackwell, yeo., at Blackwell and stole a brazen pot worth 12d. And before the felony Alice Simpson, wife of Thomas Simpson late of Blackwell, yeo., on 8 Dec. incited Gabriel to commit the crime.
[*blank of 36.5 cms*]

[*m.32d.*] 4) Order to the sheriff of Durham *non omittas* to arrest Nicholas Welton late of Thornborough, Northumberland, gen., Matthew Errington late of Stonecroft, gen., William Ridley late of Hawkhope, gen., William Shaftoe late of Hexham, gen., William Lawson late of Hexham, gen., Thomas Dobbin late of Great Burdon, co. Durham, lab., John Storie late of Rosedean, Northumberland, junior, yeo., John Storie late of the same, senior, yeo., Matthew Storie late of Garretlee, yeo., William Armstronge late of *Willeyeveysule*, lab., alias Andrew's Will late of the same, lab., William Pruddoe late of Bellbank, Cumberland, lab., Christopher Charleton late of Hatherton, Northumberland, alias Christopher Charleton late of Chopwell, co. Durham, yeo., Thomas Charleton late of Hawkhope, Northumberland, gen., alias Thomas Charleton late of Chopwell, gen., Robert Elsdon late of *Mott'*, Northumberland, yeo., alias Robert Elsdon herd of *Mott'*, yeo., Michael Hall late of Townfoot, yeo., William Hall late of *Kealees*, yeo., Anthony Pott late of *Carrocke*, yeo., and Nicholas Welton alias Weldon, late of Welton alias Weldon, gen., Richard Close late of Eggleston, co. Durham, yeo., Isabel Bee late of Billingham, spinster, Roger Fowberie late of Colepike Hall (*Colpighill*), gen., Robert Ogle late of Aydon Shiels, Northumberland, gen., Francis Blenkinsopp late of Wooley, gen., Thomas Armstrong late of Highstead Eshe, Cumberland, yeo., and Lionel Charleton late of Thornborough, Northumberland, gen., alias Lionel Charleton late of Chopwell, co. Durham, to be before the queen's justices at Durham on 21 April next to answer for divers felonies and burglaries. The sheriff of Durham, John Conyers, esq., returned that they were not to be found, and none came.

5) Robert Tailbois, attorney-general for Bp Matthew on behalf of the queen, sued against Ralph Fuister late of Newland, Northumberland, yeo., alias Ralph Fuister late of Cold Rowley, co. Durham, yeo.
[*blank of 34 cms*]

37

[*m.33*] Pleas & presentments at Durham, 30 June 38 Elizabeth [*1596*] before Bp Matthew and Thomas Calverley, chancellor of Durham, and fellow JPs.

William Todd of Herrington, gen.	John Dobson of Hutton
William Tailbois of West Auckland, gen.	Richard Kay of Hett, yeo.
Robert Farrow, gen.	Edward Hall, yeo.
George Crosier of Newbiggin, gen.	Ralph Preston, yeo.
Anthony Bailes, gen.	Henry Rickabie, yeo.
George Guy of Herrington	John Cusson, yeo.

Robert Tweddell of Hesleden   John Newton, yeo.
William Trotter of Embleton, jurors

1) William Marshall late of West Boldon, co. Durham, yeo., on 20 July 1596 broke the close of John Browne at West Boldon and stole 4 cocks of hay worth 2s.

2) Walter Caward late of West Boldon, lab., and George Caward late of the same, lab., on 29 May 1596 at West Boldon, being able bodied and not having lands, degree, licence or trade, were taken as vagrants.

3) Henry Wrey late of Langley, co. Durham, miller, on 12 Oct. 1594 entered the water corn-mill at Langley and stole 2 pecks of rye each worth 12d. belonging to John Wrangham of Langley, yeo.

4) John Swainston late of Bishop Auckland, co. Durham, yeo., and Christopher Wilson of West Auckland, yeo., on 10 June 1596 assaulted at Henknowl Thomas Tailer of West Auckland, yeo.
[blank of 47.5 cms]

33d.]   [18 cms at head illegible as used as wrapper]

5) Order to John Conyers, esq., sheriff of Durham, non omittas to arrest Jasper Read late of [...]ehaugh, Northumberland, lab., Michael Hogshon late of Harderwick, lab., Robert Fyndlee late of Darlington, co. Durham, yeo., and Roland Davison late of Allenheads, Northumberland, lab., to be before the JPs on 30 June to answer for divers felonies. On the day he returned that they were not to be found, and an order was made for their exaction at the next county court.

On 6 April 1597 Robert Tailbois, attorney for the queen, and John Conyers, esq., sheriff of Durham, returned that outlawry was pronounced at Durham on Mon. 11 Oct. 1596, Mon. 8 Nov., 13 Dec., 10 Jan. and 7 Feb. 1597. Jaspar Read and others named in the writ were pronounced outlaws by Gregory Butler and John Hawkins, coroners.
[space of 31.5 cms]

38

28]   Sessions of the peace for Durham and Sadberge at Durham, 12 Jan. 39 Elizabeth [1597] before Thomas Calverley, esq., chancellor of Durham, William James, STP and dean of Durham, George Scroope, esq., Robert Tailboys, esq., Richard Bellassis, John Heath, John Hedworth, Thomas Hilton, George Frevile and Anthony Hutton esqs., and Robert Swift, clerk, JPs.

Ralph Billingham of Crook Hall, esq., William Claxton of East Thickley, gen., Christopher Smeton of Neasham, yeo., John Shepardson of Witton, yeo., Richard Shakelock of Murton, yeo., Richard Hucheson of Durham, yeo., Robert Wawgh of Chester, yeo., Robert Cusson of Newbiggin, yeo., Anthony Stephenson of Neasham, yeo., John Snathe of Witton, yeo., John Hutcheson of Durham, yeo., Christopher Garnett of Egglescliffe, yeo., Thomas

Wood of Merrington, yeo., Christopher Foreman of Hurworth, yeo., William Ellimer of Hutton, yeo., jurors , John Conyers esq., sheriff.

1) Robert Whyte late of Eldon, co. Durham, yeo., and Robert Addamson late of the same, yeo., on 6 Sept. 1596 broke the close of John Peverell of Eldon and stole a black heifer worth 40s. and a *black spinked* heifer worth 40s.

2) Robert White and Robert Addamson [*as (1) above*] on 6 Sept. 1596 broke the close of William Farbeck of Eldon, yeo., at Eldon at Eldon Eastmoor and stole a heifer or quey worth 40s.

3) The same on 6 Sept. 1596 broke the close of Miles Case of St Andrew Auckland, clerk, called *Thirsleye feild* at St Andrew Auckland and stole a black heifer or quey worth 40s.

4) The same on 6 Sept. 1596 broke the close of John Laiton of Eldon, yeo., called *Eldon Eastmoore* at Eldon and stole two queys, each worth 40s., belonging to John Peverell.

5) Robert Hall late of Chester-le-Street, co. Durham, lab., on 11 Dec. 1596 broke the close of William Warden of Bruntoft, yeo., at Bruntoft called *Whinneyhill* and stole a bay-coloured mare worth 40s.

6) William Graye late of Durham city, lab., on 1 Nov. 1596 at Sherburn broke the close of William Stoddert of Sherburn and stole a brown ox worth 40s.

7) Robert White late of Eldon, yeo., and Robert Adamson late of the same, yeo., on 6 Sept. 1596 broke the close of Christopher Crofte of St Andrew Auckland, yeo., at Eldon at Eldon moor and stole a *black-hawk* heifer worth 20s., a *black-branded* heifer worth 20s., and a black heifer worth 20s.

8) The same on 6 Sept. 1596 broke the close of Michael Sharpe of *Brakes*, yeo., at Eldon at Eldon moor and stole a black stirk worth 20s.

9) The same on 6 Sept. 1596 broke the close of Nicholas Richardson of Eldon, yeo., at Eldon at Eldon moor and stole a black quey worth 20s.

10) The same on 6 Sept. 1596 broke the close of Martin Middleton of St Andrew Auckland at Eldon at Eldon moor and stole a brown heifer and 2 black heifers each worth 20s.

11) The same on 6 Sept. 1596 broke the close of Edward Marles of Hylton, co. Durham, yeo., at Eldon at Eldon moor and stole a stirk worth 20s.

12) Matthew Tweadell late of Old Park, co. Durham, lab., on 20 June 1596 broke into the residence of John Martindell of Old Park at Old Park and stole a cloak worth 40s. and a sword worth 3s. 4d.

13) Henry Marley of Harnisha in the parish of Wolsingham, co. Durham, yeo., on 17 Dec. 1596 at Harnisha assaulted William Stobbes, collector of fines, rents and amercements of the bishop in Wolsingham, while he was distraining on a shovel for a fine of 6d. levied at a halmote of the bishop at Wolsingham on 29 Oct. last for talking in court, and recovered the shovel.

14) Thomas Grynwell of *Newrawe*, co. Durham, yeo., on 6 Dec. 1596

at Wolsingham assaulted William Stobbes, collector of fines, rents and amercements of the bishop in Wolsingham, while distraining on a grey mare in respect of amercements levied on Grynwell at the halmote at Wolsingham on 29 Oct. for an encroachment of land (10d.) and for not mending fences (12d.), and recovered the mare.

28d.] 15) Robert Dudley late of Chopwell, co. Durham, gen., Guy Strangwishe late of the same, yeo., Thomas Todd late of the same, yeo., John Tailor late of the same, yeo., and John Grenod late of the same, yeo., on 16 Aug. 1596 assembled riotously at Chopwell in *le Eastwood* and assaulted John Ward of Chopwell, gen.

16) Robert Dudley junior late of Chopwell, gen., Guy Strangwishe late of the same, yeo., Richard Fetherston late of the same, yeo., Thomas Todd late of the same, yeo., and John Tailer late of the same, yeo., on 20 Aug. 1596 assembled riotously at Chopwell in Eastwood and assaulted Peter Ward junior, gen.

17) Robert Dudly junior late of Chopwell, gen., Guy Strangwishe late of the same, yeo., Nicholas Fetherston late of the same, yeo., John Tailer late of the same, yeo., John Grenod late of the same, yeo., and William Hoblin late of the same, yeo., on 10 Dec. 1596 assembled riotously at Chopwell at the cowfold and assaulted Peter Ward junior of Chopwell, gen.

18) Christopher Richardson late of Sunderland by the sea, co. Durham, yeo., on 5 Dec. 1596 at Seaton Carew, being a labourer and a layman, not having lands and tenements worth 40s. a year, kept ferrets and nets to catch and kill hares and rabbits, contrary to statute.

19) Thomas Brafferton late of Tunstall, co. Durham, lab., on 8 Nov. 1596, being a labourer and layman [*etc.*], kept ferrets and nets to catch and kill hares and rabbits.

20) The same on 8 Nov. 1596 broke the close of Henry Brafferton at Seaton Carew, co. Durham, and stole 20 rabbits.

21) Richard Richardson late of Seaton Carew, lab., on 1 Aug. 1597 at Seaton Carew being a labourer and layman and not having lands [*etc.*], kept ferrets and nets to take and kill hares and rabbits.

22) The same on 1 Aug. 1596 at Seaton Carew broke the close of Henry Brafferton at Seaton Carew and stole 5 couples of coneys with nets and ferrets.

23) Christopher Richardson late of Sunderland by the sea, yeo., on 5 Dec. 1596 at Seaton Carew broke the close of Henry Brafferton at Seaton Carew and stole a couple of coneys with nets and ferrets.

24) Marmaduke Spurrett of Little Eden, co. Durham, yeo., on 18 Oct. 1596 at Seaton Carew being a labourer and layman [*etc.*] kept nets for trapping rabbits.

25) The same on 18 Oct. 1596 at Seaton Carew assaulted Henry Brafferton and took and killed a couple of coneys.

26) Archibald King of Westoe, co. Durham, yeo., and Elizabeth Soothern of the same on 8 Aug. 1596 at Westoe with others

unknown assaulted Christopher Whitfeild, then bailiff of the sheriff of Durham, detailed by a writ of *capias* from the county court of Durham to arrest John Garnett and have him before the sheriff of Durham, and rescued Garnet and he is still at large.

27) Whereas by virtue of the queen's writ to the sheriff and chancellor of Durham they were ordered to distrain on Robert Parkinson of Whessoe, gen., for the sum of £100 for the queen's use, the sheriff of Durham by John Harrison, his bailiff, on 9 Dec. 1596 at Whessoe tried to seize wheat and rye and oats worth £40 and hay worth £10 to the queen's use, in part payment of the £100; but Francis Parkinson of Whessoe, gen., Thomas Linge, yeo., Agnes Parkinson and Mary Dighton and Isabel Potter of Whessoe with others unknown assembled riotously and assaulted John Harrison and recovered the wheat, rye and oats.

[*space of 12.5 cms*]

39

[*m.24*]   Sessions of the peace held at Bishop Auckland on Wed., 11 Jan. 40 Elizabeth [*1598*] before Bp Matthew, Thomas Calverley, esq., chancellor of Durham, Robert Tailbois, esq., Clement Colmore, LL.D., and fellow JPs.

Robert Farrowe of Fishburn, gen., James Watson of Sheraton, gen., Robert White of Redheugh, gen., John Cragge of Landieu, gen., Brian Emerson of Eastgate, yeo., William Scurfeild of Elstob, yeo., John Buttrie of Hesleden, yeo., Robert Tweddell of Hesleden, yeo., Thomas Wood of Merrington, yeo., John Swalwell of Ludworth, yeo., Richard Shakelock of Murton, yeo., Thomas Dobson of Redworth, yeo., William Ellinor of Hutton, yeo., John Jackson of Elstob, yeo., Richard Trotter of Auckland, yeo.

1) Anthony Culley late of Hartburn, co. Durham, yeo., on 15 Aug. 1597 between 11 p.m. and midnight burgled the residence of Jane Cliston, widow, at Longnewton and assaulted Jane, putting her in bodily fear, and stole 20s. in money, 5 gold pieces and a silver heart in a box.

2) Thomas Thorp late of Durham city, basket-maker, Christopher Hall late of Shincliffe, yeo., alias Christopher Hall late of Newcastle, yeo., William Hall late of Shincliffe, wool dealer, and Cuthbert Cheisman late of the same, yeo., alias Cuthbert Cheisman late of Woodhall, Northumberland, yeo., on 22 Aug. 1597 between 9 and 11 p.m., seduced by the devil, burgled the residence of Matthew Noble at Shincliffe mill in Shincliffe, terrifying Matthew and his whole family, and assaulted Margaret Noble late wife of Matthew, and Thorpe struck her with a bar (*solidus*) worth 2s. between her breasts to her backbone, inflicting a mortal blow 3 inches broad and 6 inches deep whereof she died immediately, thus being guilty of murder. Isabel Frissell of Newcastle, widow, harboured the accused on 1 Oct. 1597 at Newcastle.

3) Robert Bee of Easington, co. Durham, yeo., on 20 Dec. 1597 at Monkwearmouth and thereafter was a common brawler and oppressor of his neighbours and reputed a common malefactor, sower of strife [etc.].

4) John Dowthewait of Headlam, co. Durham, yeo., on 23 Dec. 1597 assaulted Christopher Crawforth at Headlam, took from him a sentence of outlawry, and tore it up.

5) Anthony Cradock of Auckland deanery, co. Durham, yeo., and Michael Langstaff of the same, servant of Anthony, on 3 Dec. 1597 assaulted Henry Gibson, a bailiff of the sheriff of Durham, while at South Church in execution of his office, namely a mandate of Bp Matthew and other JPs, and Michael Langstaffe with the aid of Cradock struck Henry on the head with a stick, inflicting a wound 2 inches wide and 1 inch deep to the peril of his life.

6) Whereas by statute of 5 Richard II against illegal entry, with pain of imprisonment and fine [etc.], Henry Tompson of Monkwearmouth, co. Durham, yeo., Christian Tomson his wife (void because –), William Carr of the same, yeo., and Gerard Wetherell of the same, yeo., on 10 Oct. 1597 broke into the tenement of Eleanor Hutton in Monkwearmouth and ejected Eleanor and remained in possession until 13 Oct. following.

7) Henry Bell late of Stockley, co. Durham, wheelwright, on 20 Dec. 1597 at Stockley assaulted William Lambton of East Brandon, yeo., on the king's highway and took from a loaded waggon 8 pieces of timber each worth 12d. belonging to Robert Marley of Stockley, yeo.

8) Whereas by statute of 5 Richard II against illegal entry [etc.], Bartholomew Cotes of Durham city, mason, John Kent of the same, blacksmith, with others unknown on 21 Dec. 1597 entered a barn of William Scaithlock at Gibbett Knowle called *the stildhouse* and ejected him from possession.

9) George Partus late of Hart, co. Durham, yeo., on 26 Oct. 1597 assaulted Roger Tyrlatt and struck him with a stick, imperilling his life.

4d.] 10) Whereas from time immemorial there was a common way between Hunwick and the parish church of St Andrew Auckland called *the Church footway* used by the inhabitants of Hunwick, Helmington and Newton Cap, George Watson of Bishop Auckland, fuller, blocked the same to their grave nuisance.

11) John Garner late of *Southfeildes*, co. Durham, yeo., on 3 Jan. 1598 at the instigation of the devil assaulted Katharine Brughe of Westoe, spinster, at Westoe, threw her to the ground and kicked her in the belly and chest so that she lingered until 6 Jan., then died of her injuries, Garner therefore was charged with her murder.

12) Andrew Raine late of Thringarth, Yorks., yeo., on 20 Sept. 1597 entered the common pasture of Langton moor in the parish of Romaldkirk, Yorks., and stole 2 stirks, one red-branded worth 40s. and the other black worth 40s., belonging to Christopher Addison of

Seaham, co. Durham, widow [*sic*].

13) John Robeson late of Boldon, co. Durham, lab., on 17 Dec. 1597 broke the close of Anthony Doddes at Ryton Woodside, co. Durham, and stole a branded-colour heifer worth 30s.

14) Anthony Dixon late of Barnard Castle, co. Durham, yeo., on 21 Dec. 1597 between 8 and 9 p.m. broke into a shop belonging to Francis Castlegaite at Barnard Castle and stole 6 girdles worth 12s. found in the shop.

15) Nicholas Freind late of Gateside, co. Durham, yeo., on 20 Aug. 1597 broke into the close of Thomas Rocke at Gateshead and stole a *broune hauled* cow worth 40s.

16) Whereas Bp Matthew, a JP, ordered the sheriff of Durham and other bailiffs, constables and other officers, especially Henry Roy and Christopher Glover, *non omittas* to attach the body of Robert Collyn late of Durham city, lab., on suspicion of felony, to be before the bishop or any other JP to answer divers charges of felony, Roy by virtue of this mandate would have arrested Collyn and taken him into custody but Cuthbert Harwood of Barnard Castle, gen., George Allanson of the same, weaver, Thomas Johnson of the same, husbandman, Thomas Langstaffe of the same, saddler, on 1 Jan. 1598 at Barnard Castle assembled riotously and assaulted Roy, putting him in fear of his life, and rescued Collyn and set him at large.

17) Thomas Thorpe late of Durham city, basket-maker, Christopher Hall late of Shincliffe, yeo., alias Christopher Hall late of Newcastle, yeo., William Hall late of Shincliffe, woolmonger, alias late of Newcastle, and Cuthbert Cheeseman, yeo., alias late of Woodhall, Northumberland, on 22 Aug. 1597 between 9 and 11 p.m. [*etc as (2) above*].

[*space of 13 cms*]

40

[*m.25*] Pleas and presentments at Durham on 5 July 40 Elizabeth [*1598*] before Bp Matthew, Thomas Calverley, esq., chancellor of Durham, George Scroope, esq., Robert Tailbois, esq., Clement Colemore and Thomas Burton, LL.D.s, Richard Bellasis, John Heath, Robert Bowes, Anthony Hutton, esqs, Robert Swift, LL.B. and George Lightfoote, JPs. Michael Pemberton, gen., Richard Heighington, gen., James Watson, gen., John Swallwell, yeo., Richard Key, yeo., Brian Stertfort, yeo., Ralph Suretesse, yeo., Thomas Emmerson, yeo., John Ferry, yeo., Christopher Ferman, yeo., William Elliner, yeo., Nicholas Hutcheson, yeo., Robert Waugh, yeo., Henry Stockden, yeo., Robert Peareson, yeo.

1) Whereas the queen ordered John Conyers, esq., sheriff of Durham, to arrest William Chilton of Newbottle, husbandman, to have his body before the queen's justices at Westminster on a day now past to satisfy Christopher Wharton in a debt of £72, and John Conyers commanded Gerard Swann, one of his bailiffs, to arrest Chilton [*etc.*],

by virtue of which warrant Swann arrested Chilton at Newbottle, but Thomas Chilton of Newbottle, yeo., Thomas Matthew of the same, yeo., and William Smith of the same, yeo., on 25 Feb. 1598 at Newbottle assembled riotously, assaulted Swann, striking him blows on his head and body that his life was despaired of, and rescued William, who is still at large.

2) Whereas John Coniers, esq., sheriff of Durham, ordered John Tailer, his bailiff, to arrest William Chilton of Newbottle, husbandman, to have him before the sheriff on 5 June 1598 to answer Richard Robinson for debt, and Tailer arrested the same, Thomas Chilton of Newbottle, yeo., George Chilton of the same, yeo., and Robert Chilton junior late of the same, yeo., on 22 May 1598 at Newbottle assembled riotously and assaulted Tailer, striking him blows on his head and body [etc.], and rescued William Chilton, who is still at large.

3) William Hall of Durham city, draper, on 6 May 1598 assaulted Barnaby Hutcheson of Durham city, yeo., a clerk of the sheriff in the Durham exchequer, inflicting wounds to the head.

[m.25d., blank]

26] 4) Order to the sheriff of Durham *non omittas* to arrest Robert Rempshawe of Choppington, *co. Durham, yeo., George Fawcon late of Staindrop, co. Durham, yeo., John Moore late of Flockton, Yorks., yeo., John Hall late of Bowes, co. Durham, yeo., Robert Walker late of Staithes, Yorks., yeo., Robert Currey late of *Barwys lonyng*, co. Durham, yeo., Thomas Browne late of Gateside, yeo., John King late of West Burdon, yeo., Robert Vasey late of the same, yeo., William Hall late of Elsdon, Northumberland, yeo., alias Mickle Will late of Elsdon, yeo., Simon Smith late of Thorpe Thewles, co. Durham, yeo., Anthony Wilkinson late of Bishopwearmouth, yeo., John Smith late of Thorpe Thewles, yeo., John Grene late of Durham city, yeo., James Lawson late of Cramlington, Northumberland, yeo., Oswin Matland late of Bedlington, yeo., Thomas Rawe late of Friarside, co. Durham, gen., Thomas Thorpe of Durham city, basket-maker, and Robert Errington late of Heaton, Northumberland, yeo., to be before the queen's justices on 5 Oct. 1597 to answer for divers trespasses, burglaries, murders and woundings; on this day the sheriff returned that Robert Rampshaue [etc.] were not to be found, and an order *sicut alias* was issued for 11 Jan. 1598. Since the defendants had been summoned at county courts held at Durham for 16 Jan. 1598, 13 Feb. 1598, 13 March 1598, 10 April 1598 and 8 May 1598 an order for the defendants to be put in exigent was issued for 15 July 1598. Rampshawe and the others were then outlawed by judgment of Michael Calverley and John Hawkins, county coroners.

5) John Derners for the queen and himself sued against Thomas Rawe late of Friarside, gen., for a felony and murder. Order to the sheriff of Durham *non omittas* to arrest Thomas Rawe late of Friarside, gen., to appear before the queen's justices on 5 Oct. 1597 to answer for

murder, for which he was indicted. The same order repeated but cancelled for 11 Jan. 1598. An order for his exactment from county court to county court to have his body was issued for 5 July 1598. The sheriff returned in court at Durham on 16 Jan. 1599 that Rawe had failed to appear on 13 Feb., 13 March, 10 April and 8 May. The sentence of outlawry was pronounced in accordance with custom by Michael Calverley and John Hawkins, county coroners.
[*space of 44 cms*]

41

[*m.29*] Sessions of the peace at Durham on Wednesday morrow [*rectius,* eve] of St Matthew 40 Elizabeth [*20 Sept. 1598*] before Bp Matthew, George Scroope, esq., William James, dean of Durham, Thomas Calverley, Robert Taylboys, Leonard Pilkington, Th.D., Clement Colemore, Thomas Burton, LL.D.s, Henry Dethick, Robert Swift, LL.B.s, Richard Belassis, Anthony Hutton, John Fetherstonhalgh, Robert Bowes, George Lightfoot esqs, JPs.

Christopher Lewen	Thomas Trotter
Thomas Middleton	Edward Tayler
Brian Downes	George Guye
Richard Trotter	Ninian Kyrsop
Ralph Suertise	Hugh Hutcheson
Richard Heighley	William Herrison
Anthony Meborne	William Corneforth
	Robert Watson, jurors

1) Whereas by statute of 2 Edward VI it was ordained that none below the rank of lord of parliament might carry crossbows in any city or town to fire at weathercocks [*etc.*], nor might they carry *hayle shott* or lead shot under pain of £10 for each offence and 3 months imprisonment, John Scott of Bishop Auckland, co. Durham, cooper, on 20 *Mercarii* 1598 carried a hand gun charged with powder and hailshot, which he discharged at a target called *a black cocke* in the common field called *Moreclose*. (fined & imprisoned according to statute)

2) Christopher Laiborne late of Coppy Crook, co. Durham, yeo., on 1 March 1598 broke the close of Richard Meborne at Coppy Crook and stole a sheep worth 10d.

3) Robert Johnson of Sedgefield, co. Durham, yeo., John Johnson of the same, Brian Gibson of the same, Mariola Johnson of the same, Robert Gibson of the same junior, Robert Hueworth of the same, Robert Noble of the same, William White junior of the same, Richard Pearson of the same, Richard Harrison of the same, William White senior of the same, Nicholas Chipchaice of the same and John Machell of Layton, yeomen, assembled riotously with others unknown in manner of new insurrection on 5 March 1598 at Sedgefield and assaulted Janet Gregson and Elizabeth Pearson.

4) Robert Smith late of Sedgefield, lab., on 27 Feb. 1598 broke the

close of Richard Turbott at Bradbury and stole *a shepe hogg* worth 10d.

5) Dorothy Peacocke of Darlington, spinster, on 8 April 1598 broke into a shop of Christopher Suertees at Durham city and stole 13 yards of *billiment* lace worth 3d.

6) John Legerton late of Smalleys, co. Durham, yeo., on 10 April 1598 broke the close of Christopher Paxton and stole – .

7) William Trewhitt of North Goswick, Northumberland, yeo., Richard Bruse of the same, yeo., and Robert Broddye of the same, yeo., on 11 March 1598 broke the close of Elizabeth Tempest, widow, at Thornley, co. Durham, and stole 17 sheep worth £5 13s. 4d.

8) Whereas Thomas Carleton late of Hawkhope, Northumberland, gen., Roger Fowbery late of Colepike Hall, co. Durham, gen., Richard Close late of Eggleston, yeo., and Lionel Charleton late of Thornborough, Northumberland, gen., on 9 Jan. 1595 were arrested at Durham on suspicion of felonies and committed to the custody of Christopher Glover of Durham city, yeo., keeper of the queen's gaol for co. Durham under John Conyers, esq., then sheriff of Durham and keeper of Durham gaol, by authority of a *mittimus* of the bishop of Durham until they were exonerated from suspicion; nevertheless Thomas, Roger, Richard and Lionel on 7 Feb. 1596 at 11 p.m. broke prison. Henry Dale late of Staindrop, yeo., harboured them at Durham later on that day.

.29d.] 9) Thomas Blaxton late of Newton, co. Durham, gen., on 20 March 1598 blocked the common way for riding to Durham from the moor of Harbour House over the field of Newton by obstructing a gate at the boundary of his land with a quickset hedge and a great ditch to the common nuisance.

10) William Johnson of Woodhouses, co. Durham, yeo., on 24 April 1598 assaulted Dorothy Trotter, wife of Robert Trotter, at Woodhouses.

11) Cuthbert Fetherston of Middle Blackdene, yeo., on 17 April 1598 assaulted Arthur Emerson at St John's Chapel in Weardale in the parish of Stanhope, co. Durham, in time of divine service.

12) Richard Welshe of West Boldon, co. Durham, yeo., William Marshall of the same, yeo., and Gerard Archer of the same, yeo., with others unknown assembled riotously on 19 Feb. 1598 and assaulted Thomas Chambers so that his life was despaired of.

13) Whereas by statute of 13 Richard II it was decreed that none should net or otherwise catch young salmon in mill dams under statutory penalties, Robert Carlell of Carlbury, co. Durham, miller, on 21 April 1598 at Carlbury mill dam fished with a *leape* or wicker net in the Tees and caught 25 young salmon.

14) Whereas by statute of 13 Richard II [*etc.*], John Turner of Piercebridge, co. Durham, miller, on 21 April 1598 at Piercebridge mill dam fished with a *leape* in the Tees and caught a young salmon.

15) Arthur Emerson of Brotherlee, co. Durham, yeo., on 17 April 1598

assaulted Cuthbert Fetherston at St John's Chapel in Weardale in the parish of Stanhope and dragged him from his place in the chapel.

16) Peter Maddison of Unthank, co. Durham, gen., on 13 Nov – at Stanhope assaulted John Fetherstonhalgh, esq., and William Watson, collectors of rents, fines and amercements due to the bishop in Stanhope, who in execution of their office had distrained on him by three stirks for arrears of rent due, and recovered the same.

[m.30]   17) Order to the sheriff *non omittas* to arrest William Parkinson late of Whessoe, co. Durham, gen., George Grene late of Henshaw, Northumberland, lab., William Shancke late of Kirkley, lab., John Readhead late of the same, lab., John Massilgen late of Ryton, co. Durham, lab., and Thomas Braie late of *Alleros* in Weardale, Northumberland [sic], yeo., to have them before the queen's justices on 12 Jan. 1597 to answer for divers felonies and burglaries. The sheriff returned that William Parkinson and others were not to be found. He was ordered *sicut alias* for 6 April, when again he returned that they were not to be found. An order that they be put in exigent was issued for 6 Oct., when the sheriff returned that proclamation had been made at Durham on 18 April, 23 May, 20 June, 18 July, and 25 Aug., when as they still failed to appear, Michael Calverley and John Hawkinis, coroners, had pronounced their outlawry.
[space of 9 cms]

42

[m.27]   Pleas and presentments at Durham on 4 Oct. 40 Elizabeth [1598] before Bp Matthew, Thomas Calverley, esq., chancellor of Durham, William James STP, dean of Durham, George Scroope, esq., Clement Colmore LL.D., George Frevile, esq., Robert Bowes, esq., John Fetherstonhalgh, esq., Robert Swift LL.B., Henry Dethick, LL.B., John Hethe, esq., and Anthony Hutton, esq., JPs.

Thomas Bainbrigg of Wheatley Hill, esq., Robert Farrowe of Fishburn, gen., John Jackson of Elstob, gen., Thomas Emmerson of Darlington, gen., John Swalwell of Ludworth, yeo., George Guy of Herrington, yeo., Anthony Shaudforth of Murton, yeo., John Shepperdson of Witton, yeo., Nicholas Hutcheson of Durham, yeo., William Elliner of Hutton, yeo., Richard Shakelock of the same, yeo., Humphrey Rippon of Aislaby, yeo., William Trotter of Embleton, yeo., John Snaithe of Witton Gilbert, yeo., Robert Waughe of Chester, yeo., jurors.

1) Phyllis Killerbie late of Bedlington, *co. Durham, widow, on 29 April 1598 broke the close of John Shawfeild of Choppington in the manor of Bedlington, gen., and stole a hen worth 3d. (whipped)

2) Peter Patteson of Chester, co. Durham, yeo., on 3 June 1595 at Durham and before and after bought and engrossed bread contrary to law and the peace. (exacted)

3) Enquiry whether Thomas Highe late of Crook mill, co. Durham, miller, on 2 July 1598 assaulted Mariota Worthie at Shildon and

struck her on the head with a stick, endangering her life and in contempt [*etc.*]. (traversed)

4) Thomas Harbotle late of Chester, co. Durham, gen., on 29 Sept. 1598 assaulted John Harrison at Chester and struck him on the face with a stick, endangering his life. (fine and pledges)

[*m.27d., blank*]

43

23]   Sessions of the peace at Durham on 18 April 41 Elizabeth [*1599*] before Bp Matthew, George Scroope, esq., Thomas Calverley, esq., chancellor of Durham, Clement Colemore, LL.D., Thomas Burton, LL.D., John Heath, Henry Anderson, George Frevile, Richard Bellassis, esqs, Henry Dethicke, Bacc. in both Laws, Robert Bowes, Anthony Hutton, John Fetherstonhalgh and George Lightfoote, esqs, JPs.

    Robert Farrow, gen., John Welburie, gen., William Blackett, gen., Robert White, gen., William Trotter, gen., Richard Trotter, yeo., John Shepardson, yeo., Thomas Denham, yeo., John Snath, yeo., Edward Tailer, yeo., William Wrenn, yeo., John Robinson, yeo., Richard Shacklocke, yeo., Anthony Younge, yeo. and Thomas Worthie, yeo., jurors.

1) Percival Mautland late of Monkwearmouth, co.Durham, yeo., on 14 Nov. 1598 entered the barn of Robert Hutton of Houghton-le-Spring, STP, in Houghton-le-Spring between the hours of 8 p.m. and midnight and there with a twist of straw maliciously set fire to a bale of straw, burning the barn and meal (*farra*) worth 40 marks.

2) Whereas by statute of 5 Richard II against illegal entry under pain of imprisonment and a fine at royal pleasure [*etc.*], Fortune Matthew of South Shields, wife of Richard Matthew of the same, yeo., on 5 April 1599 illegally entered the messuage of William Grenewaye at South Shields and assaulted Grenewaye.

3) Whereas William Batmanson of Wooley, co. Durham, yeo., on 13 April 1599 was sent by Thomas Calverley, esq., JP, to Wooley to bring John Nicholson and John Iley of *Helmeden raw*, co. Durham, yeo., before certain keepers of the peace to find surety to keep the peace with John Wall, and if they refused, to commit them to Durham gaol until they found such surety, they escaped from his custody at Wooley.

4) Whereas John Conyers, esq., sheriff of Durham, by a sealed warrant of 30 March 1599 ordered John Spaine, bailiff of Chester ward, or his deputy to distrain on the goods of Ralph Hall of Benfieldside to the use of Gabriel Walker, being a debt of £6 with costs of 13s. 4d. arising from a suit in the county court, by virtue of which John Herrison, deputy of John Spaine, took 2 cows of Hall worth £4 into custody. Robert Lee late of Shotley Bridge, yeo., on 5 March [*sic*] 1599 at Benfieldside attacked Harrison and recovered the cows.

5) William Barnes alias William Barnabey late of Whitwell, co. Durham, yeo., on 21 March 1599 and later to the present day of 18

April hunted at Cassop at *West Whinnes* with a mastiff.

[m.23d.] 6) Ralph Hall of Benfieldside, co. Durham, yeo., on 30 March 1599 assaulted John Harrison at Benfieldside and struck him on various parts of his body with a hatchet and an iron rack which Ralph and Dorothy [*sic*] held in their hands, putting him in great danger of his life.

7) Whereas by statute of 8 Henry VI against disseisin [*etc.*], Francis Trollopp of Thornley, co. Durham, gen., and John Trollopp, gen., with others unknown assembled riotously on 25 March 1599 in the fourth part of the manor or demesne of Nesbitt at Nesbitt, where John Franckland was seised in demesne and John Meburne was farmer, and assumed possession, which they retain.

8) Robert Fawcett of co. Durham, yeo., on 7 Feb. 1599 between 11 p.m. and midnight burgled the residence of Richard Fawcett, clerk, at West Boldon and stole a bay horse worth £20 belonging to Christopher Hedworth of Herrington, gen.

9) Henry Ladler of Plawsworth on 11 Dec. 1598 assaulted John Olliver at Plawsworth and struck him with a stick on various parts of the body, endangering his life.

10) Henry Reade alias Henry Dutaile late of Morpeth, Northumberland, yeo., and William Wilkinson of Tynedale, yeo., on 23 March 1599 broke the close of Robert Phillipson at Boltsburn, co. Durham, and stole 6 wethers worth 8s. each and a ewe worth 7s.

11) John Wilson late of *Bishopsside* in Allendale, Northumberland, yeo., and John Johnson late of Whitfield, yeo., on 31 July 1598 broke the close of Anthony Blarton and John Trimdon at Helme Park and stole 4 cows of various colours worth 40s. each and 2 heifers of various colours worth 30s. each and 2 stirks of various colours worth 40s. each belonging to Anthony Blarton and John Trimdon.

[m.20] 12) [*Schedule*] Writ *non omittas propter libertatem* to the sheriff of Durham to arrest Nicholas Hedley late of Lintz Green, co. Durham, gen., to have him on 18 April 1599 before the keepers of the peace to answer for certain felonies. [*endorsed*] Not found. Repeated for 22 May 1599.

44

[m.22] Pleas at special sessions at Durham on 22 May 41 Elizabeth [*1599*] before Bp Matthew, George Scrope, esq., William James, STP, dean of Durham, Thomas Calverley, esq., chancellor of Durham, Thomas Burton, Clement Colemore, LL.D.s, John Heath, Henry Anderson, John Fetherstonhalgh, esqs, Robert Swift, LL.B., George Lightfoote and Anthony Hutton esqs, JPs.

Robert Farrow, William Midleton, William Blackett, William Trotter, Richard Key, Thomas Wood, Richard Trotter, Robert Tweddle, William Elliner, Edward Emmerson, Edward Tailer, Thomas Dobbison, Nicholas Hutcheson, William Wren and John Robinson, jurors.

1) John Browne late of Stannington, Northumberland, yeo., on 18 May 1599 broke the close of Laurence Presson at St Andrew Auckland, co. Durham, and stole a black horse worth £4.

2) Whereas by statute of 8 Henry VI on novel disseisin [*etc.*], Robert Baker of Monkwearmouth, co. Durham, gen., and Agnes Bee of the same, spinster, with others unknown assembled on 18 May 1599 at Monkwearmouth on a messuage of William James, dean, and the chapter of Durham, and forcibly disseised the same with Elizabeth Wodrington, widow, farmer of the same from the dean and chapter, and remained in occupation from 18 May until the date of this enquiry.
[*space of 10 cms*]

22d.]   [*space of 10 cms*]

3) Writ to the sheriff of Durham *non omittas* to arrest Nicholas Hedley late of Lintz Green, gen., to answer before the keepers of the peace on 18 April 1599 for divers felonies, repeated for 22 May. Order to exact him from county court to county court to answer on 27 June 1599.
[*space of 22.5 cms*]

45

21]   General sessions of the peace at Durham on Wed., 27 June 41 Elizabeth [*1599*] before William James, dean of Durham, George Scrope, esq., Thomas Calverley, esq., chancellor of Durham, Clement Colemore, LL.D., John Heath, Robert Bowes, John Fetherstonhalgh, Robert Tailboyes, Henry Anderson, George Lightfoote and Anthony Hutton, esqs, JPs.

Thomas Midleton	Brian Emmerson	Wm Elliner
John Hedworth	John Swalwell	Thomas Dobson
Wm Blackett	John Shiperdson	John Robinson
Wm Trotter	Nicholas Hutcheson	John Snath
Wm Garth	John Dobson	
	Edward Emmerson	

1) Ralph Sigswick of Bellasis, co. Durham, yeo., and Richard Grene of the same, yeo., on 16 June 1599 assaulted Robert Bainbrigg at Quarrington bridge and struck him on the head with a stick held in the right hand, inflicting wounds endangering his life.

2) William Grenewaie of South Shields, co. Durham, merchant, on 4 April 1599 assaulted Fortune Mathewe wife of Richard Mathewe at South Shields, striking her with a poker held in his right hand and wounding her on the breast, endangering her life.

3) Laurence Wilkynson of Ferryhill, co. Durham, on 24 June 1599 assaulted Robert Kyrkhowse of Church Merrington at Ferryhill, striking him with a dagger held in his right hand on the left side of his head and putting him in bodily fear.
[*m.21d., blank*]

46

19]   General sessions of the peace at Durham in the counties of Durham and Sadberge on 10 Jan. 42 Elizabeth [*1600*] before Bp Matthew,

William James, dean of Durham, Thomas Calverley, esq., chancellor of Durham, George Scrope, esq., George Frevile, John Heath, John Fetherstonhalgh and Anthony Hutton, JPs.

1) Thomas Blackett of Woodcroft, co. Durham, gen., on 2 Dec. 1599 assaulted Cuthbert Morgaine in the parish church of Stanhope, seated at the time of common prayer.

2) Whereas the dean and chapter of Durham on 30 Oct. 1599 ordered Robert Massam, their itinerant bailiff to collect rents, fines and amercements, to distrain on Thomas Norton of Skirningham, co. Durham, esq., for an annual rent of £6 13s. 4d. in arrears, Massam on the last day of October seized 2 oxen, 4 cows and a heifer of Norton at Skirningham; Richard Shaffeild of Skirningham, yeo., servant of Norton, on the same day unlawfully assaulted Massam and recovered the 2 oxen, 4 cows and heifer.

3) Whereas Martin Maunger, collector of the bishop in the vill of Hamsteels, co. Durham, yeo., on 26 Nov. 1599 by virtue of an estreat distrained on Ralph Grinwell by a brass pot worth 6s. at Hollybush, but when he tried to remove the same, Ralph Grinwell and his wife assaulted Maunger and violently recovered the pot.

4) John Errington late of Bewclay, Northumberland, gen., on 12 July 1599 broke the close of Henry Anderson, esq., at Ryton, co. Durham, and stole a black-brown horse worth £5.

5) John Elrington of Northumberland, gen., and John Carr late of the same, yeo., on 24 July 1599 broke the close of Robert Whitfeilde at Allenshiel, co. Durham, and stole a grey horse worth 33s. 4d.

6) Thomas Crawe late of Lees Hill, Cumberland, yeo., on 25 Nov. 1599 broke the close of Henry Ane at Wolsingham, co. Durham, and stole 6 cows of various colours worth 40s. each.

7) John Patteson late of West Auckland, co. Durham, lab., on 20 Nov. 1597 broke into the close of George Moore at Evenwood and stole a grey gelding worth 40s.

8) John Tate late of Darlington, lab., on 11 Feb. 1599 stole 2 ewes worth 6s. each belonging to Vincent Hodgshon at Darlington.

9) William Bell late of *Furlawe*, Cumberland, yeo., alias Will of Carlisle, on 1 Sept. 1598 broke the close of Widow Marshall at Denton, co. Durham, and stole a grizzled mare worth £3 6s. 8d; and George Bell late of Bowbank, Cumberland, yeo., knowing of the theft, harboured William Bell at Bowbank on the same day.

10) William Ornesbie late of Milton, Cumberland, yeo., on – Aug. 1598 broke the close of George Bayles at Raby, co. Durham, and stole a grizzle [horse] worth £6.

11) Thomas Warmouth late of Billingham, co. Durham, lab., on –1599 broke into the house of Geoffrey Maddison at Billingham and stole a stone of iron worth 2s.

[*m.19d.*] 12) Ralph Lodge late of Cockfield, co. Durham, yeo., on 20 May 1599 and later, namely to 20 Dec., for 7 months practised the trade of tanner at Cockfield for gain, selling tanned hides without having

served an apprenticeship of seven years or being in business before
12 Jan. 5 Elizabeth [1563].

13) Presentment that Elvet and Framwellgate bridges by Durham were
in decay and a nuisance to the inhabitants of the whole country
using them; but whose was the responsibility for repair the jurors
knew not.

14) Memorandum that John Harrison of Chester, co. Durham,
chapman, being presented as trading as a mercer in Chester-le-Street
for 12 months between 1 Oct. 1598 and 1 Oct. 1599 without serving
an apprenticeship, appeared in court personally on 10 Jan. 1600 and
sought that the presentment be read to him. This done, Harrison
pleaded not guilty and proffered in court an indenture between him
and John Harrison of Allendale, Northumberland, chapman, his
father, dated 19 Sept. 1560 binding him as apprentice chapman for
seven years, wherefore the JPs dismissed the case *sine die*.
Copy of the indenture in English.

47

16] Pleas and presentments at Durham on Wed., 1 April 42 Elizabeth
[1600] before Bp Matthew, William James, STP, dean of Durham,
George Scroope, esq., Thomas Calverley, esq., chancellor of Durham,
Clement Colemore, LL.D., John Heth, John Fetherstanhaugh, George
Freville, George Lightfoote, Anthony Hutton, esqs, Thomas Burton,
LL.D., Henry Dethicke, LL.B. and Robert Swift, clerk, JPs.

Brian Townes, gen.	Edward Tayler, yeo.
Oliver Brackenburie, gen.	John Snath, yeo.
Richard Heighley, gen.	George Smith, yeo.
William Blackett, gen.	William Liddell, yeo.
Nicholas Hutchinson, yeo.	John Robinson, yeo.
William Wrenne, yeo.	Christopher Garnett, yeo.
Richard Keye, yeo.	Cuthbert Hodgesson, yeo.
	George Peacock, yeo., jurors

1) Richard Gascoigne of Kibblesworth, co. Durham, gen., and Henry
Gasc[oigne] of Hallgarth, [Durham], gen., on 25 Feb. 1600 assaulted
and wounded Robert Cuthbert of Kibblesworth, yeo., on divers parts
of the body and put him in fear.

2) William Eden late of South Shields (*South St Hyldes*), co. Durham,
gen., Abraham E[den] late of the same, gen., and Edward Hudson late
of the same, yeo., assembled riotously with 10 others unknown and
on 29 Jan. 1600 at South Shields assaulted Oswald Hucknold and
Christopher Ranson and put them in bodily fear.

3) Whereas a writ from the Durham chancery was directed to the
sheriff of Durham to remove Ambrose Dudley and all others from
possession of the manor of Chopwell and divers lands in Chopwell,
and in execution the sheriff on 26 March 1600 went to Chopwell to
remove Ambrose and the rest peacefully in order to put Sir William
Constable in possession, a Robert Dudley of [Chopwell], esq., and

Henry Dudley of the same, gen., with 30 persons unknown, by order of the same Ambrose Dudley, assembled riotously, drove off the sheriff and violently defended their possession for 3 hours, to the pernicious example of others.

4) George Lasenbie of St Helen Auckland, co. Durham, gen., Peter Lasenbye, gen., Thomas Lasenbie, gen., and Robert Lasenbye of the same, gen., being sons of the said George, on 1 April 1600, assembled riotously and assaulted Richard Vasey and Dorothy Whitmore, widow, at St Helen Auckland, and George struck with a dagger held in his right hand and inflicted on Richard a great wound in the chest an inch wide and 3 inches deep so that he was in bodily danger.

5) Whereas the queen and her council in northern parts established on 13 March 1600 ordered John Conyers, esq., sheriff of Durham and Sadberge, to attach William Brackenburie to implement an arbitration made by Nicholas Hilton and others between Henry Watson, plaintiff, and the same William as defendant, relating to a matter dependent before the queen and her council, and to have him before the queen's council at York immediately on sight of the same, by virtue of which writ a warrant was issued under his seal of office, and on 16 March a writ was sent to Lancelot Hilton, George Jackson and Anthony Tomson, bailiffs, to attach Brackenburye for non-performance. Following the issue of this precept Hilton and Jackson on 17 March took Brackenburie into custody at Langton, but a Thomas Brackenburie of Langton, yeo., and Oswald Brackenburye of the same, yeo., deliberately on 17 March assembled riotously and assaulted Hilton and Jackson, whereby Thomas Brackenburie, Oswald Brackenburie and Anthony Brackenburie rescued William Brackenburie, who is still at large.

[m.16d.] 6) George Middleton late of Killerby, co. Durham, husbandman, on 24 Nov. 1598 broke the close of Oliver Brackenburie at Killerby and stole 6 pieces of wood worth 40s.

7) Andrew Hornesbye late of Milton, Cumberland, yeo., John Johnson late of the same, lab., Robert Graime alias Hob Graime late of the same, lab., and Thomas Batie late of the same, lab., on 31 Oct. 1599 broke the close of Roger Bainbrigg at Barnard Castle, co. Durham, and stole 6 mares of divers colours worth 26s. 8d. each.

8) Andrew Hornesbie late of Milton, Cumberland, yeo., [etc. as above] on 31 Oct 1599 broke the close of Thomas Dickonson at Barnard Castle, co. Durham, and and stole 4 mares of divers colours worth 46s. 8d. each.

9) Whereas the dean and chapter of Durham on 1 Nov. 1599 ordered Robert Massam, itinerant bailiff to collect rents, fines and amercements, to distrain on the goods of Robert Finche of Wolviston, yeo., for a rent of 9s. for a cottage in Wolviston which had remained unpaid for 3 years, and Robert Massam by virtue of this mandate on 2 Nov. seized as distraint a red cow of Finche at Wolviston; the same day Finche assaulted Massam and recovered the cow.

10) Richard Haddock (12d.) of Fulwell, co. Durham, yeo., on 28 Dec. 1599 at Fulwell assaulted George Jackson and wielding a pitchfork worth 8d. prevented an ox belonging to Michael Calverley, gen., yoked to a cart or *cowpe waine* laden with muck from being taken from Fulwell to the town fields, to the injury of Jackson and Calverley and against the queen's peace.

11) Richard Haddock (12d.) of Fulwell, yeo., on 28 Dec. 1599 at Fulwell assaulted Christopher Stell and wielding a pitchfork [*etc., as (10) above*].

12) Andrew Trollope of Thornley, co. Durham, gen., on 18 Oct. 1599 at Kelloe moor assaulted John Martin on the queen's highway and struck him on the head with a sword held in his right hand, endangering his life.

13) Whereas John Conyers, esq., sheriff of Durham, ordered Edward Seamer, his bailiff in the Stockton ward, to arrest Peter Thompson if found and keep him in custody until he was secured in the gaol of Durham castle until he satified Michael Shawe for a debt of £20 principal and 8s. expenses, incurred in a suit brought by Shawe in the county court at Durham on Mon., 25 Feb. 1600, recovered by default according to the custom of the court, his action to be reported at the succeeding court on Mon., 7 April; and whereas Conyers ordered Seamer to arrest Thompson similarly to satisfy Richard Johnson for a debt of £3 8s. 4d. principal debt and 8s. 8d. in expenses from court costs in a suit brought by Johnson at Durham on Mon., 27 Sept. 1599 [*etc.*] to be certified in court on Mon., 26 March 1600, Seamer arrested Thompson and was prepared to lead him to the gaol of Durham castle but Thompson and Ralph Milborne of Wolviston, yeo, unmindful of these orders on 25 March assaulted Seamer and made an affray and Milborne rescued Thompson, who remains at large.

14) Whereas Bp Tobie Matthew, a justice of the queen's peace, at Bishop Auckland, co. Durham, on 21 Feb. 1600 ordered the sheriff, bailiffs, constables and other officers in general and Richard Matthewe in particular as deputy bailiff of South Shields and William Ranson, constable of the same, *non omittas* to attach the body of George Ogle late of South Shields, gen., to have him before the justices of the peace or one of them at the next county sessions and meanwhile to keep the peace with Oswald Hucknold of South Shields, yeo., and Mary his wife; when Richard Matthewe and William Ranson on the same day attempted to carry out these orders at South Shields, George Ogle and William Eden late of South Shields, gen., attacked them with sword, dagger and halbert, and Eden rescued Ogle, who remains at large.

17] 15) Whereas John Conyers, esq., sheriff of Durham, ordered Robert Maltbye, his bailiff of the Chester ward, to arrest Wilfrid Lawson if found and take him under custody to the gaol of Durham castle to satisfy Hugh Walton for a debt of £20 principal and 14s. court expenses incurred at the county court at Durham on Mon., 19 March 1599, as agreed by sworn verdict of twelve and by consideration of the county court, and Maltbye prepared to arrest Lawson; Robert Lawson late of Gateside, gen., Hugh Birde late of North Shields, Northumberland, gen., and Elizabeth wife of Wilfrid Lawson late of Gateside, co. Durham, gen., on 28 Nov. 1599 at Gateside assembled riotously and attacked Maltbye and rescued Lawson, who remains at large.

16) Andrew Trollope late of Harbour House, co. Durham, lab., Robert Allen late of Kelloe, yeo., John Gibson late of the same, yeo., George Armestrong late of the same, yeo., and George Armstrong late of the same, yeo. [*sic*], on 18 March 1600 on a common highway to the south of Kelloe village leading to Wingate where it crosses Kelloe *loyninge* towards Church Kelloe blocked this road with a quickset hedge and turned it into pasture from 18 March to the date of the enquiry, to the bad example and nuisance of the queen's subjects living nearby and contrary to divers statutes.

17) Nicholas Thompson late of Ushaw, co. Durham, lab., on 2 March 1600 broke into the residence of Nicholas Simpson at Ushaw between 11 p.m. and midnight and burgled a petticoat worth 5s., 3 *patletts* worth 3s., 2 girdles worth 2s. and 3 hand napkins worth 12d. belonging to Elizabeth Arrowsmith in a chest in the house.

18) Andrew Trollope of Harbour House, co. Durham, lab., Henry Ovington of Kelloe, lab., Henry Allen of the same, yeo., and George Armestrong of the same, lab., riotously broke and entered the close at Kelloe on 13 Jan. 1600 at Southfield or Middlefield, where they assembled riotously and Ovington assaulted Lancelot Richeson and struck him with a longstaff.

19) Whereas Thomas Calverley, esq., a keeper of the queen's peace, on 10 March 1600 ordered Robert Maltbie to levy from the constables and churchwardens of the county divers separate sums specified in his warrant, Maltbye distrained at Medomsley on a cow of Robert Hunter, a churchwarden there, for 28s. 8d. and was holding the same in custody. George Allenson of Medomsley, yeo., Robert Hunter of the same, yeo., and Lancelot Johnson of the same, yeo., deliberately on 20 March 1600 assembled at Medomsley, attacked Maltbie and recovered the cow.

20) Whereas the queen by the writ *fieri facias* from the Durham court of pleas, sealed with the seal of the Durham county palatine, on 4 Oct. 1599 ordered John Conyers, esq., sheriff of Durham, to distrain on the goods of Anthony Hunter for a debt of £9 9s. recovered against him by Edward Simpson in the said court; on 5 Dec. 1599 Robert Maltbye, his bailiff, by virtue of this warrant exacted 5 cows and a stirk, but Roland Hunter of Medomsley, yeo., Arthur Atkinson of the same, yeo., Robert Shawdforth of the same, Katherine Hunter wife of Thomas Hunter, and Alice Hodgshon wife of Robert Hodgshon on 8 Dec. 1599 assaulted Maltbie and recovered the cows and stirk. [*m.17d., blank*]

[8] 21) Richard Carr of Gateside, co. Durham, yeo., on 1 May 1599 and later engrossed 5 quarters of malt and 7 quarters of oats worth <£8> £25, for resale, contrary to statute.

22) John Gargrave for the same [*offence of engrossing*] 2 quarters of malt and 2 quarters of oats [worth £10].

23) Peter Greene of Hett, co. Durham, the same [*offence*] 2 quarters of malt and 2 quarters of oats worth £10.

24) Thomas Gibson the same, 2 quarters of malt and 2 quarters of oats worth £10.

25) Rowland Chambers of Seaham, co. Durham, the same, 2 quarters of oats and 2 quarters of barley worth £10.

26) Thomas Chambers of Whitburn, co. Durham, the same, 2 quarters of malt and 2 quarters of oats worth £10.

27) Cuthbert Chambers of the same, the same, 2 quarters of malt and 2 quarters of oats worth £10.

28) Rowland Chambers of Seaham, the same, 2 quarters of oats and 1 quarter of barley worth £10.

29) Henry Curtesse of Seaham, wool dealer, on 1 Sept. 1599 and afterwards for 5 months until 1 March at divers places in co. Durham practised the art of butchercraft illegally, selling meat when he had never served an apprenticeship for 7 years or been in business on 12 Jan. 1563 when the act was passed.

30) – (41) The same against Edward Browne of Wearmouth; John Simpson of Easington; William Watson of Shields; Robert Brack of Langley Park; William Lawson of Shields; Thomas Wrenn of Woodifield; Gilbert Paxton of Easington; George Herrison of Easington; Robert Bradford of Hamsterley; Richard Hazon of Easington; Richard Jackson of Hamsterley; James Wall of Escomb.

42) Reginald Fawsett of Fulwell, co. Durham, yeo., was charged with being a tracer of hares in time of snow, and that on 3 Feb. 1600 he tracked with a greyhound at Fulwell in snowtime 3 hares which he killed contrary to statute.

43) – 45) The same against Thomas Chilton of the same; William Hutchinson of Whitburn; George Demyne of Wearmouth.

46) Edward Dalton of Gateside, yeo., on 20 Sept. 1599 and later, after Martinmas, fished with nets, engines, wicker nets and *weeles* in the Tyne at Gateside and took kipper and shed salmon, contrary to statute.

47) The same against Sanders Bell of the same for fishing in the Tyne.

48) The same against George Simpson of *Law* for fishing in the Derwent.

49) The same against Robert Comyn of Shotley Bridge for fishing in the Derwent.

50) – 59) The same against Reynold Comyn of Shotley Bridge; Thomas Labourne of Chopwell wood; John Foster of Knitsley; Cuthbert Simpson of Ebchester; William Mautland of Lintzford; Andrew Joplyn of Lintzford; John Joplyn of the same; Thomas Joplyn

of the same; William Surtees of the same; John White of Blackwell.

60) The same against John Rawe junior of Chester-le-Street for fishing in the Wear.

61) – 76) The same against John Marley; William Robson of Urpeth; Saunders Purveyes; William Grinwey of Pelton; Anthony Laborne of Gibside; Nicholas Foster; Robert Foster; Richard Foster; Ralph Whitfeilde; Christopher Blacklock of Winlaton; John Storye; Charles Fletcher of Chester-[le-Street]; Percival Appleby of Chester; Anthony Halliday of Chester; Bartholomew Wadeson of Chester; Thomas Grundy. All submitted to pay 40s. and were sentenced to imprisonment for 2 months.

77) Cuthbert Bainbrigg of Whitburn, co. Durham, yeo., on 1 Jan. 1600 and later engrossed 2 quarters of barley and 2 quarters of oats worth £10 for resale, contrary to statute.

[m.18d., blank]

48

[m.15]   Sessions of the peace at Durham on 25 June 42 Elizabeth [1600] before William James, STP, dean of Durham, George Scroope, esq., Thomas Calverley, esq., chancellor of Durham, Clement Colemore, LL.D., Henry Dethicke, George Frevile, Anthony Hutton, John Fetherstonhalghe, George Lightfoote, esqs, and Thomas Burton, LL.D., JPs.

Robert Farrow, gen.	Edward Tayler	John Robinson
George Crosyer	Anthony Meborne	John Swalwell
Brian Emmerson	George Smith	Anthony Younge
George Myers	Thomas Trotter	John Hopper
Edward Robinson	Chris. Richmond	Thomas Dobbeson

1) Robert Porter late of Beamish park, co. Durham, yeo., on 1 June 1599 at Middleton[-in-Teesdale], co. Durham, stole a grey mare worth 40s. of William Kiplinge; and William Kiplinge late of Bog House, yeo., knowing that Porter had commited this felony, received and entertained him the same day at Beamish park, contrary to the peace.

2) Christopher Shawe of Cleadon, co. Durham, yeo., on 22 June 1600 assaulted John Orpeth at Cleadon and struck him with a dagger held in his right hand on divers parts of the body, putting him in mortal peril.

3) Richard Priorman of Sedgefield, co. Durham, yeo., on 24 June 1600 assaulted Robert Lavorock at Bradbury and struck him on his body with a stick held in his right hand so that his life was despaired of.

4) George Pilmer of South Shields, co. Durham, rough-mason, and Jasper Sanderson of the same, rough-mason, on 3 May 1600 and later for the space of 3 months, namely until 25 June, at divers places in the county exercised the art of rough-mason illegally for gain without having served an apprenticeship of 7 years, nor were they in business before the passage of the relevant statute on 12 Jan. 1563.

5) Whereas from time immemorial the dean and chapter of Durham

and each of their tenants inhabiting the vill of Westerton, co. Durham, had a boundary stone or *a mere stone or melderstone* on the west side of Spennymoor in Westerton defining their boundary with Coundon, Richard Peareson of Coundon, yeo., and Thomas Hopper of the same, yeo., deliberately moved the stone by night about 10 p.m. on 29 Aug. 1599, to the detriment of the dean and chapter and their tenants.

6) John Prierman of Bradbury, co. Durham, yeo., on 24 June 1600 at Bradbury assaulted Robert Lavorack with a dagger, inflicting a wound on his right hand so that his life was despaired of.

15d.] 7) John Gascoigne of Lamesley, co. Durham, gen., on 18 May 1600 assaulted Christopher Sanderson at Lamesley and struck him on divers parts of his body with a dagger, putting him in bodily fear.

8) Memo that Thomas Carlton who sued for the queen and himself came before the justices and gave the court to understand that John Tossye of Stockton, co. Durham, yeo., on 30 March 1600 and later ingrossed 20 quarters of barley worth £20 at Stockton and kept it to resell, contrary to the statute, and he asked the consideration of the court and sought an award of half the value of the barley in accordance with the statute of 5 Edward VI.

9) Memo that Thomas Carlton for the queen and himself came before the justices and laid an information that John Tossye of Stockton, yeo., on 30 March 1600 and later ingrossed 20 quarters of rye worth £30 [*etc. as above*].

10) Memo that Thomas Carlton similarly laid an information against Thomas Tayler in respect of the same day and place.

49

14] Pleas and presentments at Durham on 1 Oct. 42 Elizabeth [*1600*] before William James, dean of Durham, George Scroope, esq., Thomas Calverley, esq., chancellor of Durham, Clement Colemore, LL.D., John Heth, Anthony Hutton, George Lightfoote, esqs, Henry Dethicke, LL.B., and George Frevile, esq., JPs.

Robert Farrowe	Nicholas Hutcheson
William Scurfeilde	Christopher Richmond
William Blackett	John Godderson
William Trotter	Robert Waughe
Thomas Trotter	George Smith
Robert Tweddle	Thomas Shutwell
William Corneforde	Thomas Wood
	William Liddle, jurors

1) Nicholas Procter of Great Chilton, co. Durham, lab., on 28 Aug. 1600 broke the close of John Robinson at Great Chilton and stole a ewe worth 10d.

2) Henry Thompson of Haggerston, *co. Durham, yeo., Thomas Thompson junior of the same, yeo., and John Thompson of the same, yeo., on 26 Dec. 1599 assembled riotously in Aucklandfield

meadow and assaulted George Smith and carried away a dagger belonging to him.

3) Robert Charneley of Gateshead, draper, on 5 Jan. 1600 at Gateshead behaved as a common barrator and disturber of the peace and a spreader of gossip.

4) William Bowmer late of Lamesley, co. Durham, lab., on 27 Sept. 1600 broke the close of William Sanders at Lamesley called *le Parocke* and uprooted the hedge.

5) John Wrangham (5s.) late of Gainford, yeo., Francis Atkinson late of the same, Christopher Joyner late of the same, yeo., and Thomas Garstell late of Low Wemmergill, Yorks., yeo., on 27 Sept. 1600 broke the close of Richard Cradock at Gainford called *Westholme* and uprooted 20 feet of quickset hedge.

6) Thomas Birckbie late of Piercebridge, co. Durham, lab., and Christopher Birckbie of the same, lab., being 14 years and over and able bodied, not having land nor master nor engaged in trade whereby they might support themselves, on 5 Sept. 1600 at Piercebridge and elsewhere were vagabonds and beggars contrary to divers acts of parliament.

[*m.14d., blank*]

50

[*m.12*] Pleas and presentments at Durham on 9 Jan. 43 Elizabeth [*1601*] before George Scroope, esq., William James, STP, dean of Durham, Thomas Calverley, esq., chancellor of Durham, Clement Colemore, Thomas Burton, LL.D.s, Henry Dethicke, LL.B., John Fetherstanhaugh and George Frevile, esqs, JPs.

1) Inquest for the queen as to whether George Middleton late of Silksworth, co. Durham, gen., Adam Middleton late of the same, gen., Ralph Yonger late of the same, yeo., John Grame late of the same, yeo., and Elizabeth Brayke late of the same, spinster, on 30 Dec. 1600 at Farrington (*Fernetonhall*), co. Durham, illegally assembled and riotously broke into the close of Peter Denton of Farrington, gen., at Farrington in the parish of Bishopwearmouth called *the High Close* and tore down 10 feet of hedge and destroyed the ditch. (true bill)

2) Inquest for the queen as to whether George Middleton late of Silksworth, gen., [*etc. as (1) above*] on 2 Jan. 1601 at Farrington illegally assembled and broke into the close of Peter Dentton of Farrington, gen., called *the High Close* and broke down 10 feet of hedge and made free of the same, although it was neither common nor common way since memory, and do so to the date of the enquiry. (true bill)

3) Inquest for the queen as to whether George Atkinson of Raby, co. Durham, yeo., on 15 Sept. 1600 assaulted John Sampson with sword and dagger worth 5s. between noon and 1 p.m. in the residence of George Atkinson in Raby castle and put him in fear and violently

took from him a gold ring worth £3. (true bill)

4) William Johnson late of Woodhouses, co. Durham, yeo., John Parkyne of Auckland, yeo., Richard Robertes of the same, yeo., and Peter Walton of the same, cordwainer, on 30 Nov. 1600 at Woodhouses illegally assembled and obstructed the *feres* of the residence of Robert Trotter of Woodhouses, yeo.

5) Whereas by statute of 8 Henry VI on disseisin [*etc.*], Thomas Johnson late of Thorpe Bulmer, co. Durham, yeo., Ralph Claxton late of the same, yeo., and Tristram Wright late of the same, yeo., on 11 Dec. 1600 at Hart entered a messuage being the free holding of Sir John Lumley, Lord Lumley, and in the possession of John Browne and Janet Browne, thereby disseising Lord Lumley and expelling the Brownes his tenants, and have continued in this disseisin. (true bill)

6) Inquest for the queen as to whether William Blakey late of Cassop, co. Durham, lab., and Margaret Blakey late of the same, widow, on 10 Oct. 1600 broke into the barley field of William Middleton at Cassop and stole bigg worth 10d.

2d.] 7) Inquest for the queen as to whether Rowland Wrenn late of Wackerfield, co. Durham, lab., and John Graye late of the same, lab., on 20 Oct. 1600 entered the close of Bernard Bowes at Wackerfield and stole a bay horse worth £3. (true bill)

8) Inquest for the queen as to whether Anthony Allison late of East Brandon, co. Durham, lab., on 1 Nov. 1600 entered the close of George Pynckney at Brandon called *Westfield* and stole two sheep worth 12d. (true bill)

9) Inquest for the queen as to whether Isabel Tayler late of *Brandeslopp*, co. Durham, spinster, on 4 Nov. 1600 entered the close of William Harrison at Friarside called *the Cowclose* and stole a ewe worth 10d. (true bill)

10) Francis Coatesworth late of Eggleston, co. Durham, lab., aged 14 years and more and able bodied but without land or master or any licenced trade whereby he could support himself on 20 Dec. 1600 at Gateshead and elsewhere was found begging and a vagabond. (true bill)

11) George Massir late of Gateshead, lab., aged 14 years and more and able bodied [*etc.*] on 20 Dec. 1600 was found at Gateshead and elsewhere begging and a vagabond.

12) Inquest for the queen as to whether Rowland Wrenn late of Houghton-le-Side, co. Durham, lab., on 25 Sept. 1600 entered the close of John Hickson at Houghton-le-Side called *the Pasture* and stole a grey mare worth 40s. (true bill)

13) Inquest for the queen as to whether Rowland Wrenn late of Wackerfield, co. Durham, lab., and John Graye late of the same, lab., on 20 Oct. 1600 broke the close of Robert Bowes at Wackerfield and stole a grey mare worth £3. (true bill)

14) Inquest for the queen at to whether William Lawes late of Bedlington, *co. Durham, lab., on 13 July 1600 broke the close of

Cuthbert Watson at Bedlington called *the Park* and stole a black horse worth £7. (true bill)

15) Inquest for the queen as to whether Ludovic Ogle late of Felton, Northumberland, yeo., William Starricke late of Ovingham, yeo., and Robert Harrison late of Whickham, co. Durham, yeo., on 18 April 1600 broke the close of John Catcheside at Birtley and stole a dark-grey horse worth 40s. (true bill)

[*space of 15 cms*]

[*m.13*]   16) Inquest for the queen touching her order by writ of withernam from the court of pleas at Durham directed to John Conyers, esq., sheriff of Durham; whereas John Hedworth of the Deanery, Chester-le-Street, gen., Philip Tronhill of the same, and Edward Charlton were summoned to appear in the queen's court before the queen's justices to answer John Girlington, esq., in a plea that on 13 Sept. 1600 at Harraton or Harradon in the East Field they took livestock, namely 41 cows, 2 stots and 2 stirks belonging to John Girlington and kept them as pledge; and Hedworth sought to justify the seizure both in his own right and in that of his wife Jane, claiming that Philip Tronhill and Edward Charlton were acting as their bailiffs. Girlington although exacted could show no reason to preclude the action of Hedworth and remained silent. It was decided in the queen's court that Girlington should have nothing for his suit and that he be amerced and that Hedworth and the rest be dismissed *sine die* and that Hedworth should have the return of his livestock. The queen had several times ordered the sheriff to return the livestock to Hedworth without delay or to show cause; and the sheriff returned that the livestock had been driven to a place unknown, wherefore the queen ordered that livestock of John Girlington of an equivalent value be delivered to Hedworth until such time as Girlington returned Hedworth's livestock. On 16 Dec. 1600 the sheriff by Robert Robson, gen., undersheriff, and Robert Moorie, Gerard Swann and Robert Maltbye, bailiffs of the sheriff for this occasion, took at Harraton in the parish of Chester-le-Street in accordance with the writ of withernam a bull, 4 bullocks and 10 cows and delivered them to John Hedworth, whereupon Cuthbert Pudsay of Harraton, gen., George Vicarres of the same, yeo., and Thomas Jackson of the same, yeo., on the same day with 10 others unknown riotously assaulted Robson and his bailiffs at Harraton and recovered these.

17) Thomas Plumpton of East Boldon, co. Durham, yeo., William Jackson of the same, yeo., William Hodge of the same, yeo., John Todd of the same, yeo., William Chamber junior of the same, yeo., George Chamber of the same, yeo., William Chamber senior of the same, blacksmith, Ralph Lumley of the same, yeo., Stephen Wilkinson of the same, lab., John Ayden of the same, lab., John Saunders of the same, lab., Robert Thompson of the same, lab., Thomas Claye of the same, lab., and John Gryndye of the same, lab., on 29 June 1600 at East Boldon on a common highway at *the Fleetes*

assembled riotously and assaulted and wounded Cuthbert Bainbrigge and Thomas Matthewe.

18) Thomas Plumpton of East Boldon, yeo., William Jackson of the same, yeo., William Chamber senior of the same, blacksmith, Ralph Lumley of the same, yeo., Stephen Wilkinson of the same, lab., John Aden of the same, lab., John Saunders of the same, lab., and Thomas Claye of the same, lab., on 24 June 1600 enclosed the common highway between Whitburn and Cleadon at East Boldon moor and as far as the north-west nook of *Scrabbes Close* in East Boldon by *the Fletes* in East Boldon, thence to the Bow Bridge in East Boldon to West Boldon moor gate in West Boldon, and thence to Scotch House lane in West Boldon, and thence to Wardley *loning* in Heworth, and thence from Heworth *swardes* to Felling *loning* in Heworth, and thence to *les Fleetes* in East Boldon, this being enclosed with hedges and ditches, and it remains so fenced.

19) Anthony Ayre of Shincliffe, co. Durham, husbandman, and Christopher Skeirfeilde of the same, lab., on 20 Oct. 1600 broke the close of Lionel Martyne of Durham city, yeo., and Thomas Foster of Shincliffe, husbandman, called *le Lowfielde* in Shincliffe and depastured the grass and grain, namely maslin worth 50s., with their horses and cattle and ploughed up the ground so that Lionel and Thomas lost use of the land for a long time.

[*m.13d., blank*]

51

1] Pleas and presentments at Durham on 22 April 43 Elizabeth [*1601*] before George Scroope, esq., William James, STP, dean of Durham, Thomas Calverley, esq., chancellor of Durham, Clement Colemore, LL.D., Henry Dethicke, esq., Thomas Burton, LL.D., Anthony Huton, John Fetherstonhaughe, George Frevile and George Lightfoote, esqs, JPs.

William Scrutvile	William Corneforth
William Trotter	Hugh Hutcheson
John Hearon	Richard Trotter
Richard Heighlye	Richard Shacklocke
Edward Robinson	Anthony Meborne
Ralph Surtes	Robert Tweddle
Anthony Wilson	George Whitfeilde
	John Swalwell, jurors

1) Michael Calverley of Fulwell, co. Durham, gen., Robert Stephenson of Cleadon, lab., Ralph Bowdon of Fulwell, lab., Geoffrey Mathew of Southwick, wright, Thomas Hall of Fulwell, lab., George Jackson of the same, lab., George Atkinson of Fulwell, lab., John Robinson of the same, lab., Robert Bille of the same, yeo., and Christopher Steele of the same, lab., with others unknown in illegal conventicle on 1 July 1600 at East Boldon at *Scrabbe close nooke* assembled riotously and crushed the grain and grass of Thomas Plumpton, William Jackson and George Chamber with wains and broke with iron

implements a watercourse running from the north-west nook of *Scrabbes close*.

2) Alexander Atkinson of Cleadon, co. Durham, yeo., Richard Atkinson of Whitburn, yeo., John Urpeth of Whitburn, yeo., Robert Hyndmers of Whitburn, lab., William Jefferson of Whitburn, lab., Robert Claye of Whitburn, lab., Thomas Chambers of Whitburn, yeo., Cuthbert Baynebrigg of Whitburn, yeo., John Roxbye of the same, yeo., Thomas Hindmers of the same, lab., William Roxbye of the same, lab., Thomas Wright of the same, yeo., Michael Mathewe of Cleadon, yeo., Robert Chambers of Whitburn, yeo., Robert Wright of the same, yeo., Robert Pereson of the same, lab., Richard Heckley alias Hatherwicke of the same, lab., George Pope of the same, lab., John Turner of Cleadon, lab., Thomas Maugham of Whitburn, yeo., Thomas Thompson of the same, lab., Roger Weetherheede of the same, lab., Thomas Tynmouth of the same, lab., Anthony Jefferson of the same, lab., John Trumble of the same, lab., John Browne of the same, lab., William Bainbrig of Whitburn, lab., John Cooper of the same, lab., Robert Chaiter of the same, lab., Thomas Mathewe of the same, lab., David Simpson of the same, yeo., John Nicholson of the same, lab., Edward Dixsone of Cleadon, yeo., Richard Sharpe of Whitburn, yeo., Ralph Hepple of the same, yeo., James Mathewe of Cleadon, yeo., Cuthbert Smith of the same, yeo., Cuthbert Atkinson of the same, yeo., John Lettanie of Whitburn, lab., James Wright of the same, yeo., Richard Wake of the same, yeo., Ralph Hall of Cleadon, lab., and Ralph Snawden of the same, lab., assembled riotously in warlike fashion with others unknown on 29 June 1600 at East Boldon in *Scrabbes close nooke* and damaged the grain and grass of Thomas Plumpton, William Jackson and George Chamber with wains and broke the end of the water-sewer running from the north-west nook of *Scrabbes close*.

3) Whereas by statute of 8 Henry VI on disseisin [*etc.*], William Stobbis of Westgate, co. Durham, yeo., with 2 others unknown on 17 April 1601 expelled Nicholas Fetherston, farmer of the bishop of Durham, from a messuage called *Springe House* in Stanhope, held in the bishop's demesne.

4) Inquest for the queen as to whether John Fetherstonhalghe, esq., on 8 March 1601 impounded in the common fold at Stanhope 24 sheep belonging to George Emerson of Shipleyburn, found in a close of John at Stanhope called *le Bone*, damaging his growing grain. Ralph Maddison of Rogerley, gen., broke into the fold at Stanhope and drove away the 24 impounded sheep.

5) Inquest for the queen as to whether Anthony Allison late of East Brandon, co. Durham, lab., on 28 Oct. 1600 entered the close of Nicholas Lampton at East Brandon and stole an iron *tenamc'* worth 6d.

6) Inquest for the queen that whereas by statute of 1/2 Philip & Mary on impounded beasts none should take more than 4d. for keeping distresses and less if customary, under pain of £5, William Chamber

of East Boldon, co. Durham, yeo., with others unknown on 20 March 1601 at East Boldon moor assaulted Samuel Ayre, who was driving 42 beasts of Robert Hutton, STP, Michael Calverley of Fulwell, gen., Thomas Roxbye of Wearmouth, husbandman, George Deanham of the same, husbandman, Margaret Waike of Southwick, widow, Agnes Byers of the same, widow, and Ralph Broughe of the same, husbandman, from a pasture called *Simondside* to the vills of Fulwell, Southwick and Wearmouth. Chambers impounded the beasts and refused to release them until Michael Calverley paid him a fee of 2s. for poundage.

7) Thomas Bourne late of Durham city, yeo., on 21 Feb. 1601 broke into the stable of Simon Comyn, gen., of Durham city and stole a gelding, bay-grizzle in colour, worth £10.

8) The jurors presented that Newton bridge was in serious decay; also at Wolsingham, the New bridge, the Walkmill bridge and the Overbroom bridge; also the Browney bridge near Sunderland [Bridge]. [*m.11d., blank*]

52

J] Pleas and presentments at Durham on 8 July 43 Elizabeth [*1601*] before Bp Mathew, William James, STP, dean of Durham, George Scroope, esq., Thomas Calverley, esq., chancellor of Durham, Clement Colmore, LL.D., JPs.

Robert Farrowe	Brian Emmerson
James Watson	Christopher Richmond
William Trotter	Richard Shacklocke
Thomas Wood	John Melmerbye
Richard Trotter	Thomas Dobson
John Swalwell	Christopher Fenney
Hugh Hucheson	Robert Waughe
	James Walton, jurors

1) Robert Newton of Monkwearmouth, co. Durham, husbandman, on 30 May 1601 on the queen's highway in the township of Monkwearmouth assaulted with a stick in his hands George Collyer of Monkwearmouth.

2) William Brakenbury late of Langton, co. Durham, gen., Thomas Brakenbury of the same, yeo., and Janet his wife, John Tilborne of the same, yeo., John Cockfeilde of the same, yeo., and Dorothy his wife, Cuthbert Burrell of the same, yeo., Christopher Robinson of the same, yeo., and – his wife, Lancelot Merley of the same, yeo., Lancelot Waistell of the same, yeo., Florence Staninge of the same, widow, Anna Singleton, widow, Frances wife of Reginald Errington of the same, yeo., Elizabeth wife of John Bainbridge of the same, yeo., Margaret wife of Christopher Thompson of the same, yeo., Elizabeth wife of John Towler of the same, yeo., Katherine wife of John Stoddart of the same, yeo., Eleanor Burrell of the same, spinster, Rowland Pereson of the same, yeo., Beatrice wife of John Pereson

junior of the same, yeo., Jane wife of John Peareson of the same, yeo., the wife of John Stanebancke of the same, yeo., and the wife of John Carde of the same, yeo., with 40 others unknown riotously assembled in warlike fashion at the instigation of William Brakenbury to the terror of the lieges and on 17 June 1601 entered the close of Henry Brakinburye of Selaby, esq., called *Sellabye moore* and tore, burst, overthrew and burnt 3,000 feet of quickset hedge and flattened the ditches with mattocks and spades, contrary to the statutes against riots [*etc.*].

3) Whereas Thomas Ogle, gen., steward of Bp Matthew's court leet of Bedlington, *co. Durham, ordered John Calverley, gen., bailiff there, to distrain on the goods of Thomas Fenwick of Netherton, yeo., for the sum of 6s. 4d. due to the bishop from an amercement laid on the same in the bishop's court leet at Bedlington on 9 Oct. 1600, by virtue of which on 2 July 1601 John Calverley tried to remove at Netherton goods of Fenwick, namely a brass pot worth 10s., against payment of the fine, Thomas Fenwick assaulted Calverley in execution of his office and recovered the pot.

4) John Conyers, esq., sheriff of Durham, ordered Robert Maltbye, bailiff of the Chester ward, to arrest William Jackson if found in his bailiwick and commit him to the gaol of Durham castle until he satisfied Robert Pemberton in 20s. principal debt and 8s. 8d. court expenses arising from the suit which Pemberton brought in the county [court] held at Durham by the sheriff on Mon., 20 April 1601, and recovered from Jackson by default and by judgment of the court. The sheriff was to decree the award at the next court on Mon., 8 June. By virtue of this mandate Robert Maltbye arrested William Jaxon to take him to gaol in Durham castle, but William Jackson and William Wright of Holmside, yeo., Thomas Brigges of Whickham, yeo., and Thomas Balelye of the same, yeo., on 7 June 1601 assaulted Robert Maltbye and the latter rescued Jackson, who is still at large.

5) Whereas a statute of 1/2 Philip & Mary decreed that no person take a fee for keeping distrained goods of more than 4d. under pain of £5 [*etc.*], John Waddye of Sadberge, yeo., on 4 May 1601 took 2s. 8d. for 2 cows belonging to Richard Colman, impounded in the bishop's pound at Sadberge by William Killinghall, and refused to release the cows until Richard Colman paid poundage of 2s. 8d., refusing to take [m.10d.]   less.

6) John Lettany of Whitburn, co. Durham, yeo., collector of the bishop's rents in Whitburn, and Oswald Baker of Durham city, yeo., bailiff itinerant of the bishop for all fines and amercements, on 7 July 1601 distrained on Ralph Fell of Whitburn, yeo., by a cow for arrears of rent to the bishop at Whitsuntide past, and Ralph assaulted John and Oswald and recovered the cow.

7) Whereas by statute of 21 Henry VIII no secular or regular person might farm or take to use any manor, tenement or land for term of life or years or at will under pain of £10 for each month the land was

so occupied, Thomas Easterbye of Seaham, co. Durham, clerk, then a spiritual person and having sufficient glebe land by right of his vicarage at Seaham and leases to pasture his livestock and cultivate grain for maintenance of his family, nevertheless on 3 May 1601 leased at Cocken from Ralph Carr of Cocken, gen., divers closes of meadow and pasture estimated at 200 acres and worth £30.

8) Whereas John Barnes, esq., steward of the bishop's court leet of Stanhope, co. Durham, ordered John Stobbes, the bishop's forester, to distrain on the goods of William Emmerson of Stotfield Burn, yeo., for 2s., being the amercement laid on Thomas Fenwick in court at Stanhope on 5 May 1601, Stobbes on 2 July 1601 at Stotfield Burn tried to take 3 lambs worth together 5s. of Emmerson's goods to detain them until the amercement was paid, but Emmerson assaulted Stobbes and recovered the lambs.

9) Francis Lawson late of Thorpe Bulmer, co. Durham, gen., on 29 June 1601 diverted and blocked the common road from Nesbitt and Hesleden hall to a place called *the Oxe pasture* in Thorpe Bulmer and thence to the Northwell in this ox pasture and across to the cow close and thence to Trimdon in Thorpe Bulmer and thence to the coney warren in the vill and demesne of Hart and thence from Hart to Hartlepool; and Mary Starre, crossing the cow close, was forbidden to continue to Hartlepool, to the common nuisance of the queen's lieges [*etc.*].

10) Christopher Fuister late of Stockton, co. Durham, clerk, John Smith late of the same, tinker, Anthony Wilson late of the same, lab., Ralph Harte late of the same, lab., and William Harte late of the same, lab., assembled on 4 March 1601 at the instigation of Christopher Fuister to the terror of the lieges and entered the close of Elizabeth Buntinge, widow, at Stockton called *Hardwicke nooke* and assaulted and wounded Ralph Lambert, her servant, and destroyed 20 feet of quickset hedge.

11) MEMO that Thomas Charlton offered himself at the sessions as an informer.
[*space of 10 cms*]

53

] Pleas and presentments at Durham on 7 Oct. 43 Elizabeth [*1601*] before Bp Matthew – [*space of 6.5 cms*]

1) Whereas William Steele late of Greatham, co. Durham, lab., on 16 Sept. 1601 was bound over to keep the peace with Henry Dethicke, LL.B., a JP, at Greatham and was arrested by John Burne and Edward Sparke, constables of Greatham, by virtue of a warrant of George Lightfoot, esq., JP, to have before the same George Lightfoot or another JP to find surety, the prisoner broke custody on the same day and is still at large without having given surety.

2) William Lawson late of Felling, co. Durham, yeo., Ralph Thompson late of the same, yeo., William Franche late of the same, yeo., and

John Neden late of the same, yeo., on 11 Sept. 1601 at Gateside assembled riotously and assaulted Hugh Birde, gen., and Lawson with a rapier worth 5s. held in his right hand thrust him through the back, inflicting a mortal blow 9 inches long by 3 inches deep and wounded him elsewhere to the terror of the queen's subjects.

3) Whereas by statute of 2 April 13 Elizabeth [1571] certain articles were revived of the statute of 37 Henry VIII for reform of usury on and after 25 June 1571, including that no person(s) of whatsoever condition might take interest above the rate of 10% under pain of triple forfeiture, which sum should be shared equally between Crown and prosecutor in any royal court of record, in addition to imprisonment and restitution, Nicholas Westgarth of Shotley Bridge, co. Durham, yeo., after 2 April 1571, namely on 20 June 1592, at Shotley Bridge loaned to Thomas Colson £4 and received in gain for this loan from 20 June 1592 to 25 June following 26s. 8d.; and also Westgarth on 8 Sept. 1596 at Durham loaned to the said Thomas Colson £10 13s. 4d. for which he received 46s. 8d. for this loan from 8 Sept. 1596 to 6 Oct. following.

4) George Hackfurth late of Oakenshaw, co. Durham, yeo., – Williamson wife of William Williamson late of the same, Gerard Williamson late of the same, gen., George Bell late of the same, yeo., and James Hackfurth late of the same, yeo., on 26 Sept. 1601 assembled with 7 other persons unknown and riotously assaulted Mary Dighton, wife of Richard Dighton, in order to "appeal" her from possession of the residence of the said Richard Dighton, and discharged guns to the great terror of Mary and other lieges.

[m.9d.] 5) John Hall late of Hollingside (*Hollinbushe*), co. Durham, gen., on 2 Feb. 1601 at the instigation of the devil assaulted Robert Haswell aged 17 years at Whickham and struck him on the back and head with a gad worth 1d. held in both hands, from which blows Haswell lingered at Whickham until 2 Oct., when he died.
[*space of 55 cms*]

54

[m.8] Pleas and presentments at Durham on 13 Jan. 44 Elizabeth [1602] before William James, STP, dean of Durham, Thomas Calverley, esq., chancellor of Durham, Thomas Burton, LL.D., George Scroope, esq., Henry Dethicke, LL.B., George Frevile, John Heth, John Fetherstonhalgh and George Lightfoote, esqs, JPs.

Christopher Wharton, gen.	John Fisheborne, yeo.
William Trotter, gen.	George Cooper, yeo.
Thomas Woodd, yeo.	Cuthbert Hodgson, yeo.
Richard Key, yeo.	Hugh Hutchinson, yeo.
George Trotter, yeo.	Thomas Merley, yeo.
Nicholas Hutchinson, yeo.	John Godderson, yeo.
John Swalwell, yeo.	William Grinwell, yeo.
Richard Trotter, yeo	(John Conyers, esq., sheriff)

1) Richard Turner late of Blackwell, co. Durham, lab., and James West late of the same, lab., on 15 Dec. 1601 at Blackwell stole a ewe worth 10d. from an unknown man.

2) Henry Heardman on 15 Nov. 1601 entered the close of John Davison at Durham city and stole 2½ yards of white woollen cloth worth 12d.

3) Edward Linton late of Sedgefield, co. Durham, butcher, on 9 Dec. 1601 entered the close of Robert Swifte, clerk, at Sedgefield and stole a ewe worth 10d.

4) Ralph Collingwoode late of Newcastle, gen., on 13 Oct. [blank]

5) Whereas John Letanye of Whitburn, co. Durham, yeo., collector of rents and fines of Bp Matthew in Whitburn, by virtue of a warrant of Thomas Calverley, esq., chancellor of Durham, distrained on James Matthew of Cleadon by a mare for non-payment of 3s. 4d. for an amercement, James Matthew on 2 Dec. 1601 recovered the same mare and assaulted John Letanye.

6) Whereas George Middleton of Silksworth, co. Durham, gen., was seised in demesne of the manor of Silksworth and its appurtenances and had a customary road from Silksworth over various closes to Farrington and across a certain close called *the White Lease* and thence to *Highe Close* and thence to *the Far Meadowe Close* in Silksworth, one Peter Denton late of Farrington, gen., on 28 Dec. 1601 closed this common road at the High Close with a hedge and a ditch and Elizabeth Browne, servant of George Middleton, was prevented crossing the High Close on her master's business.

7) Mark Acheson late of Stanhope, co. Durham, yeo., on 28 Oct. 1601 entered the close of John Richardson junior at Stanhope and felled and carried away branches of whitethorn, blackthorn and hazel there growing worth 2s. and trampled the grass.
[*m.8d., blank*]

55

Pleas and presentments at the general sessions of the peace at Durham on 14 April 44 Elizabeth [*1602*] before Bp Matthew, George Scroope, esq., William James, STP, dean of Durham, Thomas Calverley, esq., chancellor of Durham, Clement Colmore, LL.D., Henry Dethicke, George Lightfoote and John Heath, esqs, JPs.

1) Robert Vasye late of Wolviston, co. Durham, yeo., on 20 Dec. 1601 broke the close of William Richardson at Merrington and stole a sheep worth 2s. 8d.

2) Alexander Barrowe late of Durham city, yeo., and Nicholas Addison late of Hexham, Northumberland, yeo., on 13 Feb. 1602 lay in ambush at Durham in a spot near *Peresbye loninge* to kill, assault or wound George Browne who was crossing a copse there, and Barrowe struck Browne twice with his hands on the head and mouth and pummelled and kicked him in the belly and guts so that he lingered from 13 Feb. until the taking of this enquiry and his life was in danger.

3) Thomas Thompson late of Haggerston in Islandshire, *co. Durham, yeo., and John Thompson late of the same, yeo., on 24 Jan. 1600 assaulted George Smith at Ancroft and inflicted various great wounds on parts of his body and in the assault stole a dagger worth 10s. and a spear worth 4s.

4) Ralph Bracke late of Chester, co. Durham, yeo., William Wallers alias Walles late of the same, yeo., and John Matthewe late of the same, yeo., on 1 Jan. 1602 and before and after that date at Chester acted without licence of the queen's JPs in Durham, namely badged bread at Gateside and Chester and elsewhere and sold bread to the queen's lieges, to evil example and contempt and contrary to statute.

5) Whereas by statute of 24 Henry VIII any selling sucking calves between 1 Jan. and 1 May were to forfeit 6s. 8d. for each calf so sold, Richard Blithman late of Gateside, butcher, on 1 Feb. 1602 and 1 May and before and after until the date of the enquiry marketed 30 calves at Gateshead to divers lieges in time of Lent.

6) Anthony White late of Shildon, co. Durham, yeo., and John White late of the same, lab., Robert Pereson late of the same, yeo., Anne White wife of John White and Margery Taylersoune wife of John Taylersoune late of Windlestone on 6 Oct. 1601 at Eldon in a close called *Northfield* assembled and assaulted Nicholas Richardson and Sitha his wife. (Anthony White bound in £20)

7) George Hubbock late of Greatham, co. Durham, yeo., and William Johnson late of the same, lab., on 10 April 1602 broke into the close of Joan Lee, widow, at Greatham and damaged grass worth 4d. by tethering a colt stag.

[m.7d.] 8) Thomas Pereson of Durham city, mercer, on 28 March 1602 ordered his servants Arthur Wright of Durham city, yeo., and William Peareson of the same, yeo., to impound livestock at Woodgarth in Durham, namely a mare, a foal, a colt and a horse, being in a meadow of 24 acres called *Barker Haugh* at Crook Hall, until he was given satisfaction for their depasturing; and Robert Hopper late of Durham, yeo., and John Hodgson late of the same, tailor, on the said day assaulted Wright and Peareson at *Souremilkedeane* and rescued the livestock on the highway near Carr House at *Sower Milke deane*.

9) Whereas by statute of 8 Henry VI any persons expelled from their tenements might sue by novel disseisin or writ of trespass, [etc.], Robert Hopper late of Durham city, yeo., Hugh Maynsforth late of the same, yeo., and Simon Hutchinson late of the same, tailor, on 26 March 1602 by order of Hugh Hopper of Durham city, draper, entered the close at Crook Hall called *Barker haugh* being the free tenement of Francis Billingham, gen., and in the possession of Thomas Pereson of Durham city, mercer, then farmer of the close, and remained in occupation for 3 years and disseised Billingham and deprived Pereson of possession from then on.

56

] Pleas and presentments at Durham on 7 July 44 Elizabeth [*1602*] before Bp Matthew, William James, STP, dean of Durham, Thomas Calverley, esq., chancellor of Durham, Clement Colmore, LL.D., George Scroope, esq., Thomas Burton, LL.D., John Heeth, esq., Henry Dethicke, LL.B., Anthony Hutton, esq., John Barnes, esq., and Hugh Wright, alderman of Durham, JPs.

James Watson	John Swainston
George Middleton	John Melmerbye
William Trotter	Robert Waughe
Cuthbert Morgan	Thomas Swainston
Richard Trotter	Hugh Hutcheson
John Swalwel	Henry Cockefeilde
Richard Shacklock	Ralph Prestone
	John Godderson, jurors.

1) John Cook late of Wetwang, Yorks., yeo., Richard Jackson late of Hutton, yeo., and Richard Darcy late of Salthaugh Grange (*Salthropp*), on 22 June 1602 stole at Durham 4 horses of divers colours at 30s. each, belonging to persons unknown.

2) Margaret Cock late of Durham city, spinster, on 1 July 1602 broke into the house of Thomas Yonger in Crossgate, Durham, and stole 2 linen pillows *(pillebers)* worth 7s. 6d., a christening cloth worth 2s., 3 bands worth 3s., a hat worth 12d., a table cloth worth 3s., 1½ yards of linen cloth worth 17d., a silken purse and belt worth 18d., 1½ yards of ribbon worth 4d., and three lengths of linen cloth worth 5d., being the goods of Thomas Yonger.

3) Thomas Carr late of Grindon, co. Durham, yeo., on 1 April 1602 broke into the residence of Ralph Brughe at Hylton between 11 and 12 in the day and stole a cloak worth 20s., a blue coat worth 20s., a silk *rashe* doublet worth 16s. and a sword worth 6s. 8d. belonging to the same.

4) Francis Dixon late of Gateside, lab., and Thomas Peareson late of the same, challon weaver, on 19 Feb. 1602 between 6 and 7 p.m. assaulted Edward Kenettie on the queen's highway at Fugar House near Whickham, and Dixon struck him on the head with a stick worth 2d. held in his right hand and stole 80s. in money in a purse belonging to the said Kenettie and to Agnes his wife.

5) Anthony Hedworth late of Whickham, co. Durham, gen., and Ralph Hedworth late of the same, gen., on 14 May 1602 assaulted John Hedworth of *Cockesclose*, gen., at Whickham, and Anthony with a stick worth 1d. and Ralph with another stick worth 1d. held in their right hands wounded John on divers parts of his body and put him in fear for his life.

6) Whereas in parliament on 8 May 1563 it was enacted that after 1 May following no persons might pursue any trade within England and Wales without apprenticeship under pain of 40s. each month in default, Henry Hawdon of Auckland, co. Durham, tailor, John White

of Brancepeth, whitesmith, Francis Tindall of Stockley, husbandman, William Sigeswicke of Hedworth, yeo., John Lawson of Heighington, lab., John Thompson of Sedgefield, lab., Henry Pattinson of Middle Merrington, yeo., William Richeson of Sedgefield, lab., Richard Penn of Chester-[le-Street], lab., and Philip Sharpe of Ferryhill, lab., pursued the trade of butcher in Durham from 1 April 1602 until the date of enquiry, namely 3 months.

7) Whereas by the above statute [etc.] and the apprenticeship should last not less than 7 years, John Borrowe of Gateside, yeo., Edward Wilson of the same, yeo., John Robson of the same, yeo., Thomas Thompson of the same, yeo., William Martocke of the same, yeo., James Twisle of the same, yeo., Richard Tode of the same, yeo., William Robson of the same, yeo., and Robert Thompson of the same, yeo., from 1 April 1602 until the enquiry, namely 3 months, pursued the trade of butcher at Gateside.

[m.6d.] 8) Whereas William James, STP, dean of Durham, Clement Colmore, LL.D., Henry Dethicke and George Lightfoot, esqs, made an order under seal to Geoffrey Mattison and John Christopher, constables of Billingham, to arrest Marmaduke Surtes and have him before them, Mattison and Christopher on 24 June 1602 seized Surtes at Billingham but the latter assaulted them and escaped custody. George Fewler of Billingham, yeo., with malice aforethought on the same day harboured him at Billingham and abetted him so that he is still at large.

9) William Thompson late of Escomb, co. Durham, yeo., John Todd of the same, yeo., and William Suddick of the same, yeo., on 25 May 1602 with 10 others unknown riotously assembled at Escomb and assaulted Cuthbert Watt and Thomas Watt at Escomb, and William Thompson wounded Cuthbert with a dagger forced from Cuthbert's hand, and John Todd wounded him on the head with another dagger, inflicting a great wound on the back of his skull an inch wide and 3 inches long.

10) Inquest taken at Durham on 3 June 1602 before George Lightfoote, esq., JP, and on the oath of Peter Denton, John Shawdforth, Richard Shacklocke, Anthony Younge, William Watson, Richard Walshe, Thomas Fatherley, William Ellyner, William Reade, William Parkin, Ralph Wilson, Thomas Trewhitt, William Atkinson and Thomas Swalwell it was testified that Richard White of Kelloe, yeo., and Jane his wife were seised in demesne of a free tenement in a messuage, 30 acres meadow and 50 acres pasture with appurtenances at Kelloe until Ralph Downes of Hardwick by the sea, gen., Anthony Maddison late of Hartlepool, yeo., Lancelot Richardson of Kelloe, yeo., and Christopher Forest of Brancepeth, yeo., and others on 18 May past disseised them violently of the same and retained the same to the date of the enquiry, contrary to the statute of 8 Henry VI.

11) Whereas by statute of 5 Elizabeth concerning apprenticeship, Adam Hodge late of [blank], co. Durham, yeo., Henry Younge of

Sheleydale, yeo., Christopher Tailer of Monkton, yeo., Robert Sym of Hylton, yeo., William Chamber of East Boldon, yeo., and Richard Lumley of Whickham, yeo., from 1 April 1602 to date, for 3 months, had pursued the trade of butcher at Gateshead.

12) Alexander Swinborne of Willington, co. Durham, yeo., Cuthbert Clerk of the same, yeo., Thomas Atkynson of the same, yeo., John Chambers of Blaydon, yeo., John Morpeth of the same, yeo., – Storye of Whickham, yeo., Christopher Blackborne of the same, yeo., Thomas Gallelye of Urpeth, yeo., Nicholas Byers of the same, yeo., Willam Robson of the same, yeo., William Grener of Pelton, yeo., – Lawes of Birtley, yeo., Richard Wilkinson of the same, yeo., John Grener of Pelton, yeo., Atkin P[...]ers of Urpeth, yeo., William Grinwell of Pelton, yeo., Robert Atkinson of Urpeth, yeo., George Simpson of the Law, yeo., Cuthbert Comeinge of Shotley Bridge, yeo., Reginald Comeinge of the same, yeo., John Fosker of the same, yeo., Roland Beates of the same, yeo., Thomas Fosker of the same, yeo., John Oltringham of the same, yeo., John Fosker of the same, yeo., Robert Richeson of Knitsley, yeo., Nicholas Hopper of Lintz Green, yeo., Andrew Joplynge of the same, yeo., Robert Comeinge of the same, yeo., and Robert Jolbye of Langley, yeo., on 1 Jan. 1602 and on many days and at many places afterwards fished in the River Derwent and other waters and took young salmon and brood spawn etc.

57

5]   Pleas and presentments at Durham on 6 Oct. 44 Elizabeth [*1602*] before William James, STP, dean of Durham, George Scroope, esq., Thomas Calverley, esq., chancellor of Durham, Clement Colmore, LL.D., William Cunstable, knt, Thomas Riddell, George Bowes, John Barnes, Henry Tonge, Thomas Chaitor, Ralph Bowes, George Freville, Robert Brandlinge, John Heath and George Lightfoote, esqs, JPs.

1) William Beseley late of Swalwell, co. Durham, yeo., and William Henderson of Whickham, yeo., on 1 March 1602 and until the date of this enquiry obstinately and without authority of any JP kept 2 common taverns or common tippling houses and sold ale and beer to the queen's subjects contrary to the statute of 5 Edward VI.

2) Whereas Thomas Ogle, esq., steward of Bp Matthew's court of Bedlington, *co. Durham, ordered John Calverley, esq., bishop's bailiff of Bedlington, by sealed and signed warrant of [*blank*] 42 Elizabeth to levy from John Skipsey of Bedlington, clerk, the sum of 2s. for [arrears of] various amercements, and Calverley on 12 June 1602 distrained on Skipsey by a [brass] pot worth 3s. 4d., Skipsey's wife recovered the same violently from Calverley and still retains it.

3) Nicholas White late of Gateside, yeo., on 26 Aug. 1602 attacked Robert Maltby, a bailiff of the sheriff of Durham, in execution of a warrant directed to him by Thomas Riddell, a JP, to arrest Nicholas and have him before the same Thomas Riddell to give surety for good

behaviour towards William Gronne, residing at Gateside. White struck Maltby on the left hand with a long sword worth 2s. 6d., inflicting a wound 3 inches long and an inch wide, and other wounds.

4) Whereas a statute of 8 Henry VI entitled ejected parties to the benefit of the assize of novel disseisin and treble damages [etc.], Simon Welburye late of Hesleden, co. Durham, gen., Cuthbert Williamson late of St Helen Auckland, gen., and Henry Newton late of Stocksfield Hall, Northumberland, yeo., forcibly ejected William Williamson of St Helen Auckland, gen., from his messuage in St Helen Auckland on 24 Sept. 1602 and are still in possession.

5) Percival Harbottle late of Tanfield, co. Durham, gen., on 20 March 1602 assaulted Thomas Browne at Tanfield, drawing blood.

6) Richard White late of Streatlam, co. Durham, yeo., on 28 Aug. 1602 at Kelloe broke the close called *West Moor* of Ralph Downes, farmer of divers lands in Kelloe, and depastured grass worth 40s. with ploughs and yoked oxen.

7) Nicholas Beesinge late of Ryton Woodside, co. Durham, yeo., on 20 March 1602 attacked Thomas Browne and struck him on the head with an iron staff worth 4d., wounding him and putting him in bodily fear.

8) Ralph Maddison late of Hylton, co. Durham, yeo., Robert Smith junior late of Waldridge, yeo., Thomas Burrell late of Chester-le-Street, yeo., John Martyne late of Birtley, yeo., and William Martyne late of Birtley, yeo., riotously assembled on 12 Sept. 1602 at Birtley and assaulted Thomas Davison and Anne his wife at Birtley in the close of Ralph Blenkynsopp and drew blood from Thomas Davison; and John Martyne and William Martyne stole 11 stooks of wheat worth 50s. belonging to Thomas Davison.

[m.5d.] 9) George Chilton late of Chester, co. Durham, yeo., and Thomas Chilton late of the same, yeo., on 24 June 1602 stole at Chester a sack worth 6d. and 3 measures (*modios*) of rye worth 6s. 8d. therein belonging to Francis Bainbridge.

10) James Mason late of Middridge, co. Durham, yeo., on 28 July 1602 stole at Brafferton a lamb worth 2s. belonging to Thomas Swalwell.

11) John Barnes for the queen sued against Robert Amorer late of Scremerston, *co. Durham, gen., for an assault committed on 24 July 1602 at Fenwick on Gilbert Selbye, gen., between 1 and 2 p.m., when he thrust at Gilbert with a sword worth 5s. held in his right hand and wounded him in the chest inflicting a mortal wound 3 inches by 6 inches. Amorer did not appear and the sheriff was ordered to arrest him to appear before the justices to answer for felony and murder. John Conyers, esq., sheriff, returned that Amorer was not to be found in his bailiwick. He was ordered to exact him from county court to county court and have him on Wed., 18 May next [1603], to answer [etc.]

58

[¶]   Pleas and presentments at the sessions of the peace at Durham on 12
Jan. 45 Elizabeth [1603] before Bp Matthew, George Scroope, esq.,
William James, STP, dean of Durham, Thomas Calverley, esq.,
chancellor of Durham, Clement Colemore, LL.D., JPs.

Peter Denton, James Shaftoe, Christopher Fenny, John Heron, John
Shaldforth, John Swainston, Richard Shacklock, Ralph Surtes,
Thomas Swainston, Robert Waughe, John Walton, Ralph Pereson
and William Parkyn, jurors.

1) Whereas John Barnes, esq., steward of the bishop's court of the
forest of Weardale, co. Durham, by sealed warrant of 23 April 1602
directed Cuthbert Fetherstonhalgh and John Westwoode, the
bishop's bailiffs to collect rents and amercements arising in the
bishop's forest, to distrain on Nicholas Bromelles for the sum of 20s.,
being an amercement laid on him at a forest court held at Stanhope
on 23 April 1603 by George Bowes, esq., deputy chief forester, and
John Barnes payable at the Durham exchequer; by virtue of which
warrant Cuthbert Fetherstonhalgh and John Westwoode on 21 Dec.
1602 distrained on Bromelles at Stanhope by goods, namely a colt or
young stag, which they wished to lead to the bishop's common fold
at Stanhope and keep until replevied, but George Pearte late of West
Blackdene in the forest of Weardale, yeo., and Nicholas Sheile of
Windyside in the same, yeo., the same day attacked them in the
execution of their office and recovered the colt.

2) – 14) Similar charges for the recovery of distresses, namely a mare
from Ralph Emerson; a horse from George Pearte; a mare from
Nicholas Sheile; a cow from Rowland Emmerson; a mare from Peter
Westwood; a colt from Nicholas Walton; a horse from Cuthbert
Emerson; a horse from Rowland Nattresse; a mare from Thomas
Emmerson; a mare from Ralph Nattresse; a mare from George
Harrison; a mare from Rowland Pattison; and a mare from John
Bainbrigg.

15) Whereas Christopher Skepper and Cuthbert Smith were deputed
by Michael Calverley, gen., the bishop's coroner in the Chester ward,
to collect among other rents 29s. 5d. from the capital messuage of
Pokerley in the parish of Chester-[le-Street] and distrained on 3 oxen
feeding at Pokerley for the arrears of the past year since Martinmas,
John Wheatly of Urhill, lab., Robert Stobbes of Pokerley, lab., and 3
others unknown assaulted Skepper and Smith at Pokerley on 9 Dec.
1602 and recovered the oxen.

16) Alice Darneton of Chilton, co. Durham, wife of John Darneton,
on 20 Dec. 1602 broke into the close of Thomas Calverley of
Littleburn, esq., at Littleburn and stole a wether worth 10d.
belonging to Calverley.

17) Whereas a writ of the queen and Star Chamber, given before the
queen and council at Westminster on 27 Nov. 1602, ordered the
sheriff of Durham to attach John Bainbrigg to be before the queen

and council at Westminster on 3 Feb. following to answer for contempt, the sheriff by warrant dated at Durham on 13 Dec. 1602 ordered Robert Moreye, William Smith, John Harreson, Christopher Skirrawe and Gregory Maison, his bailiffs, to arrest and attach Bainbrigg so that he might have him at Westminster on 3 Feb.; and John Herrison, Christopher Skirrawe and Gregory Mayson on 10 Jan. 1603 attached and arrested Bainbrigg at Billingham. When, however, they wished to take him to the sheriff to have him at Westminster, Robert Bainbrigg late of Billingham, gen., William Marshell of the same, yeo., Alice Marshell wife of William Marshell, Isabel Hodgson wife of Thomas Hodgson, Alice wife of William Jackson and Denise Legg, widow, of Billingham, with divers others on 10 Jan. 1603 assembled riotously at Billingham and in warlike fashion attacked John Herrison and Christopher Skirrawe, and Alice Marshell struck Harrison on the right of his head with a bunch of keys in her right hand and drew blood, and Robert Bainbrigg, William Marshell and Alice his wife struck Harrison and Skirrawe on their bodies so that their lives were endangered, and Robert Bainbrigg, William Marshell, Alice his wife, Isabel Hodgson alias Jackson and Denise Legg, widow, rescued John Bainbrigg from Harrison and Skirrawe with force and arms, and he is still at large.

18) Thomas Atkinson late of Thinford, co. Durham, lab., on 12 Dec. 1602 broke into the close of James Kay at Ferryhill and stole a wether worth 10d.

19) Nicholas Gray late of Eighton, co. Durham, lab., and John Williamson of the same, lab., on 25 Dec. – broke into the close of Roland Coles of Eighton at Eighton and stole a ewe worth 7d.
[m.4d., blank]

59

[m.3]   Pleas and presentments at the sessions of the peace at Durham on 8 June 1/36 James [1603] before William James, STP, dean of Durham, George Scroope, esq., Thomas Calverley, esq., chancellor of Durham, Emanuel Barnes, STP, Henry Dethicke, LL.B., Robert Tailboies, John Heath senior, Thomas Chaytor, George Lightfoote, John Barnes and Thomas Riddell, JPs.

1) Whereas George Frevile, knt, Henry Tong and John Barnes, esqs, three JPs in co. Durham, ordered the mayors, bailiffs, constables and other officers and king's ministers in co. Durham and especially the constables of St Helen Auckland to arrest Cuthbert Williamson of St Helen Auckland and have him before the justices to answer for certain felonies, John Maugham and Ralph Tailor, constables of St Helen Auckland, and Robert Corneforth and Richard Brantingham, inhabitants of the same vill, on 15 May 1603 assembled at St Helen Auckland to execute this, but Richard Scrimshawe late of West Auckland, gen., and Mary his wife, Simon Welburye late of St Helen Auckland, gen., and Jane Williamson wife of the said Cuthbert,

riotously attacked Maugham, Tailor, Corneforth and Brantingham so
that Cuthbert Williamson remains at large.

2) Thomas Lasenbye late of St Helen Auckland, co. Durham, gen., on
23 April 1603 stole at South Church a white horse worth £5
belonging to John Fell.

3) John Wilson late of Wolsingham, co. Durham, yeo., on 21 April
1603 stole at Helme Park 5 ewes worth 4s. each, and 5 lambs worth
2s. each belonging to Henry Marshell.

4) John Metcalfe late of Lynesack, co. Durham, yeo., on 12 April 1603
stole at Wolsingham a grey horse worth £3 6s. 8d. belonging to
Anthony Bessour, gen.

5) Robert Stelling late of Middleton-in-Teesdale, co. Durham, yeo., on
20 March 1603 burgled the shop of John Lampton in Durham city
about 1 p.m. and stole a piece of cloth called *sheapecoloure* being 3 1/2
yards in length at 12s. 6d. a yard, belonging to John Lampton.

6) Thomas Robertes late of Bishop Auckland, co. Durham, yeo., and
Henry Bainbrigg late of the same, yeo., on 2 May 1603 lay in wait
and assaulted John Currey on the highway called *Newgate* at Bishop
Auckland and struck Curry a blow causing a wound 4 inches in length
and an inch in depth on the left of his head with a stick worth 1d.
held in the right hand and another blow on the back of his skull an
inch long and an inch deep and another on the left ear and divers
other blows to the body to his hurt and against the king's peace.

7) Thomas Lasonbye late of St Helen Auckland, co. Durham, gen., on
4 Sept. 1602 stole at Ebchester a black bay horse worth £3 6s. 8d.
belonging to Roger Wharton.

8) Laurence Garfoote late of Middridge, co. Durham, lab., on 10
March 1603 burgled the residence of Henry Trotter at *Rootesforde*
between 10 and 11 p.m. and stole £4 in coin in a chest, a shirtband
worth 12d., 2 shirts together worth 4s., and a tawney coat worth 10s.
belonging to Henry Trotter.

9) George Emerson late of Newcastle, artificer, and Arthur Emerson of
Stotfield Burn, co. Durham, yeo., on 11 April 1603 broke into the
close of Nicholas Hedley at Tanfield and stole 8 sheep or *sheephoggs*
worth 5s. each belonging to Nicholas Hedley.

10) Whereas by statute of 8 Henry VI it was decreed that if any eject
another from his lands and continue in possession the aggrieved
party should have the assize of novel disseisin and triple damages
and the defendant should pay the king fine and redemption, Robert
Brabond late of East – in Raby, co. Durham, yeo., Francis Bainbrigg
late of the same, gen., Simon Johnson late of the same, yeo., and
[*3d.*]   Edward Watson late of Staindrop, yeo., on 3 May 1603 | took
possession of a messuage with appurtenances called *Parkewellhouse*,
co. Durham, and divers closes of which one was called *Hotsouf Field*
belonging to the king, Robert Bowes of Wackerfield, yeo, and Michael
Rayne of Shipley, yeo., being farmers thereof for three years, and
remained in possession from 3 May until the present.

[*space of 6.5 cms*]

11) John Barnes, esq., for the Crown sued Robert Armorer late of
Scremerston, *co Durham, gen., that on 24 July 1602 at Fenwick
between 1 and 2 p.m. he maliciously assaulted Gilbert Selby, gen.,
and thrust him in the chest with a sword worth 5s. held in his right
hand, giving him a mortal blow 3 inches wide and 6 inches deep
whence he died. Armorer did not answer and the sheriff was ordered
to arrest him to be before the justices on 6 Oct., when the sheriff,
John Conyers, esq., returned that Armorer was not to be found in his
bailiwick, so an order was issued for his exaction on Wed., 18 May,
when Conyers again returned that he was not found. The exaction
was published at Durham in the county court on Mon., 18 Oct. 1602,
Mon., 15 Nov., Mon., 13 Dec., Mon., 10 Jan. 1603 and Mon., 7 Feb.,
the fifth time, when on his non-appearance Michael Calverley and
John Hawkins, coroners of Bp Matthew, pronounced Armourer an
outlaw.

[*space of 36 cms*]

60

[*m.1*]   Pleas and presentments at the sessions of the peace at Durham on 11
Jan. 1/37 James [*1604*] before George Scroope, esq., William James,
STP, dean of Durham, George Frevile, knt, Thomas Calverley, esq.,
chancellor of Durham, Clement Colmore and Thomas Burton,
LL.D.s, Henry Dethicke, LL.B., George Lightfoote, Thomas Riddell,
John Heth, Henry Tonge, Robert Cooper, Thomas Chator, John
Fetherstonhalgh and John Barnes, esqs, JPs.

Richard Heighington, gen., Peter Denton, gen., Nicholas Wilson,
John Shawdforth, Edward Tayler, Ralph Surtes, Christopher
Richmond, John Swalwell, John Garmonsway, Robert Tweddle,
John Morgan, John Hutcheson, Richard Maddison, William Allen
and Thomas Dobson, jurors.

1) Whereas by statute of 5 Edward VI against riots [*etc.*] Alexander
Barrowe late of Durham city, yeo., John Barrowe late of the same,
yeo., Henry Dunne late of the same, yeo., Simon Greave late of the
same, yeo., Christopher Claxton late of the same, yeo., Thomas
Browne late of the same, yeo., and Godfrey Hucheson of the same,
yeo., on 15 Nov. 1603 assembled at Elvet in the suburbs of the city in
the parish church of St Oswald illegally, riotously and routishly and
attacked Nicholas Hobson, parish clerk there, and cast him to the
ground, and Alexander struck him on the head with a crabtree cudgel
worth 2d., and shed blood to his hurt, being a bad example to the
king's subjects and against the king's peace.

2) Whereas by statute of 1 Elizabeth against the taking or killing of
young brood spawn or fry of fish in any cateract, pipe, stew or the
like, and any stream, brook, river and salt or fresh water, and the
taking of kipper or shedder salmon, Thomas Hobson late of Gainford,
co. Durham, yeo., John Clayton late of Winston, yeo., John Hall late

of Osmond Croft, yeo., William Simpson late of Piercebridge, husbandman, John Younge of Whorlton, lab., Edward Lordman late of Barnard Castle, lab., Hugh Haggerston late of Barnard Castle, yeo., Thomas Bainbridge of Stockton, yeo., William Cotes late of the same, yeo., Roger Greateheade late of the same, yeo., George Hurworth late of the same, yeo., John Anderson late of the same, yeo., Ralph Bainbridge late of the same, yeo., Anthony Bainbrigge late of the same, yeo., Thomas Osborne late of the same, yeo., John Osborne late of the same, yeo., John Osborne junior late of the same, yeo., Thomas Swainston late of the same, yeo., John Coote late of the same, yeo., John Lukeupp late of the same, yeo., and Joshua Mayne late of the same, yeo., on 20 Nov. 1603 and on other times and occasions fished in the Tees with implements for salmon and trout out of season to the value of £100 [etc.].

3) Whereas the statute of 13 Richard II forbade the keeping of greyhounds by artificers, labourers and other laymen not having land worth 40s., together with ferrets, cords or other engines to take or destroy deer, hares, coneys and the like under pain of imprisonment for one year, John Wilkinson of Ferryhill, yeo., and John Dawson of the same, lab., being laity [etc.] on 20 Dec. 1603 at Ferryhill did use ferret and net to take and destroy coneys.

4) Whereas George Frevile, knt, authorized Matthew Thompson and Thomas Simpson, constables of the township of Cockerton, co. Durham, by warrant to remove an unknown vagrant woman at Cockerton by the highway to Newcastle out of the county they let her evade custody to the contempt [etc.].

5) Whereas the statute of 5 Elizabeth forbade trading without 7 years of apprenticeship under pain of 40s., John Ayre of Wolsingham, co. Durham, yeo., and Ralph Hodge late of West Auckland, yeo., on 1 April 1603 traded in skins at West Auckland.

6) Whereas the statute of 5 Elizabeth forbade trading without 7 years of apprenticeship [etc.], John Ayre of Wolsingham, co. Durham, yeo., and Ralph Hodge late of West Auckland, yeo., pursued on 1 April 1603 at West Auckland the trade of tanners [etc.].

7) John Ayre late of Wolsingham, yeo., and Ralph Hodge late of West Auckland, yeo., on 30 Nov. 1603 bought from unknown men at *Evensheade* in Bitchburn and elsewhere cowhides worth – , contrary to the form of the statute.

8) Whereas the statute of 2 Edward VI forbade any under the rank of lord to carry firearms, Ralph [...] late of – , co. Durham, yeo., on 20 Nov. 1603 despoiled Thomas Mayne at Hutton Henry, [...] charged with powder and hailshot.

9) Thomas R[...] late of Little Chilton, co. Durham, gen., John Heighley of Great Chilton [...], George Morton late of Little Chilton, yeo., Michael Dikkinson late of the same, yeo., and [...] yeo., riotously assembled on 20 Dec. 1603 at Ferryhill and injured John Wilkinson and John Dawson.

[*m.1d.*] 10) George Blaxton late of Blakeston, co. Durham, gen., John Trolloppe late of Kelloe, yeo., and Robert Mayre late of Hardwick, gen., on 12 Oct. 1603 riotously entered the house of Ralph Downes at Hardwick and attacked Downes and assaulted Elizabeth his wife and alarmed his household and drove them from possession until the present day.

11) Whereas by statute of 5 Edward VI any person after 1 May [*1551*] who struck anyone in church or cemetery would by verdict of twelve or confession before the justices of assize or of the peace be excommunicated, Nicholas Hobson late of Elvet in the suburbs of Durham, yeo., James Heddon late of Shincliffe, yeo., and John Syme late of the same, yeo., on 15 Nov. 1603 at Elvet in the parish church of St Oswald assembled riotously and attacked John Barrowe, and Nicholas Hobson struck Barrowe several blows with a rapier worth 5s. on several places of the body to the danger of his life.

12) Whereas by statute of 5 Edward VI [*as (11) above*], Nicholas Hobson late of Elvet in the suburbs of Durham, yeo., Robert Heddon late of Shincliffe, yeo., Hugh Ramsha late of Elvet, mason, and John Syme late of the same, yeo., on 15 Nov. 1603 at Elvet riotously assembled in St Oswald's church and assaulted Alexander Barrowe, John Barrowe, Godfrey Huchinson and Thomas Browne, and Nicholas Hobson struck John Barrowe several blows to the back of his head with a pitchfork worth 2d. to the effusion of his blood.

13) Roger Denin late of Ryhope, co. Durham, lab., on 17 Dec. 1603 at Fieldhouse by Bishopwearmouth took a wether worth 10d. belonging to John Shipperdson.

14) Laurence Wilkinson late of Ferryhill, co. Durham, yeo., on – Dec. 1603 at Ferryhill was a common brawler and disturber of the king's peace etc.

[*space of 34 cms*]

[*m.2*] 15) Writ to the sheriff of Durham *non omittas propter aliquam libertatem* to take Richard Close late of Eggleston, co. Durham, yeo., Roger Fowberie late of Colepike Hall, gen., Lionel Charleton late of Thornborough, Northumberland, gen., Thomas Charleton late of Hawkhope, gen., Nicholas Welton late of Thornborough, gen., Matthew Errington late of Stonecroft, gen., William Ridley late of Hawkhope, gen., William Shaftoe late of Hexham, gen., William Lawson late of Hexham, gen., John Nixon alias Daudel John late of Bewcastle, Cumberland, yeo., Quintin Whitehead late of the same, yeo., Robert Errington late of Darlington, co. Durham, yeo., and John Errington late of Bewclay, Northumberland, yeo., to have them before the justices of the peace at Durham on 7 Jan. 1596 to answer for divers felonies and burglaries for which they were indicted. And the sheriff returned that Close and the rest were not to be found [*etc.*] The writ *sicut alias* was issued for return at 21 April, when it was ordered on their non-appearance that they should be put in exigent from county court to county court to appear on 30 June. On that day the sheriff returned that at the county court held at Durham on Mon., 4 May 1596 the first exigent was published, with the second on 7 June, but that there were no more courts held within the time allowed, so a respite was allowed until 6 Oct., when the sheriff returned that on 5 July 1596 a further exaction was published and similarly on 2 Aug. 1596 and 30 Aug. 1596 and that they were then formally outlawed by Michael Calverley and John Hawkins, coroners of the county.

[*m.2d., blank*]

[*m.17B* This scrap of parchment has been wrongly attributed to this roll but should more properly have been attached to the next collection, namely Q/S/I 2. It is printed here as 70.]

1605-1614

Durham CRO, Q/S/I 2 The 66 membranes are ordered chronologically 65–66, 60–64, 59, 57–58, 56, 55, 54, 50–53, 47–49, 43–46,
40–42, 36–39, 34–35, 32–33, 28–31, 25B–27, 24–25, 23, 22, 20–21,
18–19, 15–17, 13–14, 8, 11–12, 9–10, 1–7. These represent sessions on
10 April and 2 October 1605; 23 April and 7 October 1606; 7 January,
8 April, 8 July and 7 October 1607; 13 January, [30 March], 29 June
and 12 October 1608; 11 January, 29 April, 12 July and 4 October
1609; 10 January, 11 April, 11 July and 3 October 1610; 9 January, 27
March, 26 June and 2 October 1611; 8 January, 15 April, 8 July and 7
October 1612; 13 January and 7 April 1613; and ?8 April 1614. The
heading of the sessions on 30 March 1608 has been derived from
Durham CRO, Q/S/I 1 m.17B.

61

[m.65]   Pleas and presentments at Durham on 10 April 3 James [1605] before
Bp Matthew, George Scroope, esq., William James, STP, dean of
Durham, William Constable, knt, Thomas Calverleye, esq.,
chancellor of Durham, George Frevile, knt, Clement Colmore, LL.D.,
Emanuel Barnes, STP, Thomas Burton, LL.D., Henry Dethick, LL.B.,
JPs.

Michael Pembarton, gen., Richard Heighington, gen., William Dod,
gen., Cuthbert Morgan, gen., William Blackett, gen., Thomas
Middleton, gen., Thomas Trotter, yeo., Robert Suerties, yeo., Richard
Trotter, yeo., John Shaldforth, yeo., Thomas Dobbison, yeo., John
Swalwell, yeo., John Braferton, yeo. and John Garmondsway, yeo.,
jurors.

1) Cuthbert Garth late of Neasham, co. Durham, yeo., on 8 Nov. 1604
at Headlam stole 8 sheep worth 5s. each from William Garth.

2) William Marshall of Elvet in the parish of St Oswald, Durham, yeo.,
being 16 years of age and over and a papist recusant, failed to attend
divine service, not being in prison since 31 March 1604, and failed to
attend at Elvet within 20 days of release from Durham gaol, nor
announced himself in person or in writing to the minister, curate,
constable, headborough or tithing as ordered by statute of 35
Elizabeth.

3) William Siggisworth late of Redworth, co. Durham, yeo., on 24 Dec.
1604 at West Newbiggin stole a branded heifer worth 30s. from
Roland Allison.

4) Robert Stockdell late of Darlington, yeo., on 8 March 1604 broke
the close of William Barnes at Darlington and stole a brown mare
worth 50s. from William Barnes.

5) William Siggisworth late of Redworth, yeo., on 24 Dec. 1604 at
West Newbiggin stole a black heifer worth 26s. 8d. from William
Allison.

6) Richard Hedworth late of Darncrook, co. Durham, gen., assembled
with others unknown and on 26 Oct. 1604 at Chester *Oakes* broke

the close of Bp Matthew and using oxen and ploughs carried off by night 6 oaks there belonging to the bishop.

7) Whereas by statute of 8 Henry VI against disseisin [etc.], John Greveson late of Woodham, co. Durham, yeo., on 30 Jan. 1604 at Woodham forcibly disseised Robert Hutton, gen., of his free tenement and continues to do so.

[space of 13 cms]

8) Whereas by statute of 1 Edward VI it was enacted that if any after 1 May [1548] spoke slighting words of the sacraments or advised others so to do they were liable to prison, fine and redemption, Robert Marley of Stockley, co. Durham, yeo., on Easter Sunday, 31 March 1605, in time of divine service in the parish church of Brancepeth irreverently approached the table and "did eat, drinke and deale" the bread and wine to Henry Horsley of Stockley, yeo., and others after they had been consecrated; and Henry Horsley irreverently ate part of the consecrated bread in church and took some away. Later on 1 April Horsley said in the presence of various trustworthy persons: "Why might wee not take it, for we paide for itt?"

9) George Emmerson late of *Craig*, Northumberland, yeo., on 10 May 1604 stole a black-brown cow at [...]*opp* in Weardale forest belonging to John Hutchinson.

[space of 8 cms]

5Sd.] 10) Order to the sheriff of Durham *non omittas* [to arrest Thomas ....] late of Kelloe, co. Durham, gen., William Claxton late of Waterhouses, gen., Cuthbert Collingwood late of Eppleton, gen., John Trollop late of [Kelloe], gen., and Philip Tayler late of Kelloe, yeo., to answer at Durham before the JPs on 27 June 1604 for divers felonies. On this date they defaulted and the sheriff, John Conyers, knt, returned that they were not to be found. The order was repeated for 10 Oct. 1604 and 9 Jan. and 10 April 1605. At the same time the sheriff was ordered to put them in exigent. The sheriff then reported that proclamation had been made at the county courts at Durham on 14 Jan., 11 Feb., 11 March and 8 April to appear at the general sessions on 2 Oct.

11) Order to the sheriff of Durham *non omittas* to arrest Thomas Forser late of Kelloe, co. Durham, gen., William Claxton late of Waterhouses, gen., Samson Trollopp late of Thornley, yeo., Robert Wilson late of Eden Dene, yeo., Robert Chilton late of Thornley, yeo., John Trollop late of Thornley, tailor, Francis Trollop late of Edenfield house, gen., Michael Garthwaite late of *Northwastes*, yeo., and George Cooke late of Sherburn, yeo., to answer at Durham before the JPs on 27 June 1604 for trespass and riot in terms of the statute against forcible entry. On default [*as above*].

12) Order to the sheriff *non omittas* to arrest John Champley late of Shotton, Northumberland, yeo., Percival Mautland late of the same, yeo., Christopher Grene late of the same, yeo., John Armstrong alias Jock Armstrong late of Coastley, yeo., William Gardiner late of Ford,

yeo., John Rotherforth alias John the Galyard late of Spittal, gen., Christopher Ridley late of Coastley, gen., and Matthew Errington late of Bewcastle, Cumberland, gen., to answer before the JPs at Durham on 10 Oct. 1604. The sheriff, John Conyers, knt, returned that they were not found and the order was repeated for 9 Jan. 1605 [etc. as above].

13) Order to the sheriff *non omittas* to arrest Francis Sayer late of Darlington, yeo., Richard Nelson late of the same, yeo., Robert – of Barnard Castle, yeo., Marmaduke Croulesse late of the same, yeo., Anthony Scott late of Gateside, yeo., Christopher Sherwood late of Grens..., James Smith alias James Braybath late of *Goswick, yeo., William Dawson late of *Buckden, yeo., Robert Davison late of the same, yeo., [...] late of the same, yeo., David Palmer late of the same, yeo., Martin Blackett late of Castle Eden, yeo., George Shaftoe late of Hamsterley, yeo., and Edward – late of Spen, yeo., to answer at Durham before the JPs on 10 Oct. 1604 [etc. as above].

62

[*m.66*] Pleas and presentments at Durham on 2 Oct. 3 James [*1605*] before Bp Matthew, Cuthbert Pepper, knt, supervisor of the king's court of wards and liveries, chancellor of Durham, George Scroope, esq., William James, STP, dean of Durham, Henry Lyndley, knt, Henry Anderson, knt, Thomas Calverley, esq., Emanuel Barnes, STP, Clement Colmore, LL.D., Robert Brandling, esq., John Barnes, esq., George Lightfoot, esq., John Fetherstonhalgh, esq., and John Heth, esq., JPs.

1) Richard Pearson of Barnard Castle, co. Durham, lorimer, Lancelot Langstaffe of the same, saddler, Edward Tobye of the same, saddler, and Thomas Johnson of the same, lab., with others riotously assembled on 30 Sept. 1605 and assaulted William Wharton.

2) Whereas John Joplyng late of Se[dgefie]ld, co. Durham, yeo., was infected with plague in parts of the county and returned to Sedgefield, Bp Matthew by warrant of 30 Sept. 1605 ordered the bailiff and constables of Sedgefield to keep Joplyng inside and away from his neighbours to prevent infection, but Joplynge went out and about to the peril of the lieges.

3) William Hogg late of Barnard Castle, co. Durham, yeo., on 24 Sept. 1605 attacked Jane Kirkley, servant of William Scrafton, at Barnard Castle.

4) Thomas Gray late of Barnard Castle, yeo., on 1 June 1605 assaulted William Scrafton at Barnard Castle.

5) Christopher Emmerson late of Durham city, lab., on 21 Aug. 1605 at Durham stole two pairs of stockings worth 2d. from Jane Carter, widow.

6) Christopher Emmerson late of Durham city, lab., on 21 Aug. 1605 at Durham stole a linen apron worth 4d. and a linen towel worth 4d. belonging to Hugh Barrow.

7) John Pattison late of Greatham, co. Durham, yeo., and Anne his wife on 6 Sept. 1605 about 11 a.m. broke into the house of Ralph Sheile at Greatham and stole a petticoat worth 10d. from Ralph Sheile.

8) Richard Pearson of Barnard Castle, lorimer, Lancelot Langstaffe of the same, saddler, and Thomas Johnson of the same, lab., with others assembled riotously on 30 Sept. 1605 and assaulted Bartholomew Mason of Barnard Castle, yeo.

9) Oswald Fenwick late of Ravensworth, co. Durham, gen., Thomas Cuthbert late of *Riding*, yeo., and Ralph Wilde late of Kibblesworth, yeo., on 22 Sept. 1605 assembled riotously at Lamesley and assaulted Christopher Sanders, king's constable of Lamesley, and Fenwick struck Sanders on the head and face with a stick worth 1d. and drew blood, and Cuthbert and Wilde struck him to the ground and kicked his guts so that he was severely battered.

10) Robert Hall alias Blewcapp late of Thornley, co. Durham, yeo., on 2 Sept. 1605 at Kelloe with malice aforethought assaulted Anthony Maddeson and Jane his wife with a drawn sword worth 2s. and buffetted Jane about the head and ears with a clenched fist.

11) John Philipp late of Harbour House, co. Durham, yeo., and Robert Hall alias Bl[ew]cap late of Thornley, lab., on 22 Sept. 1605 at Kelloe carried off 2 iron forks worth 2s. belonging to Lancelot Richardson.

6d.] 12) Robert Bellerby late of Raby castle, co. Durham, yeo., and Francis Blake alias Blackamore late of the same, yeo., on 24 July 1605 broke the close of John Sparrow at – and stole cocked hay worth 5s.

13) Richard Pearson late of Raby castle, yeo., and Francis Blake alias Blackamore late of the same, yeo., on 1 Aug. 1605 broke the close of John Sparrow at Raby and stole cocked hay worth 5s.

14) John Philipp late of Harbour House, co. Durham, yeo., on 19 Sept. 1605 and before and after deliberately lay in ambush at Kelloe to waylay Lancelot Richardson of Kelloe, yeo., and on 19 Sept. he assaulted Richardson to the danger of his life.

15) William Elrington late of [Esper] Shields, Northumberland, gen., and John Carr late of Elrington, yeo., on 8 July 1605 broke the close of John Newton at *Ridding*, co. Durham, and on divers occasions depastured with livestock corn and grass worth 2s.

16) William Elrington late of Esper Shields, Northumberland, gen., and James Johnson late of the same, lab., on 4 June 1604 at *Ridding*, co. Durham, attacked Thomas Snawball with an iron-shod stick worth 2s. 6d. and struck Snawball on the head inflicting a wound 2 inches by 1 inch and elsewhere on his body and trampled with their livestock his growing grain and grass worth 2s.

17) Whereas by statute of 13 Richard II it was enacted that artificers [*etc.*] should not keep greyhounds or other hunting dogs and ferrets, nor own hays, nets, hare-pipes, cords or other engines to take hares, rabbits or other "gentlemen's game" under pain of a year's imprisonment, Thomas Wright late of Raby castle, co. Durham, yeo.,

Robert Bellerbye late of the same, yeo., Richard Peareson late of Raby, yeo., and Francis Blake alias Blackamore late of the same, yeo., not having lands worth 40s. a year, on 16 Aug. 1605 by order of George Frevile, knt, their master, broke the king's warren in Raby east park and hunted rabbits with a *mollosse* or mastiff and net worth 6s. 8d.

18) Whereas by the above statute ... the same Wright, Peareson and Blake on 17 June 1605 hunted in the same with mastiff and net for rabbits [*omitting master's order*].

19) Whereas by the above statute ... the same Wright, Peareson and Blake on 20 June 1605 at the order of George Frevile, knt, broke the king's warren and hunted rabbits with mastiff and net worth 2s. 8d.

63

[*m.60*]   Pleas and presentments at Durham on 23 April 4 James [*1606*] before Cuthbert Pepper, knt, chancellor of Durham, George Scroope, esq., William James, STP, dean of Durham, Clement Colmore, LL.D., Emanuel Barnes, STP, John Barnes, esq., Thomas Chaitor, esq., John Heth, Thomas Riddell, George Lightfoote and Robert Brandling, esqs, JPs.

1) Whereas by statute of 8 Henry VI on disseisin [*etc.*], Isabel Lilburne late of East Thickley, co. Durham, widow, Richard Lilburne late of the same, gen. and son of the said Isabel, Toby Lilburne late of the same, gen., Joseph Lilburne late of the same, gen., William Richardson late of the same, yeo., and Robert White late of the same, yeo., on 25 March 1606 broke a close at East Thickley in the tenure of Gilbert Wharton, gen., and expelled him to the present date. The defendants had no goods [*etc.*].

2) Whereas by statute of 1 Elizabeth it was enacted that none use engines to take or kill any young brood spawn or fry of any fish in a floodgate, milltail, water, strait or stream, and salt or fresh rivers, nor take kipper or shedder salmon or trout out of season under pain of 20s. for each fish caught and confiscation of nets and engines, Nicholas Raine late of Marwood, co. Durham, yeo., and George Simpson of the same, yeo., on 20 Oct. 1605 and before and after at Marwood in the river Tees took 20 shedder and kipper salmon and trout worth 40s. out of season.

3) Whereas the king ordered by writ from the Durham chancery that John Conyers, knt, pay to the bishop of Durham certain sums of money against the relief of persons held in the king's prison at Durham as named in a schedule and that a valuation be made of their lands, goods and chattels, John Girlington or his assigns took half the profits of the manor of Harraton and lands in *Over Moor House* and Picktree amounting to £116 13s. 4d. arising from a wardship of 6 years 3 months during the minority of John Hedworth, knt. When on 19 April the sheriff ordered Robert Moorie and Robert Maltbye, his bailiffs, to attach Girlington and others named in the warrant so that the sheriff might pay the £116 13s. 4d. into the

Durham chancery these on 22 April took Girlington at Harraton and distrained on him by 40 oxen, cows and stirks for the above sum. The same day Ralph Clibborne late of Harraton, yeo., and Michael Lawson of Harraton, yeo., with 20 others unknown riotously assembled and attacked Moorie and Maltbye at Harraton and recovered the livestock.

4) William Errington late of Learchild, Northumberland, yeo., on 1 March 1606 at Egglescliffe stole a brown horse worth 40s. belonging to Robert Clavering.

5) William Franck late of Ripon, Yorks., gen., on 4 Nov. 1605 at Bishop Auckland, co. Durham, stole a dun horse worth 53s. 4d. belonging to Leonard Pickersgill.

6) William Clavering late of Alnwick, Northumberland, yeo., on 1 March 1606 at Aislaby, co. Durham, stole a bay horse worth 46s. 8d. belonging to Robert Clavering.

7) Robert Errington late of the Grange, Northumberland, gen., on 22 Jan. 1606 at Chester, co. Durham, broke into the residence of Thomas Harbotle between 11 p.m. and midnight and stole a grey horse worth £8 belonging to Andrew Clennell, gen.

8) Hugh Hutcheson late of Wydon, Northumberland, yeo., on 5 Dec. 1604 at Burn Hall, co. Durham, stole a black-grey horse worth 40s. belonging to Thomas Foster.

60d.] 9) Whereas William James, STP, dean of Durham, a JP, by sealed warrant of about 17 Dec. 1605 ordered the sheriff of Durham [etc.] and specially the constable of Cleadon to arrest Robert Merriman to answer for various trespasses, later about 20 Dec. John Calverley late of Cleadon, gen., delivered the warrant to Michael Matthew, constable of Cleadon, to arrest Merriman to have him before James [etc.], and Matthew neglected to enforce the order and Merriman is still at large.

10) Whereas by statute of 1 Elizabeth against taking fish [etc.], John Saure late of – , yeo., on 17 Oct. 1605 at Sledwick, co. Durham, fished in the Tees and caught by engine one shedder salmon out of season worth 5s.

11) Whereas by statute of 1 Elizabeth [as (10) above], John Appleby late of – , co. Durham, yeo., and George Dobison late of – , yeo., on 20 Oct. 1605 at – fished in the Tees and took by engine 6 kipper trout out of season worth 5s.

12) Whereas by statute of 1 Elizabeth [as (10) above], Gregory Turner late of Staindrop, co. Durham, yeo., on 20 Oct. 1605 at Staindrop fished in the Grant beck and took with *bleises* 6 kipper trout out of season worth 5s.

13) Whereas by statute of 1 Elizabeth [as (10) above], John Tourner late of Piercebridge mill, co. Durham, yeo., on 20 Oct. 1605 at Piercebridge mill on the Tees took with a wicker net worth 12d. in kipper time 80 smelts worth 40s.

[*space of 8.7 cms*]

[*m.61*]   14) Elsewhere at the sessions at Durham on 8 Jan. 1606 before
Cuthbert Pepper, knt, George Scroope, esq., William James, STP, dean
of Durham, and Clement Colmore, LL.D., JPs, it was presented that
whereas the justices at Chester-le-Street, co. Durham, on 20 Nov.
1605 ordered the constable of Esh to appoint two able men from
among the inhabitants to keep watches by day and two by night for
security in the township as elsewhere in the county, John Smith and
Robert Katerick, constables of Esh, gave notice to George Snagg, an
inhabitant of the constabulary, to keep watch from 25 Nov. but
Snagg refused to act. Now at the sessions on 23 April 1606 Snagg
appeared and asked for the indictment to be read. He then objected
that on 20 Nov. 1605, as on 25 Nov. when he received the order, he
was an inhabitant of Hamsteels, having a tenement called *Fyning*,
and not of Esh.
Robert Cooper for the bishop and the king alleged that George Snagg
on 20 Nov. and later was an inhabitant of Esh and sought an enquiry.
The sheriff was ordered to have jurors for Wed., 9 July, at Durham,
when no return was made, so a jury was summoned for Tues., 7 Oct.,
at 10 a.m., when again no return was made. The parties came and the
case was adjourned until 2 p.m., when Cooper as attorney-general
and Snagg appeared with the jurors. These testified that on 20 Nov.
and 25 Nov. Snagg was an inhabitant and therefore was guilty as
indicted. Judgment was given that Snagg should satisfy the king and
he sought leave to fine for his trespass. This was assessed at 5s., which
Snagg paid.
[*space of 6.5 cms*]

[*m.61d.*] 15) Copy of a certificate in English of William Bisco, mercer, and
Margery his wife, living in *Knightryderstreate* in the city of London,
that Robert Carlile son of Hugh Carlill, now or late of Wackerfield,
co. Durham, tanner, and now inhabiting Gateside and exercising the
art of mercer, served with them an apprenticeship of 7 years in
accordance with the statute of 1 Elizabeth, namely from Christmas
1591 to Christmas 1598, witnessed 3 May 1608. [*space of 17.2 cms*]

[*m.62*]   16) MEMO that William Bowes suing for the king and himself laid an
information before the JPs in general sessions at Durham on 8 Jan.
1606 that William Lounley of Edmundbyers, co. Durham, yeo.,
Thomas Snawball of the same, yeo., and William Oliver of the same,
yeo., on 30 Sept. 1605 and before and after within 2 years at
Edmundbyers took with engines in *Bawdwinhope* burn shedder and
kipper salmon and trout out of season worth 40s. contrary to statute,
and Bowes claimed 20s., being half the value.
William Lumley appeared, pleaded not guilty and put himself on the
country. Robert Cooper, esq., bishop's attorney-general on behalf of
the king, accepted that a jury be summoned. The sheriff was ordered
to empanel a jury for the next sessions on 23 April.
[*m.62d., blank*]

[*m.63*]   17) Whereas by statute of 13 Richard II artisans and labourers or other laymen having lands worth less than 40s. a year, or any priest with a living under £10, were forbidden to keep hunting dogs or greyhounds or to use ferrets, *hayes*, nets, *hare-pipes*, cords or other traps to take deer, hares, rabbits or other "gentlemen's game" under pain of imprisonment for a year, Ralph Emmerson of Shotton, co. Durham, yeo., and John Metcalfe late of Southside, yeo., on 22 Sept. 1605 by night broke into the king's warren in Raby East Park and used ferrets and nets to hunt rabbits.

18) Robert Peacock late of Greatham, co. Durham, yeo., on 24 Sept. 1605 attacked Edward Wrenn at Greatham.

19) Humphrey Toynton late of Penshaw, co. Durham, yeo., on 22 June 1605 at Little Lumley lay in wait for Thomas Niccolson and beat him all over.

20) Christopher Jackson late of Broom House, co. Durham, yeo., and Margaret Welsh late of Chester on 4 May 1605 at Chester attacked Margery Drew, and Christopher struck her on the right arm.

21) Andrew Rodham late of Blackburn mill, co. Durham, yeo., Alexander Rodham late of the same, yeo., and Anthony Dobson late of the same, yeo., on 2 Oct. 1605 at Whickham assembled riotously and attacked George Natteresse, and Alexander struck him on the head with a gad worth 1d. held in both hands, inflicting a wound 2 inches by 1 inch, and he was otherwise hit.

22) Whereas Thomas Pearson, mayor of Durham and a JP, authorised by sealed warrant of 8 Sept. 1605 George [Peareson], a constable of St Nicholas parish, [Durham], to take Edward Farales of Durham, yeo., to gaol until he found surety to keep the peace and to appear at the next sessions and not depart without licence, later on the same day George Peareson took Farales into custody, but the latter assaulted him and rescued himself and is still at large.

23) Whereas Bp Matthew, William James, STP, dean of Durham, Clement Colmore, LL.D., and Henry Dethick, LL.B., king's commissioners for ecclesiastical causes in the province of York, by warrant dated at Bishop Auckland, co. Durham, on 19 Sept. 1605 ordered all mayors, the sheriff [*etc.*] and especially Henry Maughen, messenger, or John Hutcheson his deputy *non omittas* to attach Michael Banckes of the parish of Coniscliffe to appear before the commissioners at Bishop Auckland on 10 Oct. following, to answer the king's charges, Hutchinson on 21 Sept. 1605 arrested Michael Banckes of High Coniscliffe and attached him to appear: but Nicholas Soulkeld late of High Coniscliffe, gen., Thomas Salkeld late of the same, gen., – of the same, miller, Laurence Copeland of the same, yeo., with 20 others unknown at High Coniscliffe on 21 Sept. 1605 assembled riotously and assaulted John Hutchinson and William Langstaffe his assistant and rescued Michael Banckes.

24) Whereas Bp Mathew, William James, STP, dean of Durham, Clement Colmore, LL.D., and Henry Dethick, LL.B., commissioners [*etc.*], by warrant of 27 June 1605 dated at Bishop Auckland ordered

John Conyers, knt, sheriff of Durham, *non omittas* to attach Robert Hodgshon of Hebburn, co. Durham, esq., to answer the commissioners at Bishop Auckland on 18 July, Robert Maltby, the sheriff's [*m.63d.*] bailiff, by virtue of the warrant arrested Hodgshon on 2 July I but the latter assaulted him and rescued himself.

25) Whereas the sheriff was ordered to have James Richeson late of Gateside, yeo., William Shaftoe late of Lipwood, Northumberland, yeo., Henry Charlton late of *Spittalhaugh*, Westmorland, yeo., Robert Baynbrigg late of Billingham, co. Durham, gen., William Marshall late of the same, yeo., and Denise Legg late of the same, widow, before the JPs at Durham to answer for divers felonies on – April 1604: on this day John Conyers, knt, sheriff, returned that Richeson, Shaftoe, Charlton, Baynbrigg, Marshall and Denise Legg had no goods in his bailiwick for distraint, and were not to be found. The writ *non omittas* was issued for their appearance on 27 June 1604: for their arrest for 4 Oct. 1604: *sicut pluries* for 9 Jan. 1605 and exigent in the county court for 10 April, with summonses at the county court on 14 Jan., 11 Feb., 11 March, 8 April – then respite until 2 Oct. 1605 for lack of courts. On 22 July on their non-appearance after the fifth exaction the sentence of outlawry was pronounced by William Barnes, gen., and Robert Cutter, gen., coroners of the bishop in Durham and Sadberge.

26) Whereas the sheriff was ordered to have John Richardson late of Darlington, co. Durham, lab., George Acheson late of *Miregaite*, lab., Charles Brabant late of *Skeglodge* in Raby, gen., Richard Hutchinson late of Staindrop, yeo., and John Bankes late of Shotton, yeo., to answer before the JPs at Durham on – April 1605 for crimes on which they were indicted, Conyers returned that they had no chattels [*etc. as above*]

[*space of 15 cms*]

[*m.64*]   27) Whereas the sheriff was ordered *non omittas* to have John Champley late of Shotton, Northumberland, yeo., Percival Mautland alias Jock Armstrong late of Coastley, yeo., William Gardiner late of Ford, yeo., John Rotherforth alias John the Galyard late of Spittal, gen., Christopher Ridley late of Coastley, gen., and Matthew Errington late of Bewcastle, Cumberland, gen., to answer before the JPs at Durham on 10 Oct. 1604 to the felonies on which they were indicted, the sheriff returned that they were not to be found in his bailiwick: therefore *sicut prius* for 9 Jan. 1605 and again for 10 April. Publications of the exigents were made at the county courts at Durham on 14 Jan. 1605, 11 Feb., 11 March and 8 April. On 2 Oct. 1605 the defendants again failed to appear and the sheriff returned that they had been outlawed on 22 July by William Barnes, gen., and Robert Cutter, gen., the bishop's coroners.

28) Whereas the sheriff was ordered to have Francis Sayer late of Darlington, yeo., Richard Nelson late of the same, yeo., Roland Brounlesse late of Barnard Castle, yeo., Marmaduke Brounlesse late of the same, yeo., Anthony Scott late of Gateside, yeo., Christopher

Sherwood late of Brancepeth, yeo., David Palmer late of the same, yeo., Martin Blackett late of East Boldon, yeo., George Shaftoe late of Hamsterley, yeo., and Edward Hodgshon late of Spen, yeo., to answer before the JPs at Durham on 10 Oct. 1604 for the felonies on which they were indicted, the sheriff returned that they were not to be found in his bailiwick [*etc. as above*].

29) Order to the sheriff to have James Richeson late of Gateside, yeo., William Shaftoe, [*etc. as above (25)*].

[*m.64d., blank*]

64

[9] Pleas and presentments at Durham on 7 Oct. 4 James [*1606*] before Bp James, Cuthbert Pepper, knt, supervisor of the king's court of wards and liveries, chancellor of Durham, George [Scroope, esq.], Henry Lindley, knt, Henry Anderson, knt, Thomas Calverley, esq., Clement Colmore, LL.D., John Fetherstonhalgh, John Hethe, George Lightfoote, John Barnes, Robert Cooper, esqs, JPs.

Robert Farro, gen., James Watson, gen., William Trotter, gen., Laurence Wilkinson, gen., Christopher Fulthropp, gen., James Shaftoe, gen., Christopher Fenney, gen., John Gage, gen., Thomas Lambert, Thomas Trotter, Thomas Wood, Christopher Hutcheson, Ralph Walker, John Swalwell and Richard Key, jurors.

1) William Hawdon of Bishop Auckland, co. Durham, tippler, on 28 Aug. 1606 and later at Bishop Auckland in his tippling-house allowed John Cliff, Thomas Robertes and John Benckle to play cards for gain, contrary to the statute.

2) Robert Barnes late of Whickham, co. Durham, lab., on 20 July 1606 assaulted Thomas Todd at Whickham and stole a purse worth 2d. and 12s. 6d. in money in it.

3) Janet Gregson of Sedgefield, co. Durham, widow, John Hickson of Wolviston, yeo., Robert Dickson of Wolviston, yeo., Thomas Cully of Middleton Row, yeo., James Marley of Middleton Row, yeo., Richard Colson of Hurworth-on-Tees, yeo., Peter Sayer of the same, yeo., Robert Foorde of Bishopton, yeo., Richard Wating of the same, yeo., Cuthbert Rascall of Crossgate, [Durham], yeo., Ralph Hodge of Cleadon, yeo., John Foster of Ryton, yeo., William Lightharnes of the same, yeo., Harvey Blackborne of the same, yeo., John Lawson of Chester, yeo., Alexander Emond of the same, yeo., John Kirkdene of the same, yeo., Richard Story of Gilesgate, [Durham], yeo., John Wilson of the same, yeo., John Ord of the same, yeo., Christopher Farro of Houghton, yeo., Thomas Pereson of Gateside, yeo., Edward Sanders of the same, yeo., Henry Laiborne of Whickham, yeo., Edmund Hode of Gateside, yeo., Henry Maddison of Ryton, yeo., and Richard Gowland of the same, yeo., on 10 Aug. 1606 and later until 19 Sept. kept alehouses and sold ale, bread and beer without the authority of the JPs.

4) Richard Wright late of Wolsingham, co. Durham, yeo., on 26 June

1606 broke the close of Mabel Nevill of *Denehouses* at the same and removed 2 sparrowhawks on the instruction of his master, Christopher Athie of Broadwood.

5) Whereas by statutes of 7 Henry IV and 8 Henry VIII it was forbidden to any to give liveries except to household officers, bailiffs and servants or legal members of council under pain of £5 payable by the grantor and £2 by the grantee, William Blakiston of Blakeston, co. Durham, knt, gave a blue livery to James Grene of Thorpe Thewles, yeo., who was neither officer [*etc.*] on 29 Sept. 1606 at Blakeston, and Grene wore this tunic at Thorpe Thewles and elsewhere from 29 Sept. to the date of the enquiry. Grene appeared before the JPs and pleaded not guilty. Robert Cooper, esq., bishop's attorney-general, accepted that a jury be summoned [*etc.*].
[*space of 8.5 cms*]

6) Whereas Henry Dethick, LL.B., JP, by warrant dated – authorised the sheriff of Durham and other mayors, constables and officers and especially the constables of Thorpe Thewles to arrest James Grene to be before Dethick or another JP to find surety to keep the peace and to appear at the next general session of the peace, George Swainston being constable of Thorpe Thewles arrested Grene ... was assaulted, and Grene is still at large [*partly illegible*].

7) Whereas John Barnes, esq., JP, ordered on 20 Sept. – the arrest of William Eden, gen., Nathaniel Jackson, gen., and John Eden, esq., to be before him or fellow JPs to find surety to keep the peace, especially with Hugh Wright, gen., ... I and Percival Vepon, a constable, arrested William Eden on 20 Sept. at Durham, who resisted arrest and attacked him with a sword worth 5s.

[*m.59d.*]

8) Guy Watson late of Brotherlee, co. Durham, yeo., and Richard Watson late of the same, yeo., on 18 Sept. 1606 attacked Arthur Emerson and destroyed the newly-built wall and stones surrounding his close at West Brotherlee called *the Westfeild Dale* and another called *the Horses Hill Feild* and struck Emerson with a stick worth 1d. Watson appeared before the JPs, demurred and pleaded not guilty. Robert Cooper, esq., bishop's attorney-general, accepted [*etc.*]. Jurors were summoned for 7 Jan. following.

9) Guy Watson late of Brotherlee, yeo., Richard Watson late of the same, yeo., George Lyndsey late of Fieldhead, yeo., Richard Bainbrigg late of Field Stile, yeo., and Margaret his wife, John Bainbrigg late of the same, yeo., Cuthbert Bainbrigg late of the same, yeo., Jane Lyndley late of Fieldhead, spinster, and Ann Watson late of Brotherlee, spinster, assembled riotously on 18 Sept. 1606 at West Brotherlee at the *West Feild Dale* and attacked Arthur Emmerson and Henry Emmerson and demolished a stone wall built between the West Field Dale close and the Horse Hill field close. Later at the sessions Guy Watson, Richard Watson, George Lindsey, Richard Bainbrigg and Margaret his wife, John Bainbrigg, Cuthbert Bainbrigg, Jane Lindley and Ann Watson appeared in person, demurred [*etc.*].

[space of 5.5 cms]

10) William Hawdon of Bishop Auckland, co. Durham, yeo., A[..] Smith of the same, yeo., Richard Heviside of the same, yeo., Richard Blithman of the same, yeo., Anthony – of the same, yeo., and – Currey of the same, yeo., having been authorised by the justices to keep alehouses, on 27 Aug. 1606 did sell beer and ale at excessive prices, namely 6d. a gallon. *[space of 6.5 cms]*

11) George Simpson of Staindrop, co. Durham, yeo., Lionel – of Wolsingham, yeo., George Varey of Bishop Auckland, tailor, Ralph Walker of the same, [yeo.], Nicholas Gascon of the same, yeo., Ralph Walker of the same, weaver, Ralph Wate of the same, yeo., and Brian – of the same, yeo., on 28 Aug. 1606 and until 1 Oct. were common haunters of taverns and nightwalkers.

12) Whereas Ann Tweddell late of Thorpe Thewles, co. Durham, widow, on – 1606 before the JPs took an oath denouncing Robert Tweddle of Monk Hesleden, – Barnes ordered the constable to arrest Tweddle, but he broke custody *[partly illegible]*.

65

7] Pleas at Durham on 7 Jan. 4 James [*1607*] before George Scroope, esq., Henry Lyndley, knt, Henry Anderson, knt, Thomas Calverley, esq., Clement Colmore, LL.D., Henry Dethick, LL.B., George Lightfoote, esq., Henry Ewbanck, clerk, John Fetherstonhalgh, esq., Henry Tonge, esq., Thomas Ridle, esq., and John Barnes, esq., JPs.

1) Thomas Thowbey late of Durham city, yeo., on 4 Dec. 1606 deliberately entered the residence of Richard Blithman at Durham about 7 p.m. with the purpose to kill or maim Blithman, then with his family, and assaulted Blithman and broke the house doors with shoulders and feet.

2) Ralph Skirfeild late of Kibblesworth, co. Durham, yeo., on 1 Nov. 1604 illegally felled at Pontop in the wood of Anthony Meborne saplings of ash, hazel and oak worth 40s. and carried the same away.

3) Robert Galaley late of Lintz Green, co. Durham, yeo., on 20 Oct. 1606 illegally felled in the wood of Anthony Meborne [*as (2) above*].

4) George Grimbell late of Riddyng House, co. Durham, yeo., on 1 Oct. 1606 illegally felled [*as (2) above*].

5) Percival Harbotle late of Tanfield, co. Durham, gen., on 1 Oct. 1606 at Tanfield was a common brawler and a spreader of lies.

6) Percival Harbottle late of Tanfield, gen., on 20 Sept. 1606 at Tanfield carried off with a horse and oxen yoked together 6 great cocks of hay worth 16s. belonging to Anthony Wheteley.

7) Percival Harbottle late of Tanfield, gen., on 10 Oct. 1606 at Axwell Houses lay in wait for William Carr with intent to kill or maim and attacked the same.

8) Whereas by statute of 5 Richard II it was enacted that no one enter land without leave, and then without a throng, under pain of imprisonment or fine, Richard Hackforth late of Brancepeth, co.

Durham, yeo., on 27 May 1606, sword in hand, took possession of the ox-house beside him at Brancepeth and deprived Clement Colmore, LL.D., of its possession.

[m.57d.] 9) Whereas Robert Maltbye, bailiff of Chester ward, by warrant to distrain Percival Harbottle late of Tanfield, gen., took a cow worth 20s. for amercements imposed by the king's justices itinerant in Durham and of assizes, and attempted to lead it to the common pound of the bishop at Gateside, Percival Harbottle late of Tanfield, yeo., Anne his wife, Jane Harbottle late of the same, spinster, Lionel Harbottle late of the same, yeo., and Christopher Wilde late of the same, yeo., assembled with 8 others unknown at Tanfield on 20 April 1604 and attacked Maltby and recovered the cow.

10) Hugh Storye of Great Usworth, co. Durham, yeo., Robert Hedley of Winlaton, yeo., William Joplin of the same, yeo., John Grame of the same, yeo., John Storye of the same, yeo., Richard Waster of the same, yeo., Thomas Smith of the same, yeo., John Litle of the same, yeo., Roger Oliver of the same, yeo., Oswald Pattyson of the same, yeo., Thomas Merryman of the same, yeo., Ambrose Lowther of Lamesley, clerk, John Donkin of the same, yeo., Widow Marley of the same, spinster, William Sanders of the same, yeo., Edward Kenetty of the same, yeo., Archibald Gibson of the same, yeo., Cuthbert Smith of Cleadon, yeo., Dorothy Shaw of Whitburn, widow, William Robson of the same, yeo., Richard Watson of Westoe, yeo., Robert White of Monkwearmouth, yeo., Andrew Curry of Swalwell, yeo., Anthony Scott of the same, yeo., Thomas Frame of the same, yeo., Martin Atkinson of the same, yeo., Thomas Cole of the same, yeo., William Whitlock of the same, yeo., Gillian Peterson of Middleton George, spinster, Jane Robinson of the same, spinster, Bertram Rowland of Ravensworth, yeo., George Aire of Kibblesworth, yeo., Robert Catcheside of Hedworth, yeo., Richard Bird of Chester, yeo., Robert Barkars of the same, yeo., Robert Newcome of Aycliffe, yeo., Robert Carlile of Whickham, yeo., George Smith of the same, yeo., Bartholomew Chanley of the same, yeo., Thomas Pearson of Gateside, yeo., Cuthbert Saunders of the same, yeo., Edmund Hudd of the same, yeo., Mary Hutton of the same, spinster, Edward Saunders of the same, yeo., Henry Laborne of the same, yeo., Robert Laborne of the same, yeo., Cuthbert Thompson of the same, yeo., Richard Gowland of the same, yeo., Henry Maddison of the same, yeo., Lucy Mathew of the same, widow, Richard Blithman of the same, yeo., Richard Huchinson of the same, yeo., Elizabeth Watson, widow, John Wharey of the same, yeo., Anthony Hobson of the same, yeo., William Teasdell of the same, yeo., William Dawson of the same, yeo., Thomas Dane senior of the same, yeo., George Spear of the same, yeo., Anthony Carr of the same, yeo., Robert Garbott of the same, yeo., Cuthbert Gibson of the same, yeo., Cuthbert Blacklock of the same, yeo., Thomas Stuard of the same, yeo., Ralph Sotheren of the same, yeo., Nicholas Lee of the same, yeo., Richard

Bradshea of Offerton, yeo., Henry Dickeson of the same, yeo., John Kirton of Lumley, yeo., Thomas Gowland of Ryhope, yeo., Elizabeth Moyster of the same, spinster, Anthony Browne of Hutton, John Willson of Gilesgate, Durham, yeo., Thomas Browne of the same, yeo., Cuthbert Wilson of the same, yeo., Robert Comton of Crossgate, Durham, William Clayton of Gainford, yeo., Henry Hutton of the same, yeo., Marmaduke Patteson of Stranton, yeo., John White of Great Stainton, yeo., Martin Nicholson of West Rainton, yeo., Cecily Rose of Silksworth, spinster, Widow Stanebank of Langton, William Elwen of Headlam, William Pearson of Lynesack, yeo., Nicholas Lambton of East Brandon, yeo., Lancelot Browne of Raby, yeo., Cuthbert Hartred of Barnard Castle, yeo., Thomas Day of the same, yeo., William Conyers of the same, yeo., Richard Bell of the same, yeo., Isabel Baynebrigg of the same, spinster, George Arthur of the same, yeo., William Lowish of the same, yeo., Bartholomew Mason of the same, yeo., Christopher Browne of the same, yeo., George Gaynford of Wolsingham, yeo., Ralph Maugham of the same, yeo., Clement Chapman of Frosterley, yeo., Ralph Shaw of Witton, yeo., I were indicted as common alehouse keepers since 1 Oct. 1606 without having the licence of two JPs, contrary to the statute of 5 Edward VI.

11) Whereas Abel Hocheson, collector of fines in the vills of Whitburn and Cleadon, co. Durham, was ordered to distrain upon Thomas Wright of Whitburn, yeo., for 20s. imposed at the bishop's halmote at Chester on 15 May last, in pursuance whereof on 15 Dec. he seized at Whitburn a brown stot of his worth 20s. and Wright the same day assaulted Hocheson and recovered the stot.

12) Whereas Abel Hutcheson, collector [*etc.*] in Whitburn and Cleadon, was ordered to distrain on William Hutcheson of Whitburn, yeo., for 20s. imposed at the bishop's halmote at Chester on 15 May, Hutcheson on 15 Dec. at Whitburn seized a black cow worth 20s., and on the same day Wright assaulted Hutcheson and recovered the cow.

13) Whereas Abel Hutcheson, collector [*etc.*], was ordered to distrain on John Rowsbie of Whitburn, yeo., for 20s. imposed at the bishop's halmote at Chester on 15 May, Hutcheson on 15 Dec. at Whitburn seized a red-hawked cow worth 20s. The same day Rowsbie assaulted Hutcheson at Whitburn and recovered the cow.

14) Whereas Arthur Wright, temporary itinerant bailiff of the Durham exchequer, was ordered to distrain on James Mathew of Cleadon, co. Durham, yeo., for 20s. imposed at the bishop's halmote at Chester on 15 May last, on 19 Dec. at Cleadon he seized a black horse worth 20s. The same day Mathew assaulted him at Whitburn and recovered the horse.

15) Whereas Arthur Wright, temporary itinerant bailiff of the Durham exchequer, was ordered to distrain on John Rowsbie of Whitburn, yeo., for 20s. imposed at the bishop's halmote at Chester on 15 May

last and on 19 Dec. at Whitburn he seized a black heifer worth 20s. Rowsbie on the same day assaulted Wright and recovered the heifer.

[m.58d.] 16) Whereas Arthur Wright, temporary itinerant bailiff [etc.], was ordered to distrain on Cuthbert Baunbrig of Whitburn, yeo., for 20s. imposed at the bishop's halmote at Chester on 15 May last, on 19 Dec. at Whitburn he seized a bay mare worth 20s. On the same day Baunbrig assaulted Wright and recovered the mare.

17) Whereas Michael Thompson, collector of fines in the vill of Wolsingham, co Durham, was ordered to distrain upon William Hopper of Towdy Pots, yeo., for 6s. 8d. imposed in the bishop's halmote at Wolsingham on 14 May last, on 15 Dec. Thomson seized at Wolsingham 10 sheepskins worth 6s. 8d. On the same day Hopper assaulted him at Wolsingham and recovered the skins.

18) Roger Selbie of Grindon in the liberty of Norham, gen., and William Launderel of the same, yeo., on 1 Aug. 1606 broke the close of Robert Litster at Grindon in the same county and seized a yoke and its irons and two oxbows worth – .

19) Roger Selbie of Grindonrigg, *co Durham, gen., George Selbie of the same, gen., and John Heslopp of the same, yeo., on 29 Oct. 1595 broke the close of William Woddle at Grindon and seized a brown mare and a colt together worth 50s.

20) Roger Selbie of Grindonrigg, gen., and Alexander Hunter of the same, lab., on 3 Sept. 1603 broke the close of George Ourd at Wester Newbiggin in Norhamshire and seized 4 sheep worth 4s. each.

21) Roger Selbie of Grindonrigg, gen., and Alexander Hunter of the same, lab., on 3 Sept. 1603 broke the close of Cuthbert Ourd at Wester Newbiggin, Norhamshire, and seized 2 sheep worth 8s.

22) Richard Blithman senior, late of Durham city, and Richard Blithman junior, late of Gateside, butchers, on 4 Dec. 1606 broke into the residence of Thomas Thoraby at Durham city and attacked Elizabeth Thorabey, Thomas's wife, and Richard Blithman junior punched her on the left ear and struck her to the ground.

66

[m.56] Pleas at Durham on 8 April 5 James [1607] before George Scroope, esq., Henry Lindley, knt, Henry Anderson, knt, Clement Colmore, LL.D., Thomas Calverley, esq., Emanuel Barnes, STP, Henry Ewbanck, clerk, John Fetherstonhalgh, Charles Wrenn, George Lightfoote, John Barnes, John Hethe senior, Henry Tong, Robert Brandling, Thomas Riddell and Robert Cooper, esqs, JPs.

William Scurfeild, gen., Robert Farro, gen., Ambrose Lancaster, gen., Williamm Trotter, gen., William Garth, gen., Thomas Trotter, yeo., William Cornford, yeo., Anthony Meborne, yeo., Ralph Surtes, yeo., John Swalwell, yeo., Christopher Richmond, yeo., Cuthbert Hodgson, yeo., William Parkin, yeo., Ralph Caterick, yeo. and Ralph Wilson, yeo., jurors.

1) William Compton late of Cleatlam, co. Durham, tanner, on 25 June

1606 sold to Richard Archer of Durham city, cordwainer, at the vill of Cleatlam outside time of fair or open market and without safeguards of scrutiny 10 tanned hides and 4 pieces of hide or *sticklethors*, contrary to the statute on cutting of leather of 1 James I.

2) Arthur Emmerson late of Brotherlee, co. Durham, yeo., Henry Emmerson late of the same, yeo., George Philippson late of the same, yeo., and John Emmerson late of the same, yeo., assembled with others unknown in warlike fashion on 18 Sept. 1606 at West Brotherlee at the *Westfielddale* and attacked Guy Watson: and Arthur Emmerson struck him on the head with a stick worth 1d., inflicting a wound a half inch wide, and Arthur, Henry, George and John struck Watson on various parts of the body.

3) Henry Emmerson late of Brotherlee, yeo., on 4 Feb. 1607 broke the close of Agnes Watson, widow, at Brotherlee at *Westfielddale* and drove animals across without her leave and depastured it with sheep and lambs.

4) Henry Emmerson late of Brotherlee, yeo., on 25 March 1607 broke the close of Agnes Watson, widow, at Brotherlee called *le Faw* and drove across animals without her leave and depastured it with sheep.

5) Arthur Emmerson late of Brotherlee, yeo., Henry Emmerson late of the same, yeo., and George Phillipson late of the same, yeo., on 18 Sept. 1606 at West Brotherlee at the *Westfield dale* assembled riotously, broke into the freeholding of Agnes Watson, widow, there and pulled down the wall of stones between that close and another, namely *the horses hill feild* and trampled her grass.

6) Ralph Bainbrigg late of Hill House, co. Durham, yeo., on 22 Feb. 1607 attacked Roland Emerson, infant son of Christopher Herrison, and drove with a dog the sheep of Herrison which were in Roland's custody, and frightened the sheep and caused one to abort.

7) Arthur Emmerson late of Brotherlee, yeo., on 25 March 1607 broke the close of Christopher Herrison at Swinhopeburn and tore down the fence and went through at will where there was no customary way for horseman or pedestrian.

8) John Cooke late of Medomsley, co. Durham, yeo., and James Maddeson of Ebchester, yeo., on 7 Feb. 1607 deliberately assaulted George Lawson at Redheugh on the king's highway and struck him on the head with a stick called a *bastinado* worth 1d., inflicting a wound 2 inches by 1 inch deep and another of 12 inches and other wounds to the body, so that he languished for 2 months and his life was endangered.

9) Robert Milburne late of Bedlington, *co. Durham, yeo., on 16 Feb. 1607 broke into the house of James Kirton at Bedlington and stole 6s. from a chest belonging to – Hunnam.

10) Roger Brangston late of Gateside, tailor, on – Feb. 1607 at Gateside was a common brawler and a mischief-maker.

11) John Osborne late of *Westyeate*, Northumberland, yeo., deliberately on 29 Jan. 1607 between 8 and 9 p.m. at Gateside

assaulted Michael Newcombe and wounded him with a short sword worth 20s. I so he languished until 1 Feb., when at 7 a.m. he died, so being murdered. Osborne subsequently fled.

12) Robert Thirkeld late of Richmond, Yorks., gen., on 7 March 1607 stole at Eldon, co. Durham, a mouse-coloured mare worth 33s. 4d. belonging to Anthony White.

13) William Hammour late of Bishop Auckland, co. Durham, lab., and Agnes his wife on 7 Feb. 1607 between 2 and 4 a.m. burgled the residence of Henry Wilson at Bishop Auckland and stole a gown worth 6s. 8d. and a petticoat worth 3s. 4d.

14) Gregory Hutcheson late of Durham city, tanner, between 1 May 1606 and 28 Feb. 1607 bought from William Pearson at Durham outside time of fair or open market 50 calf skins contrary to the statute of 1 James I.

15) Whereas by statute of 1 James I it was enacted that no tanner should forestall any hides coming to fair or market nor buy them outside fair or market except the beasts were killed for consumption by the owner, under pain of 6s. 8d. a hide, Gregory Hutcheson late of Durham between 1 May 1606 [as (14) above].

16) Gregory Hutcheson late of Durham, tanner, between 1 May 1606 and 28 Feb. 1607 bought from Edward Thompson at Durham outside time of fair or open market 66 calf skins contrary to the statute of 1 James I.

17) Thomas Hutcheson late of Durham, tanner, between 1 May 1605 until the present bought from William Chipchase at Durham 100 calf skins outside fair and market [etc. as (14) above].

18) MEMO that whereas Francis Pearte son of John Pearte of Hedleyclough, co. Durham, by indenture of 10 Elizabeth was apprenticed to Cuthbert Pearte as a butcher for the term of 7 years and one part of the indenture was presented before the JPs for enrolment, Roger Hutcheson of Durham, yeo., and Elizabeth his wife, lately relict of Cuthbert Pearte, acknowledged that Francis had served the late Cuthbert and Elizabeth, she being Cuthbert's executrix; done in the presence of Emanuel Barnes, STP, William Morton, archdeacon of Durham, and John Barnes, JPs.

67

Pleas at Durham on 8 July 5 James [1607] before Henry Lindley, knt, Charles Wrenn, knt, Thomas Calverley, esq., and Clement Colmore, LL.D., JPs.

1) Christopher Viccars late of Staindrop, co. Durham, yeo., constable of the same, Roger Viccars of Staindrop, yeo., James Viccars late of Staindrop, yeo., Simon Johnson late of Staindrop, yeo., William Watson late of Staindrop, yeo., Thomas Lawson late of Staindrop, yeo., Roger Cradock late of Staindrop, yeo., Oswald Lumley late of Staindrop, yeo., John Atkinson junior late of Staindrop, yeo., James Huitson late of Staindrop, yeo., William Walker late of Staindrop,

yeo., Henry Lumley late of Staindrop, yeo., and Robert Lumley late of Staindrop, yeo., assembled riotously with 60 others unknown in fashion of a new uprising on 11 May 1607 at Staindrop at the Lawhouse: and Christopher Viccars, Roger Viccars, James Viccars [*etc., as immediately above*] broke up the newly constructed house built by John Huton appurtenant to the Lawhouse and overturned the walls with iron coulters and gavelocks worth 20s. and put Katherine Hutton wife of John Hutton, then in the Lawhouse, in bodily fear and did other enormities to Hutton.

2) Enquiry on 9 May 1607 at Durham before Clement Colmore, LL.D., and John Barnes, JPs, on the oath of Robert Blaxton, John Hall, Henry Bayles, William Whitfeild, William Shawe, Richard Key, William Watson, Robert Tweddle, George Brough, John Hixson, William Lidle and John Hopper, who testified that Michael Garthwate late of *Northwastes*, co. Durham, yeo., John Phillipp alias Dand, late of Great Kelloe, tailor, Humphrey Comyn alias Cutt, late of Whickham, tailor, John Foreman late of Kelloe, tailor, George Watson late of Harbour House, yeo., and William Cooke late of Chester with 13 others unknown in warlike fashion on 7 May 1607 riotously broke into the residence of Thomas Lambe at Great Kelloe and assaulted him.

3) Whereas Henry Tonge, esq., and John Barnes, esq., JPs, on 11 May 1607 authorised the constable of Staindrop to arrest John Lawson late of Staindrop, yeo., Thomas Lawson late of Staindrop, yeo., Roger Viccars late of Staindrop, yeo., James Viccars late of Staindrop, yeo., William Watson late of Staindrop, yeo., John Atkinson junior late of Staindrop, yeo., Henry Lumley late of Staindrop, yeo., Robert Lumley late of Staindrop, yeo., Roger Cradock late of Staindrop and Simon Johnson late of Staindrop, yeo., to have them before Henry Tonge and John Barnes or other JPs to find surety to keep the peace with John Hutton, gen., and to appear at the next general sessions at Durham and not to withdraw without leave: later on 14 May 1607 John Hutton delivered the warrant to Christopher Viccars, constable of Staindrop, and Christopher on 4 May following should have arrested John Lawson, Thomas Lawson, Roger Viccars, James Viccars, William Watson, John Atkinson junior, Henry Lumley, Robert Lumley, Roger Cradock and Simon Johnson: but Christopher Viccars allowed them to escape after arrest, after which they assembled at the Lawhouse, and broke down the house of John Hutton [*etc. as above*].

d.] 4) [*Start of case illegible*] | ... 6 May 1607 at Kelloe, co. Durham, assembled riotously: and the said Michael Garthwate, Humphrey Comyn alias Cutt, Richard Whit, John Phillip alias Dann, John Foreman, George Watson, Richard Martyn and Robert Allen broke into the residence of Thomas Lambe at Kelloe and assaulted Mary Lambe his wife and drove out her and her infant son John.

5) Cuthbert Garnett late of Darlington, tinkler, Henry Browne late of the same, tailor, Blaise Tayler late of the same, tailor, William Garnett

late of Sedgefield, tinkler, John Richardson late of Bishop Auckland, yeo., James Fletcher late of Gateside, yeo., William Beton late of Gateside, embroiderer, and Arthur Smith late of Norton, tinkler, from 1 Dec. 1606 to the date of the enquiry on 8 July 1607, practised at Darlington the craft of mercer and grocer for gain without serving a 7 years' apprenticeship, contrary to statute.

6) Thomas Foggard late of Washington, co. Durham, yeo., between 1 July 1606 and 1 July 1607 at Washington engrossed from William Mallerie, esq., 5 acres of wheat and rye and 7 acres of oats worth £9 as growing crops for resale, contrary to the statute of 5 Edward VI.

7) Cuthbert Wrangham late of Cleatlam, co. Durham, yeo., between 1 Jan. 1607 and 8 July 1607 at Cleatlam engrossed 40 bushels of barley (*bigge*) worth £4 and 40 bushels of oats worth 40s. for resale, [*as (6) above*].

8) Robert Gibson late of Stranton, co. Durham, yeo., between 20 Sept. 1606 and 8 July 1607 at Stranton engrossed from Christopher Corker of Castle Eden 3 chalders of barley worth £3 and from Philip Corker of Stranton, yeo., 16 bushels of barley worth 30s. for resale, [*as (6) above*].

9) Anthony Dayle late of *Gillfeild*, Yorks., gen., Stephen Simpson late of the same, yeo., George Copperthwaite late of the same, yeo., Peter Viccars late of Shotton, co. Durham, yeo., Thomas Smith late of Staindrop, yeo., Thomas Wild late of the same, yeo., Bernard Hardin late of the same, yeo., Thomas Brathwaite late of Barnard Castle, yeo., and 10 others unknown riotously assembled on 13 May 1607 at Raby at the Southland gate to the terror of the lieges.

10) John Shawe junior of Cornforth, co. Durham, yeo., on 8 July 1606 was in possession for a term of years of an arable messuage in Cornforth and of 40 acres arable of which between then and 8 July 1607 for gain he enclosed 20 acres with a ditch and hedge and converted these to pasture.

11) Roland Brough late of Newbottle on [1] July 1607 ... [*illegible*]

[*m.54*]   12) Cuthbert Athye of Mainsforth, co. Durham, husbandman, on 8 July 1606 had a lease for term of years in Mainsforth of a messuage and 40 acres arable of which between then and 8 July 1607 he enclosed 24 acres with a ditch and hedge and converted them to pasture, contrary to law and statute.

13) Whereas George Lightfoote, esq., JP, authorized under seal on 2 July 1607 the sheriff of Durham and all bailiffs, constables and other officers of the Crown to arrest Thomas Robinson late of Stockley, yeo., to have him before George Lyghtfoote or another JP to find surety to keep the peace with Robert Marley and to appear at the general sessions and not withdraw without leave, later, on 2 July, Marley delivered the order to William Conyers, gen., bailiff of the lordship of Brancepeth, to execute. On 8 July when William Conyers attempted to take him before George Lightfoote Robinson with the aid of Arthur Colterd assaulted Conyers and rescued himself.

14) Thomas Merlay late of Hedley, co. Durham, yeo., on 28 Oct. 1606 felled at Pontop in the wood of Anthony Meborne saplings of ash, hazel and oak worth 3s. and carried the same away.

15) Whereas by statute of 5 Elizabeth it was enacted that if any tanner tanned an oxhide, horsehide or sheepskin and "put to sale exchange or depart with any of the same being tanned" he should forfeit the skin or its value: Thomas Snawball late of Durham, tanner, between 1 July 1606 and 1 July 1607 bought from unknown men 10 horsehides worth 13s. 4d. and tanned the same.

16) Presentment that the highway from Durham to Brancepeth and other villages to the west of the county at a place near Relley called *the Bullring* had been ruinous for some years past and in great decay for lack of repairs, so that the king's lieges did not dare use it for horse, cart or carriage and it was a common nuisance.

17) Whereas Anne Watson of Brotherlee, co. Durham, widow, enjoyed from time out of mind a passage on the west angle of the close called *le Faw* at Brotherlee for access at all times by ploughs and livestock, Nicholas Emmerson of Brotherlee, yeo., on 1 April 1603 without title, claim or possession blocked the passage with a hedge and ditch and so holds it to the present, 8 July 1607.

18) John Walker of Eastgate, co. Durham, miller, and Thomas

4d.] Lonsedale of the same, lab., on 25 May 1607 | broke the park of Bishop James at Stanhope and hunted hares with greyhounds.

19) Percival Harbottle late of Tanfield, co. Durham, gen., on 12 April 1607 at Tanfield was a common brawler and mischief-maker.

20) Anthony Stoker late of Durham city, litster, on – June 1607 hindered Robert Herrison of Durham, yeo., a sheriff's bailiff, in execution of his office, speaking opprobrious words publicly to the contempt of the justice's warrant.

21) John Broughe late of East Boldon, co. Durham, yeo., John Morrell late of West Boldon, gen., and Michael Granger late of Boldon mill, yeo., on 1 July 1607 at West Boldon deliberately attacked Robert Maltbie, bailiff of the Chester ward, and hurled him to the ground, buffeted him with hands and feet, drew blood and put him in bodily fear.

22) Whereas in the statute of 2 Edward VI it was enacted that none under the rank of lord of parliament should shoot in city or town at any bird on church, house or dovecote nor use hailshot under pain of £10 fine and 3 months' imprisonment, Richard Wright of Wolsingham, co. Durham, yeo., on 25 May 1607 at Sunniside shot with a handgun charged with powder and hailshot.

[*space of 26.9 cms*]

68

0] Pleas and presentments at the general sessions at Durham on 7 Oct. 5 James [*1607*] before Bp James, George Scroope, esq., Henry Lindley, Henry Anderson, Charles Wrenn, knts, Thomas Calverley, esq.,

Clement Colmore, LL.D., Henry Ewbanck, subdean of Durham, Robert Brandlinge, George Tonge, John Fetherstonhalgh, esqs, Henry Dethwick, LL.B., George Lightfoote, John Barnes, Thomas Riddle, Robert Cooper, esqs, and Francis Bunny, clerk, JPs.

1) Richard Yowton late of Whickham, co. Durham, yeo., on 1 Aug. 1607 attacked Brian Wood at Whickham and broke his head with a stick worth 1d., inflicting a wound 3 inches by 1 inch and striking him on other parts of the body.

2) Peter Denton late of Stobbilee, co. Durham, gen., on 23 Sept. 1607 broke the close of George Herrison at Stobbilee and depastured it with livestock to his damage of 20s.

3) Peter Denton late of *Rudemilne*, Northumberland, tailor, John Manie late of *Brunckhillhaugh*, yeo., William Dobson of Styford, yeo., and Richard Watson late of the same, yeo., on 3 May 1607 at Hunstanworth, co. Durham, assembled riotously at South Riddlehamhope and broke into the residence of Matthew Armstrong and attacked him and drove him from the house.

4) Richard Barloe late of Greenlaw, co. Durham, yeo., Isabel Barloe his wife, Margaret Barloe late of Greenlaw, spinster, Robert Laburne late of Greenlaw, yeo., and Robert Pye junior late of Greenlaw, yeo., assembled with 7 others unknown riotously in warlike fashion on 14 Aug. 1607 at Greenlaw and attacked Robert Maltbye, bailiff of the sheriff of Durham in the Chester ward, while in execution of a warrant of the sheriff arising from a royal writ of attachment issued from the Durham chancery against Richard Barloe, and tore off his livery coat worth 20s.

5) Robert Calverley late of Lintz Green, co. Durham, yeo., on 14 Sept. 1607 at Tanfield stole a bay mare worth £3 13s. 4d. belonging to Stephen Sotheran.

6) George Davis alias Jefferson late of Brancepeth, co. Durham, yeo., being a domestic servant of Henry Sanderson of Brancepeth, esq., on 6 Aug. 1607 broke into the king's park at Brancepeth called *the West Park* and by procurement of Sanderson shot and killed a buck worth 20s. belonging to the king with a gun charged with great shot and carried it away.

7) William Howson late of Shotton, co. Durham, yeo., between 1 May and 1 Sept. 1607 bought from William Lighton 2 stirks worth £3 and resold them within 5 weeks contrary to the statute.

[*m.50d.*] 8) George Davis alias Jefferson late of Brancepeth, yeo., being a domestic servant of Henry Sanderson of Brancepeth, esq., on 9 March 1607 [*corrected from* 6 Aug.] broke into the king's park at Brancepeth at the East [*corrected from* West] Park and killed and carried away a fawn worth 5s. belonging to the king by procurement of Henry Sanderson.

9) Whereas by statute of 33 Henry VIII it was enacted that if any kept a crossbow, handgun, hagbut or demi-hake in or out of his house he or his wife must have lands, rents or offices worth £100 a year, under

pain of £10 for each offence, George Davis alias Jefferson late of Brancepeth, yeo., domestic servant of Henry Sanderson, esq., not being so qualified, on 30 Sept. 1607 at Brancepeth in the king's West Park shot with a gun charged with hailshot and powder and killed three partridges.

10) Elizabeth Hall late of Crawcrook, co. Durham, widow, and John Hall late of the same, yeo., on 17 Sept. 1607 broke the common fold at Crawcrook and drove off their – cows and a heifer impounded for damaging sheaves of grain belonging to the inhabitants of Crawcrook in a close called *the Wheat Field*.

11) Robert Daglees late of Whickham, co. Durham, yeo., on 1 Aug. 1607 in Whickham and at other times and places was a common brawler and mischief-maker.

12) Whereas Henry Gibson, deputy bailiff of the sheriff for the western part of the Darlington ward, and Nicholas Gibson of Bishop Auckland, co. Durham, yeo., on 26 Sept. 1607 at Staindrop by virtue of a sheriff's warrant would have arrested Bernard Hardyne of Staindrop until he found sureties to appear at the next general sessions at Durham to answer divers indictments, Bernard Hardyne with Robert Hardyne late of Staindrop, yeo., and Mary his wife on the following day [27 *Sept.*] at Staindrop attacked the Gibsons in execution of their office to the effusion of blood and rescued Hardyne, who is still at large.

13) George Davis alias Jefferson late of Brancepeth, yeo., domestic servant of Henry Sanderson, esq., on 8 Oct. 1607 by procurement of Sanderson broke the East Park at Brancepeth and shot a buck worth 20s. and wounded it so it thereafter died.

14) Roger Brangston late of Gateside, tailor, on 1 Sept. 1607 smashed a churn worth 40s. belonging to Anthony Carr at Gateside.

1] 15) Whereas by statute of 33 Henry VIII against possession of fire-arms [*etc.*], George Davis alias Jefferson late of Brancepeth, domestic servant of Henry Sanderson, esq., on 28 Feb. 1607 at Brancepeth in the East Park shot 2 mallards with a gun charged with hailshot and gunpowder and killed them.

16) Whereas Miles Jefferson and Thomas Chipchase, churchwardens of the parish of Norton, co. Durham, on 4 Oct. 1607 at Blakeston by virtue of a warrant of Henry Ewbanck, clerk, prebendary of Durham, Henry Dethicke, LL.B., Robert Cooper, esq., and John Barnes, esq., four JPs, distrained on William Blakiston of Blakeston, knt, by a branded cow worth 40s. for a fine of 8s. levied on him and Alice his wife by the said justices resulting from the act of 3 James I for failure to attend Norton or a neighbouring church or preaching place on 25 July, the feast of St James, and the Sundays 26 July and 2 and 9 Aug without lawful excuse, Blakiston, however, on 4 Oct., knowing of the warrant, assaulted Miles Jefferson at Blakiston and prevented the seizure of the cow.

17) Whereas Henry Ewbanck, clerk, prebendary of Durham, Henry

Dethicke, LL.B., John Barnes, esq., and Robert Cooper, esq., JPs, ordered the proctors and churchwardens of Norton by a sealed warrant of 18 Aug. 1607 to levy goods of William Blakiston, knt, to the value of 8s. for absence from church [*as (16) above*], the money to be given to the use of the poor of the parish, and to make a return to the keepers of the peace at the next sessions, Thomas Chipchase of Norton, yeo., and Miles Jefferson of the same, yeo., being proctors, would have levied the money on 4 Oct. from the goods of Blakiston, namely a cow found at Blakeston, to be valued and sold at Norton, but Blakiston recovered the cow on the same day.

18) James Anderson late of Newcastle upon Tyne on 1 Aug. 1607 at the procurement of Anthony Carr of Gateside, yeo., and Agnes his wife assaulted Roger Brangston of Gateside, yeo., at Gateside and struck Roger with a drawn sword worth 5s. on his right arm, inflicting a wound 2½ inches by 1 inch and 1 inch deep, and also on the right [shin (?)] ½ inch in length, and also on his left hand 3 inches long and 1 inch deep with other wounds.

19) Whereas the king by letters patent under the exchequer seal of 5 James I appointed Bp James, John [Thornborough], bp of Bristol, William Morton, archdeacon of Durham, Henry Ewbanck, clerk, prebendary of Durham, John Barnes, Robert Cooper and Robert [*m.51d.*] Kellway, esqs, and any two or more I to enquire as seemed best [*etc.*] into the lands [*etc.*] of William Blakiston, knt, of Blakeston, papist recusant, held on the date of his conviction and later, value them and take his goods into the king's hand; Ewbancke, Morton, Barnes and Kellway authorised William Smith, a sheriff's bailiff, on 5 Oct. 1607, who had been detailed by John Conyers, knt, sheriff of Durham, to act with John Cooth, gen., William Guidott, gen., Toby Mooser, gen., William Collins, John Walker, George Hirst and Charles Rawlings to seize the goods and chattels of William Blaxton, knt, at Blakeston, Fulthorpe and elsewhere and deliver the same at Durham to the sheriff to the king's use: and Smith, Cooth, Guidott, Collins, Walker, Hirst and Rawlings on 6 Oct. 1607 at Fulthorpe seized 19 horses, mares and geldings, a colt and 77 oxen, cows, bullocks and stirks with other goods and chattels of William Blakiston and drove them from Fulthorpe towards Durham. William Blaxton of Blakeston, knt, however, John Blaxton junior of Blakeston, gen., and William Partus of Blakeston, yeo., later the same day [*6 Oct.*] at Sedgefield riotously attacked Smith, Cooth, Guidott, Collins, Walker, Hirst and Rawlings and recovered 18 horses, mares and geldings and the colt. It was also presented that William Partus and George Blaxton late of Blakeston, gen., later the same day at Quarrington attacked Smith, Cooth, Guidott, Collins, Walker, Hirst and Rawlings; and George Blaxton, William Partus, Robert Blaxton late of Finchale, gen., Samuel Hopper of Shincliffe, yeo., Edward Mainsford of Shincliffe, yeo., the wife of Lancelot Smith of Shincliffe and the wife of William Tutting of Shincliffe, yeo., with 12 others unknown in warlike

fashion on 6 Oct. at Shincliffe riotously assembled and attacked Smith, Guidott, Cooth, Collins, Walker, Hirst and Rawlings and recovered the 77 oxen, cows, bullocks and queys [*altered from* stirks].
[*space of 11 cms*]

68A

2] Pleas and presentments at Durham on 7 Oct. 5 James I [*1607*] before Bp James, George Scroope, esq., Henry Lyndley, Henry Anderson, Charles Wrenn, knts, Thomas Calverley, esq., Clement Colmore, LL.D., Henry Ewbanck, vice-dean <subdean> of Durham, Robert Brandling, George Tonge, John Fetherstonhalgh, Henry Dethick, LL.B., George Lightfoote, John Barnes, Thomas Riddle, Robert Cooper, esqs, and Francis Bunnye, clerk, JPs.

1) Elsewhere at the sessions held on 7 Oct. 1606 before Bp James, Cuthbert Pepper, knt, chancellor of Durham, Henry Lyndley, knt, and Henry Anderson, knt, JPs, it was presented on the oath of 12 jurors that John Claxton of West Hall, co. Durham, knt, from 27 June to 28 July 1606 at West Hall and Holywell entertained in his houses Thomas Blenkinshopp and George Johnson of West Hall, yeomen, who did not attend church for a month without lawful excuse. Later, on Wednesday 7 Oct. 1607, before Bp James, Henry Lindley, knt, and Henry Anderson, knt, JPs, John Claxton, knt, appeared, demurred and pleaded not guilty. Robert Cooper, esq., the bishop's attorney, [*etc.*]. Jurors were summoned for 13 Jan. 1608.
[*space of 13.5 cms*]

2) Elsewhere at the sessions held on 7 Oct. 1606 before Bp James, Cuthbert Pepper, knt, chancellor of Durham, George Scroope, esq., Henry Lyndley, knt, Thomas Calverley, esq., and Clement Colmore, LL.D., JPs, it was presented on the oath of 12 jurors that George Collingwood of Eppleton, esq., from 27 June to 28 July 1606 entertained at Eppleton at his home Eleanor Robinson and Alice Tayler of Eppleton, spinsters, who did not attend church for a month without lawful excuse. Later at the sessions on 7 Oct. 1607 before Bp James, Henry Lindley, Henry Anderson and Charles Wrenn, knts, JPs, Collingwood appeared in person, demurred and pleaded not guilty. Robert Cooper, esq., bishop's attorney-general, [*etc.*]. Jurors were summoned for 13 Jan 1608.

2d.] 3) Elsewhere at the sessions held on 7 Oct. 1606 before Bp James, Cuthbert Pepper, knt, chancellor of Durham, George Scroope, esq., Henry Lindley, knt, Thomas Calverley, esq., and Clement Colmore, LL.D., JPs, it was presented on the oath of 12 jurors that Francis Lawson of Thorpe Bulmer, co. Durham, esq., from 27 June to 28 July 1606 at Thorpe Bulmer entertained Margaret Forrest of Thorpe Bulmer, spinster, who failed to attend church for one month without lawful excuse. Later, on Wed., 7 Oct. 1607, before Bp James, George Scroope, esq., Henry Lindley, Henry Anderson, and Charles Wren, knts, JPs, Lawson appeared [*etc. as (1) above*].

4) Elsewhere at the sessions held on 7 Oct. 1606 before Bp James [*etc. as (3) above*] it was presented on the oath of 12 jurors that James Lawson of Neasham, esq., from 27 June to 28 July 1606 entertained Constance Bell of – , spinster, who failed to attend church for one month without lawful excuse. Later at the sessions on 7 Oct. 1607 before Bp James, George Scroope, esq., Henry Lindley, Henry Anderson and Charles Wren, knts, JPs, James Lawson appeared, demurred [*etc. as (3) above*]. [*space of 18.5 cms*]

[*m.53*] 5) Elsewhere at the general sessions at Durham on 8 April 1607 before George Scroope, esq., Henry Lindley, Henry Anderson, knts, Clement Colmore, LL.D., Thomas Calverley, esq., Emanuel Barnes, STP, Henry Ewbanck, clerk, and John Fetherstonhalgh, esq., JPs, it was presented on oath that *Arthur Emmerson late of Brotherlee, yeo., Henry Emmerson of Brotherlee, yeo., and George Phillipson late of Brotherlee, yeo., on 18 Sept. 1606 at West Brotherlee in the Westfield Dale assembled riotously* and entered the free holding of Agnes Watson, widow, in the Westfield dale and pulled down the stone wall between the same close and another called *the Horses Hill field* and trampled the grass. Now at the general sessions on 7 Oct. 1607 Arthur Emmerson and Henry Emmerson appeared before Bp James, George Scroope, esq., Henry Lindley, Henry Anderson and Charles Wrenn, knts, and Clement Colmore, LL.D., [*etc.*]
[*space of 17 cms*]

6) Elsewhere at the general sessions at Durham on 8 April 1607 before George Scroope, esq., Henry Lyndley, knt, Henry Anderson, knt, and Clement Colmore, LL.D., JPs, it was presented on oath that Arthur Emmerson [*etc. as (5) between * and *], attacked Guy Watson, and Arthur struck Watson on the head with a stick worth 1d. inflicting a wound half an inch wide; also Arthur Emmerson, Henry Emmerson, George Phillipson and John Emmerson struck Watson on divers parts of his body. Now at the sessions on 7 Oct. 1607 before Bp James, George Scroope, esq., and Clement Colmore, LL.D., JPs, Arthur and Henry Emmerson appeared [*etc. as (5) above*].

[*m.53d.*] [*space of 17.5 cms*]

7) Elsewhere at the general sessions at Durham on 8 July 1607 before Henry Lindley, Charles Wren, knts, Thomas Calverley, esq., Clement Colmore, LL.D., JPs, it was presented on oath that Cuthbert Garnett late of Darlington, tinkler, Blaise Tayler of the same, tailor, and William Beton late of Gateside, embroiderer, on 1 Dec. 1606 and until the present [*8 July*] at Darlington practised the mysteries of mercer and grocer for gain without having served 7 years of apprenticeship. Now at the sessions on 7 Oct. 1607 before Bp James, George Scroope, esq., Henry Lindley, Henry Anderson, Charles Wrenn, knts, Thomas Calverley, esq., and Clement Colmore, LL.D., JPs, Garnett, Tayler and Beton appeared [*etc.*].
[*space of 14.5 cms*]

[For the estreats of this session see Appendix 1, pp. 330–6 below]

69

7] Pleas and presentments at the general sessions of the peace at Durham on 13 Jan. 5 James [*1608*] before George Scroope, esq., Henry Lindley, Henry Anderson, Charles Wrenn, knts, Thomas Calverley, esq., Clement Colmore, LL.D., George Tonge, John Fetherstonhalgh, esq., Henry Dethwick, LL.B., George Lightfoote, John Barnes, Thomas Riddle, Robert Cooper, esqs, and Francis Bunny, clerk, JPs.

1) Whereas John Claxton, knt, of West Hall in the parish of Lanchester, co. Durham, at the general sessions at Durham on 7 Oct. 1606 before Bp James, Cuthbert Pepper, knt, chancellor of Durham, and George Scroope, esq., JPs, was indicted for being 16 years and over and in Durham from 1 May to 1 Oct. 1606 and failing to attend the parish church of Lanchester or other chapel without leave of absence, contrary to the form of the statute, a public proclamation was read at the general sessions that Claxton surrender to the sheriff before the next sessions under pain of conviction. As Claxton failed then to appear on 7 Jan. 1607 before George Scroope, esq., Henry Lindley, knt, and Clement Colmore, LL.D., JPs, he was duly convicted as a papist recusant in that being over 16 years of age, born in England and having a certain abode at West Hall in the parish of Lanchester, he failed to return home within 40 days of presentation, contrary to the act of 35 Elizabeth limiting the place of residence of such recusants.

2) Christopher Golightlie late of Hebburn, co. Durham, yeo., and William Philpe late of Great Usworth, yeo., on 29 Sept. 1607 at Bearpark stole a black cow worth 33s. 4d. from Henry Maltbie.

3) Christopher Golightlie late of Hebburn, yeo., and William Philpe of Great Usworth, lab., on 29 Sept. 1607 stole 2 black queys worth 40s. each from Samson Lever.

4) William Philpe late of Great Usworth, yeo., on 17 Sept. 1607 at Great Usworth stole a branded heifer worth 40s. from Gilbert Robinson.

5) Christopher Golightlie late of Hebburn, yeo., and William Philpe late of Great Usworth, yeo., on 29 Sept. 1607 at Bearpark stole a bullock worth 33s. 4d. from Francis Maltbie.

6) James Huntley late of Bishopton, co. Durham, lab., on 22 – 1607 about 11 p.m. burgled the residence of Thomas F[owler] at East Hartburn, and stole 2½ yards of woollen cloth worth 2s. 6d., two harden sheets worth 2s., 2 rings worth 6d. each, a whistle worth 6d. and a silver heart worth 4d. from [Thomas] Fowler.

7) Jane Storie late of Durham city, spinster, on –8 Aug. 1607 at Elvet stole 3 harden sheets from Lionel Martyne.

8) Richard Wake late of Cleadon, co. Durham, yeo., on 1 – 1607 at Cleadon attacked Elizabeth Griffon, widow, to the shedding of blood.

17d.] 9) George Simpson, bailiff of the bishop of Durham in the manor of Chester, co. Durham, and by virtue of his office collector of fines and amercements in the bishop's halmote court of Chester, on 4 Dec. 1607 at Chester took as distraint a branded ox depasturing the land of Thomas Humble, yeo., against an amercement for 6s. 8d. and drove it away for impounding at Chester until payment. Later the same day Bertram Suerties of Chester, yeo., assaulted George Simpson at Chester in execution of his office and recovered the ox.

10) George Davis alias Jefferson late of Brancepeth, co. Durham, yeo., on 20 Nov. 1607 at the instigation of the devil at Brancepeth at Page Bank attacked George Brabant and threatened him with a long gun held in both hands, putting him in bodily fear.

11) Whereas by statute of 33 Henry VIII it was enacted that any shooting with crossbow, handgun, hagbut and demi-hack must have by right of himself or his wife lands, holdings, fees, annuities or offices worth £100, under pain of forfeit of £10, George Davis alias Jefferson late of Brancepeth, yeo., being a domestic servant of Henry Sanderson, esq., who did not have the statutory requirements, did on 20 Nov. 1607 at Brancepeth at Page Bank discharge a gun loaded with hailshot and powder at 5 woodcocks and illegally killed the same.

12) Whereas by statute of 33 Henry VIII it was enacted that if any person ordered his servants to shoot with a crossbow, handgun, hagbutt or demi-hack of his master or any other at deer or fowl or anything other than a butt or bank of earth, or in time of war, he should forfeit £10 to the king for each offence, Henry Sanderson of Brancepeth, esq., on 20 Nov. 1607 at Brancepeth ordered George Davis alias Jefferson of Brancepeth, yeo., his domestic servant, to shoot wild-fowl, on the authority of which instruction Davis shot 5 woodcocks.

13) Whereas Robert Chilton of Newbottle, co. Durham, yeo., being collector of the bishop's rents and amercements in the township of Newbottle, on 10 Dec. 1607 distrained on William Chilton at Newbottle by a cow worth 40s. against an amercement imposed on Chilton in the bishop's halmote court at Houghton on 13 Oct. past, and attempted to impound the same in Newbottle; later the same day William Chilton assaulted Robert at Newbottle in the execution of his office and violently recovered the cow.

14) Arthur Emmerson late of Brotherlee, co. Durham, yeo., on 6 May 1607 broke the close of Margaret Emmerson, widow, John Emmerson, Richard Baunbrigg, William Harrison, Christopher Harrison and William Stobbes called *the Hassockes* at Swinhopeburn and used it without permission as if it were a common highway and trampled the grass with his feet.

15) Thomas Hynd late of Brotherlee, yeo., on 15 Nov. 1607 broke the close of Anne Watson called *the West field dale* at Brotherlee and by procurement of Arthur Emmerson of Brotherlee, yeo., drove Arthur's sheep across the close without Anne's leave and depastured the same and made a new path where there was no common way from time immemorial.

16) Arthur Emmerson late of Brotherlee, yeo., on 28 Sept. 1606 broke the close of Margaret Emmerson, widow, John Emmerson, Richard Baunbrigg, William Harrison, Christopher Harrison and William Stobbes called *the Fawlees* at Swinhopeburn and dug up the same with implements.

17) Mark Hull of Esp Green, co. Durham, yeo., on 5 Nov. [1605] had a son born at Esp Green which he failed to present for baptism at Lanchester church ... [*partly illegible*].

8] 18) George Fairhaire of Ford, co. Durham, gen., after 5 Nov. 1605 had a son born at Ford in the parish of Lanchester which he failed to present for baptism there within a month, contrary to the statute of 3 James I.

19) John Jenison of Walworth, co. Durham, esq., after 5 Nov. 1605 had a son born at Walworth in the parish of Heighington which he failed to present for baptism there within a month.

20) William Rawe of Luns House, co. Durham, after 5 Nov. 1605 had a son born at Luns House in the parish of Lanchester which he failed to present for baptism there within a month.

21) William Pallicer late of Cold Rowley, co. Durham, on 1 April 1607 broke the close of Michael Johnson, gen., at Twizell called *the Howners* and cut and carried undergrowth, namely 60 hazel rods.

22) Hugh Carliell late of Birtley, co. Durham, yeo., on 13 Nov. 1607 assaulted Isabel wife of John Porter of Gateside at Gateside, striking her with his clenched right hand on various parts of her body.

23) Hugh Carlill late of Birtley, yeo., on 13 Nov. 1607 at Gateside attacked John Potter with a drawn sword.

24) Hugh Carlill late of Birtley, yeo., on 13 Nov. 1607 at Gateside attacked Stephen Kitchin and punched him on the face and body.

25) John Craddock late of Gainford, co. Durham, clerk, on 20 Aug. 1607 blocked with a stone wall 120 yards long to the west of Gainford the king's highway leading from Barnard Castle by Gainford to Darlington, and still has it stopped, to the nuisance of the inhabitants.

8d.] 26) George Simpson, bishop's bailiff in the manor of Chester, co. Durham, and collector of fines and amercements imposed in the halmotes, on 4 Dec. 1607 at Chester-le-Street took a cow by way of distraint from Thomas Hyndmers for an amercement of 6s. 8d. imposed at the halmote, and intended to impound the same in Chester park until payment. Later the same day Hyndmers, a labourer, assaulted Simpson and recovered the cow.

27) George Simpson, bishop's bailiff in the manor of Chester [*etc.*] on 4 Dec. 1607 at Chester took by way of distraint a branded ox of William Punshon for a fine of 6s. 8d. imposed at the halmote, and intended to impound the same in Chester park. Later the same day Edward Stotie late of Chester, yeo., John Hodshon of the same, yeo., and Robert Smith of the same, yeo., riotously assembled at Chester, assaulted Simpson and recovered the ox.

28) Enquiry whether John Craddocke late of Gainford, co. Durham, clerk, on 20 Aug. 1607 blocked with a stone wall 20 yards long part of the king's highway from Barnard Castle to Darlington by way of Gainford and diverted the way from its ancient course to the nuisance of the inhabitants.

29) George Sympson, bishop's bailiff in the Chester manor [etc.] on 4 Dec. 1607 at Chester by way of distraint took 2 red-branded queys from Robert Suerties for an amercement of 6s. 8d. imposed [etc.] and intended to impound them. Later the same day William Moreburne of Chester, lab., by order of Surties assaulted Simpson and recovered the queys.

30) Bernard Chilton, collector of fines and amercements for the bishop in the township of Newbottle in the manor of Houghton, co. Durham, on 10 Dec. 1607 at Newbottle distrained on William Chilton senior of Newbottle by a cow for an amercement of 6s. 8d., and intended to impound the same in Newbottle pound. Later the same day William Chilton assaulted the bailiff at Newbottle and recovered the cow.

31) Thomas Ferry, collector of the bishop's rents, fines and amercements in the township of Benfieldside in the manor of Lanchester, co. Durham, on 3 Dec. 1607 at *Sumesgrave* in the township of Benfieldside took as a distraint a brass pot from John Procter for a fine of 20d. imposed at the halmote at Lanchester. Later the same day John Procter and Isabel his wife assaulted Ferry at *Sumesgrove* and recovered the pot.

[m.49]   32) Elsewhere at the general sessions of the peace at Durham on 7 Oct. 1607 before Bp James, Henry Lindley, Henry Anderson, Charles Wrenn, knts, Thomas Calverley, esq., and Clement Colmore, LL.D., JPs, information was laid by Roger Trollopp, yeo., for the king and himself that Robert Fletcher of – , yeo., between 8 Oct. 1606 and 7 Oct. 1607 illegally followed the craft of mercer and grocer by selling to the king's lieges for gain, without 7 years of apprenticeship, and he craved that forfeit of £22 at the rate of 40s. a month be shared equally. Fletcher appeared on 13 Jan. 1608 before George Scroope, esq., Henry Lindley, Henry Anderson and Charles Wrenn, knts, Thomas Calverley, esq., and Clement Colmore, LL.D., JPs, demurred and pleaded not guilty. Robert Cooper as bishop's attorney-general for the king [etc.].

[space of 9.5 cms]

33) MEMO that at the general sessions at Durham on 7 Oct. 1607 Roger Trollopp, yeo., for the king and himself laid an information against Robert Carliell late of Gateside, yeo., that between 8 Oct. 1606 and 7 Oct. 1607 he pursued the trade of mercer and grocer at Gateside illegally for gain without serving 7 years of apprenticeship, and he claimed half of the forfeit. Now at the sessions on 13 Jan. 1608 before George Scroope, esq., Henry Lindley, Henry Anderson, Charles Wrenn, knts, Thomas Calverley, esq., and Clement Colmore,

LL.D., JPs, Robert Carliell appeared, demurred, and pleaded not guilty. Robert Cooper, bishop's attorney-general [etc.].

[space of 8 cms]

9d.] 34) Elsewhere at the sessions at Durham on 7 Oct. 1607 before Bp James, George Scroope, esq., Henry Lindley, Henry Anderson, Charles Wrenn, knts, Thomas Calverley, esq., and Clement Colmore, LL.D., JPs, it was presented on oath that whereas the king by letters patent under the exchequer seal appointed Bp James of Durham, John [Thornborough], bp of Bristol, William Morton, archdeacon of Durham, Henry Ewbancke, clerk, prebendary of Durham, John Barnes, Robert Cooper and Robert Kelway, esqs, or any two or more as commissioners to enquire by oath or otherwise into lands [etc.] belonging to William Blakiston of Blakeston, knt, as held at the date he was convicted as a papist recusant as specified in schedules annexed for valuation and to seize the same into the king's hand: and whereas Henry Ewbancke, clerk, William Morton, clerk, John Barnes and Robert Kelway, esqs, by this authority deputed under seal on 5 Oct. 1607 William Smith, a sheriff's bailiff assigned to them by John Conyers, knt, sheriff, with John Cooth, gen., William Guidott, gen., Toby Moiser, gen., William Collyns, John Walker, George Hirst and Charles Rawlings the task of seizing Blakiston's goods and chattels at Blakeston, Fulthorpe and elsewhere and taking them to Durham for delivery to the king by the sheriff of Durham: these on 6 Oct. 1607 took at Fulthorpe 19 horses, mares and geldings, a colt, 77 oxen, cows, bullocks and stirks and all his personal chattels. Later, however, William Blakiston, of Blakeston, knt, John Blakiston junior of Blakeston, gen., and William Partus of Blakeston, yeo., on 6 Oct. 1607 at Sedgefield riotously attacked Smith, Cooth, Guidott, Collins, Walker, Hirst and Rawlings and recovered the 18 horses, mares, geldings and colt. Moreover, Partus and George Blakiston late of Blakeston, gen., later the same day at Quarrington attacked Smith, Cooth, Guidott, Collins, Walker, Hirst and Rawlings: and George Blakiston, William Partus, Robert Blakiston late of Finchale, gen., Samuel Hopper of Shincliffe, yeo., Edward Mainsforth of Shincliffe, yeo., the wife of Lancelot Smith of Shincliffe and the wife of William Tuttings of Shincliffe, yeo., with 12 others unknown in warlike fashion on 6 Oct. at Shincliffe riotously assembled and attacked Smith, Guidott, Cooth, Collins, Walker, Hirst and Rawlings and recovered the 77 oxen, cows, bullocks and queys. Now at the general sessions on 13 Jan. 1608 William Blakiston, John Blakiston, Robert [sic] Partus, George Blakiston, Robert Blakiston, Samuel Hopper and Edward Mainsforth appeared, demurred and pleaded not guilty [etc.]. Robert Cooper, bishop's attorney-general [etc.].

70

[Durham CRO, Q/S/I 1, *m.17B*] Sessions at Durham on 30 March 5/41 James [*1608*] before Bp James, [......] Henry Lindley, Henry Anderson and Charles Wrenn, [......] Thomas Calverley, esq., Henry Ewbank [...... John] Fetherstonhaugh, esq., Henry Dethicke, LL.D., [......] Barnes, Thomas Riddle, esq., Robert Cooper, [......], JPs.

71

[m.43] Pleas and presentments at the general sessions at Durham on 29 June 6 James [1608] before Bp James, George Scroope, esq., Henry Lindley, Henry Anderson, Charles Wrenn, knts, Clement Colmore, LL.D., and Thomas Calverley, esq., JPs.

1) Stephen Kitching late of Shieldshaugh, co. Durham, yeo., on 29 May 1608 at South Shields broke the glass windows in the residence of Richard Matthew.

2) Valentine Johnson late of Skirningham, co. Durham, gen., and John Woodmans late of Skirningham, yeo., on 6 May 1608 at Skirningham assaulted William Robinson and Philip Sadler, servants of Richard Wheitley of Darlington, yeo., and took from their custody a door worth 5s.

3) Whereas Thomas Colmore of Bedlington, *co Durham, clerk, and John Skipsee of the same, yeo., on 3 May 1608 at Bedlington took from a close called *the Marsh Close* 2 ox-stirks and 2 quey-stirks belonging to Stephen Fenwick of Netherton, gen., and impounded the same in the common pound at Bedlington for the trespass of depasturing Colmore's grass, Fenwick later on 5 May 1608 by night broke the pound and drove away the stirks.

4) Whereas Thomas Colmore of Bedlington, clerk, and John Skipsee of the same, yeo., on 3 May 1608 at Bedlington took from a close called *the Marsh Close* 2 quey-stirks belonging to William Thompson of Netherton, yeo., and impounded them at Bedlington for the trespass of depasturing Colmore's grass, William Thompson later on 5 May 1608 by night broke the pound and drove away the livestock.

5) Thomas Wall junior late of Peak Field, co. Durham, yeo., on 29 April 1608 at Woodcroft tore down 3 yards of quickset hedge belonging to William Blackett and felled and carried away an elm tree worth 2s. growing within the hedge.

6) Stephen Kitching of Shieldshaugh, co. Durham, yeo., on 29 May 1608 with malice aforethought attacked Richard Mathew of South Shields, yeo., at Shieldshaugh in the Courthouse and struck him with a great stone held in his right hand, inflicting on his head a great wound 3 inches long by 1½ inches deep, and with another blow with the stone he inflicted another wound to the head 3 inches long and 1½ inches deep, and with another blow on the left ear a further wound 3 inches by 1½ inches, and inflicted 8 further wounds to the head, and Mathew lingered from 29 May until 13 June in danger of death.

7) George Watson late of Brotherlee, co. Durham, on 22 June 1608 at Brotherlee attacked Anne Watson wife of William Watson of Brotherlee, yeo.

8) Whereas by statute of 5 Edward VI it was enacted that if any person after 1 May 1551 maliciously struck another with a stick in church or cemetery or intended to do the same, on indictment by 12 men or on the evidence of 2 legal witnesses before a justice of assize, of oyer 43d.] and terminer I or JP in sessions, he should be condemned to lose an ear, and if the offender had already lost his ears he should be branded on the cheek with the letter F, so that he might be known as a fighter, and be excommunicated; nevertheless John Hall late of Hollenbush, co. Durham, gen., on 12 June 1608 at Lamesley in its church or chapel at time of divine service assaulted Michael Porter of Lamesley, gen., and struck him on the chest with a stick worth 1/2d.

[*space of 53 cms*]

44] 9) Elsewhere at the general sessions of the peace at Durham on 13 Jan. 1608 before George Scroope, esq., Henry Lindley, Henry Anderson, Charles Wrenn, knts, Thomas Calverley, esq., and Clement Colmore, LL.D., JPs, it was presented that John Craddock late of Gainford, co. Durham, clerk, on 20 Aug. 1607 west of Gainford forcibly blocked part of the king's highway leading from Barnard Castle by Gainford to Darlington by erecting a stone wall 120 yards long, namely "hath incroched streytned and stopt upp" the king's highway until the present [*13 Jan.*] and converted it to his own use, to the damage and nuisance of the inhabitants of Gainford and other lieges; now at the sessions at Durham on 29 June 1608 before Bp James, George Scrope, esq., Henry Lindley, Henry Anderson, Charles Wrenn, knts, Thomas Calverley, esq., and Clement Colmore, LL.D., JPs, John Craddock appeared in person and having heard the indictment, demurred and pleaded not guilty. Robert Cooper, esq., bishop's attorney-general [*etc.*]. Jurors were summoned for 12 Oct.

44d.] 10) Elsewhere at the general sessions of the peace at Durham on 13 Jan. 1608 before the above it was presented that John Cradock late of Gainford, clerk, on 20 Aug. 1607 blocked the road from Barnard Castle to Darlington by Gainford with a stone wall 20 yards long and diverted the road from its ancient course and converted the same to his own use [*etc.*]; at the present sessions John Cradock appeared in person and having heard the indictment [*etc. as above*].

[*space of 10 cms*]

45] 11) Elsewhere at the general sessions of the peace at Durham on 8 July 1607 before Henry Lindley, Charles Wrenn, knts, Thomas Calverley, esq., and Clement Colmore, LL.D., JPs, it was presented on oath that Henry Browne late of Darlington, tailor, from 1 Dec. 1606 until the present 8 July 1607 at Darlington practised the crafts of mercer and grocer illegally for gain, selling grocery and mercery wares to the king's subjects without having served 7 years of apprenticeship, contrary to the statute of 5 Elizabeth. Browne appeared at the general sessions on 30 March 1608 before Bp James, George Scroope, esq., Henry Lindley, Henry Anderson, Charles Wrenn, knts, Thomas Calverley, esq., and Clement Colmore, LL.D., JPs, and having heard the indictment, demurred and pleaded not guilty. Robert Cooper, esq., bishop's attorney-general [*etc.*]. Jurors were summoned for 29 June.

[*space of 17 cms*]

12) Elsewhere at the general sessions at Durham on 8 July 1607 [*as (11) above*] it was presented that John Morrell late of West Boldon, co. Durham, gen., with others on 1 July 1607 deliberately attacked Robert Maltbye, bailiff of the Chester ward, at West Boldon, cast him to the ground and struck at him with their hands and feet to the effusion of his blood, putting him in bodily fear, and contrary to the statutes on riots. Morrell appeared on 30 March 1608 before Bp James, George Scroope, esq., Henry Lindley, Henry Anderson, Charles Wrenn, knts, Thomas Calverley, esq., and Clement Colmore, LL.D., JPs, heard the indictment, demurred and pleaded not guilty. Robert Cooper, esq., bishop's attorney-general [*etc.*]. Jurors were summoned for 29 June.

[*space of 16 cms*]

[*m.45d.*] 13) MEMO that Roger Trollopp on behalf of the king and himself appeared before the JPs in Durham at the general sessions on 7 Oct. 1607 and laid an information that John Reede of Newcastle upon Tyne, yeo., between 8 Oct. 1606 and 7 Oct. 1607 at Darlington pursued the art of mercer and grocer illegally for gain, selling grocery and mercery without serving 7 years of apprenticeship, by which action the sum of £22 accrued to the king and Trollopp at the rate of forfeiture of 40s. a month, and Trollopp claimed half in accordance with the statute and sought the advice of court and the due process of law against Reede. Reede appeared in person and having heard the information demurred and pleaded not guilty. Robert Cooper, esq., bishop's attorney-general [*etc.*]. Jurors were summoned for 29 June.

[*space of 14 cms*]

14) Elsewhere at the general sessions at Durham on 8 July 1608 before Henry Lindley, Charles Wrenn, knts, Thomas Calverley, esq., and Clement Colmore, LL.D., JPs, it was presented on oath that Robert Gibson late of Stranton, co. Durham, yeo., between 20 Sept. 1606 and 8 July 1607 at Stranton engrossed from Christopher Corker of Castle Eden, yeo., a chaldron of barley worth £3 and from Philip Corker of Stranton, yeo., 16 bushels of barley worth 30s. and resold the same, contrary to the statute of 5 Edward VI. Gibson appeared at the sessions on 30 March, heard the indictment, demurred and pleaded not guilty. Robert Cooper, esq., bishop's attorney-general [*etc.*]. Jurors were summoned for 29 June.

[*space of 19 cms*]

[*m.46*] 15) MEMO that John Trotter for the king as well as for himself appeared in person in court before the JPs at Durham on 7 Oct. 1607 and laid an information that Henry Watson late of Wolsingham, co. Durham, yeo., between 1 Jan. and 7 Oct. 1607 at Wolsingham exercised the craft of tanner illegally for gain, selling tanned hides

without having served 7 years of apprenticeship. He claimed half of
the £18 which Watson should forfeit [etc.]. Watson appeared in
person and heard the information, demurred and pleaded not guilty.
Robert Cooper, esq., bishop's attorney-general [etc.]. Jurors were
summoned for 29 June.

[space of 11 cms]

16) MEMO that John Trotter for the king as well as for himself
appeared before the JPs in court at Durham on 7 Oct. 1607 and laid
an information that William Stobbes of Westgate, co. Durham, yeo.,
between 1 Jan. and 7 Oct. 1607 at Westgate illegally exercised the
craft of glover for gain without serving an apprenticeship of 7 years.
He claimed half of the £18 which Stobbes should forfeit [etc.].
William Stobbes appeared in person, demurred and pleaded not
guilty. Robert Cooper, esq., bishop's attorney-general [etc.]. Order to
the sheriff to summon jurors for 29 June.

[space of 11 cms]

17) MEMO that John Trotter for the king as well as for himself
appeared in person in court before the JPs at Durham on 7 Oct. 1607
and laid an information that George Robinson late of Bishop
Auckland, co. Durham, yeo., between 1 June and 20 July 1607
engrossed from George Trotter 2 chaldrons of barley worth £6 for
resale, contrary to the form of the statute. Trotter claimed half of the
fine of £6 for which Robinson was liable as the value of the
commodity and sought the advice of court and due process of law.
William Stobbes [sic] appeared in person and having heard the
information [etc.]. Robert Cooper, esq., bishop's attorney-general
[etc.]. Jurors were summoned for 29 June.

[6d.] 18) MEMO that John Trotter for the king as well as for himself laid an
information before the JPs at Durham on 7 Oct. 1607 that Nicholas
Toward of Wolsingham, co. Durham, yeo., between 1 June and 20
July 1607 engrossed from William Blackett at Stanhope 2 chaldrons
of barley worth £8 for resale, and he claimed half of the £8 for which
Toward was liable in forfeiture as the value of the commodity. He
sought the advice of court and due process of law. Toward appeared
in person and having heard the information [etc.]. Robert Cooper,
esq., bishop's attorney-general [etc.]. Jurors for 29 June.

19) Elsewhere at the general sessions at Durham on 13 Jan. 1608
before George Scroope, esq., Henry Lyndley, Charles Wrenn, knts,
Thomas Calverley, esq., and Clement Colmore, LL.D., JPs, it was
presented that John Jenyson of Walworth, co. Durham, esq., after 5
Nov. 1605 had a son born at W[alworth] in the parish of Heighington
and did not have him baptised by a lawful minister in open church
within the month, in contempt of God and the king. At the sessions
on 30 March 1608 Jenison appeared in person and having heard the
indictment pleaded not guilty [etc.]. Robert Cooper [etc.]. Jurors for
29 June.

72

Pleas and presentments at the general sessions at Durham on 12 Oct. 6 James [1608] before Bp James, George Scroope, esq., Henry Lindley, Henry Anderson, Charles Wrenn, knts, Thomas Calverley, esq., Clement Colmore, LL.D., Henry Dethick, LL.B., and Henry Ewbanke, clerk, JPs.

1) Thomas Appulbie of Crossgate, [Durham], between 1 Aug. and 10 Oct. 1608 at Durham city bought and engrossed from persons unknown 5 bushels of barley worth 13s. 4d. and 5 bushels of oats worth 6s. 8d. for resale.

2) Nicholas Writer of Crossgate, [Durham], yeo., between 1 Aug. and 10 Oct. 1608 at Durham city engrossed from persons unknown 5 bushels of barley worth 13s. 4d. and 5 bushels of oats worth 6s. 8d. for resale.

3) John Dossey of Stockton, co. Durham, yeo., between 1 June and 1 Oct. 1608 at Norton engrossed from persons unknown 100 bushels of barley worth £15 and 100 bushels of oats worth £5 for resale.

4) William Newton of Gilesgate, [Durham], yeo., between 1 Aug. and 10 Oct. 1608 at Durham city bought and engrossed from persons unknown 5 bushels of barley worth 13s. 4d. and 5 bushels of oats worth £5 [corrected from 6s. 8d.] for resale.

5) Thomas Whitfeild of Framwellgate, Durham, yeo., between 1 Aug. and 10 Oct. 1608 at Durham city engrossed from persons unknown 5 bushels of barley worth 13s. 4d. and 5 bushels of oats worth 6s. 8d. for resale.

6) John Pattinson of Durham city, shoemaker, between 1 Aug. and 10 Oct. 1608 at Durham city engrossed from persons unknown 5 bushels of barley worth 13s. 4d. and 5 bushels of oats worth 6s. 8d. for resale.

7) John Ingledewe of Claypath, Durham, yeo., between 1 Aug. and 10 Oct. 1608 at Durham city engrossed from persons unknown 5 bushels of barley worth 13s. 4d. and 5 bushels of oats worth 6s. 8d. for resale.

8) Matthew Gray of Thimbleby, co. Durham, yeo., and John Coitsworth of Snowhope Close, co. Durham, yeo., on 20 July 1608 took at Bollihope from Anthony Hopper 28 sheep which were depasturing the grass of John Fetherstonhalghe and other free tenants of Bollihope and impounded them at Bollihope until Hopper made satisfaction; but Anthony Hopper late of White Kirkley House, co. Durham, yeo., and Isabel his wife, John Hopper of the same, yeo., and William Hopper of Wolsingham, yeo., on 21 July assembled riotously and broke into the pound at Bollihope and recovered the 28 sheep.

9) Thomas Joplinge of Croxdale, co. Durham, yeo., on 21 Aug. 1606 and thereafter at divers times to 29 Aug. kept for gain a tippling-house at Croxdale without licence and allowed Robert [Bucke] of Benfieldside junior, Arthur Jackson of Holmside *loninge*, lab., Percival

Harbotle of Chester, yeo., John Bainbrigg of Gellesfield, yeo., and others to play cards and drink, and John Joplinge played cards, drank and disturbed the peace.

10) Adam Hogg late of Gellesfield, co. Durham, alehouse keeper, on 21 Aug. 1608 and from then until 29 Aug. for gain allowed Robert Bucke junior of Benfieldside, Arthur Jackson of *Helmefeild loninge*, lab., Percival Harbotle of Chester, yeo., John Bainbrigg of Gellesfield, yeo., and others to play cards and drink, to the disturbance of the peace.

11) Thomas Pearson senior of Durham city, mercer, Henry Bee of Shincliffe, yeo., and Philip Cooper late of Durham city, lab., on 26 Sept. 1608 at Shincliffe assembled riotously and Cooper and Bee attacked Robert Martin, and Cooper struck him on the head with a pitchfork inflicting a wound 1 inch deep | and 1 inch broad, and Bee struck him with a rake on the face and about the ears.

12) Thomas Pearson senior of Durham city, mercer, on 26 Sept. 1608 broke into the close at Shincliffe being the free tenement of Adam Newton, esq., dean, and the chapter of Durham and ejected Lionel Martin, then farmer of the same, and disseised the dean and chapter, who remain disseised to the present [*22 Oct.*].

13) Thomas Gray late of Staindrop, co. Durham, esq., Francis Thornhill late of Staindrop, gen., John Gray late of the same, gen., Brackenburie Gray late of the same, gen., Thomas Rowbotham late of the same, yeo., George Langstaffe late of Raby, yeo., and John Richardson late of Staindrop, shoemaker, on 9 Sept. 1608 assembled riotously at Staindrop and attacked Robert Hardware and Anthony Metcalfe, servants of Francis Brackenburie, esq., and took a stook of barley worth 20s. belonging to Francis Brackenburie and in the possession of Hardware and Metcalfe.

14) Michael Thompson of Brandon walls, co. Durham, yeo., Matthew Currey late of the same, yeo., and Thomas Blumer late of the same, yeo., on 13 Sept. 1608 at Smallburn in the forest of Weardale assembled riotously and attacked Nicholas Herrison, and Thompson struck Herrison with a gavelock held in both hands on divers parts of the body to the shedding of blood.

15) Matthew Currey late of Brandon walls, yeo., and Thomas Blumer late of the same, yeo., on 13 Sept. 1608 on the order of Michael Thompson late of Brandon walls, yeo., their master, removed at Smallburn in Weardale forest a pile of stones worth 2s. belonging to George Emerson.

16) Whereas by statute of 8 Henry VI against disseisin [*etc.*], Robert Watson late of Staindrop, co. Durham, yeo., and Thomas Rowbotham late of Staindrop, yeo., on 20 June 1608 in *the twenty acres* at Raby, then the king's free tenement, ejected Francis Brackenburie, esq., and Robert Hardware, farmers, and retain the said parcel of land to the present.

17) Thomas Gray of Staindrop, esq., on 8 Sept. 1608 at Staindrop attacked Francis Brackenburie, esq.

Od.]

18) John Lancaster late of Headlam, co. Durham, gen., on 10 Sept. 1608 broke the close of Francis Brackenburie, esq., at Ingleton and removed 3¹/2 stooks of wheat worth 2s. belonging to the same in a waggon drawn by horses and oxen yoked.

[m.41]   19) John Richardson of Bishop Auckland, co. Durham, on 1 Oct. 1606, being seised of an agricultural messuage in Newton Cap and 20 acres arable, for gain converted the same to pasture by enclosing 10 acres with ditches and hedges.

20) Dorothy Grice late of Bishop Auckland, widow, on 1 Oct. 1606, being seised of an agricultural messuage in Newton Cap and 16 acres arable, for gain converted 8 acres by enclosure to pasture.

21) Roger Smirthwaite late of Pixley Hill, yeo., on 1 Oct. 1606, being seised of an agricultural messuage in Pixley Hill and 8 acres of arable, for gain enclosed 2 acres and converted them to pasture.

[space of 9 cms]

[m.41d., blank]

72A

[m.42]   Pleas and presentments at Durham on 12 Oct. 1608 before Bp James, George Scroope, esq., Henry Lindley, knt, Thomas Calverley, esq., and Clement Colmore, LL.D., JPs.

1) Elsewhere at the sessions at Durham on 7 Oct. 1606 before Bp James, Cuthbert Pepper, knt, chancellor of Durham, George Scroope, esq., Henry Lindley, knt, and Thomas Calverley, esq., JPs, it was ordered the sheriff to summon Thomas Forser late of Harbour House, co. Durham, esq., before the JPs on 7 Jan. next to answer divers indictments. At these sessions the sheriff, John Conyers, knt, returned that Thomas had nothing in his bailiwick. An order *non omittas* for Forser's arrest was issued for his appearance on 8 April 1607, when the sheriff returned that he was not to be found. *Sicut prius* then was issued for 8 July, and again for 7 Oct. and 13 Jan. 1608, when on his continued default the sheriff was ordered to exact Forser in the county court for 29 June. The sheriff then returned that the exigents had been proclaimed in the county court at Durham on 21 March, 18 April, 23 May and 20 June 1608. The series was continued for 12 Sept., when on his non-appearance the bishop's coroners, John Hawkins and John Pattinson, outlawed Forser.

[m.42d.]   2) Elsewhere at the gaol delivery at Durham on [9] Aug. 1608 before Bp James, James Altham, knt, a baron of the king's exchequer, and Edward Phelipps, knt, a king's serjeant at law, fellow justices of gaol delivery and of the peace, it was presented that Robert Tweddell late of Thorpe Thewles, co. Durham, yeo., on 1 Jan. 1606, being in possession of an agricultural messuage in Thorpe Thewles and 50 acres arable, did enclose 40 acres with a ditch and quickset hedge and for gain converted the same to pasture. Later at the sessions on 12 Oct. 1608 before Bp James, George Scroope, esq., Henry Lindley, knt, and Clement Colmore, LL.D., JPs, Tweddle appeared and demurred

[*etc.*]. Robert Cooper, esq., bishop's attorney-general [*etc.*]. Order to the sheriff to summon a jury for 11 Jan.
[*space of 11 cms*]

73

[6] Pleas and presentments at Durham on 11 Jan. 6 James [*1609*] before Bp James, George Scroope, esq., Henry Lindley, Henry Anderson, Charles Wrenn, knts, Thomas Calverley, esq., Clement Colmore, LL.D., Henry Dethicke, LL.B., Henry Ewbank, clerk, Henry Tonge, John Fetherstonhalgh, Robert Cooper and John Barnes, esqs, JPs.

1) Christopher Rawdon late of Barmpton, co. Durham, miller, and Cuthbert Graunge late of the same, yeo., on 13 Oct. 1608 being by night in the house of George Hackfurthe at Haughton[-le-Skerne], namely an alehouse, drank to excess by leave of Hackfurthe and behaved in a suspicious fashion.

2) Ralph Currey late of Bishop Auckland, co. Durham, yeo., from 1 Jan. 1608 to the date of the enquiry [*11 Jan. 1609*] at Bishop Auckland pursued the craft of glover illegally for gain and sold to the public without undergoing a 7 years' apprenticeship.

3) Edward Wall of Ryton, co. Durham, and John Litle of Winlaton, Gregory Hutcheson of Ryton and Robert Clerke of Ryton Woodside, Roger Oliver of Winlaton, John Grame of the same, Robert Clughe of the same, Thomas Merreman of the same, Henry Maddison of Ryton Woodside, Lancelot Carrocke of the same, Christopher Wilson of Whickham and Robert Carlill of the same, yeomen, on 1 Oct. 1608 kept alehouses for gain without leave of the JPs, contrary to the form of the statute.

4) Robert Duckett junior late of Great Burdon, co. Durham, yeo., on 2 Dec. 1608 at Little Burdon attacked Thomas Hutchinson and Agnes his wife.

5) Anthony Eastegate of Bishop Auckland, yeo., on 27 Nov. 1608 and before and after kept a tippling-house in Bishop Auckland without licence and allowed Robert Nichol, Henry Baldridge and Thomas Harperley to drink excessively and misconduct themselves and Nicholl and Baldridge attacked Harperley.

6) Lionel Swinborne of Gateside, yeo., on 26 Dec. 1608 attacked William Spaine and when Robert Tayler and Cuthbert Blackwell, township constables, ordered Swinborne in the name of the king to keep the peace Swinburne used scandalous and opprobrious words, namely: "Shette in the king's face and all his officers".

7) William Barwicke late of Norton, co. Durham, lab., on 11 Dec. 1608 at Norton stole 3 geese together worth 21d. from William Gaire. Matthew Corner of Wolviston, blacksmith, harboured him at his home the same day, knowing of the theft, and received the geese.

8) William Barwicke late of Norton, co. Durham, lab., on 11 Dec. 1608 at Norton stole 2 geese together worth 16d. from Thomas Chipchase. Matthew Corner of Wolviston, blacksmith, harboured him the same

day, knowing of the theft, and received the geese.

[m.36d.] 9) William Bainbrigg late of Whickham, co. Durham, yeo., on 29 June 1608 was licenced by the JPs in a bond of £10 to keep an alehouse at Whickham. Gabriel Natteresse and Anthony Acheson stood surety in £5 each. Later on 6 Oct. 1608 and before and after William allowed John Bainbrigg, Robert Comyn and Guy Bainbrigg to disturb the peace.

10) William Bainbrigg late of Whickham, yeo., on 6 Oct. 1608 at Whickham was a common brawler and disturber of the peace.

11) George Goundrie late of Darlington, yeo., on 20 Sept. 1607 at Darlington was and is a common brawler and disturber of the peace.

12) Enquiry that Anne Liddell wife of Roger Liddell of Durham city, tanner, on 11 Dec. 1608 at Crook Hall stole an iron gavelock worth 6d. from Francis Billingham, gen., from his mill.

13) Enquiry that George Hodgshon late of Bishop Auckland, co. Durham, yeo., on 24 Nov. 1608 stole a pair of leggings worth 4d., a pair of curtains worth 6d. and a shirt worth 2d. from William Bayles, being found in Bayles's house.

[m.37] 14) Elsewhere at the sessions at Durham on 7 Oct. 1607 before Bp James, George Scroope, esq., and Henry Lyndley, knt, JPs, it was presented on oath that whereas George Fairehaire late of Ford, co. Durham, gen., at the general sessions at Durham on 7 Oct. 1606 before Bp James, Cuthbert Pepper, knt, chancellor of Durham, and George Scroope, esq., JPs, was charged that he being 16 years and more from 1 May to 1 Oct. 1606 at Durham city absented himself from the parish church of Sedgefield or any other church or chapel without permission. He was ordered to surrender to the sheriff before the next sessions but failed to appear before George Scroope, esq., Henry Lyndley, knt, and Clement Colmore, LL.D., JPs, on 7 Jan. 1607, when it was shown that he was native-born, over 16, and resident at Ford in the parish of Lanchester and a recusant papist. At these sessions he was convicted of non-attendance at church, he not having cause such as imprisonment, a warrant from the king or six or more of the privy council, or sickness etc., contrary to the statute of 35 Elizabeth. Later, on Wed., 11 Jan. 1609, before Bp James, George Scroope, esq., and Henry Lyndley, knt, JPs, Fairehaire appeared, demurred and affirmed that he had been at his home at Ford on 10 Feb. 1609, within 40 days after the indictment. Robert Cooper, bishop's attorney-general [etc.]. Jurors for 19 April.
[space of 7 cms]

[m.37d.] 15) Elsewhere at the sessions on 13 Jan. 1608 before George Scroope, esq., Henry Lyndley, Henry Anderson, and Charles Wrenn, knts, JPs, it was presented on oath that George Fairehaire, a persistant papist of Ford, gen., after 5 Nov. 1605 failed to have his son, born at Ford, "baptized by a lawful minister" at Lanchester parish church or elsewhere within a month of birth, contrary to the form of the statute. Later on Wed., 11 Jan. 1609, before Bp James, George

Scroope, esq., and Henry Lyndley, knt, Fairehaire appeared in person
and demurred [etc.]. Robert Cooper [etc.] Jurors for 19 April.
[space of 10 cms]
16) Elsewhere at the general sessions on 12 Oct. 1608 before Bp James,
George Scroope, esq., Henry Lyndley, Henry Anderson, knts, Thomas
Calverley, esq., and Clement Colmore, LL.D., JPs, it was presented
that Matthew Gray of Thimbleby, co. Durham, yeo., and John
Coatsworth of Snowhope Close, yeo., on 20 July 1608 seized from
the goods of Anthony Hopper at Bollihope and took 28 sheep which
were depasturing the grass of John Fetherstonhalgh, esq., and other
free tenants of Bollihope and tried to impound them in the common
pound at Bollihope until Hopper made full satisfaction for the
trespass. Afterwards Hopper, late of White Kirkley house, yeo., Isabel
his wife, John Hopper of the same, yeo., and William Hopper of
Wolsingham, yeo,, on 21 July assembled, broke into the pound at
Bollihope and recovered the 28 sheep. Now at the sessions on 11 Jan.
1609 before Bp James, George Scroope, esq., Henry Lyndley, Henry
Anderson and Charles Wrenn, knts, Anthony Hopper appeared in
person with Isabel, John and William and demurred and pleaded not
guilty. Robert Cooper [etc.]. Jurors for 20 April [sic].
8]   17) Elsewhere at the assizes at Durham [on 9 Aug. 1608] before Bp
James, James Altham, knt, a baron of the king's exchequer, and
Edward Phelipps, knt, serjeant at law, and fellow justices of assize and
oyer and terminer, it was presented that Thomas Forser of Harbour
House, gen., at the general sessions of the peace at Durham on 7 Oct.
1606 before Bp James, Cuthbert Pepper, knt, chancellor of Durham,
and George Scroope, esq., JPs, was indicted that being over 16 years
he did live at Harbour House from 1 May to 1 Oct. 1606 but absented
himself from church at Kelloe or elsewhere, without having leave. He
was ordered to surrender to the sheriff before the next general
sessions. When Forser failed to surrender himself at the next sessions
before George Scroope, esq., Henry Lyndley, knt, and Clement
Colmore, LL.D., JPs, on 7 Jan. 1607 he was convicted as a papist
recusant, for not repairing to any church and forbearing from divine
service. Later on 29 April, and 40 days of grace following his
conviction, Forser moved from Harbour House beyond the 5-mile
limit to Neasham, contrary to the statute of 35 Elizabeth for the
restraining of popish recusants to some certain places of abode. Now
on 19 April 1609 before Bp James, George Scroope, esq., and Thomas
Calverley, esq., JPs, Forser appeared in person, demurred and denied
moving from Harbour House and put himself on his country. Robert
Cooper [etc.].
[space of 8 cms]
8d.] 18) Elsewhere at the general sessions at Durham on 12 Oct. 1608
before Bp James, George Scroope, esq., Henry Lyndley, knt, Thomas
Calverley, esq., and Clement Colmore, LL.D., JPs, it was presented on
oath that John Dossey of Stockton, co. Durham, between 1 June and

1 Oct. 1608 at Norton bought and engrossed from divers unknown 100 bushels of barley worth £15 and 5 [? *100*] bushels of oats worth £5 for resale, and on 11 Jan. 1608 before the same justices Dossey appeared in person, demurred and pleaded not guilty [*etc.*]. Robert Cooper [*etc.*]

[*space of 12.5 cms*]

19) Elsewhere at the general sessions at Durham on 11 Jan. 1609 before Bp James, George Scroope, esq., Henry Lyndley, knt, Thomas Calverley, esq., and Clement Colmore, JPs, it was presented on oath that William Bainbrigg late of Whickham, co. Durham, yeo., on 6 Oct. 1608 at Whickham was a common brawler and disturber of the king's peace and a trouble-maker. On the same day Bainbrigg appeared in person, demurred and pleaded not guilty [*etc.*]. Robert Cooper [*etc.*].

[*m.39*]   20) Elsewhere at the general sessions at Durham on 11 Jan. 1609 before the above it was presented on oath that on 29 June 1608 William Bainbrigg, yeo., late of Whickham, was licenced as an alehouse keeper in a bond of £10, his sureties, Gabriel Nattres and Anthony Acheson, standing in bond of £5 each. Later Bainbrigg on 6 Oct. 1608 and later allowed John Bainbrigg, Robert Comyn and Guy Bainbrigg and others to play cards, drink and misconduct themselves to the disturbance of the peace. William appeared the same day [*11 Jan.*], demurred and pleaded not guilty [*etc.*]. Robert Cooper [*etc.*].

[*space of 15 cms*]

21) Elsewhere at the general sessions at Durham on 11 Jan. 1609 before Bp James, George Scroope, esq., Henry Lindley, Charles Wrenn, knts, Thomas Calverley, esq., and Clement Colmore, LL.D., JPs in Durham and Sadberge, it was presented on oath that George Goundrie late of Darlington, yeo., on 20 Sept. 1607 at Darlington was a common brawler and disturber of the peace and a common mischief-maker. Goundrie appeared the same day, demurred and pleaded not guilty [*etc.*]. Robert Cooper [*etc.*].

[*m.39d., blank*]

74

[*m.34*]   Pleas and presentments at the general sessions of the peace at Durham on 29 April 7 James [*1609*] before Bp James, Richard Hutton, serjeant at law, chancellor of Durham, George Scroope, esq., Henry Lindley, Charles Wren, knts, Thomas Calverley, esq., Emanuel Barnes, STP, Clement Colemore, LL.D., Henry Dethicke, LL.B., George Tonge, George Lightefote, John Heathe, John Barnes and Robert Cooper, esqs, JPs.

1) Enquiry whether John Cooke late of Medomsley, co. Durham, yeo., and James Maddinson late of Ebchester, yeo., on 9 Nov. 1608 at Medomsley stole a brown cow worth 50s. from Thomas Wakefeilde.

2) John Machel late of Layton, co. Durham, yeo., Margaret his wife, John Harborne late of Layton, lab., and Elizabeth Henman late of

Layton, spinster, with others unknown assembled riotously to the terror of the lieges on 26 March 1609 at Layton and made an affray against William L[ynn], John Lynn, William Wilkinson and Ralph Waun, and John Machol struck William Lynn, he being lame and impotent and riding on a mare, and wounded him with a long fork and threw him from his mare to the ground; and John Machel and Margaret his wife, John Hartborne and Elizabeth Henman recovered 120 sheep, 10 cows and 2 stirks which William Lynn, John Lynn, William Wilkinson and Ralph Waun had tried to impound for damage to their closes at Layton.

3) John Machel late of Layton, yeo., Margaret his wife, and Elizabeth Henman of the same, spinster, on 5 April 1609 at Layton riotously attacked Cuthbert Smithe and Robert Smithe his son and recovered 6 cows which they had tried to impound for damage to a close at Layton called *the Bowgarthes*.

4) William Watson late of Thorpe Thewles, co. Durham, yeo., on 2 Feb. 1609 at Thorpe Thewles attacked Matthew Gray, striking him on the mouth.

5) John Machell late of Layton, yeo., Margaret his wife, Anthony Snawden late of the same, lab., and Elizabeth Henman late of the same, spinster, with others unknown assembled to the terror of the lieges on 28 March 1609 at Layton and attacked William Wilkinson, Ralph Waun and Robert Wilkinson junior; and Margaret struck Ralph Waun with an implement and with her hands and tore his clothes and Elizabeth struck Robert Wilkinson with a stick.

6) John Machell late of Layton, yeo., Anthony Snawden late of the same, lab., and Thomas Robinson late of the same, with others unknown, assembled to the terror of the lieges on 29 March 1609 at Layton and assaulted Robert Wilkinson, William Wilkinson and William Lynn and recovered 80 sheep which they were trying to impound for damage done in a close at Layton called *Milne pele*.

7) Robert Cuthbert late of Kibblesworth, co. Durham, yeo., on 4 April 1609 at Lamesley attacked Martin Wheatley and struck him with a coal-gad worth 2d. on various parts of the body and threw him to the ground.

8) John Machel late of Layton, yeo., and John Harborne late of the same, lab., on Sun. 26 March 1609 violently broke the close of William Lynn, John Lynn, William Wilkinson and Ralph Waun at *lee Milnehill outlying* and Deanham close at Layton and destroyed the newly-repaired fences and ditches.

34d.] 9) Enquiry whether Anthony Snawdon late of Layton, lab., and John Harborne late of Sedgefield, yeo., on 25 March 1609 violently entered the close of Robert Wilkinson at Layton called *Greenehills* and destroyed 100 feet of newly-erected fence with picks and mattocks and attacked Robert, and Snawden wounded Wilkinson with a fork.

10) Enquiry whether John Machell late of Layton, yeo., and John Harburne late of the same, lab., on Sun., 26 March 1609, during the

time of divine service broke the close of Robert Wilkinson senior at Layton at *Greenehills* and destroyed 100 feet of fence and ditch with picks and forks.

11) Enquiry whether Anthony Snawden late of Layton, lab., on 24 March 1609 broke into the close of William Lynn, John Lynn, William Wilkinson and Ralph Waun at Layton called *lee Milnehill* and depastured it with his cows, sheep and other livestock, joined by animals of John Machell, his master.

12) Enquiry whether Anthony Snawden late of Layton, lab., on 24 March 1609 broke the close of Robert Wilkinson senior called *Greenehills* at Layton at the instance of John Machell and destroyed 100 feet of fence with picks and mattocks and depastured it with 20 sheep belonging to John Machell.

13) Enquiry whether John Machell late of Layton, yeo., on 24 March 1609 broke the close of Robert Wilkinson senior called *Greenehills* at Layton and destroyed 100 feet of newly-built fences and ditches with picks and mattocks.

14) Enquiry whether John Machell late of Layton, yeo., and John Harborne late of the same, lab., on Sun., 26 March 1609, in time of divine service, broke the closes of William Lynn, John Lynn and Richard Waun at Layton called *Thorneclose, Coweclose and Calfeclose*, and destroyed the fences and ditches with picks and mattocks.

15) Matthew Gray late of Thimbleby, co. Durham, yeo., John Sigswicke late of Thorpe Thewles, yeo., and George Iley late of the same, yeo., on 2 Feb. 1609 riotously assembled at Thorpe Thewles at Stonyhirst and attacked William Watson, and George Iley struck him on the back of the head with a sword worth 4s., giving him a mortal wound 4 inches long by 2 inches deep; and John Sigswicke ran him through the left arm with a sword worth 4s., inflicting a wound 2 inches by 1 inch deep; and Mathew Gray struck him on the right little finger with a dagger worth 12s., inflicting a wound 1 inch by a half inch. Furthermore, Gray, Sigswicke and Iley struck Watson on other parts of the body so that he lingered from 2 Feb. to 2 March 1609 and his life was despaired of.

16) Ralph Harbotle late of Chester[-le-Street], co. Durham, gen., and Ralph Midelton of Seaton, gen., on 3 April 1609 at Ravensworth at the White house assembled riotously and attacked Thomas Marley, cast him to the ground and kicked his guts.

[m.35] 17) Whereas John Fetherstonhalghe, a JP in co. Durham, ordered by warrant of 17 April 1609 that George Emmerson, bailiff of Stanhope park, and all other bailiffs and officers arrest Edward Emmerson late of Gate Castle, yeo., and have him in safe custody to answer before him for divers trespasses committed in the park: later on 18 April 1609 by virtue of this warrant Richard Emmerson as bailiff arrested Edward in Stanhope park and tried to take him before the magistrate, but Edward attacked Richard and freed himself.
[*m.35d., blank*]

75

[2] Pleas and presentments at the general sessions of the peace at Durham on 12 July 7 James [1609] before George Scroope, esq., Henry Lindley, George Selbye, Charles Wrenn, knts, Thomas Calverley, esq., Clement Colmore, LL.D., Henry Dethick, LL.B., John Barnes and Robert Cooper, esqs, JPs.

1) Robert Middleton late of Thorpe Thewles, co. Durham, yeo., between 1 Sept. and 30 Nov. 1608 at Thorpe Thewles bought from John Siggesworth 6 stirks worth 60s. each and 10 cows worth £4 each and resold the same within 5 weeks.

2) Robert Kitchin late of Newton Hansard, co. Durham, yeo., between 14 July and 31 Aug. 1608 at Hartburn bought from William Garre 25 stirks worth 40s. each and resold the same within 5 weeks.

3) John Hickson late of Hurworth, co. Durham, yeo., between 1 Sept. and 31 Dec. 1608 at Stotfold bought from William Mosse 20 oxen worth £5 each and resold the same within 5 weeks.

4) Guy Watson late of Brotherlee, co. Durham, yeo., on 25 March 1608 with force and arms broke the close of the bishop of Durham at Stanhope and cut down in the wood and carried away an ash tree worth – .

5) Richard Hall late of Black Dene, co. Durham, yeo., on 25 March 1608 broke the close of the bishop of Durham at Stanhope and cut down in the wood and carried away an ash tree worth – .

6) Roger Fetherstonhalgh late of – , co. Durham, yeo., on 25 March 1608 broke the close of the bishop of Durham at Stanhope and cut down in the wood and carried away 2 ash trees worth – .

7) Peter Wright late of Billing Shield, co. Durham, yeo., on 25 March 1608 broke the close of the bishop of Durham at Stanhope and cut down in the wood and carried away an ash tree worth – .

8) Robert Kitchin late of Newton Hansard, co. Durham, yeo., on 4 June 1608 carried a gun loaded with shot and gunpowder at Newton Hansard and shot and killed a hare.

9) The same on 25 March 1609 at Newton Hansard shot and killed a hare.

10) The same on 11 June 1609 at Newton Hansard shot and killed a hare.

11) John Wethereld late of Middleton Row, co. Durham, yeo., between 1 May 1609 and the date of enquiry [12 July] bought at Durham city from various persons unknown 100 stones of wool at 10s. a stone, contrary to the statute of 5 Edward VI.

12) John Tuting late of – , co. Durham, yeo., on 1 Dec. 1608 at Stanhope hunted 10 partridges with a setting dog and killed the same.

13) Whereas John Conyers, knt, sheriff of Durham, by sealed warrant of – April 1609 ordered Robert Maltby, his bailiff of the Chester ward, to arrest William Browne to appear at Durham county court on 1 May to answer Richard Mathew for a debt of 35s.; later on 31 May

1609 at South Shields Maltby would have taken Browne to gaol until he found sureties to appear in the county court, but [*illegible...*], lab., and Denise his wife with 6 others unknown assembled riotously and attacked Maltby and rescued Browne.

[*m.32d.*] 14) John Bradley of Staindrop, co. Durham, miller, Robert Dickson of the same, yeo., and Francis Baley of the same, yeo., between 8 Sept. and Martinmas [*11 Nov. 1608*] took and killed salmon and fry worth 10s. in the River Tees and elsewhere, contrary to the form of the statute.

15) Richard Owde late of Ravensworth, co. Durham, yeo., Thomas Owde late of Ryton, yeo., Thomas Cuthbert late of Ravensworth, yeo., and Anthony Cuthbert late of Ryton, yeo., malefactors, on 5 June 1609 with sticks and gads assembled illegally at Whickham at the washing pool and attacked Robert Foster, servant of Thomas Merley, wounded him and put him in fear for his life.

16) George Herrington late of – in the demesne of Staindrop, co. Durham, yeo., and Christopher Finley late of – in the same, between 8 Sept. and Martinmas 1608 took and killed salmon and fry worth – in the River Tees and elsewhere, contrary to the form of the statute.

17) William Blacket late of Lynesack, co. Durham, yeo., on 1 May 1609 and before and since namely from 1 Jan. 1609 to 1 July following, at Stanhope in Weardale, Lynesack, Bedlam, Bishopley, Wolsingham, Burnhope, Rookhope and elsewhere in the forest of Weardale broke into the free warren of the bishop of Durham and hunted with setting dogs, nets and other engines and killed partridges, pheasants and other game birds, contrary to the form of the statute.

18) John Robson of Chester-le-Street, co. Durham, yeo., on 3 Feb. 1609 broke the close of the bishop of Durham at Chester-le-Street called *Chester Oaks* and cut down and carried off an oak tree.

19) William Wheateley late of Chester-le-Street, yeo., on 11 Nov. 1608 broke the close of the bishop of Durham at Chester called *Chester Oaks* and felled and removed 2 oak trees.

20) William Penn late of Chester-le-Street, yeo., on 13 Nov. 1608 broke the close of the bishop of Durham at *Chester Oaks* and felled and removed 2 oak trees.

21) Thomas Stowle late of – , yeo., on – 1608 broke the close of the bishop of Durham at Chester and felled and carried off 2 oak trees worth 40s.

22) Cuthbert Midleton of Hetton-le-Hill, co. Durham, gen., on 6 July 1609 at Pittington in the house of Henry Anderson, knt, attacked Robert Dearham, gen., and slapped him twice on the face.

23) James Greene late of Thorpe Thewles, co. Durham, yeo., on 1 June 1609 and before and after at Thorpe Thewles obstinately on his own authority, without leave of any magistrates, kept a common tippling-house and allowed John Kendell to drink immoderately and permitted unlawful games.

24) William Jackson junior late of Broom House, co. Durham, yeo., on

24 June 1609 at Stanhope in open market assaulted William Snathe and struck him on the chest.

'] 25) Whereas the vills of Hilton, Ingleton, Killerby, Morton, Summerhouse, Denton and Darlington were ancient townships and from time immemorial their inhabitants had a common way for horse and foot, carriage and droving at all times of the year, the said road leading to Wackerfield and thence by the common king's highway to the coal pits called *Grewborne* and *Ganles pitt* and thence to Wackerfield; and whereas Bernard Bowes late of Wackerfield, yeo., George Bowes late of Wackerfield, yeo., John Bassnet late of Wackerfield, yeo., Henry Morecock late of Wackerfield, yeo., Bartholomew Morfote of Wackerfield, yeo., Christopher Foreman late of Wackerfield, yeo., John Simson late of Wackerfield, yeo., and Christopher Sigswicke late of Wackerfield, yeo., assembled riotously with 20 other unknown malefactors on 30 April 1609 in a close called *the East Field of Wackerfield* and blocked with fences and ditches the common highway from Wackerfield to the common way to *Spitlefeilde* and thence to the coalpits; and John Hutcheson of Killerby, John Carlile of Denton, Peter Merley of Hilton, yeomen, and Richard Birckbecke of Morton, gen., Richard Herreson of Summerhouse, yeo., and Christopher Shawe of Ingleton, yeo., going with their carts from these several places to the East Field at Wackerfield with the intent to proceed with their carts by the common ways to the coal pits of *Grewborne* and *Ganlespitts* and back were impeded against prescription, to the great injury of all the inhabitants of Hilton, Ingleton, Killerby, Morton, Summerhouse, Denton and Darlington and all the other townships accustomed to use these roads to the coal pits, contrary to the form of the statute against riots.

26) William Jackson junior late of Broom House, yeo., and Christopher Jackson late of the same, yeo., on 1 July 1609 with force and arms at Durham city in open market attacked William Snathe.

27) Whereas John Startforth sued in the king's court at Durham a writ of *capias* directed to the sheriff to arrest Percival Harbotle late of Tanfield, co. Durham, gen., to have him to answer before the justices at Durham on 13 July in a plea of debt for £80, and by virtue of a writ of John Conyers, knt, sheriff of Durham, dated – 1609 an order was issued to Robert Maltbie, bailiff of Chester ward, together with Ralph Suerties of Ravensworth, gen., George Wheatley of Ravensworth, yeo., Robert Robson of Urpeth, yeo., and Richard Bell of Durham, yeo., his special bailiffs, to arrest Harbotle and have him in custody to appear on 13 July; accordingly Robert Maltbie, Ralph Suertes, George Wheatley and Robert Robson on 9 June 1609 arrested Harbotle at Ravensworth and would have led him to Durham gaol until he found sureties to appear at Durham. Harbotle, however, on the same day attacked Maltbie, Suerties, Wheateley and Robson at Ravensworth and hit Wheateley on the head with a stick and maltreated Maltbie, [*etc.*], to the delay of the execution of their office.

28) Christopher Hudspeth late of Durham city, yeo., on 5 June 1609 at Durham city for his own gain and without leave of the JPs on 5 June between midnight and 1 a.m. permitted Hugh Rowle of Durham city, waller, George Blithman of the same, yeo., Toby Hudspeth of the same, yeo., and John Harrison of the same, yeo., to tipple and drink in his house at Durham, contrary to the form of the statute.

29) Ingram Maugham of Durham city, yeo., on 5 June 1609 at Durham city for his own gain and without licence kept a convivial house and allowed Hugh Rowle of Durham, waller, George Blithman of the same, yeo., Toby Hudspeth of the same, yeo., and John Herrison of the same, yeo., to tipple and drink between 10 p.m. and midnight [etc.].

30) William Nicholson late of Bishop Auckland, co. Durham, lab., on 4 May 1609 with force and arms broke into the house of Robert Read of Bishop Auckland at Bishop Auckland and stole 10d. in money found in a sideboard (abaco).

[m.33d., blank]

76

[m.28]   Pleas and presentments at Durham on 4 Oct. 7 James [1609] before George Scroope, esq., Henry Linley [?cancelled], George Selby, Charles Wrenn, knts, Thomas Calverley, esq., Clement Colemore, LL.D., Henry Dethicke, LL.B., John Barnes and Robert Cooper, esqs, JPs.

1) Edward Collyn late of Cleasby, co. Durham, yeo., Marmaduke Bawmer late of Dabholme, Yorks., yeo., and John Langstaffe late of Blackwell, co. Durham, yeo., on 14 July 1608 at West Hartburn riotously attacked Robert Mawre and Eleanor his wife, contrary to the statutes of riot and rout.

2) Isabel Wilson of Westoe, co. Durham, spinster, on 16 Sept. 1609 at Monkton stole an apron of green say worth 4d. from Eleanor Brumpton.

3) Thomas Lacy late of Penshaw, co. Durham, yeo., Henry Hall late of the same, yeo., and Richard Homes late of the same, yeo., on 28 Aug. 1609 at Penshaw riotously attacked Humphrey Toynton and wounded him, contrary to the statutes of riot and rout.

4) John Shawe of Cornforth, co. Durham, yeo., between 5 Oct. and 31 Dec. 1608 at Elwick bought of Toby Ewbanck, gen., 20 oxen at £5 each and 10 cows at 40s. each outside open market and fair and not in a place where sales should be conducted, contrary to the form of the statute.

5) Robert Harbottle late of Chester-le-Street, co. Durham, gen., on 2 Oct. 1609 in Durham city in the North Bailey assaulted John Pilkington, gen., constable of the same North Bailey, and punched him twice under the left eye.

6) Thomas Hopper of Hole Row, Northumberland, yeo., and Alison Hopper of the same, spinster, on 13 Sept. 1609 at Benfieldside, co. Durham, at Bishophaugh alias Thristlehaugh distrained on 2 cows worth 40s. each and a stirk worth 20s. of George Currey and

Cuthbert Currey and drove them out of the Chester ward to Hole Row in Northumberland, outside co. Durham, and impounded them.

7) Robert White late of Monkwearmouth, co. Durham, yeo., Thomas Hutchinson late of the same, yeo., Richard Haddocke late of the same, yeo., and John Hindmer late of the same, yeo., on 9 Sept. 1609 at Monkwearmouth in a certain close called *the East Field* assembled, disturbed the peace, and broke the close of William Pearson at Monkwearmouth in the East Field and forcibly carried away 10 cartloads of wreck of sea deposited on Pearson's land.

8) Whereas Brian Kiersbie of Byers Green, co. Durham, yeo., collector of the bishop's rents [*etc.*] in the vill of Byers Green, by virtue of a warrant distrained on Thomas Nicholl on 11 Aug. 1609 at Byers Green by 6 sheep worth 2s. each for an amercement imposed in the halmote court at Bishop Auckland on 8 June past, and would have impounded the same at Byers Green; later in the day Nicholl assaulted Kiersbie and recovered the sheep.

9) Adam Blaxton late of Little Burdon, co. Durham, yeo., and Christopher Davison of Hetton-le-Hill, yeo., between 10 May 1609 and the date of the enquiry bought at Billingham and elsewhere for resale 20 quarters of butter at 26s. 8d. a quarter.

d.] 10) Thomas Snawball late of Crossgate, [Durham], tanner, on 10 Sept. 1609 at Durham, outside open market or other place for scrutiny and sealing of hides, did sell to William Coussing of Durham city, cordwainer, a tanned ox-hide before it was scrutinised and sealed in accordance with the statute of 1 James I, namely an act concerning tanners, curriers, shoemakers and other artificers occupied with the cutting of leather.

11) William Tailer late of Durham city, butcher, Anthony Tailer late of the same, cordwainer, Robert Tailer late of the same, cordwainer, and Robert Scathlocke late of the same, butcher, on 1 Oct. 1609 assembled riotously at Chester-le-Street, disturbed the peace, and attacked George Pearson of Durham city, cordwainer, at Chester-le-Street; and William Tailer struck him on the face with a horse-rod, and Robert Tailer struck him on the crown of the head with a dagger worth 6d. to the proffuse shedding of blood, while Anthony Tailer struck him on the same place with a cudgel which also drew blood, and Scathlocke struck him with a sword. The jurors also presented that the defendants struck Pearson on other parts of the body so that his life was despaired of.

[*space of 37 cms*]

] 12) Elsewhere, namely at the general gaol delivery at Durham on 21 Aug. 1609 before Bp James, James Altham, knt, a baron of the king's exchequer, Edward Phelipps, knt, serjeant at law, Richard Hutton, serjeant at law, chancellor of Durham, George Scroope, esq., Henry Lindley, Charles Wrenn, knts, Thomas Calverley, esq., and Clement Colmore, LL.D., and fellow justices to deliver the gaols of Durham and Sadberge, as also JPs and justices of oyer and terminer, it was presented that Michael Sawghell late of Hylton, co. Durham, gen., Peter Hodgshon of the same, yeo., and other malefactors unknown assembled at the instigation of Henry Hilton of Hylton, esq., to the terror of the lieges on 16 Aug. 1609 with pitchforks and other implements and broke the close of John Holliday and Reginald Fawcett at Monkwearmouth and trampled grass worth 20s. and depastured it with cattle and horses and carried off with oxen 2 waggonloads of hay belonging to John Holliday and Reginald Fawcett, which was mown and dried and won. The defendants appeared at the general sessions of the peace on 4 Oct. 1609 before Bp James, George Scroope, esq., George Selbye, Charles Wrenn, knts, Thomas Calverley, esq., and Clement Colmore, LL.D., JPs, demurred and pleaded not guilty. Robert Cooper [etc.]. Jurors for 10 Jan. next.

[space of 11 cms]

13) MEMO that Roger Trollopp who sued for the king and himself appeared in court before the king's justices of the peace and oyer and terminer at the general sessions at Durham on 13 Jan. 1608 and informed the court that Henry Marley late of Hylton, yeo., between 10 Jan. 1606 and the date of the information [13 Jan. 1608] engrossed from various persons unknown 5 chalders of wheat worth £10 and 5 chalders of rye worth £5 with the intent to resell, contrary to the statute of 5 Edward VI. By this act £10 of the value of the grain was forfeit to the king and to Trolloppe by the terms of the statute, and Trolloppe claimed half. The court was to advise on his claim and Marley was summoned to answer the charge. Later at Durham at the general sessions on 4 Oct. 1609 before Bp James, George Scroope, esq., George Selbye, Charles Wrenn, knts, Thomas Calverley, esq., Clement Colmore, LL.D., George Tonge and John Barnes, esqs., JPs, Marley appeared in person, demurred and pleaded not guilty. Robert Cooper [etc.]. Jurors for 10 Jan. next.

[space of 10 cms]

[m.29d.] [space of 6.5 cms]

14) Elsewhere at the general gaol delivery at Durham on 21 Aug. 1609 before Bp James, James Altham, knt, a baron of the king's exchequer, Edward Phelipps, knt, serjeant at law, Richard Hutton, serjeant at law, chancellor of Durham, George Scroope, esq., Henry Lindley, George Selby, Charles Wrenn, knts, Thomas Calverley, esq., and Clement Colmore, LL.D., [etc.] it was presented that William Pattisone late of Bishopwearmouth, yeo., Thomas Hilton late of Bishopwearmouth, yeo., Nicholas Bryan late of the same, yeo., William Robinson late of the same, yeo., Thomas Roxbye late of the same, yeo., John Thompson late of the same, yeo., and John Shiperdson late of the same, yeo., on 24 July 1609 at Bishopwearmouth in a close called Hollow Crosse assembled riotously and broke into the same and seized 3 measures of hay worth 12d. of Francis Burgoyne, clerk, rector of Bishopwearmouth, in right of his rectory. Later at the general

sessions of the peace at Durham on 4 Oct. 1609 before Bp James, George Scroope, esq., Charles Wrenn, knt, Thomas Calverley, esq., and Clement Colmore, LL.D., JPs, the defendants appeared in person, demurred and pleaded not guilty. Robert Cooper [etc.]. Jurors for 11 Jan.

[space of 39 cms]

] 15) Elsewhere at the general sessions of the peace at Durham on 4 Oct. 1609 before Bp James, George Scroope, esq., George Selby, Charles Wren, knts, Thomas Calverley, esq., and Clement Colmore, LL.D., JPs, it was presented that Thomas Lacy late of Penshaw, co. Durham, yeo., Henry Hall late of Penshaw, yeo., and Richard Homes late of Penshaw, yeo., on 28 Aug. 1609 with force and arms at Penshaw attacked Humphrey Toynton and wounded him in various parts, contrary to the form of the statute on riots. The defendants appeared on the same day, demurred and pleaded not guilty. Robert Cooper [etc.]. Jurors for 10 Jan.

[space of 13.5 cms]

16) Elsewhere at the general sessions at Durham on 12 July 1609 before Bp James, George Scroope, esq., Thomas Calverley, esq., and Clement Colmore, LL.D., JPs, it was presented that Christopher Finley late of – in Staindrop demesne, co. Durham, yeo., between 8 Sept. and Martinmas [11 Nov. 1608] took and killed salmon and fry worth – in the River Tees and elsewhere, contrary to the form of the statute. Finley appeared on 10 Jan. 1610 before Bp James, Richard Hutton, serjeant at law, chancellor of Durham, George Scroope, Thomas Calverley, esqs, and Clement Colmore, LL.D., JPs, demurred and pleaded not guilty. Robert Cooper [etc.]. Jurors for – April.

d.] [space of 14.5 cms]

17) Elsewhere at the general sessions at Durham on 12 July 1609 before George Scroope, esq., Henry Lindley, George Selby, Charles Wrenn, knts, Thomas Calverley, esq., and Clement Colmore, LL.D., JPs, it was presented that James Grene late of Thorpe Thewles, co. Durham, yeo., on 1 June 1609 and before and after until the date of the enquiry, obstinately and by his own authority and without leave of the JPs took it on himself at Thorpe Thewles to keep a common tippling-house and allowed John Kendall to drink there immoderately and continually allowed unlawful games, contrary to the form of the statute. Grene appeared on 4 Oct. 1609 before Bp James, George Scroope, esq., George Selby, Charles Wren, knts, Thomas Calverley, esq., and Clement Colmore, LL.D, JPs, demurred and pleaded not guilty. Robert Cooper [etc.]. Jurors for 10 Jan.

[space of 19.3 cms]

] 18) Elsewhere at the general gaol delivery at Durham on – Aug. 1609 before Bp James, James Altham, knt, a baron of the king's exchequer, Edward Phelipps, knt, serjeant at law, Richard Hutton, serjeant at law, chancellor of Durham, George Scroope, esq., Henry Lindley, knt, Thomas Calverley, esq., and Clement Colmore, LL.D, JPs, it was presented on oath that Thomas Hopper late of Hole Row, Northumberland, yeo., and Margaret his wife and Cuthbert Hopper of the same, yeo., with many others unknown assembled riotously at the instigation of Thomas Middleton of Belsay, Northumberland, esq., to the terror of the lieges on 25 July 1609 and with force and arms broke the close of George Currey and Cuthbert Currey at Benfieldside in the parish of Lanchester at *Bushophaugh* and cut down the undergrowth called *allers* growing in the hedges and destroyed them and assaulted George Currey and carried off with oxen 2 waggon-loads of hay belonging to the same, having been won and dried, and did other damage to the close, contrary to the form of the statute on riots. The defendants appeared at the general sessions on 4 Oct. 1609 before Bp James, George Scroope, esq., Thomas Calverley, esq., Clement Colmore, LL.D., John Fetherstonhalgh and John Barnes, esqs, JPs, and pleaded not guilty to trespass and riot [*etc.*]. Robert Cooper [*etc.*]. Jurors for 10 Jan.

[*space of 13 cms*]

19) Elsewhere at the general sessions of the peace at Durham on 4 Oct. 1609 before Bp James, George Scroope, esq., George Selbye, Charles Wrenn, knts, Thomas Calverley, esq., Clement Colmore, LL.D., Henry Dethick, LL.B., a master in the king's court of chancery, John Barnes, esq., and Robert Cooper, esq., JPs, it was presented on oath that Thomas Hopper of Hole Row, Northumberland, yeo., and Alison Hopper of the same, spinster, on 13 Sept. 1609 at Benfieldside at Bishophaugh alias Thrislehaugh took as distress 2 cows worth 40s. each and a stirk worth 20s. from George Currey and Cuthbert Currey and drove them out of the Chester ward and impounded and detained them, contrary to the form of the statute. The defendants appeared at the same sessions on 4 Oct. 1609 and demurred that their offence was not against the statute. Robert Cooper [*etc*]. Jurors for 10 Jan.

[*m.31d.*]   [*space of 16 cms*]

20) Elsewhere at the general sessions of the peace at Durham on 12 Oct. 1608 before Bp James, George Scrope, esq., Henry Lindley, Henry Anderson, Charles Wrenn, knts, Thomas Calverley, esq., and Clement Colmore, LL.D., JPs, it was presented on oath that Dorothy Grice late of Bishop Auckland, widow, on 1 Oct. 1606, being seised in demesne as of fee of an agricultural messuage in Newton Cap and of 16 acres in Newton Cap did convert 8 acres from grain to pasture and persevered with the same to the date of the enquiry [*12 Oct. 1608*] and surrounded them with hedges and ditches. Later at the general sessions on 10 Jan. 1610 before Bp James, Richard Hutton, serjeant at law, chancellor of Durham, George Scroope, esq., and Clement Colmore, LL.D., JPs, Dorothy Grice appeared in person and denied that on 1 Oct. 1606 and between then and 1 Oct. 1608 she for her own gain and convenience did hedge and ditch 8 of the 16 acres of arable [*etc.*]. Robert Cooper [*etc.*]. Jurors for – April.

[*space of 22.5 cms*]

77

5B] Pleas and presentments at the general sessions at Durham on 10 Jan. 7 James [1610] before Bp James, Richard Hutton, serjeant at law, chancellor of Durham, Edward Talbot, esq., George Scroope, esq., Charles Wrenn, knt, Thomas Calverley, esq., and Clement Colmore, LL.D., JPs in Durham and Sadberge.

1) Robert Browne late of Durham city, barber, Anne Browne wife of the same, and George Browne servant of the same on 30 Nov. 1609 at Durham in the North Bailey attacked William Greene, gen., constable of the North Bailey, and Robert punched his head and all three broke the stick which William carried in his hands and struck him with it.

2) George Pearson late of Durham city, cordwainer, on 1 Oct. 1609 at Chester-le-Street attacked William Taylor and thrust him many times on the head with a dagger worth 2s.

3) John Eden late of West Auckland, co. Durham, esq., and William Eden late of the same, gen., on 2 Jan. 1610 at Lutterington in the close called *the Croftes* attacked George Garth as he was passing on the king's highway.

4) Whereas John Lancaster late of Swalwell, co. Durham, yeo., was licenced by the JPs to keep a tippling-house at Swalwell park, Lancaster on 17 Dec. 1609 in contempt of the laws and ordinances governing common alehouses allowed Thomas Anderson in time of divine service to drink there immoderately and drank with him and also allowed Edward Reade and Edward Simpson to assault Anderson.

5) Richard Heviside late of Bishop Auckland, co. Durham, yeo., licenced by the JPs to keep a common alehouse in Bishop Auckland, was bound in £10, with two sureties in £5 each, to observe the regulations governing alehouses, and on 25 Sept. 1609 at Bishop Auckland he allowed Ambrose Vint and Robert Trotter by night to play cards and drink excessively.

6) Robert Trotter late of Shipley, co. Durham, yeo., and Ambrose Vint late of Barnard Castle, yeo., on 25 Sept. 1609 at Bishop Auckland attacked George Ayrie.

7) Hugh Hutchinson late of Durham city, tanner, between 12 and 25 Oct. 1609 at Durham city engrossed by purchase from Robert Grenay of Bishop Middleham and not by lease, grant or farming of land or tithes 2 measures of barley at 26s. 8d. a *verge* to a total of 40s. with an intent to resell.

8) Enquiry whether Henry Maltbye late of Durham city, yeo., on 28 Oct. 1609 at Ebchester attacked Agnes Simpson wife of John Simpson and struck her on the face and other parts of the body.

9) Thomas Wilson late of Darlington, yeo., from 20 July 1609 to the date of the enquiry [10 Jan.] practised for gain at Darlington the craft of weaver without having served 7 years' apprenticeship.

Bd.] 10) Richard Storey late of Durham and Gilbert Dixon of Durham, litsters, William Storke late of Bishop Auckland, yeo., George Robinson late of the same, yeo., Thomas Hodgshon late of the same, yeo., Thomas Sivelltopp late of Chester-le-Street, yeo., Richard Fletcher late of the same, yeo., Roger Haswell late of the same, yeo., Anthony Alanday of the same, yeo., Richard Thompson late of Hylton, yeo., Robert Hilton late of the same, yeo., Richard Gibson late of the same, yeo., George Bargell late of Hetton-le-Hole, yeo., Richard Sharp late of Whitburn, yeo., Thomas Wright late of the same, yeo., Cuthbert Hutchinson late of the same, yeo., John Letony late of the same, yeo., James Mathew late of Cleadon, yeo., John Dossye late of Longnewton, yeo., Anthony Dossey late of Stockton, yeo., William Thompson late of the same, yeo., Richard Harparley late of Elton, yeo., John Gibson late of the same, yeo., Robert Finche late of Wolviston, yeo., Percival Watson late of the same, yeo., John Mainsforth late of the same, yeo., Robert Hixson late of Kirk Merrington, yeo., and Ralph Johnson late of Piercebridge, yeo., between 1 May 1609 and the date of enquiry [10 Jan.] at Darlington and elsewhere bought and engrossed from divers persons a chalder of barley at £5 with an intent to resell, contrary to the form of the statute.

11) Whereas the king by writ of *capias ad satisfaciendum* from the court of pleas at Durham ordered John Conyers, knt, sheriff of Durham, to arrest Anthony Kirsopp late of Whickham, co. Durham, yeo., alias Antonine Kirshopp of Whickham, yeo., and have him in safe custody to answer the king's justices at Durham on 11 Jan. next to satisfy Samuel Rawlyn in a debt of £80 which he had recovered in that court with 88s. damages; and the sheriff on 18 Dec. 1609 ordered Robert Maltby, his bailiff in the Chester ward, Robert Harryson, his bailiff in Durham city, and John Crooke, Nicholas Rawlinge, John Humfrey and Cuthbert Armestrong, his special bailiffs, to take Antonine Kirsopp [*etc.*]; later John Humfrey, a special bailiff, by virtue of the warrant of 12 Dec. 1609 arrested Kirsopp at Whickham and would have taken him to gaol at Durham castle [*etc.*], but Andrew Rodham late of Whickham, yeo., Andrew Barras late of Whickham, yeo., and Robert Kirsopp late of Whickham, yeo., on 22 Dec. 1609 assembled riotously at Whickham and attacked John Humfrey in the execution of his warrant and rescued Kirsopp.

12) Archibald Gibson late of Fugar House, co. Durham, yeo., licenced by the JPs to keep a common alehouse at Fugar House, on 7 Jan. 1610, being a Sunday, permitted certain persons unknown to play at cards the whole night, contrary to his recognizance.

13) William Hardcastle late of Sunderland by the sea, co. Durham, yeo., William Shipperdson late of Sunderland, yeo., William Thompson late of the same, blacksmith, Edward Anderson late of the same, shipwright, Robert Barkas late of the same, yeo., Brian Jackson late of the same, yeo., and Richard Morgan late of the same, sailor, assembled riotously at Sunderland with 30 others unknown at the instigation of William Hardcastle and William Shepperdson to the terror of the lieges on 2 Dec. 1609 and assaulted John Chrusoe and Thomas Richardson.

14) Enquiry whether James Hodgshon late of Birtley, Northumberland, yeo., on 1 Jan. 1605 at Durham city stole 13 yards of linen cloth at 2s. a yard from Gilbert Camberle.

5] 15) Whereas John Conyers, knt, sheriff of Durham, by warrant of 8 Jan. 1610 ordered William Sonkey, bailiff of the Darlington ward, to collect all fines [etc.] which had been entered in the estreat rolls and especially to collect a fine of 8s. 8d. due from Richard Lilborne of Thickley, co. Durham, gen., William Sonkey as sheriff's bailiff deputed Henry Gibson of Bishop Auckland, yeo., and Simon Sonkey of the same, yeo., who on 9 Jan. 1610 at East Thickley took a mare and attempted to lead it to the bishop's pound at Bishop Auckland; but Lilborne and Edward Blackett late of Shildon, yeo., the same day attacked Gibson in the execution of his office and recovered the mare.

16) Enquiry whether John Grenes late of Holmside *loning*, co. Durham, yeo., on 5 Nov. 1609 at Thickley stole a wether worth – from Nicholas Johnson.

17) Enquiry whether John Humble late of Whickham, co. Durham, lab., on 10 Nov. 1609 at Hunstanworth stole a wether hogg worth 10d. from Christopher Redshaw. (admission)

18) Enquiry whether William Lawson late of Gateshead, yeo., on 7 Dec. 1609 at Durham stole 2 sheep worth 6s. 8d. each from Ralph Cliborne.

19) William Lawson late of Gateside, yeo., on 3 Jan. 1610 at Harraton stole 3 sheep worth 6s. 8d. each from Ralph Cliborne.

20) Enquiry whether Thomas Hudspeth late of Darlington, yeo., on 5 Oct. 1609 at Coniscliffe stole from Cuthbert Stobbert a cow of branded colour worth 40s., 2 heifers of divers colours worth 30s. each and a calf worth 18s.

21) Enquiry whether James Hodgson late of Birtley, Northumberland, yeo., on 1 June 1606 at Durham city stole from James Fletcher a sword worth 20s.
[*m.26d., blank*]

7] 22) Elsewhere at the general sessions at Durham on 10 Jan. 1610 before Bp James, Richard Hutton, serjeant at law, chancellor of Durham, George Scroope, esq., Thomas Calverley, esq., and Clement Colmore, LL.D., JPs, it was presented that George Pearson late of Durham city, cordwainer, on 1 Oct. 1609 at Chester-le-Street attacked William Tayler and struck him violently on the head several times with a dagger worth 2s. Now at the same sessions Pearson appeared in person, demurred and pleaded not guilty. Robert Cooper, esq., bishop's attorney-general [*etc.*]. Order to the sheriff to have a jury for 11 April.
[*m.27d., blank*]

78

4] Pleas and presentments at Durham on 11 April 8 James [*1610*] before Richard Hutton, serjeant at law and chancellor of Durham, George Scroope, esq., Charles Wrenn, knt, Thomas Calverley, esq., and Clement Colmore, LL.D., JPs.

1) Robert Milner late of Monkwearmouth, co. Durham, yeo., deliberately on 27 Dec. 1609 between 9 a.m. and 11 a.m. at Monkwearmouth attacked Adam Watson, cast him to the ground and knee'd him so that he languished from his injuries from 27 Dec. to 5 March following, when he died at Sunderland by the sea.

2) George Ovington late of Barnard Castle, co. Durham, tanner, on 30 Jan. 1610 at Barnard Castle stole from a lime pit a cow-hide worth 15s. belonging to John Dobson.

3) Enquiry whether Michael Briggs late of Headingley, Yorks., yeo., on 21 March 1610 at Chester-le-Street stole a grizzle mare worth £5 from John Netherwood.

4) Whereas at the halmote court of the bishop at Chester on 7 Jan. 1610 a fine of 6s. 8d. was set on Thomas Wright of Whitburn, co. Durham, yeo., for leasing a half husbandland for a term of 6 years from Stephen Kitchen without leave of the court and contrary to custom, later Christopher Skepper, gen., clerk of the bishop's halmote courts, delivered the estreat to William Atcheson, collector of rent and amercements in Whitburn, who on 3 April 1610 distrained on Wright by a cow to impound at Whitburn but Wright on 4 April broke the pound and recovered the cow.

5) The same for Robert Chamber, in respect of the recovery of a stirk.

6) The same for Anthony Johnson, in respect of the recovery of a cow.

7) Enquiry whether John Shawe of Cornforth, co. Durham, yeo., on 1 April 1609 being seised as in demesne of a messuage of arable in Cornforth of 20 acres and being a husbandman did enclose the same with ditch and hedge and convert it to pasture.

8) William Jackson late of Broom House, co. Durham, yeo., on 16 Dec. 1609 at *Riding* near the park of Adam Newton, esq., dean, and the chapter of Durham, hunted at Bearpark by night with a greyhound and killed deer belonging to the dean and chapter and assaulted Thomas Herrison, servant of John Walton, parkkeeper, putting him in bodily fear.

9) Enquiry whether James Atkinson late of Monkwearmouth, co. Durham, yeo., on 2 Feb. 1610 and before and after was a common brawler, disturber of the peace and a trouble-maker, contrary to the form of the statute.

10) Walter Watkyns of North Bailey in Durham city, yeo., from 1 Jan. 1610 to the date of enquiry [*11 April*] on his own authority and without the leave of the county JPs conducted a tippling-house at Durham for the sale of ale and beer.

[*m.24d., blank*]

[*m.25*]　11) Henry Slinger of Staindrop, co. Durham, yeo., William Temple of the same, yeo., Robert Dawson of the same, yeo., George Viccars of the same, yeo., Ralph Awder of the same, yeo., – Browne of the same, widow, John Ewbancke of the same, yeo., Christopher Dixon of the same, yeo., James Ward of the same, yeo., Anne Harrison of the same, widow, – Rotheram of the same, yeo., Thomas South of the same, yeo., and Robert Watson of the same, yeo., from 1 March 1610 to 10 April following on their own authority kept a common alehouse at Staindrop for the sale of ale and beer.

12) Whereas by statute of 2 Edward VI it was ordained that none less than a lord of parliament should shoot at birds in a city [*etc.*], nor might they use hailshot nor more than one lead pellet at a time under penalty of £10 for each offence, Robert Kitchin of Newton House, co. Durham, yeo., on 22 Dec. [*1609*] at Newton House shot with a handgun charged with lead shot and powder.

13) Brian Wall late of St Helen Auckland, co. Durham, yeo., on 1 March 1610 and before and after was a common brawler [*etc.*], contrary to the form of the statute.

14) Whereas Robert Warwicke appeared in person before the sheriff of Durham in his county court at Durham on 9 April 1610 and was committed to the safe custody of Christopher Glover, keeper of Durham gaol, until he found sureties to answer Alice Arrowsmith, widow, administratrix of the goods and chattels of Christopher Arrowsmith her late husband in a plea of recovery of £16; and James Dobson as deputy for Glover took Warwicke into custody and would have led him to gaol to remain there until he found sureties; Thomas Banckes of Durham city, yeo., on the same day assaulted Dobson in the cemetery of Bow church and rescued Warwicke, who is still at large.

15) Enquiry whether Stephen Wilkinson late of Bowden, co. Durham, yeo., on 5 April 1610 at Quarrington stole a tunic worth 9d., a cap worth 1d. and an apron worth 1d. from Margaret Smith at her home.

16) Thomas Deanham late of Darlington, yeo., on 21 Feb. 1610 at Darlington on the king's highway near the *Spitle* assaulted Marmaduke – and James Rookby, constables of Darlington then keeping the peace, and stabbed Ralph Atkinson with a drawn sword to the peril of his life.

17) William Punshon of Herrington, co. Durham, yeo., between 1 March 1610 and the date of the enquiry [*11 April*] was a common frequenter of tables and did so play during church time at Haughton-le-Skerne.

[*m.25d., blank*]

79

3]   Pleas and presentments at the Durham sessions on 11 July 8 James [*1610*] before George Scroope, esq., Thomas Calverley, esq., Clement Colmore, LL.D., Henry Tonge, Robert Cooper, John Heth, and John Fetherstonhalgh, esqs, JPs.

1) Edward Lightley late of Blackwell, co. Durham, yeo., on 5 April 1610 at Longnewton stole 3 pecks of unwinnowed wheat worth 6d. and 1½ pecks of unwinnowed oats worth 2d. from William Sober in his barn; and Richard Collyn late of Longnewton, yeo., knowingly harboured him on the same day after the felony.

2) Christopher Corner late of Sedgefield, co. Durham, yeo., on 4 April 1610 broke the close of George Frevile, knt, at *Close,* co. Durham, and felled 16 ash saplings each worth 4d. growing therein.

3) Whereas John Barnes, esq. and JP, by warrant of 1 May 1610 ordered Lancelot Davison of Chester, co. Durham, yeo., and Edward Stoker of Chester, yeo., then constables of Chester, to arrest James Fawside late of Chester, yeo., and have him before him or another JP to answer for certain trespasses impugned to him by Ralph Nattres his master, namely, illegal withdrawal from Nattres's service at Harraton without notice or leave, and to receive such punishment as after examination the JPs might agree upon; this warrant was delivered by the hands of John Nattres and John Ladler to Davison and Stoker, constables, on 2 July 1610, but these refused to undertake its execution in contempt of the king's law and a bad and pernicious example to others.

4) Elsewhere at the general sessions at Durham on 11 April 1610 before Richard Hutton, serjeant at law and chancellor of Durham, George Scroope, esq., and Charles Wrenn, knt, JPs, it was presented on oath that James Atkinson late of Monkwearmouth, co. Durham, yeo., on 2 Feb. 1610 and before and after was a common brawler, disturber of the peace and a trouble-maker, contrary to the form of the statute; at these sessions on 11 July 1610 before the above JPs James Atkinson appeared in person, demurred and pleaded not guilty. Robert Cooper, esq., [*etc.*].

5) Elsewhere at the general sessions at Durham on 11 April 1610 before Richard Hutton, serjeant at law, chancellor of Durham, George Scroope, esq., Charles Wrenn, knt, Thomas Calverley, esq., and Clement Colmore, LL.D., JPs, it was presented on oath that whereas at the halmote court of Bp James at Chester, co. Durham, on 7 June 1609 a fine of 6s. 8d. was assessed on Thomas Wright of Whitburn, yeo., for taking a lease of 6 years on half a husbandland from Stephen Kitchin without licence, outside the bishop's halmote at Chester and contrary to the custom of the court; later Christopher Skepper, gen., clerk of the bishop's halmote, delivered to William Atcheson, then collector of the bishop's rents and fines in Whitburn, an estreat of the amercements of the bishop's tenants there and elsewhere to levy and collect and pay to the bishop's receiver. Later, [*m.23d.*] on 3 April 1610, William Atcheson distrained on Wright by a | cow and took it to the bishop's common pound, from which on 4 April Wright recovered it. Later at the general sessions at Durham on 11 July 1610 before George Scroope, esq., Thomas Calverley, esq., and Clement Colmore, LL.D., JPs, Wright appeared in person, demurred and pleaded not guilty. Robert Cooper, esq., [*etc.*].

6) Elsewhere at the general sessions at Durham on 11 April 1610 before Richard Hutton, serjeant at law and chancellor of Durham, George Scroope, Thomas Calverley, esqs, and Clement Colmore, LL.D., JPs, it was presented on oath that whereas at the bishop's

halmote court at Chester on 7 June 1609 a fine of 6s. 8d. was
imposed on Robert Chamber of Whitburn, yeo., for leasing a half
husbandland for the term of 6 years from Stephen Kitchin without
licence, out of the halmote and contrary to custom; later Christopher
Skepper, gen., clerk of the halmote courts, delivered to William
Atcheson, then collector [etc.], an estreat of amercements [etc.], and
on 4 April 1610 Atcheson distrained on Chamber by a stirk for the
same and led it to the bishop's pound in Whitburn, whence
Chamber on the same day recovered it. Later at the general sessions
at Durham on 11 July 1610 before George Scroope, esq., Thomas
Calverley, esq., and Clement Colmore, LL.D., JPs, Chamber appeared
in person, demurred and pleaded not guilty. Robert Cooper, esq., [etc.].

80

[2] Pleas and presentments at the general sessions at Durham on 3 Oct. 8
James [1610] before Bp James, George Scroope, esq., Charles Wrenn,
knt, Thomas Calverley, esq., Clement Colmore, LL.D., Emanuel
Barnes, STP, William Murton, archdeacon of Durham, Henry
Ewbanck, a prebendary of Durham, Henry Dethick, a master of the
king's chancery, John Barnes, John Heth, John Calverley, Robert
Cooper, esqs, and Francis Bunny, clerk, JPs.
  Robert Farrow, gen., Thomas Tunstall, gen., Robert White, gen.,
John Storie, gen., Anthony Meborne, gen., Thomas Wood, Richard
Robinson, Thomas Whitfeild, Ralph Katherick, Francis Kay, William
Cornforth, Cuthbert Hodgshon, Cuthbert Chambers, Robert Guy,
Richard Welsh, William Watson and John Atkinson, yeomen, jurors.
1) Thomas Dobbyson late of Woodifield, co. Durham, yeo., and
Thomas Wren of Woodifield, yeo., on 20 April 1610 threw down the
newly-erected fences of Thomas Humble and Thomas Hutchinson at
North Bedburn.
2) George Gundrie late of Darlington, yeo., on 23 Sept. 1610 at
Darlington assaulted Edward Coates, shed his blood and struck
him on the body with a cudgel worth 1/2d., putting him in fear of his
life.
3) Anthony Smith of Tweedmouth, *co. Durham, yeo., Ralph Smith
late of Berwick-upon-Tweed, yeo., and Thomas Harrett late of
Berwick, yeo., on 6 July 1610 about 10 a.m. at Tweedmouth
deliberately attacked James Anderson; and Ralph [sic] Smith hacked
at him with a short sword worth 2s. 6d. on the left arm, which he
severed. Anderson lingered at Tweedmouth from 26 to 29 July, when
at 7 p.m. he died. Ralph Smith also struck him on the left shin with a
sword held in both hands. Anthony Smyth on 26 July attacked
Anderson with a dagger worth 1s. and struck him on the right of the
head, inflicting a mortal wound 5 inches by 1 inch, from which he
lingered [etc.] and would have been the cause of his death if the
blows inflicted by Ralph [etc.]. Thomas Harret on 26 July aided and
abetted Anthony and Ralph in their felony in that they murdered

George [sic] Anderson. Also Andrew Eviott of Spittal, *co Durham, yeo., and Matthew Gray late of Berwick, yeo., on 26 July 1610 at Spittal comforted Anthony, Ralph and Thomas after the felony.

4) John Dent late of Darlington, tanner, and Christopher Harrison late of Yarm, Yorks., pedlar, on 7 Aug. 1610 before Bp James, Richard Hutton, serjeant at law, and other JPs were asked to take the oath of allegiance as laid down by the statute of 3 Elizabeth cap. 4 and refused. They were committed to Durham gaol the same day, and now on 3 Oct. in full session before Bp James, George Scroope, esq., and Charles Wrenn, knt, JPs, were again required to take the oath and again refused.

5) John Gilbert late of Gateside, glover, Francis Glover late of the same, glover, and Thomas Gilbert late of the same, petty chapman, on 5 July 1610 attacked Edward Moore, constable of Gateside, putting him in bodily fear.

[m.22d., blank]

81

[m.20]   Pleas and presentments at the general sessions at Durham on 9 Jan. 8 James [1611] before Clement Colmore, LL.D., Henry Dethick, LL.B., a master in the king's chancery, John Heath, John Barnes, Robert Cooper and John Lyons, esqs, JPs.

1) Whereas the king by writ of *fieri facias* from the court of king's pleas at Durham dated 4 Oct. 1610 ordered George Selbye, knt, sheriff of Durham, to levy £8 from the lands and chattels of Cuthbert Holte late of Wardley, co. Durham, yeo., and William Bradley late of the same, yeo., being the damages awarded in court before the king's justices at Durham at the suit of Timothy Comyn, gen., arising from their disseising Comyn of a half messuage, 300 acres arable, 200 acres meadow and 400 acres pasture in Wardley which John Mathew, gen., on 3 April 1605 had leased to Comyn at Wardley to hold from the previous Michaelmas for 7 years, which term was not yet expired; and the sheriff was to have the money before the king's justices at Durham on 10 Jan. following, to render to Comyn; later, on 12 Oct. 1610, Robert Maltbye, sheriff's bailiff in the Chester ward, and Henry Maltbye, on the strength of the sheriff's warrant of 8 Oct., took at Wardley 5 cows belonging to Cuthbert Holt and William Bradley to raise the £8 [etc.], but John Smith late of Wardley, yeo., on the same day attacked the Maltbyes with an iron-shod staff and recovered the cows.

2) John Browne late of Staindrop, co. Durham, esq., alias John Broune late of Newcastle, "utter barester", on 19 Oct. 1610, claiming to be under-steward of the manor court of Staindrop, for his own gain and under colour of his office illegally assumed the power and authority to grant licences to several inhabitants in Staindrop to keep alehouses without any admission from the JPs authorized to take sureties from persons so licenced. And Browne on the said day at Staindrop under colour of his office gave licence under his own authority to William

Temple, keeper of an alehouse in Staindrop, and took the bond from him illegally and in contempt of the king and the JPs and took from Temple a fee of 2s. 6d. for the same.

3) Nicholas Hutcheson late of Durham city, tanner, Roland Dawson late of the same, cobbler, and Anthony Areson late of the same, yeo., on 20 Dec. 1610 at Durham traced hares in the snow and killed one, contrary to the statute of 1 James I.

4) Anthony Hutcheson late of Durham city, tanner, Leonard Sanders late of *Intack*, co. Durham, lab., George Sommer late of Durham city, yeo., Edward Cragges late of Gilesgate, [Durham], yeo., Robert Heighington late of Durham city, yeo., Ralph Welfoote late of Bishopton, yeo., Christopher Shaw late of the same, yeo., Lionel Trotter late of Winlaton, yeo., and William Herrison late of Durham city, yeo., on 2 Jan. 1611 at divers places of habitation traced hares in the snow and each killed one hare.

5) Whereas John Barnes, esq., steward of the bishop's forest court of Weardale, by sealed warrant of – 1610 ordered Cuthbert Fetherstonhalgh, a bailiff and officer of the bishop in the forest to collect rents, fines and amercements arising in the forest, to distrain on John Pearte of the *Intack* in the forest for 6s. 8d., being an amercement or fine imposed by the forest jurors at the court held on – 1610 before Henry Blakiston, gen., chief forester of Weardale, and John Barnes, assessor of rents, to be paid at the Durham exchequer on a date specified in the warrant; later on 18 Dec. 1610 at Stanhope in the forest of Weardale Fetherstonhalgh distrained on Pearte by a caldron, and Pearte on the same day at Stanhope attacked Fetherstonhalgh and recovered the caldron.

6) Whereas John Barnes, bishop's steward in the forest of Weardale, authorized Cuthbert Fetherstonhalgh by warrant to distrain on Thomas Faraleis of Ireshopeburn in Weardale forest for a fine of 5s. imposed by the jurors at the court held on – 1610 before Henry Blakiston, gen., chief forester, and John Barnes [etc.], Fetherstonhalgh on 16 Dec. 1610 distrained on Faraleis at Stanhope by a mare and would have led it to the bishop's common fold at Stanhope until Faraleis had satisfied the bishop but Faraleis attacked him the same day and recovered the mare.

)d.] 7) George Donne late of the *Quarrell'*, co. Durham, yeo., Percival Cooke late of the same, yeo., William – late of Gateshead, yeo., William Robinson late of the same, yeo., Margaret Carr late of the same, widow, Roger Harbottle late of the same, yeo., Thomas Shipley late of the same, yeo., Richard Blithman late of the same, yeo., William Ranyet late of the same, yeo., John Freind late of the same, yeo., Patrick Purvent late of the same, yeo., Edmund Ellynor late of Hutton Henry, yeo., and Lionel Trotter late of Winlaton, yeo., from 3 Oct. 1610 to the date of enquiry [9 Jan.] on their own authority and without licence of the JPs kept at their several homes a tippling-house for sale of ale and beer to the king's lieges.

8) John Machell late of Thorpe Thewles, co. Durham, yeo., on 17 Sept. 1610 at Carlton bought from John Siggesworth outside fair and market 4 heifers at 30s. each, which he resold within 5 weeks.

9) Ralph Welfoote late of Bishopton, yeo., co. Durham, between 1 April and 30 June 1610 bought at Dalton from John Comyn and others unknown outside fair and market 100 hoggs at 4s. each which he resold within 5 weeks.

10) George Pearson late of Brancepeth, co. Durham, yeo., and Mark Hedley late of the same, yeo., from 1 Jan. 1610 to the date of the enquiry [9 *Jan. 1611*] practised at Brancepeth the craft of websters without having been apprenticed for 7 years.

11) George Craw late of Elwick, co. Durham, yeo., between 1 Sept. and 30 Nov. 1610 at Hart bought from Gerard Mebourne 3 cows at £2 6s. 8d. each outside fair and market and resold the same within 5 weeks.

12) Isaac Anderson late of Wingate, co. Durham, gen., on 1 Jan. 1610 was seised as of fee of 2 arable messuages with appurtenances in Wingate and 86 acres arable, and for his own gain he enclosed 60 acres with hedges and ditches and converted them to pasture until 1 Jan. 1611.

13) Whereas by statute of 8 Henry VI against disseisin [*etc.*], Peter Driden late of Riding, Northumberland, yeo., Richard Teasdale late of Slaley, yeo., John Mayne late of *Brunchellhaugh*, yeo., Richard Carr late of Hexham, yeo., and William French late of the same, yeo., at the instance of Claudius Forster late of Bamburgh, esq., on 1 Sept. 1610 forcibly entered a messuage, 40 acres arable, 40 acres meadow and 40 acres pasture with appurtenances in Riddlehamhope, co. Durham, being the freehold of John Heth senior, esq., and ejected Matthew Armstronge, tenant for 3 years, thereby disseising Heth until the date of the enquiry [9 *Jan.*].

14) Robert Herrison late of Whickham, co. Durham, lab., Henry Herreson late of the same, yeo., Matthew Werill late of the same, lab., and Anne Herrison late of the same, widow, on 13 Oct. 1610 at Whickham assembled riotously, disturbed the peace, and attacked Henry Maltbye, a bailiff of George Selbye, knt, sheriff of Durham, in the execution of his office so that his life was despaired of.

15) Christopher Corner late of Sedgefield, co. Durham, yeo., Laurence Corner of the same, weaver, John Emmerson of the same, yeo., Marmaduke Merrington of Murton, yeo., and Richard Smith of Hutton Henry, yeo., with others at the instance of Richard Smith assembled riotously on 30 Oct. 1610 and broke the common fold at Hutton Henry and recovered a bay mare belonging to Richard Smith, impounded by Henry Jilson.

[*m.21*]   16) Previously at the general sessions of the peace at Durham on 9 Jan. 1611 before Clement Colmore, LL.D., Henry Dethick, LL.B., a master in the king's chancery, John Heth, Robert Cooper, John Barnes, and John Lyons, esqs, JPs, it was presented on oath that whereas the king by writ of *fieri facias* from the king's court of pleas at Durham dated 4 Oct. 1610 ordered George Selbye, knt, sheriff of Durham, to levy on the lands and goods of Cuthbert Holte late of Wardley, yeo., and William Bradley late of the same for £8 awarded in damages to Timothy Comyn, gen., for his ejection on 3 April 1605 from his tenancy at Wardley, and on 12 Oct. 1610 Robert and Henry Maltbye seized at Wardley 5 cows against the £8; John Smith late of Wardley, yeo., assaulted the bailiffs and recovered the same. Now at the general sessions on 9 Jan. 1611 Smith appeared in person, demurred and pleaded not guilty. Robert Cooper, esq., for the king [*written over* bishop]. Jurors for 27 March.

17) Previously at the general sessions at Durham on 9 Jan. 1611 before the above it was presented on oath that Robert Herrison late of Whickham, co. Durham, lab., Henry Herrison late of Whickham, yeo., Matthew Werill late of Whickham, lab., and Anne Herrison late of Whickham, widow, on 13 Oct. 1610 at Whickham assembled riotously, disturbed the peace, and attacked Henry Maltbye, a bailiff of George Selbye, knt, sheriff of Durham, in the execution of his office so that his life was despaired of. Henry and Anne Herrison appeared on 9 Jan. before the JPs, demurred and pleaded not guilty. Robert Cooper, esq., the bishop's attorney-general [*etc.*]. Order for the sheriff to have the jurors for 27 March.

21d.] 18) Previously at the general sessions at Durham on 9 Jan. 1611 before Clement Colmore, LL.D., [*etc. as above*] it was presented on oath that Christopher Corner late of Sedgefield, co. Durham, yeo., Laurence Corner of the same, weaver, John Emerson of the same, yeo., Marmaduke Merrington of Murton, yeo., and Richard Smith of Hutton Henry, yeo., assembled with other malefactors at the instance of Richard Smith on 30 Oct. 1610 and broke into the common fold at Hutton Henry and abstracted a bay mare belonging to Smith, impounded there by Henry Jilson. Christopher and Laurence Corner appeared at the general sessions at Durham on 9 Jan. before the JPs, demurred and pleaded not guilty. Robert Cooper, esq., [*etc.*]. Jurors for 27 March.

82

18] Pleas and presentments at the general sessions at Durham on 27 March 9 James [*1611*] before Richard Hutton, serjeant at law, chancellor of Durham, George Scroope, esq., Charles Wrenn, knt, Thomas Calverley, esq., Clement Colmore, LL.D., Henry Dethick, LL.B., a master in the king's chancery, William Murton, archdeacon of Durham, John Calverley, Henry Tonge, John Heth, George Lightfoote, Robert Cooper and John Barnes, esqs, JPs.

1) Anthony Eastgate late of Bishop Auckland, co. Durham, smith, on 17 Dec. 1610 at Bishop Auckland in the residence of William Billop, common-alehouse keeper for the sale of ale and beer, drank to excess with William Bavye and incited Bavye to overdrink and attacked Bavye.

2) William Bavye late of Darlington, yeo., on 17 Dec. 1610 at Bishop Auckland attacked Anthony Eastgate.

3) Hugh Hutchinson junior late of Durham city, tanner, on 26 March 1611 bought from an unknown man in Durham city outside fair or market 12 calf-skins worth 10s., contrary to the form of the statute of 1 James I.

4) Thomas Moore late of Durham city, tanner, on 23 March 1611 at Durham city outside market and fair bought 12 calf-skins for 21s., contrary to the form of the statute.

5) Simon Groume late of Fellside, co. Durham, lab., on 27 Jan. 1611 at Fellside attacked Thomas Gilson and "bett out" his left eye with a pole or *stang* held in his two hands, so that he remains blind in that eye.

6) George Pearson late of Bishop Auckland, co. Durham, yeo., on 1 March 1611 obstructed a common way from Bishop Auckland to a parcel of land called *the Bishop's Demesnes* in Bishop Auckland by closing it with a fence and a ditch and holds it separate from the remaining common way to the harm of and pernicious example to others and as a common nuisance.

7) Thomas Freind late of Bishop Auckland, yeo., on 6 Jan. 1611 at Bishop Auckland did fire a gun in the residence of Thomas Ramforth in the presence of him and his wife Elizabeth which overcame Elizabeth with the sulphur fumes and put both in great danger.

8) William Bayles late of Bishop Auckland, apothecary, at devilish instigation at Darlington in the residence of John Wood on 13 Feb. 1611 about midday assaulted Henry Browne and stabbed him with a knife worth 4d. held in his right hand, Browne being without any drawn weapon and not having first struck Bayles. This entered the right of his chest near the throat, giving him a mortal wound 5 inches deep by 1½ inches, of which he died instantly.

9) Whereas George Selbye, knt, sheriff of Durham and Sadberge, by sealed warrant dated Durham 15 June 1610, authorized Robert Maltbye, his bailiff in the Chester ward, to arrest John Hedworth of Harraton, co. Durham, knt, that the sheriff might have him at Westminster before the king's judges to satisfy Hugh [?Wa]lton for a debt of £100; when Maltbye on 15 Jan. 1611 tried to arrest Hedworth, he and George Liddell late of Harraton, yeo., John Buckham late of the same, yeo., and Thomas Toft of the same, [m.18d.]   servants of Hedworth, riotously I assembled and attacked Maltbye in the execution of his office and rescued Hedworth.

10) Whereas George Selbie, knt, sheriff of Durham, by warrant of 29 Jan. 1611 ordered Henry Maltbye his bailiff to take the goods of Christopher Hedworth, gen., to the use of Richard Faraleis, namely 40s. 9d. for debt and 10s. 8d. costs, so that he had the money at the next county court at Durham on Mon., 11 Feb., to render to Richard Farales, which sum was recovered at the county court before the sheriff at Durham on Mon., 19 Nov., by default; Maltbye on 7 Feb.

1611 at Pokerley took goods, namely a branded ox, in satisfaction. The same day Richard Hedworth late of Pokerley, gen., and Ralph Hedworth of the same, gen., assaulted Maltbye and recovered the ox.

11) John Fenwick late of Wallington, Northumberland, knt, Richard Carr late of – , Northumberland, gen., William French late of Wallington, yeo., and Richard Parker late of Wallington, yeo., on 22 March 1611 forcibly entered the messuage, 40 acres arable, 40 acres meadow and 40 acres pasture with appurtenances in Riddlehamhope, co. Durham, being the freehold of John Heth senior, esq., and riotously ejected Matthew Armstrong, farmer for 3 years, and retained possession from 22 March 1611 to the date of the enquiry [27 March], so disseising John Heth senior.

12) George Craw late of Elwick, co. Durham, yeo., between 1 Sept. and 30 Nov. 1610 at Amerston, bought from William Smith outside fair or market 4 cows at 45s. each and resold them within 5 weeks.

13) William Guy late of Murton, co. Durham, yeo., between 1 Sept. and 30 Nov. 1610 at Chester bought from Richard Reade, gen., outside fair or market 20 oxen at £4 each and resold them within 5 weeks.

14) The same between the same dates at Pelton Grange, co. Durham, bought from Thomas Heath, gen., 20 oxen at £4 each and resold them within 5 weeks.

15) Elizabeth Brompton late of Harton, co. Durham, spinster, at Martinmas 1610 at Harton, being retained in the service of John Emmerson at Harton at an agreed competent salary to serve for a year, left his service at Harton on 9 March 1611 without permission or giving due warning, contrary to the form of the statute. Christopher Brompton late of Monkton, yeo., knowing that Elizabeth had left service, harboured her at Monkton on 9 March until the date of the enquiry [27 March], contrary to the form of the statute.

16) William Grinwell late of Huller Bush, co. Durham, yeo., Christabel wife of Ralph Grinwell late of the same, yeo., and Isabel Grinwell late of the same, spinster, on 2 Nov. 1610 at Huller Bush riotously attacked George Harrison so that his life was despaired of, and carried off pieces of timber worth 5s. in his keeping.

17) Anthony Dossy late of Stockton, co. Durham, yeo., between 1 Sept. and 31 Dec. 1610 at Little Newton, bought from Eleazor Wallys of Durham city 48 bushels of barley at 3s. 4d. a bushel to the sum of £8, with the intention of resale, contrary to the form of the statute.

18) Edward Stoddert late of Darlington, cordwainer, on 12 March 1611 at Darlington attacked John Trotter, cast him to the ground, jumped on him and kicked him in the backbone.

19) John Wrenn late of Woodifield, co. Durham, yeo., bachelor, on 1 Dec. 1610 and thereafter to the date of the enquiry did at Darlington and elsewhere badge and buy corn and grain, contrary to the form of the statute of 5 Elizabeth.

19] 20) Elsewhere at the general sessions held at Durham on 3 Oct. 1610 before Bp Matthew, George Scroope, esq., Charles Wrenn, knt, Thomas Calverley, esq., Clement Colmore, LL.D., and Emanuel Barnes, STP, JPs, it was presented that Peter Finche of Wolviston, co. Durham, yeo., between 1 March and 1 May 1610 at Stotfold bought from William Mosse outside open fair and market 5 score hoggs for £25 and resold the same within 5 weeks, contrary to the form of the statute; at the general sessions on 27 March 1611 he appeared before Richard Hutton, serjeant at law, chancellor of Durham, Charles Wrenn, knt, Thomas Calverley, esq., and Clement Colmore, LL.D., JPs, demurred and pleaded not guilty. Robert Cooper, esq., the bishop's attorney-general, for the king [etc.]. Order to the sheriff to summon jurors for 26 June next.

21) Elsewhere at the general sessions at Durham on 9 Jan. 1611 before Clement Colmore, LL.D., Henry Dethick, LL.B., a master in the king's chancery, John Heth, John Barnes, Robert Cooper and John Lyons, esqs, JPs, it was presented that John Machell late of Thorpe Thewles, co. Durham, yeo., on 17 Sept. 1610 at Carlton bought from John Siggesworth outside open fair and market 4 heifers at 30s. each and resold them within 5 weeks, contrary to the form of the statute; now at the general sessions at Durham on 27 March before Richard Hutton, serjeant at law, chancellor of Durham, Charles Wrenn, knt, Thomas Calverley, esq., and Clement Colmore, LL.D., JPs, Machell appeared, demurred and pleaded not guilty. Robert Cooper, esq., [etc.]. Jurors for 26 June.

[m.19d.] 22) Anthony Dossye late of Stockton, co. Durham, yeo., between 1 Sept. and 31 Dec. 1610 at Greatham outside open fair and market bought from Valentine Dunne of Greatham, yeo., 3 chalders of barley at £4 16s. to the sum of £14 8s., intending to resell, contrary to the form of the statute.

23) Thomas Forser late of Harbour House, co. Durham, esq., on 1 Jan. 1610 was seised as in demesne of 8 agricultural messuages in Kelloe and 400 acres arable with appurtenances there customarily sown, and between then and 1 March 1611 he enclosed 100 acres with ditches and quickset hedges and converted the same to pasture.

24) Dorothy Grice late of Bishop Auckland, co. Durham, widow, on 1 Jan. 1610 was seised of an agricultural messuage in Pixley Hill and 40 acres arable there, and between then and 1 March 1611 enclosed 6 acres with ditches and quickset hedges and converted the same to pasture.

25) Hugh Wright late of Durham city, gen., John Walton late of Durham city, draper, Christopher Surties late of Durham city, mercer, Robert Blunt late of Durham city, dyer, and William Wright of Durham city, mercer, with 7 other unknown malefactors assembled riotously on 20 March 1611 at Durham city in Claypath on the orders of Hugh Wright in disturbance of the king's peace, to molest and hinder Edward Hutton LL.B., the bishop's bailiff of Durham city, from ordaining the bishop's fair in Durham city. They riotously broke

into the residence of Richard Farales and threatened him, and Hugh Wright uttered threats and insults against Edward Hutton, bailiff, namely: "You shall not beare a staffe in this Citty but att your perill and therefore lay it downe or I will make yow and rule you all". These words were said publicly in contempt of Edward Hutton, bailiff, as of Robert Cooper, esq., and John Barnes, esq., two JPs there present in execution of their office of keeping the peace in the city at time of fair, to the terror of the king's lieges in the city to attend the fair.

26) Hugh Wright late of Durham city, gen., Richard Wright late of Durham city, mercer, Charles Hall late of Durham city, yeo., William Key late of Durham city, yeo., William Baker late of Durham city, yeo., William Wright late of Durham city, mercer, and Miles White late of Durham city, lab., assembled with 12 others unknown and on 20 March 1611 at Durham city riotously prevented Edward Hutton, LL.B., bishop's bailiff of Durham city, in the execution of his office touching proclamation of the fair, and Richard Wright attacked Robert Herrison, a bailiff of George Selby, knt, sheriff of Durham, in the market-place in the execution of his duty.

27) Thomas Wrenn late of Woodifield, co. Durham, yeo., on 15 March 1611 cast down 60 yards of fence at North Bedburn lately erected around his close by Thomas Hutcheson.

83

15] Pleas and presentments at the general sessions at Durham on 26 June 9 James [1611] before Bp James, George Scroope, esq., George Frevile, knt, Charles Wrenn, knt, Clement Colmore, LL.D., William Murton, archdeacon of Durham, Henry Dethick, LL.B., a master of the king's chancery, George Tonge, Christopher Place, John Fetherstonhalgh, John Barnes, John Heth, John Calverley, esqs, Francis Bunny, clerk, and Henry Ewbanke, subdean of Durham, JPs.

James Watson, Thomas Tunstall, William Skirfeild, George Crosier, William Whitfeild, John Buttre, John Shadforth, John Warde, Thomas Wood, George Trotter, Richard Barle, William Corneforth, John Garmontsway, Richard Jefferson and Thomas Emerson, jurors.

1) James Davison late of Durham city, yeo,, not being a merchant of staple nor apprenticed to nor living with any such as "shall make yarne, any kinds of clothes, chamlett, woolsteed, sayes, stamyne, knithose, knit peticoots, knit gloves, knit sleeves, hattes, coifes, cappes, Arras tapestrie, coverlets, girdles" or other woollen articles, did on 30 March 1611 at Durham city buy from Christopher Whitfeild 128 stones of wool worth £44, contrary to the form of the statute.

2) Thomas Cuthbert late of *Riding*, co. Durham, yeo., Thomas Cuthbert junior late of Ravensworth, yeo., John Leigh late of Ravensworth, yeo., Richard Sotheren late of Ravensworth, yeo., and Anthony Cuthbert late of Ravensworth, yeo., on 17 March 1611 at

Ravensworth assaulted Andrew Rodham and put him in fear for his life.

3) Robert Emerson late of Sunderland in Weardale, co. Durham, yeo., on 7 June 1611 at Stanhope at Hangingwells Fell disturbed the peace and there assaulted George Emerson junior, Humphrey Bell, John Rutter and Thomas Emerson.

4) George Emerson late of Eastgate, co. Durham, yeo., Thomas Emerson late of the same, lab., Humphrey Bell late of the same, lab., and John Rutter late of the same, lab., on 7 June 1611 assembled riotously at Sunderland in Stanhope at *Grenehole head* and disturbed the peace and there assaulted Robert Emerson.

5) Robert Davison late of Darlington, gardener, alias Robert Davison of Norwich, yeo., on 17 Nov. 1610 at Darlington stole a black horse worth 40s. from a person unknown.

6) Robert Drydon late of Whickham, co. Durham, yeo., on 15 June 1611 at Whickham stole 4 geese worth 8d. each from Cuthbert Nattres.

7) George Emerson late of Eastgate, co. Durham, yeo., Thomas Emerson late of the same, lab., Humphrey Bell late of the same, lab., and John Rutter late of the same, lab., on 7 June 1611 at Sunderland in Stanhope at Blackhill assembled riotously and disturbed the peace and there assaulted John Alleson.

8) Thomas Harperley late of Bishop Auckland, co. Durham, lab., and Matthew Wilson late of the same, lab., were indicted as common night-walkers, drunkards, of bad fame, and disturbers of the peace, and that on 27 May 1611 at Bishop Auckland in the residence of Robert Reade after 9 p.m. they drank illegally, got drunk and misbehaved, using obscene and opprobrious words, in contempt of the law and the king's officers in Durham.

9) John Rosse late of *Helmeden Raw,* co. Durham, yeo., between 1 May and 26 June 1611 purchased from men unknown 3 score stone of butter at – with the intention of resale, contrary to the form of the statute.

10) Robert Pearson junior late of Durham city, cordwainer, between 1 Nov. 1610 and 28 Feb. 1611 at Sherburn out of open fair or market engrossed by purchase and not by lease or farm from Anthony Maxwell, clerk, 2 chalders of barley at – and 2 chalders of oats at – , with the intention of resale, contrary to the form of the statute.

11) William Sympson late of Aycliffe, co. Durham, yeo., from 1 Jan. 1611 to the date of the enquiry [*26 June*] at Aycliffe exercised the craft of glover without serving 7 years' apprenticeship, contrary to the form of the statute of 5 Elizabeth.

12) Whereas George Selby, knt, sheriff of Durham and Sadberge, by virtue of a royal writ of 20 May 1611 ordered Robert Maltby, his bailiff of the Chester ward, and John Johnson and Nathaniel Richeson, his special bailiffs, to arrest George Marshall if in his bailiwick so that the sheriff should have him before the barons of the

exchequer at Westminster in the octave of Trinity [26 May] to answer
Daniel Brader, the king's debtor, in a plea of trespass *quominus*; on 23
May 1611 Johnson and Richeson, bailiffs, took Marshall at
Bedlington, *co. Durham, to lead him to the king's gaol at Durham
until he found sureties to appear to answer Daniel Brader at
Westminster. The said George Marshall late of Bedlington, yeo., John
Bell late of the same, yeo., Andrew Bell late of the same, yeo.,
Anthony Potts late of the same, yeo., and Anne Ellett wife of John
Ellett late of the same, yeo., on 23 May 1611 at Bedlington riotously
assembled and assaulted Johnson and Richeson in the execution of
their duty, | putting them in peril of their lives, and rescued Marshall,
who is still at large.

5d.]

13) Whereas Bp James for the king ordered Henry Maugham,
messenger for the king's commissioners for ecclesiastical causes in the
diocese of Durham, to attach Anne Garnett wife of Robert Garnett of
Blackwell, gen., to appear before the king's commissioners on a given
day, and Maugham on 24 June 1611 attached Anne at Darlington to
be before the king's commissioners; Anthony Denham late of
Darlington, yeo., and Michael Garnett late of Blackwell, gen., on the
same day at Darlington attacked Maugham in the execution of his
duty and rescued Anne from his custody.

14) Stephen Kitchen late of Fieldhouses, yeo., on 31 May 1611
attacked Thomas Perkin at Harton so that his life was despaired of.

15) Previously at the general sessions on 26 June 1611 before Bp
James, George Scroope, esq., George Frevile, Charles Wrenn, knts,
Clement Colmore, LL.D., William Murton, archdeacon of Durham,
Henry Dethick, LL.B., a master in the king's chancery, George Tonge,
Christopher Place, John Fetherstonhalgh and John Barnes, JPs,
Stephen Kitchin late of Fieldhouses, yeo., was indicted that on 31
May 1611 he assaulted Thomas Perkin at Harton [*as (14) above*]. Now
at the same sessions he appeared in person, demurred and pleaded
not guilty. Robert Cooper, esq., [*etc.*]. The sheriff was ordered to have
a jury before the JPs at Durham on 2 Oct.

84

6]

Pleas and presentments at Durham on 2 Oct. 9 James [*1611*] before
George Scroope, esq., Henry Anderson, knt, Charles Wrenn, knt,
Thomas Calverley, esq., George Tonge, esq., Clement Colmore, LL.D.,
John Calverley, John Barnes, and Robert Cooper, esqs, JPs.

William Blackett, gen., Cuthbert Morgan, gen., John Stephenson,
gen., Thomas Burden, John Shadforth, Richard Robinson, Thomas
Dobbyson, Richard Jefferson, Richard Welshe, Henry Dobbison,
Robert Tweddle, William Kitchin, William Watson, Ralph Davison
and Thomas Hunter, yeomen, jurors.

1) Whereas John Heth, esq., a JP in Durham and Sadberge, by sealed
warrant of – Sept. 1611 ordered John Atcheson, constable of Lumley,
co. Durham, to arrest Ralph Fatherlye of Lumley, yeo., to be before

him or another JP to find sureties to keep the peace, especially towards Alice Lowson, widow, Ralph Lowson her son, and Margaret Lowson her daughter and to appear at the next sessions at Durham; Atcheson on 18 Sept. 1611 arrested Fatherlye at Lumley, who uttered malicious, opprobrious and seditious words, namely: "he would come before no Justice, nether cared he for any Justice and what constable soever offered to arrest him, he should come upon his sythe". Furthermore Fatherlye attacked him with scythe and pitchfork, thereby rescuing himself.

2) Robert Emerson late of Sunderland, co. Durham, yeo., Cuthbert Acheson late of the same, yeo., and John Allanson late of the same, yeo., on 7 June 1611 at Stanhope at Hangingwells Fell assembled riotously and there assaulted George Emerson.

3) Robert Emmerson late of Sunderland, yeo., [etc. as (2) above] on 7 June 1611 at Stanhope [etc.] assembled and assaulted John Rutter.

4) Whereas Christopher Ewbanck of Durham, yeo., and Isabel Ewbanck his wife on 25 Sept. 1611 at Darlington before Henry Tonge, esq., and John Barnes, esq., JPs, refused to take the oath of allegiance as laid down by parliament by 3 James I cap. 4, and were committed to gaol at Durham, there to remain until the next sessions, namely 2 Oct. 1611, these now in full and open sessions before George Scroope, esq., Henry Anderson, knt, Charles Wrenn, knt, and Robert Cooper, esq., persevered in their refusal, contrary to the form of the statute.

5) Anthony Rodham late of Farnacres, co. Durham, yeo., and John Rodham late of Farnacres, yeo., on 14 Sept. 1611 broke into the common pound or fold at Whickham and drove off 6 oxen and 2 heifers belonging to Anthony, contrary to the form of the statute.

6) John Berriman late of South Church, co. Durham, yeo., on 25 July 1611 at South Church was a common brawler, disturber of the peace and oppressor of his neighbours, a mischief-maker and spreader of discord.

7) Ralph Hedworth late of Whickham, co. Durham, yeo., on 25 Aug. 1611 at Whickham broke the common pound and took a horse of his.

8) Andrew Rodham late of Whickham, yeo., between 1 Aug. 1611 and the date of enquiry [2 Oct.] broke the fold of Dorothy Dalton, widow, at Whickham and blocked it with wains and carts and trampled it with livestock so that it could not be sown.

[m.16d.] 9) William Thursby late of Brafferton, co. Durham, yeo., on 2 Oct. 1610, being seised of an agricultural messuage at Brafferton and 42 acres of arable, enclosed the same with ditches and quickset hedges and converted the same to pasture.

10) James Blades late of Foxton, co. Durham, yeo., on 18 July 1611 forcibly entered the close at Foxton being the freehold of John Elstobb, gen., and ejected Elstobb and took possession from 18 July to the date of enquiry [2 Oct.].

11) Thomas Robinson late of Gateside, yeo., between 1 and 30 June 1611 at Durham bought from an unknown man 6 heifers at 32s. each and resold them within 5 weeks.

12) William Gibson late of Billingham, co. Durham, yeo., since 1 Sept. 1610 bought at Billingham out of open fair or market from Thomas Shipperd and others unknown a chalder of barley for £4 16s. with the intention of resale.

13) Peter Harreson late of Whickham, co. Durham, yeo., and Christopher Watson late of Whickham, on 18 Aug. 1611, being a Sunday, before mattins in the parish church of Whickham and in time of divine service, entered the church in an unseemly manner and behaved irreverently and prevented John Allison, STB, rector of Whickham, from celebrating divine service, prayers and sermon.

14) Patrick Young late of Ryton, co.Durham, yeo., on – Aug. 1611 at Ryton uttered the following opprobrious words: "God save the Pope. The Pope of Rome is a better man than the Kinge": and other scandalous and seditious words.

15) Alexander Blenkinsop late of Whickham, yeo., on 19 Sept. 1611 at Whickham wounded with an axe worth 2s. 6d. an ox worth £3 belonging to Robert Crawforth.

16) Robert Gray late of Allenshiel, co. Durham, yeo., on 24 June 1611 stole at Allenshiel a black horse worth £3 6s. 8d. belonging to John Whitfeild.

17) Ralph Archbald late of Morton, co. Durham, yeo., on 30 July 1611 at Unthank attacked Patrick Hughe.

18) Thomas Mathew late of Newbottle, co. Durham, yeo., on 20 July 1611 at Houghton set fire to 3 wainloads of whins belonging to Robert Hutton, STP, rector of Houghton-le-Spring and lying cut, and completely destroyed the same.

7] 19) Elsewhere at the general sessions at Durham on 9 Jan. 1611 before Bp Matthew, George Scroope, esq., Charles Wrenn, knt, Thomas Calverley, esq., and Clement Colmore, LL.D., JPs, it was presented on oath that Isaac Anderson late of Wingate, gen., on 1 Jan. 1610 was seised of 2 agricultural messuages with appurtenances and 86 acres arable in Wingate and enclosed and converted 60 acres to pasture. Now on 2 Oct. 1611 before George Scroope, esq., Henry Anderson, Charles Wrenn, knts, and Clement Colmore, LL.D., JPs, Anderson appeared in person, demurred and pleaded not guilty, and Robert Cooper, bishop's attorney-general [etc.].

20) Previously at the general sessions at Durham on 2 Oct. 1611 before George Scroope, esq., Henry Anderson, Charles Wrenn, kts, and Clement Colmore, LL.D., JPs, it was presented that Ralph Archibald late of Morton, yeo., [etc. as (17) above]. Archibald appeared in person, demurred and pleaded not guilty. Robert Cooper [etc.].

21) Elsewhere at the general sessions at Durham on 27 March 1611 before George Scroope, esq., Charles Wrenn, knt, Thomas Calverley, esq., Clement Colmore, LL.D., William Murton, archdeacon of

Durham, and Henry Dethick, LL.B., a master in the king's chancery, JPs, it was presented on oath that William Guy late of Murton, co. Durham, yeo., between 1 Sept. and 30 Nov. 1610 at Chester bought from Richard Reede, gen., outside open fair or market 20 oxen at £4 [m.17d.] each and resold the same within 5 weeks. | Later at the general sessions at Durham on 2 Oct. 1611 before the JPs William Guy appeared in person, demurred and pleaded not guilty. Robert Cooper, esq., [etc.].

22) Elsewhere at the general sessions at Durham on 27 March 1611 before George Scroope, esq., Henry Anderson, Charles Wrenn, knts, Thomas Calverley, esq., Clement Colmore, LL.D., and William Murton, archdeacon of Durham, JPs, it was presented that William Guy late of Murton, yeo., between 1 Sept. and 30 Nov. 1610 at Pelton grange bought from Thomas Heath, gen., 20 oxen at £4 each and resold the same within 5 weeks. Now at the general sessions at Durham on 2 Oct. 1611 Guy appeared in person, demurred and pleaded not guilty. Robert Cooper [etc.].

23) At the general sessions at Durham on 2 Oct. 1611 before George Scroope, esq., Henry Anderson, Charles Wrenn, knts, and Clement Colmore, LL.D., JPs, it was presented that John Berriman late of South Church, co. Durham, yeo., on – July 1611 at South Church was a common brawler [etc.]. He appeared in person, demurred and pleaded not guilty. Robert Cooper [etc.].

24) At the general sessions at Durham on 2 Oct. 1611 before George Scroope, esq., [etc. as (23) above] it was presented that [Alexander] Blenkinsopp late of Whickham, co. Durham, yeo., on 19 Sept. 1611 at Whickham wounded an ox worth £3 of Robert Crawforth with an axe worth 2s. 6d. Blenkinsopp appeared in person, demurred and pleaded not guilty. Robert Cooper [etc.].

85

[m.13] Pleas and presentments at the general sessions of the peace at Durham on 8 Jan. 9 James [1612] before George Scroope, esq., Clement Colmore, LL.D., William Morton, archdeacon of Durham, Henry Dethick, LL.B., a master in the king's chancery, Henry Ewbanck, subdean of Durham, John Heth, Christopher Place, John Fetherstonhalgh, George Lightfoote, John Barnes and Robert Cooper, esqs, JPs.

1) Whereas George Selbye, knt, sheriff of Durham and Sadberge, by warrant of – Dec. 1611 ordered Nicholas Hodgshon, sheriff's bailiff, to distrain on the goods of Roger Metcalfe in his bailiwick for a debt of 21s. which Richard Elstob recovered in the Durham county court, namely 15s. and costs of 4d., and Hodgshon and Simon Sonkey and George Browne, the sheriff's bailiffs and servants, on 10 Dec. 1611 at Darlington seized a cow against the debt; Samuel Elstobb late of Darlington, yeo., Robert Shaw late of the same, yeo., Elizabeth Elstobb wife of Richard Elstobb, Anne Elstobb late of the same,

spinster, and Elizabeth Elstobb late of Darlington, spinster, riotously assembled with 8 others unknown with pitchforks and stones and the same day at Darlington attacked Hodgshon, Sonkey and Browne and wounded Browne so that his life was despaired of and recovered the cow, which is still at large.

2) Christopher Hall late of Hetton-le-Hole, co. Durham, yeo., and Nicholas Tunstall late of Rainton, yeo., on 23 Dec. 1611 at Hetton-le-Hole hunted and killed 3 hares with greyhounds.

3) Thomas Rawlyn of Highwood, co. Durham, yeo., Toby alias Talbott Jackson of Shotton, yeo., Francis Jackson of the same, yeo., and Charles Jackson of Baldersdale, Yorks., yeo., on 8 Oct. 1611 at Mayland, co. Durham, riotously assembled and attacked Thomas Gibbon, striking him on the head and other parts of the body.

4) Anthony Wheitlaw late of Bishop Auckland, co. Durham, yeo., and John Brasse late of Bishop Auckland, yeo., on 12 Dec. 1611 at Bishop Auckland stole an ash tree worth 5s. belonging to Ralph Walker.

5) Robert Smith late of Carr House, co. Durham, yeo., on 11 Aug. 1611 at Preston-le-Skerne impounded livestock, namely 2 oxen, a cow and 4 bullocks belonging to William Bowser, for a supposed trespass on Smith's land at Preston-le-Skerne until Bowser redeemed the same by paying 2s. 4d., namely 4d. an animal, whereas Smith should have received only 4d. for the whole, contrary to the form of the statute.

6) Michael Dent late of Thornley, co. Durham, yeo., on 16 Dec. 1611 stole 2 wethers together worth 13s. 4d. from William Rippon at Stanley.

7) John Smith late of Carr House, co. Durham, yeo., on 28 Oct. 1611 at Crook Hall stole in *the Ryefeild* 2 sheep worth 3s. each belonging to Thomas Stott.

8) John Ewyns late of West Herrington, co. Durham, lab., on 11 Nov. 1611 broke into the residence of Robert Skirfeild at West Herrington and stole 3 shirts together worth 2s. from the same.

9) Whereas George Selbye, knt, sheriff of Durham and Sadberge, ordered by warrant of – Oct. 1611 Nicholas Hodgshon his bailiff to arrest Anthony Coward of Langley, co. Durham, and have him in the gaol of Durham castle until he satisfied Robert Coundell for £4 7s.
3d.]   1d. as debt and 16s. 4d. in costs I recovered before the sheriff in the county court at Durham; on 18 Oct. 1611 John Snawdon late of St Helen Auckland, yeo., and Edward Bigland late of Bishop Auckland, yeo., were deputed by Hodgshon at Little Stainton to arrest Coward [*etc.*]; and Anthony Coward late of Little Stainton, yeo., William Binckes late of the same, yeo., Ralph Bend late of the same, yeo., and William Cow[herd] late of the same, yeo., assembled with 8 others and riotously attacked Snawdon and Bigland in execution of their office at Little Stainton; and Binckes, Bend and Cowherd rescued Anthony the same day and he is still at large.

10) Ralph Cole late of Gateshead, butcher, Robert Thompson late of Gateshead, lab., Robert Collingwood late of Gateshead, lab., Henry

Pearson late of Gateshead, lab., and James Trumble late of Gateshead, lab., assembled with 7 others unknown and on 8 Nov. 1611 at Gateshead at the Back *Lonning* in Gateside disturbed the peace and attacked Thomas Herrison, Thomas Gray and Gavin Clifton, servants of Thomas Riddell of Gateshead.

11) John Simpson late of Middleton-in-Teesdale, co. Durham, yeo., on 1 May 1610 at Middleton-in-Teesdale and at other dates and places was a common brawler and disturber of the peace and a trouble-maker.

12) Christopher Kirkbride alias Kirkbreade late of Chester, co. Durham, lab., and George Leigh late of Chester, lab., on 7 Jan. 1612 between midnight and 2 a.m. broke the close of Elizabeth, Lady Lumley, widow, at Lumley park in the parish of Chester-le-Street and hunted deer with 2 greyhounds and killed 3 does.

13) Elsewhere at the sessions on 8 Jan. 1612 before George Scroope, esq., Clement Colmore, LL.D., William Murton, archdeacon of Durham, Henry Dethick, LL.B., a master of the king's chancery, Henry Ewbanck, subdean of Durham, and John Heth, esq., JPs, Ralph Cole late of Gateshead, butcher, Robert Thompson late of the same, lab., Robert Collingwood late of Gateshead, lab., Henry Pearson late of Gateshead, lab., and James Trumble late of Gateshead, lab., [*etc. as (10) above*]; and Cole, Thompson, Collingwood, Pearson and Trumble appeared in person, demurred and pleaded not guilty. Robert Cooper, esq., [*etc.*].

[*m.14*]   14) Elsewhere at the sessions on 8 Jan. 1612 before the above JPs Thomas Ogle of Bedlington, *co Durham, gen., Gavin Milbourne of the same, yeo., Lancelot Ogle of the same, gen., John Skipsey senior of the same, yeo., John Moodie of the same, yeo., William Hunter of the same, yeo., George Marshall of the same, yeo., Oswald White of the same, yeo., Thomas White of the same, yeo., William Watson of the same, yeo., William Spittell of the same, yeo., Robert Mill of the same, yeo., Robert Browne of the same, yeo., Thomas Potts of the same, yeo., John Donne of the same, yeo., Robert Donn senior of the same, yeo., and George Milles of the same, yeo., assembled at the instance of Thomas Ogle with 30 others unknown on 5 Nov. 1611 at Bedlington in the manner of an uprising to the terror of the lieges to celebrate the day or festival dedicated to the deliverance of the king, queen and nobility from the Gunpowder Treason, and they tore down the stone walls 6 feet high and 18 feet long of a house in building and demolished it to the ground and smashed up 60 waggon-loads of stone lying on the site to build a house at Bedlington for Daniel Brader to his damage. At the general sessions at Durham the same day Lancelot Ogle appeared and pleaded not guilty. Robert Cooper, esq., the bishop's attorney-general [*etc.*].

15) Elsewhere at the general sessions at Durham on 2 Oct. 1611 before George Scroope, esq., Henry Anderson, Charles Wrenn, knts, Thomas Calverley, George Tonge and John Barnes, esqs., JPs, it was presented

that Robert Emerson late of Sunderland, co. Durham, yeo., Cuthbert Achesone late of the same, yeo., and John Allanson late of the same, yeo., on 7 June 1611 assembled riotously at Hangingwells Fell, Stanhope, and there assaulted George Emmerson, to his grievous harm; now at the general sessions at Durham on 8 Jan. 1612 before George Scroope, esq., Clement Colmore, LL.D., William Murton, archdeacon of Durham, and John Heth, esq., JPs, Robert Emerson appeared, demurred and pleaded not guilty. Robert Cooper, esq., [etc.].

4d.] 16) Elsewhere at the general sessions at Durham on 2 Oct. 1611 before George Scroope, esq., Henry Anderson [etc. as (15) above], it was presented that Robert Emerson late of Sunderland, yeo., Cuthbert Acheson late of Sunderland, yeo., and John Allenson late of Sunderland, yeo., on 7 June 1611 at Hangingwells Fell, Stanhope, assembled riotously and there assaulted John Rutter, to his grievous harm. Now at the general sessions at Durham on 8 Jan. 1612 before the said JPs Emerson appeared, demurred and pleaded not guilty. Robert Cooper, esq., [etc.].

17) Elsewhere at the general sessions at Durham on 2 Oct. 1611 before George Scroope, esq., Henry Anderson [etc. as (15) above], it was presented that Thomas Robinson late of Gateside, yeo., between 1 and 30 June 1611 at Durham bought from a person unknown 6 heifers at 32s. each and resold the same within 5 weeks of purchase, contrary to the form of the statute. Now at the general sessions on 8 Jan. 1612 Robinson appeared, demurred and pleaded not guilty. Robert Cooper [etc.].

?] 18) MEMO that Francis Bunny, clerk, a prebendary of Durham cathedral, for the king and himself sued before the keepers of the peace and justices of oyer and terminer at the general sessions at Durham on 8 Jan. 1612 that whereas Edward Hixon of Preston-le-Skerne, co. Durham, gen., was seised in demesne of 200 acres of land in Preston-le-Skerne which on 24 Oct. 1597 were arable and had been so for 12 years, Hixon on 1 Oct. 1610 converted the same to sheep pasture. Bunny sought that the court impose a fine of 20s. per acre so converted, namely £200, and claimed a third part.

19) MEMO that Francis Bunny, clerk [etc.] sued before the justices [etc.] that whereas -- of Preston-le-Skerne, gen., was seised of – acres arable on 24 Oct. 1597 which had been arable for the previous 12 years, on 1 Oct. 1610 and thereafter had converted the same to sheep pasture and fattening and grazing of cattle: he asked for the imposition of the fine at the rate of 20s. a acre and claimed a third of the same.

20) [the same]

21) Simon Gifford, gen., farmer or proprietor of the corn tithes in the deanery of Darlington, sued for the king before the keepers of the peace on 8 Jan. 1612 that Philip Gregorie late of Darlington, yeo., for the past 3 years converted to pasture 20 acres out of 40 acres in
3d.] Darlington which were arable on 24 Oct. 1597 I for which he should

be fined at 20s. an acre to a total of £20, of which he claimed a third.

22) Simon Gifford, gen., farmer [etc.], sued against Thomas Gregorie of Darlington, yeo., who for the past 3 years converted 20 acres out of 40 acres being arable on 24 Oct. 1597 for sheep pasture and cattle fattening. The fine should be £20, at the rate of 20s. an acre, of which he claimed a third.

86

[m.11]   Pleas and presentments at the general sessions of the peace at Durham on 15 April 10 James [1612] before Bp James, Charles Wren, knt, Clement Colemore, LL.D., William Murton, archdeacon of Durham, Henry Dethick, LL.B., a master in chancery, John Heath, George Tong, John Fetherstonhalgh, John Barnes and Robert Cooper, esqs, JPs.

1) Robert Tweddell late of Monk Hesleden, co. Durham, yeo., on 15 Jan. 1612 attacked Francis Tweddell at Monk Hesleden.

2) George Dunlopp late of Gateside, yeo., on 31 Dec. 1611 about 2 p.m. at devilish instigation attacked Mary Swann at Gateside and struck her on the head with a poker worth 6d. held in his right hand, inflicting a mortal blow 3 inches long by 2 inches deep from which she lingered from 31 Dec. until 14 March, when at 2 p.m. she died in Gateside.

3) George Damforte late of Hett, co. Durham, yeo., on 5 Feb. 1612 at Byers garth stole half a bushel of barley worth 10d. from Thomas Murrey, esq., master, and the brethren of Sherburn Hospital, in a barn at Byers garth.

4) Thomas Thomson late of Morpeth, Northumberland, yeo., on 25 Jan. 1612 at Brandon, co. Durham, at the Biggin stole a cambric shirt worth 10d. from Oswald Richardson.

5) Whereas George Selbie, knt, sheriff of Durham and Sadberge, by a sealed warrant of 5 March 1612 ordered Robert Harrison, Henry Maltbye and Peter Hannon, his special bailiffs, to arrest John Blaikeston, gen., to appear before the barons of the king's exchequer in a plea of trespass brought by John Swinstoe to recover a debt, Henry Maltbie on 9 March at Durham city attempted to arrest Blaikeston and take him to gaol until he found sufficient surety to appear at Westminster: and George Blaikeston late of Durham city, gen., and John Blaikeston late of Newton, gen., attacked Maltbie in the execution of his duty, and rescued Blaikeston, who is still at large.

6) Whereas George Leigh late of Chester-le-Street, co. Durham, lab., was indicted that he and Christopher Kirkebride alias Kirkebroode late of Chester, co. Durham, lab., on – Jan. 1612 between noon and 2 p.m. broke into the park of Elizabeth, Lady Lumley, widow, at Lumley park in the parish of Chester-le-Street and took deer with 2 greyhounds; since Leigh defaulted an order was issued to the sheriff of Durham non omittas to arrest Leigh to appear before the JPs at general sessions at Durham on 15 April to answer [etc.]. Later on 19

Feb. past John Hall, Thomas Lawson and John Rutter arrested Leigh at Chester-le-Street to take him to gaol at Durham until he found sureties, but Leigh broke custody, assaulted the 3 bailiffs, and is still at large.

1d.] 7) Daniel Brader late of Bedlington, *co. Durham, gen., Nathaniel Richardson late of Newcastle, yeo., and John Johnson late of Newcastle, yeo., on 22 May 1611 assembled riotously at Bedlington and assaulted George Marshall.

8) Eleanor Waite late of Raby, co. Durham, widow, George Bayles late of the same, yeo., John Bayles late of the same, yeo., John Crawforth late of the same, yeo., and Richard Pickering late of the same, yeo., on 2 April 1612 forcibly entered the messuage and close in Heighington being the freehold of Bp James and expelled Matthew Dobson, farmer for the previous 3 years, and disseised him from 2 April to the date of the enquiry [*15 April*], contrary to the statute of 8 Henry VI.

9) Ralph Walker late of Bishop Auckland, co. Durham, yeo., and John Walker late of the same, yeo., on 24 March 1612 at divers times and places at Bishop Auckland took with a wicker net or *leape* worth 5s. shedder and kipper salmon and trout worth 40s. out of season.

10) Gregory Hutchinson late of Durham city, tanner, John Dixson late of the same, yeo., and Peter Dobbisonn late of the same, yeo., on 7 April 1612 at Framwellgate [Durham] assembled riotously and attacked Gilbert Hall so that his life was despaired of.

11) Arthur Ellott late of Fishburn, co. Durham, lab., on 25 Feb. 1612 stole at Fishburn a cow worth 22s.(?) from John Graves.

2] 12) Previously at the general sessions on 15 April 1612 before Bp James, Charles Wrenn, knt, Clement Colmore, LL.D., Robert Cooper, and John Barnes, esqs, JPs, it was presented that Daniel Brader late of Bedlington, *co. Durham, gen., Nathaniel Richardson late of Newcastle, yeo., and John Johnson late of Newcastle, yeo., on 22 May 1611 at Bedlington assembled riotously and assaulted George Marshall. Now at the general sessions on 15 July Brader appeared in person before the JPs and having heard the indictment demurred and pleaded not guilty. Robert Cooper as bishop's attorney, sued for the king. The sheriff was ordered to have the jurors for 10 July following.

13) Previously at the general sessions on 15 April 1612 before Bp James [*etc. as (12) above*], Ralph Walker late of Bishop Auckland, yeo., and John Walker late of the same, yeo., were indicted that on 24 March 1612 they fished with a wicker net worth 5s. at Bishop Auckland at divers times and places for shedder and kipper salmon and trout worth 40s. At the same sessions Ralph Walker appeared in person and pleaded not guilty. Robert Cooper [*etc.*]

2d.] 14) Elsewhere at the general sessions on 27 March 1611 before Richard Hutton, serjeant at law, chancellor of Durham, George Scroope, esq., Charles Wrenn, knt, Thomas Calverley, esq., and Clement Colmore, LL.D., JPs, Thomas Forser late of Harbour House, co. Durham, esq., was indicted that on 1 Jan. 1610 he being seised in demesne as of fee of 8 messuages under agriculture and 400 acres arable in Kelloe customarily sown, did enclose 100 acres out of the 400 with ditches and quickset hedges and converted them to pasture until 1 March 1611. Now at the general sessions of 15 April 1612 before Bp James, Charles Wrenn, knt, Clement Colmore, LL.D., John Barnes, esq., and Robert Cooper, esq., JPs, Forser appeared in person and demurred [*etc.*].

15) Elsewhere at the general sessions at Durham on 2 Oct. 1612 [*sic*] before George Scroope, esq., Henry Anderson, knt, Charles Wrenn, knt, and Thomas Calverley, esq., JPs, it was presented that William Thuresbye lately of Brafferton, co. Durham, yeo., being seised of an agricultural messuage in Brafferton and 42 acres arable customarily sown, on 2 Oct 1610 did enclose the same with ditches and quickset hedges and converted it pasture until 2 Oct. 1611. Now at the sessions on 15 April 1612 before Bp James, Charles Wrenn, knt, and Clement Colmore, LL.D., JPs, Thuresbye appeared in person, demurred and pleaded not guilty. Robert Cooper [*etc.*].

87

[*m.9*]   Pleas and presentments at the general sessions at Durham on 8 July 10 James [*1612*] before Bp James and Clement Colmore, LL.D., –

1) Christopher Atcheson late of Hamsterley, co. Durham, yeo., on 25 April 1612 at Pontop broke the close and wood of Anthony Meaborne and felled 40 ash tres, 60 hazel wands and 20 oak saplings worth 40s.

2) James Swinborne late of Lintz Green, co. Durham, yeo., on 25 April 1612 at Pontop broke the close and wood of Anthony Meaborne and felled 80 ash trees, 80 hazel wands and 80 oak saplings worth £4.

3) Richard Hedworth late of Pokerley, co. Durham, gen., and Alice his wife, he being in fee by right of his wife, held 90 acres arable in West Boldon on 1 Oct. 1611 and between 8 July 1611 and the date of enquiry they converted 66 acres to sheep pasture and cattle grazing.

4) William Gascoigne late of Darlington, knt, alias William Gascoigne of Sedbury, Yorks., knt, John Eden late of Belasis, co. Durham, esq., Nathaniel Jackson late of Darlington, yeo., and William Eastegate late of Darlington, yeo., assembled with 20 others unknown on 23 Sept. 1611 at Darlington and caused a tumult to the terror of the lieges.

5) John Bradley late of Darlington, yeo., on 2 June 1612 being an innkeeper at the *Bull* at Darlington sold ale and beer without licence from the magistrates and at a greater price, namely 4d. a quart.

6) George Ellison of Tudhoe, co. Durham, yeo., George Lilborne of the same, yeo., Isabel Bussey late of Coundon, Jane Crawe wife of Francis Crawe late of the same, and Eleanor Pearson late of the same, on 10 June 1612 broke into the park of the bishop of Durham at Bishop Auckland and peeled 200 elms.

7) Archibald Gibsonn late of Fugar House, co. Durham, yeo., on 20

May 1612 at Fugar House in the parish of Lamesley assaulted Thomas Robinson, servant of Isaac Anderson, gen., as he was about to clean a watercourse at Fugar House at *the wood* at his master's command and prevented him from so doing.

8) Toby Ewbank of Durham city, gen., on 20 June 1612 in Durham city attacked Timothy Comyn, gen., and struck him on the lips with the pommel of his sword to the effusion of his blood.

9) William Michesoun late of East Boldon, co. Durham, yeo., on 27 April 1612 at West Boldon attacked John Thompson.

10) John Thompson late of West Boldon, co. Durham, on 26 April 1612 at West Boldon attacked W[illiam Michesoun].

.] 11) John Laurence late of Cowpen, co. Durham, yeo., John Jeekell late of the same, yeo., Robert Cooke late of the same, John Winde late of the same, yeo., Thomas Pickering late of the same, yeo., Richard Fleck late of the same, yeo., James Mann late of the same, yeo., Henry Mann late of the same, yeo., Ralph Hutchinson late of the same, yeo., Robert Davison late of the same, yeo., George Trotter late of the same, yeo., James Rasheld late of the same, yeo., Roger Nullakyn late of the same, yeo., William Chilton late of the same, yeo., Robert Hutton late of the same, yeo., Charles Blackett late of the same, yeo., Matthew Rickaby late of the same, yeo., Robert Browne late of the same, yeo., and Thomas Nicholson late of the same, yeo., on 10 May 1612 at Billingham at *Crykeholme* assembled riotously in the bishop's close and dug a trench 30 yards long.

12) Isabel Hedworth late of Middleton [One] Row, co. Durham, widow, being seised in demesne of 100 acres there which were tilled lands on 24 Oct. 1597, converted 60 acres to sheep pasture [*etc.*] between 1 Oct. 1611 and 8 July 1612.

13) Thomas Wethereld late of Middleton [One] Row, yeo., being seised in demesne in 60 acres arable in Middleton [One] Row which were in tillage on 24 Oct. 1597, did convert 40 acres to pasture [*etc.*].

14) Henry Andrew late of Middleton [One] Row, yeo., being seised in demesne in 50 acres arable at Middleton [One] Row [*etc.*] did convert 30 acres to pasture [*etc.*].

15) James Dale late of Middleton [One] Row, yeo., being seised in demesne in 50 acres arable at Middleton [One] Row [*etc.*] did convert 30 acres to pasture [*etc.*].

16) Thomas Morgan of Wolsingham, co. Durham, gen., between 1 Dec. 1611 and 1 Feb. following sold at Wolsingham outside open fair and market a quarter of barley worth 20s. and a quarter of oats worth 10s. to men unknown passing through the village to Bishop Auckland, so forestalling the market there.

17–21) The same against John Wheteley of Wolsingham, yeo.; William Garthorne of Wolsingham, yeo.; William Tenesworth of Wolsingham, yeo., and two more ... [*corner of MS missing*].

] 22) Presentment that part of the king's highway from Durham city to Hexham, Northumberland, by Framwellgate [Durham] at Dryburn was on the date of enquiry [8 July 1612] in decayed condition for lack of repairs, so that travellers in winter with horses, carts and carriages could barely cross without danger. The jurors testified that the site was in the parish of St Oswald in the suburbs of Durham and that the inhabitants of the parish with lands adjoining the way should repair it.

23) Isabel Procter late of Benfieldside, co. Durham, widow, on 4 May 1612 at Benfieldside in the parish of Lanchester at *Netherwood* felled 2 oaks worth 6s. 8d. each in the bishop's wood.

24) John Waugh late of *Snawes grene*, co. Durham, yeo., and Cuthbert Smith late of *Lawe*, yeo., on 4 May 1612 at Highwood in the parish of Lanchester felled an oak worth 6s. 8d. in the bishop's wood.

25) Nicholas Atcheson late of Ebchester, co. Durham, on 4 May 1612 at Ebchester felled 3 oaks worth 6s. 8d. each from the bishop's forest.

26) Cuthbert Smyth late of the *Lawe*, yeo., on 4 May 1612 at Benfieldside at *le Lawe* felled an oak worth 6s. 8d. from the bishop's wood.

27) Robert Lee late of Shotley Bridge, co. Durham, yeo., on 4 May 1612 at Benfieldside felled 2 oaks worth – each in the bishop's wood.

28) Cuthbert Comyn late of Tinker Hills, co. Durham, yeo., on 4 May 1612 at Benfieldside at Tinker Hills felled an oak worth 6s. 8d. in the bishop's wood.

29) Nicholas Hopper late of Benfieldside, co. Durham, yeo., on 4 May 1612 at Benfieldside felled an oak worth 6s. 8d. in the bishop's wood.

30) Thomas Walker late of Aldin Grange, co. Durham, yeo., on 4 May 1612 at Broom in Billingham wood felled 6 oaks worth 6s. 8d. each and 2 ash trees worth 3s. 4d. in the bishop's wood.

[m.10d.] 31) Whereas at the general sessions of the peace at Durham on 15 April 1612 before Bp James, Charles Wrenn, knt, and Clement Colmore, LL.D., JPs, it was presented that Robert Tweddell late of Monk Hesleden, co. Durham, yeo., on 15 Jan. 1612 attacked Francis Tweddell at Hesleden Hall in Monk Hesleden; at the general sessions at Durham on 8 July 1612 before Bp James, Henry Hilton, esq., and Henry Dethick, LL.B., a master in chancery, JPs, Tweddell appeared in person and pleaded not guilty. Robert Cooper [etc.]. The sheriff to have the jurors for 7 Oct.

32) Similarly at the general sessions of 15 April 1612 before the above, it was presented that George Selbye, knt, sheriff of the county palatine of Durham and Sadberge, authorized by sealed warrant of 5 March 1612 Robert Herrison, Henry Maltbye and Peter Hammon as his special bailiffs to arrest John Blakiston, gen., to have him at Durham gaol so that the sheriff might produce him before the king's barons of the exchequer at Westminster to answer John Swinstoe in a plea of trespass *quo minus* to satisfy debts owed by Swinstoe to the Crown. Maltbye on 9 March would have arrested Blakiston in Durham city and taken him to Durham gaol to await bail, but George Blakiston late of Durham city, gen., and the said John Blakiston late

of Newton, gen., the same day attacked Maltbye in the execution of his office, and George rescued John, who is still at large. Now at the sessions of 8 July 1612 before Bp James, Henry Hilton, esq., Henry Dethick, LL.B., a master in chancery, and John Barnes, esq., JPs, George Blakiston appeared in person, demurred and pleaded not guilty [*etc.*]. Robert Cooper [*etc.*]. Jurors for the next general sessions.

88

Pleas and presentments at the general sessions of the peace at Durham on 7 Oct. 10 James [*1612*] before Bp James, Charles Wrenn, Timothy Whittingham, knts, Clement Colemore, LL.D., Henry Dethick, LL.B., a master in chancery, William Murton, archdeacon of Durham, George Tonge, John Heth senior, John Calverley, John Fetherstonhalgh, John Barnes and Robert Cooper, esqs, JPs in Durham and Sadberge.

1) Henry Siggeswick late of [Whorlton], co. Durham, miller, on 15 Sept. 1612 at Whorlton mill fished with a wicker net worth 2s. 6d. in the Tees and caught divers shedder and kipper salmon and trout worth 10s. out of season to the detriment of the inhabitants of Durham and Sadberge and contrary to the form of the statute.

2) John Applebye late of Whorlton, yeo., on 15 Sept. 1612 at Whorlton [*as above*].

3) Robert Darnton late of Whorlton, yeo., on 15 Sept. 1612 at Whorlton [*as above*].

4) Thomas Wastering of Barnard Castle, co. Durham, yeo., on 29 Sept. 1612 at Barnard Castle fished with a wicker net worth 2s. 6d. in the Tees and caught 3 shedder and kipper salmon out of season [*etc.*].

5) Edward Ledeman late of Barnard Castle, yeo,. on 29 Sept. 1612 at Barnard Castle fished in the Tees with a wicker net worth 2s. 6d. and caught 2 shedder and kipper salmon out of season [*etc.*].

6) Whereas John Shaw late of Cornforth, co. Durham, yeo., was seised of 100 acres in Cornforth which on 24 Oct. 1597 and the previous 12 years had been tilled, and between 1 Oct. 1611 and 12 Oct. 1612 converted 20 acres to sheep pasture and cattle fattening.

7) Thomas Forcer late of Harbour House, co. Durham, esq., on 1 Oct. 1611 was seised of 60 acres which were arable on 24 Oct. 1597 [*etc.*], and converted the same to sheep pasture [*etc.*].

8) [*one case illegible*]

9) ... John Smith, constable, allowed Ralph Searle, a prisoner committed to him on 27 Sept. 1612 at Bishopwearmouth, co. Durham, to break custody.

10) Elizabeth Hall late of Crawcrook, co. Durham, widow, and John Hall late of the same, yeo., on 20 April 1611 enclosed 2 acres of pasture at Crawcrook where rights of common pasture were held by John Lyons, esq., Thomas Humble, Nicholas Newton, John Baite, William Thompson, Arthur Humble, Richard Walker, Cecily Grene, widow, Thomas Pickering, Anthony Dodd, Robert Sanderson, William Jolley, William Foggert, John Hauxley, John Grene, George

Newton, Thomas Grene, John Barloe, Richard Laverock, John Humble, Anthony Humble, Roger Grene, Andrew Copland and Thomas Walker, as free tenants and farmers of Crawcrook from time immemorial, and between then and 23 April 1612 enclosed the same with fences and ditches and prevented common pasture.

11) Laurence Brigham late of Durham city, tailor, on 11 Aug. 1612 attacked Henry Reay, struck him with a drawn sword and bit the index finger of his right hand.

12) Thomas Rawlynge late of Gibbsneese, co. Durham, and John Niccolson late of Winston, yeo., on 15 Sept. 1612 at Winston attacked William Bunting in his residence.

13) Henry Rea late of Durham city, yeo., on 12 Aug. 1612 attacked Laurence Brigham in Durham city, putting him in fear of his life.

14) Nicholas Newton of Crawcrook, yeo., and William Thompson late of the same, yeo., on 30 Sept. 1612 at Crawcrook tore down 60 yards of hedge on the free tenement of Elizabeth Hall.

15) Elizabeth Hall late of Crawcrook, widow, on 4 Oct. 1612 broke the common pound at Crawcrook and took from it 2 horses and a mare belonging to her.

16) John Robinson late of Frosterley, co. Durham, yeo., on 1 Nov. 1611 broke the close of William Chapman at Frosterley at Easter Rogerley and depastured it with horses, cattle, cows, pigs, sheep and muttons until 1 Jan. 1612.

17) Richard Adamson late of Eldon, co. Durham, yeo., and John Adamson late of Eldon, yeo., on 10 Dec. 1611 at Windlestone broke the close called *the Com Gapp* belonging to Thomas Robinson and ploughed the ground.

18) Whereas Henry Hilton, esq., JP, by sealed warrant of 27 Sept. 1612 directed William Patterson and Robert Wilkison, constables of Bishopwearmouth, co. Durham, to have Ralph Searle late of Bishop-wearmouth, yeo., before him or any fellow JP to answer for suspicion of felony, by virtue of which they tried to take Searle but he escaped the custody of Wilkison and is still at large.

19) Robert Garnett late of Blackwell, co. Durham, gen., Anthony Garnett – , gen., Laurence Hewitson late of Darlington, yeo., Robert Watson late of Blackwell, lab., Richard Brackyn late of Darlington, lab., and Robert – , yeo., on 3 Oct. 1612 at Hurworth-on-Tees broke the close ... 2 wainloads of whins [*illegible*].

[*m.2*]   20) Whereas John Barnes, esq., JP, by sealed warrant of 1 Sept. 1612 ordered all bailiffs, constables and other officers to arrest Edward Errington and Thomas March and have them before him or another JP to find sureties to appear to answer at the next quarter sessions and to keep the peace, this warrant was given to Thomas Pereson, parish constable of St Nicholas, Durham. Later the same day Pereson tried to arrest the same at Durham, but they broke custody and are still at large.

21) Whereas Bp James and fellow JPs in full sessions at Durham on 8 July 1612 by sealed warrant of the same date ordered all bailiffs [*etc.*]

to attach John Law late of Billingham, co. Durham, yeo., and have him before the JPs to find surety to keep the peace with Christopher Boick, clerk, vicar of Billingham; Thomas Chapman of Billingham, yeo., and Francis Chapman of the same, yeo., being constables of Billingham, having received the warrant from Christopher on 3 Aug. 1612 failed to execute it although Law was within their sight at Billingham.

22) George Laurence late of Cowpen, co. Durham, yeo., on 4 Oct. 1611 and until the date of enquiry [7 Oct. 1612] carried on at Cowpen the trade of weaver without having been apprenticed for 7 years.

23) John Meborne late of Hett, co. Durham, yeo., John Wood late of Merrington, yeo., Robert Suddick late of Croxdale, yeo., Thomas Hobson late of Hett, yeo., Thomas Woddifeild late of Hett, yeo., John Kirkley late of Hett, yeo., Henry Ferrey late of Hett, yeo., Matthew Wood late of Hett, yeo., and Cuthbert Swynburne late of Hett, yeo., on 7 May 1612 at Hett at *Chamberlaine Medowes* assembled and ploughed up the soil of Lionel Martyn there and depastured his grass with yoked oxen.

24) Whereas George Selbye, knt, sheriff of Durham, by sealed warrant of 16 Sept. 1612 ordered Robert Harrison, his bailiff, to have Thomas Brigham of Durham city in safe custody in the gaol of Durham castle until he satisfied William Key and Elizabeth his wife in £5 8s. principal debt and costs of 9s. as recovered in county court before the sheriff; Henry Maltbye of Durham city, yeo., sworn deputy of Harrison, on 19 Sept. 1612 tried to arrest Brigham in Durham, but when he attempted to lead him to gaol to satisfy the debt Thomas Brigham late of Durham, smith, and Robert Brigham late of Durham, smith, the same day attacked Maltbye in the execution of his office and rescued Thomas Brigham, who is still at large.

] 25) Marmaduke Myers of Middleham, co. Durham, clerk, rector of Middleton [One] Row and vicar of Middleham, between 1 May and 30 June 1612 bought at Darlington from unknown men 20 cows worth 50s. each, 2 heifers at 50s. each and 11 oxen at 50s. each and resold the same contrary to statute.

26) Whereas at the general sessions of the peace at Durham on 8 July 1612 before Bp James, Henry Anderson, knt, Clement Colmore, LL.D., Henry Dethick, LL.B., a master in chancery, John Heeth senior, esq., William Murton, archdeacon of Durham, George Tonge, John Calverley and John Barnes, esqs, JPs, it was presented on oath that William Gascoigne late of Darlington, knt, alias William Gascoigne of Sedbury, Yorks., knt, John Eden late of Belasis, esq., Nathaniel Jackson late of Darlington, yeo., and William Eastgate late of Darlington, yeo., assembled with 20 others unknown on 23 Sept. 1611 at Darlington in a conventicle and started fighting to the terror of the lieges; now at the general sessions at Durham on 7 Oct. 1612 John Eden appeared and challenged the evidence on which he had been indicted and pleaded not guilty. Robert Cooper, esq., bishop's

attorney-general, on behalf of the king accepted trial by a jury which the sheriff was ordered to empanel for the next sessions on 13 Jan.

27) Whereas at the previous gaol delivery at Durham on Mon., 3 Aug. 1612 before Bp James, James Altham, knt, a baron of the king's exchequer, and Edward Bromley, knt, another baron, fellow justices of oyer and terminer and gaol delivery, it was presented that Richard Richardson of Seaton Carew, co. Durham, yeo., on 3 Aug. 1612 between 1 and 2 a.m. broke the warren of John Welburie, esq., at Seaton and with a net worth 5s. took and killed 3 rabbits worth 6d. each; now at the general sessions on 7 Oct. 1612 before Bp James, Charles Wrenn, knt, Timothy Whittingham, knt, and Henry Dethick, LL.D., a master in chancery, JPs, the record was examined and Richardson appeared, demurred and pleaded not guilty [etc.].

28) Whereas at the previous gaol delivery at Durham on Mon., 3 Aug. 1612, [etc. as (27) above] Michael Johnson of Twizell, co. Durham, gen., being seised as of fee of 54 acres arable in Brafferton [etc.], between 1 Aug. 1611 and 4 Aug. 1612 converted 40 acres to sheep pasture and fattening and grazing of cattle; now at the general sessions of the peace on 7 Oct. 1612 [etc.].

[m.3d]   29) Whereas at the previous gaol delivery at Durham on Mon., 3 Aug. 1612, [etc. as (27) above] it was presented that Jane Robinson late of Windlestone, co. Durham, widow, Thomas Robinson late of Windlestone, yeo., and Cuthbert Robinson late of Windlestone, yeo., on 11 Dec. 1611 assembled illegally at Windlestone and attacked Richard Adamson; now at the general sessions at Durham on 7 Oct. 1612 before Bp James, Charles Wrenn, Timothy Whittingham, knts, and John Barnes, esq., JPs, Jane, Thomas and Cuthbert appeared, demurred and pleaded not guilty. Robert Cooper [etc.].

30) Whereas at the previous general sessions of the peace at Durham on 7 Oct. 1612 before Bp James, Charles Wrenn, Timothy Whittingham, knts, Henry Dethick, LL.B. a master in chancery, William Murton, archdeacon of Durham, and John Barnes, esq., JPs, it was presented that Nicholas Newton of Crawcrook, co. Durham, yeo., and William Thompson late of the same, yeo., on 30 Sept. 1612 at Crawcrook destroyed 60 yards of fence belonging to Elizabeth Hall on her free tenement; now at the general sessions on 3 Jan. 1613 before the JPs Newton and Thompson appeared, demurred and pleaded not guilty. Robert Cooper [etc.]. A jury was summoned for 19 April 1616 when, before Bp James, George Frevile, Charles Wrenn, knts, Clement Colmore, LL.D., and Talbot Bowes, esq., JPs, the sheriff of Durham, George Selbye, knt, returned the writ and the jurors testified that Newton and Thompson were guilty. It was judged that they be fined 5s., which was paid in court to the use of the bishop.

89

[m.4]   Pleas at the general sessions at Durham on 13 Jan. 10 James [1613] before Bp James, Henry Anderson, Charles Wrenn, Timothy

Whittingham, knts, Clement Colmore, LL.D., Henry Dethicke, LL.B., a master in chancery, William Murton, archdeacon of Durham, Henry Tonge, John Heth and John Barnes, esqs, JPs.

1) John Pickering late of Willington, co. Durham, yeo., and Thomas Nicholl late of the same, yeo., on 24 March 1612 at Byers Green lopped boughs of oak and underwood worth 3s. 4d. belonging to the bishop on his waste without licence.

2) John Pickering late of Willington, yeo., and Thomas Nicholl late of the same, yeo., on 30 April 1611 at Byers Green dug up 5 yards of ground on the bishop's waste.

3) Henry Swainston late of Coppy Crook, co. Durham, yeo., on 10 June 1612 stole a wether worth 8s. belonging to Robert Vasey at Shildon.

4) John Appelby of Winlaton, co. Durham, yeo., (submitted) and Alice his wife and Bernard Tiers of Winlaton, yeo., and Isabel his wife on 28 Oct. 1612 at Winlaton assaulted Percival Clugh, sworn deputy of Christopher Clugh, the sheriff's bailiff in the Chester ward, in the execution of his office.

5) William Swallwell senior of Ludworth, co. Durham, yeo., on 30 Sept. 1612 tore down the fence around the close of John Rutter at Ludworth and depastured his ground with livestock.

6) Anthony Farrowe (submitted) late of Little White, co. Durham, yeo., and Thomas Hackworth (submitted) late of Morley, yeo., on 19 Nov. 1612 broke the close of John Harrison senior at *Sideburne* House in the parish of Brancepeth, containing 6 acres in severalty enclosed with a rabbit fence, and hunted rabbits by night with nets worth 5s., taking one rabbit worth 8d.

7) Robert Fell late of Dalton, co. Durham, yeo., (traversed) on 29 Oct. 1612 at Dalton impounded a mare belonging to Richard Clement, clerk, found trespassing on Fell's soil at Dalton and detained it until Clement paid poundage of 6d., whereas he should have received only 4d., contrary to the form of the statute.

8) Richard Hilton late of Durham city, cordwainer, (submitted) on 16 Nov. 1612 attacked Christopher Coleman at Durham and imperilled his life.

9) Ralph Skirfeld of Kibblesworth, co. Durham, yeo., on 28 Nov. 1612 at Kibblesworth fished with a fish spear (*leaster*) worth 12d. in the Team and caught 6 salmon, being shed and kipper salmon out of season worth 10s., to the prejudice of the inhabitants [*etc.*].

.] 10) [*illegible....*] at Kibblesworth fished with a fish spear worth 12d. in the Team and caught 6 salmon [*etc.*] worth 10s.

11) Matthew Cuthbert of Kibblesworth, yeo., on 28 Nov. 1612 at Kibblesworth fished in the Team and caught and killed 6 salmon [*etc.*].

12) Thomas Hutcheson of Kibblesworth, yeo, on 28 Nov. 1612 at Kibblesworth fished with a fish spear in the Team and caught 6 salmon [*etc.*].

13) Robert Bell of Durham city, cordwainer, on 9 Jan. 1613 at Crook

Hall in the parish of St Margaret at *Whamsley loning* attacked Thomas Herrison with a stick held in both hands.

14) Edward Tailor late of Harton, co. Durham, yeo., on 10 Jan. 1613 attacked John Wallis at South Shields and hit him with a candlestick.

15) John Greveson (traversed) late of Woodham, co. Durham, yeo., Robert Simpson (submitted) late of Woodham, yeo., George Simpson late of Woodham, yeo., and William Simpson late of Longnewton, yeo., on 15 Nov. 1612 attacked Lancelot Maire at Woodham and damaged his left arm.

16) Anthony Farrowe (submitted) late of Little White, co. Durham, yeo., and Thomas Hackworth late of *Morley*, yeo., on 19 Nov. 1612 broke a close at *Sideburne* House in the parish of Brancepeth belonging to John Herrison senior and attacked John Herrison and William Herrison, the sons of John.

17) Michael Richardson of Durham city on 5 Jan. 1613 attacked William Hubbocke of Durham city, yeo., at Bishop Auckland.

18) Margaret Watson of Bishop Auckland, co. Durham, spinster, on 6 Jan. 1613 at Bishop Auckland stole a basin worth 10d. from John Rudley.

19) John Lawson late of Heighington, co. Durham, yeo., keeper of a common tavern in Heighington, on 21 Nov. 1612 at Heighington sold 5 gallons of ale to Mark Hobson at 12d. a gallon instead of 1d.

20) John Somer (submitted) late of Bishop Auckland, yeo., and John Welshe (submitted) late of the same, yeo., being alehouse keepers in Bishop Auckland licenced by the JPs on divers occasions between 1 Oct. 1612 and 1 Jan. 1613 allowed Richard Slatter, John Hillis, John Key and others to play at cards by night.

21) Robert Watson late of Staindrop, co. Durham, yeo., on 24 Dec. 1612 at Staindrop stole a grey mare worth 40s. from an unknown man.

[m.5] 22) Whereas George Selbie, knt, sheriff of Durham, ordered Richard Hivisid, bailiff of the west ward of Darlington, and also Robert Todd, Thomas Worthie, and Edward Ward, special bailiffs, to take Thomas Clayton to appear in the county court at Durham on 11 Jan. to answer William Bunting in a plea of debt; Worthie and Todd arrested Clayton at Staindrop on 9 Jan. 1613. Later the same day William Newcome late of Winston, yeo., attacked Worthie and Todd and rescued Clayton, who is still at large.

23) Michael Richardson of Durham city, yeo., on 24 Nov. 1610 attacked Thomas Watson of Little Kepier, yeo., in Durham city.

24) The same on 4 Sept. 1612 attacked William Hubbock of Durham city, yeo.

25) Alan Achison late of Whickham, co. Durham, yeo., between 1 Jan. and 31 Dec. 1612 at Whickham practised the craft of cordwainer and sold shoes and boots without having served an apprenticeship of 7 years, contrary to the statute of 5 Elizabeth.

26) William Thompson (traversed) of Crawcrook, co. Durham, yeo., from 1 Jan. to 31 Dec. 1612 was drunk at Crawcrook at various times and places, frequented taverns and drank to excess.

27) Elizabeth Hall (submitted) late of Crawcrook, widow, on 30 Nov. 1612 attacked Andrew Copeland, then a constable in Ryton, in the execution in Crawcrook of a warrant directed to him and John Bates, the other constable, issued by Francis Bunny, clerk, JP.

28) John Morrey late of Gateside, yeo., practised at Gateside from 1 Jan. 1612 until the date of enquiry [13 Jan. 1613] the craft of rope-maker without having served an apprenticeship of 7 years.

29) Peter Denton of East Stobbilee, co. Durham, gen., on 5 Aug. 1610 at Durham city loaned usuriously to Thomas Arrowsmith £3 from 5 Aug. 1609 to 5 Aug. following and required 9s. profit, thus receiving 10%, contrary to the form of the statute.

[m.5d., blank]

90

Pleas and presentments at the general sessions at Durham on 7 April 11 James [1613] before Bp James, Richard Hutton, serjeant at law, chancellor of Durham, Henry Anderson, Charles Wrenn, Timothy Whittingham, knts, Clement Colmore, LL.D., William Murton, archdeacon of Durham, Henry Dethick, LL.B., a master in chancery, John Heth senior, George Tonge, John Fetherstonhalgh, John Calverley, Robert Cooper and John Barnes, esqs, JPs.

1) Henry Franckeland late of Woodhouses, co. Durham, gen., and Isabel his wife, and George Franckland late of Lealholm Hall, Yorks., gen., on 3 April 1613 and on divers days and places before and after at Woodhouses in the parish of St Andrew Auckland, co. Durham, broke the close of Michael Morton and tore down 3 perches of fence at the Lady Closes alias Salcotes and depastured therein with their livestock.

2) The same on 31 March 1613 forcibly entered a kiln on the freehold of the bishop of Durham and ejected Michael Morton, then farmer, and disseised the same of possession from 31 March until the date of enquiry, contrary to the statute of 8 Henry VI.

3) Stephen Gray late of Woodham, co. Durham, yeo., on 23 March 1613 at Woodham assaulted Thomas Worthye and surreptitiously stole a purse worth 2d. containing 40s. 10d. from his person.

4) John Hall late of Middleton Row, co. Durham, yeo., on 30 Dec. 1612 at Middleton Row stole a peck of rye meal worth 6d. from Henry Killinghall. Henry Mason late of Middleton Row, yeo., harboured him there on the same day, knowing of his felony.

5) The same on 20 Oct. 1612 at Middleton Row stole half a peck of rye meal worth 3d. from Henry Killinghall, and Thomas Wilson late of Middleton Row harboured him there, knowing of his felony.

6) George Storye late of Durham city, yeo., on 8 Jan. 1612 attacked Cuthbert Pattyson at Durham.

7) Brian Acheson late of Hag House, co. Durham, yeo., and William Fletcher late of the same, yeo., on 4 March 1613 and before and after broke the close of George Parkinson, gen., called the South Feild and Pasture at Hag House in the parish of St Margaret, Durham, and

trampled the same at will, using it as a common footpath.

8) Christopher Hodgshon late of Wales Moor, co. Durham, yeo., on 18 March 1613 at Lynesack at Dodds Close tore down 6 yards of fence built on the free holding of Ralph Singleton.

9) Mark Owde late of Chester, co. Durham, yeo., on 1 April 1612 at Cocken in the parish of Houghton-le-Spring attacked Nicholas Carr.

[m.6d.] 10) Charles Hall junior of Durham city, yeo., on 21 March 1613 attacked John Davyes, clerk, at Durham city.

11) Ralph Fell late of Dalton, co. Durham, yeo., on 29 Oct. 1612 about midnight broke into the common bakehouse at Dalton and stole a bowl of oats worth 4s. belonging to Richard Clement.

12) Samuel Johnson late of Sedgefield, co. Durham, yeo., on 3 April 1613 at Sedgefield broke into an orchard of Christopher Da[...] and uprooted 2 cherry trees, 3 apple trees and a plum tree together worth 10s. and removed the same.

13) Philip Bainbrigg late of *Sowingburne*, co. Durham, yeo., on 8 Jan. 1613 at Stanhope at Thimbleby Hill broke a gate and tore down 3½ yards of fence belonging to Robert Joplyn.

14) Brian Acheson late of Hag House, yeo., and William Fletcher late of the same, yeo., on 4 March 1613 and on divers days and places before and since broke the close of George Parkinson, gen., called *the Southfield and Pasture* at Hag House in the parish of St Margaret and trampled the grass and came and went at will. (void as before [7])

90A

[m.7]   ? 7/8 April 11/12 James [1613/4]]

1) Elsewhere at the general sessions of the peace at Durham on 13 Jan. 1613 before Bp James, George Frevile, Henry Anderson, Charles Wren, Timothy Whittingham, knts, Clement Colmore, LL.D., and William Murton, archdeacon of Durham, JPs, it was presented that William Thompson of Crawcrook, co. Durham, yeo., from 1 Jan. to 30 Dec. 1612 was drunk at Crawcrook at various times and places, a common frequenter of taverns, and an excessive drinker, contrary to the form of the statute. The same day Thompson appeared before the JPs, demurred and pleaded not guilty. Robert Cooper, esq., [etc.]. Jurors for 8 April, when the parties appeared but the sheriff failed to return the writ. The case was adjourned to 11 Jan. 1615, when the sheriff was ordered to have a jury for 19 April, when the 12 jurors testified that Thompson was sometimes drunk. He was fined 5s. to the use of the bishop, which he paid.

2) Elsewhere [as (1) above] it was presented that Robert Fell late of Dalton, co. Durham, yeo., on 29 Oct. 1612 at Dalton impounded a mare belonging to Richard Clement, clerk, for an alleged trespass committed against him at Dalton and refused to release the mare until Clement paid 6d. as poundage, whereas the permitted fee was only 4d. The same day Fell appeared before the JPs, demurred and pleaded not guilty. Robert Cooper, esq., [etc.]. The sheriff was ordered to have jurors for 8 April.

3) Elsewhere [as (1) above] it was presented that John Greveson late of
Woodham, co. Durham, yeo., Robert Simpson late of the same, yeo.,
and George Simpson late of Longnewton, yeo., on 15 Nov. 1612 at
Woodham attacked Lancelot Maire and struck him divers blows to
the body and damaged his left arm. The same day Greveson appeared
before the JPs and denied the guilt of himself and his fellows and the
sheriff was ordered to have a jury for 7 April. Robert Cooper [etc.].

.]   4) John Barnes sued on behalf of the king against Henry Swanston of
Coppy Crook, co. Durham, yeo., [as 89/3 above]. The sheriff was
ordered to have Swanston before the JPs on 7 April to answer for
divers felonies. On the day the sheriff returned that he was not to be
found in his bailiwick.

Durham CRO, Q/S/I 4 The 10 membranes are filed in chronological order and cover sessions on 11 January and 19 April 1615.

[*m.1*]   Pleas and presentments at Durham on 11 Jan. 12 James [*1615*] before Bp James, George Frevile, Timothy Whittingham, Charles Wrenn, knts, Talbot Bowes, esq., Clement Colmore, LL.D., John Calverley, esq., Marmaduke Blakiston, a prebendary of Durham, Ralph Conyers, Christopher Place, John Fetherstonhalgh, Robert Cooper, esqs, Ferdinando Moorecroft, master of Greatham Hospital, and Francis Bunny, a prebendary of Durham, JPs.

Marmaduke Wivell, gen., John Wortley, gen., James Shaftoe, gen., John Shaudforth, gen., Christopher Hutchinson, gen., Edward Wandlasse, gen., Thomas Wood, Thomas Heighington, George Cooper, Anthony Buckle, John Hopper, John Layton, Thomas Shutwell, Henry Dobbison and William Pearson, yeomen, jurors.

1) Michael Mathew late of Cleadon, co. Durham, yeo., Anthony Mathew late of the same, yeo., and George Mathew late of the same, yeo., on 15 Aug. 1614 at Cleadon riotously attacked John Hayton and drew blood.

[*1A*] Later on 19 April 1615 before Bp James, George Frevile, Charles Wrenn, knts, Clement Colmore, LL.D, John Calverley, Christopher Place and Robert Cooper, esqs, JPs, the defendants appeared and put themselves on the court's mercy without admitting any guilt. They were collectively amerced 6s., which Michael paid on their behalf.

2) Richard Wake late of Cleadon, yeo., and John Cowherd late of the same, yeo., on 15 Aug. 1614 at Cleadon attacked John Haton and drew blood. [*continuation schedule lost but sewing holes visible*]

3) John Sowerby late of Barnard Castle, co. Durham, mercer, on 12 Oct. 1614 at Barnard Castle attacked Ambrose Mason.

[*1B*] Later at the same sessions he appeared, admitted the charge, and sought leave to fine. This was assessed at 20s., which he paid. It was judged that Sowerby should be committed to the gaol of Durham castle until he found sureties to appear at the next sessions and to keep the peace and not withdraw without leave of the JPs.

4) John Sowerby late of Barnard Castle, mercer, on 30 Dec. 1614 at Barnard Castle attacked William Walker.

5) Elizabeth Thompson of Escomb, co. Durham, widow, on 11 Dec. 1614 broke the close of Richard Hodgshon at Escomb and flattened the ditch and uprooted 60 yards of quickset hedge growing on the same.

[*1C*] Later on 19 April 1615 before the JPs she appeared, admitted the charge, and was amerced 20s. and discharged.

6) Whereas George Selby, knt, sheriff of Durham, by sealed warrant of 10 Nov. 1614 ordered Edward Bigland, yeo., and John Siggeswick, yeo., his bailiffs, to arrest John Robinson of Windlestone, yeo., if he

was found in their bailiwick, to have him in the gaol of Durham castle until he satisfied Ralph Siggeswick for £3 7s. 4d. principal debt and 12s. 4d. in interest and costs, as recovered by Ralph before the sheriff in the Durham county court; John Siggeswicke on 27 Nov. 1614 arrested Robinson at Windlestone, to hold him until he made repayment, but Cuthbert Robinson late of Windlestone, yeo., and Elizabeth his wife, and Margery Taylerson of the same, widow, attacked John Siggeswicke there in the execution of his office and rescued Robinson.

7) Roger Simpson late of Swalwell, co. Durham, yeo., Edward Simpson late of the same, yeo., George Colson alias Sanders late of the same, yeo., Robert Smith late of Clockburn in the parish of Whickham, yeo., and William Thompson late of *Newfeild*, yeo., on 1 Oct. 1614 at Axwell houses in the parish of Whickham assembled riotously to disturb the peace and broke the close of William Blakiston, esq., at Axwell houses called *Bromefeild* and dug up a watercourse running through this close 30 perches in length and diverted it from its usual course.

8) Thomas Readheade late of Wolviston, co. Durham, yeo., John Coward late of Newton, yeo., William Denison late of Wolviston, yeo., Christopher Eldon late of Wolviston, yeo., Henry Haswell late of Wolviston, yeo., Ralph Smithson late of Wolviston, yeo., Toby Sharpe late of Wolviston, yeo., and Marmaduke Merley late of Newton, yeo., on 22 Aug. 1614 at Bruntoft assembled riotously to disturb the peace and broke the close called *the Stackclose* belonging to Hugh Bolt and mowed and carried 16 acres of meadow worth £6 belonging to Hugh Bolt.

9) Hugh Mason of Brancepeth, co. Durham, weaver, John Farrow late of the same, joiner, and Thomas Cooper late of the same, spurrier, on 11 March 1614 at – *brigge* broke into the park of Robert [Carr], earl of Somerset, called the East Park and depastured [*illegible*].

10) The same on a similar charge. [*illegible*]

1.] 11) Whereas John Shipperd and Humphrey Davison, constables of Wolviston, on 9 Jan. 1615 distrained on Peter Finche of Wolviston, yeo., at Wolviston for refusal to pay 3d. in cess as assessed on the tenants of Wolviston for the salaries of the master and governor of the Durham house of correction and the muster-master, namely by a tin plate or doubler worth 3d., and purposed to sell the same, Finch and Elizabeth his wife assaulted the bailiffs and recovered the plate.

12) George Richardson of Hutton Henry, co. Durham, yeo., on 1 Jan. 1614 held 60 acres arable in Hutton Henry which had been in tillage for 12 years before 24 Oct. 1597, and between 1 Jan. 1614 and 8 Jan. 1615 converted the same to sheep pasture and the feeding and grazing of cattle.

13) George Wheteley late of Ravensworth, co. Durham, yeo., Martin Wheitley late of the same, yeo., Richard Sotheron late of the same, yeo., George Wascer alias Wascall late of the same, yeo., and Thomas

Cuthbert junior, late of the same, yeo., on 3 Nov. 1614 assembled riotously at Ravensworth to disturb the peace and entered the residence of Michael Thompson at Ravensworth by night and put Michael and his family in bodily fear and carried away 2 yards of linen cloth worth 2s. and half a stone of woollen yarn worth 5s. George, Martin, Richard and George appeared and without admitting guilt put themselves on the court's mercy. They were amerced 6s. 8d. each, which they paid.

[1D] Later on 5 July 1615 Thomas Cuthbert appeared, denied any guilt but to save the expense of a trial put himself on the mercy of the court. He was amerced 6s. 8d., which he paid, and was dismissed.

14) Christopher Sanders of Lamesley, co. Durham, yeo., Robert Carr of *Hurwood Loning* in the parish of Whickham, yeo., John Hinson of Ravensworth, yeo., Gregory Hynson of the same, yeo., William Sanders of Eighton, yeo., Thomas Huntergroome of Lamesley, yeo., Lionel Hynson of the same, yeo., Robert Hogg of the same, yeo., John Wilson of the same, yeo., Richard Hope of the same, yeo., William Wrenn of the same, yeo., Robert Dacon of the same, yeo., John Sanders of the same, yeo., John Dobyson of the same, yeo., George Browell of the same, yeo., John Horner of the same, yeo., Andrew Mann of the same, yeo., William Wilson of the same, yeo., and William Haddock of North End by Gateside, yeo., with 28 others unknown assembled riotously by night in warlike fashion on 27 Aug. 1614 at Gateside on Gateside Moor at the order of Thomas Liddell of Ravensworth, gen., and dug up with iron implements 80 yards of gutter taking water from a spring in *Seamor Moss* on Gateside Moor across the moor to Gateside for the public good of the inhabitants, so that the water could not be conveyed.

15) Whereas Ralph Jarvies, collector of the bishop's fines and amercements in the manor of Bishopwearmouth, co. Durham, distrained by virtue of his office on certain tenants in the same, and on 10 Jan. 1615 distrained at Bishopwearmouth on Robert Stephenson of Bishopwearmouth, yeo., by a heifer for an amercement of 2s. 6d.; John Fletcher late of Bishopwearmouth, yeo., the same day at Bishopwearmouth assaulted Jarvies and recovered the heifer.

16) Whereas Ralph Jarvies, collector [*as (15) above*] on 11 Jan. 1615 distrained at Bishopwearmouth on John Browne of Bishopwear-mouth, yeo., by a mare worth 40s. for an amercement of 10s., Browne assaulted Jarvies the same day and recovered his mare.

[1E] Later on 19 April 1614 before Bp James, George Frevile, Charles Wrenn, knts, Clement Colmore, LL.D., John Calverley, Christopher Place and Robert Cooper, esqs, Browne appeared, admitted the charge, and put himself on the court's mercy. He was amerced 3s. 4d., which he paid.

17) Whereas Thomas Wheitley, collector of the bishop's fines [*as (15) above*] in the manor of Benfieldside, co. Durham, on 30 Nov. 1614 at

the Law in Benfieldside distrained on George Simpson of the Law, yeo., by a cow worth 30s. for an amercement of – ; Isabel Simpson his wife assaulted Wheitley and recovered the cow.

18) Presentment [*virtually illegible*] touching the New bridge.

19) William Porter of Shield Row, co. Durham, gen., a month after 27 May 1606, namely between 1 Oct. and 3 Nov. 1614, harboured in his house at Shield Row Isabel alias Bella Carnaby, Margaret Davison and Mary wife of William Dunne, who had absented themselves from divine service from 1 Oct. to 3 Nov. 1614.

20) George Collingwood of Eppleton, co. Durham, esq., a month after 27 May 1606, namely between 1 Oct. and 3 Nov. 1614, harboured at Eppleton Alice Tayler, who had absented [*etc. as (19) above*].

21) Elizabeth Hedley of Lintz Green, co. Durham, widow, [*as (19) above*] harboured John Walker and Magdalen Kirkely [*etc. as above*].

22) Richard Hegson of – , co. Durham, yeo., harboured Frances Claxton [*etc. as (19) above*].

[2A] Later at the sessions on 10 April 1616 before Bp James, Timothy Whittingham, knt, Clement Colmore, LL.D., Talbot Bowes, John Calverley and Robert Cooper, esqs, JPs, Richard Hickson of Preston-le-Skerne, co. Durham, gen., appeared and having heard the indictment denied identity with the accused and sought a jury. As Robert Cooper, the bishop's attorney-general, could not deny the different names Hickson was exonerated.

23) Robert Hodgshon of Hebburn, co. Durham, esq., harboured from 1 Oct. to 3 Nov. 1614 Margaret Lasenby, Anne Carlell, Robert Colson, Richard Walker and Robert Stoddert, who failed to attend divine service for a month.

24) John Hodgshon of Manor House, co. Durham, gen., harboured from 1 Oct. to 3 Nov. 1614 Isabel North and Margaret Tall [*etc. as (19) above*].

25) Thomas Blakiston of Blakeston, co. Durham, esq., harboured from 1 Oct. to 3 Nov. 1614 James Anderson, Henry Pickering, Mary Blaxton, Mary Wickliffe, Margaret Johnson, Isabel White and Mary Wheatley [*etc. as (19) above*].

26) William Blakiston of Wynyard, co. Durham, knt, between 1 Oct. and 3 Nov. 1614 harboured Eleanor Leadam, Mary Leadam and William Partus [*etc. as (19) above*].

.] 27) John Trollopp of Little Eden, co. Durham, esq., between 1 Oct. and 3 Nov. 1614 harboured John Trollopp, William Andrew, John Simpson, John Whitfeild and Jane Phillipp [*etc. as (19) above*].

28) William Clopton of Sledwick, co. Durham, esq., from 1 Oct. to 3 Nov. 1614 harboured Robert Middleton [*etc. as (19) above*].

29) Francis Dakers of Whitehill Hall, co. Durham, esq., commonly called "the Lord Dakers", from 1 Oct. to 3 Nov. 1614 harboured Robert Beuley and Margaret – , who failed to attend divine service for a month.

30) Ralph Hall late of Greencroft, co. Durham, gen., being a papist

recusant failed after 5 Nov. 1605 to have his son, born at Greencroft, baptised in the parish church of Lanchester within the month.

31) John Blaxton junior late of Coxhoe, co. Durham, gen., being a papist recusant, failed to have his daughter, born at Coxhoe, baptised in Kelloe parish church within the month.

32) Robert Merriman late of Trimdon, co. Durham, yeo., being a papist recusant, failed to have his daughter baptised at Trimdon parish church within the month.

33) Order to the sheriff *non omittas* to arrest James Hunter late of Durham city, fuller, to answer before the JPs at Durham on 5 Oct. following for divers felonies. When it was returned that he was not to be found the date for appearance was extended to 11 Jan., when on default an order to compel appearance under pain of outlawry was issued for 19 April.

[m.3]   34) Elsewhere at the general sessions at Durham on 5 Oct. 1614 before Bp James, George Frevile, Timothy Whittingham, Charles Wrenn, knts, Clement Colmore, LL.D., John Calverley, Christopher Place and Robert Cooper, esqs, JPs, it was presented that John Sowerby of Barnard Castle, co. Durham, yeo., on 1 Aug. 1614 at Barnard Castle was a common brawler and mischief-maker. Later on 11 Jan. 1615 before the JPs Sowerby appeared, demurred and pleaded not guilty. Robert Cooper [[*etc*.]. Jurors for 19 April.

35) Elsewhere at the general sessions at Durham on 5 Oct. 1614 before the same JPs [*as (34)*)] William Wharton late of Barnard Castle, yeo., was presented together with William Sowerby late of Barnard Castle, yeo., and John Sowerby late of Barnard Castle, yeo., and charged that on 20 Sept. 1614 at Barnard Castle they attacked Nicholas Gibson, deputy of Michael Atkinson, a bailiff of George Selby, knt, sheriff of Durham, in the Darlington ward, while in the execution of his office. Later on 11 Jan. 1615 John Sowerby appeared, demurred and pleaded not guilty [*etc*.]. Robert Cooper [*etc*.]. Jurors for 19 April.

36) Elsewhere at the general sessions at Durham on 8 July 1612 before Bp James, Clement Colmore, LL.D., John Barnes, esq., and Robert Cooper, esq., JPs, it was presented that Christopher Atcheson late of Hamsterley, co. Durham, yeo., on 25 April 1612 at Pontop broke the close of Anthony Meaborne and felled and carried away wood, namely 40 ashes, 60 hazel wands and 20 oak saplings worth 40s. Later at the sessions on 11 Jan. 1615 before Bp James, George Frevile, Timothy Whittingham, Charles Wrenn, knts, Clement Colmore, LL.D., Talbot Bowes, John Calverley, Christopher Place, William Bellasis and Robert Cooper, esqs, JPs, Christopher Atcheson appeared, demurred and pleaded not guilty. Robert Cooper [*etc*.]. Jurors for 19 April. On that day Atcheson appeared before Bp James, George Frevile, Charles Wrenn, knts, Clement Colmore, LL.D., John Calverley and Robert Cooper, esqs, JPs, and to save expense sought leave to make fine. This was assessed by the justices at 6s. 8d., to the use of the bishop.

3d.] 37) Elsewhere at the general sessions on 11 Jan. 1615 before Bp James,
Timothy Whittingham, Charles Wrenn, knts, Clement Colmore,
LL.D., John Calverley, *custos rotulorum*, William Bellasys and Robert
Cooper, esqs, JPs, it was presented on oath that John Sowerby late of
Barnard Castle, mercer, on 30 Dec. 1614 at Barnard Castle attacked
William Walker. Sowerby appeared the same day, demurred and
pleaded not guilty [*etc.*]. Robert Cooper [*etc.*]. Jurors for 19 April.

38) William Yonge late of Hetton, co. Durham, yeo., Robert Yonge of
the same, yeo., and Thomas Clarke of Moorsley, yeo., on 10 Oct.
1614 at Pittington stole two hoggs worth 6d. each and a sheep worth
6d. from John Barkus.

39) James Fawside late of Whickham, co. Durham, lab., and Rebecca
Unthank late of Rainton, spinster, on 9 Sept. 1614 about 11 p.m.
burgled the residence of Thomas Snawball in Durham city and stole a
hat worth 2s. 6d. and 2 green aprons worth 3s., a waistcoat worth 2s.
6d. and other linen cloth worth 2s. 6d. from Thomas Snawball.

40) Cuthbert Viccars late of Lynesack, co. Durham, yeo., on 15 Nov.
1613 at Lynesack stole 4 sheep worth 5s. each from Robert
Stephenson: and Henry Watson late of Lynesack, yeo., knowingly
harboured him after the felony.

41) James Fauside late of Chester, co. Durham, lab., on 15 Oct. 1614
between 11 p.m. and midnight burgled the residence of Richard
Hunter at Elvet and stole a hat worth 2s. 6d. and a red petticoat
worth 10s. belonging to Hunter.

42) William Yonge late of Hetton-le-Hole, co. Durham, lab., on 21
Dec. 1614 at Murton stole a ewe worth 12d. from John Shaudforth of
Murton.

43) James Fawside of Chester-le-Street, co. Durham, lab., on 17 Oct.
1614 burgled the residence of George Silvertopp at Chester and stole
4 yards of black russet worth 20d. a yard from Alice Silvertopp of
Chester.

44) Robert Morgin late of Bishop Auckland, co. Durham, lab., on 23
Oct. 1614 about 11 p.m. burgled the residence of William Brasse at
Bishop Auckland and stole linen clothes worth 6d.

45) Robert Cowart late of Billingham, co. Durham, yeo., arrested
because on 12 Oct. 1614 he stole at Billingham certain sheaves of
peas worth 6d. from George Marckham, appeared before the JPs on
11 Jan. 1615 and was led to the bar of the court by the sheriff. Asked
how he pleaded, he admitted his guilt. It was adjudged that he be
whipped in Durham market-place in open market and thence taken
to Billingham and be put in the stocks for four hours.

4] 46) Elsewhere at the general sessions on 11 Jan. 1615 before Bp James,
Timothy Whittingham, Charles Wrenn, knts, Clement Colmore,
LL.D., John Calverley, William Bellasys, Christopher Place, Robert
Cooper and Ralph Conyers, esqs, JPs, it was presented that Hugh
Mason late of Brancepeth, co. Durham, weaver, John Farrow late of
the same, joiner, and Thomas Cooper late of the same, spurrier, on

14 Sept. 1614 about 11 p.m. broke into the paled park of Robert, earl of Somerset, at Brancepeth called *the East Park* against his pleasure and without authority, and hunted deer and took a buck worth 20s. and a doe worth 10s. with cords called *snerles* worth 6d., strangling them: Mason, Farrow and Cooper appeared, and Mason and Farrow admitted their guilt and put themselves on the mercy of the court, where it was judged that they be imprisoned in Durham castle for 3 months in accordance with the statute and pay to the earl of Somerset triple damages and costs after imprisonment, and that they find sureties for their good behaviour for 7 years, and that they remain in prison until their sureties were found. Thomas Cooper pleaded not guilty [*etc.*]. Robert Cooper, the bishop's attorney-general [*etc.*]. Jurors for 19 April.

47) Elsewhere at the general sessions on 11 Jan. 1615 before [*the above, as (46)*] it was presented that Hugh Mason [*etc. as above, (46)*] on 11 March 1614 about 11 p.m. broke into the East Park of Robert, earl of Somerset, at Brancepeth and hunted deer and took a buck worth 20s. with cords worth 6d. Mason, Farrow and Cooper appeared, and Mason and Farrow admitted the charge and put themselves on the mercy of the court [*sentence of 3 months' imprisonment, etc.*]. Thomas Cooper pleaded not guilty [*etc.*]. Robert Cooper [*etc.*]. Jurors for 19 April.

[*m.4d.*] 48) Elsewhere at the general sessions at Durham on 11 Jan. 1615 before Bp James, Timothy Whittingham, Charles Wrenn, knts, Clement Colmore, LL.D., Talbot Bowes, John Calverley, Ralph Conyers, Christopher Place, William Bellasys and Robert Cooper, esqs, JPs, it was presented on oath that Christopher*Sanders of Lamesley, yeo., Robert*Carr of *Norwood Loninge* by Whickham, yeo., John*Hinson of Ravensworth, yeo., Gregory*Hinson of the same, yeo., William*Sanders of Eighton, yeo., Thomas*Huntergroome of Lamesley, yeo., Lionel*Hinson of the same, yeo., Robert*Hogg of the same, yeo., John*Wilson of the same, yeo., Richard*Hope of the same, yeo., William*Wrenn of the same, yeo., Robert*Dacon of the same, yeo., John*Sanders of the same, yeo., John*Dobyson of the same, yeo., George*Browell of the same, yeo., John*Horner of the same, yeo., Andrew*Mane of the same, yeo., William*Wilson of the same, yeo., John*Hedworth of Ravensworth castle, yeo., and William *Haddocke of Northend by Gateside, yeo., with 28 others unknown assembled riotously on 27 Aug. 1614 at Gateside on Gateside moor at the instance of Thomas Liddell junior of Ravensworth, gen., and broke 80 yards of gutter lately made to lead water from a spring on *Seamor Mosse* in Gateside moor to the town of Gateside for the common good and dug up the same, so that it could not convey water. The defendants appeared, demurred and pleaded not guilty [*etc.*]. Robert Cooper [*etc.*]. Jurors for 19 April, when the sheriff failed to make a return. The case was adjourned until 5 July. Then Robert Cooper, the bishop's attorney-general, appeared with Thomas Liddell, who had bailed his tenants. Liddell sought the mercy of the court for the same, and the justices were reminded that he had been previously fined £50 on an indictment and a fine of £10 assessed on his bailiffs. It was judged that the tenants named * should be acquitted of payment of the fines but that they should be imprisoned during the pleasure of the justices.

49) Elsewhere at the general sessions on 5 Oct. 1614 before Bp James, Timothy Whittingham, Charles Wrenn, knts, Clement Colmore, LL.D., Talbot Bowes, John Calverley, Ralph Conyers and Robert Cooper, esqs, JPs, it was presented on the oath of 12 that Robert Saunders late of Lamesley, co. Durham, yeo., Ralph Palliser late of the same, yeo., Robert Liddell late of Ravensworth, yeo., and Richard Lawes late of the same, yeo., with 12 others unknown assembled riotously on 28 Aug. 1614 at Gateside on the moor at the order of Thomas Liddell junior late of Ravensworth castle, gen., and during the night destroyed 100 yards of gutter from the spring on *Seamor Mosse* to Gateside [*etc.*]. Later at the sessions on 11. Jan 1615 the defendants all appeared, demurred and pleaded not guilty [*etc.*]. Robert Cooper [*etc.*]. Jurors for 19 April, when the sheriff made no return. The case was adjourned until 5 July, when Cooper and Thomas Liddell appeared [*as above*]. The fines were remitted but the defendants were to be imprisoned during the pleasure of the justices.

5] 50) MEMO that John Walker, who sued for the king and himself, came before the JPs on 11 Jan. 1615 and laid an information that Thomas Cornforth late of Gilesgate, [Durham], yeo., between 1 Sept. and 30 Oct. 1614 at Durham city bought from persons unknown 6 cows, 6 stirks or *runts* and 6 heifers at 20s. each and sold them alive within 5 weeks. He claimed his share of the forfeiture of double value, namely £36.

Cornforth appeared before Bp James, George Frevile, Timothy Whittingham, Charles Wrenn, knts, Clement Colmore, LL.D., Talbot Bowes, John Calverley, Christopher Place, William Bellasys and Robert Cooper, esqs, JPs, demurred and pleaded not guilty. John Walker agreed to a jury, which was summoned for 19 April.

51) MEMO that John Walker for the king and himself laid an information before the JPs on 5 Oct. 1614 that Thomas Cornforth of Gilesgate, [Durham], yeo., between 1 May and 20 Aug. 1614 at Durham city bought from persons unknown 10 cows, 10 runts, 10 steers and 10 queys at 20s. each and sold them alive within 5 weeks, thereby being liable to forfeit £80.

At the sessions on 11 Jan. before Bp James, [*etc., as (50) above*], Cornforth appeared, demurred and pleaded not guilty [*as above*].

52) MEMO that John Walker for the king and himself laid an information before the JPs on 27 April 1614 against George Thompson of Trimdon, co. Durham, yeo., that between 1 April 1613 and 10 April 1614, being possessed for a term of years of 10 acres arable in West Hurworth which had been under tillage on 24 Oct.

1597, he converted the same to pasture for grazing sheep and cattle | instead of growing corn according to the local system of agriculture. Walker claimed his third share in the forfeiture of £10, at the rate of 20s. for each acre so converted.

Later on 11 Jan. 1615 before Bp James, George Frevile [etc., as (50) above], Thompson appeared, demurred and pleaded not guilty [etc.]. Walker agreed to a jury, which was summoned for 19 April.

53) MEMO that John Walker for the king and himself laid an information before the JPs on 27 April 1614 that Richard Morley of Stainton-in-the-Street, co. Durham, yeo., on 1 April 1613 was in possession for a term of years of 30 acres arable in Stainton-le-Street which had been in tillage [etc.], and between then and 10 April 1614 converted the same to pasture; and Walker claimed a third of the forfeiture of £30.

Later on 11 Jan. 1615 before Bp James [etc., as (50) above], Morley appeared, demurred and pleaded not guilty [etc.].

54) MEMO that Hugh Porter for the king and himself laid an information before the JPs on 5 Oct. 1614 that William Lawes late of Lintzford, co. Durham, yeo., between 1 May and 27 July 1614 at Durham city and elsewhere bought from persons unknown 20 cows at 40s. each, 20 stots at 5s. [sic] each and 14 queys at 38s. each and resold the same alive within 5 weeks [etc.]. He claimed his share of the forfeiture of double value, namely £233 4s.

Later on 11 Jan. 1614 before Bp James [etc., as (50) above], Lawes appeared, demurred | and pleaded not guilty [etc.]. John Walker [sic] agreed to the procedure. Jurors for 19 April.

55) MEMO that Hugh Porter for the king and himself laid an information before the JPs on 5 Oct. 1614 that Thomas Fayrer late of Hunstanworth, co. Durham, clerk, between 1 May and 20 June 1614 at Durham and elsewhere bought from persons unknown 40 stone of wool at 7s. a stone, not having wife nor apprentice to require wool nor being a staple merchant [etc.]. This made him liable to a forfeiture of double value, namely £28, of which Porter claimed half.

Later on 11 Jan. 1615 before Bp James [etc., as (50) above], Fayrer appeared, demurred and pleaded not guilty [etc.]. Jurors for 19 April.

56) MEMO that Hugh Porter for the king and himself laid an information before the justices on 5 Oct. 1614 that William Jackson late of East Boldon, co. Durham, yeo., between 1 July and 31 Aug. 1614 at East Boldon engrossed 30 bolls of wheat at 14s. and 30 bolls of pease at 8s. for resale, contrary to 5 Edward VI, for which first offence he was liable to forfeit £33, being the value of the same, and 2 months' imprisonment without bail.

Later on 11 Jan. 1615 before Bp James [etc., as (50) above], Jackson appeared, demurred and pleaded not guilty [etc.]. Jurors for 19 April.

57) MEMO that Hugh Porter for the king and himself laid an information before the JPs on 5 Oct. 1614 that Robert Thompson late of East Boldon, yeo., between 1 July and 31 Aug. 1614 [as (56) above].

Later on 11 Jan. 1615 before Bp James [*etc., as (50) above*] Thompson
[*etc. as above*]. As the sheriff made no return on 19 April the case was
adjourned to 5 July, when George Selbye, knt, sheriff of Durham,
brought the empanelled jury, which testified as to Thompson's
innocence. It was judged that Thompson be acquitted and recover
costs of 30s. against Porter.

58) MEMO that Hugh Porter for the king and himself laid an
information before the JPs on 5 Oct. 1614 that Richard Raw late of
East Boldon, yeo., between 1 July and 31 Aug. 1614 at East Boldon
engrossed from divers persons unknown 30 bolls of wheat at 14s. and
30 bolls of pease at 8s. for resale, for which he was liable to forfeit
£33 [*etc.*].
Later on 11 Jan. 1615 before Bp James [*etc., as (50) above*] Raw
appeared, demurred and pleaded not guilty [*etc.*]. Jurors for 19 April.

59) Elsewhere at the general sessions on 5 Oct. 1614 before Bp James,
George Frevile, Timothy Whittingham, Charles Wrenn, knts,
Clement Colmore, LL.D., John Calverley, Christopher Place and
Robert Cooper, esqs, JPs, it was presented that George Athye late of
Wolsingham, co. Durham, yeo., was licenced by the JPs to keep an
alehouse at Wolsingham and did on 29 Aug. 1614 and before and
after permit divers unknown persons to play at cards and tables.
Later on 11 Jan. 1615 Athye appeared before the JPs and pleaded not
guilty [*etc.*]. Robert Cooper [*etc.*]. Jurors for 19 April. On the day
Athye appeared before Bp James, George Frevile, Charles Wrenn, knts,
Clement Colmore, LL.D., John Calverley and Robert Cooper, esqs,
JPs, and to reduce expense asked the court that he be admitted to
fine. This was assessed at 5s., which Atheye paid and was dismissed.

7] 60) Elsewhere at the general sessions on 5 Oct. 1614 before Bp James,
Timothy Whittingham, Charles Wrenn, knts, Clement Colmore,
LL.D., John Calverley, Christopher Place, William Bellasys, Ralph
Conyers, esqs, Ferdinando Moorecroft, master of Greatham Hospital,
and Robert Cooper, esq., JPs, it was presented that Ralph Palliser late
of Lamesley, co. Durham, yeo., with 28 others unknown riotously
assembled on 27 Aug. 1614 at Gateside on the moor by order of
Thomas Liddell junior late of Ravensworth castle, gen., and by night
destroyed 80 yards of gutter [*etc.*]. Later at the sessions on 11 Jan.
1615 Palliser appeared, demurred and pleaded not guilty [*etc.*]. Robert
Cooper [*etc.*]. Jurors for 19 April. On 19 April the sheriff made no
return and the case was adjourned to 5 July, when Robert Cooper
appeared, as did Thomas Liddell as surety for Palliser, who was his
tenant. Liddell on behalf of Palliser put himself on the mercy of the
court. Because at the same sessions a fine of £50 had been assessed
for Liddell and a fine of £10 on his bailiff for the same trespass and
riot the fine was remitted but it was judged that Palliser be
imprisoned during the justices' pleasure.
MEMO that the indictment was entered on page 36, 12 James [*sic*]

61) Elsewhere at the general sessions on 11 Jan. 1615 before Bp James,

Timothy Whittingham, Charles Wrenn, knts, Clement Colmore, LL.D., Talbot Bowes, John Calverley, esqs, Ferdinando Moorecroft, master of Greatham Hospital, Ralph Conyers, Christopher Place, and Robert Cooper, esqs, JPs, it was presented that Roger Simpson late of Swalwell, co. Durham, yeo., Edward Simpson late of the same, yeo., George Colson alias Sanders late of the same, yeo., Robert Smyth late of Clockburn in the parish of Whickham, yeo., and William Thompson late of *Newfeild*, yeo., on 1 Oct. 1614 assembled riotously at Axwell houses in the parish of Whickham and broke the close of William Blakiston, esq., at Axwell houses called *Broomefeild* and dug up 30 perches of watercourse running through the close and diverted it. Roger and Edward Simpson appeared, demurred and pleaded not guilty. Robert Cooper [*etc.*]. Jurors for 19 April.

62) MEMO that Hugh Porter for the king and himself laid an information before the JPs on 5 Oct. 1614 that George Swainston late of Thorpe Thewles, co. Durham, yeo., between 24 June and 31 Aug. 1614 at Durham city and elsewhere bought from divers persons unknown 30 stots at 50s. each and resold the same alive within 5 weeks, for which he was liable to forfeit £150 [*etc.*], of which Porter claimed half.

Later on 11 Jan. 1615 before Bp James, George Frevile, Timothy Whittingham, Charles Wrenn, knts, Clement Colmore, LL.D., John Calverley, *custos rotulorum* for Durham and Sadberge, John Fetherstonhalgh and Robert Cooper, esqs., JPs, Swainston appeared and admitted the resale of one stot within 5 weeks and sought leave to fine, which in consideration of his poverty was assessed at 30s. This was divided between the bishop and Porter. He was dismissed as to the remaining 29 animals.

[*m.7d.*] 63) MEMO that Hugh Porter for the king and himself laid an information before the JPs on 5 Oct. 1614 that Thomas Maland late of *Halnth'*, yeo., between 1 May and 30 June 1614 at Durham city and elsewhere bought from divers persons unknown 5 oxen, 3 cows and 8 heifers at 50s. each and 30 ewes at 5s. each and resold the same within 5 weeks, for which he was liable to forfeit £95 [*etc.*].

Later on 11 Jan. 1615 before the JPs Maland appeared, admitted the charge, and put himself on the mercy of the court. He was fined 20s. on the grounds of poverty and ignorance of the statute, of which half was paid to the bishop's receiver and half to Porter.

64) MEMO that John Walker for the king and himself laid an information before the JPs on 27 April 1614 that Christopher Staward late of Leadgate in the parish of Ryton, co. Durham, yeo., on 28 Dec. 1613 at Leadgate did discharge a fowling-piece charged with hailshot and powder at rabbits contrary to the form of the statute, for which he was liable to a fine of £10, with half payable to the informer, and to 2 months' imprisonment without bail.

Later on 11 Jan. 1615 before Bp James, George Frevile, Timothy Whittingham, Charles Wrenn, knts, Clement Colmore, LL.D., Talbot

Bowes, John Calverley, *custos rotulorum*, William Bellasys and Robert Cooper, esqs, JPs, Staward appeared and admitted he was a servant of Ambrose Dudley, esq., and about 27 April at Chopwell on the several soil of Dudley and at his order he shot rabbits on his master's responsibility. He put himself on the mercy of the court as to the amount of fine, which was assessed at 13s. 4d., and paid half to the bishop's receiver and half to Walker.

65) MEMO that John Walker for the king and himself laid an information before the JPs on 12 Jan. 1614 that Robert Smith of Newcastle upon Tyne, yeo., between 1 Aug. and 30 Oct. 1613 at Gateside bought from divers persons unknown 100 stone of butter at 4s. 8d. a stone to sell at Newcastle in fair or market, contrary to the statute of 5 Edward VI against forestalling, whereby he was liable for a first offence to forfeit according to value £23 6s. 8d., to be shared equally between the bishop and the informer.

Later on 11 Jan. 1615 before Bp James, George Frevile, Timothy Whittingham, Charles Wrenn, knts, Clement Colmore, LL.D., Talbot Bowes, William Bellasys and Robert Cooper, esqs, JPs, Smith appeared and admitted buying 6 stones of butter, which he denied was coming by land to sell in fair or market at Newcastle, but he put himself on the court's mercy. It was judged that he be held for a forestaller and be fined on the 6 stones at 26s. 8d., which he paid. Walker gave notice that he had no intention to prosecute as regards the residue, which recognition Smith asked to be recorded. Walker was exonerated for this withdrawal and discharged.

92

] Pleas and presentments at the general sessions at Durham on 19 April 13 James [*1615*] before Bp James, George Frevile, Henry Anderson, Charles Wrenn, knts, Clement Colmore, LL.D., John Calverley, Christopher Place, Ralph Coniers, William Bellasis, John Fetherstonhalgh and Robert Cooper, esqs, JPs.

Robert Farrowe, gen., Thomas Tunstall, gen., Richard Heighington, gen., John Buttrie, gen., John Shaudforth, gen., John Stephenson, gen., Miles Dawson, gen., William Whitfeild, gen., Peter Wright, John Bales, Anthony Yong, Edward Serle, William Grinwell, Thomas Robinson and Ralph Wilde, yeomen, jurors.

1) George Reveley of Ancroft, *co. Durham, gen., Richard Steele of the same, yeo., Henry Chanley of the same, yeo., Edward Steele of the same, yeo., William Dynnys senior of the same, yeo., James Nicholson of the same, yeo., Martin Skelley of the same, yeo., Edmund Crosby of the same, yeo., John Thompson of the same, yeo., Richard Peate of the same, yeo., Willam Dinnys junior of the same, yeo., Thomas Grayme of the same, yeo., Peter Grayme of the same, yeo., and Henry Harrett of the same, yeo., on 22 Feb. 1614 at Goswick assembled riotously and broke down and diverted the ancient watercourse of Haggerston Mill called *Haggerstonbrigg Milne*

so that the water went another way.

2) George Reveley of Ancroft, *co. Durham, gen., Richard Steele of the same, yeo., Henry Chanley of the same, yeo., Edward Steele of the same, yeo., William Dinnys senior of the same, yeo., James Nicholson of the same, yeo., Martin Skelley of the same, yeo., and Edmund Crosby of the same, yeo., assembled riotously on 15 Feb. 1615 at Goswick and broke down the aquaduct to Goswick Mill called *Haggerstonbrigg Milne* so that the water was lost before it reached the mill.

3) Humphrey Stevenson late of Bishop Auckland, co. Durham, yeo., Thomas Ellyson late of the same, yeo., Ralph Currey of the same, yeo., and Henry Ellyson of the same, yeo., on 8 April 1615 at Bishop Auckland assembled riotously and broke the close of Henry Maugham at Bishop Auckland called *Panne Myre* and trampled and turned the same with yoked horses and cattle when it was sown with oats.

4) Robert Finche of Wolviston, co. Durham, yeo., licensed by the JPs to keep an alehouse at Wolviston, between 18 and 19 Dec. 1614 allowed William Mosse of Stotfield to drink and play for a day and a night, he not being a traveller nor a labourer nor a handyman taking his hour off for lunch nor for the better following of his work needing lodging and food in a tavern, nor being allocated there in an emergency by 2 JPs, contrary to the form of the statute of 4 James I.

[*8A*] Later at the sessions on 5 July 1615 before Bp James, George Frevile, Henry Anderson, Charles Wrenn, knts, Clement Colmore, LL.D., and Talbot Bowes, esq., JPs, William Mosse admitted his guilt and most humbly sought leave to fine. This was assessed at 10s., according to the statute, and was to be paid to the use of the poor of Elwick in which parish he offended, to be levied by the constable and churchwardens, to be distributed equally among the poor by the churchwardens and supervisors of the poor.

5) William Hawdon of Bishop Auckland, yeo., on divers days and at divers places between 11 Jan. and 4 April 1615 kept a common tavern at Bishop Auckland and sold ale and beer at a price greater than 1d. an *alequart*.

[*8B*] Later on 4 Oct. 1615 before Bp James, Timothy Whittingham, knt, Clement Colmore, LL.D., John Calverley and Talbot Bowes, esqs., JPs, Hawdon appeared in person, admitted the offence and sought leave to fine. This was assessed at 20s., to the use of the poor of St Andrew Auckland parish, to be levied by the constable and churchwardens and divided equally. It was further judged that Hawdon henceforth be barred from keeping an alehouse there for 3 years without special leave of any 2 JPs.

6) Robert Readshawe of Pedam's Oak, co. Durham, yeo., on 1 Aug. 1614 broke the close of Cuthbert Warde at Pedam's Oak and mowed and carried away grass worth 12d.

[*8C*] Later on 10 Jan. 1616 before Henry Anderson, knt, Clement Colmore, LL.D., Robert Cooper and Ralph Conyers, esqs, JPs,

Readshawe appeared in person and without admitting guilt sought leave to fine. This was assessed at 2s., forfeited to the bishop's use, which was paid.

3d.] 7) John Eden junior of West Auckland, co. Durham, gen., on 30 March 1615 at Evenwood attacked Jane West, wife of Ralph West of Evenwood.

8) Christopher Whelpden of Wolsingham, co. Durham, yeo., on 20 March 1615 at Wolsingham broke glass windows in the residence of Thomas Bainbrigg.

9) The same on the same day broke glass windows in the residence of Ralph Simpson at Wolsingham.

10) MEMO that on 6 March 1615 Clement Colmore and Robert Cooper, JPs, were informed by John Booth of Gilesgate [Durham] that Edward Ewbancke of Old Durham, gen., and others unknown broke into a barn at Old Durham where they found 100 bolls of barley belonging to Booth unwinnowed, and about 60 sheaves of unthreshed oats, and they prevented him from threshing and winnowing the same; and Booth sought a remedy. Having heard his petition Colmore and Cooper went immediately to the barn and an outer fold where they found Ewbanck holding a pitchfork, and several *hanglocks* had been affixed by Ewbanck to the doors of the barn. They ordered him to lay down the pitchfork and open the hanglocks lest he be regarded as a breaker of the peace. Ewbanck declared that the pitchfork was his usual walking-stick. He was ordered to appear at the next quarter-sessions, but he declared that he would rather give his beasts straw and grain from the barn than that they should perish. They reported that they found Booth's barley and oats among the chaff in the barn, and more oats unthreshed in the yard, and some had been carried off before the JPs' arrival at Maiden Castle.

11) William Hopper of Wolsingham, co. Durham, yeo., being licenced to keep a common alehouse at Wolsingham, on 30 March 1615 allowed unknown men to remain 6 hours playing cards and drinking without recognized justification. Hopper appeared in person, admitted the charge and sought leave to fine. This was assessed at 10s., to the use of the poor of Wolsingham [etc.], and Hopper was not to keep a tavern for 3 years without special leave of any 2 JPs.

12) Walter Teneswood of Wolsingham, yeo., being licenced to keep a common alehouse at Wolsingham, on 12 Feb. 1615 allowed unknown men to remain 6 hours playing cards and drinking [etc.]. Teneswood appeared in person, admitted the charge and sought leave to fine. This was assessed at 10s., to the use of the poor of Wolsingham [etc. as (11) above].

13) John Pattison of Claypath, [Durham], yeo., keeper of a common tavern in Durham city, on 20 March 1615 and at other times and places sold ale and beer at more than 1d. a quart. He appeared, admitted the charge and sought leave to fine. This was assessed at

20s. to the use of the poor of St Nicholas's parish. Pattison was not to keep a tavern for 3 years without special leave of any two JPs.

[m.9] 14) John Horne of Wolsingham, yeo., being licenced to keep an alehouse at Wolsingham, allowed men unknown to remain from 20 to 22 Feb. 1615 for two and a half days, playing cards and drinking [etc.]. Horne appeared and admitted the charge and put himself on the mercy of the court. The fine was assessed at 10s., forfeited to the use of the poor of Wolsingham [etc.] and he was debarred for 3 years from keeping an alehouse.

15) George Chapman of Wolsingham, yeo., being licenced to keep an alehouse at Wolsingham, on 10 Feb. 1615 allowed for 2 days men unknown to play cards and drink [etc.]. He appeared and admitted the charge [etc.]. The fine was assessed at 10s., forfeited to the use of the poor of Wolsingham [etc.].

16) Richard Simpson of Durham city, yeo., on 20 March 1615 kept a common alehouse at Durham and sold ale without any licence, contrary to the statute of 5 Edward VI. He also allowed John Pattinson of Durham city, cordwainer, and Robert Rotherforth of the same, cordwainer, to remain drinking for 3 hours. He appeared and denied the charge as to keeping a common alehouse, but admitted the remainder and sought leave to fine. This was assessed at 10s. for the use of the poor of the parish of St Nicholas. He was required to enter into a bond not to keep an alehouse in Durham for 3 years. Meanwhile the sheriff was to summon a jury on 5 July next [etc.].

17) Richard Simpson late of Claypath, yeo., on 20 March 1615 in Durham sold ale [at more than 1d.] an ale-quart. He admitted the charge [etc.]. The fine was assessed [at 10s.] and he was debarred [etc.].

18) Otwell Cooke of Richmond, Yorks., on – April 1615 assaulted Isabel Mautland wife of Richard Mautland [illegible]. He put himself on the mercy of the court and his fine was assessed at – to the bishop's use [semi-legible].

[m.9d.] 19) James Hobson of Lumley, co. Durham, yeo., and Edward Dixon of the same, yeo., on 17 March 1615 kept a common alehouse at Lumley and sold ale and beer at more than 1d. a quart. They appeared and admitted the charge. The fine was assessed at 20s., to the use of the poor of the parish of Chester-le-Street [etc.], and they were debarred for 3 years [etc.].

20) Ralph Brough of Herrington, co. Durham, yeo., and John Stobbes of Streteyate, yeo., between 11 Jan. and 17 March 1615 kept a common alehouse and sold [etc.]. They appeared, admitted the charge [etc.]. The fine was assessed at 20s., to the use of the poor of the parish of Houghton-le-Spring and chapel of Lamesley.

21) Elizabeth Thompson late of Escomb, co. Durham, widow, William Thompson late of the same, yeo., and John Thompson late of the same, yeo., on 20 March 1615 at Escomb assembled riotously and attacked John Todd and struck him on the head with stones to the effusion of his blood. The defendants appeared, admitted the charge,

and sought leave to fine. This was assessed at 100s., to the use of the
bishop. They were dismissed as regards any other action.

22) Thomas Allyson of Cleadon, co. Durham, yeo., Thomas Pearson of
Gateside, yeo., Cuthbert Nattres of Whickham, yeo., Ralph Maugham
of Wolsingham, yeo., Percival Chapman of the same, yeo., John
Snow of the same, yeo., William Grinwell of the same, yeo., Robert
Grinwell of the same, yeo., Edward Feildes of the same, yeo., William
Bowes of Sunderland by the sea, yeo., Anthony Reynold of
Darlington, yeo., Thomas Cowton of the same, yeo., William Allen of
the same, yeo., Christopher Fawsett of the same, yeo., Jane Sober of
the same, widow, John Aycrigg of the same, yeo., Vincent Milner of
the same, yeo., George Blackett of Urpeth, yeo., William Lawes of the
same, yeo., and Anthony Gray of the same, yeo., from 5 Oct. 1614 to
11 Jan. 1615 at their several homes kept alehouses and sold ale and
beer without licence. William Grinwell and John Aycrigg appeared,
admitted the charge and sought leave to fine. Both were committed
to the gaol of Durham castle for 3 days, and each fined 20s. to the
use of the bishop.
[9A] Later at the general sessions on 5 July 1615 before Bp James,
George Frevile, Henry Anderson, Charles Wrenn, knts, Clement
Colmore, LL.D., and Talbot Bowes, esq., JPs, Ralph Maugham,
Percival Chapman and John Snaw appeared, admitted the charges
[etc.]. Each fined 20s. and all three were committed to Durham gaol.
[9B] Later at the general sessions on 4 Oct. 1615 before Bp James,
Timothy Whittingham, knt, Clement Colmore, LL.D., John Calverley
and Talbot Bowes, esqs, JPs, Edward Feildes appeared, demurred and
pleaded not guilty [etc.]. Robert Cooper, bishop's attorney [etc.],
withdrew proceedings and Feildes was dismissed.

23) John Baynbrigg late of Wolsingham, co. Durham, yeo., George
Potter late of the same, yeo., Lionel Thompson late of the same, yeo.,
Thomas Bainbrigg junior late of the same, yeo., and Thomas Grinwell
late of Bowlees, yeo., on 4 April 1615 and before and after were
drunkards. [illegible] appeared and admitted the charge. A fine of 5s.
was assessed on each, to the use of the poor of Wolsingham.
Later at the general sessions on 10 April 1616 before Bp James,
Timothy Whittingham, knt, Clement Colmore, LL.D., John
Calverley, Ralph Conyers and Robert Cooper, esqs, JPs, Lionel
Thompson and Thomas Grinwell appeared and admitted the charge
[etc., partly illegible].

10]   24) Elsewhere at the general sessions on 11 Jan. 1615 before Bp James,
George Frevile, Charles Wrenn, knts, Clement Colmore, LL.D., Talbot
Bowes, John Calverley, Robert Cooper, William Bellasis and Ralph
Conyers, esqs, JPs, it was presented that Christopher Batmanson of
Broom, gen., and his wife, Margaret Swinburne wife of Thomas
Swinburne of Elvet, esq., Jane Horsley of the same, widow, Jane
Hopper of the same, widow, Robert Hopper of the same, draper, John
Johnson of Elvet, weaver, Thomas Forcer of Harbour House, esq., and

Margaret his wife, Margery Parkinson of Hag House, spinster, Margery Doddes of – , spinster, Helen Richardson wife of William Richardson of Moor House, yeo., Francis Dakers of Whitehill, esq., and his wife, John Claxton of Nettlesworth, knt, and Mary his wife, Jane Hedworth wife of John Hedworth of Harraton, knt, Agnes Lambton wife of William Lambton of Tribley, gen., Robert Bulie of Whitehill, yeo., Margaret – of the same, – , Katherine Johnson of Twizell, widow, Michael Johnson of the same, gen., and his wife, George Johnson of the same, gen., Ralph Johnson of the same, gen., Nicholas Johnson of the same, gen., Peter Witham of Twizell, gen., Katherine Lowrie of Fawside, widow, Katherine Lowrie of the same, spinster, Margaret Byermoor, spinster, – Johnson of Broomyholm, widow, William Marlie of Whitehill, yeo., Gerard Liddle of Lambton Woodside, lab., and Barbara his wife, Joan Wrey wife of William Wrey of Beamish, esq., Jane Hodgshon of the same, spinster, Dorothy Hodgshon of the same, spinster, Margaret Wrey wife of Robert Wrey of the same, miller, Anne Dernall of – , widow, Janet Darnall wife of George Dernall of – , lab., Christopher Blackett of – , yeo., and Jane his wife, Henry Browne of – , yeo., and Barbara his wife, Anne Porter of Shield Row, widow, Anne Porter wife of William Porter, gen., Muriel Eden of the same, spinster, Isabel alias Bilha Carnaby of the same, spinster, Margaret Davison of the same, spinster, Mary Dunne wife of William Dunne, yeo., Clara Carnaby wife of Nicholas Carnaby of the same, gen., Elizabeth Hedley of Lintz Green, widow, John Walker of the same, lab., Magdalen Kirkley of the same, spinster, Margaret Kirkley wife of Anthony Kirkley of – , lab., Robert Kirkley son of Anthony, yeo., Margaret Cooke wife of George Cooke of – , yeo., Eleanor Swinburne of – , widow, Elizabeth Story wife of John Story of – , lab., Frances Claxton of – , spinster, Anne Joplin wife of Thomas Joplin of – , yeo., Eleanor Joplin of the same, spinster, Elizabeth Lawes wife of Robert Lawes of Urpeth, yeo., – Harrott wife of Thomas Harrott of *Cockesclose*, – , John Johnson of Stella, gen., and Dorothy his wife, Christopher Denton of Blaydon, – , and Cecily his wife, Ralph Harding of Hollingside, gen., Isabel Harding of the same, spinster, Barbara Blaxton of Gibside, widow, Jane Blaxton wife of William Blaxton of the same, esq., Charles Hedworth of Little Usworth, gen., and Elizabeth his wife, Dorothy Constable of Biddick, widow, Frances Constable of the same, spinster, Dorothy Lisle wife of James Lisle of Barmston, gen., Margaret Merriman of Boldon, widow, Robert Hodgshon of Hebburn, esq., and Anne his wife, Nicholas Tempest of the same, gen., William Hodgshon of the same, gen., Margaret Lasenby of the same, spinster, Anne Carlell of the same, spinster, Robert Coolson of the same, yeo., Richard Waller of the same, yeo., Robert Stoddart of the same, yeo., Anne Manners wife of Robert Manners of the same, lab., Elizabeth Riddell wife of Thomas Riddell of Gateside, esq., Katherine Kennet wife of William Kennet of Saltwellside, gen., John Hodgshon of Manor House, gen., and Jane his wife, George Fairhaire of Ford, gen., and Elizabeth his wife, Jane Hildyeard of the same, widow, Agnes Atcheson of – , widow, Elizabeth Fairhaire of Ford, spinster, William Rawe of Luns House, yeo., and Emmot his wife, Margaret Brigges wife of Cuthbert Brigges of Ford, yeo., Elizabeth Eley wife of John Eley of – , yeo., Mary Byerslie of Cornsay, widow, George Kirkley of Broomshiels, yeo., Isabel Kirkley of Butsfield, spinster, Isabel Carr wife of George Carr of Esp Green, yeo., Agnes Hull wife of William Hull of Hurbuck, yeo., Elizabeth Wilkinson wife of Rowland Wilkinson of Moorside, yeo., Agnes Wheatlie of the same, spinster, Alison Hutchinson wife of John Hutchinson of Burn House, yeo., Agnes Jackson wife of John Jackson of – , yeo., Thomas Darnall of Moorside, yeo., Ralph Hall of Greencroft, gen., and Alice his wife, Christopher Tayler of the same, yeo., and Isabel his wife, Isabel North of Manor House, spinster, Margaret Tall of the same, spinster, Margaret Brasse of Morralee, spinster, Christopher Hopper of Iveston, yeo., Margaret Joplin wife of John Joplin of Hag House, tailor, John Pooleson of – , lab., and Mary his wife, Frances Stevenson wife of William Stevenson of Knitsley, husbandman, Thomas Buck of *Stonyford*, hoop-maker, and Alice his wife, Barbara Newton wife of William Newton of Bradley, gen., John Johnson of Fulforth, tailor, Katherine Porter of – , widow, Mary Mallam wife of John Mallam of – , yeo., – Mallam of the same, widow, Elizabeth Hart of – , widow, Charles Ratcliffe of Tunstall, gen., and Katherine his wife, William Forrest of – , – , Elizabeth Lawson wife of Francis Lawson of Thorpe Bulmer, esq., William Blaxton of Wynyard, knt, and Alice his wife, Ralph Blaxton his son, gen., Eleanor Leadam of the same, spinster, Mary Leadam of the same, spinster, William Partus of the same, yeo., Margaret Bone wife of John Bone of Billingham, yeo., Francis Bone his son, yeo., Joan Bone of the same, spinster, Cecily Swalwell of Wolviston, widow, Francis Blakiston of Blakeston, gen., M[ary] Blaxton wife of Thomas Blaxton of the same, esq., James Anderson of the same, yeo., Henry Pukers of the same, yeo., Mary Blaxton of the same, spinster, Mary Wickliffe of the same, spinster, Margaret Johnson of the same, spinster, Isabel White of the same, spinster, Margaret Wheatley of the same, spinster, Margaret Hall of Neasham, widow, – Tunstall of the same, widow, Dorothy Gibson wife of John Gibson of the same, yeo., John Willie of – , – , and Elizabeth his wife, Jane Simme wife of John Simme of Elton, gen., Elizabeth Ray wife of John Ray of – , husbandman, Anne Baines of – , widow, Alice Robinson of – , widow, Richard Wating of – , lab., Thomas Archer of – , tailor, and Emmot his wife, Beatrice Wilson of – , widow, Lancelot Mason of Sedgefield, yeo., and Susan his wife, Robert Mason his son, yeo., Mary Mason his daughter, spinster, – Woodroope of the same, widow, Denise Bulmer of Embleton, widow, Anne Salvin of Butterwick, widow, William Salvin her son, gen., Roger Richardson of the same, yeo., Elizabeth Bailes of Fishburn, widow, Grace Hussy of Bradbury, widow, Margaret Laverock

wife of Robert Laverock of the same, yeo., Anne Ovington wife of
Peter Ovington of the same, yeo., Elizabeth Smith wife of George
Smith of Foxton, yeo., Anne Hickson of Mordon, widow, William
Hickson her son, yeo., Eleanor Hickson her daughter, spinster,
Margaret Hickson her daughter, spinster, Anne Shawe wife of John
Shawe of Cornforth, yeo., Mary Lawson of – , – , John Hackforth of – ,
– , Anne Killinghall wife of Henry Killinghall of – , gen., Anne Cully
wife of Thomas Cully of – , lab., Henry Moore of Mordon, gen., and
Eleanor his wife, Katherine Conyers wife of George Conyers of
Sockburn, knt, Susan Killinghall wife of William Killinghall of – ,
gen., George Stockdaile of – , gen., Anne Wilson wife of Richard
Wilson of – , Margaret Herrison of – , widow, Thomas Kilborne of – ,
tailor, Mary Wilkinson of – , spinster, Eleanor Hodgshon of – ,
spinster, Ralph Appleby of – , weaver, James Wilson of – , weaver,
George Collingwood of Eppleton, esq., and Jane his wife, Alice Tailer
of the same, spinster, Thomas Smith of the same, mason, Mabel
Mason of the same, spinster, Christopher Turner of Houghton, lab.,
Henry Wight of Shadforth, husbandman, and Emmot his wife, Anne
Parker of the same, – , Agnes Robinson of the same, widow, Dorothy
Todd wife of Nicholas Todd of the same, yeo., John Trollopp of the
same, esq., John Trollopp, his son, gen., Francis Trollopp his son,
gen., John Trollopp of the same, yeo., William Andrew of the same,
yeo., John Simpson of the same, yeo., John Whitfeild of the same,
yeo., Jane Phillipp of the same, spinster, – Welburie of Little Eden,
widow, Elizabeth Chilton wife of Robert Chilton of the same, yeo.,
Elizabeth Trollopp wife of Francis Trollopp of the same, gen., Samson
Trollopp of – , gen., and his wife, Grace Wilson wife of Robert Wilson
of Thornley, yeo., Anne Trollopp wife of John Trollopp of the same, – ,
Margaret Heafeild of – , spinster, Eleanor Wilson wife of Henry
Wilson of the same, tailor, – Potter wife of John Potter, tailor, – Clarke
of – , widow, Grace Trollopp of – , widow, Robert Hunter of – , lab.,
and his wife, – Bulmer wife of [Henry] Bulmer of Tursdale, knt,
Thomas Awde of the same, smith, John Blaxton of Coxhoe, gen., and
Anne his wife, Margaret Garfoote wife of Michael Garfoote of – ,
wheelwright, Richard B[...] of Hurworth, gen., and his wife, – Hickson
wife of John Hickson of – , yeo., Barbara Warde wife of Robert Warde
of Trimdon, gen., Robert Merriman of the same, yeo., and Muriel his
wife, William Thompson of – , yeo., Jane Chaytor wife of Thomas
Chaytor of Butterby, esq., Jane Simpson wife of Thomas Simpson of
Croxdale, yeo., Henry Harrington of Harperley, gen., and Petronella
his wife, Thomas Harrington of the same, gen., Margery Eden wife of
John Eden of West Auckland, esq., Muriel Eden of the same, spinster,
Margaret Athie of the same, widow, Anne Fennicke wife of Luke
Fennicke of – , – , William – of – , – , Margaret Iley of – , widow, Anne
Iley of the same, – , Margaret Metcalfe of – , spinster, Eleanor
Metcalfe of the same, spinster, Dorothy Claxton wife of John Claxton
of – , carpenter, Margaret Lancaster wife of Ambrose Lancaster of

Headlam, – , Margaret Garth wife of William Garth of the same, yeo., Christopher Crawforth of the same, yeo., and Dorothy his wife, Ambrose Crawforth of the same, yeo., and Mary his wife, Anne Pears wife of William Pears of – , Anne Swainston of Gainford, widow, Mary Hildreth of – , widow, – – of the same, spinster, Thomas Watson of Bolam, lab., and his wife, – – of the same, pedlar, William Morton of the same, pedlar, and Juliana his wife, Gabriel Thompson of the same, gen., John Edforth of Shawes, tailor, and Eleanor his wife, Thomas Edforth of – , – , William Clapton of Sledwick, esq., and Anne his wife, Robert Middleton of the same, – , I William Bayley of – , carpenter, and Isabel his wife, Jane Yonge of – , widow, Roberta Salvin of Thornton, widow, Jane Tockett wife of Roger Tockett of Ornsby Hill, esq., Katherine Bailes of High Coniscliffe, widow, William Branson of – , gardener, Jane Teuer wife of Robert Teuer of Heighington, yeo., Elizabeth Oswold wife of Henry Oswold of – , – , Agnes Robinson of – , widow, Jane Dent of – , spinster, Jane Wales wife of John Wales of – , chandler, John Weatherell of – , – , Thomas Towers of Preston-le-Skerne, gen., and Elizabeth his wife, Thomas Towers of the same, gen., and Anne his wife, Thomas Blenkensopp of the same, yeo., Anne Cotsworth of Newton, widow, – Fleming wife of John Fleming of Burtree House, yeo., Jane Barnes of Burdon, widow, William Claxton of Waterhouses, gen., Thomas Claxton of the same, gen., and Elizabeth his wife, Elizabeth Boode of the same, spinster, Isabel Brigges wife of Nicholas Brigges of *Haram*, – , Margaret Richardson of Tuddoe, widow, Jane Underwoodd of the same, widow, – Morland of the same, widow, Barbara Colman wife of Thomas Colman of the same, yeo., James Greene of Billy Row, gen., and Margaret his wife, John Ayre of Wolsingham, weaver, and Mary Pemberton wife of Michael Pemberton of Landieu, yeo., being aged 16 years and more on 1 Sept. 1614 failed to attend their parish church for the space of 3 months, contrary to the statutes of 1 and 23 Elizabeth. It was publicly proclaimed at the general sessions that they should each surrender to the sheriff of Durham to appear on 19 April 1615, which they failed to do.

0d.]

25) John Barnesfather late of Houghton-le-Spring, co. Durham, yeo., on 2 Feb. 1615 about 11 p.m. broke into the impaled park of Elizabeth Lumley, widow, Lady Lumley, at Lumley, hunted deer without her authority and killed a doe with a greyhound. Barnesfather appeared, demurred and pleaded not guilty. Robert Cooper [*etc.*]. Jurors for 5 July.

26) Elsewhere at the general sessions on 11 Jan. 1615 before Bp James, George Frevile, Timothy Whittingham, Charles Wrenn, knts, Clement Colmore, LL.D., Talbot Bowes, John Calverley, esqs, Ferdinando Moorecroft, master of Greatham Hospital, Ralph Conyers, Christopher Place and Robert Cooper, esqs, JPs, it was presented that William Porter of Shield Row, gen., for a month after 27 May 1606, namely from 1 Oct. to 3 Nov. 1614 at Shield Row

harboured Isabel alias Bilha Carnaby, Margaret Davison and Mary wife of William [Dunne], who failed to attend church or chapel. Porter appeared on 19 April 1615, demurred and pleaded not guilty [*etc.*]. Robert Cooper [*etc.*]. Jurors for 5 July.

1615

Durham CRO, Q/S/I 5 The 6 membranes are filed in chronological order and cover the sessions of 5 July 1615.

93

Pleas and presentments at Durham on 5 July 13 James [1615] before Bp James, George Frevile, Henry Anderson, Charles Wrenn, knts, Clement Colmore, LL.D., Talbot Bowes, William Bellasis, Ralph Conyers, Christopher Place, Robert Cooper and John Fetherstonhalgh, esqs, JPs in Durham and Sadberge.

Thomas Tunstall, gen., Anthony Vasey, gen., Richard Birbeck, gen., George Crosier, gen., John Shaudforth, gen., Christopher Fenny, gen., William Whitfeild, gen., John Garthorne, Robert Lang, Anthony Yong, John Atkinson, Nicholas Hall, John Swalwell, George Craggs and Ralph Wilde, yeomen, jurors.

1) Robert Benison late of Sunderland by the sea, co. Durham, yeo., from 1 Jan. to 23 June 1615 at Sunderland practised the art of butchery without having served a 7 years' apprenticeship.

2) William Swinburne late of Barley, co. Durham, yeo., on 8 June 1615 at Darlington at *Westfeildbancke* attacked Robert Hall.

[1A] Later on 8 Jan. 1617 before Bp James, Clement Colmore, LL.D., William Murton, archdeacon of Durham, John Calverley, William Bellasis, Robert Cooper and Ralph Conyers, esqs, JPs, William Swinburne appeared in person, pleaded not guilty and put himself on the mercy of the court. His fine was assessed at 3s. 4d., forfeited to the bishop's use, which he paid.

3) William Herrison late of Eldon, co. Durham, yeo., Robert Herrison of the same, yeo., and John Barnes of the same, yeo., on 30 March 1615 at Coundon Grange in the parish of St Andrew Auckland assembled and *digged up* the ground of Robert Hopper in a close called *the Sunnerfeild*.

[1B] Later on 10 April 1616 before Bp James, Timothy Whittingham, knt, Clement Colmore, LL.D., Talbot Bowes, John Calverley and Robert Cooper, esqs, JPs, Herrison appeared, pleaded guilty and put himself on the mercy of the court. His fine was assessed at 6s. 8d., to the bishop's use, which he paid.

4) Matthew Short late of Elvet, co. Durham, fuller, on 29 May 1611 at Burn Hall in the parish of St Oswald at *Saltwellheugh* carried away an oak worth 6s. belonging to William Snath of Burn Hall.

[1C] Later on 10 Jan. 1616 before Henry Anderson, knt, Clement Colmore, LL.D., John Calverley, Robert Cooper and Ralph Conyers, esqs, JPs, Short appeared and pleaded guilty. His fine was assessed at 2s., which he paid.

5) Cuthbert Hutchinson of Framwellgate, [Durham], yeo., and Robert Yonger late of the same, yeo., on 27 May 1615 at Cocken in the parish of Houghton-le-Spring broke the close of George Parkinson called *Pond Close* and trampled the grass.

[*1D*] Later on 4 Oct. 1615 before Bp James, Timothy Whittingham, knt, John Calverley and Talbot Bowes, esqs, JPs, Hutchinson appeared and pleaded guilty. His fine was assessed at 2s.

6) William Brasse of *Stockwelhewgh*, co. Durham, yeo., on 17 May 1615 at Cocken in the parish of Houghton-le-Spring broke the close of George Parkinson called *the Ring and Broome Close* and depastured it with livestock.

[*1D dorse*] Later on 4 Oct. 1615 before Bp James [*etc. as (5) above*], Brasse appeared and pleaded guilty. His fine was assessed at 2s., which he paid.

7) Christopher Pattison late of Whickham, co. Durham, yeo., being a papist recusant convicted after 5 Nov. 1605, namely 2 Feb. 1615, failed to have his child, born at Whickham, baptized at Whickham parish church or elsewhere within the month.

8) Robert Merriman of White Hurworth, co. Durham, yeo., being a papist recusant [*etc.*] on 1 March 1615 failed to bring his daughter born at White Hurworth in the parish of Trimdon for baptism at the parish church or elsewhere within a month of birth.

9) John Elstobb of Foxton, co. Durham, gen., on 30 June 1615 at Foxton broke down the common pinfold, to the general nuisance. Elstobb appeared and pleaded guilty. His fine was assessed at 6s. 8d., which he paid.

10) Adam Reede late of Wolsingham Parkhead, co. Durham, yeo., on 11 June 1615 at Wolsingham assaulted Anthony Horne, causing bodily fear. He appeared, denied the charge, but put himself on the court's mercy. His fine was assessed at 3s. 4d., which he paid.

11) Anne Bowden wife of Bertram Bowden of Gateside, yeo., on 5 March 1615 at Gateside assaulted Thomas Bi[rd], then a constable of Gateside, and recovered a candlestick and a quart pot taken as distraint by Bird for a cess at 2s. assessed on Bertram Bowden for poor relief in Gateside. Anne appeared in person and pleaded guilty, but because she was old and Bird was negligent the JPs dismissed her without any fine.

12) Thomas Cuthbert late of Ravensworth, co. Durham, yeo., on 27 Dec. 1612 broke into the residence of Ralph Surtesse of – and attacked William Franch of Hedley, lab., with a knife worth 1d. [*illegible*]

[*m.1d.*]   13) Whereas John Robinson, itinerant bailiff of Bp James to collect rents, fines and amercements from the tenants of the manor of East Boldon, co. Durham, on 27 June 1615 seized at East Boldon 5 oxen for arrears of rents in the vill owed by the tenants to a total of £4 15s. 1d.; William Atkinson late of East Boldon, yeo., Jane Arras of the same, spinster, and Margaret Arras of the same, spinster, assaulted Robinson and recovered the cattle. Later on 10 Jan. 1616 before Henry Anderson, knt, Clement Colmore, LL.D., John Calverley, Robert Cooper and Ralph Conyers, esqs, JPs, Jane Arras appeared, pleaded not guilty, but put herself on the court's mercy. Her fine was assessed at 3s. 4d., which she paid.

14) Whereas John Burdus, constable of the borough of Gilesgate in the parish of St Giles, [Durham], on 15 May 1615 took Ralph Jackson of Gilesgate, glover, for divers trespasses, assaults, and affrays in the said borough, to put him in the stocks as a breaker of the peace, Cuthbert Cornforth of Gilesgate, yeo., refused later the same day to help Burdus in the execution of his office. Later Cornforth appeared, pleaded not guilty, and put himself on his country. Robert Cooper, the bishop's attorney-general [etc.]. Jurors for 4 Oct. On this day Cornforth appeared, admitted the charge, and put himself on the mercy of the court. His fine was assessed at 20s., which Cornforth paid to John Richardson, esq., the bishop's receiver.

15) Ralph Jackson late of Gilesgate, [Durham], glover, on 15 May 1615 at Gilesgate assaulted John Burdus, then constable of Gilesgate. Jackson appeared in person, demurred and pleaded not guilty. Robert Cooper [etc.]. Jurors for 4 Oct. On this day Jackson appeared, admitted the charge, and put himself on the court's mercy. His fine was assessed at £3 6s. 8d., which Jackson paid to Richardson [as (14) above], and he was dismissed from the court.

16) Anthony Vasey late of Newland, co. Durham, gen., and Nicholas Vasey of the same, gen., on 22 May 1615 in Wolsingham at Wolsingham Parkhead attacked Ambrose Carlton, gen. They appeared, demurred and pleaded not guilty [etc.]. Robert Cooper [etc.]. Jurors for 4 Oct., when Anthony and Nicholas appeared, admitted the charge [etc.]. Their fine was assessed at 3s. 4d. each, which was paid to Richardson [as (14) above].

17) Thomas Halliman late of Bewley Grange, co. Durham, yeo., on 4 – 1615 and before and after was a drunkard there [illegible].

18) Edward Punshon of Shincliffe, co. Durham, yeo., on 3 July 1615 at Shincliffe attacked Anthony Ayre, bailiff of Elvet, in the execution of his duty. Punshon appeared, demurred and pleaded not guilty. Robert Cooper [etc.]. Jurors for 4 Oct. On that day George Selby, knt, sheriff of Durham, certified the return of the writs, and the jurors testified on oath that Punshon was not guilty.

19) William Burnopp late of *Townsallhouse*, co. Durham, yeo., John Colson late of the same, yeo., and Francis Carlton late of Wolsingham Park, gen., on 21 April 1615 at Wolsingham at *Sawtre Gate* assembled riotously and attacked Anthony Vasey. Burnopp and John Colson appeared, demurred and pleaded not guilty [etc.]. Robert Cooper [etc.]. Jurors for 4 Oct. On this day all 3 defendants appeared and admitted the charges. The fines were assessed at 10s. each, which were paid to John Richardson [etc.].

20) Ambrose Carlton of Wolsingham Park, co. Durham, gen., Thomas Carlton late of the same, gen., Lancelot Carlton late of the same, gen., and Adam Reede late of the same, yeo., on 4 June 1615 at Wolsingham assembled riotously and attacked Nicholas Vasey, gen. They appeared, demurred, and pleaded not guilty [etc.]. Robert

Cooper [etc.]. Jurors for 4 Oct., when the defendants admitted the charge and the fines were assessed at 13s. 4d., which Thomas paid on behalf of all to John Richardson.

21) Thomas Carlton late of *Townsteadhowse*, co. Durham, gen., Ambrose Carlton late of the same, gen., Robert Burnopp late of Hollin Hall, yeo., and Elizabeth Thompson late of *Townsteadhowse*, spinster, on 22 April 1615 at Wolsingham at *Peates Ca*[...] assembled riotously and assaulted Anthony Vasey, gen., and Nicholas Vasey, gen. They appeared and pleaded not guilty [etc.]. Robert Cooper [etc.].

[m.2d.] [illegible] | Later they admitted their guilt and were fined 13s. 4d. each, which was paid by Thomas Carlton.

22) John Simpson of Cockerton, co. Durham, yeo., Gabriel Wilson of Wolsingham, yeo., John Linsey of Wolsingham, yeo., and William Hopper of Wolsingham, yeo., on 24 May 1615 at *Wisell* alias Wiserley in the parish of Wolsingham at *le Stott i' the Milne* assembled riotously and assaulted George Lampson and broke down an aquaduct leading water from the Wear to the mill called *the Stott i' le Milne* at *Wisell* alias Wiserley in the same parish, so that the water found another course. All but Hopper appeared, demurred and pleaded not guilty [etc.]. Robert Cooper [etc.]. Jurors for 4 Oct.

23) John Simpson of Cockerton, yeo., on 30 June 1615 at *Wisell* alias Wiserley at the *Stott i' le Milne* assaulted George Marshall and threw him to the ground. He appeared, demurred and pleaded not guilty. Robert Cooper [etc.]. Jurors for 4 Oct.

24) John Simpson of Cockerton, yeo., Gabriel Wilson of Wolsingham, yeo., and Ralph Wall of the same, yeo., on 25 May 1615 at *Wisell* alias Wiserley at the *Stott i' le Milne* assembled riotously and assaulted George Lampson in the same mill, putting him in bodily fear, and pulled up the wooden *milne cloure* to retain the water in the mill-pond and removed planks in the pond. They appeared, demurred and pleaded not guilty [etc.]. Robert Cooper [etc.].

[m.3] 25) Ralph Moyser of Ryhope, co. Durham, yeo., on 6 June 1615 at Houghton-le-Spring in the residence of John Barking attacked John Pattison of Durham city, cordwainer, and struck him on the head and left ear with a dagger worth 12d., inflicting wounds. Moyser appeared, demurred and pleaded not guilty [etc.]. Robert Cooper [etc.]. Jurors for 4 Oct. On that day Moyser admitted the charge. His fine was assessed at 40s., which he paid to John Richardson.

26) MEMO that Henry Anderson, knt, JP, at the general sessions at Durham on 5 July 1615 before Bp James, George Frevile, Charles Wrenn, knts, Clement Colmore, LL.D. and Talbot Bowes, esq., JPs, returned the following record: MEMO that on 31 May 1615 I, Henry Anderson, knt, a JP, at the suit of John Trumble of Gateside, yeo., went in person to Trumble's residence in Gateside, where I found Ralph Thompson of Gateside, yeo., George Caruddes of the same, yeo., and Richard Bradshawe of the same, yeo., with other malefactors who had entered into Trumble's messuage and

appurtenances to expel him and there remained until my [*Anderson's*] coming: who ordered the arrest of Thompson, Carruddes and Bradshaw and their removal to Durham gaol until they fined for their release. The record was sealed and dated the same day at Gateside. The defendants appeared and put themselves on the mercy of the court. Their fines were assessed, namely Thompson at £3 6s. 8d.; Caruddes at 20s.; and Bradshaw at 20s.

27) Elsewhere at the sessions at Durham on 11 Jan. 1615 before Bp James, George Frevile, Timothy Whittingham, Charles Wrenn, knts, Clement Colmore, LL.D., John Calverley, Ralph Conyers, Christopher Place, John Fetherstonhalgh and Robert Cooper, esqs, JPs, it was presented that Thomas Readhead late of Wolviston, co. Durham, yeo., John Coward late of Newton, yeo., William Denison late of Wolviston, yeo., Christopher Eldon late of Wolviston, yeo., Henry Haswell late of Wolviston, yeo., Ralph Smithson late of the same, yeo., Toby Sharpe late of the same, yeo., and Marmaduke Marley late of Newton, yeo., on 22 Aug. 1614 at Bruntoft assembled riotously at *Stackclose* and broke the close of Hugh Bolt and mowed and carried 16 acres of meadow there, worth £6. Later on 5 July 1615 before Bp James, George Frevile, Henry Anderson, Charles Wrenn, knts, Clement Colmore, LL.D., and Talbot Bowes, esq., JPs, the defendants appeared, demurred and pleaded not guilty [*etc.*]. Robert Cooper [*etc.*]. Jurors for 4 Oct. On that day the defendants, without admitting their guilt, humbly put themselves on the mercy of the court. The fines were assessed at 15s. each, which were paid to John Richardson, esq., the bishop's receiver-general.

] 28) Elsewhere at the general sessions at Durham on 11 Jan. 1615 before Bp James, George Frevile, Timothy Whittingham, Charles Wrenn, knts, Clement Colmore, LL.D., John Calverley, Ralph Conyers, Christopher Place, John Fetherstonhalgh and Robert Cooper, esqs, JPs, it was presented that whereas John Shipperd and Humphrey Davison, constables of Wolviston, on 9 Jan. 1615 at Wolviston distrained on Peter Finche of Wolviston, yeo., for refusal to pay 3d. as the rate usually assessed on him and similar tenants in Wolviston for the salary and fee of the master and governor of the house of correction in Durham, lately built, as also for the stipend of the muster-master, namely by a tin plate worth 3d., which would be sold to raise the necessary money; Finche and Elizabeth his wife later the same day assaulted Shipperd and Davison and violently recovered the plate. Later on 5 July 1615 they appeared before Bp James, George Freville, Henry Anderson, Charles Wrenn, knts, Clement Colmore, LL.D., and Talbot Bowes, esq., JPs, demurred and pleaded not guilty. Robert Cooper [*etc.*]. Jurors for 4 Oct. [*etc.*].

29) MEMO that Richard Hall sued for the king and himself before the JPs at Durham on 11 Jan. 1615 in person and laid an information that John Hinde of Blackburn, co. Durham, yeo., between 4 Oct. and 30 Nov. 1614 at Blackburn by the Browney took 20 salmon out of

season and killed them with a fork and 2 daggers worth 2s., contrary to the statute of 1 Elizabeth, and he claimed his share in the value of the fish worth 20s., the fork and the daggers.

Later at the sessions on 5 July 1615 before Bp James, [etc., as (28) above] Hinde appeared in person, demurred and pleaded not guilty [etc.]. The jurors were summoned for 4 Oct., when the sheriff failed to return the writ and the case was adjourned to 10 Jan., when Hall withdrew his information and Hinde was acquitted. Hinde released his claim of expenses against Hall and the court pardoned his own costs.

30) MEMO that Hugh Porter sued for the king and himself before the JPs at Durham on 5 Oct. 1614 and laid an information that Abraham Wilkes late of – , Yorks., yeo., from 31 May to 20 Sept. 1614 bought at Darlington and elsewhere 120 stones of wool at 8s. a stone without being himself or his wife or domestic apprentices workers in wool or cloth, stocking or glove knitters, or other textile workers that "did make of the said wool and yarn any kinde of clothes, chanlett, wollsteedes, sayes, stamyne, knithose, knit pettescot, knit gloves, knitsleves, hattes, coifes, cappes, arras tapestrie, coverliddes, girdels etc." nor being a merchant of the staple, contrary to the statute of 5 Edward VI. He claimed his share in a forfeiture of double value. |

[m.4]

Later on 5 July 1615 before Bp James, [etc., as (28) above] Wilkes appeared, demurred and pleaded not guilty [etc.]. Jurors for 4 Oct.

31) MEMO that John Walker sued for himself and the king before the JPs on 11 Jan. 1615 and laid an information that Cuthbert Cheasearne alias Cheasbrough late of Killerby, co. Durham, yeo., on 1 Nov. 1613 possessed for a term of years 40 acres arable in Killerby which for 12 years and more before 24 Oct. 1597 were under tillage, and between 1 Nov. 1613 and 11 Nov. 1614 converted the same to sheep pasture and the feeding of cattle. Walker claimed his third in the fine of 20s. an acre, namely £40.

Later on 5 July 1615 before Bp James [etc., as (28) above] Cheasearne appeared, demurred and pleaded not guilty. A jury was summoned for 4 Oct., when Walker withdrew his suit. Cheasearne waived his costs, and Walker was exonerated by the court.

32) MEMO that John Walker for the king and himself laid an information before the JPs on 27 April 1614 that Gavin Ogle late of Eland Hall, Northumberland, yeo., between 1 May and 30 Sept. 1613 at Durham city bought from unknown men 10 cows, 10 stirks or runts and 10 heifers at 20s. each and resold the same within 5 weeks, contrary to the form of the statute. Walker claimed his third of the forfeiture of double value, namely £60.

Later on 5 July 1615 before Bp James [etc., as (28) above], Ogle appeared, demurred and pleaded not guilty. [illegible]

[m.4d.]

33) MEMO that John Walker for the king and himself laid an information before the JPs on 27 April 1614 that Richard Booth of White Hurworth, gen., on 1 April 1613 was in possession of 20 acres

arable in White Hurworth which for 12 years and more before 24 Oct. 1597 had been in tillage; and between 1 April 1613 and 10 April 1614 he converted the same to sheep pasture and grazing and feeding of cattle. Walker claimed a third of the fine of £20.

Later on 5 July 1615 before Bp James [*etc., as (28) above*], Booth appeared, demurred and pleaded not guilty. Jurors for 4 Oct.

(removed by *certiorari*)

34) MEMO that Hugh Porter for the king and himself laid an information before the JPs on 11 Jan. 1615 against Thomas Stott of Framwellgate, [Durham], yeo., that between 1 May and 31 Aug. 1614 at Durham city, he bought 120 sheep hoggs at 3s. 4d. each and resold the same within 5 weeks, so rendering himself liable to the forfeiture of £40, of which he claimed half.

Later on 5 July 1615 before Bp James [*etc., as (28) above*], Stott appeared, demurred and pleaded not guilty. Jurors for 4 Oct.

35) Presentments of responsibilities for public bridges and common sites on the king's highway, namely, over the Team in the parish of Lamesley, Lamesley bridge, Upper Team bridge and Nether Team bridge, Whickham Bridge; over the Derwent in the parish of Medomsley, 3 public bridges over Smallhope called Lanchester three bridges; over the Wear in the parish of Chester-le-Street, called *Head*; over the Browney, called *Relley bridge* in the parish of St Oswald [Durham]; over Chester burn, called *Chesterbridge* in the parish of Chester-le-Street; over the – , Hylton bridge in the parishes of Monkwearmouth and Boldon; over the Wear, Framwellgate bridge, Elvet bridge, Shincliffe bridge; over the – , Eastbridge in the parish of Longnewton; over the – , Whit[...]bridge in the parish of Bishopton; over the – , Coxhoe bridge and Four mile bridge in the parish of St Oswald [Durham]; over the – , Butterwick bridge; over the – , Fishburn bridge, Bradbury bridge; half of Croft Bridge, half of Piercebridge; Greta bridge; over the Wear, Newbridge in the parish of Stanhope, Witton bridge in the parish of Witton; over the Gaunless, *Dentburn* bridge, South Church in the parish of St Andrew Auckland, St Andrew Auckland bridge, Filton bridge, West Auckland bridge; over the Skerne, *Oxenfeild* bridge in the parish of Darlington, Darlington and Norgate bridges, Haughton bridge; over the Gaunless, Burdon bridge; over the Skerne, Woodham bridge in the parish of Aycliffe, and Rushyford bridge; Gate.. bridge in the parish of Darlington. All these were very ruinous and in need of repair for wheeled traffic. Responsibility for repair of Elvet and Framwellgate bridges lay with the inhabitants of Durham city and the revenues from *Briggland*. Shincliffe bridge was the responsibility of Adam Newton, dean, and the chapter of Durham. The remainder were repaired by cess at the charge of the county.

Other public bridges were situated at West Boldon, over the Browney at *Hirdehousebridge* and at *Aldernage* bridge, *Floters Milne* bridge in the parish of Houghton, *Howliforth* bridge in the parish of Sedgefield;

joint bridges over the Tees at Barnard Castle and Eggleston; over the Wear at Wolsingham, Newton in the parish of St Andrew Auckland, Sunderland bridge in the chapelry of Croxdale, and Wascrop; and over the Skerne at Shadforth. These were in good and sufficient repair and anciently supported by cess. The half bridge at Allenford in the parish of Medomsley over the Derwent was chargeable on the chief messuage at Greencroft in the parish of Lanchester, the other half being repaired by Northumberland.

Other bridges were Hedworth in the parish of Jarrow, Bow bridge on the road to East Boldon in the parish of Boldon; over the Deerness, Deerness bridge by Nevill Oak in the parish of St Oswald, [Durham], Sherburn house bridge in the parish of Pittington, the bridge on the road between Pittington and Sherburn Hospital, Ramside bridge in the parish of Pittington, Woodstonehouse bridge in the parish of Houghton, East Hartburn bridge and *Oxenbridge* in the parish of Longnewton, and Browney bridge in the parish of Hart, Billingham [m.5d.] bridge, the bridge by Blakeston mill, | Cow Bridge in the parish of Billingham, *Clockbridge* in the parish of Greatham, Claxton bridge in the same, Coatham west bridge in the parish of Longnewton, Longnewton bridge, Stillington bridge in the parish of Redmarshall, Bishopton bridge, Eastgate bridge over Rookhope burn in the parish of Stanhope, West Auckland; over the Gaunless, Greenwood bridge, Gordon bridge in the parish of St Helen Auckland, Bedburn bridge in the parish of Hamsterley, *Howlet* bridge in the parish of Middleton; Headlam bridge over Headlam Beck in the parish of Gainford, a second bridge over the same on the road between Headlam and Langton, Killerby Mill bridge in the parish of Heighington, Ritton bridge over the Skerne in the parish of Haughton, the bridge over the same on the road between Blackwell and *Brankinmoore* in the parish of Darlington. The bridges at Cockerton, Barmpton, Coatham, Brafferton and Isle in the parish of Sedgefield were unsafe and a common nuisance.

Allenford bridge was chargeable half on the inhabitants of the parish of Medomsley and half on the chief messuage of Greencroft by grant of Ralph Hall, gen. Hedworth was chargeable on the inhabitants of the same. Bow bridge was chargeable on the inhabitants of Boldon; Deerness on the parish of St Oswald, Sherburn house bridge on the master and brethren of Sherburn Hospital. The bridge by Sherburn Hospital was chargeable jointly on the hospital and the township of Sherburn; Ramside bridge on the inhabitants of Pittington parish; Woodham house bridge on Lady Lumley and the heirs of Lord Lumley; East Hartburn and *Oxenbridge* on the parish: Browney bridge on the township of Hart; Billingham on the parishes of Billingham and Norton; Blakeston mill on William Blakiston, knt; Cow bridge on Billingham parish; *Clockbridge* and Claxton bridge on Greatham parish; Coatham west bridge and Longnewton bridge on Longnewton parish. Stillington bridge was chargeable on Redmarshall parish;

Bishopton bridge on its parish; Eastgate on Stanhope parish; West Auckland bridge on the parish of St Helen Auckland; Evenwood bridge and Burdon bridge on the same parish; Bedburn bridge on Hamsterley parish; *Howlete* bridge on the parish of Middleton-in-Teesdale; Headlam bridge and Langton bridge on the parish of Winston; Killerby Mill bridge on the mill proprietor; Ketton bridge on Marmaduke Wilde, being chargeable on the chief messuage of Ketton, and on James Bellingham, knt, being chargeable on the chief messuage of Beaumont Hill. The bridge between Blackwell and *Brankinmoore* was chargeable on the township of Blackwell. The bridge of West Cockerton was chargeable on the township; Barmston bridge on the township; Coatham and Brafferton bridges on their respective townships; Isle bridge on the chief messuage of the Isle. The bridges at Swalwell, Lintzford and Ebchester were shared with Northumberland, as were Eddys Bridge, Monkbridge by Jarrow, and the Tyne Bridge.

Other bridges were Houghall bridge alias Tanfield bridge, Giles bridge in the parish of St Giles, [Durham], Sherburn town bridge, Littletown bridge, Rainton bridge, Houghton bridge and Newbottle bridge, Bow bridge, Hutton bridge, Norton stone bridge, *Dires* bridge in the parish of Norton, Billingham Mill bridge, the bridge-in-the-street in the parish of Billingham, the middle bridge in the same, Bruntoft bridge in the parish of Elwick, Greatham bridge, *Carle* bridge in the parish of Egglescliffe | the Milne bridge and Kent bridge in the same parish, Stillington bridge in the parish of Redmarshall, Shotton bridge in the parish of Sedgefield, Cornforth bridge in the parish of Middleham, Stanhope bridge over Stanhope burn, Middleton bridge over the Egglesburn, Ricknall bridge over the Skerne, Aycliffe bridge, the bridge between Houghton-le-Side and Denton in the parish of Denton. All these were in good repair.

The bridge at Swalwell was the responsibility of the parish of Whickham, and Lintzford was the same. Ebchester bridge was the parish responsibility. Eddys Bridge was the responsibility of (Muggleswick) parish. Monk bridge was the responsibility of the dean and chapter of Durham. Half of the Tyne bridge was the responsibility of the bishop. Houghall and Tanfield bridges were the responsibility of the chapelry of Tanfield. Giles bridge was the responsibility of the parish. Sherburn town bridge was the responsibility of Pittington parish. The bridge between Hallgarth and Littletown was the responsibility of Pittington parish. The bridges at Rainton, Houghton and Newbottle were the responsibility of Houghton parish. Bow bridge was the responsibility of the parishes of St Oswald's, [Durham], Kelloe and Middleham. Hutton bridge was the responsibility of the parishes of Norton and Castle Eden. The bridges at Norton and *Dinefield* were the responsibility of the parish of Norton. Billingham over-mill-race, the bridge-in-the-street and the middle bridge were the responsibility of Billingham parish. Bruntoft bridge was the responsibility of the parish of Elwick. Greatham bridge was the responsibility of the parish. *Carle* bridge was the responsibility of Egglescliffe parish. The mill bridge was the responsibility of – Garnett, gen. Kent bridge was the responsibility of Egglescliffe parish. Stillington bridge was the responsibility of the township. Shotton bridge was the responsibility of Sedgefield parish. Cornforth bridge was the responsibility of Middleham parish. Stanhope bridge was the responsibility of its parish, as was Middleton bridge. Ricknall bridge was the responsibility of – parish. Aycliffe bridge was the responsibility of the parish. The bridge between Houghton-le-Side and Denton was the responsibility of Denton parish.

[6A] Later at the sessions on 10 Jan. 1616 before Bp James, Timothy Whittingham, knt, Clement Colmore, LL.D., Talbot Bowes, John Calverley and Robert Cooper, esqs, JPs, John Humfrey of Bishopton, co. Durham, and other inhabitants of the same parish appeared and admitted that Bishopton bridge was ruinous and that they were liable for its repair. The sheriff was ordered to distrain for payment by 10 April, at which date George Selby, knt, sheriff of Durham, certified that the bridge was repaired sufficiently.

36) It was presented that the common highway from Stockton to the *angle* or common street called *Long Loning* in the parish of Norton and thence to Yarm bridge, where half was the responsibility of Durham and half of Yorkshire, and to Yarm, a market town, and back to Stockton was on 4 July 1615 in bad repair for foot, horse and wheeled traffic, and that it was the responsibility of the inhabitants of Norton parish to repair.

37) John Litster late of Coppy Crook, co. Durham, yeo., on 4 July 1615 blocked the highway from Bishop Auckland to Fildon bridge and thence to Brusselton *Loning* and *Legg' Cross* as far as Denton township and elsewhere with a fence and ditch at St Helen Auckland at the low end of Brusselton *Loning* so that none might pass.

[6B] Later on 10 April 1616 before Bp James, Timothy Whittingham, knt, Clement Colmore, LL.D., Talbot Bowes, John Calverley and Robert Cooper, esqs, JPs, Litster appeared, admitted the charge, and put himself on the mercy of the court. His fine was assessed at 5s., which was paid to John Richardson.

[m.6d.] 38) MEMO that John Walker for the king and himself laid an information before the JPs on 11 Jan. 1615 that John Fuister late of Ebchester, co. Durham, yeo., between 30 Sept. and 1 Dec. 1614 at Ebchester took in Derwent water 20 salmon out of season with a *leaster* or salmon spear worth 12d.; and he claimed a half share of the forfeit of 20s. in respect of the kipper salmon and 10d. [sic] for the spear. Later on 5 July 1615 before Bp James, George Frevile, Charles Wrenn, knts, Clement Colmore, LL.D., and Talbot Bowes, esq., JPs, Fuister appeared, admitted the charge as to killing one salmon, and put himself on the court's mercy. His fine was assessed at 10s., of which half was paid to Walker and half to the bishop's receiver. Walker withdrew any residual suit.

39) MEMO that John Walker for the king and himself laid an information before the JPs on 11 Jan. 1615 that John Pattison late of Stanhope, co. Durham, yeo., between 1 Sept. and 11 Nov. 1614 at Darlington and elsewhere bought 6 queys at 40s. each and resold them within 5 weeks, contrary to the form of the statute, and he claimed a half share of the double forfeiture of £24.

Later on 5 July 1615 before Bp James [*etc., as (28) above*], Pattison appeared, admitted the charge as to buying 5 and selling one quey, and put himself [*etc.*]. His fine was assessed at 20s., which was paid half to the bishop's receiver and half to Walker, who withdrew any residual suit.

40) John Walker for the king and himself laid an information before the JPs on 11 Jan. 1615 that William Gargrave late of St Helen Auckland, co. Durham, yeo., between 30 Sept. and 1 Dec. 1614 at Durham city and elsewhere bought from unknown men 10 stots at 40s. each and resold them within 5 weeks, contrary to the form of the statute, and Walker claimed half of the forfeiture of £40. Later on 5 July 1615 before Bp James [*etc., as (28) above*], Gargrave appeared, admitted the charge [*with a quibble as to 3 stots – written in a very cramped hand*], and his fine was assessed at 20s., which he paid, half to the bishop's receiver and half to Walker, who withdrew any residual suit.

41) MEMO that Hugh Porter for the king and himself laid an information before the JPs on 5 Oct. 1614 that William Lawes late of Lintzford, co. Durham, yeo., between 1 May and 27 July 1614 at Durham city and elsewhere bought from unknown men 20 cows at 40s. each, 20 stots at 50s. each and 14 queys at 38s. each and resold them within 5 weeks, contrary to the form of the statute. Porter claimed his half share in the forfeiture of £233 4s.

Durham CRO, Q/S/I 6 This consists of 21 membranes arranged chronologically 1–6, 8–16, 7 (double dated as 30 April 1617/ 8 April 1618), 17–18, 21, and 19–20. These represent part of the sessions on 10 April and (?) 2 October 1616; 8 January, 30 April and 1 October 1617; and part of the sessions for 7 January, ?8 April and ?8 July 1618.

94

[*m.1*]

Pleas and presentments at Durham on 10 April 14 James [*1616*] before Bp James, Timothy Whittingham, knt, Clement Colmore, LL.D., Henry Hilton, Talbot Bowes, John Calverley, esqs, Marmaduke Blakiston, prebendary of Durham, William Bellasis, Christopher Place, John Fetherstonhalgh, Ralph Conyers, Robert Cooper, esqs, and Francis Bunny, clerk, JPs.

Henry Bales [of Newton Cap], gen., Gilbert Frevill [of Redworth], gen., Christopher Hutchinson [of Durham], gen., Nicholas Hutchinson [of Durham], yeo., William Pereson [of Sherburn], yeo., John Hunter [of Medomsley], yeo., John Morgan [of Frosterley], yeo., Thomas Willson [of Brafferton], yeo., John Richardson [of Tudhoe], yeo., John Sparke [of the same], yeo., Nicholas Morley [of Pelton], yeo., Edward Searle [of Brafferton], yeo., John Cook [of Pelton], yeo., Thomas High[e of Tudhoe], yeo., John Shipperdson [of Wearmouth], yeo., jurors.

1) Robert Smith late of Ebchester, co. Durham, yeo., John Joplin late of the same, yeo., and Thomas Joplin late of the same, yeo., on 17 March 1616 at Medomsley at Broom hill assembled riotously and destroyed a fence 60 yards in length separating the free tenement of Thomas Murray, esq., the master, and the brethren of Sherburn Hospital, and broke up the ditch.

2) Whereas by a statute of 4 Henry VII it was forbidden that any butcher or his servant kill any beast within the walls of London or of any city, borough or walled town within England, or in Cambridge, Berwick or Carlisle, under pain of 12d. for each ox, or 8d. each cow or other animal, payable to the king and the informant; Robert Peacock late of Durham city, butcher, between 12 Jan. and 5 April 1616 killed within the walls of Durham 8 calves, 10 sheep and 3 sows.

3) Whereas by the above statute ..., Richard Foster late of Durham city, butcher, between 12 Jan. and 5 April 1616 killed within the walls of Durham 28 calves, 14 sheep and 8 sows.

4) Whereas by the above statute ..., William Dawson late of Durham city, butcher, between 12 Jan. and 5 April 1616 killed within the walls of Durham 7 calves and 9 sows.

5) Whereas by the above statute ..., Robert Fawell late of Durham city, butcher, between 12 Jan. and 5 April 1616 killed within the walls of Durham 10 calves, 2 sheep and 5 sows.

6) Whereas by the above statute ..., Nicholas Ladley late of Durham city, butcher, between 12 Jan. and 5 April 1616 killed within the walls of Durham 12 calves and 7 sows.

7) Whereas by the above statute ..., Thomas Williamson late of Durham city, butcher, between 12 Jan. and 5 April 1616 killed within the walls of Durham 17 calves, 4 sheep and 4 sows.

[d.] 8) George Lasenby late of Beamish, co. Durham, yeo., on 10 Feb. 1616 about 8 p.m. broke into the residence of William Stephenson at Beamish and stole 4 yards of woollen cloth worth 13s. 4d., 3 shirts at 2s. each, 3 shirtbands at 4d. each, and 8s. in a purse within a cupboard (*abacum*) in the house.

9) Elsewhere at the general sessions on 11 Jan. 1615 before Bp James, George Frevile, knt, Talbot Bowes, esq., Clement Colmore, LL.D., John Calverley, Ralph Conyers and Robert Cooper, esqs, JPs, it was presented that John Hodgshon of Manor House, gen., harboured there for a month after 27 May 1606 Isabel North and Margaret Tall, who absented themselves from divine service from 1 Oct. to 3 Nov. 1614 without reasonable excuse; Hodgshon appeared on 10 April 1616 before Bp James, Timothy Whittingham, knt, Talbot Bowes, John Calverley and Robert Cooper, esqs, JPs, demurred and pleaded not guilty. Robert Cooper as the bishop's attorney-general [*etc.*]. Jurors for 10 July.

10) Elsewhere at the general sessions on 11 Jan. 1615 before Bp James, George Frevile, knt, Talbot Bowes, esq., Clement Colmore, LL.D., John Calverley and Robert Cooper, esqs, JPs, it was presented that Robert Hodgshon of Hebburn, esq., harboured there for a month Margaret Lasenby, Anne Carlell, Robert Colson, Richard Waller and Robert Stoddert who between 1 Oct. and 3 Nov. 1614 absented themselves [*etc.*]. Later on 10 April 1616 before [*the above as (9) with Clement Colmore, LL.D.*], JPs, Hodgshon appeared, demurred and pleaded not guilty. Robert Cooper [*etc.*]. Jurors for 10 July. (removed by *certiorari*)

11) Elsewhere at the general sessions on 11 Jan. 1615 before Bp James, George Frevile, knt, Talbot Bowes, esq., Clement Colmore, LL.D., John Calverley and Robert Cooper, esqs, JPs, it was presented that George Collingwood of Eppleton, esq., harboured there for a month Alice Tayler, who absented herself from divine service from 1 Oct. to 3 Nov. 1615. Later on 10 April 1616 before Bp James, Timothy Whittingham, knt, Talbot Bowes, esq., Clement Colmore, LL.D., John Calverley and Robert Cooper, esqs, JPs, Collingwood appeared, [*following membrane missing*]

95

[*no heading, but apparently the sessions held on 2 Oct. 1616*]

1) Francis Cotesworth late of Blackwell, co. Durham, lab., and Thomas Mounty late of the same, lab., on 14 Aug. 1616 at Blackwell stole 3 pecks of rye or maslin worth 11d. from Jane Cornforth of Blackwell,

widow. Cotesworth and Mounty appeared at the bar of the court with the sheriff and admitted the charge. It was judged that they be whipped in the Durham market-place at the next open market and should then be dismissed.

2) Oswald Huckneld late of South Shields, co. Durham, yeo., and Tobias Hucknold late of the same, yeo., the latter being the king's constable in South Shields, with others unknown, on 14 July 1616 assembled riotously at South Shields and attacked Cuthbert Hall and Elizabeth his wife to the effusion of Elizabeth's blood and illegally put Cuthbert in the stocks. Tobias appeared at the same general sessions and while affirming his innocence put himself on the mercy of the court to save expense. A fine of 3s. 4d. was imposed, to the bishop's use, and he was dismissed. Later on 9 July 1617 before John Calverley, Talbot Bowes and Ralph Bowes, knts, JPs, Oswald appeared, admitted the charge, and paid a fine of 2s. to the king's use as the bishopric was vacant. The case was dismissed *sine die*.

3) Elizabeth Siggsewick wife of Robert Siggswick late of Darlington, co. Durham, yeo., on 20 Aug. 1616 at Darlington attacked Eleanor Kilborne and struck her on the head with a rake worth 1d., inflicting a wound 1 inch long by a half inch deep to the back of the head and another wound 1 inch by a half inch to the forehead and elsewhere. Elizabeth appeared and admitted the charge. A fine of 3s. 4d. was imposed to the use of the bishop by reason of his regalian rights in the county palatine of Durham and Sadberge, which she paid and was dismissed.

4) Thomas Cherneside late of Cheswick, *co. Durham, gen., with 13 others unknown, on 23 July 1616 entered a messuage and 2 acres with appurtenances in Cheswick, being the freeholding of Thomas Hudson, and disseised the same and there remains. Thomas Hudson appeared at the general sessions before the king's justices on 2 Oct. 1616 and sought a writ of restitution to be directed to the sheriff of Durham, which was granted after mature consideration. Thomas Chernyside also appeared and sought that the indictment be pleaded, notwithstanding the writ.

5) Thomas Churneside late of Cheswick, *co. Durham, gen., with 13 others unknown on 23 July 1616 broke the close of Thomas Hudson, gen., at Cheswick and reaped and took a *macram* of barley worth 100s. Thomas Chernysyde appeared, demurred and pleaded not guilty. Robert Cooper as attorney-general of Bp James [*etc.*]. Jurors for 8 Jan.

6) Henry Jackson late of Woodifield, co. Durham, yeo., Henry Jackson junior of the same, yeo., Edward Greame of the same, lab., William Robinson of the same, yeo., and William Glen of Steel House, co. Durham., lab., on 16 Sept. 1616 at Wheatbottom in the parish of – riotously assembled in the close called *the Ley* and stole 22 stooks of oats of Anthony Nicholson of Wheatbottom. The defendants appeared, demurred and pleaded not guilty. I Robert Cooper as attorney-general [*etc.*]. Jurors for 8 Jan.

[*m.2d.*]

7) Whereas George Selby, knt, sheriff of Durham and Sadberge, by
virtue of a writ from the court of pleas at Durham authorised on 12
July 1616 Robert Errington and Richard Vasey as special bailiffs to
arrest Henry Gibson of Sunderland, co. Durham, yeo., and William
Punshon late of Herrington, gen., to be before the king's justices at
Durham on 22 July at 8 a.m. to answer Henry Hilton, gen., in a plea
that each return £100, and on 16 July 1616 Errington and Vasey
arrested Punshon at Houghton-le-Spring to take him to Durham gaol
until he found surety to appear; Percival Thompson of Houghton,
yeo., William Tayler of the same, yeo., and Alexander Blacklock of
the same, yeo., with 7 others unknown attacked Errington and Vasey
at Houghton in the execution of their duty and rescued Punshon,
who had engineered the same rescue. Thompson and Tayler
appeared, demurred and pleaded not guilty [etc.]. Robert Cooper
[etc.]. Jurors for 8 Jan., when both parties appeared and the jury
testified that Taylor was guilty but that Thompson was not guilty. It
was judged that Tayler be arrested to make satisfaction for his
trespass. He asked leave to fine, which was assessed at £6 13s. 4d.,
assigned to the bishop's use from time immemorial, and he was
committed to prison in Durham castle until the fine was paid.
Thompson was dismissed.
8) Thomas Cherneside late of Goswick, *co. Durham, gen., with 13
others unknown on 23 July 1616 entered the messuage and 2 acres
with appurtenances in Cheswick belonging to Thomas Hudson, gen.,
and disseised him of his free tenement. Cherneside appeared,
demurred and pleaded not guilty. Robert Cooper [etc.]. Jurors for 8
Jan.
9) Edward Robinson late of Kimblesworth, co. Durham, yeo., after 1
Aug. 1613, namely on 4 Aug. 1616, while not having lands [etc.], kept
a greyhound.
10) Elsewhere at the general sessions on 5 July 1615 before Bp James,
George Frevile, Henry Anderson, Charles Wrenn, knts, Clement
Colmore, LL.D., John Calverley and Christopher Place, esqs, JPs, it
was presented that Gordon bridge on the king's highway over the
Gaunless in the parish of St Helen Auckland was in great decay, a
danger to the lieges and a common nuisance. The jurors testified that
its repair was the responsibility of the parishioners. Now on 2 Oct.
1616 before Bp James, Henry Anderson, Timothy Whittingham, knts,
Clement Colmore, LL.D., Henry Hilton, Talbot Bowes, John
Calverley, Ralph Conyers and Robert Cooper, esqs, JPs, William
Dixon, an inhabitant, was distrained and appeared, demurred and
argued that the bridge was not a parochial but a county
responsibility. The contrary was affirmed by Robert Cooper. It was
ordered that an inquest be taken.
11) Elsewhere at the general sessions on 10 July 1616 before Bp James,
Henry Anderson, knt, Clement Colmore, LL.D., Talbot Bowes, esq.,
William Murton, archdeacon of Durham, Christopher Place, Ralph

Conyers, Robert Cooper, esqs, and Francis Bunney, clerk, JPs, it was
presented that Robert Millott of Cocken, co. Durham, esq., and his
wife, Mabel Smith of Eppleton, – , Jane Carleton of Easington,
spinster, Margaret Todd of Hawthorn, - , William Hanson of Trimdon,
yeo., Elizabeth Suddick wife of Robert Suddick of Croxdale, yeo.,
Bridget Cockson wife of Anthony Cockson of Pittington parish, gen.,
Denise Blakey of Kelloe parish, widow, Janet Frend of Elvet in the
parish of St Oswald, [Durham], spinster, Margaret Comyn of the
same, widow, John Hedworth of Harraton, knt, Mary Rookeby wife of
Robert Rookeby of the same, gen., – Jackson wife of Thomas Jackson
of the same, yeo., John Floure of Witton Gilbert parish, yeo., and
Elizabeth his wife, Clara Walker of the same, widow, Isabel Walker of
the same, spinster, Alice Hopper wife of Christopher Hopper of the
same, yeo., Jane Kirkley of Butsfield, spinster, Alice Skurrey of the
same, widow, Isabel Darnall wife of Thomas Darnall in the parish of
Lanchester, yeo., Isabel Claxton of Ford, spinster, Agnes Claxton of
the same, spinster, Thomas Bowes of Langley Hall, gen., and Mary his
wife, Janet Tayler wife of William Tayler of Cornsay Row, yeo.,
Christopher Hopper of Newbiggin, yeo., Jane Bainbrigg in the parish
of Lanchester, – , Margaret Taylor of the same, spinster, Elizabeth Hull
of the same, widow, George Wrey of Langley mill, yeo., and Elizabeth
his wife, Robert Carudders of Lanchester, yeo., Jane wife of John
Atkinson of the same, yeo., Robert Atkinson of the same, yeo., John
Joplyn of Hag House, yeo., and Margaret his wife, Anne Musgrave of
Medomsley parish, widow, George Shaftoe of the same, yeo., and
Isabel his wife, Anne Kirkley wife of Richard Kirkley of Medomsley,
yeo., Barbara wife of Willam Newton of the same, yeo., Thomas
Grinwell of the same, yeo., Leonard Grinwell of the same, yeo.,
[m.3d.]   Agnes wife of William Proude of | Hunstanworth, yeo., Isabel Ayden
of the same, widow, Isabel Potts wife of Thomas Potts of the same,
yeo., Charles Forrest of Whickham parish, yeo., and Jane his wife,
Jane Lawes of Gateside, spinster, Marmaduke Squire of the same,
yeo., Margaret wife of John Raffe of the same, yeo., Marmaduke
Constable of Biddick, gen., Anne Browne of the same, spinster,
Anthony Todd of Great Usworth, yeo., Christopher Sotheron of
Hebburn, yeo., Frances Jackson of the same, spinster, James King of
the same, yeo., William Tempest of Jarrow parish, gen., Anne wife of
Robert Manners of the same, yeo., David Birtley of the same, yeo.,
Robert Slator of the same, yeo., Katherine Rawe of the same, – ,
Margaret wife of John Rutor of the same, yeo., John Dand of the
same, yeo., and Isabel his wife, George Watson of the same, yeo., and
Anne his wife, Jane Carr wife of Robert Carr of Tanfield, yeo., Jane
Foreman of the same, widow, George North of the same, – and – his
wife, Jane wife of Michael Hopper of the same, yeo., William Curey
of Wolsingham, knt, and Katherine his wife, Agnes Forwick of
Hamsterley parish, – , Robert Reynison of Mayland, yeo., and – his
wife, Henry Dale of Staindrop, yeo., Charles Brabant junior of the

same, yeo., Grace wife of Francis Brakenbury of Osmond Croft, esq., Dorothy Clayton late of Winston, widow, Margaret wife of Thomas Watson of Gainford parish, yeo., Thomas Hode of the same, yeo., Katherine Gray of Selaby, widow, William Clopton junior of Sledwick, gen., Eleanor Colton of Whorlton, widow, Robert Hickson of Aycliffe parish, gen., Elizabeth Barnes of the same, widow, Thomas Strangwish of the same, yeo., Jane Waite of the same, spinster, Katherine Speck of the same, – , Margaret Baxter wife of William Baxter of Whitworth, gen., – Stoddart of Brancepeth parish, widow, – Tunstall wife of Francis Tunstall of the same, esq., John Claxton junior of Nettlesworth, esq., Jane wife of William Wilkinson of the parish of Hartlepool, yeo., William Wilkinson his son, yeo., Anthony Grame of the same, yeo., Isabel wife of Robert Porrett of Hartlepool, gen., Anne Porrett of the same, spinster, Margery Thompson of the same, spinster, Robert Harrington of North Bedburn, yeo., and Mary his wife, Agnes Beanes of Bishopton parish, widow, Elizabeth wife of Richard Peacock of the same, yeo., Agnes Fletcher of Norton parish, spinster, William Blakiston junior of Blakeston, gen., Francis Hodgshon of the same, yeo., Margaret wife of John Skurrey of Preston, yeo., Mary wife of James Anderson of Grindon, yeo., Margaret wife of Lancelot Todd of Stillington, yeo., Margaret Cully of Sadberge, – , Eleanor wife of William Weatherell of Girsby in the parish of Sockburn, yeo., George Hodgshon of the same, yeo., and Mary his wife, Mary Emerson of Tunstall, – , Katherine Lasenby of Wynyard, spinster, Helen Partus wife of William Partus of – , yeo., Anne wife of William Kirkley of Knitsley, yeo., Janet Faireman of Beamish, John Winter of Thornley, yeo., and Eleanor Simpson of the same, spinster, being on 10 May 1616 of 16 years or more, failed to attend their parish churches for the space of 2 months. Being summoned by public proclamation to present themselves at the general sessions on 2 Oct. 1616 they defaulted and were convicted of contempt.

96

Pleas and presentments at the general sessions at Durham on 8 Jan. 14 James [1617] before Bp James, Clement Colmore, LL.D., John Calverley, esq., William Murton, archdeacon of Durham, William Bellasys, esq., Ferdinando Moorecroft, master of Greatham Hospital, Robert Cooper and Ralph Conyers, esqs, JPs.

Robert Farrowe, gen., William Whitfeild, gen., Christopher Fenny, gen., William Peres, John Shipperdson, John Hopper, John Swalwell, Robert Pye, William Marley, George Smith, Simon Lackenby, Thomas Stott, Ralph Catherick, George Lawes and Thomas Heighington, yeomen, jurors

1) Whereas Thomas Litster, collector of the bishop's rents, fines and amercements in Cornforth, co. Durham, by virtue of his office to raise estreats as delivered to him on 1 Dec. 1615 distrained on certain

tenants of the bishop and especially on John Shawe junior of Cornforth by an ox for an amercement of 3s. 6d. imposed at Sedgefield halmote court on 24 Oct. 1615; on the same day Shawe assaulted Litster and recovered the ox.

[4A] Later at Durham on 8 April 1618 before Richard Hutton, knt, a judge of Common Pleas and chancellor of Durham, William Bellasis, John Calverley, George Tonge, Ralph Conyers, knts, Christopher Place and Robert Cooper, esqs, JPs, Shawe appeared, admitted the charge, and sought leave to fine. This was assessed at 6s. 8d., to the bishop's use, which he paid.

2) Whereas Thomas Ettis, collector of the bishop's rents, fines and amercements in Cornforth, on 4 Dec. 1616 distrained [etc.] on John Shaw junior of Cornforth by a cow for an amercement of 2s. imposed at the Sedgefield halmote court on 25 April 1616; later on the same day William Watters of Cornforth, yeo., assaulted Ettys and recovered the cow.

3) Thomas Nicholson of Redmires, co. Durham, tailor, on 6 Oct. 1616 at Witton-le-Wear stole a sword worth 6s. from Cuthbert Snath of Witton-le-Wear.

4) Thomas Wardell late of Heworth, co. Durham, yeo., on 14 Oct. 1616 at Heworth in the parish of Jarrow stole 3 heifers, one being black-hawk and two red-branded, at 26s. 8d. each, from Barbara Almond, widow.

5) Thomas Wardell late of Heworth, yeo., on 14 Oct. 1616 at Heworth stole by night a red-branded heifer worth 26s. 8d. from Edward Robinson.

6) George Dun late of Eighton *Loningend*, co. Durham, yeo., on 2 Dec. 1616 at Chester-le-Street stole a sad-branded cow worth 51s. from John Gallely of Chester.

7) Thomas Gent of Newton Bewley, co. Durham, yeo., on 11 Aug. 1616 at Wolviston attacked Thomas Davison, clerk. Gent appeared, admitted the charge, and sought leave to fine, which was assessed at 40s., which he paid.

8) John Farrowe of Brancepeth, co. Durham, yeo., being a licenced alehouse keeper at Brancepeth, on 7 Nov. 1616 allowed ill-conditioned men to drink and fight. Farrowe appeared and admitted the charge. His fine was assessed at 6s. 8d., which he paid.

[m.4d.] 9) James Robson late of Carlton, co. Durham, yeo., on 6 Jan. 1617 broke the close of Robert Chipchaise at Whitton and stabbed a mare of Robert Chipchaise worth £4 in the belly and neck with a knife worth 6d. to its great harm.

Later Robson appeared and admitted the charge. The fine was assessed at 40s., and he was to be sent to the house of correction at Durham for 3 days. He was then to be taken to Norton, his present dwelling, and put in the stocks for 6 hours. By special grace the fine was remitted on petition as Robson was a poor man and because he was to receive bodily punishment.

10) John Brigges late of Preston in Amounderness, Lancs., lab., being aged 16 years and more and healthy, but without land, master or trade and being a loiterer, on 3 Jan. 1617 at West Rainton, co. Durham, and elsewhere begged and pretended to have suffered great harm at Preston by fire, and was found by William Bellasys, esq., JP, begging at Lambton on the same day, and was apprehended by Bellasys as a sturdy beggar. Brigges appeared at the bar in the custody of the sheriff and admitted the charge. It was judged that he be branded with the letter R on the left arm, according to the statute, and that he be returned from township to township by constable until he reached Preston as his last home.

11) Whereas George Selby, knt, sheriff of Durham and Sadberge, by warrant of 16 Dec. 1616 ordered Robert Maltby, his bailiff in the Chester ward, or his deputy, together with Thomas Teasdale, Thomas Watson and Robert White, special bailiffs, to arrest John Halliday and have him before the justices at Durham on 11 Jan. following to satisfy Robert Errington, Richard Vasey and John Watson in £12 13s. 4d. as adjudged to them as damages in the king's court at Durham for his failure to prosecute against them in a plea of wrongful distraint of livestock; Thomas Teasdale on 22 Dec. 1616 arrested Halliday at Sunderland by the sea: but George Halliday late of Sunderland by the sea, yeo., and Alice his wife, and Margaret Stafford wife of Thomas Stafford late of the same, yeo., the same day assaulted Teasdale there and rescued John Halliday. Now George, Alice and Margaret appeared, demurred and pleaded not guilty. Robert Cooper as bishop's attorney-general [etc.]. Jurors for 30 April.

] 12) MEMO that at the general sessions on 8 Jan. 1617 before Bp James, Clement Colmore, LL.D., John Calverley, esq., William Murton, archdeacon of Durham, William Bellasys, esq., Ferdinando Moorecroft, master of Greatham Hospital, Robert Cooper and Ralph Conyers, esqs, JPs, it was presented that the common way from Stockton to Norton was very delapidated at Norton *Plancks* and dangerous so as to be a common nuisance. Responsibility for repair lay on the parishioners of Norton whose lands were in the vicinity. The JPs assessed a fine of £10 on the inhabitants unless the repair was made before the sessions on 30 April next. On this day Robert Cooper, esq., appeared as the bishop's attorney-general and sued for the king against the inhabitants, who defaulted. The sheriff was ordered to distrain on the same and have them for 9 July. On this day they again defaulted and the sheriff returned that they had not been distrained upon. Later on 1 Oct. Cooper appeared, as did Thomas Lambart, an inhabitant; and Cooper as a JP certified that the inhabitants had properly repaired part of the highway at their own expense. The case was dismissed *sine die*.

13) Elsewhere at the general sessions on 2 Oct. 1616 before Bp James, Henry Anderson, Timothy Whittingham, knts, Clement Colmore, LL.D., Henry Hilton, Talbot Bowes, esqs, William Murton,

archdeacon of Durham, John Calverley and Robert Cooper, esqs, JPs, it was presented that Edward Robinson late of Kimblesworth, co. Durham, yeo., after 1 Aug. 1613, namely on 4 Aug. 1616 and before and after kept a greyhound for deer coursing at Kimblesworth without having the necessary property qualifications. He appeared on 8 Jan. before Bp James, Clement Colmore, LL.D., John Calverley, esq., William Murton, archdeacon of Durham, William Bellasys, Robert Cooper and Ralph Conyers, esqs, JPs, and pleaded not guilty. Robert Cooper [etc.]. Jurors for 30 April.

14) Elsewhere at the general sessions on 2 Oct. 1616 before the above it was presented that Thomas Widdyfeild late of Hett, co. Durham, yeo., John Hobson junior late of the same, yeo., Matthew Wood late of the same, yeo., Ralph Adamson late of the same, yeo., and Richard Meaburne late of the same, yeo., on 29 Sept. 1616, being a Sabbath, broke the close of William Herrison called *the Long Moores* at Hett and overcast 20 yards of fence. Later on 8 Jan. before the above JPs the

[m.5d.] defendants appeared, I demurred and pleaded not guilty [etc.]. Robert Cooper [etc.]. Jurors for 30 April. On this day the sheriff failed to return the writ and the case was adjourned to 9 July, when George Selby, knt, sheriff of Durham, produced a jury which affirmed the innocence of the accused. The case was adjourned *sine die*.

15) MEMO that Hugh Porter for the king and himself appeared before the JPs on 10 April 1616 and laid an information that George Raulyn late of *Hedgbanck*, co. Durham, yeo., between 20 Feb. and 8 April 1616 at Durham city and elsewhere bought from men unknown 40 wethers at 10s. each and sold them alive within 5 weeks. He claimed half of the double fine of £40. Later on 8 Jan. 1617 before Bp James, Clement Colmore, LL.D., William Murton, archdeacon of Durham, John Calverley, William Bellasis, Robert Cooper and Ralph Conyers, esqs, JPs, Rawlyn appeared and pleaded not guilty. Hugh Porter agreed to this procedure. Jurors for 30 April.

16) MEMO that John Litster for the king and himself appeared before the JPs on 11 Jan. 1615 and laid an information that Richard Bates late of Biddick, co. Durham, gen., between 29 Sept. and 11 Nov. 1614 at Herrington engrossed 120 loads of wheat at 20s. each, 120 loads of peas at 16s. each and 120 loads of oats at 8s. each for resale, for which he should forfeit £264 and suffer 2 months' imprisonment without bail. Later on 8 Jan. 1617 before Bp James, Clement Colmore, LL.D., William Murton, archdeacon of Durham, John Calverley, William Bellasis, Robert Cooper and Ralph Conyers, esqs, JPs, Bates appeared, demurred and pleaded not guilty. Litster agreed to this procedure. Jurors for 30 April.

[m.6] 17) MEMO that Robert Atkinson for the king and himself appeared before the JPs on 10 July 1616 and laid an information that John Machell late of Pitfield in the parish of Bishopton, co. Durham, gen., on 1 May 1615 was seised in demesne of 40 acres arable in Pitfield which had been in tillage for 12 years before 24 Oct. 1597, and between 1 May 1615 and 10 May 1616 he converted the same to pasture of sheep and cattle instead of corn and grain, as was the usage of the country, for which he was liable to forfeit £40, of which he claimed a third. Later on 8 Jan. 1617 before Bp James, Clement Colmore, LL.D., William Murton, archdeacon of Durham, John Calverley, William Bellasys, Robert Cooper and Ralph Conyers, esqs., JPs, Machell appeared, demurred and pleaded not guilty [etc.]. Atkinson agreed to this procedure. Jurors for 30 April.

18) MEMO that Robert Atkinson for the king and himself appeared before the JPs on 10 July 1616 and laid an information that William Blakey late of Little Stainton, co. Durham, yeo., on 1 May 1615 held for a term of years 40 acres arable in Little Stainton which had been in tillage for 12 years [etc.], and between 1 May 1615 and 10 May 1616 he converted the same to pasture [etc.], for which he was liable to forfeit £40, of which he claimed a third.

Later on 8 Jan. 1617 before the above JPs Blakey appeared, demurred and pleaded not guilty [etc.]. Atkinson agreed to this procedure. Jurors for 30 April.

5d.] 19) MEMO that Robert Atkinson for the king and himself appeared on 10 July 1616 before the JPs and laid an information that Hugh Simpson late of Haughton, co. Durham, yeo., on 1 May 1615 held for a term of years 50 acres arable in Little Stainton [etc.] and converted the same to pasture, for which he was liable to forfeit £50 [etc.]. Later on 8 Jan. 1617 before the above JPs Simpson appeared, demurred and pleaded not guilty [etc.]. Atkinson agreed to this procedure. Jurors for 30 April.

20) MEMO that Robert Atkinson for the king and himself appeared before the JPs on 10 July 1616 and laid an information that Anthony Smithson late of Fulthorpe, co. Durham, yeo., on 1 May 1615 held for a term of years 100 acres arable in Fulthorpe [etc.], and between 1 May 1615 and 10 May 1616 converted the same to pasture [etc.] for which he was liable to forfeit £100, of which he claimed a third. Later on 8 Jan. 1617 before the above JPs Smythson appeared, demurred and pleaded not guilty. Atkinson agreed to ths procedure. Jurors for 30 April.

97

3] Pleas and presentments at the general sessions on 30 April 15 James [1617] before Bp James, George Frevile, Charles Wren, John Calverley, Talbot Bowes, Ralph Conyers, knts, Clement Colmore, LL.D., Christopher Place, esq., Marmaduke Blakiston, prebendary of Durham, Robert Cooper, esq., JPs.

John Wortley [of Langley], esq., Ambrose Lancaster [of Headlam], gen., William Garth [of Headlam], gen., Laurence Wilkinson [of Kyo], gen., Christopher Gaynes [of School Aycliffe], gen., William Whitfeild [of Newton], gen., John Ward [of Hurworth], yeo., Peter Wright [of Langley], yeo., Richard Morley [of Stainton], yeo., Thomas Todd [of Redworth], yeo, Thomas Thursby [of School Aycliffe], yeo., Thomas Tweddle [of Hesleden], yeo., Anthony Wilkinson [of Hesleden], yeo., Nicholas Tewer [of Heighington], yeo., George Cragg [of Durham], yeo., jurors.

1) Tobias Oswald late of Wolsingham, co. Durham, gen., and Hugh Porter late of Durham city, yeo., on 5 Feb. 1617 broke the close of John Walker at Bishop Auckland called *Entwynes close* and depastured hay worth 13s. 4d. with a horse.

2) Cuthbert Simpson late of Burtree House in the parish of Haughton, co. Durham, yeo., on 7 April 1617 at Coatsay Moor in the parish of Heighington attacked William Gaines with a long stick worth 1d. on the forefinger of his left hand so that he nearly lost its use, and elsewhere on his body.

3) Richard Baxter late of Barnard Castle, co. Durham, yeo., on 20 Oct. 1616 and before and after fished in the Tees at Barnard Castle with *a lock and a leap* worth 4s. for salmon out of season.

4) Henry Hugison late of Barnard Castle, yeo., on 20 Oct. 1616 and before and after fished in the Tees at Barnard Castle with a wicker net worth 2s. for shedder salmon and fry.

5) Ambrose Clement late of Winston, co. Durham, yeo., on 20 Oct. 1616 and before and after fished in the Tees at Winston with 2 locks and a wicker net worth 4s. for shedder and kipper salmon and fry.

6) Robert Hardware late of Alwent in the parish of Gainford, co. Durham, yeo., on 20 Oct. 1616 and before and after fished in Grant beck at Alwent with devices worth 2s. and took 16 shedder salmon worth 32s.

7) John Hambleton late of Alwent in the parish of Gainford, yeo., on 20 Oct. 1616 and before and after fished in Grant beck at Alwent with devices worth 2s. and took 7 shedder salmon worth 14s.

8) Luke Finley late of Alwent in the parish of Gainford, yeo,. on 20 Oct. 1616 and before and after fished in Grant beck at Alwent with devices worth 2s. and took 3 shedder salmon worth 6s.

9) Edward Lodoman late of Barnard Castle, yeo., on 20 Oct. 1616 and before and after fished in the Tees at Barnard Castle with a lock and a wicker net worth 4s. for shedder salmon and fry.

[m.8d.]   10) Nicholas Thompson late of Ryhope, co. Durham, yeo., George Thompson late of the same, yeo., William Thompson late of the same, yeo., Richard Thompson late of the same, yeo., Robert Easterby late of the same, yeo., John Liddell late of the same, yeo., and Thomas Roxbye late of Ryhope, yeo., assembled riotously with 14 others unknown on 7 Feb. 1617 at Sunderland by the sea at *Cargate* and assaulted John Shipperdson; and Nicholas Thompson and Robert Easterby beat him and all put him in fear for his life.

[8A] Later on 1 Oct. 1617 before Henry Anderson, Timothy Whittingham, William Bellasys, John Calverley, George Tonge and Ralph Conyers, kts, JPs, Nicholas, George, William, Richard and Thomas appeared and while they did not admit their guilt, to save expense they put themselves on the mercy of the court. They were fined 16s. 8d. collectively, which was paid.

[8B] Later on 7 Jan. 1618 before Timothy Whittingham, William Bellasis, John Calverley, George Tonge, knts, and Robert Cooper, esq., JPs, Robert Easterby appeared and [as above] put himself on the court's mercy. He was fined 3s. 4d. to the use of the bishop, which he paid.

11) William Crook late of Wolsingham, co. Durham, yeo., and Hugh Hodgshon junior late of Softley, yeo., on 30 Aug. 1616 about 6 p.m. broke into the bishop's empaled park at Stanhope and unlawfully hunted with greyhounds and killed a doe worth 10s.

12) John Liddell late of Choppington in the parish of Bedlington, *co. Durham, yeo., from 8 Jan. to 30 April 1617 kept an alehouse at Choppington without licence and sold ale and beer to the public.

13) Ralph Dawson of Cambois in the parish of Bedlington, *co. Durham, yeo., from 8 Jan to 30 April 1617 kept an alehouse at Cambois without licence and sold ale and beer.

14) Whereas John Bainbrigg of Wheatley Hill, co. Durham, gen., and Thomas Heeth of Kepier East Grange, gen., having been appointed in the general sessions collectors of a cess of 12d. in the pound assessed by the king's JPs in the Easington ward and levied in the Easington ward among other wards for the repair of all common bridges in the county, by virtue of an estreat dated 5 July 1615, did on 18 Oct. 1617 distrain by a cow at Whitwell house in the parish of Kelloe within the Easington ward on Robert Lorrell, gen., for 13s. 4d. which he had refused to pay them as his rate for Whitwell house, which used to be worth £13 6s. 8d. On the same day Lorrell assaulted Bainbrigg and Heeth and recovered his cow.

15) MEMO that on 19 Feb. 1617 John Calverley, esq., Marmaduke Blakiston, subdean of Durham, and Robert Cooper, esq., being three JPs, at the petition of Clement Colmore, LL.D., of Durham city went to a messuage called Quarrell hill in Brancepeth, where the magistrates found Charles Hackforth, John Hackforth and Christopher Robinson of Brancepeth, labs., and Mary Sanderson wife of Henry Sanderson of Brancepeth, gen., Jane Sanderson his daughter and Mary Hackforth of Brancepeth, spinster, in forcible possession. The JPs arrested Charles Hackforth, John Hackforth, Christopher Robinson, Mary Sanderson, Jane Sanderson and Mary Hackforth for their trespass and held them in Durham gaol until they fined with the king's justices. Dated at Brancepeth.

16) Robert Mason late of Trimdon, co. Durham, lab., on 26 April 1617 burgled the residence of Ralph Willye at Merrington between 9 and 11 a.m. and stole 6s. in money, 2 pies worth 4d. in a cupboard (abaco) and 37s. in cash in a chest.

98

'] Pleas and presentments on 1 Oct. 15 James [1617] before George Frevile, Henry Anderson, Timothy Whittingham, William Bellasis, John Calverley, George Tonge, Ralph Conyers, knts, Marmaduke

Blakiston, prebendary of Durham, William Murton, archdeacon of Durham, Robert Cooper, Christopher Place and Ambrose Dudley, esqs, JPs *sede vacante*.

Robert Ward [of Trimdon], gen., William Whitfeild [of Durham], gen., Christopher Hutchinson [of Durham], gen., John Hopper [of Collierley], yeo., Robert Pye [of Collierley], yeo, Edward Blackett [of Hillhouse], yeo., John Swalwell [of Ludworth], yeo., Nicholas Marley [of Pelton], yeo., William Pearson [of Whitehall], yeo., Thomas Stott [of Bitchburn], yeo., George Hutchinson, yeo., Thomas Wrenn [of Woodifield], yeo., Martin Lawes [of Kibblesworth], yeo., Anthony Robinson [of Hawthorn], yeo., Richard Morton [of Morton], yeo., jurors

1) Elizabeth Kearton wife of Simon Kearton late of Cornforth, co. Durham, yeo., on 26 Aug. 1617 at Cornforth broke into the garden of Peter Blakiston, gen., and overturned a fence.

[9A] Later at the general sessions on 7 Jan. 1618 before Timothy Whittingham, William Bellasis, John Calverley, George Tonge, knts, and Robert Cooper, esq., JPs, Elizabeth appeared, demurred and pleaded not guilty. Robert Cooper withdrew the charge and the case was dismissed.

2) John Ridley late of Shotley Bridge, co. Durham, yeo., on 3 July 1617 at Benfieldside attacked William Johnson.

[9B] Later on 12 Jan. 1620 before William Bellasis, John Calverley, George Tonge, knts, Robert Cooper and William Smith, esqs, JPs, Ridley appeared and admitted the charge. He was fined 5s. to the use of Bishop Richard [Neile], which he paid.

3) Richard Smith late of Hesleden Hall, co. Durham, yeo., on 20 Sept. 1617 broke the close of Christopher Mitforth, esq., at East Hulam called *Batterslay* and tore down 2 gates there.

[9C] Later on 7 Jan. 1618 before Timothy Whittingham, William Bellasis, John Calverley, George Tonge, knts, Clement Colmore, LL.D., Francis Burgoyne, subdean of Durham, and Robert Cooper, esq., JPs, Smith appeared, admitted the charge and put himself on the mercy of the court. He was fined 3s. 4d. to the use of the bishop, which he paid.

4) Nicholas Sparke late of Tudhoe, co. Durham, yeo., on 2 Sept. 1617 at Tudhoe was a common brawler [*etc.*]

5) George Swalwell late of Wolviston, co. Durham, yeo., Alice Davison wife of Ralph Davison of the same, yeo., Richard Caterick of the same, yeo., Laurence Brewell late of the same, yeo., and Anne Swalwell daughter of the aforesaid George, spinster, on 26 Aug. 1616 at Wolviston at the Fogg Close assembled riotously and attacked William Marckham, Margaret Marckham and Henry Eldon and mowed and carried in a waggon hay of Margaret Marckham worth 26s. 8d.

[9D] Later on 8 April 1618 before Richard Hutton, knt, a justice of Common Pleas and chancellor of Durham, William Bellasis, John

Calverley, George Tonge, Ralph Conyers, knts, Christopher Place and Robert Cooper, esqs, JPs, George and Anne Swalwell appeared, admitted the charge and put themselves on the mercy of the court. They were fined jointly 5s. 10d., which was paid by George for both to the bishop's use.

6) Whereas by common law every township in England should have stocks in the local place of punishment to correct malefactors, breakers of the peace, sturdy beggars, vagabonds, etc., the village of Neasham, co. Durham, although an ancient township, failed to provide the same, contrary to the ordinance of 20 Sept. 1617.

7) Whereas Reginald Fawcett of Fulwell, co. Durham, gen., who was appointed collector in the Chester ward, by virtue of an indented estreat for a cess of 12d. in the pound assessed in the Chester ward by JPs in the Durham sessions of 10 July 1616 for the repair of common bridges, on 4 Aug. 1616 at Jarrow distrained on a cow of – Bavington, gen., for 12s., based on the ancient rate of £12 for the manor of Jarrow held by him and other tenants, which Mr Bavington refused to pay: Edward Blithman late of – , yeo., on the same day assaulted Fawcett and recovered the cow.

[9E] Later on 8 July 1618 before George Frevile, Henry Anderson, John Calverley, George Tonge, Ralph Conyers, knts, Clement Colmore, LL.D., Robert Cooper and William Carr, esqs, JPs, Blithman appeared and admitted the charge. Because the court knew that he was proprietor of the manor of Jarrow and cell of Farne it was agreed that his punishment should provide an example to all liable to pay taxes who now submitted, therefore he was ordered to pay the 12s. for which he had been distrained and 3s. 4d. for the offence, which he paid.

8) Whereas Edward Williamson and Oswald Johnson, bailiffs of Thomas Swinburne of Durham city, esq., and Margaret his wife, on 19 Aug. 1617 at Redmarshall, co. Durham, distrained on the manor and lands being held by Thomas Swinburne in right of Margaret his wife by 6 cows and 4 oxen for £24 owed to Thomas and Margaret as from the previous 1 Aug., intending to impound the same I Humphrey Elstob of Redmarshall, gen., assembled with 9 other persons unknown the same day and attacked Williamson and Johnson and recovered the livestock.

[9F] Later on 8 April 1618 before Richard Hutton, knt [etc.], William Bellasis, John Calverley, George Tonge, Ralph Conyers, knts, Christopher Place and Robert Cooper, esqs, JPs, Elstobb appeared, admitted the charge and put himself on the mercy of the court. He was fined 20s. to the use of the bishop, which he paid.

9) Whereas Reginald Fawcett of Fulwell, co. Durham, gen., [etc. as (7) above] on 3 Aug. 1617 at East Boldon distrained on 3 tin candlesticks belonging to John Brough of East Boldon, yeo., for the rate of 21d. according to the ancient valuation of 35s., which he refused to pay; Brough assaulted Fawcett the same day and recovered the 3 candlesticks.

10) Robert Smith late of Durham city, lab., on 31 Aug. 1617 at Durham stole a tanned hide worth 6s. from Nicholas Tayler.

11) Cuthbert Wright late of Shadforth, co. Durham, yeo., Ralph Huntley junior late of the same, yeo., and Cuthbert Wilkinson late of Bishopwearmouth, yeo., on 28 Sept. 1617 assembled riotously by night at Shadforth and attacked Henry Hull to the effusion of his blood. Huntley and Wilkinson appeared, admitted the charge and sought leave to fine. This was assessed at 10s. on Huntley and 13s. 4d. on Wilkinson, which was paid to the use of the king, *sede vacante*. [9G] Later on 7 Jan. 1618 before Timothy Whittingham, William Bellasis, John Calverley, George Tonge, knts, Clement Colmore, LL.D., Francis Burgoyne, subdean of Durham, and Robert Cooper, esq., JPs, Cuthbert Wright appeared, admitted the charge, and his fine was assessed at 13s. 4d. to the use of Bp Neile, which he paid.

12) Robert Steele late of Tudhoe, co. Durham, yeo., on 28 Aug. 1617 at Tudhoe attacked Nicholas Sparke of Tudhoe and struck him over the head with a wooden implement worth 2d. Steele appeared and admitted the charge. His fine was assessed at 40s., paid to the king's use *sede vacante*, which he paid.

13) Francis Fawell late of West Auckland, co. Durham, yeo., on 24 Aug. 1617, being the Sabbath, at St Helen Auckland attacked Brian Colson with a stick worth 1d., inflicting 2 great wounds on his head. Fawell appeared, demurred and pleaded not guilty. Robert Cooper as the king's attorney-general in the palatinate of Durham and Sadberge agreed to the procedure. Fawell further stated that on the said day Brian had assaulted him and any blows were inflicted in self-defence. Cooper countered that Fawell assaulted Colson and sought a trial. The jurors were to be summoned for 7 Jan. 1618. On this day Fawell appeared and admitted the charge. His fine was assessed at 10s., to the bishop's use.

[m.10] 14) John Colson late of St Helen Auckland, co. Durham, yeo., and Magdalen his wife, Brian Colson of the same, yeo., John Colson junior of the same, lab., Mary Colson of the same, spinster, Henry Swainston late of the same, yeo., and Margaret his wife, on 24 Aug. 1617, being the Sabbath, assembled riotously at St Helen Auckland and attacked Francis Fawell. Brian Colson struck Fawell over the head with a forked staff worth 2d., inflicting 2 great wounds, and John Colson senior and Magdalen his wife, John Colson junior, Mary Colson, Henry Swainston and Margaret his wife, struck him elsewhere on the body.

The defendants appeared, demurred and pleaded not guilty. Robert Cooper [etc.]. The jury was summoned for 7 Jan. 1618, when the defendants admitted the charge and each was fined 2s. 6d. at a total of 17s. 6d. to the use of the bishop.

15) MEMO that Hugh Porter for the king and himself laid an information before the JPs on 8 Jan. 1617 that Charles Fletcher late of Chester, co. Durham, yeo., between 4 Oct. and 30 Nov. 1616 at Chester

netted in the River Wear 50 kipper salmon, for which he should forfeit 20s. per salmon and his gear, and Porter should have half the fine. Later on 1 Oct. 1617 before George Frevile, Henry Anderson, Timothy Whittingham, William Bellasis, John Calverley, George Tonge, Ralph Conyers, knts, Robert Cooper and Ambrose Dudley, esqs, JPs, Fletcher appeared, demurred and pleaded not guilty. Porter agreed to the procedure [etc.]. Jurors for 7 Jan.

16) MEMO that Hugh Porter for the king and himself laid an information before the JPs on 30 April 1617 that contrary to the usury acts of 2 April 13 Elizabeth and 37 Henry VIII which ordained that after 25 June 1571 none might lend for gain at more than 10% under pain of triple forfeiture of the value of the goods with [0d.] imprisonment and fine | to be divided equally between the king and the informant, Ralph Marley late of Urpeth, co. Durham, yeo., on 26 March 1613 at Urpeth loaned to George Blackett 40s. for repayment on 28 Feb. the following year, for which he gained 8s. This should incur a forfeiture of £6, of which Porter claimed a half share. Later Marley appeared on 1 Oct. 1617 before George Frevile, Henry Anderson, Timothy Whittingham, William Bellasis, John Calverley, George Tonge, Ralph Conyers, knts, Robert Cooper, Christopher Place and Ambrose Dudley, esqs, JPs, demurred and pleaded not guilty. Porter agreed to the procedure and a jury was summoned for 7 Jan.

17) MEMO that Hugh Porter for the king and himself laid an information on 30 April 1617 before the JPs that contrary to the laws on usury Ralph Marley late of Urpeth, yeo., on 26 March 1614 loaned to George Jackson £3 until 28 Feb. following and thereby gained 12s. This incurred a forfeiture of £9 [etc.]. Later on 1 Oct. 1617 before George Frevile, Henry Anderson, Timothy Whittingham, William Bellasis, John Calverley, George Tonge, Ralph Conyers, knts, Robert Cooper and Ambrose Dudley, esqs, JPs, Marley appeared, demurred, and pleaded not guilty. Porter agreed [etc.]. Jurors for 7 Jan.

[11] 18) MEMO that Hugh Porter for the king and himself laid an information before the JPs on 5 July 1615 against John Heighington of Hillhouse, co. Durham, yeo., that between 1 May and 24 June 1615 at Durham city and elsewhere he bought from persons unknown 50 stones of wool at 10s. a stone, not being a wool merchant or manufacturer [etc.], for which offence he should incur double forfeit of £50. Later Heighington appeared on 1 Oct. 1617 before George Frevile, Henry Anderson, Timothy Whittingham, William Bellasis, John Calverley, George Tonge, Ralph Conyers, knts, Robert Cooper and Ambrose Dudley, esqs, JPs, and without prejudice sought leave to fine. This was assessed at 13s. 4d., to be shared equally to the use of the king, sede vacante, and Porter and was paid.

19) MEMO that Hugh Porter for the king and himself laid an information before the JPs on 10 July 1616 that John Heighington late of Whinhouse in the parish of Aycliffe, co. Durham, yeo., between 1 May and 24 June 1616 at Darlington and elsewhere

bought from persons unknown 120 stones of wool at 10s. a stone. Later on 1 Oct. 1617 before George Frevile, Henry Anderson, Timothy Whittingham, William Bellasis, John Calverley, George Tonge, Ralph Conyers, knts, Robert Cooper and Ambrose Dudley, esqs, JPs, Heighington appeared and without prejudice sought leave to fine. This was assessed by Cooper at 13s. 4d., which was shared equally to the use of the king, *sede vacante,* and Porter and was paid.

20) MEMO that Hugh Porter for the king and himself laid an information before the JPs on 8 Jan. 1617 against George Paxton junior late of Hulam, co. Durham, yeo., that between 1 Aug. and 11 Nov. 1616 at Durham city and elsewhere he bought from persons unknown 20 kine at £3 each and resold them alive within 5 weeks, thereby incurring a double forfeit amounting to £120.

Later on 1 Oct. 1617 before George Frevile, Henry Anderson, Timothy Whittingham, William Bellasis, John Calverley, George Tonge, Ralph Conyers, knts, Robert Cooper and Ambrose Dudley, esqs, JPs, Paxton appeared and Porter withdrew the charge. Paxton was acquitted and relaxed to Porter all costs arising from his defence. The court also exonerated Porter for his non-prosecution.

[m.11d.] 21) MEMO that John Walker for the king and himself laid an information on 10 Jan. 1616 against John Adamson of Eldon, co. Durham, yeo., that on 1 April 1614 he held by lease 60 acres arable in Eldon, being in tillage [etc.] and between 1 April 1614 and 10 April 1615 did convert the same to sheep and cattle pasture, thereby incurring a forfeit of £60 at 20s. an acre.

Later on 1 Oct. 1617 before George Frevile, Henry Anderson, Timothy Whittingham, William Bellasis, John Calverley, George Tonge, Ralph Conyers, knts, Robert Cooper and Ambrose Dudley, esqs, JPs, Adamson appeared, and Walker withdrew the charge. Adamson was acquitted and relaxed to Walker all costs [etc.].

22) Whereas within the county palatine of Durham and Sadberge it was the custom from time immemorial that at every general sessions of the peace a bailiff or other officer of the sheriff of Durham should impanel jurors from time to time to enquire into felonies, trespasses and the like without requiring any fee for attendance, Robert Maltby late of Gateside, yeo., at the sessions at Durham on 1 Oct. 1617 before George Frevile, Henry Anderson, Timothy Whittingham, William Bellasis, John Calverley, George Tonge, Ralph Conyers, knts, and Robert Cooper, esq., JPs, being a bailiff of George Selby, knt, sheriff of Durham, empanelled a jury by colour of his office and unjustly took from Edward Williamson of Elvet, [Durham], gen., servant of Thomas Swinburne, esq., being a juror to give evidence for the king in an indictment against Humphrey Elstobb of Redmarshall, gen., [? his share] of a fee of 8d. which Maltby averred was the responsibility of the jurors for his attendance on them. On 1 Oct. 1617 Maltby appeared and denied the charge. Robert Cooper [etc.]. The jurors for 7 Jan.

] 23) MEMO that on 8 Jan. 1617 before Bp James, Clement Colmore, LL.D., John Calverley, esq., William Murton, archdeacon of Durham, William Bellasis, esq., Ferdinando Moorecroft, master of Greatham Hospital, Robert Cooper and Ralph Conyers, esqs, JPs, it was presented by William Bellasis, esq., that of his certain knowledge the king's highway at Gilesgate in the parish of St Giles, Durham, leading from Durham to Moor House and other townships was badly in need of repair at the lane beside Ramside on 6 Jan. 1617, the responsibility lying on the neighbouring parishioners. It was agreed to levy a fine of £10, unless a repair was affected before the next sessions on 30 April. The sheriff was to summon the inhabitants to appear at this sessions to answer.

Later on 1 Oct. 1617 before George Frevile, Henry Anderson, Timothy Whittingham, William Bellasis, John Calverley, George Tonge, Ralph Conyers, knts, Robert Cooper and Ambrose Dudley, esqs, JPs, William Hilton and John Hall, two inhabitants of the parish, having been distrained to appear, objected that the costs of repair should be borne by John Heath senior, esq., denied any customary parochial responsibility, and asked for the lifting of the distraint.

Robert Cooper [etc.] objected to the traverse and with the agreement of Hilton and Hall a jury was to be summoned.

24) Elsewhere on 9 July 1617 before John Calverley, Talbot Bowes, Ralph Conyers, knts, Clement Colmore, LL.D., Marmaduke Blakiston, subdean of Durham, Christopher Place, John Fetherstonhalgh, Robert Cooper and Ambrose Dudley, esqs, JPs, it was presented that Ralph Howe late of Carterthorne, yeo., John Simpson late of Escomb, yeo., Richard Smith late of Toft Hill, yeo., William Grene late of Carterthorne, yeo., Margaret Howe wife of Thomas Howe late of the same, yeo., Anne Garbett wife of – Garbett of West Auckland, yeo., who was lately called Anne Waugh of the same, spinster, and Anne Barnes late of Carterthorne, spinster, on 15 April 1617 assembled riotously with 10 others unknown at Carterthorne in the parish of St Helen [Auckland] and attacked Ralph Wheitley; and John Simpson struck him on the head with a dagger worth 6d., inflicting 5 wounds; and Ralph Howe, Richard Smith, William Grene, Margaret Howe, Anne Garbett and Anne Barnes threw stones at him. Later on 9 July

d.] before the JPs the defendants appeared, I demurred and pleaded not guilty. Robert Cooper [etc.]. The defendants objected that Wheitley had made the first assault, which was denied by Cooper. The jury was summoned for 1 Oct., when the sheriff failed to return the writ. The case was adjourned to 7 Jan., when the jurors found the defendants not guilty and testified that any damage caused to Wheitley was by his own fault and through self-defence.

25) Elsewhere on 9 July 1617 before John Calverley, Talbot Bowes, Ralph Conyers, knts, Clement Colmore, LL.D., Marmaduke Blakiston, subdean of Durham, Christopher Place, John Fetherstonhalgh, Robert

Cooper and Ambrose Dudley, esqs, JPs, it was presented that Ralph Howe late of Carterthorne, yeo., John Simpson late of Escomb, Richard Smith late of Toft Hill, yeo., William Grene late of Carterthorne, yeo., Margaret Howe wife of Thomas Howe late of the same, yeo., Anne Garbatt wife of – Garbatt of West Auckland, yeo., lately called Anne Waugh late of the same, spinster, and Anne Barnes late of Carterthorne, spinster, on 15 April 1617 assembled riotously with 10 others unknown at Carterthorne and attacked William Willson; and John Simpson struck him on the head with a dagger worth 6d., inflicting 4 wounds, and the rest threw stones. The defendants appeared on 9 July 1617, demurred and pleaded not guilty and alleged self-defence.

Robert Cooper rejected the allegation and the jury was summoned for 1 Oct., when the sheriff failed to return the writ. The case was adjourned until 7 Jan., when the jurors found the defendants not guilty, and testified that any damage suffered by Willson was the result of his own act.

[*m.13*]   26) MEMO that on 1 Oct. 1617 before George Frevile, Henry Anderson, Timothy Whittingham, William Bellasis, John Calverley, George Tonge, Ralph Conyers, knts, Christopher Place and Robert Cooper, esqs, JPs, it was presented by William Bellasis, knt, of his certain knowledge that part of the king's highway at Claypath in the parish of St Nicholas, Durham, from Durham to Kepier and beyond at the lane by the bishop's bakehouse and especially the stretch between the bakehouse and the bishop's mills was in dangerous decay on 29 Sept. 1617 and should be repaired by the parishioners of St Nicholas. The JPs assessed a fine of 20s., to be levied unless sufficient repairs were effected before the next sessions on 7 Jan.; and the sheriff was to have the inhabitants present in court to answer the case.

27) MEMO that on 1 Oct. 1617 before Henry Anderson, Timothy Whittingham, William Bellasis, John Calverley, George Tonge, Ralph Conyers, knts, William Murton, archdeacon of Durham, and Robert Cooper, esq., JPs, it was presented by Ralph Conyers, knt, of his certain knowledge that the king's highway at Layton in the parish of Sedgefield, co. Durham, leading from Sedgefield to Layton and beyond was in decay at Layton *Lonnen* on 28 Sept. 1617 and the responsibility of the parishioners of Sedgefield. A fine of £10 was to be levied unless the repairs were effected before the July sessions, when they were to answer.

[*m.13d.*]   28) MEMO that on 1 Oct. 1617 before Henry Anderson, Timothy Whittingham, William Bellasis, John Calverley, George Tonge, Ralph Conyers, knts, William Murton, archdeacon of Durham, and Robert Cooper, esq., JPs, it was presented by William Murton of his certain knowledge that the king's highway at Picktree in the parish of Chester, co. Durham, called Picktree *Lonnen* from Gateside by Gateside moor to Picktree was in decay at the Long *Loning* on 29

Sept. 1617 and was the responsibility of the parishioners of Chester. A fine of £10 was to be levied unless repaired before the Michaelmas sessions [etc.].

29) Order *non omittas* to the sheriff of Durham to summon William Hutchinson of *Leighlezees* in the parish of Whickham, co. Durham, yeo., George Hodgshon of Hollybush, yeo., Robert Kirkham of Staindrop, yeo., John Viccars junior of the same, yeo., John Brasse of the same, yeo., John Bird of the same, yeo., Henry Bawcock of Winston, yeo., William Drummer of Alwent, yeo., Richard Peacock of the same, miller, Gerard Fletcher of Lumley, yeo., William Thompson of Bishopwearmouth, yeo., Arthur Grayme of Ford, yeo., John Hutchinson of Burn House in the parish of Lanchester, yeo., Cuthbert Briggs of Ford, yeo., Jane Iley of Hamsteels, spinster, Christopher Wheitley of Wolsingham, yeo., John Dixon of the same, yeo., and Robert Wright of the same, yeo., to be before the JPs at the sessions on 1 Oct. to answer for divers felonies. When they did not come George Selby, knt, sheriff of Durham, was ordered to have them for 7 Jan. At this sessions the sheriff returned that they were not to be found. The order was renewed for 8 April, when the sheriff returned that he had arrested John Dixon, but the remainder were not to be found. The order was renewed for 8 July, when the sheriff returned that he had arrested John Hutchinson and Cuthbert Briggs. Renewal for 30 Sept., when no return was made, 13 Jan., [etc.] until their outlawry was proclaimed by the coroners. [*almost illegible through cramped hand*]

99

[4] Pleas and presentments on 7 Jan. 15 James [*1618*] before Timothy Whittingham, William Bellasis, John Calverley, George Tonge, knts, Clement Colmore, LL.D., Francis Burgoyne, subdean of Durham, and Robert Cooper, esq., JPs.

Christopher Hutchinson [of Durham], gen., William Whitfeild [of Durham], gen., Thomas Gregson [of Murton], yeo., John Hopper [of Collierley], yeo., William Pearson [of Sherburn], yeo., Simon Lackenby [of Morton], yeo., William Hallyman [of Murton], yeo., Ralph Davison [of Morton], yeo., Nicholas Tewer [of Heighington], yeo., George Highe [of Wolviston], yeo., George Craggs [of Durham], yeo., Robert Punshon [of Pelton], yeo., Thomas Robinson [of Morton], yeo., Robert Pye [of Collierley], yeo., Anthony Yonge [of Morton], yeo., jurors.

1) Whereas Rowland Watson, collector of fines, [etc.] of the king *sede vacante* in Wolsingham, co. Durham, by virtue of his office was to levy various fines from tenants, on 20 Nov. 1617 he distrained at Wolsingham on William Todd of Wolsingham, yeo., by a pewter doubler for an amercement of 12d. imposed at the halmote at Wolsingham on 26 June 1617, and Todd assaulted Watson the same day and recovered the pewter doubler.

2) Whereas Rowland Watson, collector of fines, [etc.] of Bp Neile in Wolsingham, by virtue of his office was to levy various fines from the tenants, on 20 Nov. 1617 he distrained at Wolsingham on Dorothy Colson of Wolsingham, widow, by a pewter doubler for an amercement of 6d. imposed at the halmote at Wolsingham on 27 Oct. 1617 and she assaulted Watson the same day and recovered the doubler.

[14A] Later on 30 Sept. 1619 before Bp Neile, Timothy Whittingham, John Calverley, Ralph Conyers, knts, Robert Cooper and William Smith, esqs, JPs, Dorothy appeared and admitted the charge. She was fined 6s. 8d., to the use of the bishop, which was paid.

3) Whereas Rowland Watson, collector [etc.] in Wolsingham [etc.], on 29 Nov. 1617 distrained at Wolsingham on George Thompson of Wolsingham, yeo., by a mare for amercements of 10s. imposed at the halmote at Wolsingham on 27 Oct. 1617 Thompson assaulted Watson the same day and recovered the same.

[14B] Later on 8 July 1618 before George Frevile, Henry Anderson, John Calverley, George Tonge, Ralph Conyers, knts, Clement Colmore, LL.D., Robert Cooper and William Carr, esqs, JPs, Thompson appeared and admitted the charge. He was fined 10s. to the bishop's use, which he paid. It was judged that he pay the original 10s. for which he was distrained and be discharged.

4) Whereas Richard Gargrave, collector for Bp Neile in West Auckland, co. Durham, on 6 Dec. 1617 distrained at West Auckland on John Eden of West Auckland, esq., by a cow for arrears of rent amounting to 7s. 8d. owed at Martinmas and also for amercements of 7s. imposed at the halmote at Evenwood on 24 Oct. 1617, Thomas Hewittson late of the same, lab., assaulted Gargrave the same day at West Auckland and recovered the cow.

5) Cecily Fetherston late of Gilesgate, [Durham], spinster, on 1 Dec. 1617 at Gilesgate attacked Anne Niccolson and cast her to the ground.

6) Richard Foster of Gilesgate, [Durham], yeo., and Janet Foster of the same, widow, on 18 Dec. 1617 at Gilesgate attacked Cecily Fetherston, spinster.

[14C] Later on 13 Jan. 1619 before Henry Anderson, William Bellasis, John Calverley, George Tonge, knts, Clement Colmore, LL.D., and Robert Cooper, esq., JPs, the defendants appeared and admitted the charge. They were fined 6s. 8d. to the bishop's use, which they paid.

7) William Shaftoe late of Whickham, co. Durham, gen., on 6 Dec. 1617 and before and after at Whickham was a frequenter of taverns and a drunkard.

8) Ralph Wheitley late of Bishop Auckland, co. Durham, yeo., and William Willson late of the same, yeo., on 15 April 1617 at Carterthorne in the parish of St Helen [Auckland] demolished 38 perches of stone wall newly built on his land by Thomas Howe.

[m.14d.] 9) William Willson late of Bishop Auckland, yeo., and Ralph Wheatley late of the same, yeo., on 15 April 1617 at Carterthorne in the parish of St Helen [Auckland] attacked Ralph Howe, and Willson struck Howe with an iron-shod stick worth 18d. held in both hands and *did ripple* the skin of his shin.

10) Ralph Wheitley late of Bishop Auckland, yeo., and William Willson late of the same, yeo., on 15 April 1617 at Carterthorne attacked Richard Smith, and Wheitley struck him with a pitchfork 2 yards long worth 10d. held in his right hand.

11) William Swalwell junior late of Ludworth, co. Durham, yeo., John Swalwell junior late of the same, yeo., and William Swalwell late of the same, yeo., on 26 Aug. 1617 at Ludworth assembled riotously and attacked Robert Haswell and depastured his grass worth 5s. in a close called *the Fence* with yoked oxen pulling a plough.

[*14D*] Later on 8 April 1618 before Richard Hutton, knt, a judge of Common Pleas and chancellor of Durham, William Bellasis, John Calverley, George Tonge, Ralph Conyers, knts, Christopher Place and Robert Cooper, esqs, JPs, the defendants appeared and admitted the charge. They was fined jointly £3 to the use of the bishop, which they paid.

12) William Punshon late of West Herrington, co. Durham, gen., and John Litster late of the same, yeo., on 24 Aug. 1617 at West Herrington in the tavern of Edward Milles fought together and Punshon maltreated Litster.

[*14E*] Later on 7 April 1619 before Henry Anderson, William Bellasis, John Calverley, Talbot Bowes, George Tonge, Ralph Conyers, knts, Clement Colmore, LL.D., and Robert Cooper, esq., JPs, Punshon appeared and admitted his guilt. He was fined 6s. 8d., which was paid to the bishop's use.

[*14F*] Later on 12 Jan. 1620 before Willam Bellasis, John Calverley, George Tonge, knts, Robert Cooper and William Smith, esqs, JPs, Litster appeared and admitted the charge. He was fined 3s. 4d., but this was remitted on account of his poverty.

13) William Punshon late of West Herrington, co. Durham, gen., and John Litster late of the same, yeo., living at West Herrington, on 24 Aug. 1617 remained at night drinking and playing cards for an hour or more in the residence of Edward Milles in West Herrington, being a common alehouse, not having been invited there by any traveller, not being workmen [*etc.*].

[*14G*] Later on 7 April 1619 before Henry Anderson, William Bellasis, John Calverley, Talbot Bowes, George Tonge, Ralph Conyers, knts, and Robert Cooper, esq., JPs, Punshon appeared and admitted the charge. He was fined 3s. 4d., to the use of the poor of Houghton parish, co. Durham, for equal distribution by the churchwardens.

[*14H*] Later on 12 Jan. 1620 before William Bellasis, John Calverley, George Tonge, knts, Robert Cooper and William Smith, esqs, JPs, Litster appeared and admitted the charge. He was fined 3s. 4d. to the use of the poor of the parish of Houghton [*etc.*].

14) Cuthbert Porter late of Winlaton, co. Durham, yeo., Christopher Clugh late of the same, yeo., and Nicholas Soulby late of the same, yeo., living at Ryton, on 7 Dec. 1617, being the Sabbath and at the time of divine service, stayed drinking for 2 hours and more in the residence of William Foggart in Ryton, being a common tavern, not being invited by a traveller [etc.].

[14l] Later the same day Clugh appeared before the JPs, demurred and pleaded not guilty. Robert Cooper [etc.]. Jurors for 8 April.

15) John Ellinor late of Hutton Henry, co. Durham, yeo., on 1 Jan. 1617 was in possession by lease of 30 acres arable at Hutton Henry [etc.] and between 1 Jan. 1617 and 1 Jan. 1618 converted the same to sheep and cattle pasture.

16) Arthur Blith late of Durham city, lab., on 27 Dec. 1617 at Durham stole from John Walker a shirt worth 3s. 6d., a girdle worth 6d., a handkerchief worth 4d., and a walling hammer worth 12d.

[m.15]   17) John Dowglasse late of Gateside, yeo., on 20 Aug. 1617 at Gateside stole a tunic worth 5s. from a person unknown.

18) John Dowglasse late of Gateside, yeo., on 20 Aug. 1617 at Gateside stole a tanning kettle *(tanneam patinam)* worth 6d. from Widow Stephenson.

19) Margaret Hogg wife of Adam Hogg late of Whickham, co. Durham, yeo., on 3 Nov. 1617 at Kibblesworth stole a sheepskin worth 4d. from Jane Lawes, widow. She was brought to the bar by the sheriff and admitted the charge. It was judged that she be whipped in open market at Durham and be discharged.

20) John Turbatt late of St Andrew Auckland, co. Durham, lab., and Janet his wife on 20 Oct. 1617 at South Church stole a bushel of rye worth 4d. and 2 pecks of wheat worth 6d. from Christopher Glover; and Robert White late of Auckland Deanery, lab., knowingly received the same at Auckland Deanery. John was brought to the bar and admitted the charge. It was judged that he be whipped in open market at Auckland and be discharged.

21) William Heddon of Bishop Auckland, co. Durham, yeo., on 15 Dec. 1617 attacked William Gargrave at Bishop Auckland. He appeared and admitted the charge. His fine was assessed by the JPs at 40s., to the bishop's use, which he paid. It was judged that he find surety both to appear at the next sessions and to keep the peace.

22) William Laycock late of South Shields mill, co. Durham, miller, on 17 Dec. 1617 at Durham city in the New Place attacked George Beecroft. Laycock appeared and admitted the charge. He was fined 3s. 4d. to the bishop's use, which he paid.

23) William Foggart late of Ryton, co. Durham, yeo., licenced to keep an alehouse at Ryton, on 7 Dec. 1617 allowed Cuthbert Porter, Christopher Clugh and Nicholas Soulby of Winlaton, yeomen, to stay drinking for over 2 hours, uninvited by any traveller [etc.], contrary to the statute of 1 James. Foggart appeared and admitted the charge. He was fined 10s. to the use of the poor of Ryton [etc.].

24) Christopher Clugh late of Winlaton, co. Durham, yeo., on 7 Dec. 1617 at Ryton attacked Roger Colson, a king's constable in Ryton, and cast him to the ground. He appeared, demurred and pleaded not guilty. Robert Cooper [*etc.*]. Jurors for 8 April.

5d.] 25) John Smith late of Crook in the parish of Ryton, co. Durham, yeo., and Anne his wife, William Smith of the same, yeo., Isabel Smith of the same, spinster, John Humble of Crawcrook, yeo., George Humble late of Daniel in the parish of Ryton, yeo., Richard Hareson of the same, lab., Richard Walker of the same, lab., and George Swinburne late of Rickless in the parish of Ryton, yeo., on 30 Nov. 1617 at Ryton assembled riotously to waylay George Chaytor of Winlaton and attacked him to his grievous harm. The defendants appeared, demurred and pleaded not guilty [*etc.*]. Robert Cooper [*etc.*]. Jurors for 8 April, when the sheriff failed to return the writ. The case was adjourned to 8 July when the parties appeared and George Selby, knt, sheriff of Durham, impanelled jurors who testified that John Smith and William Smith were guilty and the remainder innocent. It was judged that the latter be acquitted. John Smith fined £3 6s. 8d., and William Smith fined 33s. 4d. to the use of the bishop, and both were committed to gaol until the fines were paid.

26) John Grinwell late of Winlaton, yeo., Christopher Clugh late of the same, yeo., William Pickering of the same, yeo., William Dodds late of the same, yeo., and Robert Readhead late of the same, yeo., with 16 others unknown on 7 Dec. 1617 being the Sabbath assembled riotously at Ryton to murder or maim George Humble of Daniel, yeo., and attacked him at Ryton. Grinwell struck Humble on the left hand and forehead with a drawn sword worth 4s., inflicting 2 great wounds on his hand and one on the side of his head, and the remainder hit him to his grievous harm. Pickering, Clugh and Readhead appeared, demurred and pleaded not guilty. Robert Cooper [*etc.*]. Jurors for 8 April, when Clugh, Pickering and Dodds appeared, but the sheriff failed to return the writ. The case was called for 8 July. Meanwhile on 8 April Grinwell appeared and admitted the charge [*etc.*] and was fined 60s. to the bishop's use. It was adjudged that he find sureties to keep the peace with George Humble and Richard Humble and that he appear at the next sessions. Meanwhile he was committed to Durham castle until [*etc.*]. Later on 12 Jan. 1620 before William Bellasis, John Calverley, George Tonge, knts, Robert Cooper and William Smith, esqs, JPs, Doddes appeared and admitted the charge. He was fined 6s. 8d., which he paid.

27) John Grinwell late of Winlaton, yeo., Christopher Clugh of the same, yeo., William Pickering of the same, yeo., William Dodds late of the same, yeo., and Robert Readhead late of the same, yeo., assembled at Ryton with 16 others unknown on 7 Dec. 1617, being the Sabbath, with the intention of murdering or maiming Richard Humble of Daniel, yeo., and they attacked Humble at Ryton, and Grinwell struck him on the head with a drawn sword worth 4s.,

[*m.16*]   inflicting a great wound, and the remainder hit him I on the head, to his grievous harm. Pickering, Clugh and Readhead appeared, demurred and pleaded not guilty [*etc.*]. Robert Cooper [*etc.*]. Jurors for 8 April, when the defendants appeared but the sheriff failed to return his writ, which was renewed for 8 July. Meanwhile on 8 April Grinwell appeared and admitted the charge. He was fined 40s., which he paid. Later on 12 Jan. 1620 before William Bellasis, John Calverley, George Tonge, knts, Robert Cooper and Willam Smith, esqs., JPs, Dodds appeared and admitted the charge. He was fined 6s. 8d., which he paid.

28) George Chayter late of Winlaton, yeo., William Dodds of Ryton Woodside, yeo., and John Grinwell of Winlaton, yeo., on 30 Nov. 1617, being the Sabbath, assembled riotously at Ryton and attacked William Smith, and Chaytor drew his blood, to his grievous harm. Chayter appeared before the JPs, demurred and pleaded not guilty. Robert Cooper [*etc.*]. Chayter pleaded self-defence, but Cooper denied the allegation. The jurors were summoned for 8 April, when all parties appeared but the court decided that for divers reasons no jurymen should be impanelled to try the issue and that the defendants should be acquitted without fine.

29) Elsewhere on 30 April 1617 before Bp James, George Frevile, Charles Wrenn, John Calverley, Talbot Bowes, Ralph Conyers, knts, Clement Colmore, LL.D., Christopher Place, esq., Marmaduke Blakiston, a prebendary of Durham, and Robert Cooper, esq., JPs, it was presented that Luke Finley late of Alwent in the parish of Gainford, co. Durham, yeo., on 20 Oct. 1616 and before and after at Alwent took 3 kipper salmon worth 6s. in Grant beck with devices worth 2s.

Later on 7 Jan. 1618 before Timothy Whittingham, William Bellasis, John Calverley, George Tonge, knts, Clement Colmore, LL.D., Francis Burgoyne, subdean of Durham, and Robert Cooper, esq., JPs, Finley appeared, demurred and pleaded not guilty. Robert Cooper [*etc.*]. Jurors for 8 April.

[*m.16d.*]   30) MEMO that Hugh Porter for the king and himself laid an information before the JPs on 30 April 1617 against Luke Finley late of Alwent, yeo., that between 20 Sept. and 30 Nov. 1616 at Alwent he took in the [Grant beck] 5 kipper salmon with a device worth 12d. for which offence he should forfeit the salmon, the implement and 20s. and Porter claimed half the fine.

Later on 7 Jan. 1618 before Timothy Whittingham, William Bellasis, John Calverley, George Tonge, knts, Clement Colmore, LL.D., Francis Burgoyne, subdean of Durham, and Robert Cooper, esq., JPs, Finley appeared, demurred and pleaded not guilty. Porter agreed to the procedure. Jurors for 8 April.

31) MEMO that Hugh Porter for the king and himself laid an information before the JPs on 8 Jan. 1617 that Cuthbert Smith senior late of the Law in the parish of Ebchester, co. Durham, yeo., between

4 Oct. and 30 Nov. 1616 at Ebchester took in the Derwent 100 kipper
salmon with a fish spear worth 12d. For this Smith should be fined
20s. and forfeit the salmon and the fishspear.

Later on 7 Jan. 1618 before the above Smith appeared, demurred and
pleaded not guilty [*etc.*]. Porter agreed to the procedure. The jury was
summoned for 8 April, when George Selby, knt, sheriff of Durham,
failed to return the writ, and the case was adjourned to 8 July. He
again failed to return the writ and the case was adjourned to 30 Sept.
On this day the jurors testified that Smith took 20 salmon in one
night within the given dates but was not guilty of killing more. It was
judged that Smith fine with the king for his trespass, assessed by the
JPs at 20s., to the use of Bp Neile.

32) MEMO that Michael Watson for the king and himself laid an
information before the JPs on 9 July 1617 that George Swainston late
of Thorpe Thewles, co. Durham, yeo., on 1 June 1616 possessed for a
term of years 200 acres arable in Fulthorpe and between then and 10
June 1617 converted the same to sheep and cattle pasture [*etc., but
continuation missing.*]

100

(?) 8 April 16 James [*1618*]

1) Edward Short late of Burn Hall, co. Durham, yeo., on 10 Feb. 1618
at Burn Hall in the parish of St Oswald, [Durham], in a certain close
attacked Nicholas Head and cast him to the ground. Short appeared
on 8 April, demurred and pleaded not guilty. Robert Cooper, esq.,
attorney-general of Bp Neile [*etc.*]. Jurors for 8 July, when Short
admitted the charge. He was fined 5s. to the bishop's use.

2) Ralph Wren of Framwellgate, [Durham], yeo., on 14 March 1618 at
Durham attacked Cecily Cartington and cast her to the ground. He
appeared on 8 April, demurred and pleaded not guilty. Robert Cooper
[*etc.*]. Jurors for 8 July.

3) William Holt late of Gateshead, yeo., and Patrick Sivill alias Savage
late of the same, yeo., on 14 Feb. 1618 at Gateshead attacked Robert
Maltby and cast him to the ground. They appeared on 8 April,
demurred and pleaded not guilty. Robert Cooper [*etc.*]. Jurors for 8
July, when the defendants appeared and admitted the charge. They
were fined jointly 26s. 8d., which they paid.

4) Brian Wall late of Wheatbottom, co. Durham, yeo., on 4 April 1618
at Wheatbottom attacked Alice Bussie wife of William Bussie. Wall
appeared on 8 April, demurred and pleaded not guilty. Robert Cooper
[*etc.*]. Jurors for 8 July.

5) Nicholas Head late of Croxdale Mill, co. Durham, miller, on 6 Jan.
1618 at Sunderland [Bridge] in the residence of Ralph Yonge attacked
Edward Short to the effusion of his blood. Head appeared on 8 April,
demurred and pleaded not guilty [*etc.*]. Robert Cooper [*etc.*]. Head
counter-alleged that Short on the same day assaulted him at
Sunderland [Bridge] and any blows were in self-defence. This was

rebutted by Cooper. Jurors for 8 July, when Head admitted the charge and was fined 3s. 4d., which he paid.

6) Nicholas Head late of Croxdale Mill, miller, on 20 Feb. 1618 at Whitehouse attacked Edward Short, to the effusion of his blood. Head appeared on 8 April, demurred and pleaded not guilty [*etc.*]. Robert Cooper [*etc.*]. Head counter-alleged self-defence, which was rebutted by Cooper [*etc.*]. Jurors for 8 July, when Head admitted the charge. He was fined 3s. 4d., which he paid.

[*m.17*]   7) Elsewhere at the general sessions on 10 July 1616 before Bp James, Henry Anderson, knt, Clement Colmore, LL.D., Talbot Bowes, Christopher Place, Ralph Conyers and Robert Cooper, esqs, JPs, it was presented that Ralph Hardyng of Hollingside, co. Durham, esq., a month after 27 May 1606, namely from 1 May to 3 June 1616 at Hollingside harboured Charles Forrest, who failed to attend divine service for a month.

Later on 8 April 1618 before Richard Hutton, knt, a judge of Common Pleas and chancellor of Durham, William Bellasis, John Calverley, George Tonge, Ralph Conyers, knts, Clement Colmore, LL.D., Robert Cooper, Christopher Place and Ralph Fetherstonhalgh, esqs, JPs, Hardyng appeared, demurred and pleaded not guilty [*etc.*]. Robert Cooper [*etc.*]. Jurors for 8 July. (removed by *certiorari*)

8) Elsewhere at the general sessions on 10 July 1616 before [*the above as (7)*] it was presented that Ralph Rookeby of Saltwellside, esq., after 27 May 1606, namely between 1 May and 3 June 1616, at Saltwellside harboured Marmaduke Squire, who absented himself from church for a month.

Later on 8 April 1618 before Richard Hutton, knt, a judge of Common Pleas and chancellor of Durham, William Bellasis, John Calverley, George Tonge, Ralph Conyers, knts, Clement Colmore, LL.D., Robert Cooper and Christopher Place, esqs, JPs, Rookeby appeared, demurred and pleaded not guilty [*etc.*]. Robert Cooper [*etc.*]. Jurors for 8 July. (removed by *certiorari*)

9) Elsewhere on 10 July 1616 before [*the above as (7)*] it was presented that John Blakiston of Little Eden, co. Durham, gen., between 1 May and 3 June 1616 harboured Anne Carleton and Jane Phillipp, who [*etc.*].

Later on 8 April 1618 before Richard Hutton, knt, [*etc., as (8) above*] Blakiston appeared, demurred and pleaded not guilty [*etc.*]. Robert Cooper [*etc.*]. Jurors for 8 July.

[*m.17d.*]   10) Elsewhere on 10 July 1616 before [*the above as (7)*] it was presented that Charles Ratcliffe of Tunstall, co. Durham, gen., [*etc.*] between 1 May and 3 June 1616 harboured at Tunstall William Forrest and Mary Emerson [*etc.*].

Later on 8 April 1618 before Richard Hutton, knt, [*etc., as (8) above*] Ratcliffe appeared, demurred and pleaded not guilty [*etc.*]. Robert Cooper [*etc.*]. Jurors for 8 July. (removed by *certiorari*)

11) Elsewhere on 2 Oct. 1616 before Bp James, Henry Anderson,

Timothy Whittingham, knts, Clement Colmore, LL.D., Henry Hilton, Talbot Bowes, John Calverley and William Bellasis, esqs, JPs, it was presented that George Collingwood late of Eppleton, co. Durham, esq., [etc.] between 20 June and 20 Aug. 1616 harboured Margery Harbotle, Katherine Hedworth and Eleanor Johnson [etc.].

Later on 8 April before Richard Hutton, knt, [as (8) above] Collingwood appeared, demurred and pleaded not guilty [etc.]. Robert Cooper [etc.]. Jurors for 8 July.

12) Elsewhere on 10 Jan. 1616 before Henry Anderson, knt, Clement Colmore, LL.D., John Calverley, Robert Cooper, Ralph Conyers, Ambrose Dudley and John Fetherstonhalgh, esqs, JPs, it was presented that whereas John Bainbrigg of Wheatley Hill, co. Durham, gen., and Thomas Heath of Kepier East Grange, gen., in virtue of an estreat of a cess of 12d. in the pound in Easington ward, as had been assessed for the whole county palatine of Durham and Sadberge in the sessions at Durham on 5 July 1615 for the repair of bridges, did distrain on 18 Oct. 1615 in the lands of Lady Lumley by a cow belonging to her for 10s., being the rate for the castle and park according to the ancient valuation of £10; and Martin Halliman of Lumley, gen., on 18 Oct. 1615 assaulted Bainbrigg and Heath and recovered the cow.

Later on 8 April before Richard Hutton, knt, [etc., as (8) above] Halliman appeared, demurred and pleaded not guilty. Robert Cooper [etc.]. Jurors for 8 July.

13) [continuing from a previous membrane, now missing] an information laid by Thomas Thompson against John Watson for the reselling of sheep and wethers [etc.] incurring a forfeit of £90.

Later on 8 April Watson appeared before Richard Hutton, knt, [etc., as (8) above], and admitted the charge. He was fined 10s., half to the use of the bishop and half to Thompson, which he paid.

14) MEMO that Thomas Thompson for the king and himself laid an information before the JPs on 9 July 1617 that John Bainbrigg of Field Stile, co. Durham, yeo., between 1 May and 24 June 1617 at Darlington and elsewhere bought from divers persons unknown 60 hoggs at 7s. each and 60 wethers at 8s. each and resold them alive within 5 weeks, incurring thereby a forfeiture of £90, being double value.

Later on 8 April 1618 before Richard Hutton, knt, [etc., as (8) above], Bainbrigg appeared and admitted the charge. He was fined 10s. on the assessment of Robert Cooper, which he paid to the bishop's receiver and to Thompson.

15) MEMO that Hugh Porter for the king and himself laid an information before the JPs on 1 Oct. 1617 that William Punshon of Chester, co. Durham, yeo., between 1 May and 1 Aug. 1617 at Chester and elsewhere bought and engrossed from divers persons unknown 100 stones of butter at 4s. each for resale. Punshon for this first offence should forfeit the value of the butter, namely £20, of

which he claimed half, and be imprisoned for 2 months without bail. Later on 8 April 1618 before Richard Hutton, knt, [*etc.*, *as (8) above*], William Bellasis, John Calverley, George Tonge, Ralph Conyers, knts, Christopher Place and Robert Cooper, esqs, JPs, Punshon appeared and Porter withdrew his charge. The costs of defence were remitted by Punshon against Porter, while the court waived any expenses arising from the non-prosecution.

16) MEMO that on 8 April 1618 before Richard Hutton, knt, [*etc.*], William Bellasys, John Calverley, George Tonge, Ralph Conyers, knts, Ferdinando Moorecroft, master of Greatham Hospital, Christopher Place and Ralph Fetherstonhalgh, esqs, JPs, it was presented by a JP of his own knowledge that the common bridge over the – , known as Billingham bridge, was in decay for some years and that the responsibility for its repair belonged to the inhabitants of the parish holding lands nearest thereto. A fine of 66s. 8d. was assessed, to be levied if it was not repaired before Midsummer, and the sheriff was to have these parishioners before the JPs to answer on 8 July.

17) MEMO that on 8 April 1618 before [*the above as (16)*] it was presented that the watercourse, *letch or stell* at *Blankinmoore* as on 1 March 1618 ran along the king's highway between the parishes of Darlington and Hurworth, crossing it at divers places, and should be scoured. It was a parochial responsibility. A fine of 40s. was assessed, to be levied unless the repair to the watercourse was effected before Midsummer etc. The sheriff was to have the inhabitants before the JPs on 8 July following.

[*m.18d.*] 18) MEMO that on 8 April 1618 before Richard Hutton, knt, [*etc.*], William Bellasys, John Calverley, George Tonge, Ralph Conyers, knts, Clement Colmore, LL.D., Ferdinando Moorecroft, master of Greatham Hospital, Robert Cooper, Christopher Place and Ralph Fetherstonhalgh, esqs, JPs, it was presented that the king's highway at Langley called Langley *Loninge* in the parish of Brancepeth from Brancepeth to Durham was on 1 March 1618 in decay in several places and the responsibility of John Wortley of Langley, gen., and Peter Wright of the same, yeo., by reason of their tenure of land near the highway. Order to the sheriff to have the same before the JPs on 8 July.

19) MEMO that on 8 April 1618 before Richard Hutton, knt, [*etc.*], William Bellasys, John Calverley, George Tonge, Ralph Conyers, knts, Clement Colmore, LL.D., Ferdinando Moorecroft, master of Greatham Hospital, Robert Cooper and Ralph Fetherstonhalgh, esqs, JPs, it was presented that the king's highway at Brancepeth in the Long *Loning* of Brancepeth from Brancepeth to Langley *Loning* in Langley and thence to Durham city was in decay in divers places on 1 March 1618 and the responsibility of the men of Brancepeth and East Brandon. A fine of £ – was assessed to be levied unless it was repaired before Midsummer. The sheriff was to have the inhabitants before the JPs on 8 July.

20) MEMO that on 8 April 1618 before Richard Hutton, knt, [etc., as (19) above] it was presented by the 12 jurors that the public bridge over – in the parish of Brancepeth commonly called the Wood bridge and a smaller bridge called Stotley bridge were on 1 Feb. 1518 in great decay and the responsibility of parishioners of Brancepeth having land near the road. A fine of £10 was assessed unless they were repaired before the Midsummer sessions [etc.].

21) MEMO that on 8 April 1618 before Richard Hutton, knt, [etc., as (19) above] it was presented on the oath of the 12 jurors that the king's highway at Sherburn at Sherburn House Loane between Sherburn Hospital and Byers garth was on 1 Feb. 1618 in decay in divers places and the responsibility of Thomas Murrey, esq., master, and the brethren of Sherburn Hospital by reason of tenure of land near the road. A fine of £10 was assessed, to be levied unless [etc.]. Order to the sheriff to have the master and brethren to answer on 8 July.

22) MEMO that on 8 April 1618 before [the above as (19)] it was presented that the little bridge over the – on the road from Durham to Witton Gilbert by Fieldhouse in the parish of St Margaret, [Durham], was on 1 Feb. 1618 in great decay and a responsibility of parishioners who by reason [etc.]. A fine of 20s. was assessed to be levied unless the bridge was repaired before the Midsummer sessions.

1]   23) [Case continuing from a membrane now missing – rebuttal of information laid by Hugh Porter]. Jurors for 8 July.

24) MEMO that John Walker for the king and himself laid an information before the JPs on 10 Jan. 1616 that John Lightley of Middleton St George, yeo., between 11 Nov. and 20 Dec. 1615 at Middleton St George engrossed from divers persons unknown 40 bushels of wheat at 6s. a bushel and 40 bushels of barley (bigge) at 4s. a bushel for resale, incurring a forfeit of £20 and 2 months' imprisonment without bail.
Later on 8 April before Richard Hutton, knt, [etc., as (19) above] Lightley appeared, demurred and pleaded not guilty [etc.]. Jurors for 8 July.

25) MEMO that Hugh Porter for the king and himself laid an information before the JPs on 1 Oct. 1617 that John Story of Gateshead, butcher, between 24 June and 30 Sept. 1617 at Gateside forestalled from persons unknown 100 stones of butter at 4s. a stone coming by land to Newcastle for sale in the market, thereby incurring a forfeiture of the butter, a fine of £20 and 2 months' imprisonment without bail.
Later on 8 April 1618 before Richard Hutton, knt, [etc., as (19) above], Story appeared, demurred and pleaded not guilty [etc.]. Jurors for 8 July.

1d.] 26) Elsewhere on 7 Jan. 1618 before Timothy Whittingham, William Bellasis, John Calverley, George Tonge, knts, Clement Colmore, LL.D., Francis Burgoyne, subdean of Durham, and Robert Cooper, esq., JPs, it was presented that Ralph Wheatley late of Bishop Auckland, co. Durham, yeo., and William Willson late of the same, yeo., on 15 April 1617 at Carterthorne in the parish of St Helen [Auckland] tore down 38 perches of stone wall belonging to Thomas Howe and lately built on his soil.

Later on 8 April 1618 before Richard Hutton, knt, a judge of Common Pleas, chancellor of Durham, William Bellasis, John Calverley, George Tonge, Ralph Conyers, knts, Clement Colmore, LL.D., and Robert Cooper, esq., JPs, the defendants appeared, demurred and pleaded not guilty [etc.]. Robert Cooper [etc.]. Jurors for 8 July.

27) Elsewhere on 10 July 1616 before Bp James, Henry Anderson, knt, Clement Colmore, LL.D., Talbot Bowes, Christopher Place, Ralph Conyers and Robert Cooper, esqs., JPs, it was presented that William Hodgshon of Hebburn, co. Durham, gen., between 1 May and 3 June 1616 harboured in his house David Birtley, who absented himself from church [etc.].

Later on 8 April before Richard Hutton, knt, [etc., as (26) above] Hodgson appeared, demurred and pleaded not guilty [etc.]. Robert Cooper [etc.]. Jurors for 8 July. (removed by certiorari)

28) Elsewhere on 10 July 1616 before Bp James [etc., as (27) above], it was presented that Robert Hodgshon of Hebburn, co. Durham, esq., between 1 May and 3 June 1616 harboured in his houses Christopher Sotheron, Francis Jackson and James King, who failed to attend church [etc.].

Later on 8 April 1618 before Richard Hutton, knt, [etc., as (26) above], Hodgson appeared, demurred and pleaded not guilty [etc.]. Robert Cooper [etc.]. Jurors for 8 July. (removed by certiorari)

101

[m.19]   [(?) 8 July 16 James [1618]]

1) Whereas Ralph Conyers, knt, JP, by a sealed warrant of 2 July 1618 ordered the king's constable of Wolviston, co. Durham, to arrest Peter Finch of Wolviston, Frithimand Finch of the same, and others named in the warrant to appear before the magistrates, by virtue of which Ralph Davison and William Chilton, constables of Wolviston, on 2 July 1618 at Wolviston arrested Peter and Frithimand until they found surety to appear at the next sessions; and Peter resisted arrest and rescued Frithimand.

On 8 July Peter Finche appeared, demurred and pleaded not guilty [etc.]. Robert Cooper [etc.]. Jurors for 30 Sept., when the sheriff failed to return the writ. The case was adjourned to 13 Jan., when the sheriff again made no return. The case was further adjourned to 7 April, when Finche admitted the charge and was fined 3s. 4d.

2) John Shipperd late of Wolviston, yeo., Ralph Davison of the same, yeo., Matthew Corner late of the same, blacksmith, Thomas Corner of the same, lab., and William Corner late of the same, blacksmith,

son of Matthew, on 26 June 1618 at Wolviston at Wolviston North Field assembled riotously and attacked Robert Finch son of Peter Finch of Wolviston, yeo.

Now on 8 July before the JPs Shipperd, Davison, and Matthew and William Corner appeared, demurred and pleaded not guilty [etc.]. Robert Cooper [etc.]. Jurors for 30 Sept., when the sheriff failed to return the writ. The case was adjourned to 13 Jan., when the sheriff again failed to return the writ. It was further adjourned to 7 April, when Shipperd admitted the charge and was fined 2s. 6d.

3) Whereas Mary Finch wife of Robert Finch of Wolviston, yeo., and James Robinson of the same, tailor, on 7 July 1618 at Wolviston in Northfield Close took 20 sheep of Ralph Davison of Wolviston which were depasturing the grain of Robert Finch and tried to impound them at Wolviston; Davison with Matthew Corner of Wolviston, yeo., and Alice his wife, Ralph Davison of the same, yeo., William Chilton of the same, yeo., Stephen Watson of the same, yeo., Mary Shipperd wife of John Shipperd of the same, yeo., and William Shipperd of the same, yeo., assaulted Mary Finch and James Robinson and recovered the 20 sheep. On 8 July Corner and Alice his wife, Davison, Chilton, Watson, Mary and William Shipperd
9d.] appeared in court, demurred | and pleaded not guilty [etc.]. Robert Cooper [etc.]. Jurors for 30 Sept., when the sheriff failed to return the writ. The case was adjourned to 13 Jan., when again there was no writ returned. The case was further adjourned to 7 April, when Chilton, Watson, and Mary and William Shipperd admitted the charges and paid fines of 3s. 4d. each to a total of 13s. 4d. The sheriff was ordered to have the rest in court on 7 July.

4) MEMO that at the general sessions on 8 July 1618 before George Frevile, Henry Anderson, William Bellasis, John Calverley, George Tonge, Ralph Conyers, knts, Clement Colmore, LL.D., Robert Cooper and William Carr, esqs, JPs, it was presented by Ralph Conyers, knt, of his certain knowledge that the public bridge over the Skerne called Ketton bridge was ruinous and the responsibility of the parishioners of Haughton and Aycliffe with lands adjacent. The fine was assessed at £13 6s. 8d., to be levied unless the bridge was repaired before the general sessions to be held on 30 Sept. [etc.].

5) MEMO that on 8 July 1618 before [the above as (4)] it was presented by Robert Cooper, esq., of his certain knowledge that the Old Acres Loaning from Oldacres to – was on 1 June 1618 in decay and the responsibility of the parishioners of Sedgefield [etc.]. A fine of £5 was assessed, to be levied unless the road was repaired before the general sessions on 30 Sept. [etc.].

6) MEMO that on 8 July 1618 before [the above as (4)] it was presented by William Bellasis, knt, of his certain knowledge that part of the highway from Durham to Kepier at Claypath [Durham] on the lane between the bishop's bakehouse and his mills was in decay. The fine was assessed at £5, to be levied [etc.].

[m.20] 7) MEMO that Hugh Porter for himself and the king laid an information before the JPs on 1 Oct. 1617 that Laurence Cowpland of High Coniscliffe, co. Durham, yeo., between 30 May and 1 Aug. 1617 at Darlington and elsewhere bought from divers persons unknown 5 cows at £3 each, 3 stots at 50s. each and a bull at 50s., and sold the same alive within 5 weeks, incurring a double forfeit of £38 [etc.].

Later on 8 July 1618 before George Frevile, Henry Anderson, William Bellasis, John Calverley, George Tonge, Ralph Conyers, knts, Clement Colmore, LL.D., Robert Cooper and William Carr, esqs, JPs, Cowpland appeared and pleaded not guilty, except to the sale of 2 stots. His fine was assessed by Robert Cooper at 40s., which was paid half to the bishop's receiver and half to Porter.

8) MEMO that Hugh Porter for the king and himself laid an information before the JPs on 7 Jan. 1618 that Miles Bell late of Coniscliffe, yeo., and Nicholas Haddock of the same, yeo., between 1 Feb. and 3 May 1617 at Darlington and elsewhere bought from persons unknown 40 hoggs at 8s. each and resold them alive within 5 weeks, incurring a forfeiture of £320.

Later on 8 July before George Frevile, [etc., as (7) above], the defendants appeared, admitted the charge, and testified that they had fined before the Council of the North. It was adjudged that as they were poor they should pay only 10s.

9) MEMO that Thomas Thompson for the king and himself laid an information before the JPs on 7 Jan. 1618 that Lancelot Darnell late of Satley, co. Durham, yeo., between 29 Sept. and 30 Nov. 1617 at Darlington and elsewhere bought from persons unknown 3 stots at 30s. each and 3 queys at 30s. each and resold them alive within 5 weeks, incurring a forfeit of £18.

Later on 8 July before George Frevile [etc., as (7) above], Darnell appeared and pleaded not guilty save for a quey. His fine was assessed by Robert Cooper as attorney-general for the bishop at 6s. 8d., half to the bishop's use and half to Thompson.

10) MEMO that Thomas Thompson for the king and himself laid an information before the JPs on 7 Jan. 1618 against Martin Rippon late of Satley, yeo., that between 29 Sept. and 30 Nov. 1617 he bought at [(?) Darlington] and elsewhere from persons unknown 3 stots at 30s. each and 3 queys at 30s. each and resold them alive within 5 weeks, incurring a forfeit of £18.

Later on 8 July before George Frevile [etc., as (7) above], Rippon
[m.20d.] appeared and Thompson withdrew the charge I and was exonerated by both parties.

11) MEMO that Thomas Thompson for the king and himself laid an information before the JPs on 7 Jan. 1618 against Thomas Jefferson of Bowrum house in the parish of St Helen Auckland, co. Durham, yeo., that between 1 May and 1 Sept. 1617 at Darlington and elsewhere he bought from persons unknown 80 wethers at 8s. each

and 80 hoggs at 8s. each and resold the same within 5 weeks, incurring a forfeit of £128.

Later on 8 July 1618 before George Frevile, [etc., as (7) above], Jefferson appeared and Thompson withdrew the charges and was exonerated by both parties.

12) MEMO that Thomas Thompson for the king and himself laid an information before the JPs on 8 July 1618 that Thomas Jefferson of *Bowramhouse* in the parish of St Helen Auckland, yeo., between 1 April and 10 May 1618 at Darlington bought from unknown persons 90 hoggs at 8s. each which he resold alive within 5 weeks, incurring a forfeit of £72.

Later at the same sessions before George Frevile, [etc., as (7) above], Jefferson appeared and Thompson withdrew the charge [etc.].

13) MEMO that Thomas Thompson for the king and himself laid an information before the JPs on 7 Jan. 1618 that Cuthbert Sanderson of Darlington, yeo., between 29 Sept. and 20 Dec. 1617 at Darlington and elsewhere bought from persons unknown 20 stones of wool at 9s. a stone, not being a manufacturer or stapler [etc.], so incurring a forfeit of £18.

Later on 8 July 1618 before George Frevile, [etc., as (7) above], Thompson withdrew his charge [etc.].

14) MEMO that Hugh Porter for the king and himself laid an information before the JPs on 7 Jan. 1618 against John Chilton late of Chester, co. Durham, yeo., that between 4 Oct. and 30 Nov. 1617 he fished at Chester in the Chester burn and took 100 kipper salmon with a device worth 6d. Later on 8 July 1618 before George Frevile, [etc., as (7) above], Porter withdrew his charge and was exonerated.

[*The cover to the roll is an index to the Sessions Roll from 13 Jan. 1619 to 12 Jan. 1620, with a subsidiary index of recusants – defective.*]

1622

Durham CRO, Q/S/I 7 This roll of 11 membranes, filed in correct chronological order, consists of the sessions for 9 January, 2 May, 10 July and 3 October 1622.

102

[*m.1*] Pleas and presentments at Durham on 9 Jan. 19 James [*1622*] before [Richard] Hunt, dean of Durham, John Calverley, George Tonge, Ralph Conyers, knts, [John] Cradock, STD, chancellor of the diocese of Durham, Daniel Birkhead, STP, Francis [Burgoyne], archdeacon of Northumberland, Gabriel Clerke, archdeacon of Durham, Ferdinando Moorecroft, M.A., Robert Cooper, William Smith and James Lawson, esqs, JPs.

Henry Bailes [of Newton Cap], gen., Christopher Hutchinson [of Durham], gen., Humphrey Elstobb [of Bishopton], gen., Arthur Walton [of Lanchester], William Hallyman [of Murton], Ralph Davison [of Murton], Thomas Colson [of Bishopton], John Richardson [of Tudhoe], Ralph Maddison [of Birtley], Robert Pye [of Collierley], Nicholas Marley [of Pelton], Richard Maddison [of Pelaw], Thomas Dobyson [of Woodifield], John Cooke [of Pelton], Richard Sampson [of Pelaw], yeomen, jurors.

1) Robert Finch senior of Wolviston, co. Durham, yeo., Edith Finch wife of Peter Finch of the same, yeo., Frithimond Finch late of the same, spinster, Anne Finch late of the same, spinster, and John Chilton late of the same, miller, on 15 Dec. 1621 in a mill at Wolviston, the freeholding of Richard Hunt, dean, and the chapter of Durham, ejected John Smart, farmer of the mill, and disseised the dean and chapter from 15 Dec. to the present. The dean and chapter and John Smart sued for a king's writ of restitution before the JPs, which was granted after mature consideration. Order to the sheriff to use the *posse comitatus* to restore Smart.

2) Peter Finch late of Wolviston, yeo., Hugh Finch late of the same, yeo., John Chilton late of the same, miller, and Ralph Fetherston late of the same, lab., on 14 Nov. 1621 in a mill at Wolviston, being the freehold of Richard Hunt, dean, and the chapter of Durham, ejected John Smart, then farmer, and remained in possession until 15 Dec.

3) Whereas John Robinson, being travelling bailiff of Bp Neile to collect rents and arrears of tenants and farmers remaining unpaid at Durham as listed by Timothy Comyn, gen., auditor-general, and given to Robinson, on 6 Dec. 1621 distrained at Crayke, *co Durham, within the manor demesne by 3 cows to impound them for a year's rent of the demesne unpaid for the period ending Martinmas 1619, namely £51 23½d.; but Christopher Johnson late of Crayke, yeo., on the same day assaulted Robinson and recovered the animals.

[*1A*] Later on 3 Oct. 1622 before Bp Neile, William Bellasis, John Calverley, George Tonge, knts, John Cradock, STD, Ralph Fetherstonhalgh and William Smyth, esqs, JPs, Johnson appeared and admitted the charge. His fine was assessed at 10s., which he paid.

4) Whereas John Robinson [*etc., as (3) above*] on 6 Dec. 1621 at Crayke distrained by 16 cows to impound them for a year's rent unpaid on the demesne for the period ending Martinmas 1621, namely £51 23½d., Thomas Johnson late of Crayke, yeo., and Anne his wife, – Johnson late of the same, spinster, Anne Johnson late of the same, spinster, Katherine Cookson wife of Timothy – of the same, yeo., and Mary Cookson of the same, spinster, assembled riotously and recovered the animals the same day.

[*1B*] Later on 3 Oct. 1622 before the above JPs [some of] the defendants appeared and admitted the charge. They were fined 20s. jointly. [*semi-legible*]

d.] 5) Whereas John Robinson, travelling bailiff [*etc.*], on 6 Dec. 1621 at Crayke distrained by 12 stots and 10 queys to impound for a year's rent unpaid on the demesne for the period ending Martinmas 1620, namely £51 23½d., being rent in arrears, John Browne late of Crayke, yeo., assaulted Robinson and recovered the cattle.

6) Hugh Barrowe late of Beamish, co. Durham, yeo., on 30 Aug. 1621 at Ravensworth at the Fell attacked Emanuel Skirfeild and struck him with a drawn sword worth 5s. on divers parts of the body, inflicting a grave wound on the right arm near the wrist (*shacle bone*) so that the veins and nerves of the right arm "dried and mortified", another blow on the right shin 3 inches long by one inch deep, 3 wounds on his left arm and one on his left knee one inch long by a half inch deep, imperilling his life.

7) George Simpson late of Birkby, Yorks., yeo., on 10 Dec. 1621 at Darlington attacked Margaret Atkinson wife of Michael Atkinson.

8) John Eden of Belasis, co. Durham, esq., on 26 Nov. 1621 at Darlington attacked George Parkinson, gen.

9) Robert Johnson of Seaton Carew, co. Durham, yeo., on 24 Oct. 1621 at Seaton Carew attacked Nicholas Laing and cast him to the ground.

10) Thomas Stevenson late of Neasham, co. Durham, yeo., on 7 Nov. 1621 broke the close of James Lawson, esq., called *the Garthends* at Neasham and depastured the same with his pigs to the value of 10s.

11) Anthony Allen late of Neasham, yeo., on 7 Nov. 1621 broke the close of James Lawson, esq., at the Garthends at Neasham, disturbed the ground with his pigs, and let them eat grass worth 10s.

12) Stephen Chamber late of Blackwell, co. Durham, yeo., John Chamber senior of the same, yeo., and John Chambers junior late of the same, yeo., on 12 Dec. 1621 at Blackwell assembled riotously and attacked Henry Bailes. Stephen appeared on 2 May 1622 before Richard Hunt, dean of Durham, William Bellasis, John Calverley, knts, John Cradock, STD, Robert Cooper and William Smith, esqs, JPs, and admitted the charge. He was fined 20s.

13) John Chamber senior of Blackwell, yeo., and Stephen Chambers of the same, yeo., on 8 Jan. 1622 broke the gate of the common pound at Darlington and removed 16 cows and 60 sheep. On 2 May before

the above JPs – Chambers appeared and admitted the charge. He was fined 5s.

[*1A dorse*] Later on 23 April 1623 before John Calverley, George Tonge, William Muschamp, knts, John Cradock, STD, diocesan chancellor, William Smith and Christopher Place, esqs, JPs, the other appeared, admitted the charge and was fined 5s.

[*m.2*] 14) Stephen Chambers late of Blackwell, yeo., on 5 Jan. 1622 at Darlington attacked Henry Bailes. On 2 May Chambers appeared before Richard Hunt, dean of Durham, William Bellasis, John Calverley, knts, John Cradock, STD, Robert Cooper and William Smith, esqs, JPs, and admitted the charge. He was fined 10s.

15) Whereas George Selby, knt, sheriff of Durham, by a sealed writ of 26 Nov. 1621 ordered Michael Atkinson, the sheriff's bailiff in the Darlington ward, or his deputy, to arrest William Allenson of *Readhouse* if found within his bailiwick to be before the sheriff at the county court at Durham on Mon., 3 Dec., to answer Philip Wharton in a plea of debt of £6; Henry Bailes was deputed to effect this order. On 26 Nov. 1621 at Darlington Bailes took Allenson until he found surety to appear in court, but Ralph Jackson of Darlington, draper, Laurence Jackson of the same, yeo., and George Jackson of Elstob, yeo., riotously attacked Bailes on the same day and rescued Allenson.

16) Philip Flappiday late of Ragby, Yorks., lab., William Jackson late of the same, lab., William King late of Bishop Auckland, co. Durham, lab., Cuthbert Carse late of the same, lab., Elizabeth Jackson late of the same, spinster, and Jane Bowes late of the same, spinster, on 25 Oct. 1621 assaulted Henry Viccers at Bishop Auckland and purloined from him 19s. 6d. in a purse without his knowledge.

17) Philip Flappiday [*etc., as (16) above*] on 25 Oct. 1621 at Bishop Auckland assaulted Francis Newby and purloined 19s. 9d. in a purse [*etc.*].

18) Philip Flappiday [*etc., as (16) above*] on 25 Oct. 1621 at Bishop Auckland assaulted Henry Jackson and purloined 45s. 5d. in money and 2 brass farthings in a purse [*etc.*].

19) William King late of Gateside, lab., on 21 Oct. 1621 at Gateside stole a bay mare worth 53s. 4d. and a bridle and saddle worth 10s. from John Hedworth.

20) Robert Judison late of Longnewton, co. Durham, lab., on 10 Dec. 1621 at Longnewton stole a sheep worth 10d. from a person unknown. He was brought to the bar by the sheriff and admitted the charge. It was judged that he be whipped in the next open market at Durham.

21) George Tuggall late of Whickham, co. Durham, lab., on 14 Dec. 1621 at Whickham stole a sheep worth 10d. from a person unknown. Henry Foster late of Whickham received him at Whickham on 15 Dec. They were brought to the bar by the sheriff and admitted the charge. It was judged that they be whipped at Whickham on the following Monday.

22) William Vasey late of Wolsingham, co. Durham, lab., on 24 [...]ember 1621 at Wolsingham stole from John Wheitley 3 measures of malt at 10d. a measure; and John Grinwell late of Wolsingham, yeo., and Isabel Welforte late of the same, spinster, received him on the following day. All three appeared and admitted the charge. It was judged that they be whipped at Wolsingham at the next open market.

'd.] 23) Ralph Walker late of Bishop Auckland, co. Durham, tanner, on 3 Jan. 1622 at Bishop Auckland attacked Anthony Eastgate in the execution of the sheriff's warrant for his arrest. Walker appeared and admitted the charge. His fine was assessed at 3s. 4d., on payment of which with fees he should go *sine die.*

24) Anne Tutopp wife of Matthew Tutopp of Fellside, co. Durham, lab., on 4 Dec. 1621 at Fellside in the parish of Whickham attacked Eppie Earsmith wife of John Earsmith and cast her to the ground. Anne appeared and admitted the charge. Her fine was assessed at 20s., to the king's use. It was judged that she be imprisoned for the following 7 days, and that Matthew Tutopp should not henceforth keep a common alehouse in co. Durham.

25) William Tunbridge of Bishop Middleham, co. Durham, yeo., on 11 Dec. 1621 at Sedgefield attacked John Valyon in the latter's residence and held him tight by the throat. He appeared and admitted the charge. He was fined 20s. to the king's use and committed to Durham gaol until the fine was paid.

26) William Tunbridge of Bishop Middleham, yeo., on 3 Dec. 1621 attacked Margaret Valyon wife of John Valyon in his residence and cast her to the ground and bruised her. Tunbridge appeared and admitted the charge. His fine was assessed at 10s. to the king's use and he was committed to gaol [*etc.*].

27) William Tunbridge of Bishop Middleham, yeo., on 11 Dec. 1621 between 8 and 9 p.m., being in the custody of William Elstobb, a constable in Sedgefield, on a warrant of Ralph Conyers, knt, JP, to find surety to keep the peace in the counties of Durham and Sadberge with Margaret Valyon wife of John Valyon and to appear at the next sessions, did attack John Valyon and shed his blood. Tunbridge appeared and admitted the charge. His fine was assessed at 10s. to the king's use and he was committed to gaol [*etc.*].

28) George Niccolson late of Gateside, smith, and Richard Gascoigne late of the same, gen., with 10 others unknown on 2 Oct. 1621 at Gateside assembled riotously and attacked Hugh Barrowe: and Niccolson struck him with a drawn sword worth 5s. inflicting 2 wounds on his left arm and Gascoigne struck him on divers parts of his body. Niccolson appeared and admitted the charge. His fine was assessed at £10 to the king's use and he was committed to gaol until its payment and until surety was found by him to keep the peace and to appear at the next general sessions and not withdraw without licence.

[m.3]   29) Roger Branxton late of Gateside, yeo., after 1 Aug. 1604, namely on 7 Dec. 1621 at Gateside took and killed a hare in the snow with 2 greyhounds. Branxton appeared, demurred and pleaded not guilty [etc.]. Robert Cooper [etc.]. Jurors for 2 May.

30) Roger Branxton late of Gateside, yeo., after 1 Aug. 1604, namely on 7 Dec. 1621, at Gateside took a hare in the snow with 2 greyhounds. He appeared, demurred and pleaded not guilty [etc.]. Robert Cooper [etc.]. Jurors for 2 May.

31) Thomas Billopp of Gateside, yeo., after 1 Aug. 1604, namely on 18 Dec. 1621, at Farnacres took a hare in the snow with a greyhound. He appeared, demurred and pleaded not guilty [etc.]. Robert Cooper [etc.]. Jurors for 2 May.

32) Whereas the JPs on 3 Oct. 1621 ordered the king's constables of Gateside to attach George Niccolson of Gateside, smith, Robert Niccolson of the same, mariner, Richard Gascoigne of the same, gen., and William Heworth of the same, yeo., to be before the JPs at the next gaol delivery, and warrants were delivered the same day to John Atkinson and John Chamber, two constables of Gateside, Atkinson and Chamber refused to act. They appeared, demurred and pleaded not guilty. Robert Cooper [etc.]. Jurors for 2 May, when they found the accused not guilty and they were dismissed.

[m.3d.]   33) Elsewhere on 11 July 1621 before Richard Hunt, dean of Durham, John Calverley, Talbot Bowes, Ralph Conyers, knts, John Cradock, diocesan chancellor, Daniel Birkhead, STP, Robert Cooper and William Smyth, esqs, JPs, it was presented that William Grene of Monkwearmouth, co. Durham, yeo., and Isabel his wife, and Elizabeth Grene of the same, spinster, on 12 June 1621 at Monkwearmouth in the cemetery of the parish church assaulted Henry Robinson and seized 5 cows of his as bailiff of Francis Todd, clerk, which were grazing in the cemetery, and drove them to the common pound at Hylton. Later on 9 Jan. 1622 before Richard Hunt, dean of Durham, John Calverley, George Tonge, Ralph Conyers, kts, John Cradock, diocesan chancellor, Robert Cooper, William Smith and James Lawson, esqs, JPs, Greene appeared with his wife, demurred and pleaded not guilty [etc.]. Robert Cooper [etc.]. Jurors for 2 May.

34) MEMO that Nicholas Porter for the king and himself on 12 July 1620 laid an information before the JPs that John Trumble late of Gateside, cordwainer, between 1 May and 24 June 1620 at Gateside forestalled from persons unknown 100 stones of butter at 3s. 8d. a stone, coming by land for sale in Newcastle market, contrary to the statute of 5 Edward VI, and thereby incurred as a first offender a forfeit of £18 6s. 8d. and two months' imprisonment without bail. Trumble appeared on 9 Jan. 1622 before the above JPs, when Porter withdrew his charge and was exonerated.

103

¶] Pleas and presentments at Durham on 2 May 20 James [*1622*] before Richard Hunt, dean of Durham, William Bellasis, John Calverley, George Tonge, knts, John Cradock, STD, Daniel Birkhead, STP, Robert Cooper, William Smith, Ralph Fetherstonhalgh and Christopher Place, esqs, JPs.

George Crosier [of Newbiggin], gen., Thomas Middleton [of Seaton], gen., William Eden [of Whitton], gen., Christopher Hutchinson [of Durham], gen., Christopher Gaynes [of School Aycliffe], gen., George Trotter [of Byers], James Shaudforth [of Trimdon], Thomas Dobbyson [of Woodifield], Cuthbert Welsh [of Hetton], Richard Maddeson [of Pelaw], William Parker [of Collierley], Anthony Hopper [of Towdy Pots], Robert Hopper [of Witton], Roger Pearson [of Gateside], Arthur Walton [of Lanchester], jurors.

1) John Blakiston of Blakeston, co. Durham, gen., Francis Blakiston of the same, gen., Marmaduke Blakiston of the same, gen., and William Blakiston of the same, gen., on 29 March 1621 broke into the capital messuage at Blakeston, being the freehold of Marmaduke Blakiston, clerk, and ejected him to the present date. Marmaduke Blakiston appeared and sued the king's writ of restitution, which was granted. Order to the sheriff to use the *posse comitatus* if necessary.

2) George Wardell senior of Mainsforth, co. Durham, yeo., and Christine his wife on 1 March 1622 forcibly entered an acre of arable at Mainsforth in the possession of John Lee, gen., and expelled Lee to the present date. Wardele and his wife appeared, demurred and pleaded not guilty [*etc.*]. Robert Cooper [*etc.*]. Jurors for 10 July, who pronounced a verdict of not-guilty.

3) John Chamber late of Darlington, pedlar, on 6 Feb. 1622 stole at Darlington 2 pecks of barley worth 2s. from Thomas Soter.

4) Elizabeth Robinson late of Darlington, widow, on 6 Feb. 1622 at Darlington stole a boll of barley worth 3s. 4d. from Thomas Soter.

5) Richard White of Seaton, co. Durham, yeo., and Robert Johnson son of George Johnson of the same, yeo., on 26 July 1621 at Owton took away in ox-waggons a fother of lime worth 10s. belonging to James Bellasis without his leave.

6) Robert Johnson son of George Johnson of Seaton, yeo., on 22 May 1621 at Owton attacked Thomas Skilbeck and prevented him from performing the business of James Bellasis, esq., his master.

4d.] 7) Brian Potter of Hutton Henry, co. Durham, yeo., and Matthew Curry of Greatham, yeo., on 22 Aug. 1621 at Owton seized lime of James Bellasis, esq., worth £9 in a lime kiln and removed it in ox-carts.

8) Edward Hodgshon late of Framwellgate, [Durham], glazier, on 25 April 1622 in Durham city stole a greyhound with a collar together worth 20s. from John Stevenson.

9) Whereas George Selby, knt, sheriff of Durham, by virtue of a warrant from the JPs at the sessions of 9 Jan. 1622 to arrest Peter Finch and Edith his wife, Frithimond Finch, Robert Finch senior and Mary his

wife and John Chilton, ordered Robert Moore and William Moore, his bailiffs in the Stockton ward, with Samson Stobbert, William Fosse and William Savage by his sealed warrant of 4 Feb. to take and hold them until they found sureties for good behaviour; later on 17 March 1622 William Fosse arrested at Wolviston Robert Finch senior, who assaulted him and escaped.

10) Bernard Longstaffe late of Blackwell, co. Durham, piper, on 20 Nov. 1621 and thereabouts at Blackwell put nets worth 4s. in the Tees and took 10 kipper salmon worth 20s. He appeared and admitted the charge. A fine of 20s. was assessed to the king's use, which he paid.

11) William [Laver]ock of Ryton, co. Durham, yeo., on 19 Feb. 1622 at Ryton attacked Thomas Hudson and cast him to the ground. He appeared and admitted the charge. His fine of 20s. was assessed to the king's use, and he was committed to Durham castle gaol until its payment and until he found surety for his good behaviour and for his appearance at the next sessions.

12) Whereas Robert Cooper, esq., steward of the bishop's halmotes in Durham and Sadberge, by warrant of 1 Jan. 1622 ordered William Jolly to levy from the goods of William Laverock £23 6s. 10d. as debt and 2s. costs to the use of John Hudson, as recovered by him in the halmote at Chester on 16 Oct. 1621 by Laverock's default: Jolly on 19 Feb. 1622 at Ryton took an ox of Laverock, but Laverock assaulted him the same day and recovered the animal. Laverock appeared and admitted the charge [etc.]. His fine was assessed at 40s. and he was committed to gaol until its payment.

13) Christine alias Katherine Wardale, wife of George Wardale senior of Mainsforth, co. Durham, yeo., and George Wardale late of the same, yeo., on 1 March 1622 at Mainsforth assembled with others unknown and attacked Ann Farrowe. They appeared and it being found that George was an infant under 7 years of age he was discharged. Christine admitted the charge and was fined 10s. to the king's use and was committed to gaol until she paid.

[m.5]

14) Christine Wardall wife of George Wardall senior of Mainsforth, yeo., on 1 March 1622 at Mainsforth assaulted Margaret Farrow, widow, and cast her to the ground. She appeared and admitted the charge. Her fine was assessed at 10s., which she paid.

15) Margaret Farrowe of Mainsforth, widow, Anne Farrowe of the same, spinster, and Thomas Tedcastle of the same, yeo., on 1 March 1622 at Mainsforth attacked George Wardale junior and threw stones at him. They appeared and admitted the charge. They were fined 3s. 4d. each, to a total of 10s., to the king's use, which they paid.

16) Margaret Farrowe of Mainsforth, widow, Anne Farrowe of the same, spinster, and Thomas Tedcastle of the same, yeo., on 1 March 1622 at Mainsforth attacked Christine Wardale wife of George Wardale to the effusion of her blood and bruised her with stones. They appeared and admitted the charge [etc.]. They were fined 3s. 4d. each to a total of 10s. to the king's use.

17) John Corsby late of Buckton in the county palatine of Durham, lab., on 16 March 1622 at Buckton assaulted William Briggs and drove William's finger with a wedge into the bore of a cart-axletree, thereby bruising it. He appeared and admitted the charge. His fine was assessed at 20s. to the king's use, and he was committed to gaol until he made payment. It was judged that he also be imprisoned for 10 days.

18) Elsewhere on 3 Oct. 1621 before Bp Neile, Richard Hunt, dean of Durham, Timothy Whittingham, William Bellasis, John Calverley, Talbot Bowes, George Tonge, knts, John Cradock, Robert Cooper, William Smyth and James Lawson, esqs, JPs, it was presented that William Eden late of Whitton, co. Durham, gen., on 12 Sept. 1621 at Elvet attacked Sarah Metcalfe wife of Ralph Metcalfe in the residence of the latter, struck her on the face and head, and cast her to the ground. Eden appeared on 2 May before Richard Hunt, dean of Durham, William Bellasis, John Calverley, George Tonge, knts, John Cradock, STD, Robert Cooper and William Smith, esqs, JPs, demurred and pleaded not guilty [etc.]. Robert Cooper [etc.]. Jurors for 10 July, when Eden sought leave to fine. This was assessed at 10s., which he paid.

19) Elsewhere on 9 Jan. 1622 before Richard Hunt, dean of Durham, John Calverley, George Tonge, Ralph Conyers, knts, John Cradock, STD, diocesan chancellor, Robert Cooper, William Smith and James Lawson, esqs, JPs, it was presented that George Niccolson late of Gateside, smith, and Richard Gascoigne I of the same, gen., with 10 others unknown assembled riotously on 2 Oct. 1621 at Gateside and attacked Hugh Barrowe; and George Niccolson inflicted 2 wounds on his left arm with a sword worth 5s. and Richard Gascoigne struck him on divers parts of his body. They appeared on 2 May before Richard Hunt [etc., as (18) above], demurred and pleaded not guilty [etc.]. Robert Cooper [etc.]. Jurors for 10 July.

5d.]

20) Elsewhere on 9 Jan. 1622 before Richard Hunt [etc., as (19) above] it was presented that whereas George Selby, knt, sheriff of Durham, by order of the county court of Durham of 26 Nov. 1621 authorized Michael Atkinson, his bailiff in the Darlington ward, to arrest William Allenson of Readhouse to have him at Durham before the sheriff on Mon., 3 Dec., to answer Philip Wharton for a debt of £6; Henry Bailes, being sworn deputy for Atkinson, on 26 Nov. at Darlington arrested Allenson to find surety for his appearance. On the same day Ralph Jackson of Darlington, draper, Laurence Jackson of the same, yeo., and George Jackson of Elstob, yeo., attacked Bailes at Darlington and freed Allenson. On 2 May Ralph Jackson appeared before Richard Hunt [etc., as (18) above], demurred and pleaded not guilty [etc.]. Robert Cooper [etc.]. Jurors for 10 July. On that day the sheriff returned a panel of jurors that testified that Ralph Jackson was innocent. It was judged that Laurence and George Jackson be similarly discharged.

21) Elsewhere on 9 Jan. 1622 before Richard Hunt [*etc., as (19) above*] it
was presented that Peter Finch late of Wolviston, co. Durham, yeo.,
Hugh Finch late of the same, yeo., John Chilton late of the same,
miller, and Ralph Fetherston late of the same, lab., on 14 Nov. 1621
in a mill at Wolviston, being the freehold of Richard Hunt, dean, and
the chapter of Durham, ejected John Smart, then its farmer, and
remained there until 15 Dec. following.
On 2 May Hugh Finch and John Chilton appeared before [*the JPs as
(18) above*], demurred and pleaded not guilty [*etc.*]. Robert Cooper
[*etc.*]. Jurors for 10 July, when the sheriff failed to return the writ. The
case was adjourned until 3 Oct., when Hugh sought leave to fine.
This was assessed at 3s. 4d. to the king's use, which he paid.

[*m.6*] 22) Elsewhere on 9 Jan. 1622 before Richard Hunt, [*etc., as (19) above*]
it was presented that Robert Finch senior of Wolviston, co. Durham,
yeo., Edith Finch wife of Peter Finch of the same, yeo., Frithimund
Finch late of the same, spinster, Anne Finch late of the same,
spinster, and John Chilton late of the same, miller, on 15 Dec. 1621
at a mill at Wolviston being the freehold [*etc.*] ejected John Smart and
were still in possession [*etc.*]. The dean and chapter with John Smart
sued a writ of restitution to be directed to the sheriff of Durham,
which was granted by the JPs. Now on 2 May 1622 John Chilton
appeared before Richard Hunt [*etc., as (18) above*], demurred and
pleaded not guilty [*etc.*]. Robert Cooper [*etc.*]. Jurors for 10 July.

23) MEMO that Nicholas Porter for the king and himself laid an
information before the JPs on 9 Jan. 1622 that John Garthorne of
Landieu in the parish of Wolsingham, co. Durham, yeo., after 1 June
1559, namely between 20 Sept. and 29 Nov. 1621, did fish in the
River Wear at Wolsingham with a fish spear worth 10d. and a net
worth 4s. at *Boyley* burn and took and killed 100 kipper salmon, so
incurring a forfeit of 20s. for the salmon together with the
implements [*etc.*].
Later on 2 May Garthorne appeared before Richard Hunt, [*etc., as
(18) above*], demurred and pleaded not guilty. Porter agreed to the
procedure [*etc.*]. Jurors for 10 July.

104

[*m.6d.*] Pleas and presentments at Durham on 10 July 20 James [*1622*] before
William Bellasis, John Calverley, George Tonge, Ralph Conyers, knts,
John Cradock, STD, diocesan chancellor, Daniel Birkhead, STD,
William Smith and Ralph Fetherstanhalgh, esqs, JPs.
Thomas Middleton [of Seaton], gen., John Brasse [of Edderacres],
gen., Thomas Gregson [of Murton], Thomas Robinson [of Murton],
William Halliman [of Murton], George Garth [of Newbiggin], Richard
Maddeson [of Pelaw], John Casson [of Sadberge], Christopher
Richardson [of Archdeacon Newton], Ralph Maddeson [of Birtley],
Anthony Yonge [of Murton], James Shaudforth [of Trimdon], John
Atkinson [of *Farleis*], William Shacklock [of Morton], Leonard

Somerside [of Chester], yeomen, jurors.

1) John Thornton late of Fulthorpe, co. Durham, yeo., and Francis Cooper of the same, yeo., on 18 May 1622 at a mill at Wynyard being the freehold of Marmaduke Blakiston, clerk, ejected Ralph Blakiston, gen., its farmer, and still retain possession. Marmaduke and Ralph Blakiston sued before the JPs a writ of restitution directed to the sheriff, which was granted.

2) Anthony Pearson late of Hartington, Northumberland, lab., on 12 Nov. 1621 at Crawcrook, co. Durham, stole a branded stot worth 33s. 4d. from Thomas Newton.

3) William Grinway late of South Shields, co. Durham, yeo., on 15 June 1622 at South Shields attacked Robert Walles, a constable of the township.

4) Whereas John Robinson, travelling bailiff of the bishop to collect rents and arrears of tenants and farmers as listed upaid at the Durham exchequer, on 3 July 1622 at East Thickley alias Old Thickley, co. Durham, distrained on a cow on the same manor for a rent of 13s. 4d. due on 4 Sept. past and tried to impound it at Bishop Auckland; Joseph Lilborne late of East Thickley, gen., on the same day assaulted Robinson and recovered the cow.

5) Francis Welfoote late of Bishopton, co. Durham, yeo., Thomas Welfoote late of the same, yeo., Francis Mawer late of the same, yeo., and Bartholomew Jackson late of the same, yeo., on 22 July 1621 at Bishopton assembled riotously and assaulted John Simpson.

6) Richard Sowerby late of Alwent, co. Durham, yeo., John Bartle late of Longnewton, yeo., and Richard Moody late of the same, yeo., on 28 June 1622 entered the mill at Longnewton and ejected John Simpson and hold it to the present.

7) Whereas Cuthbert Henderson, a collector of rents, fines and amercements for the bishop in Stanhope, co. Durham, by virtue of an estreat sent to him and George Dacues, gen., and delivered on 26 June 1622 did distrain at Stanhope on the goods of William Blackett of Stanhope senior, gen., namely 4 doublers and 2 pans, for amercements totalling 3s. 10d. imposed at the halmote in Wolsingham on 21 May 1622; on the same day Blackett assaulted Henderson at Stanhope and recovered the goods.

[7A] Later on 8 Jan. 1623 before Timothy Whittingham, William Bellasis, John Calverley, knts, John Cradock, STD, and William Smith, esq., JPs, Blackett appeared and admitted the charge. His fine was assessed at 6s. 8d., to the king's use.

8) Whereas George Selby, knt, sheriff of Durham, by sealed precept of the county court of 28 June 1622 ordered Michael Atkinson, his bailiff in the Darlington ward, with Cuthbert Comyn, special bailiff, to take John Widdowes senior of Cornforth and have him before the sheriff in the county court at Durham on Mon., 1 July next, to answer Thomas Humble for a debt of £40, by which authority Cuthbert Comyn on the same 1 July took Widdowes at Cornforth to

find surety to answer; on the same 1 July Robert Scathlock late of Durham city, yeo., and Janet Readhead wife of William Readhead of Cornforth, yeo., attacked Comyn and rescued Widdowes with his active assistance.

9) Whereas the king by a writ of the Durham chancery ordered Robert Moorye, William Moorye, Humphrey Farrowe, John Warde, Robert Pereth and Roger Corner to make public proclamation that Peter Finch, who should have appeared in person in the Durham chancery, had defied the order and should be declared a rebel, and that they should have him in the Durham chancery on 30 May past to answer; John Warde and Roger Corner, two of the commissioners named, on 6 May 1622 with Christopher Arrowsmith and William Siggeswick their assistants, attached Finch at Wolviston and had him in custody: and on the same 6 May Peter Finch of Wolviston, yeo., Toby Finch of the same, yeo., Frithimond Finch of the same, spinster, Anne Finch of the same, spinster, Mary Finch wife of Robert Finch of the same, yeo., Jane Robinson wife of James Robinson of Hartlepool, yeo., Anne Sharpe of Wolviston, widow, Grace Sharpe of the same, spinster, Elizabeth Cawood wife of William Cawood of Wolviston, yeo., Katherine Woodroff wife of Thomas Woodroff of the same, yeo., and Margaret Hall wife of Ralph Hall of the same, yeo., assembled riotously with knives and stones at Wolviston and attacked Warde, Corner, Arrowsmith and Siggeswick and drew blood, and Peter Finch wounded Warde in the right hand with a knife worth 2s., and rescued himself, aided and abetted by the rest.

10) Nicholas Robinson late of Durham city, lab., on 18 May 1622 at Stanhope stole a lamb worth 10d. from Elizabeth Fetherston, widow. He was produced at the bar by the sheriff and admitted the charge. It was judged that he be whipped in the next market at Durham.

11) Anthony Foggan of Brancepeth, co. Durham, lab., and Edward Lambert of the same, lab., on 9 June 1622 about 1 a.m. broke into the fenced park of the Prince of Wales at Brancepeth East Park and hunted deer, and Foggan shot a pregnant fallow doe worth 20s. with a gun loaded with a slug. The defendants appeared and admitted the charge. It was judged that they be committed to the gaol of Durham castle for 3 months without bail and remain there until they paid a fine of £10 to the king's use and triple damages to the use of the prince, and they were to find sureties for good behaviour for 7 years.

[m.7d.] 12) Robert Graves of Heighley Hall, co. Durham, gen., on 7 May 1622 at Heighley Hall in the parish of Winston attacked William Browne and struck him on divers parts with a pitchfork worth 2d., inflicting such a wound on his right hand that he almost lost the use of a finger. Graves appeared, demurred and pleaded not guilty [etc.]. Robert Cooper [etc.]. Jurors for 3 Oct.

13) Thomas Browne late of Durham city, yeo., on 4 July 1622 at Durham city attacked Thomas Thoraby, struck him with a stick worth 1d., and cast him to the ground and knee'd him. Browne appeared,

demurred and pleaded not guilty [*etc.*]. Robert Cooper [*etc.*]. Jurors for 3 Oct. (removed by *certiorari*)

14) Gavin Whally late of Darlington, haberdasher, on 26 June 1622 at Darlington attacked Edmund Whally. He appeared, demurred and pleaded not guilty [*etc.*]. Robert Cooper [*etc.*]. Jurors for 3 Oct., when both parties appeared and the empanelled jury pronounced Gavin not guilty. He was dismissed *sine die*.

15) Elsewhere on 3 Oct. 1621 before Bp Neile, Richard Hunt, dean of Durham, Timothy Whittingham, William Bellasis, John Calverley, Talbot Bowes, George Tonge, knts, John Cradock, diocesan chancellor, Robert Cooper, William Smyth and James Lawson, esqs, JPs, it was presented that Valentine Cotes late of Stockton, co. Durham, yeo., William Anderson late of the same, yeo., John Anderson late of the same, yeo., Matthew Hearon late of the same, yeo., and William Crasley late of the same, yeo., on 10 Sept. 1621 at Stockton took with nets in the Tees 2 kipper salmon worth 2s. Later on 10 July before the above JPs the defendants appeared, demurred and pleaded not guilty [*etc.*]. Robert Cooper [*etc.*]. Jurors for 3 Oct., when the panel testified as to their innocence and they were dismissed *sine die*.

16) MEMO that Richard Husband for the king and himself appeared before the JPs on 9 Jan. 1622 and laid an information against James Dale late of Middleton Row, co. Durham, yeo., that on 26 Dec. 1620 he was seised of 13 acres arable at Middleton Row in tillage on 24 Oct. 1597 [*etc.*], and between 26 Dec. 1620 and 1 Jan. 1622 he converted the same to sheep pasture [*etc.*]. For this offence he should forfeit £13, of which Husband claimed a third. Dale appeared on 10 July 1622 before the JPs, demurred and pleaded not guilty [*etc.*]. Husband agreed to the procedure [*etc.*]. Jurors for 3 Oct. [*etc.*], when the sheriff failed to return the writ. The case was adjourned to 8 Jan., when the empanelled jury found Dale not guilty. He was dismissed *sine die*.

17) MEMO that Richard Husband for the king and himself on 9 Jan. 1622 laid an information before the JPs that Roger Wilson of Kelloe, clerk, on 26 Dec. 1620 was seised in demesne of 40 acres arable in Middleton Row [*etc.*] which he converted to sheep and cattle pasture [*etc.*]. Wilson appeared on 10 July 1622 before the JPs, demurred and pleaded not guilty. Richard Husband [*etc.*]. Jurors for 3 Oct. [*etc.*]. The empanelled jury found Wilson not guilty [*etc.*].

18) MEMO that Richard Husband for the king and himself on 9 Jan. 1622 laid an information before the JPs that Henry Andrew late of Middleton Row, yeo., was seised on 26 Dec. 1620 of 13 acres arable in Middleton Row | which he converted to sheep and cattle pasture, thereby incurring a forfeit of £13 [*etc.*].

Later on 10 July 1622 before the JPs Andrew appeared, demurred and pleaded not guilty. Richard Husband [*etc.*]. Jurors for 3 Oct.

19) MEMO that Nicholas Porter for the king and himself on 9 Jan.

1622 laid an information before the JPs that George Mowbrey of Bishopley, co. Durham, yeo., after 1 June 1559, namely on several occasions between 30 Oct. and 29 Nov. 1621 at Bishopley fished with a net worth 20s. in Dryburn and took 4 kipper salmon, for which he should forfeit 20s., the fish and the net, and he claimed a half. Later on 10 July 1622 before the above JPs Mowbrey appeared and admitted the charge. His fine was assessed at 20s., half to the king and half to Porter, and he was dismissed.

105

[m.9]   Pleas and presentments at Durham on 3 Oct. 20 James [1622] before Bp Neile, William Bellasis, George Tonge, Ralph Conyers, knts, John Cradock, STD, Daniel Birkhead, STD Francis Burgoyne, STB, Ralph Fetherstonhalgh, William Smith, James Lawson, esqs, JPs.

John Wortley [of Langley], esq., George Parkinson [of Hag House], gen., Thomas Middleton [of Durham], gen., Christopher Hutchinson [of Durham], gen., Christopher Hall [of Trimdon], gen., Thomas Emerson [of Darlington], gen., John Morgan [of *Milnehouses*], gen., John Vasey [of Coniscliffe], gen., Peter Blackett [of Greenhead], Thomas Richardson [of Hunwick], Richard Cornforth [of *Aykes Raw*], John Shacklock [of Murton], Cuthbert Johnson [of Hetton], Lionel Ayre [of Wiserley], John Atkinson [of Embleton], yeomen, jurors.

1) William Johnson late of Seaton Carew, co. Durham, yeo., William Partus of Wynyard, yeo., and Eleanor his wife, William Middleton of Fulthorpe, yeo., and Francis Cooper of the same, lab., on 26 May 1622 entered closes of meadow and pasture called *Great Brigg flatt, Little Brigg flatt, Bottom* and *the Lowe meadows* nearby and 2 closes called *the Shipdounes* and 2 closes of pasture and one of meadow adjoining Wynyard mill at Wynyard, being the freehold of Marmaduke Blakiston, clerk, and ejected Ralph Blakiston, gen., the farmer, from 26 May to the present, thereby disseising Marmaduke and Ralph, who appeared and sought a writ of restitution from the JPs. This was granted after consideration, with authority to the sheriff to use the *posse comitatus*.

2) William Johnson late of Seaton Carew, co. Durham, yeo., and William Partus late of Wynyard, yeo., on 10 Aug. 1622 at Wolviston attacked Ralph Blakiston, gen., and Partus felled him to the ground with a stick worth 2d. and both "bruised" him.

3) Thomas Samson of Pelaw, co. Durham, yeo., and Leonard Samson of the same, yeo., on 11 Sept. 1622 at Pelaw in the parish of Chester[-le-Street] attacked Anthony White on the king's highway. They appeared on 23 April 1623 before John Calverley, George Tonge, William Muschampe, knts, John Cradock, STD, William Smyth and Christopher Place, esqs, JPs, and admitted the charge. They were jointly fined 6s. 8d. to the king's use and dismissed *sine die*.

4) Thomas Samson of Pelaw, yeo., and Leonard Samson of the same, yeo., on 11 Sept. 1622 at Pelaw in the parish of Chester attacked

Robert Trotter on the king's highway. They appeared on 23 April 1623 before the above and admitted the charge. They were fined jointly 6s. 8d. to the king's use [etc.].

5) Robert Walles of South Shields, yeo., on 15 July 1622 at South Shields assaulted Margaret Greneway wife of William Greneway and Grace Turner. Walles appeared on 8 Jan. 1623 before Timothy Whittingham, William Bellasis, John Calverley, knts, John Cradock, STD, and William S[mith], esqs, JPs, and admitted the charge. His fine was assessed at 6s. 8d., which he paid.

6) William Liddell late of Gateside, lab., on 27 Aug. 1622 at Whickham, co. Durham, at Allerdene attacked Archibald Carrudders and bruised him. He appeared on 23 April 1623 before [etc. as (3) above] and admitted the charge. His fine was assessed at 3s. 4d., paid to the king's use [etc.].

7) John Halliday late of Sunderland by the sea, co. Durham, miller, on 20 Aug 1622 at Barmston illegally "did cut insunder" an oak worth 20s. in the wood of Henry Hilton, esq., and removed a part worth 4d.

8) John Reede of Barmston, co. Durham, yeo., and Matthew Foggart of Washington, yeo., on 20 May 1622 at Hylton in Hylton Wood illegally lopped the branches of an oak worth 20d. in the wood of Henry Hilton, esq., and carted the same.

9) John Douthwhaite late of Willington, co. Durham, yeo., on 22 Aug. 1622 assaulted George Sheiffeild, gen., at Brancepeth. He appeared on 3 Oct. and admitted the charge. His fine was assessed at 40s., to the king's use, which he paid. He was dismissed *sine die*.

10) John Walker of Elvet, co. Durham, yeo., being a collector of money for the relief of lepers, soldiers and sailors in co. Durham by warrant of the king's justices in Durham and Sadberge, on 26 April 1622 broke into the residence of William Pickering at Houghton-le-Side, and under colour of his office seized 13 yards of harden cloth worth 12s. against 13s. 4d. assessed on the parishioners of Denton for the same relief in 1621 and remaining unpaid. Such action was extortionate and unjust and contrary to law and ordinance, and against the peace. Walker appeared and admitted the charge. His fine was assessed at 10s. to the king's use, which he paid.

11) Whereas Richard Hunt, STP, dean of Durham, John Cradock, STD, and Henry Ewbank, MA, three JPs, by sealed warrant dated 1 April ordered John Walker, William Hutchinson, George Anderson, Brian Potter and Nicholas Porter to distrain on and levy 13s. from the parishioners of Hurworth, co. Durham, for relief [as above] in respect of the year 1621, Walker seized unjustly at Hurworth 2s. for arrears [etc.]. Walker appeared and pleaded guilty. His fine was assessed at 10s. to the king's use, which he paid.

12) Whereas Anne Herrison wife of Richard Herrison of Woodhouses, yeo., on 18 Sept. 1622 at Woodhouses in the parish of St Andrew Auckland broke the close of William Middleton there called *the Intack* and took a mare of George Moore of Escomb and tried to

impound it at Bishop Auckland for trespass, George Moore late of Escomb, yeo., and Jane his wife the same day attacked Anne at Woodhouses, cast her to the ground, and recovered the mare. George and Jane Moore appeared on 3 Oct. and admitted the charge. They were fined jointly 20s. to the king's use, which they paid.

13) Whereas John Gordan by sealed warrant of Bp Neile, John Cradock, STD, and Francis Burgoyne, STB, three commissioners of the king to assess and levy the first payment of the second subsidy in the parishes of Norham and Islandshire, directed to him and the parish constables and delivered to him on 22 Aug. 1622, did distrain at Grindon in the parish of Norham on a mare for 5s. assessed on John Selbye of Grindon for the first instalment and tried to impound the same, Robert Litster late of Grindon, yeo., assaulted Gordon the same day at Grindon and recovered the mare. Also Thomas Burne, a parish constable of Norham, refused to accompany Gordon in the execution of his office. Litster and Burne appeared on 3 Oct. and admitted the charge. They were jointly fined 40s. to the king's use [etc.].

[m.10] 14) Elsewhere at the general sessions on 2 May 1622 before Richard Hunt, dean of Durham, William Bellasis, John Calverley, George Tonge, knts, John Cradock, STD, Daniel Birkhead, STP, Robert Cooper, William Smyth, Ralph Fetherstonhalgh and Christopher Place, esqs, JPs, it was presented that Richard White of Seaton, yeo., and Robert Johnson son of George Johnson of Seaton, yeo., on 26 July 1621 at Owton took in an ox-waggon a fother of lime worth 10s. belonging to James Bellasis, esq.
White appeared on 3 Oct. before Bp Neile, William Bellasis, John Calverley, George Tonge, knts, John Cradock, STD, Ralph Fetherstonhalgh, William Smyth and James Lawson, esqs, JPs, demurred and pleaded not guilty [etc.]. Robert Cooper [etc.]. Jurors for 8 Jan. (removed by certiorari)

15) Elsewhere at the general sessions on 2 May 1622 before [the above as (14)] it was presented that Brian Potter of Hutton Henry, co. Durham, yeo., and Matthew Currye of Greatham, yeo., on 22 Aug. 1621 at Owton took from his lime-kiln lime belonging to James Bellasis, esq., worth £9 and took it away in an ox-waggon. They appeared on 3 Oct. before [the above as (14)], demurred and pleaded not guilty [etc.]. Robert Cooper [etc.]. Jurors for 8 Jan. (removed by certiorari)

16) Elsewhere at the general sessions on 10 July 1622 before William Bellasis, John Calverley, George Tonge, Ralph Conyers, knts, John Cradock, STD, Daniel Birkhead, STD, William Smyth and Ralph Fetherstonhalgh, esqs, JPs, it was presented that Richard Sowerby late of Alwent, co. Durham, yeo., John Bartle late of Longnewton, yeo., and Richard Moory late of the same, yeo., on 28 June 1622 entered a messuage in Longnewton possessed by John Simpson whom they ejected, and remain in occupation.

Now on 3 Oct. 1622 before [*the above as (14)*] Sowerby, Bartle and Moorey appeared, demurred and pleaded not guilty [*etc.*]. Robert Cooper [*etc.*]. Jurors for 8 Jan, when the defendants were found not guilty [*etc.*].

17) Elsewhere at the general sessions on 10 July 1622 before [*the above as (16)*] it was presented that William Grinway late of South Shields, co. Durham, yeo., on 15 June 1622 at South Shields attacked Robert Walles, a king's constable in South Shields, in the execution of his office. Grinway appeared on 3 Oct. before [*the above as (14)*], demurred and pleaded not guilty [*etc.*]. Robert Cooper [*etc.*]. Jurors for 8 Jan., when Grinway put himself on the mercy of the court. His fine was assessed at 6s. 8d. to the king's use, which he paid.

18) Elsewhere at the general sessions on 10 July 1622 before [*the above as (16)*] it was presented that Francis Welfoote late of Bishopton, co. Durham, yeo., Thomas Welfoote late of the same, yeo., Francis Mawer late of the same, yeo., and Bartholomew Jackson late of the same, yeo., on 22 July 1621 at Bishopton assembled riotously and attacked John Simpson.
The defendants appeared on 3 Oct. before [*the above as (14), less James Lawson*], demurred and pleaded not guilty [*etc.*]. Robert Cooper [*etc.*]. Jurors for 8 Jan., when the panel found the defendants innocent [*etc.*].

19) MEMO that Francis Milburne for the king and himself on 2 May 1622 laid an information before the JPs that John Robinson of Gateside, yeo., from 2 Feb. to 1 May 1622 practised the craft of shoemaker and sold shoes without serving an apprenticeship of 7 years. For this he should forfeit 40s. a month, of which Milburne claimed half.
Later on 3 Oct. 1622 Robinson appeared before [*the above as (14), less James Lawson*], demurred and pleaded not guilty. Milburne agreed [*etc.*]. Jurors for 8 Jan.

20) MEMO that Richard Husband for the king and himself on 9 Jan. 1622 laid an information before the JPs that George Gailes late of Middleton Row, co. Durham, yeo., on 26 Dec. 1620 held by term of years 13 acres in Middleton Row which were in tillage on 24 Oct. 1597, and between 26 Dec. 1620 and 1 Jan. 1622 converted the same to sheep and cattle pasture, for which he should forfeit £13 at 20s. an acre, of which he claimed a third. On 3 Oct. 1622 he appeared before [*the above as (14), less George Tonge*], and Husband withdrew his charge. Gailes was dismissed and Husband exonerated.

21) MEMO that Richard Husband for the king and himself on 9 Jan. 1622 laid an information before the JPs that John Browne late of Middleton Row, yeo., on 26 Dec. 1620 held by term of years 21 acres arable at Middleton Row and between 26 Dec. 1620 and 1 Jan. 1622 converted the same to sheep and cattle pasture. For this he should forfeit £21 [*etc.*].
Later on 3 Oct. before [*the above as (14), less George Tonge*] Browne

appeared and Husband withdrew his charges [*etc.*].

22) MEMO that Richard Husband for the king and himself on 9 Jan. 1622 laid an information before the JPs that Cuthbert Middleton late of Middleton Row, yeo., and Henry Hull late of the same, yeo., on 26 Dec. 1620 held by term of years 13 acres arable in Middleton Row [*etc.*] and between 26 Dec. 1620 and 1 Jan. 1622 converted them to sheep and cattle pasture for which he should forfeit £13 [*etc.*]. Later on 3 Oct. before [*the above as (14), less George Tonge*], the defendants appeared and Husband withdrew his charges [*etc*].

[*m.11d.*] 23) MEMO that Nicholas Porter for the king and himself on 9 Jan. 1622 laid an information before the JPs against Philip Hildreth late of Piercebridge, co. Durham, yeo., that between 20 Sept. and 29 Nov. 1621 he did take with a fish spear worth 10d. at Piercebridge in the water of Tees 100 kipper salmon, for which he should forfeit 20s., the fish and the fish spear, and Porter claimed his half share.

Later on 3 Oct. 1622 before [*the above as (14), less George Tonge*] Hildreth appeared and Porter withdrew his charge [*etc.*].

24) MEMO that it was presented in general sessions on 3 Oct. before Bp Neile, Henry Anderson, John Calverley, George Tonge, Ralph Conyers, knts, John Cradock, STD, diocesan chancellor, Ralph Fetherstonhalgh, William Smyth and James Lawson, esqs, JPs, by Ralph Fetherstonhalgh, esq., JP, of his own knowledge, that part of the king's highway at Brancepeth over the moor called *the Fell* to Witton-le-Wear was dangerous and needed repair. A fine of 20s. was assessed, to be levied from parishioners with land adjacent, unless they repaired the same at their own expense before the following Martinmas.

Durham CRO, Q/S/I 8 The 14 membranes are in chronological order, recording the sessions held on 7 January, 7 April, 14 July and 30 September 1624; and 12 January 1625.

106

Pleas and presentments at Durham on 7 Jan. 21 James [*1624*] before Thomas Riddell, William Bellasis, John Calverley, Ralph Conyers, knts, John Cradock, STD, diocesan chancellor, Francis Burgoyne, STB, William Smyth, esq., and Hugh Wright, mayor of Durham, JPs.

Thomas Middleton [of Seaton], gen., Peter Denton [of Stobbilee], gen., Christopher Hutchinson [of Durham], gen., Anthony Allenson [of Bishop Auckland], Thomas Fatherley [of Lumley], John Atkinson [of Embleton], Richard Cornforth [of *Akes Raw*], Bernard Robinson [of Herrington], Thomas Atkinson [of Boldon], Robert Paxton [of Easington], John Gargrave [of Hetton], William Shacklock [of Murton], John Cook [of Pelton], Leonard Somerside [of Chester], George Lawes [of Kibblesworth], yeomen, jurors.

1) William Langley late of Lumley Castle, co. Durham, gen., John Lumley of the same, gen., John Hallyman of Lumley, yeo., Richard Short of the same, yeo., Thomas Short of the same, yeo., Richard Darling of Chester, yeo., Robert Atkinson of Lumley Castle, yeo., John Hodgson late of the same, yeo., and William Wheldon late of the same, yeo., on 5 Nov. 1623 assembled riotously at Lumley and drew up coal from a pit of William Essington, gen., at Lumley in a close called *Stobclose* so that Thomas Hodshon and Richard Hodgshon, being underground at the time, were in danger of suffocation. The defendants appeared, demurred, and pleaded not guilty. William Smyth, esq., as attorney-general of the bishop [*etc.*]. Jurors for 7 April. (removed by *certiorari*)

2) Arthur French late of Pelton, co. Durham, yeo., on 24 Aug. 1623 at Pelton in the residence of the same attacked Edward Asmell and Anne his wife and felled Edward to the ground and inflicted further harm on Anne. French appeared, demurred and pleaded not guilty. William Smyth [*etc.*]. Jurors for 7 April, when the panel found French innocent and he was discharged.

3) Cuthbert Spence late of Durham city, joiner, on 8 Aug. 1623 burst open the house-door of Christopher Hutchinson, gen., at Durham and broke into the house and opened a Flanders chest, 2 cupboards and a press and took 2 hats, a linen sheet and a green curtain, worth together 3s., belonging to Ralph Dun.

4) John Crawforth late of Whickham, co. Durham, yeo., Robert Smyth late of the same, lab., and Richard Emerson of the same, lab., after 1 Aug. 1604, namely on 24 Dec. 1623, at Whickham hunted a hare in the snow with a greyhound.

5) Robert Harbotle late of Ravensworth, co. Durham, yeo., after 1 Aug. 1604, namely on 28 Dec. 1623, at Ravensworth hunted a hare in the

snow with a greyhound.

6) Roger Brankston late of Gateside, yeo., after 1 Aug. 1604, namely on 28 Dec. 1623, at Gateside hunted a hare in the snow with a greyhound.

7) Thomas Sonkey late of Durham city, yeo., William Grinwell late of the same, yeo., Anthony Kidd late of the same, lab., Matthew Corner late of the same, yeo., Thomas Thorpe late of the same, yeo., William Corner late of the same, [yeo.], and Henry Corner late of the same, yeo., on 17 May [*year illegible*] at Wolviston assembled with 100 others unknown and assaulted William Hugh.

[*m.1d.*] 8) Samuel Bell late of Hetton-le-Hole, co. Durham, fuller, from 24 June 1623 for 6 months practised at Hetton the craft of fulling without serving a 7 years' apprenticeship.

9) Thomas Roper late of Pittington, co. Durham, fuller, was charged with the same at Pittington.

10) Eleanor Smyth of South Street, Durham, widow, and Jane Applebye of the same, widow, on 28 Oct. 1623 at Houghall stole a ewe and a wether jointly valued at 12[(?)d.] from John Farrowe of Houghall.

11) Charles Wren late of Langley mill, co. Durham, yeo., on 26 Sept. 1623 at Esh stole 3 sheep worth together 8s. from John Rennyson.

12) Francis Clugh late of Darlington, lab., on 19 Nov. 1623 at Darlington stole a sheep hogg worth 10d. from George Stevenson.

13) Thomas Maugham late of Harperley, co. Durham, yeo., on 23 Dec. 1623 at Wolsingham Park in the parish of Wolsingham stole a wether worth 2s. from William Colson.

14) John Pope late of Easington, co. Durham, lab., and Thomas Redchester of the same, lab., on 21 Dec. 1623 at Pespool stole 2 ewes worth together 16d. from George Wilkinson.

15) John Drummell late of Bishop Auckland, co. Durham, lab., on 26 Dec. 1623 broke into the residence of John Walker at Bishop Middleham by night and stole a pair of garters worth 12d., 2 knives, a bodkin and a pair of scissors worth 10d., a jerkin worth 8d., a pair of stockings worth 6d., a pair of shoes worth 6d., a bed-ticking worth 12d. and wool yarn worth 12d. belonging to the same.

16) Matthew Rogerson late of South Shields, co. Durham, lab., on 27 Dec. 1623 at East Boldon stole a ewe worth 10d. from John Todd. He appeared at the bar of the court and admitted his guilt. It was judged that he be whipped in the next open market at Durham.

17) Henry Simpson late of West Sleekburn, *co. Durham, lab., on 7 Oct. 1623 at West Sleekburn stole a ewe worth 10d. from Cuthbert Preist. He appeared at the bar of the court and admitted the charge. It was judged that he be whipped in the next open market at Durham.

18) Christopher Cock late of Houghton-le-Spring, co. Durham, yeo., and Archibald Hobkirke of the same, lab., on 31 Dec. 1623 stole by night at Hetton-le-Hole a sheep hogg worth 6d. from Dorothy Gargrave. They appeared at the bar of the court and admitted the charge. It was judged that they be whipped in the next open market at Durham.

19) Thomas Bower late of Sunderland [Bridge], co. Durham, lab., and Richard Hutchinson of the same, lab., on 8 Oct. 1623 at Ferryhill stole 6 pecks of unwinnowed wheat worth 10d. from Thomas Kirkhouse. They appeared at the bar of the court and admitted the charge. It was judged that they be whipped in the next open market at Durham.

20) Thomas Bower late of Sunderland [Bridge], lab., and Richard Hutchinson of the same, lab., on 6 Oct. 1623 at Sunderland stole 2 pecks and a measure of unwinnowed rye worth 10d. from Gerard Salvyn, esq. They appeared at the bar of the court and admitted the charge. It was judged that they be whipped in the next open market at Durham.

21) Stephen Bauwhinney late of South Shields, yeo., on 20 Oct. 1622 at South Shields attacked Elizabeth Watson wife of Robert Watson. He appeared and without admitting his guilt, in order to save expense, sought leave to fine. This was assessed at 3s. 4d., to the king's use, which he paid.

22) Helen Bawwhinney wife of Stephen Bawwhinney late of South Shields, yeo., on 20 April 1623 at South Shields attacked Elizabeth Watson wife of Robert Watson. She appeared and pleaded not guilty, but to save expense sought leave to fine. This was assessed at 3s. 4d. to the king's use, which she paid.

23) John Colson late of Sunderland by the sea, co. Durham, yeo., William Dossee late of the same, yeo., and Henry Gibson of the same, yeo., after 1 Aug. 1604, namely on 12 Dec. 1623 at Sunderland hunted 3 hares in the snow with greyhounds. Colson and Dosie appeared, admitted the charge, and sought leave to fine. The fines were assessed at 40s. to the use of the poor of Bishopwearmouth parish and they were discharged.

24) MEMO that Nicholas Porter for the king and himself on 9 July 1623 laid an information before the JPs that William Hirdman late of Monk Hesleden, yeo., having been born a subject of the late Edward VI and the present king, between 1 May and 24 June 1623 at Darlington bought from divers persons unknown 100 stones of wool at 7s. a stone, not being a merchant [etc.], for which he should incur a forfeit of £70 [etc.].
Later on 7 Jan. before Thomas Riddell, William Bellasis, John Calverley, Ralph Conyers, knts, John Cradock, STD, diocesan chancellor, and William Smyth, esq., JPs, Herdman appeared, demurred and pleaded not guilty. Porter agreed to the procedure. Jurors for 7 April.

25) MEMO that Nicholas Porter for the king and himself on 9 July 1623 laid an information before the JPs that Thomas Johnson late of Crook in the parish of Brancepeth, co. Durham, yeo., between 20 Sept. and 20 Nov. 1622 at Brancepeth shot with a fowling piece loaded with hailshot and powder on 13 several occasions at 13 woodcocks, for which he should forfeit £130 at £10 an offence of

which he claimed half, and incur 39 months' imprisonment without bail at 3 months for each offence.

He appeared on 7 Jan. before [*the above JPs as (24)*], demurred and pleaded not guilty. Jurors for 7 April.

[*m.2d.*] 26) MEMO that John Shaw of Cornforth, yeo., for the king and himself on 9 Jan. 1622 laid an information before the JPs that George Swainston of Thorpe Thewles, co. Durham, yeo., on 1 May 1620 held 50 acres arable at Fulthorpe for the term of one year and converted the same to pasture for a year from that date, for which he should forfeit £50 of which he claimed a third.

Later on 7 Jan. 1624 before [*the above JPs as (24)*] Swainston appeared, demurred and pleaded not guilty. Porter agreed to the procedure. Jurors for 7 April. (removed by *certiorari*)

27) MEMO that John Shawe for the king and himself on 30 Sept. 1623 laid an information before the JPs that George Swainston late of Norton, co. Durham, yeo., on 30 May 1622 held for a term of years 300 acres arable in Fulthorpe and converted the same to grazing, for which he should forfeit £300 [*etc.*]. Later on 7 Jan. 1624 before [*the above JPs as (24)*] Swainston appeared, demurred and pleaded not guilty [*etc.*]. Jurors for 7 April. (removed by *certiorari*)

28) Elsewhere on 9 July 1623 before Timothy Whittingham, John Calverley, George Tonge, knts, John Cradock, STD, diocesan chancellor, Daniel Birkhead, STD, Ralph Fetherstonhalgh, William Smith and Christopher Place, esqs, JPs, it was presented that whereas George Marshall of Bedlington, *co. Durham, gen., and John Foster late of Morpeth, Northumberland, yeo., on 6 March 1623 as bailiffs of Thomas Ogle, esq., and at his order, distrained at Bedlington by a cow on Ambrose Swynburne for a sum of 14s. owed to Ogle by Swinburne for rent in arrears since the previous feast of the Purification [*2 Feb. 1623*]; when they tried to take the cow to the common pound George Creswell late of Bedlington, yeo., Edward Milborne late of the same, yeo., Robert Horsley late of the same, lab., Henry Hall late of the same, lab., Isabel Hall late of the same, spinster, and Rose Mil[borne] alias – late of the same, widow, assaulted them the same day at Bedlington park, assembling riotously, assaulting John Foster and recovering the cow. On 7 Jan. 1624 before [*the above JPs as (24)*] the defendants appeared, |
[*m.3*] demurred and pleaded not guilty. William Smyth as bishop's attorney-general [*etc.*]. Jurors for 7 April, when the panel found the defendants innocent of riot and recovery.

29) Elsewhere at the general sessions on 9 July 1623 before Timothy Whittingham, John Calverley, George Tonge, knts, John Cradock, STD, diocesan chancellor, Daniel Birkhead, STD, Ralph Fetherstonhalgh, William Smyth and Christopher Place, esqs, JPs, it was presented that Gavin Milborne late of Bedlington, gen., and George Creswell late of the same, yeo., on 3 May 1623 entered a cottage and an acre at Bedlington, the freehold of Elizabeth Spittle,

widow, and ejected Robert Makenea, the farmer, and retain possession. At the general sessions Elizabeth Spittle and Robert Makenea sued for a writ of restitution, which was granted by the JPs, with authority to the sheriff to use the *posse comitatus*.

Now on 7 Jan. 1624 before Thomas Riddell, [*etc. as (24) above*] Milburne and Creswell appeared, demurred and pleaded not guilty. William Smyth as bishop's attorney-general [*etc.*]. Jurors for 7 April, when the panel found them not guilty [*etc.*].

30) Elsewhere at Durham on 30 Sept. 1623 before Bp Neile, Timothy Whittingham, Thomas Riddell, John Calverley, George Tonge, knts, John Cradock, STD, diocesan chancellor, Ralph Fetherstonhalgh, William Smyth and James Lawson, esqs, JPs, it was presented that the common highway at Piercebridge in the parish of Gainford, co. Durham, on Piercebridge moor on the road between Staindrop and Darlington was in ruin for lack of repair and a common nuisance. The JPs assessed a fine of £10 on the villagers of Piercebridge, and the way was to be repaired before Martinmas, and the sheriff was to have the inhabitants to answer at the sessions. Now on 7 Jan. 1624 before [*the above as (24)*] Peter Carter, an inhabitant of the village, appeared following distraint, demurred and denied that the moor road was a common way from Staindrop to Darlington, nor was it the responsibility of the inhabitants of Piercebridge, and sought trial.

31) MEMO that Nicholas Porter for the king and himself on 9 July 1623 laid an information before the JPs that Nicholas Comyn late of *Helmedon Raw,* co. Durham, yeo., between 1 May and 24 June 1622 at Durham bought from persons unknown 20 sheep hoggs at 3s. 4d. each and 20 wethers at 4s. 6d. each and did not put them to grass but resold them within 5 weeks, contrary to the statute, thereby incurring a double forfeit of £15 12s. 4d., of which he claimed half. Later on 7 Jan. 1624 before Thomas Riddell [*etc. as (24) above*], Comyn appeared and admitted selling 2 sheep hoggs. His fine was assessed at 2s. 6d. to the king's use. He sought a jury for the remainder of the charge. Porter agreed to the procedure. Jurors for 7 April.

107

Pleas and presentments at Durham on 7 April 22 James [*1624*] before Timothy Whittingham, Thomas Riddell, William Bellasis, John Calverley, George Tonge, knts, John Cradock, STD, diocesan chancellor, William Smyth and James Lawson, esqs, JPs.

Thomas Middleton [of Seaton], gen., Christopher Hutchinson [of Durham], gen., Robert Farrowe [of Fishburn], gen., Samuel Sayer [of Mordon], gen., John Stephenson [of Byerside], gen., William Shipperson [of Wearmouth], Anthony Hopper [of Towdy Pots], Robert Goodchild [of Pallion], Ralph Reede [of Cassop], John Sparke [of Tudhoe], John Jackson [of Embleton], William Pearson [of Whitehall], John Gargrave [of Hetton], Leonard Somerside [of Chester], Lionel Ayre [of Wiserley], yeomen, jurors.

1) Roger Akerman alias Trewwhitt late of Durham city, lab., on 1 April 1624 at Crossgate, [Durham], attacked Margaret Allison wife of Ralph Allison and felled her to the ground.

2) Richard Browell late of Witton Gilbert, co. Durham, yeo., on 13 Jan. 1624 at Witton Gilbert assaulted John Snath, a king's constable in Witton Gilbert, while in execution of his office.

3) William Tewer late of Chester, co. Durham, yeo., on 18 March 1624 at Bishop Auckland assaulted George Pryorman.

4) John Douglas late of Lamesley, co. Durham, yeo., and Ralph Skirfeild late of Kibblesworth, yeo., after 1 Aug. 1604, namely on 20 Dec. 1623, at Kibblesworth hunted a hare in the snow with a greyhound.

5) Robert Harbotle late of Ravensworth, co. Durham, yeo., and Richard Sotheron junior late of the same, yeo., after 1 Aug. 1604, namely on 20 Dec. 1623, at Whickham at *Rydingfeild* hunted 2 hares in the snow with a greyhound.

6) Robert Johnson late of Elstob, co. Durham, yeo., on divers occasions between 1 Aug. 1623 and 1 Jan. 1624 at Elstob in the parish of Great Stainton shot with a fowling piece loaded with hailshot and powder at 5 pigeons on 5 separate occasions.

7) Richard Browell late of Witton Gilbert, co. Durham, yeo., on 13 Jan. 1624 at Bearpark in the parish of St Oswald, [Durham], took away 2 pales of wood worth 2d. belonging to Richard Hunt, dean, and the chapter of Durham.

8) Whereas Thomas Woller and Brian Emerson, collectors of the bishop's rents, fines and amercements in Stanhope, co. Durham, by virtue of an estreat assessed on certain tenants and delivered to them on 6 Dec. 1623 at Stanhope, distrained on Thomas Whitfeild by a kettle for an amercement of 2s. imposed at the halmote at Wolsingham on 25 June 1623; whereupon Dorothy Whitfeild wife of Thomas Whitfeild of Stanhope, yeo., the same day assaulted Woller and Emerson and recovered the kettle.

9) It was presented that the stretch of king's highway at Choppington in the parish of Bedlington called *Chappington Loaning*, running from Newbiggin to Morpeth, required repair and Thomas Ogle of Choppington, esq., was responsible for its upkeep by reason of his lands adjoining.

[*m.4d.*] 10) Isabel Carr late of Cornforth, co. Durham, widow, on 18 March 1624 at Whitwell House in the parish of Kelloe stole a turkey cock worth 2s. 6d., a capon worth 12d., 2 hens worth 8d. and a coverlet worth 2s. 6d. from John Hilton, esq.

11) Anne Stevenson wife of Robert Stevenson late of Hylton, co. Durham, yeo., on 14 March 1624 at Hylton stole from its body the wool of a wether worth 6d. belonging to John Heighley.

12) Anne Stevenson wife of Robert Stevenson of Hylton, yeo., on 14 March 1624 at Snotterton sheared and stole the wool of a wether worth 6d. belonging to Toby Ewbank, gen.

13) Thomas Allen late of Bishopley, co. Durham, lab., on 27 March 1624 at Bishopley stole a frieze coat worth 6d. and a pair of garters worth 4d. from Cuthbert Nevey. Allen appeared at the bar of the court and admitted the charge. It was judged that he be whipped in the next open market at Durham.

14) Elizabeth Jackson late of Richmond, Yorks., widow, on 1 April 1624 at Durham city stole a petticoat and a woman's smock worth 10d. from Anthony Sparke. She appeared at the bar of the court and admitted the charge. It was judged that she be whipped in the next open market at Durham.

15) Timothy Yonger late of Durham city, lab., and Robert Yonger late of the same, lab., on 29 March 1624 at Ferryhill stole a goose worth 4d. from a person unknown. They appeared at the bar of the court and admitted the charge. It was judged that they be whipped in the next open market at Durham.

16) Dorothy Dixon late of Durham city, spinster, and Elizabeth Battison late of the same, spinster, on 27 March 1624 at Ulnaby in the parish of Coniscliffe, co. Durham, stole a lamb worth 6d. from Richard Smith. They appeared at the bar of the court and admitted the felony. It was judged that they be whipped in the next open market at Durham.

17) Ralph Willye late of Rainton Pits, co. Durham, lab., on 23 March 1624 at Cocken in the parish of Houghton-le-Spring stole a *hoope* of wheat worth 6d. from William Carr, esq. He appeared at the bar of the court and admitted the felony. It was judged that he be whipped in the next open market at Durham.

18) Willam Frisell late of Cornforth, co. Durham, yeo., on 21 March 1624 at the time of divine service at the parish church of Bishop Middleham assaulted Francis Maltbye at Bishop Middleham. He appeared and admitted the charge. His fine was assessed at 20s. to the king's use, which he paid.

19) MEMO that Nicholas Porter for the king and himself on 9 July 1623 laid an information before the JPs against George Tayler late of Gilesgate, [Durham], tanner, that on 20 April 1622 and from then to now he bought at Gilesgate from divers persons unknown 40 untanned ox-hides at 18s. each l coming by land for sale at Durham market, for which he should forfeit the value of the skins, namely £36, of which Porter should receive half.
Later on 7 April 1624 Tayler appeared before the JPs, demurred and pleaded not guilty. Porter agreed to the procedure. Jurors for 14 July.

20) MEMO that Nicholas Porter for the king and himself on 30 Sept. 1623 laid an information before the JPs that Edward Lee late of Sunderland by the sea, gen., between 20 June and 20 Sept. 1623 at Sunderland and elsewhere engrossed 400 bolls of malt at 10s. a boll for resale, incurring a forfeit of £200 of which he claimed half, and imprisonment for 2 months without bail. Later on 7 April 1624 Lee appeared before the JPs, demurred and pleaded not guilty. Jurors for 14 July.

21) MEMO that Nicholas Porter for the king and himself on 30 Sept. 1623 laid an information before the JPs that Robert Bambrough late of Gilesgate, [Durham], yeo., between 1 May and 20 Aug. 1623 bought from persons unknown 5 cows at 33s. 4d. each, 5 queys at 26s. 8d. each, and 5 runts at 30s. each, and did not put the same to grass and resold them at Durham within 5 weeks to persons unknown, incurring a forfeit of £45 at their double value, of which he claimed half.

Later on 7 April 1624 Bambrough appeared before the JPs, demurred and pleaded not guilty [etc.]. Porter agreed to the procedure [etc.]. Jurors for 14 July.

22) MEMO that Nicholas Porter for the king and himself on 9 July 1623 laid an information before the JPs that Nicholas Metcalfe late of Harton, co. Durham, yeo., between 1 May 1622 and 24 June 1623 at

[m.5d.]

Harton engrossed I from persons unknown 100 measures of wheat at 8s., 100 measures of barley at 5s., 40 bushels of peas at 4s. and 100 bushels of oats at 2s. 6d. for resale, incurring for a first offence a forfeit of £85 10s., of which he claimed half, and 2 months' imprisonment without bail. Later on 7 April 1624 Metcalfe appeared before the above JPs, demurred and pleaded not guilty [etc.]. Porter agreed to the procedure [etc.]. Jurors for 14 July.

23) MEMO that Nicholas Porter for the king and himself on 10 July 1622 laid an information before the JPs that Cuthbert Bell late of Whitburn, co. Durham, yeo., between 20 April and 24 June 1622 at Whitburn and elsewhere engrossed from persons unknown 100 stones of butter at 3s. 4d. a stone for resale, for which first offence he should forfeit £16 13s. 4d., of which he claimed half, with 2 months' imprisonment without bail.

Later on 7 April 1624 Bell appeared before the JPs, demurred and pleaded not guilty. Porter [etc.]. Jurors for 14 July.

24) Elsewhere at the sessions at Durham on 8 Jan. 1623 before Timothy Whittingham, William Bellasis, John Calverley, George Tonge, Ralph Conyers, knts, John Cradock, STD, diocesan chancellor, Gabriel Clarke, archdeacon of Durham, Ferdinando Moorecroft, MA, William Smyth, esq., and William Hall, mayor of Durham, JPs, it was presented that whereas a commission of rebellion was sealed under the king's seal at York on 26 June 1622 by the king's Council of the North, and it was ordered that Samuel Johnson, Henry Gibson, William Armstrong, George Stockton, James Wilson and Cuthbert Comyn should attach Marmaduke Robinson, who had been summoned by the sheriff at divers places to appear before the king's Council of the North under pain of the oath of allegiance, and since Marmaduke had defaulted he was to be committed to gaol to be before the Council of the North at York by 30 Sept. By virtue of this writ Cuthbert Comyn and a Robert Robinson, king's commissioners, on 20 Sept. 1622 attached Marmaduke at Norton: but John Robinson of Norton, yeo., Bartholomew Robinson of the same, yeo., Alison

Robinson [wife] of Marmaduke Robinson of the same, yeo., John
Keirton of the same, yeo., William Pattison of the same, yeo., and
Thomas Wright of the same, yeo., on the same day [20 Sept. 1622]
assembled riotously at Norton, assaulted Comyn and Robert and
rescued Marmaduke. Now on 7 April 1624 before Timothy
Whittingham, Thomas Riddell, William Bellasis, John Calverley,
George Tonge, knts, John Cradock, STD, diocesan chancellor, William
Smyth and James Lawson, esqs, JPs, Marmaduke appeared, demurred
and pleaded not guilty. William Smyth [etc.]. Jurors for 14 July.

25) Elsewhere on 3 Oct. 1622 before Bp Neile, William Bellasis, George
Tonge, Ralph Conyers, knts, John Cradock, STD, Daniel Birkhead,
STD, Francis Burgoyne, STB, Ralph Fetherstonhalgh, William Smyth
and James Lawson, esqs, JPs, it was presented that William Johnson
late of Seaton Carew, co. Durham, yeo., William Partus of Wynyard,
yeo., and Eleanor his wife, William Middleton of Fulthorpe, yeo., and
Francis Cooper of the same, lab., on 26 May 1622 broke the closes of
meadow and pasture called *Great Briggflatt, Littlebrigg Bottom* and *the
Low Meadowes* adjoining, and 2 closes called *the Shipdounes* and 2
closes of pasture and a close of meadow by Wynyard Mill, being the
freeholds of Marmaduke Blakiston, clerk, and ejected Ralph Blakiston
the farmer and disseised both to the present date, for which they
sued the king's writ of restitution, for the sheriff to take the *posse
comitatus* [etc.]. Now on 7 April 1624 before [*the above JPs as (24)*]
William Johnson appeared, demurred and pleaded not guilty [etc.].
William Smyth [etc.]. Jurors for 14 July.

26) Elsewhere on 3 Oct. 1622 before [*the above as (25)*] it was presented
that William Johnson late of Seaton Carew, yeo., and William Partus
late of Wynyard, yeo., on 10 Aug. 1622 at Wolviston attacked Ralph
Blakiston, gen., and Partus struck him with a stick worth 2d. held in
both hands and felled him to the ground, and both bruised him.
Now on 7 April 1624 before Timothy Whittingham, William Bellasis,
John Calverley, George Tonge, knts, John Cradock, STD, diocesan
chancellor, William Smyth and James Lawson, esqs, JPs, Johnson
appeared, demurred and pleaded not guilty [etc.]. William Smyth
[etc.]. Jurors for 14 July.
[*m.6d., blank*]

108

Pleas and presentments at Durham on 14 July 22 James [*1624*] before
William Bellasis, Thomas Riddell, John Calverley, George Tonge, knts,
John Cradock, STD, diocesan chancellor, Daniel Birkhead, STD, Hugh
Wright, mayor of Durham, and William Smyth, esq., JPs.
Thomas Middleton [of Seaton], gen., Peter Denton [of Stobbilee],
gen., William Eden [of Whitton], gen., John Morgan [of *Milnehouses*],
gen., John Machell [of Pitfield], gen., Miles Dawson [of Unthank],
gen., William Pearson [of Whitehall], Thomas Tayler [of *Newhouses*],
Edward Dale [of Dalton], John Todd [of Dalton], Martin Niccolson

[of Willington], William Shacklock [of Murton], Lancelot Todd [of Stillington], Anthony Fewler [of Hartburn], John Jackson [of Billy Row], yeomen, jurors.

1) George Partus late of Newton, co. Durham, yeo., on 28 June 1624 at Sedgefield attacked Magdalen Spedling, widow.

2) The public bridge called Haughton Bridge over the Skerne on the king's highway required repair and was the responsibility of the county.

3) William Carrudders late of Darncrook in the parish of Gateside, yeo., from 3 May to 24 June 1624 at Darncrook obstinately and without licence from the JPs kept a common alehouse and sold ale and beer.

4) George Partus late of Newton, co. Durham, yeo., and John Partus late of the same, yeo., on 28 June 1624 broke into a messuage at Sedgefield being the freehold of John Woodroffe and disseised him to the present date.

5) Richard Foster late of Easington, co. Durham, lab., on 3 June 1624 at Easington stole 3 lbs of bread worth 6d. from John Draver. He appeared at the bar of the court and admitted the felony. It was judged that he be whipped in the next open market at Durham.

6) Jane Armestronge late of Piercebridge, co. Durham, spinster, on 5 June 1624 at Piercebridge stole 3/4 peck of rye worth 6d. from John Witham, esq. She appeared at the bar of the court and admitted the felony. It was judged that she be whipped in the next open market at Durham.

7) Janet Pickering wife of Nicholas Pickering late of Woodifield, co. Durham, yeo., on 18 May 1624 at Durham city stole a brass pan worth 10d. from James Browne. She appeared at the bar of the court and admitted the felony. It was judged that she be whipped in the next open market at Durham.

8) William Maddison late of Billingham, co. Durham, yeo., Nicholas Maddison late of the same, yeo., Luke Nelson late of Tollesby, Yorks., yeo., and George Nelson late of Marton, on 7 July 1624 at Elvet in the parish of St Oswald, [Durham], assembled riotously and assaulted [m.7d.]   Robert Parkyn I and took 4 cows of John Browne, clerk, vicar of St Oswald, which were in Parkyn's custody.

9) William Surtees late of Whickham, co. Durham, yeo., on 6 June 1624 at Whickham discharged a fowling piece loaded with hailshot and powder and shot a hare.
He appeared in court, demurred and pleaded not guilty [etc.]. William Smyth [etc.]. Jurors for 30 Sept.

10) Isabel Hall late of Framwellgate, [Durham], widow, and William Hutchinson late of the same, tanner, on 22 April 1624 at Framwellgate attacked Christopher Robinson, and Hutchinson dashed him to the ground and both bruised him.
They appeared in court, demurred and pleaded not guilty. William Smyth [etc.]. Jurors for 30 Sept.

11) William Haddock of Lamesley, co. Durham, yeo., John Haddock of the same, yeo., and Robert Haddock of the same, yeo., on 9 May 1624 at Lamesley assembled riotously and attacked William Carrudders and bruised him. William Haddock appeared, demurred, [*etc.*].

On 30 Sept. before Thomas Riddell, William Bellasis, John Calverley, George Tonge, Ralph Conyers, knts, John Cradock, William Smyth and James Lawson, esqs, JPs, John and Robert Haddock appeared, demurred and pleaded not guilty, alleging that Carrudders had attacked them and that it was self-defence. (removed by *certiorari*)

12) Thomas Craggs late of Whickham, yeo., William Craggs late of the same, yeo., and Robert Swynhoe late of the same, lab., on 23 May 1624 being a Sunday between 7 and 8 p.m. at Whickham assembled riotously at *Whickhamhaughe* and attacked William Laycock, thrice felled him to the ground and inflicted divers wounds to his head, shedding much blood.

Robert Swynhoe appeared in court, demurred and pleaded not guilty [*etc.*]. William Smyth [*etc.*]. Jurors for 30 Sept.

Later on 12 Jan. 1625 before Richard Hunt, dean of Durham, Thomas Riddell, William Bellasis, John Calverley, George Tonge, knts, John Cradock, STD, diocesan chancellor, William Smyth and James Lawson, esqs, JPs, Thomas and William Craggs appeared, demurred and pleaded not guilty [*etc.*]. William Smyth [*etc.*]. Jurors for 27 April.

109

.] Pleas and presentments at Durham on 30 Sept. 22 James [*1624*] before Thomas Riddell, William Bellasis, John Calverley, George Tonge, Ralph Conyers, knts, John Cradock, STD, William Smyth and James Lawson, esqs, JPs.

Thomas Middleton [of Durham <Seaton>], gen., Michael Porter [of *Wagyate*], gen., Robert Ayton [of West Herrington], gen., Nicholas Hutchinson [of Durham], gen., Thomas Richardson [of Hunwick], yeo., Christopher Wright [of Hunwick], yeo., John Atkinson [of Embleton], yeo., Thomas Wilson [of Brafferton], yeo., Edward Searle [of Brafferton], yeo., John Jackson [of Middridge], yeo., Thomas Robinson [of Murton], yeo., William Shacklock [of Murton], yeo., Richard Cornforth [of *Aykes Raw*], yeo., Leonard Somerside [of Chester], yeo., Roger Pearson [of Gateside], yeo., jurors.

1) John Grice late of Bishop Auckland, co. Durham, yeo., on 24 Sept. 1624 at Durham city attacked Thomas Bullock, gen., with a drawn sword. Later on 12 Jan. 1625 he appeared and admitted the charge. His fine was assessed at 20s. and he was committed to gaol until he found sureties for good behaviour.

2) Thomas Browne late of Durham city, barber, on 20 Sept. 1624 kept an alehouse at Durham and sold ale and beer at a higher rate than 1d. for an ale-quart.

3) Anne Pilkington late of Middlestone, co. Durham, widow, Thomas

Pilkington late of the same, gen., and Ralph Loxon late of the same, yeo., on 25 Aug. 1624 at Kirk Merrington assembled by the highway in a close called *the Fogg Close* and attacked Philip Heighington with hoes and stones.

4) Anne Pilkington late of Middlestone, widow, Thomas Pilkington late of the same, gen., and Ralph Loxon late of the same, yeo., on 25 Aug. 1624 at Kirk Merrington assembled in the Fogg Close and attacked Robert Blunt with stones.

5) Richard Hixon late of Preston-le-Skerne, co. Durham, gen., between 1 Jan. 1625 [sic] and to date at Preston-le-Skerne allowed 80 yards of bank, sewer and ditch of the Skerne to fall into disrepair at the *Fleetes*, which he should have kept in order by the terms of his tenure, but rather the river had become choked with mud, muck and other matter so that the channel became blocked and the water flooded the land of divers neighbours.

[8A] Later on 10 Jan. 1627 before John Calverley, George Tonge, knts, John Cradock, STD, diocesan chancellor, Francis Burgoine, archdeacon of Northumberland, and William Smyth, esq., JPs, Hixon appeared and alleged a charter of pardon from the king, dated 10 Feb. 1626 to "Robert Hixon of Lumley Park, gen.", covering offences committed before 27 March 1625. It was judged that the royal pardon should be accepted.

6) It was presented that the king's highway at Binchester in the parish of St Andrew Auckland, co. Durham, by Bishop Auckland required repair at the spot by Binchester bridge leading to Bishop Auckland and that Lindley Wrenn of Binchester, esq., had diverted the ancient course of the water towards a mill he had built by the highway, thereby flooding the road, which could not be mended until the channel was redirected.

110

[m.9]   Pleas and presentments at Durham on 12 Jan. 22 James [1625] before Richard Hunt, dean of Durham, Thomas Riddell, William Bellasis, John Calverley, George Tonge, knts, John Cradock, STD, diocesan chancellor, William Smyth and James Lawson, esqs, JPs.

Thomas Middleton [of Durham], gen., Christopher Hutchinson [of Durham], gen., Robert Farrow [of Fishburn], gen., Thomas Richardson [of Hunwick], gen., Ralph Cattrick [of Fishburn], Ralph Maddison [of Birtley], William Pearson [of Whitehall], Nicholas Hall [of Elwick], George Wardell [of West Morton], Richard Hopper [of Coundon], Peter Blackett [of Greenhead], Richard Jurdison [of Shotton], Thomas Robinson [of Morton], Thomas Greggson [of Morton], George Trotter [of Byers], yeomen, jurors.

1) Philip Heighington late of East Merrington, co. Durham, yeo., on 25 Aug. 1624 at East Merrington assaulted Anne Pilkinton, widow.

[9A] Later on 30 Sept. 1625 before Bp Neile, Richard Hunt, dean of Durham, Thomas Riddell, John Calverley, knts, and William Smyth, esq., JPs, he appeared and admitted the charge. His fine was assessed at 10s. to the king's use, which he paid.

2) Robert Blunt late of East Merrington, lab., on 25 Aug. 1624 at East Merrington attacked Thomas Pilkinton and drew blood.

3) William Heighington late of East Merrington, yeo., on 20 Aug. 1624 broke the close of Anne Pilkinton, widow, at the *Foggclose* and depastured the same of grass worth 5s. and damaged it with ox-waggons.

[9B] Later on 30 Sept. 1625 before [*the above as (1)*] Heighington appeared and admitted the charge. His fine was assessed at 2s. to the king's use, which he paid.

4) Ralph Henderson late of Harraton, co. Durham, yeo., on 27 Nov. 1624 at Harraton in the parish of Chester[-le-Street] in the residence of Robert Waster assaulted Robert Waster and Margaret his wife.

[9C] Later on 13 July 1625 before Richard Hunt, dean of Durham, Timothy Whittingham, William Bellasis, John Calverley, knts, John Cradock, STD, and William Smyth, esq., JPs, Henderson appeared and admitted the charge. His fine was assessed at 20s. to the king's use, which he paid.

5) Thomas Softley late of Gateside, yeo., between 1 Aug. 1624 and 11 Jan. 1625 at Gateside was a night walker.

[9D] Later on 11 Jan. 1626 before Richard Hunt, dean of Durham, Timothy Whittingham, John Calverley, George Tonge, knts, John Cradock, STD, and William Smyth, esq., JPs, he appeared and admitted the charge. His fine was assessed at 6s. 8d. to the king's use, which he paid.

6) Ralph Emerson late of Eastgate in the parish of Stanhope, co. Durham, yeo., was 16 years and more on 1 Oct. 1624 but failed to attend church within 3 months.

7) Ralph Davison late of Billingham, co. Durham, yeo., on 7 July 1624 at Elvet assaulted Robert Parkyn and seized 4 cows of John Browne, clerk, vicar of St Oswald, in his custody.

d.] 8) Thomas Atkinson late of Hag House, co. Durham, yeo., on 10 Nov. 1624 at Bearpark in the parish of Witton Gilbert at the Old Spring assaulted George Walton with a hatchet.

9) John Bussie late of Cornforth, co. Durham, on 2 Jan. 1625 broke the close of John Shaw at Quarrington called *Standlin* and overturned 3 yards of fence erected by Shaw and also a *hirsell* for livestock.

10) Anthony Fenwick late of Coatham, co. Durham, lab., on 16 Dec. 1624 at Aycliffe stole a wether worth 7s. from George Pryorman.

11) John Hall late of Chester, co. Durham, lab., on 5 Jan. 1625 at Lamesley stole 6 fir deals worth 6d. from Thomas Suerties, gen. He appeared at the bar of the court and admitted the felony. It was judged that he be whipped on Sat. in open market at Durham and be sent to his last place of residence.

12) Alice Armestrong late of Durham city, spinster, on 5 Nov. 1624 at Ferryhill stole 2 cheeses worth 6d. from Robert Farrow. She appeared

at the bar of the court and admitted the felony. It was judged that she be whipped on Sat. in open market at Durham and sent to her last place of residence.

13) Richard Davison late of Hurworth, co. Durham, lab., on 20 Oct. 1624 at Hurworth stole a ewe worth 6d. from William Foreman. He appeared at the bar of the court and admitted the felony. It was judged that he be whipped on Sat. in open market at Durham and sent to his last place of residence.

14) Margaret Bell late of Durham city, spinster, and Dorothy Pattinson late of the same, spinster, on 23 Dec. 1624 at Longnewton stole a sheep worth 6d. from a person unknown. They appeared at the bar of the court and admitted the felony. It was judged that they be whipped on Sat. in open market at Durham and sent to their last place of residence.

[m.10] 15) Margaret Turner late of Middleton-in-Teesdale, co. Durham, widow, and John Turner of the same, yeo., on 16 Dec. 1624 at Middleton-in-Teesdale stole a wether worth 10d. from John Johnson. They appeared at the bar of the court and admitted the felony. It was judged that they be whipped in open market at Durham on Sat. and sent back to their last place of residence.

16) John Vasey late of Stanhope, co. Durham, yeo., and Peter Blackett of Greenhead, gen., on 1 Nov. 1624 at Stanhope assaulted William Skepper. Blackett appeared and admitted the charge. His fine was assessed at 20s. to the king's use, which he paid.

17) Miles Tayler late of Crossgate, [Durham], tanner, on 19 Nov. 1624 at Gateside on Gateside moor on the king's highway laid in wait for William Johnson with intent to kill and assaulted him with a drawn sword worth 3s. 4d. Taylor appeared and admitted the charge. It was judged that he fine £3 6s. 8d. to the king's use and be committed to gaol in Durham castle for a month and until he found surety for his good behaviour and for his appearance at the next sessions.

18) Wilfrid Lambe late of North Bailey, Durham city, plumber, on 31 Dec. 1624 at Durham city assaulted William Hawdon, a constable in the parish of St Nicholas. He appeared and admitted the charge. It was judged that he be fined 3s. 4d. to the king's use, which he paid.

19) Roger Akerman late of Durham city, lab., seeking to defraud the king's lieges on 10 Jan. 1625 at Gateside posed as the representative of William March of Durham city, saddler, and obtained from Peter Foster 2 lbs of tobacco worth 6s., which he converted to his own use by exposing for sale, contrary to the statute of 33 Henry VIII.

[m.10d.] 20) George Gray late of Lambton, co. Durham, yeo., on 27 Oct. 1624 attacked Robert Clarke with sticks and stones at Lumley. Gray appeared on 12 Jan,, demurred and pleaded not guilty. William Smyth, the bishop's attorney-general [etc.]. Jurors for 27 April.

21) Elsewhere on 30 Sept. 1624 before Thomas Riddell, William Bellasis, John Calverley, George Tonge, Ralph Conyers, knts, John Cradock, STD, William Smyth and James Lawson, esqs, JPs, it was

presented that Richard Hixon late of Preston-le-Skerne, co. Durham, gen., between 1 Jan. 1625 [*sic*] and to date at Preston-le-Skerne failed to keep in repair 80 yards of river bank of the Skerne at the *Fleetes* as his tenure required, so that the channel was blocked and land flooded during this period.

22) Elsewhere on 30 Sept. 1624 before [*the above as (21)*] it was presented that the king's highway at Binchester in the parish of St Andrew Auckland I near Bishop Auckland by the bridge leading to Bishop Auckland was in great decay because Lindley Wrenn of Binchester, esq., had blocked the ancient course of the water and diverted it over the road to his mill, and the road could not be repaired until the water was restored to its old channel.

23) Elsewhere on 14 July 1624 before William Bellasis, Thomas Riddell, John Calverley, George Tonge, knts, John Cradock, STD, diocesan chancellor, Daniel Birkhead, STD, Hugh Wright, mayor of Durham, and William Smyth, esq., JPs, it was presented that William Maddison late of Billingham, co. Durham, yeo., Nicholas Maddison late of the same, yeo., Luke Nelson late of Tollesby, Yorks., yeo., and George Nelson late of Marton, yeo., on 7 July 1624 with drawn swords assembled riotously at Elvet and assaulted Robert Parkyn and seized and drove off 4 cows belonging to John Browne, clerk, vicar of St Oswald's.

Later on 12 Jan. 1625 before Richard Hunt, dean of Durham, Thomas Riddell, William Bellasis, John Calverley, George Tonge, knts, John Cradock, STD, diocesan chancellor, William Smyth and James Lawson, esqs, JPs, Nicholas Maddison appeared, demurred and pleaded not guilty. William Smyth [*etc.*]. Jurors for 27 April, when the sheriff failed to return the writ. The case was adjourned until 13 July, then to 30 Sept., then 11 Jan., then 19 April, when Nicholas Mattison and William Mattison appeared, demurred and pleaded not guilty, but asked leave to fine. This was assessed at 5s. each, which was paid to the king's use.

24) Anne Pilkington late of Middlestone, co. Durham, widow, Thomas Pilkington late of the same, gen., and Ralph Loxson late of the same, yeo., on 25 Aug. 1624 assembled riotously with hoes and stones at Kirk Merrington in the king's highway at the *Fogg Close* and attacked Philip Heighington.

[d.] Later on 12 Jan. 1625 before [*the above as (23)*] – [*blank*].

25) The same were charged with a similar assault the same day on Robert Blount, [*with a similar sequel*].

26) MEMO that Nicholas Porter for the king and himself on 14 July 1625 laid an information before the JPs in accordance with the act of 2 April 1571 confirming an act of 37 Henry VIII against lending at usury above 10% I that Thomas Nicholson late of Witton-le-Wear, co. Durham, tailor, on 24 Dec. 1623 at Darlington loaned to Thomas Wrenn 70s., and 6 months later received 9s. in gain. He claimed that Nicholson should forfeit £10 10s., namely triple the sum loaned, of

which he should have half, with imprisonment until he made fine and redemption at the king's will.

Later on 12 Jan. before [*the above as (23)*] Nicholson appeared, demurred and pleaded not guilty. Porter agreed to the procedure. Jurors for 27 April.

27) MEMO that Nicholas Porter for the king and himself laid an information before the JPs on 14 July 1624 that Edward Middleton late of Ingleton, co. Durham, yeo., between 1 May and 24 June 1624 at Durham city bought from persons unknown 3 runts at 40s. each, 3 cows at 33s. 4d. each and 3 heifers at 26s. 8d. each without putting them to grass and resold them at Durham within 5 weeks for which he should forfeit their double value at £30, of which he claimed half.

Later on 12 Jan. before [*the above as (23)*] Middleton appeared, demurred and pleaded not guilty. Porter [*etc.*]. Jurors for 27 April.

[*m.12d.*] 28) MEMO that Nicholas Porter for the king and himself on 30 Sept. 1624 laid an information before the JPs that Geoffrey Todd late of Denton, co. Durham, yeo., between 1 Aug. and 29 Sept. 1624 at Darlington and elsewhere engrossed from divers persons unknown 40 stones of butter at 4s. a stone for resale, thereby incurring a forfeit of £8 of which he claimed half, and 2 months' imprisonment. Later on 12 Jan. before [*the above as (23)*] Todd appeared, demurred and pleaded not guilty, [*etc.*]. Jurors for 27 April.

29) MEMO that Nicholas Porter for the king and himself on 30 Sept. 1624 laid an information before the JPs that Ralph Widowes late of Coundon, co. Durham, yeo., between 1 Aug. and 29 Sept. 1624 at Darlington and elsewhere engrossed from divers unknown persons

[*m.13*] 40 stones of butter l thereby incurring a forfeit of £8 [*etc., as (28) above*]. Later on 12 Jan. 1625 before [*the above as (23)*] Widdowes appeared, demurred and pleaded not guilty. Porter agreed to the procedure. Jurors for 27 April.

30) MEMO that Nicholas Porter for the king and himself on 30 Sept. 1624 laid an information before the JPs that Giles Weatherell late of Stockton, co. Durham, yeo., between 23 April and 29 Sept. 1624 at Stockton and elsewhere engrossed from divers unknown persons 100 stones of butter at 4s. a stone for resale, thereby incurring a forfeit of £20 for a first offence, of which he claimed half, and 2 months' imprisonment without bail.

Later on 12 Jan. 1625 before [*the above as (23)*] Weatherell appeared, demurred and pleaded not guilty [*etc.*]. Jurors for 27 April.

[*m.13d.*] 31) MEMO that Nicholas Porter for the king and himself on 30 Sept. 1624 laid an information before the JPs that Thomas Cowley late of Ricknall Grange, co. Durham, yeo., between 20 April and 29 Sept. 1624 at Darlington and elsewhere engrossed from divers persons unknown 100 stones of butter at 4s. a stone for resale, thereby incurring a forfeit of £20 [*etc.*].

Later on 12 Jan. 1625 before [*the above as (23)*] Cowley appeared, demurred and pleaded not guilty. Porter agreed to the procedure and a jury was summoned for 27 April.

4]   An alphabetical index of the names of those indicted on the roll, 7
Jan. 1624 to 27 April 1625. [*endorsed*] Pleas and presentments before
the justices of the peace, 7 Jan. 1624 to 27 April 1625.
[*The sessions for 27 April 1625 is now filed with that for 11 January
1626, all the record that survives for 1 Charles I, listed as Durham CRO,
Q/S/I 9.*]

APPENDIX 1

1607

Durham CRO, Q/S/I 3. This roll of 5 membranes is not an indictment roll but a record of recusancy fines imposed at the sessions held on 7 January 1607. There is no reference to such cases on the membranes filed as Q/S/I 2, mm. 57–58.

[m.1]   Estreats from sessions held at Durham on 7 Jan. 4 James I [1607] before George Scroope, esq., Henry Lindley, Henry Anderson, knts, Thomas Calverley, esq., Clement Colmore, LL.D., George Lightfoote, John Barnes and Thomas Riddell, esqs, JPs.

1) Charles Radcliffe of Tunstall in the parish of Stainton, indicted that being 16 years and more he did at Tunstall from 1 May until 17 Sept. 1606 absent himself from church without lawful excuse, wherefore he should forfeit to the king for each month of absence £25 Sum total £100.

2) The same for Elizabeth his wife. 3) Mary Booth of Tunstall, spinster. 4) William Blakiston of Blakeston in the parish of Norton, knt. 5) Alice his wife. 6) John Blakiston of Blakeston. 7) Katherine Lasonbie of the same, spinster. 8) Katherine Wicliffe of the same, spinster. 9) Margaret Hall, wife of Francis Hall of Neasham in the parish of Egglescliffe. 10) Eleanor Grimston of the same, widow. 11) Josiana Tunstall of the same, widow. 12) John Hall of the same, gen. 13) John Willey of Fieldhouse, yeo. 14) John Pallacer of Egglescliffe, yeo. 15) Phyllis his wife. 16) Katherine Buck of the same, spinster. 17) Lancelot Mason of Sedgefield, yeo. 18) Susan his wife. 19) Margaret Laverock, wife of Robert Laverock of Bradbury in the parish of Sedgefield. 20) Elizabeth Laverock of the same, spinster. 21) Anne, wife of Thomas Chapman of the same, yeo. 22) Anne Salvin of Butterwick, widow. 23) Janet, wife of Thomas Wilkinson of Butterwick, yeo. 24) Alice Scathlock of the same, widow. 25) Roger Richardson of the same, yeo. 26) Robert Elstob of Foxton, gen. 27) William Wating of Neasham, yeo. 28) Jane his wife. 29) John Wating of Neasham, yeo. 30) Elizabeth Wating of the same, widow. 31) Thomas Kilburne of the same, tailor. 32) Dorothy his wife. 33) John Hackforth senior of the same, yeo. 34) Katherine Conyers, wife of George Conyers of Sockburn, knt. 35) Alice Skepper of the same, spinster. 36) George Stockdale of Girsby, Yorks., yeo. 37) Juliana Hodgshon of the same, widow. 38) Mary Storey, wife of Francis Storey of Morton in the parish of Haughton[-le-Skerne]. 39) Jane Barnes of Great Burdon, widow. 40) [duplicated] Beatrice Wilson of Longnewton, widow. 41) Joan, wife of John Sim of Middleton St George, yeo. 42) Helen Sim of the same, spinster. 43) Christopher Ewbanck of the same, gen. 44) Isabel his wife. 45) Katherine Ewbanck of the same, spinster. 46) Anne Culley, wife of Thomas Culley of the same, yeo. 47) Anne Marley, wife of James Marley of the same, yeo.

48) Elizabeth Fewler of the same, spinster. 49) Margaret Harvie of the same, widow. 50) Anne Killinghall, wife of Henry Killinghall of the same, gen. 51) Alice Shaw of Cornforth in the parish of Bishop Middleham, widow. 52) Anne, wife of John Shaw junior of the same, yeo. 53) Isabel, wife of Robert Morpett of Stillington in the parish of Redmarshall. 54) Isabel Aire, wife of Richard Ayre of Bishopton, yeo. 55) Elizabeth, wife of John Rey of the same, yeo. 56) Alison Robinson of the same, widow. 57) Anne Beanes of the same, widow. 58) Susan Killinghall, wife of William Killinghall of Sadberge, gen. 59) Andrew Browne of the same, yeo. 60) Isabel his wife. 61) Anthony Burne of the same, tailor. 62) Edith his wife. 63) John Metcalfe of the same, yeo. 64) Ralph Appelbie of the same, yeo. 65) James Wilson of the same, yeo. 66) Janet Hall late of Hesleden in the parish of Monk Hesleden, widow. 67) Alice Booth of Thorpe Bulmer, spinster. 68) Margaret Forrest of the same, spinster. 69) Elizabeth Forwood, wife of Michael Forwood of Hart, gen. 70) Margaret Heyfeild of the same, spinster. 71) Elizabeth Lawson, wife of James Lawson of Hartlepool, gen. 72) Constance Bell of the same, servant of the same James Lawson. 73) Margaret, wife of John Bone of Billingham, yeo. 74) Margery, wife of John Eden of Belasis, gen. 75) Margaret Todd of *Stoddry* in the parish of Dinsdale. 76) Cuthbert Thornele of Darlington, gen.

2]   77) John Dent of Darlington, yeo. 78) Janet Dent of the same, spinster. 79) Eleanor Storie of the same, widow. 80) John [*sic*] Wetherelt of the same, spinster. 81) – wife of John Wethereld. 82) Jane, wife of John Wall of the same, yeo. 83) Christopher Potter of the same, yeo. 84) – wife of the same. 85) Anne, wife of Thomas Robinson of Cockerton, yeo. 86) Katherine Bales of Coniscliffe, widow. 87) Richard Bargie late of the same, yeo. 88) John Emmerson late of the same, yeo. 89) Richard Marshall of Denton, gen. 90) Anne his wife. 91) Janet Garth of the same, widow. 92) Margaret Athie of Broadwood in the parish of Stanhope, widow. 93) Elizabeth Liddle of Westerton, widow. 94) – wife of Richard Meaburne of Woodhouses, yeo. 95) Jane, wife of John Waad of Wolsingham. 96) Margaret, wife of George Thompson of Wolsingham, yeo. 97) John Aire now or late of the same, yeo. 98) Dorothy, wife of John Claton of Winston, wright. 99) Jane Wall of St Helen Auckland, spinster. 100) Elizabeth Wall of the same, spinster. 101) Ralph Cotesforth of Harperley in the parish of Witton-le-Wear. 102) Jane his wife. 103) Robert Rackwood of Rackwood Hill, gen. 104) Margaret his wife. 105) Anne Rackwood of the same, spinster. 106) John Appleby senior of Hamsterley, yeo. 107) John Appleby junior of the same, yeo. 108) Charles Banckes of Langley in the parish of Staindrop, yeo. 109) William Ridley of Staindrop, yeo. 110) Thomas March of the same, yeo. 111) – his wife. 112) John Hildreth of Piercebridge in the parish of Gainford. 113) Mary his wife. 114) Robert Hawdon of the same, yeo. 115) Barbara his wife. 116) Barbara, wife of George Sisson. 117) Peter Walbancke of the same, yeo. 118)

Florence his wife. 119) John Helcott of the same, yeo. 120) Agnes his wife. 121) John Swainston of the same, yeo. 122) Eleanor Thompson of the same, widow. 123) Isabel Morland of the same, widow. 124) Ambrose Crawforth of Headlam, yeo. 125) Mary his wife. 126) William Helcot of the same, yeo. 127) Anne Helcott of the same, spinster. 128) Margaret Garth, wife of William Garth of the same, gen. 129) Ninian Watson of Summerhouse, gen. 130) Eleanor his wife. 131) William Morton of Bolam, yeo. 132) Jane his wife. 133) Frances Morton of the same, spinster. 134) Thomas Watson of the same, yeo. 135) Margaret his wife. 136) Janet Gibson of the same, spinster. 137) Eleanor Simpson of the same, spinster. 138) Elizabeth Robson of the same, spinster. 139) Eleanor Alder of the same, spinster. 140) Mary Saire of the same, spinster. 141) Janet Young of Whorlton, spinster. 142) Eleanor Colton, wife of Francis Colton of – , yeo. 143) Anne, wife of Henry Weare now or late of Piercebridge, yeo. 144) Alice, wife of John Langstaffe of Barnard Castle, saddler. 145) William Clopton of Sledwick, esq. 146) Anne his wife. 147) William Yonge of the same, yeo. 148) Robert Middleton of the same, yeo. 149) Robert Lounsdale of the same, yeo. 150) Isabel Dubdill of the same, spinster. 151) John Claxton of Holywell in the parish of Brancepeth, knt. 152) Mary his wife. 153) Thomas Blenkensopp of the same, yeo. 154) George Johnson of the same, yeo. 155) Charles Hedworth of East Brandon, gen. 156) Elizabeth his wife. 157) William Claxton of Waterhouses, gen. 158) Grace his wife. 159) Alice, wife of David Ladley of Willington, yeo. 160) William Herrison of Tudhoe, yeo. 161) Margaret Richardson, wife of Robert Richardson of the same, yeo. 162) Agnes Trewhitt, wife of Henry Trewhitt of the same, yeo. 163) Mary Watson of Stockley, spinster. 164) Jane Tewer, wife of Robert Tewer of Heighington. 165) Cecily Priorman of the same, spinster. 166) Isabel Jackson, wife of William Jackson of the same, yeo. 167) – wife of Thomas Shortred of the same, yeo. 168) Isabel, wife of Nicholas Brigges of *Haran*, yeo. 169) Martin Denham of the same, tailor.

[m.3]   170) Thomas Towers of Preston-le-Skerne, yeo. 171) Elizabeth his wife. 172) George Swalwell of Carr House, yeo. 173) – his wife. 174) Isabel Parkinson of Nunstainton, spinster. 175) Anne Gibson, wife of Thomas Gibson of Whitworth, yeo. 176) Anne Malam, wife of Bartholomew Malam of the same. 177) – wife of John Dodds now or late of the same. 178) George Collingwood of Eppleton in the parish of Houghton-le-Spring, esq. 179) Jane his wife. 180) Eleanor Robinson of the same, spinster. 181) Alison Tayler of the same, spinster. 182) Christopher Turner of Haughton, lab. 183) Margaret Merriman, wife of John Merriman of Newton *Garthes*, yeo. 184) Anne Linsey of Little Haswell, spinster. 185) Elizabeth, wife of Robert Chilton of Eden Dene, yeo. 186) Mary wife of Anthony Whitfeild of Little Eden, yeo. 187) Elizabeth, wife of Francis Trollopp of *Warroint house* near Little Eden. 188) George Browne of Durham city, barber.

189) Mary, wife of Richard Middleton of Tunstall, gen. 190) John Middleton of the same, gen. 191) Barbara Ward, wife of Robert Warde of Trimdon, gen. 192) John Trollopp senior of Thornley in the parish of Kelloe, esq. 193) Magdalen his wife. 194) John Trollop junior of the same, esq. 195) Elizabeth his wife. 196) Samson Trollopp of the same, gen. 197) Margaret Trollopp of the same, spinster. 198) [twice] Dorothy Trollopp of the same, spinster. 199) Elizabeth Welburie of Kelloe, widow. 200) Agnes Welburie of the same, spinster. 201) Jane Fetherston of Thornley, spinster. 202) Margaret Browne of the same, spinster. 203) Margery Burstall of the same, spinster. 204) Richard White of Thornley, yeo. 205) John Winter of the same, yeo. 206) John Trollopp of the same, servingman. 207) Grace his wife. 208) Grace, wife of Robert Wilson of the same, yeo. 209) Cecily Balye of Hurworth, widow. 210) Thomas Awde of Tursdale, blacksmith. 211) – his wife. 212) Margery Burstall, wife of Anthony Burstall of Thornley, yeo. 213) John Tayler of Thornley, yeo. 214) Janet, wife of Thomas Forman of the same, yeo. 215) Anne, wife of John Trolloppe of the same, tailor. 216) – wife of Robert Clerk of the same, lab. 217) Margaret, wife of Philip Tayler of the same, blacksmith. 218) Robert Hunter of the same, yeo. 219) Mary Biggins of Sunderland, widow. 220) Elizabeth Suddick, wife of Robert Suddick of *Sotheron Closes*, yeo. 221) Anne Yonge, wife of Ralph Yonge of the parish of Croxdale, yeo. 222) Margaret Browne, wife of John Browne of Croxdale, yeo. 223) Eleanor, wife of George Pickering of the same, yeo. 224) Isabel Underwood of the same, widow. 225) Robert Maire of Hardwick, gen. 226) Grace his wife. 227) Christopher Weare of the same, gen. 228) Margaret Maire of the same in the parish of Monk Hesleden. 229) John Heighington of Hutton Henry, gen. 230) Alice his wife. 231) Alice, wife of John Welburie of Monk Hesleden, gen. 232) Dorothy Welburie of the same, spinster. 233) Jane Welburie of the same, spinster. 234) Thomas Blakiston of the same, esq. 235) Mary his wife. 236) Anne Blakiston of the same, widow. 237) Katherine Wall of the same, spinster. 238) Cecily Coxon of Little Pittington, widow. 239) Henry Wright of Shadforth, yeo. 240) Emmot his wife. 241) Alison Heddrington, wife of Roland Heddrington of the same, husbandman. 242) George Johnson of Twizell in the parish of Chester-le-Street, gen. 243) Katherine his wife. 244) Michael Johnson of the same, gen. 245) Margaret Johnson of the same, spinster. 246) Margaret Bennett of the same, spinster. 247) Isabel Davidson of Urpeth, spinster. 248) John Lowrie of Woodend, yeo. 249) Margaret Forster of Pelton, widow. 250) Joan Lawes, wife of James Lawes of the same, yeo. 251) Jane, wife of Thomas Bainbrigg of Whitehall, yeo. 252) John Tempest of Lambton, gen. 253) Margery his wife. 254) Gerard Liddle of the same. 255) Barbara Jackson of the same, spinster.

.4]   256) Roger Lambton of Lambton, gen. 257) Alice, wife of William Lambton. 258) John Applebie of the same, yeo. 259) Thomas Jackson of the same, yeo. 260) Robert Hartburne of the same, yeo. 261)

Elizabeth, wife of Robert Lawes of Urpeth, yeo. 262) Dorothy Lumley of Woodsend House, widow. 263) Susan, wife of John Halliman of Lumley, yeo. 264) Mabel Smith of Chester, spinster. 265) Ralph Harding of Hollingside in the parish of Whickham, gen. 266) Isabel Harding of the same, spinster. 267) Barbara Blakiston of Gibside, gen. [*sic*] 268) – wife of William Wrey of *Ravenshelme*, esq. 269) – wife of Thomas Gascoigne of Hillhead, gen. 270) Dorothy Constable of Biddick in the parish of Washington, widow. 271) Frances Constable of the same, spinster. 272) Dorothy Lisle, wife of James Lisle of Barmston, esq. 273) Elizabeth Hedley of Lintz Green in the parish of Tanfield, widow. 274) Elizabeth Mush of the same, spinster. 275) Richard Gregson of the same, yeo. 276) Elizabeth Atkinson of the same, spinster. 277) – wife of John Storie of Low Friarside, yeo. 278) – wife of Anthony Kirkley of Tanfield, yeo. 279) Magdalen Kirkeley of the same, spinster. 280) Robert Holtbie of Stanley, gen. 281) – his wife. 282) – wife of Robert Joplin of Stanley, yeo. 283) Mary Joplin of the same, spinster. 284) John Powleson now or late of Medomsley, yeo. 285) Mary his wife. 286) Isabel, wife of George Shaftoe of Hamsterley, gen. 287) Ralph Spoore of Esh, yeo. 288) Margaret his wife. 289) Robert Merriman of Cleadon in the parish of Whitburn, yeo. 290) Ann – of the same, servant of the same Robert Merriman. 291) Agnes Manners, wife of Robert Manners of the same, yeo. 292) Henry Browne of Whitburn, blacksmith. 293) William Fenwick of Newton *Garthes*, gen. 294) – wife of John Peareson of the same, yeo. 295) Elizabeth, wife of Robert Forster of Gateshead. 296) Jane Browne of the same, spinster. 297) John Hodgshon of Manor House in the parish of Lanchester, gen. 298) Jane his wife. 299) George Fairehare of Ford, gen. 300) – his wife. 301) William Raw of Luns House, yeo. 302) Eleanor his wife. 303) Mark Hull of Esp, carpenter. 304) Elizabeth his wife. 305) Agnes Walton of Whitehouse, widow. 306) Agnes Atkinson of the Deanery House of Lanchester, widow. 307) Margaret, wife of Christopher Hopper of Newbiggin, yeo. 308) Humphrey Snawdon of Mawsfield, yeo. 309) Jane his wife. 310) Janet Kirkley of West Butsfield, spinster. 311) Isabel Kirkley of the same, spinster. 312) Agnes Kirkley of the same, spinster. 313) Agnes, wife of John Jackson of Billingside, yeo. 314) Nicholas Winter senior now or lately of Fulforth, yeo. 315) Janet, wife of John Rackett of West Butsfield, yeo. 316) Agnes Lowrie of Greencroft, spinster. 317) Cuthbert Brigges of Ford, yeo. 318) Margaret his wife. 319) Elizabeth, wife of John Ealye of Hamsteels, yeo. 320) Christopher Taylor of Greencroft, yeo. 321) Isabel his wife. 322) Richard Darnell of the same, yeo. 323) – his wife. 324) William Darnell of the same, yeo. 325) Elizabeth Darnell of the same, spinster. 326) Margaret, wife of Cuthbert Hopper of *Lawtowne* in Greencroft. 327) Margaret Jackson of Newbiggin, spinster. 328) Margaret Talor now or late of Cornsay, spinster. 329) Margaret Brasse of Mawsfield, spinster. 330) Margaret – alias Old Margerett of the same, <widow>. 331) Alice, wife of John Hutchinson of Burn House, yeo. 332) Isabel Crooke of Butsfield, widow. 333) Alison Comyng of Lanchester, widow. 334) Alison, wife of Christopher Hopper of West Hall, yeo. 335) Isabel Carr, wife of George Carr of Moorside, yeo. 336) Thomas Forcer of Harbour House in the parish of St Margaret, Durham. 337) Margaret his wife. 338) George Littlephaire of the same, yeo. 339) Margaret wife of Michael Garfoote of the same. 340) Isabel Tempest, wife of Nicholas Tempest of Stella, knt. 341) Dorothy, wife of John Sowlebye of the same, yeo. 342) Henry Gascoigne of *Hill*, gen.

5]   343) John Willey of – . 344) Ralph Emmerson of Witton Gilbert, yeo. 345) John Thompson of the same, yeo. 346) Dorothy Hodgshon of Whitehill, spinster. 347) Jane Hodgshon of the same, spinster. 348) Anthony Trotter of the same, yeo. 349) Thomas Taler of the same, yeo. 350) Mabel Smith of the same, spinster. 351) Robert Hodgshon of Hebburn, esq. 352) Anne his wife. 353) William Hodgshon of the same, gen. 354) Margaret Lasinbye of the same, spinster. 355) Barbara Blunt of the same, spinster. 356) Thomas Medomston alias Medomesley of the same, yeo. 357) Cuthbert Sutton alias Sotheron of the same, yeo. 358) Thomas Powle of the same, schoolmaster. 359) John Awde of Heworth, yeo. 360) Elizabeth his wife. 361) Thomas Horsley of Old Elvet, gen. 362) Jane his wife. 363) Robert Whitfeild of the same, draper. 364) Elizabeth his wife. 365) Janet Hopper of the same, widow. 366) Jane Marshall, wife of William Marshall of the same, yeo. 367) Christabel Nickson of the same, widow. 368) Robert Hopper of the same, draper. 369) John Rutter of New Elvet, pewterer. 370) – wife of John Bussie senior of the same, gen. 371) John Bussie junior of the same, gen. 372) Mary Bussie of the same, spinster. 373) Ralph Lambert of the same, yeo. 374) Elizabeth Hall of the same, spinster. 375) John Tempest of the same, gen. 376) Margaret, wife of Brian Bellassis of the same, esq. 377) Jane Hopper of the same, widow. 378) Christopher Batmanson of Broom, yeo. 379) Helen his wife. 380) Henry Haggerston of Haggerston, esq. 381) Henry Haggerston of the same, gen. 382) Mary Haggerston of the same, spinster. 383) Helen Haggerston of the same, spinster. 384) – wife of George Reiveley of Ancroft, esq. 385) James Lawson of Hartlepool, gen. 386) – wife of John Watson of Eighton, yeo. 387) John Crawforth of Bolam, yeo. 388) Margaret his wife. 389) Janet Wetherell of Bolam, spinster. 390) Margaret Alwen of the same, spinster. 391) Grace Law, wife of Gregory Law of Coniscliffe, yeo. 392) Anne Browne of the same, spinster. 393) Richard Morgan of Stanhope, yeo. 394) Margaret Robinson of Bishopton, [*illegible*]. 395) Anthony Whitfeild of Little Eden, yeo. 396) – wife of Thomas Joplyng of Stanley, yeo. 397) Katherine Hedworth of Chester, spinster. 398) Beatrice Wilson alias Butcher of Longnewton, widow. 399) Jane Hilyard now or late of Fulforth, widow. 400) Christopher Hilyard of the same, gen. 401) Mary, wife of John Jenison of Walworth, esq. 402) Thomas Nypkin alias Welden of the same, yeo. 403) Elizabeth

Jenison of the same, spinster. 404) John Fletcher of the same, yeo. 405) Christopher Potter of the same, yeo. 406) Francis Lawson of Thorpe Bulmer, esq. 407) Elizabeth his wife. 408) Richard Booth of Great Chilton, gen. 409) Barbara his wife. 410) Isabel, wife of Bertram Bulmer, knt, of Tursdale. 411) – Constable of Biddick, gen. 412) William [illegible]. 413) Katherine his wife. 414) Jane, wife of Thomas Chaytor of Butterby, esq. 415) William Hixon of [...]stone, yeo. 416) Anne Hixon of Preston, spinster. 417) Edward Corby of Elvet, yeo. 418) Isabel his wife. 419) Barbara Hall of the same, spinster.
[signed] George Scroope I Thomas Calverley I Clement Colmore I Henry Ewbanck I John Barnes [other signatures illegible]

APPENDIX 2

ALTHAM, James, kt., son of James Altham, sheriff of London (1557); admitted Gray's Inn, 1575, reader 1600 and 1603 (*Reg.* 48); serjeant at law, 1603; baron of Exchequer, 1607–17, kt, 1607; d. 21 Feb. 1617 (Baker, *Serjeants,* 496: Foss, 12–13).

ANDERSON, Henry, esq./kt of Haswell Grange, the estate being acquired pre–1571; son of Bertram Anderson of Newcastle upon Tyne (d. 1571) and Alice Carr of Cocken; married firstly Isabel Morland of Pittington and secondly Fortune Collingwood of Dalden, co. Durham, and Eslington, Northumberland. Admitted Gray's Inn, 1566 *(Reg.* 35); sheriff of Newcastle, 1571; alderman, 1575; mayor, 1575, 1583, 1594; MP, 1584–93. Kt, 1603. With William Selby he was the first local beneficiary of the Grand Lease of the manors of Gateshead and Whickham and their coal mines from Bishop Barnes, 1583; founder member of the Newcastle Hostmen's Company, 1600; on commission of the peace for Durham, 1583; a commissioner for musters in the palatinate of Durham, 1595; d. 6 Aug. 1605 (Surtees I, 122: AA 4 XVIII [1940], 41: *Cal. Border Papers II,* 73: Metcalfe, 148: Welford *M* i, 67–73).

ASHTON, Hugh, chancellor of Durham, appted 28 July 1509 (Durham 3/70, m. 1); protégé of Lady Margaret Beaufort, countess of Derby, and comptroller of her household; archdeacon of Winchester, 1511–19; archdeacon of Cornwall, 1515; archdeacon of York, 1516; benefactor of St John's Coll., Cambridge; d. 1522 (DNB I, 648); appted Durham justice of assize, 1509 (Durham 13/231, m. 4).

BAINBRIDGE, Richard, of Wheatley Hill, married Alice, daughter of John Rodes and niece and heiress of Robert Rodes of Little Eden (Surtees I, 101); appted justice of gaol delivery in Durham, 1471, with Henry Gillowe, clerk, Thomas Middleton and William and John Raket (DK *Report* xxxv [1874], 99).

BARNES, Emanuel, DD, son of Bishop Barnes; matric. Magdalen Coll., Oxford, 1577, BA 1579, MA 1581, incept. Cambridge, MA 1586; preb. of Durham, 5th stall, 1585, 4th stall, 1607; rector of Houghton-le-Spring, 1584; of Wolsingham, 1585–1614; of Crayke, 1612; preb. of York, 1602; d. 1614 (Venn I i, 92; Hutchinson ii, 182–83, 187; Surtees I, lxxxii and note).

BARNES, John, esq., son of Bishop Barnes, his mother re-married Dr Leonard Pilkington (see below); of the Middle Temple (DK *Report* xxxvii [1876], 85); master of Greatham Hospital, 1585–1610; protonotary in Durham, 1584 (Mickleton MS 2 f. 66); granted for life the office of clerk of peace for Durham; clerk of the bishop's chancery and keeper of the rolls on surrender of same by Richard Scott, survivor of three from the previous grant, 1610; d. July 1613 *(Reg. Cath. D.,* 82 and note; DK *Report* xl [1879], 482; Surtees I, lxxxii note: III, 136).

BELLASIS, Richard, esq., of Ludworth and Great Haswell, younger son of Richard Bellasis of Henknoll and Margery Errington of Cockle Park, Northumberland; admitted Gray's Inn, 1564, *(Reg.* 36); on commission of peace for Durham, 1583; assessed at muster at Spennymoor on 30 Sept. 1584 at a light horseman, able and well furnished *(Cal. Border*

Papers I, 162), d. 12 Jan. 1600/1 without issue (Surtees I, 203; *W & I* ii, 315).

BELLASIS, William, esq./kt of Morton House, son and heir of Brian Bellasis and of his great-uncle Richard Bellasis (see above), married Margaret Selby of Whitehouse (Winlaton); kt, 1617; justice of assize in Durham, 1624, 1625 (Durham 13/25); sheriff of Durham, 1625-40; d. 3 Dec. 1641 aged 48 *(W & I* iv, 31n.; AA 4 XXII [1944], 52; Metcalfe, 170).

BENTLEY, John, attorney in Durham court of pleas, 1498 (Durham 13/230, m. 2); justice of gaol delivery at Durham, 1502 (Durham 13/229); protonotary in Durham (Mickleton MS 2, f. 66); justice of assize, 1503, of quorum, 1504, 1505 (Durham 13/230); justice of gaol delivery and of quorum, 1509 (ib., 13/231); bishop's attorney-general, 1510, 1521 (ib., 13/232 m. 2d., 242); escheator in Durham, 1518; clerk of peace (Mickleton MS 2 f. 67v.: Hutchinson i, 399); justice of assize, 1531 (Durham 13/252).

BIRKHEAD (alias Birkett), Daniel, STP, married Alice Place of Dinsdale *(Reg. Cath. D.,* 86n.); adm. pensioner Emmanuel Coll., Cambridge, 1595/6, BA, 1599/1600, MA (Trinity), 1603, BD, 1610, DD, 1618, incorp. Oxford, 1605; rector of Langton, Yorks., 1610; of Egglescliffe, 1611-24; of Winston, 1617-24; preb. of Durham, 6th stall, 1619-20, 10th stall, 1620-24; d. 1624 (Venn I i, 158; Hutchinson ii, 191, 210; CJ 198 n. 29).

BLAKISTON, Marmaduke, 5th son of John Blakiston and Elizabeth Bowes of Dalden and Streatlam; rector of Redmarshall, 1585; of Sedgefield, 1599-1631; vicar of Woodhorn, Northumberland, 1606; preb. of Durham, 7th stall, 1601, and treasurer, 1606; preb. of York (Wistow) and archdeacon of East Riding, 1615; d. 1639 (Hutchinson ii, 196-7; CJ 195-6).

BLAXTON, Thomas, esq., of Blakiston, son and heir of William Blakiston and Anne Conyers of Wynyard, married Elizabeth Place of Halnaby, co-heiress of her mother Catherine, née Surtees of Dinsdale; d. 1559. (His sister Margery married John Trollop of Thornley.) (Surtees III, 162).

BOWES, George, esq., of Biddick Waterville, 3rd son of Sir George Bowes of Bradley and Dorothy Mallory of Studley, Yorks., married Magdalen Bray; d. 1606 (Surtees IV i, 110).

BOWES, Ralph, esq., son and heir of Robert Bowes of Aske and Anne Bowes of Dalden, married Joan Headlam of Nunthorpe, Cleveland; granted jointly with son Robert the office of coroner of Chester ward on the surrender of John King, 1613; d. 1622 (DK *Report* xl, 482; Surtees IV, 112).

BOWES, Robert, esq., of Raby, 2nd son of Sir George Bowes of Bradley and Dorothy Mallory of Studley; d. c. 1600 in mining accident at Keswick (Surtees IV i, 110).

BOWES, Talbot, esq./kt of Aske, Yorks., and Streatlam, 2nd son of Sir George Bowes of Streatlam and Jane Talbot, married Agnes Warcop of Smardale, Westmorland; admitted Gray's Inn, 1579 *(Reg.* 54); MP for Richmond, 1603, 1614, 1620, 1625; kt, 1617; d. 1638 (Surtees IV i, 108; Metcalfe, 170).

BRANDLING, Robert, esq., of Felling and North Gosforth, Northumberland, son and heir of William Brandling (d. 1575) and Anne Heley, married firstly Jane Wortley of Wortley, Yorks., and secondly Mary Hilton of Hylton; sheriff of Northumberland, 1617; MP for Morpeth, 1620; cited before the court of High Commission at Durham for obstruction and abuse at Alnwick and Lesbury parish churches, adultery, etc., 1633; d. c. 1636 (Surtees II, 90: Welford *M* i, 374–8).

BULMER, William, esq., 3rd son of Sir William Bulmer of Wilton in Cleveland, married Elizabeth Elmedon of Embleton and Tursdale and had livery of her lands in 1508; commanded the Durham contingent at Flodden, 1513 (Surtees I, lxv, 79); justice of assize in Durham, 1501, 1503, of quorum 1504, justice of gaol delivery, 1505 (Durham 13/1); re-appted justice of gaol delivery in Durham, 1509 (ib., 3/70, m. 1).

BUNNY, Francis, clerk, (JP 1584) 3rd son of Richard Bunny of Newland near Wakefield, Yorks., married Mary Wortley; matric. Magdalen Coll., Oxford, 1564/5; preb. of Durham, 8th stall, 1572; archdeacon of Northumberland, 1573–8; rector of Ryton, 1578–1617; assessed at Spennymoor muster on 30 Sept. 1584 at a light horseman but defaulted; d. 1617 (Surtees II, 262; Clark II ii, 17: iii, 78; *Cal. Border Papers II*, 163).

BURGOYNE, Francis, BA, matric. Peterhouse, Cambridge, 1579, BA 1581/2, MA (Jesus) 1585; rector of Carlton, Cambs., 1587–97; of Bishop Wearmouth, 1595–33; of Spofforth, Yorks., 1598–1633; of Howick, Northumberland, 1621–33; preb. of Southwell, 1590; of Durham, 8th stall, 1617; subdean, 1618; archdeacon of Northumberland, 1621–33; justice of assize in Durham, 1625 (Durham 13/25); d. 1633 (Venn I i, 258; Hutchinson ii, 201, 225; CJ 193).

BURTON, Thomas, LLD educ. Eton, matric. King's Coll., Cambridge, 1553, BA 1557/8, LLB 1572, LLD 1581; preb. of Carlisle, 1574; vicar of St Michael, Appleby, Westmorland, 1576–9; diocesan chancellor of Carlisle, 1576–7; rector of Stanhope, 1577–1608; vicar-general and official to bishop of Durham; vicar of Kirk Merrington, 1583–1606; assessed at Spennymoor muster on 30 Sept. 1584 at an able horse and man, well furnished (*Cal. Border Papers I*, 162); preb. of York; d. 1608 (Venn I i, 268).

CALVERLEY, John, esq./kt, of Littleburn, eldest son of Thomas Calverley (see below), married Anne, daughter of Bishop Hutton; matric. University Coll., Oxford, 1588; admitted Lincoln's Inn at request of father, 1590 (*Reg.* 110); justice of assize in Durham, 1614 (Durham 13/16); *custos rotulorum*, 1615; kt, 1617 (Surtees I, lxxxv; CJ, 196; Metcalfe, 170).

CALVERLEY, Thomas, esq., (JP 1584) of Littleburn, son of Sir William Calverley of Calverley, Yorks., married Isabel Anderson, sister of Henry Anderson of Haswell Grange and Newcastle upon Tyne (see above); admitted Lincoln's Inn, 1552 (*Reg.* 60); chancellor of Durham, 1563–1605; steward of Durham, 1565–1613 (DK *Report* xxxvii [1876], 68); justice of assize in Durham, 1569 (Durham 13/284); commissioner for survey of Borders on East and Middle Marches, 1580; assessed at Spennymoor muster on 30 Sept. 1584 at a light horseman and apparel (*Cal. Border Papers I*, 34–5, 162); recorder of Newcastle 1582–(?)1600

(AA 4 XLIX [1971], 147–9; Hutchinson i, 458, 460).

CARR, William, esq. (JP 1618), of Cocken, son and heir of Ralph Carr (d. 1605); acquired Derwentcote and Blackhall from Philip Constable, 1614 (Surtees I, 208: II, 292).

CATRIK, John, possibly the same John Catterick who at his death in 1478 held a messuage and a carucate of land at Stanwick, N. Yorks., from the Knights Hospitallers (*VCH, N. Yorks.* I, 129; cf. *York. Vis.* 255–56). Appointed justice of gaol delivery in Durham, 1465, in 1468 he was arbiter in a suit of dower brought by Matilda, widow of Sir William Bowes of Streatlam (DK *Report* xxxv, 86, 106).

CHAYTOR, Christopher, esq. (JP 1589), son of John Chater of Newcastle upon Tyne, merchant, married Elizabeth Clervaux of Croft, Yorks.; bought Butterby from John, Lord Lumley; sometime servant to Protector Somerset; registrar of consistory court of Durham; surveyor-general for queen in Northern Counties; justice of gaol delivery in Durham, 1562 (Durham 13/2 m. 8); d. 17 Apr. 1592, aged 98 (*W & I* ii, 203 and note; Surtees IV ii, 111).

CHAYTOR, Thomas, esq., of Butterby, son of Christopher Chaytor (see above); married firstly Eleanor Thornell of East Newton, Yorks., and secondly Jane Tempest of Stella; notary public; joint appt with father for life as registrar of Durham consistory court, 1583; deputy escheator, 1595 (Mickleton MS 2, f. 72); surveyor-general for queen in Northern Counties (Hutchinson i, 444; Surtees IV ii, 111).

CLARKE, Gabriel, BD, educ. Christ Church Coll., Oxford, 1606, BA, 1612, Pembroke Coll., Cambridge, BD; preb. of Lincoln, 1615; chaplain to Bishop Neile; rector of Howick, 1619–21; archdeacon of Northumberland, 1619–20; of Durham, 1620–62; rector of Elwick, 1620–24; master of Greatham Hospital, 1624–44; preb. of Durham, 6th stall, 1620–23, 3rd stall 1623–38, 1st stall, 1638; justice of assize in Durham, 1627 (Durham 13/34); subdean of Durham, 1662; d. 1662 (Hutchinson ii, 171–2, 180; Surtees III, 137; CJ 194).

CLAXTON, Ralph, esq., of Wynyard, son and heir of Ralph Claxton and Sybil Conyers of Wynyard, married Elizabeth Hebburn of Hardwick; d. 1549 (Surtees III, 79).

CLAXTON, William, esq., of Burn Hall, son of William Claxton of Burn Hall and Joan Leyburn, married firstly Joan Kirkby and secondly Elizabeth Storday; d. 1566 (Surtees IV ii, 97; *W & I* i, 252–53).

COLMORE, Clement, LLD, incorp. from Oxford (matric. 1566, BA 1569/70, MA 1572/3, proctor, 1578, fellow of Brasenose), MA 1579, BCL 1580, DCL 1582; diocesan chancellor; rector of Brancepeth, 1584; of Gateshead, 1588–95; of Middleton-in-Teesdale, 1599; preb. of Lichfield, 1586; of Durham, 11th stall, 1590; master of St Edmund's Hospital, Gateshead, 1587; on commission of the peace for Durham, 1583; assessed at the Spennymoor muster on 30 Sept. 1584 at a light horseman but defaulted; legal adviser to the commissioners on Border disputes, 1585; commissioner under Bishop Matthew and others to treat with Scots on Border matters, 1595–7; justice of assize at Durham, 1601; d. 18 June 1619 (Durham 13/299; *Cal. Border Papers I,* 162, 195–6, 203: *II,* 80, 199, 262; Venn I i, 375; *W & I* iii, 145n.).

COMYN, Timothy (JP 1620), son and heir of Simon Comyn (bishop's receiver-general, 1595) and Alice Robson; matric. pensioner, St John's Coll., Cambridge, c. 1594; joint grant with father of office of bishop's auditor for 2 lives at £20 a year, 1605 (DK *Report* xxxvii, 127, 162); mayor of Durham, 1620 (Venn I i, 377; Surtees IV ii, 18; *Dur. Vis.* 81; CJ 198).

CONSTABLE, William, kt, of Chopwell, son and heir of Sir Robert Constable of Flamborough "the spy"; kted by Lord Lieutenant of Ireland at Dublin, 1599 (Metcalfe, 209). When he sold Chopwell in 1608 he received Derwentcote from James I (Surtees II, 277, 292).

CONYERS, John, esq., of Butterwick, 2nd son of Cuthbert Conyers of Layton; married Jane Oglethorpe, widow; sheriff of Durham, 1576–(?)87 (Surtees III, 37; AA 4 XXII, 50).

CONYERS, Ralph, esq./kt, of Layton, son and heir of John Conyers (as above) and heir to his uncle Ralph, attainted after Rising of the North, 1570; kted 1617; d. c. 1639 (Surtees III, 37; Metcalfe, 170).

COOPER, Robert, esq., of Durham, married Margaret Pateson; of Inner Temple; appted arbiter with John Savile, serjeant at law, in dispute wherein Lord Lumley repudiated the regalian rights of the bishop of Durham over Hartlepool, which was decided in 1598 in the bishop's favour (DK *Report* xxxvii, 135); feodary of Durham (Mickleton MS 2, f. 72); bishop's attorney-general, 1606; appted bailiff of Stockton, 1607; joint grant for life with Francis James, DD, of office of steward of Durham at £20 a year, 1609 (DK *Report* xl, 484, 497, 507); master in chancery, (Hutchinson i, 478; Surtees III, 102: IV ii, 150; *VCH, Durham* III, 267).

CRADOCKE, John, DD, married Margaret Bateman of Wensleydale; MA (Peterhouse, Cambridge) 1601, DD 1620; admitted Gray's Inn, 1584 *(Reg.* 66); diocesan chancellor and vicar-general, 1619; vicar of Gainford, 1594–1627; archdeacon of Northumberland, 1604–19; preb. of Durham, 5th stall, 1619; vicar of Woodhorn; rector of Northallerton, 1624–27; justice of assize in Durham, 1625 (Durham 13/25); d. 1627 (Venn I i, 411: Surtees IV, 12–3: CJ 192–3).

DALLYSON, William, educ. Cambridge and Gray's Inn, reader, 1548, 1552; serjeant at law, 1552; justice of Common Pleas in Lancashire, 1554; MP for Lincolnshire, 1554; justice of Queen's Bench, 1556–9; d. 1559 (Baker, 507; Foss, 211).

DALTON, Ralph, esq., of West Auckland, surveyor of works to Bishop Tunstall; escheator in Durham; executor of Robert Hyndmer, 1558 (Mickleton MS 2 f.1v.; *W & I*, i, 161: iii, 23n.).

DETHICK, Henry, LLB, 3rd son of Sir Gilbert Dethick, Garter King-of-Arms, married Jane Bowes of London; MA (Corpus Christi Coll., Oxford) 1572, BCL 1573/4; admitted Gray's Inn, 1607 *(Reg.* 114); master in chancery; diocesan chancellor of Carlisle, 1596 *(Cal. Border Papers II*, 219); master of Greatham Hospital, 1610; d. 1613 (Clark II iii, 20; Surtees III, 137).

DUDLEY, Ambrose, esq., of Chopwell, son and heir of Robert Dudley (a customer of Newcastle) and Anne Wood, married Isabel Greenfield of Wooton, Bucks.; alderman of Newcastle; d. May 1613 (Surtees II, 277; Welford *H* 198; cf. *Cal. Border Papers II*, 330, 535).

EWBANK, Henry, MA, married Anne, daughter of Thomas Sampson, dean of Christ Church, Oxford; matric. Queen's Coll., Oxford 1573, BA 1576, MA 1579; rector of Washington, 1583; of Winston, 1588; of Whickham, 1620; master of St Mary's Hospital, Newcastle, 1585–1615; preb. of Durham, 12th stall, 1596–1620; subdean, 1607; admitted Gray's Inn, 1610; preb. of Lichfield; d. 1628 (Surtees IV, 141; Clark II ii, 56: iii, 61; CJ 198-9 n. 40).

FETHERSTONHAUGH, John, esq., of Stanhope Hall, married Margaret Radcliff of Blanchland; commissioner for musters in palatinate, 1595; threatened by bishop with fine of £10 for failure to attend Easter quarter sessions, 1596 (*Cal. Border Papers II*, 73, 146); d. 1620 (DK *Report* xliv [1883], 393; *Dur. Vis.* 119).

FETHERSTONHAUGH, Ralph, esq., of Stanhope Hall, son and heir of above, married Jane Appleyard of Burstwick in Holderness, Yorks.; matric. Oriel Coll., Oxford, 1586/7, BA 1590; admitted Gray's Inn, 1591 (*Reg.* 78); justice of assize in Durham, 1625 (Durham 13/25); d. Nov. 1636 (Clark II ii, 156: iii, 160; *W & I* iv, 270–1).

FORSTER, Claudius, esq., of Bamburgh, son and heir of Nicholas Forster and Jane Radclyffe of Blanchland, married Elizabeth Fenwick of Wallington, Northumberland; sheriff of Northumberland, 1612; kt, 1614; cr. bart, 1619; d. 1623 (AA 4 XXI [1943], 5; CJ 198).

FREVILLE, George, esq./kt, of Hardwick, married Elizabeth Jenison of Walworth; clerk of ordnance under earl of Sussex, 1569; admitted Gray's Inn, 1580 (*Reg.* 58); on commission of peace for Durham and of quorum, 1583; assessed on 100 marks of land at Spennymoor muster on 30 Sept. 1584 for a light horseman, but horse judged unsuitable, the man "course", armour "good" (*Cal. Border Papers I*, 162); grantee of forfeited Hebburn lands at Hardwick, 1590; kt, 1603; keeper of Raby; constable of Raby castle, 1608 (*Cal. State Papers Dom. 1603–10*, 581); justice of assize in Durham, 1614 (Durham 13/16); d. Nov. 1619 (Surtees III, 34, 36; *W & I* iv, 223n.).

GILLOWE, Henry, clerk, chancellor of Durham, appointed receiver-general, 1464; rector of Stocking Pelham (Herts.), 1451; Gilling, N. Yorks., 1467–79; Houghton-le-Spring, 1470–83; canon of York, 1476–82, and subdean, 1478; d. 1483 (*Fasti*, 51).

HALL, William, ?of Barnard's Inn, admitted Gray's Inn, 1603 (*Reg.* 105); mayor of Durham, 1605, 1613, 1617–19 (Surtees IV ii, 18; CJ 198).

HEATH, John, esq., of Kepier, son and heir of John Heath (warden of the Fleet prison) and Thomasin Dearham of Cremplesham, Norfolk, married Elizabeth Parker of Norwich; on commission of peace for Durham and of quorum, 1583; assessed at Spennymoor muster on 30 Sept. 1584 at a light horseman, able and well furnished (*Cal. Border Papers I*, 162); d. Jan 1618 (Surtees IV, 70; *W & I* iv, 65–70).

HEBBURN, Richard, esq., son of John Hebburn of Hardwick and Alice Harbottle of Beamish, married Ann Metcalfe of Nappa, Yorks.; d. May 1560. Following the attainder of his son Anthony in 1570, after the Rising of the North, the estate passed to George Freville (Surtees III, 34, 35).

HEDWORTH, John, esq., of Harraton, son and heir of Ralph Hedworth (see below) and Anne Hilton, married Jane Bellasis of Murton House, divorced, 1549; of quorum of Durham JPs, 1583; assessed at Spennymoor muster on 30 Sept. 1584 on lands worth £100 at a light horseman, able and well furnished *(Cal. Border Papers I*, 162); d. Jan 1601 (Surtees II, 184).

HEDWORTH, Ralph, kt, of Harraton, son and heir of John Hedworth and Ellen Hoton of Hardwick. His first wife was Anne Hilton, his second Dorothy Gascoigne, and his third Catherine Constable (Surtees II, 184).

HILTON, Henry, esq., of Hylton, son of Thomas Hilton (see below) and Ann Bowes of Streatlam, had livery of his grandfather's lands in March 1608, married Mary Wortley of Wortley, Yorks.; d. 1663 (Surtees II, 27).

HILTON, Thomas, esq., of Hylton, son and heir of Sir William Hilton and Anne Yorke of Gowlethwaite, Yorks., dying in father's lifetime, Feb. 1598 (Surtees II, 27).

HILTON, William, esq., son and heir of Sir William Hilton and Margery Bowes of Streatlam, married Sybil, daughter of Thomas Lumley, son and heir of George, 1st Lord Lumley; high forester of Weardale, 1509 (Durham 3/70, m. 5); justice of gaol delivery in Durham, 1510 (ib., 13/232, m. 6). In 1526 he conveyed his estates in Northumberland, Durham, Cumberland and Yorkshire in trust to Sir William Bulmer, Sir Ralph Hedworth, Robert Bowes of Cowton, George Bowes of Dalden, Robert Bowes of Aske, John Hedworth and John Lambton for himself for life with remainder to his son and heir, Sir Thomas Hilton, William his second son, etc.; d. pre-1537 (Surtees II, 27, 31-2).

HUNT, Richard, matric. Trinity Coll., Cambridge, 1582, BA 1585/6, MA 1589, DD 1608; rector of Foulsham, Norfolk, 1603; vicar of Terrington, Norfolk, 1609; chaplain to James I; preb. of Canterbury, 1614; installed dean of Durham, May 1620; justice of assize in Durham, 1624, 1625 (Durham 13/25); preb. of Lichfield, 1636; d. 1638 (Hutchinson ii, 154-55; Venn I ii, 434).

HUTTON, Anthony, esq., 2nd son of William Hutton of Hunwick and Anne Simpson of Henknoll, married Anne Carr of Sherburn House; on commission of peace for Durham, 1583; assessed at Spennymoor muster on 30 Sept. 1584 for an able horse and man, well furnished; commissioner for musters in palatinate of Durham, 1595 *(Cal. Border Papers I*, 162: II, 73); d. March 1603 *(W & I* iv, 125n.).

HUTTON, Richard, chancellor, married Ann Briggs of Canmire, Westmorland; matric. Jesus Coll., Cambridge, c. 1565/6; of Staple Inn, admitted Gray's Inn, 1580, *(Reg.* 57); barrister, 1586; member of Council of North, 1599-1619; serjeant, 1603; recorder of York, 1608; appted chancellor of Durham with receivership-general of lands in county, 1610; kt, 1617; king's justice of Common Pleas, 1617-39; queried legality of imposition by Charles I of "Ship money"; d. 26 Feb. 1639 (Venn I ii, 443; Baker, 520; DK *Report* xl, 433; Foss 360-1).

HYNDE, John, serjeant at law, 1531, king's serjeant, 1535-45, king's justice of Common Pleas, 1545-50; kt; educ. Cambridge and Gray's Inn; reader at Gray's Inn, 1517, 1527, 1531; member of Council of North; d. 1550 (Baker, 520: Foss, 365-6).

HYNDMER, Robert, clerk, last dean of Lanchester, 1532; last dean of St

Andrew Auckland, 1541; rector of Stanhope, 1545–58; rector of Sedgefield, (?)1551–58; appted temporal and diocesan chancellor of Durham, 26 Mar 1530; executor of Bishop Tunstall, 1558; d. 1558 (*Fasti*, 66, 106: Hutchinson i, 444). Will printed *W & I* i, 160–4 (executors Ralph Dalton, Reginald Hindmer, Michael Myers and John Hindmer).

JAMES, William, educ. Christ Church Coll., Oxford, BA, 1563, MA, 1565, BD, 1571, DD, 1574; master of University Coll., Oxford, 1572; archdeacon of Coventry, 1577–84; dean of Christ Church, Oxford, 1584; dean of Durham, 1596; chaplain to earl of Leicester; bishop of Durham, 1606; d. May 1617 (DNB x, 662).

KAY, Thomas, clerk, LLB, rector of Wolsingham, 1521–33; dean of Chester, 1532–33; canon of Lanchester, 1535; LLD *(Fasti*, 71); justice of gaol delivery at Durham, 1511; keeper of great seal at Durham (Durham 13/232B, m. 1).

LAWSON, James, esq., of Neasham, son and heir of Henry Lawson and Frances Conyers of Layton, married Jane Conyers of Sockburn; d. 1631 (Surtees III, 264).

LIGHTFOOT, George, esq., of Greystone, counsellor at law; admitted Gray's Inn, 1567 (*Reg.* 37); recommended by Sir Ralph Eure to Lord Burghley as "a lawyere of whom we stand great need, who lyeth in Bishoppricke and none nearer hand" for a place on the Northumberland commission of the peace, 1596 (*Cal. Border Papers II*, 94). He left £20 to found a school at Barnard Castle; d. Mar. 1616 (*Reg. Cath. D.*, 82–3).

LINDLEY, Henry, kt, clerk of Durham county court; constable of Durham castle, 1582, 1606; escheator of Durham, 1595; kted by Lord Lieutenant of Ireland at Dublin, 1599 (Mickleton MS 2, f. 70v.; DK *Report* xl, 507; Metcalfe, 209; Hutchinson i, 460, 478).

LYONS, John, esq., of Bradley, deputy receiver of the queen's revenues in North, 1597 (*Cal. Border Papers II*, 234); receiver for the crown at Newcastle; attended show of arms at Durham, Oct. 1618; d. 1629 (Mickleton MS 2 f. 262v.; DK *Report* xliv [1883], 459; Surtees II, 268).

MATTHEW, Toby, BA, Christ Church Coll., Oxford, 1564, MA, 1566, "much respected for his great learning, eloquence, sweet conversation, friendly disposition, and the sharpness of his wit"; public orator, 1569–72; preb. of Christ Church, Oxford, 2nd stall, 1570; archdeacon of Bath, 1572; preb. of Salisbury, 1572; pres. St John's Coll., Oxford, 1572–77; a queen's chaplain in ordinary, 1572; BD, 1573, DD, 1574; dean of Christ Church, Oxford, 1576–84; vice-chancellor of Oxford, 1579; precentor of Salisbury, 1583; dean of Durham, 1583; rector of Bishopwearmouth, 1590; bishop of Durham, 1595; archbishop of York, 1606; d. 29 Mar. 1628 (DNB xiii, 60–62).

MEYNELL, Robert, serjeant at law, 1547; member of Lincoln's Inn, (Baker, 169, 526); appted steward of Durham, 12 Mar. 1547; protonotary at Durham; bishop's attorney-general; clerk of peace; d. 1563 (Mickleton

MS 2 ff. 66, 67v.; Hutchinson, i, 444).

MILLOTT, Thomas, esq., (JP 1618) of Whitehill, son and heir of Robert Millott (d. c. 1565) and Grace Wyclyffe, married Jane Rokeby of Mortham, Yorks.; d. 1620 (Durham QS Order Book 1, p. 63; Surtees II, 153).

MOLYNEUX, Edmund, serjeant at law, 1540; king's serjeant, 1542–50; kt, 1547; king's justice of Common Pleas, 1550–52; educ. Gray's Inn, reader at Gray's Inn, 1532, 1536; member of Council of North; d. 1552 (Baker, 526; Foss, 447).

MOORECROFT, Ferdinando, MA, grad. Christ Church, Oxford; married Margaret James, niece of Bishop James; rector of Stanhope, 1608; vicar of Heighington, 1625; master of Greatham Hospital, 1613–19; preb. of Durham, 6th stall, 1619, 11th stall, 1619; justice of assize in Durham, 1627 (Durham 13/34); d. c. 1641 (Hutchinson ii, 212; CJ 194–5).

MORESLAWE, Thomas, married Elizabeth, widow of Sir William Lumley, with land in Farnacres; appted commissioner for control of salmon fishing, 1468; justice of gaol delivery, 1471; of assize, 1472 (DK *Report* xxxv, 98, 123).

MURTON (alias Morton), William, BD, matric. pensioner Christ's Coll., Cambridge, 1575, BA (Corpus) 1575, MA 1582; rector of Longnewton, 1588; vicar of Newcastle, 1596–1620; archdeacon of Northumberland, 1599–1603; of Durham, 1603–20; d. 1620 (Venn I iii, 219; Hutchinson ii, 221; Welford *H* iii, 107, 231).

MUSCHAMP, William, kt, of Barmoor, son and heir of George Muschamp and Elizabeth Selby of Twizell, married Elizabeth Gilborne of Charing, Kent; kted at Berwick, 1617; sheriff of Northumberland, 1622; admitted burgess of Berwick, 1627; d. 1631 (AA 4 XXI [1943], 6; Metcalfe, 170).

NEILE, Richard, educ. Westminster School, matric. St John's Coll., Cambridge, 1580; chaplain to Lord Burghley and his son, Robert Cecil, 1st earl of Salisbury; bishop of Rochester, 1603; of Lichfield, 1610; of Lincoln, 1614; of Durham, 1617; of Winchester, 1628; archbishop of York, 1631; d. 1640 (CJ 191).

NEVILLE, Henry, earl of Westmorland, lord of Raby, etc. Implicated in Rising of the North, 1569, when his lands were confiscated and he was forced into exile (Sharp, *Memorials of the Rebellion of 1569*, 289–304).

NEVILLE, Ralph, nephew of Ralph, earl of Westmorland, son of John Lord Neville, (younger brother of 2nd earl of Westmorland), married Isabel Booth, niece of Bp Booth, before 1473; attainted after battle of Towton, 1461, where father killed; restored, 1472, and knted 1475; succeeded to earldom of Westmorland on uncle's death on 3 Nov. 1484 (*Complete Peerage* xii, 551).

PEPPER, Cuthbert, kt, of East Cowton, Yorks., married Margaret Wylde of East Cowton, Yorks.; admitted Gray's Inn, 1570; reader, (?)1602 (*Reg.* 41); commissioner for gaol delivery at Hexham and co. Durham, 1596 (*Cal. Border Papers II*, 119); surveyor of king's court of wards and liveries; licenced to serve as attorney before Council at York, 1598 (*Cal. State Papers Dom. 1598–1601*, 5); kted at Whitehall, 1604; appted chancellor of Durham, 1605; d. 1608 (DK *Report* xxxvii, 168: xl, 507; *Yorks. Vis.* 560; *VCH, N. Yorks i*, 161; Metcalfe, 153).

PHELIPPS, Edward, kt, 4th son of Thomas Phelipps of Barrington, Somerset; admitted Middle Temple, 1571, reader, 1596 (*Reg.* 88); serjeant, 1603; kt, 1603; justice of Common Pleas in county palatine of Lancaster, 1604; speaker of House of Commons, 1604–11; Master of the Rolls, 1611–14; builder of Montacute House, Somerset; d. 11 Sept. 1614 (Baker, 530: Foss, 513–14).

PILKINGTON, Leonard, ThD, (JP 1584) brother of Bishop Pilkington, master of St John's Coll., Cambridge, 1561–2; rector of Middleton, 1561–2; of Whitburn, 1563–1616; preb. of Durham, 7th stall, 1567; treasurer of Durham cathedral; of quorum of Durham JPs, 1573/4; assessed at Spennymoor muster at a light horseman, able and well furnished (*Cal. Border Papers I*, 163; Hutchinson ii, 196).

PLACE, Christopher, esq., of Dinsdale, son and heir of Robert Place and Mary Allenson of Cleasby, Yorks., married Mary Tattersall of Cambs.; d. 1624 (Surtees III, 236).

RAKET, John, attorney in Durham court of pleas, 1498, (?) coroner of Chester ward, 1498 (Durham 13/230); clerk of peace (Mickleton MS 2 f. 67v.); justice of gaol delivery at Durham, 1501 (Durham 13/229, 13/230); coroner of Chester ward, 1504 (ib., 13/1); justice of assize at Durham, 1508 (ib., 13/1 m. 22); appted justice of gaol delivery at Durham, 1509, 1512 (ib., 3/70).

RAKET, Richard, clerk of the crown, of assize, of the peace, of halmotes and protonotary at Durham "in the time of Bp Neville" (Mickleton MS 2, ff. 66–67v.); keeper of Frankleyn park and a commissioner for control of salmon fishing (DK *Report* xxxiii [1872], 142: xxxv, 98).

RAKET, William, probably son of above Richard Raket, appted clerk in the Durham chancery, 20 June 1437, and keeper of its rolls for life, appointed justice of assize in Durham, 1446 and 1455. In 1476 he was confirmed jointly with John Raket as clerk of chancery and keeper of the chancery rolls (DK *Report* xxxiii, 142, 199: xxxiv, 176, 210–1: xxxv, 99, 103).

RASTELL, WIlliam, admitted Lincoln's Inn, 1532, reader, 1547; serjeant, 1555; JQB, 1558–63; d. Louvain, 1565 (Foss, 546–47).

RICHARDSON, John, sen., esq., (JP 1619) of Durham, admitted Gray's Inn, 1598 (*Reg.* 93); appted bishop's remembrancer and solicitor in all courts and receiver of fines at an annual fee of 40s., 1607; surveyor of the bishop's lands; bailiff of Howdenshire; steward of the courts at Sunderland; protonotary at Durham, 1613; clerk of assizes; d. c. 1640 (DK, *Report* xl, 508; Mickleton MS 2 f. 66v.; Durham QS Order Book 1, p. 90; CJ 199 n. 43).

RIDDELL, Thomas, esq./kt, of Gateshead, married Elizabeth Conyers of Sockburn; sheriff of Newcastle, 1601; mayor, 1619, 1635; MP, 1624, 1628; kt, 1616; justice of assize in Durham, 1625 (Durham 13/25); d. March 1650 (Surtees II, 128; AA 4 XVIII [1940], 50, 65; Welford *H* iii, 209).

SALVAYN, Gerard, esq., of Croxdale, son and heir of Gerard Salvayn senior and Joan ...; married Eleanor Wrenn of Billy Hall; justice of gaol delivery in Durham, 1556 (Durham 13/274 mm. 1–2); justice of assize in Durham and on quorum, 1569. (His sister Anne was step-mother of William Claxton of Burn Hall, while his brother Anthony, BD, was master of University Coll., Oxford, rector of Winston, 1545, of Sedgefield, 1558, and of Ryton, 1558, master of Sherburn Hospital, 1552–9, preb. of Durham, 12th stall, 1556, and vicar-general of Bishop Tunstall.) (Durham 13/284); d. 1571 (Surtees IV ii, 97, 119: *VCH, Durham* II, 116)). Will and inventory printed *W & I* i, 345–51.

SANDERS, Edward, son of Thomas Saunders, esq., of Harrington, Northants.; admitted Middle Temple, reader, 1525, 1533, 1539; serjeant at law, 1540; king's serjeant, 1547–53; MP for Coventry, Lostwithiel and Saltash, recorder of Coventry, pre–1553; justice of Common Pleas, 1553–57; kt, 1555; chief justice of Queen's Bench, 1557–59; chief baron of the Exchequer, 1559–76. Helped to frustrate the attempt to proclaim Lady Jane Grey as queen (Baker, 535: Foss, 587).

SCROOPE, George, esq., of Langley, son of John, 8th Lord Scrope of Bolton in Wensleydale (d. 1549), brother to Henry, 9th Lord Scrope (d. 1592) and uncle of Thomas, 10th Lord Scrope (d. 1609) (*Complete Peerage* xi, 547–9: DK *Report* xliv, 506, 507); admitted Lincoln's Inn, 1561 (*Reg.* 69); at the Spennymoor muster on 30 Sept. 1584 assessed at a light horseman, which he presented but disclaimed liability (*Cal. Border Papers I*, 163). He appears to have had no son, only two daughters, Eleanor, and Mary, who married John Dowthwaite of Westholme (*W & I* iv, 175 and note).

SELBY, George, kt, of Winlaton and Newcastle, "the king's host", married Margaret Selby of Twizell; sheriff of Newcastle, 1594; mayor, 1600, 1606, 1611, 1622; MP, 1601, 1604; governor of Hostmen's Company, 1601; kt, 1603; sheriff of Northumberland, 1607; of Durham, 1608–25; d. 1625 (AA 4 XVIII [1940], 47, 49, 50, 52, 54: XXII [1944], 51; Surtees II, 274).

SMITH, William, esq., of Durham, son and heir of Thomas Smith and Margaret Lightfoot, married Mary Heron of Chipchase; counsellor at law; of Gray's Inn; recorder of Durham city, 1603; bishop's attorney-general; steward of Durham, 1623 (*Reg. Cath. D.*, 82n.; Hutchinson i, 490; Surtees IV ii, 20; CJ 199 n. 42).

SWIFT, Robert, LLB, married Anne Lever of Sherburn Hospital; matric. St John's Coll., Cambridge, BA 1552/3, LLB (from Louvain); justice of assize in Durham, 1562 (Durham 13/2); diocesan chancellor, 1561–1577; preb. of Durham, 1st stall, 1562; rector of Sedgefield, 1562–99; of quorum of Durham JPs, 1573/4; co-founder of Sedgefield school, 1596; d. 1599 (Venn I iv, 192; Hutchinson ii, 171; *W & I* iii, 174n.; Surtees III, 32, 419).

TAILEBOIS, Robert, esq., of Thornton Hall, son and heir of Ralph Tailebois of Thornton and Eleanor Killinghall of Middleton St George, married Elizabeth, daughter of Bishop Barnes; as "late of Clifford's Inn" was admitted to Middle Temple, 1580 (*Reg.* 126); clerk of peace (Mickleton MS 2 f. 68); escheator in Durham, 1594; (?) *custos rotulorum*, 1596 (*Cal. Border Papers II*, 220); bishop's attorney-general; justice of assize in Durham, 1600 (Durham 13/299); d. in Durham gaol and was buried at St Mary le Bow, Durham, in Jan. 1605 (Surtees III, 382; Hutchinson i, 471).

TALBOT, Edward esq., brother of Gilbert, 7th earl of Shrewsbury, married Jane Ogle, co-heiress of Ogle barony with her sister (who married Sir Charles Cavendish); MP for Northumberland, 1584, 1586; sheriff of Northumberland, 1601, 1609; *custos rotulorum* for Northumberland, 1603; JP in West Riding, Yorks.; succ. as 8th earl of Shrewsbury, 1616; d. 1618 (AA 4 XX [1942], 89).

TEMPEST, Robert, esq., of Holmside, nephew and heir of Sir Thomas Tempest of Holmside (see below), brother-in-law of George Smith of Nunstainton, and cousin of Thomas Trollop; sheriff of Durham, 1558–61; a guardian of the temporalities of Durham, 1560; implicated in the Rising of the North, 1569 (AA4 XXII [1944], 49: Surtees II, 327).

TEMPEST, Thomas, 2nd son of Robert Tempest of Holmside (sheriff of Durham, 1476–82, on council of bishop and a JP); sued in Durham court of pleas, 1503 (Durham 13/1); justice of assize at Durham on quorum, 1508 (ib., m. 22); of gaol delivery at Durham, 1508 (ib., m. 24); appted justice of gaol delivery at Durham on quorum, 1509 (ib., 3/70, m. 1); steward of Durham, 1510–44; recorder of Newcastle upon Tyne, (?)1517–(?)36; JP for Northumberland, 1537; member of Council of North, 1537–43; founded chantry in Lanchester parish church, 1540; d. 1543. His estates, forfeited through the implication of his nephew and heir, Robert in the Rising of the North, 1569, were eventually acquired in 1613 by Sir Timothy Whittingham (Hutchinson i, 400, 409; Surtees II, 325–7; AA 4 XLIX [1971], 142–7).

TONGE, George, esq./kt, son of Henry Tonge of West Thickley and Denton, married Elizabeth Blakiston of Newton Hall; matric. Christ Church Coll., Oxford, 1602; kt, 1617; justice of assize in Durham, 1627 (Durham 13/25); d. 1640 (Clark II ii, 259; Surtees IV i, 4).

TONGE, Henry, esq., son and heir of George Tonge and Helen Lambton of Lambton, father of above (Surtees IV, 4).

TROLLOP, Thomas, esq., of Thornley, son and heir of John Trollop and Margery Blakiston, succeeding his father in 1555 and dying about 1558. His first wife was Anne Lumley of Ludworth and Seaton Carew and his second wife Grace Pudsey. His son was attainted following the Rising of the North (Surtees I, 92). His will is printed *W & I* i, 174–76.

WHITTINGHAM, Timothy, kt, of Cowling, Yorks., and Holmside, son and heir of William Whittingham, (dean of Durham, 1563–79), and Catherine Jaquemans of Orleans, married Elizabeth Ascough of Osgodby, Lincs.; matric. Christ's Coll., Cambridge, 1572, BA 1575/6, MA 1579, incorp. Oxford 1577; admitted Middle Temple, 1576; kt, 1603; justice of assize in Durham, 1614 (Durham 13/16); owned Fountains Abbey, 1622–25; d. 1638 (Venn I iv, 397; Surtees II, 330).

WRENN, Charles, esq./kt, of Binchester, married Gertrude Thornhaugh of Fenton, Notts.; matric. Brasenose, Oxford, 1580, admitted Gray's Inn, 1584 (*Reg.* 64); laid information before William James as dean of Durham, William Murton, Robert Cooper and John Barnes, JPs, on plotting by Catholics prior to 5 Nov. 1605 (*Cal. State Papers Dom.,*

Addenda, 1580–1625, 469); constable of Durham castle, 1606, and re–appted jointly with his son Lindley, 1611; steward of Raby and Brancepeth, 1608 (*Cal. State Papers Dom., 1603–10,* 461); justice of assize in Durham, 1613 (Durham 13/15); kt, 1607; d. 1621 (Clark II 94; Hutchinson i, 481; Metcalfe, 158; *W & I* iv, 147–8).

WRIGHT, Hugh, alderman of Durham, son of William Wright (mayor of Durham, 1581), married firstly Thomasine Theobald of Rushall, Staffs., and secondly Hilda Chomley of Whitby; attorney in Durham court of pleas (Durham 13/299); mayor of Durham, 1601, 1610, 1614, 1623, 1632; receiver and feodary of Durham; solicitor-general to Bp Howson, 1628; d.1654 (Mickleton MS 2, ff. 72v., 73v.; Surtees IV ii, 18, 153; Hutchinson i, 495)

INDEX

The Index combines people, places and a few key themes. Where these occur in the edited text numbering refers to the session (in bold) and the section (normally the indictment) in the roll. Where they occur in the introductions or biographies the **page** reference is marked by a following asterisk. Names of magistrates and/or their designations are printed in **bold**. Grand jurors have an asterisk preceding the surname and for ease of identification where a family has more than one representative in this category an asterisk precedes the entry. Persons and places in the recusants' roll (Appendix 1) are numbered individually, preceded by App. An attempt has been made to group within semi-colons references which appear to relate to one person. Otherwise persons of the same name are listed alphabetically by status followed by place of residence. Where nicknames are cited, or alternative names, these are given in square brackets and not listed separately. Surnames are grouped under the most common spelling, with one variant where there are many examples. No special notice is taken of doubled consonants or the interchangeability of vowels, such as i/y. Places are to be considered as located in co. Durham unless otherwise indicated. Where these are obscure they are given their parish or district in square brackets. The names of closes are not normally listed.

Allenheads, Northd 37/5

Allensford 1/3

Allenshiel 46/5: 84/16

Alleros, Weardale, Northd 41/17

Alleyn, William, late of Egglescliffe, yeo. 20/3,4

Allison (Allyson), Anthony, late of East Brandon, lab. 50/8: 51/5; John, STB, rector of Whickham 84/13; Margaret, wife of Ralph 107/1; Roland 61/3; Thomas, of Cleadon, yeo. 92/22; William 61/5 (and see Alanson)

Almond, Barbara, widow 96/4

Alnwick, Northd 63/6

Alston, lordship of 7*

Altham, James, kt, baron of Exchequer 72A/2: 73/17: 76/12,14,18: 88/27: 337*

Alwen, Margaret, spinster App. 390

Alwent [Gainford] 97/6–8: 98/28: 99/29,30: 104/6: 105/16

Alwent, *Peter 33

Amerston 82/12

Amorer, Robert, late of Scremerston, gen. 57/11: 59/11

Ancroft [Northd] 55/3: 92/1,2

Anderson, Edward, shipwright 77/13; George, collector 105/11; Henry, esq. 337*: 43–45: 46/4: kt 62,64–66, 68/A: 68A/1,3–7: 69: 69/32–34: 70,71: 71/9,12: 72,73: 73/15,16: 75/22: 76/20: 84: 84/4,19,22,23: 85/15–17: 88/26: 89,90: 91A/1: 92: 92/4,6,22: 93: 93/4,13,26,27: 95/10: 96/13: 97/10: 98: 98/7,15–23,26–28: 99/3,6,12,13: 100/7,11,12,27: 101/4,7: 105/24; Isaac, late of Wingate, gen. 81/12: 84/19: 87/7; James 80/3: late of Newcastle upon Tyne 68/18: 91/25: yeo. 92/24: of Grindon, yeo. 95/11: Mary, wife of 95/11; John, yeo. 60/2; yeo. 104/15; Thomas 77/4; William, yeo. 104/15

Andrew(e), Anthony, late of Ebchester, yeo. 24/1; Edward, late of Satley, lab. 11/21; Henry, late of Middleton Row, yeo. 87/14: 104/18; John, of Shotley Bridge, yeo. 33/9; Robert, of Blackburn mill, lab. 22/4; William 91/27: yeo. 92/24

Ane, Henry 46/6

Anton, Ald' Suddle, husbandman 25/8

Appleby(e) (Appulbie), Jane, widow

106/10; John, yeo. App. 258; junior, yeo. App. 107: senior, of Hamsterley, yeo. App. 106; yeo. 63/11: late of Whorlton, yeo. 88/2; of Winlaton, yeo. 89/4: Alice, wife of 89/4; Percival, of Chester 47/73; Ralph, weaver 92/24: yeo. App. 64; Thomas, of Crossgate 72/1

Archdeacon Newton 104

Archebaude (Arch(i)bald), George, lab. 26/2; Ralph, late of Morton, yeo. 84/17,20

Archer, Adam, late of Hartley, Westd, lab 9/6; George 25*: 28/7; Gerard, yeo. 41/12; Richard, of Durham, cordwainer 66/1; Robert, yeo. 28/3,7: husbandman/esq. 29/3,6(bis): Agnes, wife of 29/6; Thomas, tailor 92/24; Emmot, wife of 92/24

Areke, Thomas, of Easington, chaplain 10/3

Areson, Anthony, yeo. 81/3

Armestrong(e), Alice, late of Durham, spinster 110/12; Cuthbert, sp. bailiff 77/11; George, yeo. 47/16(bis),18; Jane, late of Piercebridge, spinster 108/6; John [Jock], late of Coastley, yeo. 61/12; Matthew 68/3: tenant-farmer 81/13: 82/11; Thomas, late of Highstead Eshe, yeo. 36/4; William 107/24; [Andrew's Will], late of *Willeyeveysule*, lab. 36/4

Arnold, James, lab. 29/16

Arras, Jane, spinster 93/13; Margaret, spinster 93/13

Arrowe, John, lab. 26/3

Arrowsmith, Alice, widow 78/14; Christopher 104/9: deceased 78/14; Elizabeth 47/17; Thomas 89/29

Arthur, George, yeo. 65/10

Asmell, Edward 106/2: Anne, wife of 106/2

Asshton, Hugh, clerk, chancellor of Durham 21*: 12: 337*

Aston, *John 12

Atcheson (Atchynson), Agnes, widow 92/24; Christopher, late of Hamsterley, yeo. 87/1; John, constable of Lumley 84/1; Nicholas, late of Ebchester 87/25; Robert 26/3; Thomas, yeo. 26/1; William, collector 78/4: 79/5,6 (and see Acheson, Atkinson)

Athie (Athye), Christopher, of Broadwood 64/4; Cuthbert, of Mainsforth,
husbandman 67/12; George, late of
Wolsingham, yeo. 91/59; Margaret,
widow 92/24: of Broadwood, widow
App. 92 (and see Addye)
Athirton, John, esq., sheriff of Durham
21*: 6/5
Atkinson, Agnes, of Deanery House,
Lanchester, widow App. 306; Alexander, of Cleadon, yeo. 51/2; Arthur,
yeo. 47/20; Cuthbert, lab. 26/2: yeo.
51/2; Elizabeth, spinster App. 276;
Francis 49/5; George, of Fulwell,
lab. 51/1: of Raby, yeo. 50/3; James,
late of Monkwearmouth, yeo. 78/9:
79/4; *John 19: yeo. 80,93: of
Farleis, 104: of Embleton, 105,106,
109; constable 102/32; of Rowley
Gilett, husbandman 8/2; junior,
late of Staindrop, yeo. 67/1,3; yeo.
95/11: Jane, wife of 95/11; Martin,
yeo. 65/10; Michael, bailiff 91/35:
102/15: 103/20: 104/8: Margaret,
wife of 102/7; Ralph 28/3: 78/16;
Richard 17/3: of Whitburn, yeo.
51/2; Robert, informer 96/17–20;
yeo. 95/11; of Hedworth, husbandman 26/2; of Lumley Castle, yeo.
106/1; of Urpeth, yeo. 56/12;
*Thomas, of Boldon, yeo. 106: late
of Hag House, 110/8; yeo. 56/12:
late of Thinford, lab. 58/18; William,
juror 56/10; late of East Boldon,
yeo. 93/13; of *Hallhill* 8/7: of
Rowley Gilett, lab. 8/8 (and see
Acheson, Atcheson)
Atkynson [Kerber], John, husbandman 7/4,5
Auckland 16* 39: 50/4: 56/6; bailiff
of 18/4; Baron *16; deanery 39/5:
99/20; park at 10/4 (see also Bishop
Auckland, North Auckland and
West Auckland)
Aucklandfield 49/2
Awde, John, of Heworth, yeo. App.
359: Elizabeth, wife of App. 360;
Thomas, smith 92/24: of Tursdale,
blacksmith App. 210: wife of App.
211 (and see O(u)rd)
Awder, Ralph, yeo. 78/11
Awderson, George, late of Durham,
yeo. 28/6: 29/2

Axwell Houses 32*: 65/7: 91/7,61
Aycliffe 3/5,6: 7/4,5: 8/1: 9/9: 11/6:
29/5,6: 65/10: 83/11: 95/11: 110/10;
parish of 98/19: bridges in 93/35;
parishioners of 101/4
Aycrigg, John, yeo. 92/22
Ayden, Isabel, widow 95/11; John,
lab. 50/17,18
Aydon Shiels, Northd 36/4
Aykes Raw 105
Ayre, Anthony, bailiff 93/18: of Shincliffe, husbandman 50/19; John, of
Wolsingham, yeo. 60/5–7: weaver
92/24; *Lionel, of Wiserley, yeo.
105,107; Richard, of Bishopton,
yeo., Isabel wife of App. 54; Robert,
husbandman 26/2; Samuel 51/6;
William, of Tunstall, yeo. 10/2 (and
see Aire)
*Ayton, *John 15*: 13,16,19; *Robert,
gen. 15*,16*: 20,22,32: of West
Herrington, gen. 109

*Bailes, *Anthony, gen. 37; Elizabeth,
of Fishburn, widow 92/24; George
46/10: yeo. 86/8; *Henry, of Newton
Cap, gen. 102: 102/12,14,15: 103/20:
juror 67/2; John, yeo. 86/8; Katherine, of Upper Coniscliffe, widow
92/24: App. 86; William 73/13:
apothecary 82/8
Bailey, see Bayley
Bailiffs of the county court 11*: of
the sheriff 12*
*Bainbrigg(e), *Anthony, yeo. 60/2;
Cuthbert, yeo. 64/9: of Whitburn,
yeo. 47/77: 50/17: 51/2: 65/16;
Francis 57/9: gen. 59/10; Gregory,
yeo. 26/2; Guy 12*: 73/9,20; Henry,
yeo. 59/6; Isabel, spinster 65/10;
Jane, of Lanchester 95/11; John,
yeo. 92/23: of Field Stile, yeo.
100/14; 58/14,17: yeo. 52/2: yeo.
64/9: Elizabeth, wife of 52/2; of
Gellesfield, yeo. 72/9,10: 73/9,20;
of Wheatley Hill, gen. 13*: 100/12:
collector 97/14; *Matthew 15*: 17;
Philip, gen. 15: 20,25,29; late of
Sowingburne, yeo. 90/13; Ralph, yeo.
60/2: late of Hill House, yeo. 66/6;
Richard 20*: 1,4,5,7,10: 337*; 69/14,
16; late of Field stile, yeo. 64/9:

Margaret, wife of 64/9; Robert 45/1: late of Billingham, gen. 58/17: 63/25; Roger 11/18: 47/7: of Wearhead, yeo. 17/5; *Thomas, of Wheatley Hill, esq. 42; of Stockton, yeo. 60/2; of Whitehall. yeo., Jane wife of App. 251; 92/8: Junior, late of Wolsingham, yeo. 92/23; William, late of Whickham, yeo. 73/9,10,19,20; of Whitburn, lab. 51/2

Baines (Banes), Anne, widow 92/24; Richard 10/5 (and see Beanes)

Baite, John, 88/10

Baker, Oswald, of Durham, yeo. bailiff 52/6; Robert, of Monkwearmouth, gen. 44/2; William, late of Durham, yeo. 82/26

Bakworthe, John, yeo. 33/9

Baldersdale, N. Yorks. 85/3

Baldridge, Henry 73/5

*Bales, *Henry, of Newton Cap, gen. 94; *John, yeo. 92

Bambrough, Robert, late of Gilesgate, yeo. 107/21

Bamburgh, Northd 81/13

Ban(c)kes, Charles, of Langley, yeo. App. 108; John, late of Shotton, yeo. 63/26; Michael, of Over Coniscliffe 63/23; Thomas, of Durham, yeo. 78/14

Bancroft, see Bayncrofte

Barburn, Christopher 17/1

Bargell, George, late of Hetton-le-Hole, yeo. 77/10

Bargie, Richard, yeo. App. 87

Barka(r)s, Robert, yeo. 65/10: 77/13 (and see Berker)

Barking, John 93/25

Bark(o)us, John 91/38; Thomas, of Hedleywood, yeo. 12/3 (and see Berkhouse)

Barle, *Richard 83

Barley 93/2

Barloe, John 88/10; Margaret, late of Greenlaw, spinster 68/4; Richard, late of Greenlaw, yeo. 68/4: Isabel, wife of 68/4

Barmpton 73/1

Barmston 92/24: 105/7,8: App. 272: township of 93/35

Barnard Castle 26*,27*,31*: 29/20: 33/2: 39/14,16: 47/7,8: 60/2: 62/1,3,4,8: 63/28: 65/10: 69/25,28: 71/9: 77/6:

78/2: 88/4,5: 91/3,4,34,35: 97/3,4,9: 109/1: App. 144; demesne of 12/5

Barnard Castle, Richard of 9*

Barnes, Anne, late of Carterthorne, spinster 98/24,25; Elizabeth, widow 95/11; Emanuel, STP 59,61–63,66: 66/18: 68/24: 74,80: 82/20: 337*; Jane, of (Great) Burdon, widow 92/24: App. 39; John, esq. 56,57: 57/11: 59: 59/1,11: 60,62–64: 64/7,12: 65,66: 66/18: 67/2,3: 68/16,17,19: 68/A: 69: 69/34: 70,73–76: 76/13,18,19: 79/3: 80: 81: 81/16: 82: 82/21,25: 83: 83/15: 84: 84/4: 85: 85/15: 86: 86/12,14: 87/32: 88: 88/20,26,29,30: 89,90: 90A/4: 91/36: 337*: esq., steward 52/8: 58/1: steward of forest court 81/5,6; yeo. 93/3; Miles, wright 31/7; Robert, late of Whickham, lab. 64/2; William 61/4: gen. coroner 63/25,27

Barnes [Barnabey], William, late of Whitwell, yeo. 43/5

Barnsfather, John, late of Houghton-le-Spring, yeo. 92/25

Barras, Andrew, late of Whickham, yeo. 77/11

Barrow(e), Alexander, late of Durham, yeo. 55/2: 60/1,12; Hugh 62/6: late of Beamish, yeo. 102/6,28: 103/19; John, yeo. 60/1,11,12; Nicholas, of Woodcroft, lab. 25/5,6

Bartle, John, late of Longnewton, yeo. 104/6: 105/16

Barton, N. Yorks. 24/4

*Barton, *Conan, of Durham, gen. 26/3: 31,32,34; *Thomas 3

Barwicke, William, late of Norton, lab. 73/7,8

Barwys lonyng 40/4

Bassnet, John, late of Wackerfield, yeo. 75/25

Basworth, *Thomas 11

Bates, John, constable 89/27; Richard, late of Biddick, gen. 96/16 (and see Beates)

Batie, Thomas, lab. 47/7,8

Batmanson, Christopher, of Broom, gen./yeo. 92/24: App. 378: Helen, wife of 92/24: App. 379; John 21*; Marmaduke, of Little Smeaton, gen. 26*: 31/7; Robert, senior 10/8–10: of Langley 6/6; Batemanson, William, of Wooley, yeo. 43/3

Berkhouse, Thomas 22* (and see Bark(o)us)

Bernardstede, Robert, of Newburgh, yeo. 8/4

Berriman, John, late of South Church, yeo. 84/6,23

Berrington, [Northd] 25/9

Berwick Hill, Northd 30/5,6

Berwick-upon-Tweed [Northd] 26/1: 28/1: 80/3

Berwyk, *Richard 17

Beseley, William, late of Swalwell, yeo. 57/1

Bessour, Anthony, gen. 59/4

Besyn, John, of *Shirwenthousez*, yeo. 18/2

Beton, William, late of Gateside, embroiderer 67/5: 68A/7

Beuley, Robert 91/29

Beverley, provost of 21*

Bewcastle [Tynedale] 8/3: Cumbd 15/2: 17/2: 33/3,4,6: 60/15: 61/12: 63/27

Bewclay, Northd 46/4: 60/15

Bewley Grange 31/5: 93/17

Biddick 11/16: 92/24: 95/11: 96/16: App. 270,271

Biddyke, Robert, husbandman 28/2(*bis*)

Biggins, Mary, of Sunderland, widow App. 219

Bigland, Edward, yeo., bailiff 91/6: late of Bishop Auckland, yeo. 85/9

Bill, see Bylle

Billing Shield 75/7

Billingham 33/1: 36/4: 46/11: 56/8: 58/17: 63/25: 76/9: 84/12: 87/11,30: 88/21: 91/45: 92/24: 108/8: 110/7,23: App. 73; bridge 100/16; bridges in parish of 93/35; constables of 56/8: 88/21; wood 87/30

*Billingham, Francis, gen. 55/9: 73/12; *John 15*: 25,29; *Ralph, of Crook Hall, esq. 38

Billingside 20/5: App. 313

Billop(p), Thomas, of Gateside, yeo. 102/31; William, alehouse keeper 82/1

Billy Row (*Billelawes*) 10/6: 92/24: 108

Binchester 10*,26*,35*: 29/5: 34/5; bridge 109/6: 110/22; highway at 109/6: 110/22; mill at 109/6

Binckes, William, yeo. 85/9

Bir(ck)beck, *Richard, gen. 93: of Mor-

ton, gen. 75/25

Birckbie, Christopher, lab. 49/6; Thomas, late of Piercebridge, lab. 49/6

Bird, Anthony, late of Whickham, gen. 23/6; Hugh, late of North Shields, gen. 47/15: 53/2; John, yeo. 98/29; Richard, of Chester, yeo. 65/10; Thomas, constable 93/11

Birden, Robert, of Durham 3/9

Birkby, N. Yorks. 102/7

Birkhead, Daniel, STP 34*: 102: 102/33: 103–105: 105/14,16: 106/28, 29: 107/25: 108: 110/23: 338*

Birtley 16*: 50/15: 57/8: 69/22–24: 102,104,110; [Northd] 77/14,21

Birtley, David, yeo. 95/11: 100/27

Bisco, William, of London, mercer 63/15: Margery, wife of 63/15

Bishop Auckland 9*,28*,35*: 7: 26/3: 37/4: 39: 39/10: 41/1: 47/14: 59/6: 63/5,23,24: 64/1,10: 66/13: 67/5: 68/12: 71/17: 72/19,20: 73/1,5,13: 75/30: 76/20: 77/5,6,10,15: 82/1,2, 6–8,24: 83/8: 85/4,9: 86/9,13: 87/16: 89/17,18,20: 91/44: 92/3,5: 97/1: 99/8–10,21: 100/26: 102/16–18,23: 104/1: 105/12: 106: 106/15: 107/3: 109/6: 110/22; division of 24n *: halmote at 76/8: highway 93/37; park at 87/76 (see also North Auckland)

Bishop Field, Allendale, Northd 43/11

Bishop Middleham 77/7: 102/25–27: 106/15: 107/18

Bishopley 75/17: 104/19: 107/13

Bishopton 3/2: 4/5: 64/3: 69/6: 81/4,9: 95/11: 102: 104/5: 105/18: App. 54–57,394; parish of 96/17: bridges in 93/35

Bishopwearmouth 40/4: 50/1: 60/13: 76/14: 88/9: 91/15,16: 98/11,29; constables of 88/18; poor of parish of 106/23; rector of 76/14

Bitchburn 3/7,8: 6/3: 10/1: 60/7: 98

Black Dene 75/5

Blackburn mill 22/4: 63/21

Bla(c)kburn(e), Christopher, yeo. 56/12; Edward, of Carlisle, yeo. 29/12; Harvey, yeo. 64/3; John, late of *Lukkous*, lab. 25/12; Rinian, lab. 25/12

*Bla(c)kett, *Alexander 15*: 17; Charles,

Carnaby, Isabel [Bilha] 91/19: 92/26: spinster 92/24; Nicholas, gen. 92/24: Clara, wife of 92/24
Carr House [Durham] 55/8: App. 172, 173
Carr, Anthony, yeo. 65/10: 68/14: of Gateside, yeo. 68/18: Agnes, wife of 68/18; George, of Esp Green, yeo. 92/24: Isabel, wife of 92/24; of Moorside, yeo., Isabel wife of App. 335; Isabel, late of Cornforth, widow 34*: 107/10; John, husbandman 30/1: yeo. 46/5: late of Elrington 62/15; Margaret, widow 81/7; Nicholas 90/9; Ralph, of Cocken, gen. 52/7; Richard, of Ford, gen. 26/1: of Gateside, yeo. 47/21; late of Hexham, yeo. 81/13: gen. 82/11; Robert, earl of Somerset 91/9,46,47; of *Hurwood Loning*, yeo. 91/14; of *Norwood loninge* by Whickham, yeo. 91/48; of Tanfield, yeo. 95/11: Jane, wife of 95/11; Thomas, late of Grindon, yeo. 56/3; William 65/7: yeo. 39/6: esq. 98/7: 99/3: 101/4,7: 107/17: 340*
Carrocke, Northd 36/4
Carrocke, Lancelot, yeo. 73/3
Carrudde(r)s, Archibald 105/6; George, yeo. 93/26; Robert, of Lanchester, yeo. 95/11; William, late of Darncrook, yeo. 108/2,11
Carse, Cuthbert, lab. 102/16–18
Carter, Joan, widow 62/5; Peter 12*: 106/30
Carterthorne [St Helen Auckland] 98/24,25: 99/8–10: 100/26
Cartington, Cecily 100/2
Case, Miles, of St Andrew Auckland, clerk 38/3
Casson, *John, of Sadberge, yeo. 104
Cassop 43/5: 50/6: 107
Castell, Thomas, prior of Durham 21*
Castle Eden 31*: 61/13: 71/14: bridges in parish of 93/35
Castlegaite, Francis 39/14
Catcheside, John 50/15; Robert, of Hedworth, yeo. 65/10
Catrik, John 20*: 3: 9/11: 340*
Caterick*, Ralph, yeo. 66,80,96: of Fishburn, yeo. 110; Richard, yeo. 98/5; Robert, constable 63/14 (and see Katerik)

Caward, George, lab. 37/2; Walter, late of West Boldon, lab. 37/2
Cawood, William, of Wolviston, yeo. 104/9: Elizabeth, wife of 104/9
Chamber(s), *Cuthbert, yeo. 80: of Whitburn 47/27; George, yeo. 50/17: 51/1,2; John, constable 102/32: of Blaydon, yeo. 56/12; John, junior, yeo. 102/12: senior, yeo. 102/12,13; John, late of Darlington, pedlar 103/3; Richard. lab. 26/2; Robert, of Whitburn, yeo. 51/2: 78/5: 79/6; Rowland, of Seaham 47/25,28; Stephen, late of Blackwell, yeo. 102/12–4; Thomas 41/12: gen. 13*: of Whitburn 47/26: yeo. 51/2; William, junior, yeo. 50/17: senior, blacksmith 50/17,18; lab. 26/2: of East Boldon, yeo. 51/6: 56/11
Chamerlen, Edward, yeo. 26/1
Chamerley, Robert, lab. 26/1
Champley, John, late of Shotton, yeo. 61/12: 63/27
Chanley, Bartholomew, yeo. 65/10; Henry, yeo. 92/1,2
Chanlez, John, yeo. 26/1
Chapman, Clement, of Frosterley, yeo. 65/10; *Cuthbert 27; Francis, yeo., constable 88/21; George, of Wolsingham, yeo., alehouse-keeper 92/15; James, lab. 25/2: yeo. 26/4; Lancelot, of Frosterley, yeo. 29/16 (*bis*); Percival, yeo. 92/22; Robert, of Frosterley, yeo. 6/5; Thomas, yeo., Anne wife of App. 21; of Billingham, yeo., constable 88/21; William 88/16
Charles I 35*
Charl(e)ton, Christopher, late of Hatherton/Chopwell, yeo. 36/4; Edward, bailiff 50/16; Henry, late of *Spittalhaugh*, yeo. 63/25; Lionel, late of Thornborough/Chopwell, gen. 36/4: 41/8: 60/15; Thomas, late of Hawkhope/Chopwell, gen. 36/4: 60/15: informer 52/11; William, yeo. 26/1: late of the Eales, 34/2,4,6
Charneley, Robert, of Gateshead, draper 49/3
Chaytour, Christopher, of Durham, gen., JP 27*: 28/8: 340*; George, late of Whittonstall, yeo. 11/16: of Winlaton 99/25,28; Robert, lab.

Claye, Robert, of Whitburn, lab. 51/2; Thomas, lab. 50/17,18

Cla(y)ton, Dorothy, late of Winston, widow 95/11; John, late of Winston, yeo. 60/2; wright, Dorothy wife of App. 98; Thomas 89/22; William, of Gainford, yeo. 65/10

Cleadon 13*: 26/2: 47/2: 50/18: 51/1,2: 54/5: 63/9: 64/3: 65/10,11,14: 69/8: 77/10: 91/1,2: 92/22: App. 289–91; constable of 63/9; fines in 65/11,12

Cleasby 76/1

Cleatlam 31*: 66/1: 67/7; division of 24n.*

Clement, Ambrose, late of Winston, yeo. 97/5; Richard, clerk 89/7: 90/11: 90A/2

Clemet, John, of Ravensworth, trumpeter 4/2

Clennell, Andrew, gen. 63/7

Clerk, see Clarke

Clerkson, William, late of Jarrowclyff, yeo. 29/4

Clervaw, Richard 11/20

Clibborne, Ralph, late of Harraton, yeo. 63/3: 77/18,19

Cliff, John 64/1

Clifton, Gavin, servant 85/10

Cliston, Jane, widow 39/1

Clockburn in parish of Whickham 91/7,61

Clopton, William, of Sledwick, esq. 91/28: App. 145: Anne, wife of App. 146; junior, of Sledwick, gen. 95/11

Close, Richard, lab. 29/17: late of Eggleston, yeo. 36/4: 41/8: 60/15

Clugh, Christopher, bailiff 89/4: yeo. 99/14,23,24,26,27; Francis, late of Darlington, lab. 106/12; John, of Durham, shoemaker 1/5; Percival, deputy bailiff 89/4; Robert, yeo. 73/3

Coastley, Northd 61/12: 63/27

Coates, Edward 80/2

Coatham 13*: 34/4: 110/10: township of 93/35

Coatsworth, John, of Snowhope Close, yeo. 72/8: 73/16

Cock, Christopher, late of Houghton-le-Spring, yeo. 106/18; Margaret, late of Durham, spinster 56/2 (and see Cook)

Cockefeilde, *Henry 56

Cocken, Houghton-le-Spring 30*: 2/1: 52/7: 90/9: 93/5,6: 95/10: 107/17

Cockerton 2/3: 7/2,3: 93/22–24: App. 85; division of 24n.*; West, township of 93/35; constables of 60/4

Cockfield 3/4: 46/12

Cockfeilde, John, yeo. 52/2: Dorothy, wife of 52/2

Cockson, Anthony, of Pittington, gen. 95/11: Bridget, wife of 95/11 (and see Cookson)

Cokden, John 29/18

Coke, Richard, sheriff's bailiff 6/5

Cokkeclose [Lamesley] 22/4: 92/24

Cold Rowley 1/3: 36/5: 69/21

Cole, Ralph, late of Gateshead, butcher 85/10,13; Thomas, yeo. 65/10

Coleman, Christopher 89/8

Colepike Hall 36/4: 41/8: 60/15

Coles, Roland, of Eighton 58/19

Colleyrawe [Cockfield] 3/4

Collierley 7/1: 98,99,102,103

Collingwood, Cuthbert, late of Eppleton, gen. 61/1; George, of Eppleton, esq. 31*: 68A/2: 91/20: 92/24: 94/11: 100/11: App. 178: Jane, wife of 92/24: App. 179; Ralph, late of Newcastle, gen. 54/4; Robert, late of Gateshead, lab. 85/10,13 (and see Colynwod)

Collins (Collyns), William 68/19; William 69/34

Collyer, George, of Monkwearmouth 52/1

Collyn(g), Edward, late of Cleasby, yeo. 76/1; Richard, late of Longnewton, yeo. 29/13: 79/1; Robert, late of Durham, lab. 39/16

Colman, Richard 52/5; Thomas, yeo. 92/24: Barbara, wife of 92/24

Colmore, Clement, LLD 27*: 39–45, 47–52,55,56: 56/8: 57,58,60–63: 63/14, 23,24: 64,65: 65/8: 66,67: 67/2: 68/A: 68A/2, 3,5–7: 69: 69/1,32–34: 71: 71/9, 11,12,14,19: 72/A: 72A/2: 73: 73/14,16–21: 74–76: 76/12–20: 77: 77/22: 78,79: 79/5,6: 80,81: 81/16–18: 82: 82/20,21: 83: 83/15: 84: 84/19–23: 85: 85/13,15: 86: 86/12–15: 87: 87/31: 88: 88/26,30: 89,90: 90A/1: 91: 91/1,16,22,34,36,

Dabholme, N. Yorks. 76/1

Dacon, Robert, yeo. 91/14,48

Dacues, George, gen. 104/7

Daglees, Robert, late of Whickham, yeo. 68/11

Dakers [the Lord Dakers], Francis, of Whitehill Hall, esq. 91/29: 92/24: wife of 92/24

*Dale, *Edward, of Dalton, yeo. 108; Henry, late of Staindrop, yeo. 41/8: 95/11; James, late of Middleton Row, yeo. 87/15: 104/16; *John 7,11 (and see Dayle)

Dallyson, William, serjeant at law/JCP 24*: 25,29: 341*

Dalton 81/9: 89/7: 90/11: 90A/2: 108: common bakehouse at 90/11; division of 24n.*

Dalton, Dorothy, widow 84/8: Edward, of Gateside, yeo. 47/46; Ralph 26,30: 341*; William, yeo. 6/6

Damforte, George, late of Hett, yeo. 86/3

Danby on Wiske, N. Riding, Yorks. 26*: 31/1,3: Little 29/16

Dand, John, yeo. 95/11: Isabel, wife of 95/11

Dane, Thomas, senior, yeo. 65/10

Daniel [Ryton] 36/2: 99/25–27

Danyell, John 4/1

Darcy, Richard, late of Salthaugh [Grange] 56/1

Darley, John, late of Billingside, husbandman 20/5

Darling, Richard, of Chester, yeo. 106/1

Darlington, 17*,20*,24*,25*,26*,31*, 32*,35*: 2/3: 5/1: 7/5: 11/20: 12/2: 19/1,2: 25/4: 27/6–9: 28/7: 29/6,15: 31/7: 32/1,2: 37/5: 41/5: 42: 46/8: 60/15: 61/4,13: 63/26,28: 67/5: 68A/7: 69/25,28: 71/2,9–11,13: 73/11,21: 77/9, 10,20: 78/16: 80/2,4: 82/2,8,18,19: 83/5,13: 84/4: 85/1,21,22: 87/4,5: 88/19,25,26: 92/22: 93/2,30,39: 95/3: 98/19: 100/14: 101/7–13: 102/7,8,13–15: 103/3,4,20: 104/14: 105: 106/12,24: 110/26,28,29,31: App. 76–84; *Bull* at 87/5; division of 24n.*; market at 2/3; parish church at 12/2; road to 106/30; township of 75/25

Darlington, deanery of 85/21; parish of 100/17: bridges in 93/35; ward

8*,12*,13*,14*: 68/12: 77/15: 91/35: 102/15: 103/20: 104/8: west ward of 89/22

Darmansteid [Gilsland], Cumbd 25/10,11

Darnall, Anne, widow 92/24; Elizabeth, spinster App. 325; George, lab. 92/24: Janet, wife of 92/24; Lancelot, late of Satley, yeo. 101/9; Richard, yeo. App. 322: wife of App. 323; Thomas, of Lanchester, yeo. 95/11: Isabel, wife of 95/11; of Moorside, yeo. 92/24; William, yeo. App. 324

Darncrook [Gateshead] 23/7: 61/6: 108/2

Darn(e)ton, Alice, of Chilton, wife of John 58/16; Robert, husbandman 25/1: late of Whorlton, yeo. 88/3; Thomas, husbandman 25/1; William, lab. 25/1

Davis [Jefferson], George, late of Brancepeth, yeo. 69/10–12: servant 68/6,8,9,13,14

Davison (Davidson), Christopher, of Hetton-le-Hill, yeo. 76/9; Humphrey, constable 91/11: 93/28; Isabel,of Urpeth, spinster App. 247; James, late of Durham, yeo. 83/1; John 54/2; Lancelot, of Chester, yeo., constable 79/3; Margaret 91/19: 92/26: spinster 92/24; *Ralph, yeo. 84: of Morton/Norton, yeo. 99,102: constable 101/1,3: late of Billingham, yeo. 110/7: of Wolviston, yeo. 98/5: 101/2,3: Alice, wife of 98/5; of Bewley grange, yeo. 31/5; Richard, late of Hurworth, lab. 110/13; Robert, yeo. 61/13; late of Darlington/Norwich, gardener/yeo. 83/5; yeo. 87/11; Roland, late of Allenheads, lab. 37/5; Thomas 57/8: Anne, wife of 57/8; clerk 96/7

Davye, George, of Sigston, yeo. 27/7–9

Davyes, John, clerk 90/10

Dawson, John 60/9: lab. 60/3; *Miles, gen. 92: of Unthank, gen. 108; Ralph, of Cambois, yeo. 97/13; Richard, late of Durham, yeo. 29/1; Robert, yeo. 78/11; Roland, cobbler 81/3; William, late of Buckden, yeo. 61/13: yeo. 65/10; William, late of Durham, butcher 94/4

Day, John, lab. 29/17; Stephen, of

Dossey, Anthony, late of Stockton, yeo. 77/10: 82/17,22; John, late of Longnewton, yeo. 77/10: of Stockton, yeo. 72/3: 73/18; William, yeo. 106/23 (and see Tossye)

Dotchon, Anthony, yeo. 31/1,3

Douglas, John, late of Gateside, yeo. 99/17,18: late of Lamesley, yeo. 107/4

*Downes, *Brian 41; Ralph, of Hardwick, gen. 56/10: 60/10: Elizabeth, wife of 60/10; farmer 57/6; *Richard 14,15,22

Douthwhaite, John, of Headlam, yeo. 39/4; late of Willington, yeo. 105/9

Doxford, Northd 29/16

Draver, John 108/5

Drew, Margery 63/20

Drummell, John, late of Bishop Auckland, lab. 106/15

Drummer, William, of Alwent, yeo. 98/29

Dryburn [Durham] 87/22: 104/19

Dryburnhalgh, Northd 18/1

Drydon, Peter, late of Riding, yeo. 81/13; Robert, late of Whickham, yeo. 83/6

Dubdill, Isabel, spinster App. 150

Duddoe [Norham], [Northd] 26/1

Dudley, Ambrose, 28*,29*: 47/3: esq. 91/64: 98: 98/15–21,23–25: 100/12: 341*; Henry, gen. 47/3; Robert, of Chopwell, esq. 28*: 47/3: gen. 38/15: junior, gen. 38/16,17

Duffeilde, Stephen 27/3

Dukk, Robert, lab. 23*: 20/3,4

Dukket(t), John, chaplain 30/4; Richard, kt 11/23; Robert, junior, late of Great Burdon, yeo. 73/4

Dunlopp, George, late of Gateside, yeo. 86/2

Dunne (Donn), George, late of the Quarrell', yeo. 81/7; late of Eighton lane end, yeo. 96/6; Henry, yeo. 60/1; John, yeo. 85/14; Ralph 106/3; Robert, senior, yeo. 85/14; Valentine, of Greatham, yeo. 82/22; William, yeo. 92/24: Mary, wife of 91/19: 92/24,26

Dunsforth, John, of Plawsworth, husbandman 11/1

Durham city 9*,10*,11*,13*,16*,19*,21*, 22*,30*,31*,35*: 1/5: 2/2,4–6: 3/9: 4/3:

11/4,7,14: 12/4: 17/4: 18/3: 22/2: 23/2,7: 24/3: 25/2: 26/3,4: 27/1: 28/6,8: 29/2,16: 30/4: 31/4,6: 36/1: 38: 38/6: 39/8,16: 40/4: 41/5,8,9: 42: 42/2: 50/19: 51/7: 54/2: 55/2,8: 56/1,2,6,10: 59/5: 60/1,11, 12: 61/2,10–13: 62/56: 63/22: 64/3: 65/1,10,22: 66/2, 14–18: 67/2,15,16, 20: 68/12, 19: 69/1,7,34: 72/1,2,4–7, 11,12: 73/12: 75/11,26–29: 76/10,11: 77/1,2,7,8,10,11,14,18,21,22: 78/10, 14: 81/3,4: 82/3,4,17,25,26: 83/1,10, 12: 84/4,11: 86/5,10: 87/8,32: 88/11, 13,24: 89/8,13,17,23,24,29: 90/6,10: 91/33,39,50,51,54,55,62, 63: 92/16: 93/25,32,34,35,40,41: 94: 94/2–7: 96/15: 97: 97/1: 98: 98/8,10,18,20,26: 99: 99/16,22: 100/2: 102,103: 103/8: 104/8,10,13: 105,106: 106/3,7,10,31: 107/1, 14–16,21: 108/7: 109: 109/1,2: 110/12,14,17–19,27: App. 188; alderman of 56; bailiff of 12/5: 18/3; bp's bakehouse at 98/26: 101/6; bridges at 46/13; fair at 82/25,26; castle at 9*,12*; Claypath In 72/7: 82/25: 92/13,16: 101/6: highways 87/22: 98/26: 100/18, 19,22: 101/6; House of Correction at 18*,33*: 91/11: 93/28: 96/9; market at 1/1; market place at 91/45; mayor of 63/22: 106: 107/24: 108: 110/23; North Bailey in 76/5: 77/1: 78/10: 110/18; Saddlergate in 6/6: South Street in 21*: 11/14: 106/10; stocks at 93/14 (see also Elvet, Framwellgate, Gilesgate, Kepier)

Durham, county of (palatinate) 11*,20*, 22*,28*; assizes at 9*,11*, 18*,23*; attorney-general of 10*, 24*,34* (see also Cooper, Robert; Smith, William); chancellor of 9*,19*,20*,21*,23*,24*, 27*,28*,32*: 38/27: 54/5: chancery at 7*,9*, 23n.13*; coroners of 11*,12*,18* (see also under Coroner); county court 11*,18*: 47/13,15 (see also under sheriff); court of pleas 7*, 8*,9*,11*,32*: 47/20: 50/16; exchequer at 11*: 58/1: 65/14,15; gaol at 10/1: 41/8: 43/3: 47/13,15: 52/4: 63/3,22: 75/27: 78/14: 80/4: 83/12: 84/4: 86/5,6: 87/32: 93/26: 95/7: 97/15: 102/25,26: in castle of 18*,19*: 77/11: 85/9: 88/24: 91/3,6,46: 92/22: 103/11: 104/11: 110/17; gaol delivery

bandman 22/1: juror 56/10; *William, of Hutton, yeo. 38–40,42,44,45

Elizabeth I 28*

Ellison, George, of Tudhoe, yeo. 87/6; Henry, yeo. 92/3; John, of Chilton field, yeo. 29/16: of Shield Row, yeo. 29/16: 33/8; Robert, of Durham, yeo. 29/16; Thomas, yeo. 92/3

Ellott, Arthur, late of Fishburn, lab. 86/11; John, yeo. 83/12: Anne, wife of 83/12

Elrington, Northd 62/15

Elrington, John, of Northumberland, gen. 46/5; yeo. 12/3; Thomas, of Espershields, gen. 12/4; William, late of Esper Shields, gen. 62/15,16

Elsdon, Northd 40/4

Elsdon, Robert, late of /herd of *Mott'*, yeo. 36/4

Elstob 39,42: 102/15: 107/6

*Elstobb, Anne, spinster 85/1; Elizabeth, late of Darlington, spinster 85/1; *Humphrey, of Bishopton, gen. 102: of Redmarshall 98/8,22; John, gen. 84/10: of Foxton, gen. 93/9; *Ralph 26,27; Richard 85/1: Elizabeth, wife of 85/1; Robert, of Foxton, gen. App. 26; Samuel, late of Darlington, yeo. 85/1; *William 11; constable 102/27; lab. 20/3,4

Elton 77/10

Elvet [Durham] 30*: 98/22: 103/18: 105/10: 108/8: 110/7,23: App. 417–19; New App. 369–77; Elvet, Old App. 361–68; bridge 18*,29*: 46/13: 93/35; par. St Oswald, 60/1,11,12: 61/2: 87/22: 91/41: 92/24: 93/4,18,35: 95/11: 100/1: 107/7: 108/8: 110/7,23; bridges, 93/35

Elwen, William, of Headlam 65/10

Elwick 10/2: 76/4: 81/11: 82/12: 110: bridges in parish of 93/35

Ely, liberty of 7*

Embleton 16*: 37,42: 92/24: 105–107, 109

Embleton, William, chancellor of Durham 9*

*Em(m)erson, Adam, of Gatecastle, yeo. 26/5; Arthur, late of Brotherlee, yeo. 41/11,15: 64/8,9: 66/2,5,7: 68A/,5,6: 69/14–16: of Stotfield Burn, yeo. 59/9; *Brian, of Eastgate, yeo. 16*: 39,45,48,52: collector

107/8; Christopher, late of Durham, lab. 62/5,6; Cuthbert 58/8; *Edward 16*: 17,44,45: late of Gate Castle, yeo. 7/17; George 72/15: bailiff 74/17: late of *Craig*, yeo. 61/9; junior 83/3: late of Eastgate, yeo. 83/4,7: 84/2:85/15: of Shipleyburn 51/4: late of Newcastle, artificer 59/9; Henry, late of Bradley, yeo. 13/1: 14/1: late of Stanhope 17/1; 64/9: late of Brotherlee, yeo. 66/2–5: 68A/5,6; Hugh, of Weardale 17/5; John 69/14,16: yeo. 66/2: 68A/6: 82/15: yeo. 81/15,18: yeo. App. 88; Margaret, widow of John 69/14,16; Mary, of Tunstall 95/11: 100/10; Nicholas, of Brotherlee, yeo. 67/17; Ralph 58/2: son of Hugh, yeo. 17/5: of Shotton, yeo. 63/17: late of Eastgate, yeo. 110/6: of Witton Gilbert, yeo. App. 344; *Richard 17: 6/2: 25/8: bailiff 74/17: lab. 106/4; *Robert, of Eastgate 17: of Ireshopeburn 17; *of Willington 10,11: late of Esh 1/3; husbandman 25/1,4; of Ludwell, yeo. 26/5: of Stanhope, yeo. 17/5; late of Sunderland, yeo. 83/3,4: 84/2,3: 85/15,16; Roland, yeo. 32/5: of Rookhope, yeo. 28/9: 58/5; *Thomas, yeo. 16*: 40,83: of Darlington, gen. 42,105; 25/8: 58/10: lab. 83/3,4,7; *William, senior, 17: of Esh, yeo. 31/2: of Stotfield Burn, yeo. 52/8

Emond, Alexander, yeo. 64/3

Eppleton [Houghton-le-Spring] 31*: 10/2: 61/10: 68A/2: 91/20: 92/24: 94/11: 95/11: 100/11: App. 178–81

Erle, Robert, husbandman 29/3

Errington, Edward 88/20; John, late of Bewclay, gen. 46/4: yeo. 60/15; Matthew, late of Bewcastle, gen. 61/12: 63/27; late of Stonecroft, gen. 36/4: 60/15; Reginald 52/2; Frances, wife of 52/2; Robert, late of Heaton, yeo. 40/4: late of Darlington, yeo. 60/15; 96/11; late of the Grange, gen. 63/7; sp. bailiff 95/7; William, late of Learchild, yeo. 63/4

Errisdell, William, yeo. 26/1

Eryholme, N. Riding, Yorks. 31/7

Escomb 47/41: 56/9: 91/5: 92/21:

Ferman, *Christopher, yeo. 40
Ferrefeilde [Stanhope] 27/5
*Ferrour, *John 15*: 13,18,19; *Nicholas 2,10; William 1/2: of Wiserley, husbandman 6/5
*Fer(r)y (Ferrey), Henry, late of Hett, yeo. 88/23; *John, yeo. 40; *Thomas 15*: 1,3,6,9,11; husbandman 25/1: collector 69/31
Ferryhill 25/1: 32/1: 45/3: 56/6: 58/18: 60/3,9,14; 106/19: 107/15
Fetherston, Cecily, late of Gilesgate, spinster 99/5,6; Cuthbert, of Middle Blackdene, yeo. 41/11,15; Elizabeth, widow 104/10; Jane, of Thornley, spinster App. 201; Nicholas, farmer 51/3: yeo. 38/17; Ralph, lab. 102/2: 103/21; Richard, yeo. 38/16
Fetherstonhaugh (Fethirstanehalgh), Cuthbert, bailiff 58/1: 81/5,6; family 16; *Guy 17; Henry, cousin of William Claxton 12/5: Eleanor, dau. of 12/5; *John, esq. 12,17: of Stanhope Hall, esq. 15/2; collector 41/16; esq. 41–48,50,51: 51/4: 54,60,62,64–66,68/A: 68A/5: 69,70: 72/8: 73: 73/16: 74/17: 76/18: 79: 83: 83/15: 85,86,88,90,91: 91/62: 92,93: 93/27,28: 94: 98/24,25: 100/12: 342*; late of Stanhope, yeo. 11/20; Ralph, esq. 10*: 100/7,16, 18,19: 102/3: 103–105: 105/14,16, 24: 106/28–30: 107/25: 342*; Richard, late of Stanhope, yeo. 11/19,20; of Wolsingham, yeo. 33/1; Roger, yeo. 75/6; William, of Stanhope 11/10
Fett, John, yeo. 26/1
Fewler, *Anthony, of Hartburn, yeo. 108; Elizabeth, spinster App. 48; George, of Billingham, yeo. 56/8
Fewster, Roland, of Durham, saddler 23/2 (and see Fuister)
Field Stile [Brotherlee] 64/9: 100/14
Fieldhead 64/9
Fieldhouse by Bishopwearmouth 60/13: 83/14,15: App. 13
Fields, see Feildes
Fildon Bridge 93/37
Finch(e), Anne, spinster 102/1: 103/22: 104/9; Elizabeth, wife of Peter 91/11: 93/28; Frithimond, spinster 100/1: 102/1: 103/9,22: 104/9; Hugh, yeo. 102/2: 103/21; Peter, of Wolviston,

yeo. 82/20: 91/11: 93/28: 101/1,2: 102/1,2: 103/9,21: 104/9: Edith, wife of 102/1: 103/9,22; Robert, son of 101/2,3; of Wolviston, yeo. 47/9: 77/10: 92/4: 101/3: senior, 102/1: 103/9,22; Mary, wife of 101/3: 103/9: 104/9; Toby, yeo. 104/9
Finchale 69/34
Findlay, see Fyndlee
Finley, Christopher 75/16: late of Staindrop demesne, yeo. 76/16; Luke, late of Alwent, yeo. 97/8: 99/29,30
Fishburn 14*,16*: 39,42: 86/11: 92/24: 107,110
*Fisheborne, *John, yeo. 54; *Lionel 23; *Thomas 12,19
Fitz William, Ralph 9*
Flamborough, E. Yorks. 28*
Flappiday, Philip, late of Ragby, lab. 102/16–18
Fleck, Richard, yeo. 87/11
Fleming, John, of Burtree House, yeo. 92/24: wife of 92/24
Fletcher, Agnes, of Norton, spinster 95/11; Charles, of Chester 47/72: yeo. 98/15; Gerard, of Lumley, yeo. 98/29; James 77/21: late of Gateside, yeo. 67/5; John, late of Bishopwearmouth, yeo. 91/15: yeo. App. 404; Richard, yeo. 77/10; Robert, yeo. 69/32; William, yeo. 90/7,14
Flockton, N. Yorks. 40/4
Floure, John, of Witton Gilbert, yeo. 95/11: Elizabeth, wife of 95/11
Foggan, Anthony, of Brancepeth, lab. 104/11
Foggart, Matthew, of Washington, yeo. 105/8; Thomas, late of Washington, yeo. 67/6; William 88/10: late of Ryton, yeo. 99/14,23
*Follancebye, *Henry 29,31,34; *Thomas 7
Follingsby 26/3
Foorde, Robert, of Bishopton, yeo. 64/3
Forcer, Thomas, of Harbour House, esq. 92/24: App. 336: Margaret, wife of 92/24: App. 337
Ford [Lanchester] 69/18: 73/14,15: 92/24: 95/11: 98/29: App. 299,300,317,318
Ford, Northd. 9/1,2: 26/1: 61/12: 63/27
For(e)man, *Christopher, of Hurworth, yeo. 38; late of Wackerfield, yeo. 75/25; Jane, widow 95/11; John,

Gainford 29*,31*: 49/5: 60/2: 65/10: 69/25,28: 71/9,10: 92/24: 95/11; parish of 97/6–8: 99/29; 106/30: bridges in 93/35

Gaire, William 73/7: 75/2

Galleley (Galile), James, of Gateshead, butcher 19/5; John, of Chester 96/6; Robert, late of Lintz Green, yeo. 65/3; Thomas, of Urpeth, yeo. 56/12; William, of Bradbury, lab. 28/3

*Gamylsby (Gamylsey), *John 1; senior 8: 11/17

Gaole, Thomas, lab. 32/2

Garbett, — , of West Auckland, yeo. 98/24; Garbett/Waugh, Anne, wife of — /spinster 98/24,25; Robert, yeo. 65/10

Gardiner, William, late of Ford, yeo. 61/12: 63/27

Garfoote, Laurence, late of Midd-ridge, lab. 59/8; Michael, wheel-wright 92/24: Margaret, wife of 92/24: App. 339

Gargrave, Dorothy 106/18; *John, of Helton, yeo. 106,107; 47/22; Richard, collector 99/4; William 99/21: late of St Helen Auckland, yeo. 93/40

*Garmond(i)sway, *John, yeo. 60,61,83; *Richard 12

Garner, John, late of *Southfeildes*, yeo. 39/10

*Garnett, — , gen. 93/35; Anthony, gen. 88/19; *Christopher, of Eggles-cliffe, yeo. 38,47; Cuthbert, late of Darlington, tinkler 67/5: 68A/7; *Henry, yeo. 20; James 30/2; John 38/26; Michael, late of Blackwell, gen. 83/13; Robert, of Blackwell, gen. 83/13: 88/19: Anne, wife of 83/13; William, late of Sedgefield, tinkler 67/5

Garretlee, Northd 36/4

Garrys, *Ralph 22–24,26

Garshopp, Gerard, late of Lintz 18/2

Garstell, Thomas, late of Low Wem-mergill, yeo. 49/5

*Garth, Cuthbert, late of Neasham, yeo. 61/1; *George, of Newbiggin, yeo. 104: 77/3; Janet, widow App. 91; *William 45: gen. 66: 61/1: of Headlam, gen. 97; yeo./gen. 92/24: Margaret, wife of 92/24: App. 128

Garthorne, *John 36,93: of Landieu, yeo. 103/23; William, of Wolsing-ham, yeo. 87/18

Garthwaite, Michael, late of *North-wastes*, yeo. 61/11: 67/2,4

Gascoigne, Henry, of Hallgarth, gen. 47/1: of *Hill*, gen. App. 342; John, of Lamesley, gen. 48/7; Richard, of Kibblesworth, gen. 47/1: 102/28,32: 103/19; Thomas, of Hillhead, gen., wife of App. 269; William, late of Darlington/Sedbury, kt 87/4: 88/26

Gascon, Nicholas, yeo. 64/11

Gate Castle 74/17

Gateshead/Gateside 10*,12*,17*,24*, 28*,32*,35*: 7/6: 16/1: 19/5: 22/3,4: 23/6,7: 29/8,10: 39/15: 40/4: 47/15, 21,46: 49/3: 50/10,11: 52/2: 55/4,5: 56/4,7,11: 57/3: 61/13: 63/15,25,28,29: 64/3: 65/10,22: 66/10,11: 67/5: 68/14, 18: 68A/7: 69/22–24,33: 73/6: 77/18,19: 80/5: 81/7: 85/10,13,17: 86/2: 89/28: 91/14,48,49,65: 92/22,24: 93/11,26: 95/11: 98/22,28: 99/17,18: 100/3,25: 102/19,28–32,34: 103: 103/19: 105/6, 19: 106/6: 109: 110/5,17,19: App. 295,296; alehouse keepers at 28*; bailiff of 18/5; constables at 102/32; moor 98/28: highway on 110/17; parish of 108/2

Gaunless, coal-pit at 75/25; river 95/10: bridges over 93/35

Gaynes, *Christopher, of School Aycliffe, gen. 97,103; William 97/2

Gaynford, George, of Wolsingham, yeo. 65/10

Gellesfield [Whickham] 72/9,10

Gent, Thomas, of Newton Bewley, yeo. 96/7

Gibbett Knowle 39/8

Gibbon, cf Gybon

Gibbsneese 88/12

Gibside 47/65: 92/24: App. 267

*Gibson, Agnes, servant 6/8; Archi-bald, yeo. 65/10: late of Fugar House, yeo. 77/12: 87/7; Brian, yeo. 41/3; Cuthbert, yeo. 65/10; Henry, 107/24: yeo. 106/23; sheriff's bailiff 39/5: deputy bailiff 68/12; of Bishop Auckland, yeo. 77/15; Henry, of Sunderland, yeo. 95/7; Janet, spinster App. 136; John, lab. 6/8; yeo. 47/16: yeo. 77/10: yeo. 92/24: Dorothy,

Haggerston, Helen, spinster App. 383; Henry, of Haggerston, esq. App. 380; gen. App. 381; Hugh, late of Barnard Castle, yeo. 60/2; Mary, spinster App. 382

*Hagthroppe, *John 15*,16*: 24,25, 28–31; *Robert 15*: 13,18,19

Haley (Hayle), Laurence, late of Durham, yeo. 25/7: 28/8

*Hall, Barbara, spinster App. 419; Charles, late of Durham, yeo. 82/26: junior, yeo. 90/10; *Christopher, of Trimdon, gen. 105; late of Hetton-le-Hole, yeo. 85/2; late of Shincliffe/Newcastle, yeo. 39/2,17; of Wingate Grange 25/10,11: John son of 25/11; Cuthbert 95/2: Elizabeth, wife of 95/2; Dorothy 43/6; *Edward, yeo. 28*: 36,37; Elizabeth, spinster App. 374; late of Crawcrook, widow 68/10: 88/10,14,15,30: 89/27; Francis,of Neasham, Margaret, wife of App. 9; Gilbert 86/10; Henry, lab. 106/28; late of Penshaw, yeo. 76/3,15; Isabel, spinster 106/28: late of Framwellgate, widow 108/10; James, tailor 34/1; Janet, late of Hesleden, widow App. 66; *John, of Greencroft, gen 26,27,30,31,33: of Birtley, gen. 34: juror 67/2: yeo. 68/10; John 98/23: late of Bowes, yeo. 40/4: late of Osmond Croft, yeo. 60/2; late of Chester, lab. 110/11; of Finchale, yeo., bailiff 28/2; bailiff 86/6: yeo. 88/10; late of Hollingside, gen. 53/5: 71/8: gen. App. 12; late of Middleton Row, yeo. 90/4,5; Margaret, of Neasham, widow 92/24; Michael, late of Townfoot, yeo. 36/4; *Nicholas, yeo. 93: of Elwick, yeo. 110; Ralph, of Benfieldside 43/4,6: of Cleadon, lab. 51/2; of Greencroft, gen. 91/30: 92/24: 93/35: Alice, wife of 92/24; yeo. 104/9: Margaret, wife of 104/9; Richard, informer 93/29; late of Black Dene, yeo. 75/5; Robert 93/2; late of Chester-le-Street, lab. 38/5; [Blewcapp], late of Thornley, yeo. 62/10,11; Thomas, of Fulwell, lab. 51/1: of Stranton, lab. 29/17; William, of Durham, draper 40/3: mayor of Durham, JP 107/24: 342*;

[Mickle Will], late of Elsdon, yeo. 40/4; late of Shincliffe/Newcastle, woolmonger 39/2,17; late of Kealees, yeo. 36/4

Hallgarth [Durham] 47/1

Halliday, Anthony, of Chester 47/74; George, late of Sunderland by the sea, yeo. 96/11: Alice, wife of 96/11; John 96/11: late of Sunderland by the sea, miller 105/7

Halliman, John, of Lumley, yeo. 106/1: Susan wife of App. 263; Martin, of Lumley, gen. 100/12; Thomas, late of Bewley Grange, yeo. 93/17; *William, of Morton/Norton, yeo. 99,102,104

Halmote courts 11* (see also under Chester-le-Street, Evenwood, Houghton-le-Spring, Lanchester and Wolsingham)

Halnth' 91/63

Hambleton, John, late of Alwent, yeo. 97/7

Hammour, William, late of Bishop Auckland, lab. 66/13: Agnes, wife of 66/13

Hamsteels 46/3: 63/14: 98/29: App. 319

Hamsterley 47/38,40: 61/13: 63/28: 87/1: 95/11: App. 106,107,286; bridges in parish of 93/35

Hangingwells Fell [Stanhope] 83/3: 84/2: 85/15,16

Hannon, Peter, sp. bailiff 86/5: 87/32

Hanson, William, of Trimdon, yeo. 95/11

Haram 92/24: App. 168,169

Harbottle, Guygerd 16/2; Jane, spinster 65/9; John, lab. 25/2: of Prudhoe, yeo. 31/3; John, of Tughall Hall, gen. 26*: 29/16: gen. 31/1: junior of Beckley 31/3; Lionel, yeo. 65/9; Margery 100/11; Michael, late of Tughall hall, yeo. 33/7; Percival, of Chester, yeo. 72/9,10; of Glendale, gen. 29/16; late of Tanfield, gen. 57/5: 65/5–7,9: 67/19: 75/27: Anne, wife of 65/9; Ralph, late of Chester, gen. 74/16; of Danby on Wiske, gen. 27*: 31/1,3: yeo. 33/7,9; Richard, yeo. 26/2; Robert [Sodron Robert], of Prudhoe, gen. 23*: 16/1; late of Chester-le- Street, gen. 76/5;

late of Ravensworth, yeo. 106/5: 107/5; Roger, of Beckley, gen. 26*: 29/16: 31/1; yeo. 81/7; Roland, gen. 26*: 29/16; Thomas, late of Chester, gen. 42/4: 63/7

Harbour House [Durham] 41/9: 47/16,18: 62/11,14: 67/2: 72A/1: 73/17: 82/23: 86/14: 88/7: 92/24: App. 336–39

Hardcastle, William, late of Sunderland by the sea, yeo. 77/13

Harderwick, Northd 37/5

Harding, Isabel, spinster 92/24: App. 266; Ralph, of Hollingside, esq./gen. 100/7: gen. 92/24: App. 265 (and see Hardyn)

Hardware, Robert, servant 72/13,16: late of Alwent, yeo. 97/6

Hardwick by the sea [Monk Hesleden] 56/10: 60/9: App. 225–28

Hardyn(e), Bernard, yeo. 67/9: of Staindrop 68/12; Robert, late of Staindrop, yeo. 68/12: Mary, wife of 68/12 (and see Harding)

Harnisha [Wolsingham] 38/13

Harper, John 27/1: husbandman 25/1

Harperhill [Gilsland] 25/10,11

Harperley [Witton-le-Wear] 92/24; 106/13: App. 101,102

Harperley, Richard, late of Elton, yeo. 77/10; Thomas 73/5: late of Bishop Auckland, lab. 83/8

Harraton 23*: 26/2: 29/2: 50/16: 63/3: 77/19: 79/3: 82/9: 92/24: 95/11: 110/4

Harrett, Henry, yeo. 92/1; Thomas, late of Berwick, yeo. 80/3; of *Cockesclose* 92/24: wife of 92/24

Harrington, Henry, of Harperley, gen. 92/24; Petronella, wife of 92/24; Robert, of North Bedburn, yeo. 95/11: Mary, wife of 95/11; Thomas, gen. 92/24

Ha(y)ton, John 91/1,2

*Harrison (Herryson), — , yeo. 29/16(*bis*); Anne, widow 78/11: widow 81/14,17; *Anthony 17; Christopher 29/19: late of Lumley, husbandman 29/4,7; 66/7: 69/14,16: late of Yarm, pedlar 80/4; George 58/12: 68/2: 82/16: of Easington 47/37; Henry, yeo. 81/14,17; John, 42/4: sheriff's bailiff 38/27: 58/17; deputy bailiff 43/4,6; yeo. 75/28,29: senior 89/6,16 (*bis*): John,

son of 89/16: William son of 86/16; of Allendale, chapman 46/14: of Chester, chapman 46/14; of Whickham, yeo. 29/16; Lancelot, yeo. 29/16; Margaret, widow 92/24; Nicholas, yeo. 29/16: 72/14; Peter, late of Whickham, yeo. 84/13; Richard, lab. 99/25: yeo. 26/2: yeo. 41/3; yeo. 29/16: of Summerhouse, yeo. 75/25; of Woodhouses, yeo. 105/12: Anne, wife of 105/12; Robert, yeo. 93/3; of Durham, yeo., bailiff 67/20: 82/26: 87/32: 88/24; bailiff 77/11: 86/5: late of Whickham, yeo. 50/15: lab. 81/14,17; *Roland 17; Thomas, of Northumberland, yeo. 25/3: yeo., bailiff 28/2; 32/2: 34/2: 89/13: servant 78/8: servant 85/10: yeo. 26/2; *William 41; 50/9: 69/14,16; late of Durham, yeo. 81/4; late of Eldon, yeo. 93/3; 96/14: of Tudhoe, yeo. App. 160

Hart 39/9: 50/5: 52/9: App. 69,70; bridges in parish of 93/35

Hart(e), Elizabeth, widow 92/24; Ralph, lab. 52/10; William, lab. 52/10

Hartburn 39/1: 75/2: 108; East 69/6; West 76/1

Har(t)borne, John, late of Layton, lab. 74/2,8,10,14; late of Sedgefield, yeo. 74/9; Robert, yeo. App. 260

Hartington, Northd 104/2

Hartlepool 52/9: 56/10: 95/11; 104/9: App. 71,72,385

Harton 82/15: 83/14,15: 89/14: 107/22

Hartred, Cuthbert, of Barnard Castle, yeo. 65/10

Harvie, Margaret, widow App. 49

Harwood [Teesdale forest] 29/12

Harwood, Cuthbert, of Barnard Castle, gen. 39/16

Haswell, Little App. 184

Haswell, Henry, late of Wolviston, yeo. 91/8: 93/27; Robert 53/5: 99/11; Roger, yeo. 77/10

Hatfield, Thomas, bishop 7*,8*

Hatherton, Northd 36/4

Hattersgyll, Cumbd 29/11

Haughton 96/19: App. 182; bridge 108/2

Haughton field 32/2: 34/2,6

Haughton-le-Skerne 73/1: 78/17; division of 24n.*; parish of 97/2: bridges 93/35; parishioners of 101/4

Hauxley (Haukesley), John 88/10; of Smalleys, yeo. 29/16

Haveloke, John, late of Melkridge, yeo. 29/11

Haward, Charles, yeo. 26/1

Hawdon, Henry, of Auckland, tailor 56/6; Robert, yeo. App. 114: Barbara, wife of App. 115; William, constable 110/18; of Bishop Auckland, tippler 64/1,10: yeo. 92/5

Hawick, Walter 9*

Hawkhope, Northd 36/4: 41/8: 60/15

Hawkins, John, coroner 35/1: 37/5: 40/4,5: 59/11: 60/15: 72A/1

Hawkwell, John, coroner 41/17

Hawthorn 95/11

Haydon Bridge, Northd 26*: 31/1,3: 34/2,4,6

Hazon, Richard, of Easington 47/39

Head, Nicholas 100/1: late of Croxdale Mill, miller 100/5,6

Headingley, Yorks. 78/3

Headlam 39/3: 61/1: 65/10: 92/24: 97: App. 124–28

Heafeild, Margaret, spinster 92/24

Heardman, Henry 54/2

Hearon, *John 51; Matthew, yeo. 104/15 (and see Heron)

He(a)th, John, esq. 27*: 38,40, 42–47, 49,54–57: senior 59,60, 62–64,66,74, 79–81: 81/16: 82: 82/21: 83: 84/1: 85: 85/13,15: 86,89: esq. senior 81/13: 82/11: 88: 88/26: 90: 98/23: 342*; Thomas, gen. 82/14: 84/22: of Kepier East Grange, collector 97/14: 100/12

Heaton, Northd 40/4

Heaviside, see Heviside

Heawe, Gerard, lab. 28/3

Hebburn 63/24: 69/2,3,5: 91/23: 92/24: 94/10: 95/11: 100/27,28: App. 351–58

Hebburn, family 27*; Richard, esq. 24,26,27,31: 342*

Heckley [Hatherwicke], Richard, lab. 51/2

Heddon, James, late of Shincliffe, yeo. 60/11; Robert, late of Shincliffe, yeo. 60/12; William, of Bishop Auckland, yeo. 99/21

Heddrington, Roland, husbandman, Alison wife of App. 241; Thomas, late of Edyssgil, lab. 25/12

Hedgbanck 96/15

Hedley 31/1: 67/14: Hall 29/16

Hedley, Elizabeth, of Lintz Green, widow 91/21: 92/24: App. 273; Mark, yeo. 81/10; Nicholas 59/9: late of Lintz Green, gen. 43/12: 44/3; Robert, yeo. 29/1: of Winlaton, yeo. 65/10; Roland, lab. 30/1

Hedleyclough 66/18

Hedleywood, Northd 22*: 12/3

Hedworth 26/2: 56/6: 65/10

Hedworth, Anthony, late of Whickham, gen. 56/5; Charles, of East Brandon, gen. App. 155: Elizabeth, wife of App. 156; of Little Usworth, gen. 92/24: Elizabeth, wife of 92/24; Christopher, gen. 82/10: of Herrington, gen. 43/8; Isabel, late of Middleton Row, widow 87/12; John, esq. 27*: 38: 343*; kt 63/3: of Harraton, kt 82/9: 92/24: 95/11: Jane, wife of 92/24; of Harraton, gen. 26/2; of Cockesclose, gen. 56/5; of the Deanery, Chester, gen. 50/16: Jane, wife of 50/16; of Ryton Woodside, gen. 36/2: *John 28*: 45: 102/19: of Ravensworth castle, yeo. 91/48; Katherine 100/11: of Chester, spinster App. 397; Ralph 23*: 30,31: 343*; gen. 56/5: 82/10: late of Whickham, yeo. 84/7; Richard, late of Darncrook, gen. 61/6; late of Pokerley, gen. 82/10: 87/3: Alice, wife of 87/3

Heighington 56/6: 86/8: 89/19: 92/24: 99: App. 164–67; bridges in parish of 93/35: church of 69/19: 71/19; moor 24n.*

*Heighington, John, of Hillhouse, yeo. 98/18; of Hutton Henry, gen. App. 229: Alice, wife of App. 230; late of Whinhouse, yeo. 98/19; Philip, late of East Merrington, yeo. 109/3: 110/1,24; *Richard, gen. 13*,14*: 40,60,61,92; Robert, late of Durham, yeo. 81/4; *Thomas, yeo. 91,96; William, late of East Merrington, yeo. 110/3

Heighley Hall [Winston] 104/12

H(e)ighley, John 107/11: of Great Chilton 60/9; *Richard 41,47,51; William, of Whorlton, yeo. 29/20

Helco(t)t, Anne, spinster App. 127; John, yeo. App. 119: Agnes, wife of

App. 120; William, yeo. App. 126

Helme Park [Wolsingham] 43/11: 59/3

Helmeden raw 43/3: 83/9: 106/31

Helmington [Newton Cap] 39/10

Helmysley, William, lab. 25/1

Henderson, Cuthbert, collector 104/7; Ralph, late of Harraton, yeo. 110/4; William, of Whickham, yeo. 57/1

Hendrie, George, of Lemington, lab. 30/5,6; Robert, of Walbottle, husbandman 30/5,6; William, lab. 30/5,6: of Berwick Hill, lab. 30/5,6

Henknowl 13*: 37/4

Henman, Elizabeth, late of Layton, spinster 74/2,3,5

Henry II 7*; VI 21*; VIII 25n.*

Henshaw, Northd 41/17

Hepple, Ralph, yeo. 51/2

Heron, *John 58 (and see Hearon)

Herrington 37,42: 43/8: 78/17: 92/20: 95/7: 96/16; 106; West 85/8: 99/12,13: 109; division of 24n.*

Herrington, George, late of Staindrop 75/16

Hesleden 37,39: 57/4: 97: App. 66: hall 52/9: 87/31: 98/3

Heslopp, John, yeo. 26/1: yeo. 65/19

Hett 47/23: 86/3: 88/23: 96/14; division of 24n.*

Hetton 103,105–107

Hetton-le-Hill 75/22: 76/9

Hetton-le-Hole 77/10: 85/2: 91/38,42; 106/8,18; division of 24n.*

Heugh [Lanchester] 31/2

Heviside, Richard, of Bishop Auckland, yeo. 64/10: 77/5: bailiff 89/22

*Hewitson, James, late of Staindrop, yeo. 67/1; *John 15*: 2,3,5,7,9; Laurence, late of Darlington, yeo. 88/19; Thomas, lab. 99/4; *William 15*: 13,19 (cf. Hugison)

Heworth 29/6: 50/18: 96/4,5: App. 359,360

Heworth, William, yeo. 102/32 (and see Hueworth)

Hexham, Northd 36/4: 60/15: 81/13: 87/22; liberty of 7*

Heyfeild, Margaret, spinster App. 70

Hickson, Anne, of Mordon, widow 92/24: Eleanor, daughter of, spinster 92/24: Margaret, daughter of, spinster 92/24: William, son of, yeo. 92/24; Edward, of Preston-le-

Skerne, yeo. 28/6; John 50/12: late of Hurworth, yeo. 75/3: of Wolviston, yeo. 64/3; yeo. 92/24: wife of 92/24; Robert, of Aycliffe, gen. 95/11 (and see Hixon)

Hickson/Hegson, Richard, of Preston-le-Skerne, yeo./gen. 34*: 91/22: 110/21

High constables 12*,14*,17*; oath of 12–13*

*Highe, *George, of Wolviston, yeo. 99; *Thomas, of Tudhoe, yeo. 94; late of Crook mill, miller 42/3

Highstead Eshe, Cumbd 36/4

Highwood, Lanchester 85/3: 87/24

Hilderton, Thomas, of Whitehouse, gen. 25/2: 26/4

Hildreth, John, of Piercebridge App. 112: Mary, wife of App. 113; Mary, widow 92/24; Philip, late of Piercebridge, yeo. 105/23

Hill App. 342: House 66/6: 98: 98/18

Hillhead App. 269

Hillis, John 89/20

Hilton, township of 75/25

Hilton, George, of Hylton, gen. 23*: 16/2; Henry, of Hylton, esq. 94: 76/12: 87/31,32: 88/18: 95/7,10: 96/13: 100/11; 105/7,8: 343*; John, esq. 107/10; Lancelot, bailiff 47/5; Nicholas 47/5; Richard, late of Durham, cordwainer 89/8; Robert, yeo. 77/10; Roger 26*: 31/2: Christabel, wife of 26*: 31/2; Thomas, esq. 23*: 38: 343*; late of Bishopwearmouth, yeo. 76/14; William, esq. 22*,23*: 16,17: of Hylton, esq. 15/1,2: 16/1: 343*; 98/23 (and see Hylton)

Hil(d)y(e)ard, Christopher, gen. App. 400; Jane, widow 92/24: of Fulforth, widow App. 399

Hinde, John, of Blackburn 93/29 (and see Hynde)

Hinson, Gregory, yeo. 91/14,48; John, of Ravensworth, yeo. 91/14,48; Lionel, yeo. 91/14,48

Hinton, *John 30

Hirdman, William, late of Monk Hesleden, yeo. 106/24

Hirst, George 68/19: 69/34

Hixon, Anne of Preston, spinster App. 416; Edward, of Preston-le-Skerne, gen. 85/18: yeo. 28/3: 29/1,2; John, juror **67**/2; late of Preston-le-Skerne, husbandman **29**/3; Richard, late of Preston-le-Skerne/Lumley Park, gen. **109**/5: **110**/21; Robert, late of Kirk Merrington, yeo. **77**/10; William, of [...]stone, yeo. App. 415 (see also Hickson)

Hobkirke, Archibald, lab. **106**/18

Hoblin, William, yeo. **38**/17

Hobson, Anthony, yeo. **65**/10; James, of Lumley, yeo. **92**/19; John, junior, yeo. **96**/14; Mark **89**/19; Nicholas, parish clerk **60**/1,11: late of Elvet, yeo. **60**/12; Thomas, late of Gainford, yeo. **60**/2; late of Hett **88**/23

Hode, Edmund, of Gateside, yeo. **64**/3; Thomas, yeo. **95**/11 (and see Hudd)

Hodge, Adam, yeo. **56**/11; Ralph, late of West Auckland, yeo. **60**/5–7; of Cleadon, yeo. **64**/3; William, yeo. **50**/17

*Hod(g)shon (Hogeson), *Christopher, late of Wales Moor, yeo. **90**/8; *Cuthbert, yeo. **47,54,66,80**; Dorothy, spinster **92**/24: of Whitehill, spinster App. 346; Edmund, of Fenham, yeo. **16**/1; Edward, late of Framwellgate, glazier **103**/8; late of Spen **63**/28; Eleanor, spinster **92**/24; Francis, yeo. **95**/11; George, yeo. **95**/11: Mary, wife of **95**/11; late of Bishop Auckland, yeo. **73**/13; of Hollybush, yeo. **98**/29; Guy, of Prudhoe, yeo. **16**/1; Hugh, junior, late of Softley, yeo. **97**/11; James, late of Birtley, yeo. **77**/14,21; Jane, spinster **92**/24: App. 347; John, of Manor House, gen. **91**/24: **92**/24: **94**/9: App. 297: Jane, wife of **92**/24: App. 298; tailor **55**/8; yeo. **69**/27; yeo. **106**/1; Juliana, widow App. 37; Michael, late of *Harderwick*, lab. **37**/5 Nicholas, bailiff **85**/1,9; Peter, yeo. **76**/12; Richard **91**/5: **106**/1; Robert **47**/20: Alice, wife of **47**/20; of Hebburn, esq. **63**/24: **91**/23: **92**/24: **94**/10: **100**/28: App. 351: Anne, wife of **92**/24: App. 352; Samson, of West Boldon, — **26**/2; Thomas **106**/1; yeo. **77**/10; Vincent **46**/8; William, gen. **92**/24: of Hebburn, gen. **100**/27: App. 353

Hodgson [Jackson], Isabel, wife of Thomas **58**/17

Hogg, Adam, late of Gellesfield, alehouse keeper **72**/10; late of Whickham, yeo. **99**/19: Margaret, wife of **99**/19; Robert, yeo. **91**/14,48; William, late of Barnard Castle, yeo. **62**/3

Hole Row, Northd **76**/6,18,19

Holland, Henry, of Beamish, gen. **24***: **23**/1

Holliday, John **76**/12

Hollingside **53**/5: **71**/8: **92**/24: App. 265,266

Hollin Hall [Stanhope] **93**/21

Holly Bush [Lanchester] **46**/3: **98**/29

Holmside **10***: **52**/4; lane **72**/9: **77**/16

Holte, Cuthbert, late of Wardley, yeo. **81**/1,16; William, late of Gateshead, yeo. **100**/3

Holtbie, Robert, of Stanley, gen. App. 280: wife of App. 281

Holywell **68A**/1: App. 151–54

Homes, Richard, late of Penshaw, yeo. **76**/3,15

Hood, see Hode, Hudd

Ho(o)pe, Richard, yeo. **91**/14,48; Robert, of Moorsholm, yeo. **28**/3

Hopkirk, William, lab., Scot **26**/1

*Hopper, Alison, spinster **76**/6,19; *Anthony, of Towdy Pots **103**: yeo. **107**; late of White Kirkley House, yeo. **72**/8: **73**/16: Isabel, wife of **72**/8: **73**/16; Christopher, yeo. **95**/11: Alice, wife of **95**/11; of Iveston, yeo. **92**/24; of Newbiggin, yeo. **95**/11: Margaret wife of App. 307; of West Hall, yeo., Alison wife of App. 334; Cuthbert, yeo. **76**/18: of *Lawtowne*, Margaret wife of App. 326; Hugh, of Durham, draper **55**/9; Jane, widow **92**/24: App. 377; Janet, widow App. 365; *John **48,91**: yeo. **96**: of Collierley **98,99**: juror **67**/2: yeo. **72**/8: **73**/16; Michael, yeo. **95**/11: Jane, wife of **95**/11; Nicholas, late of Benfieldside, yeo. **87**/29: of Lintz Green, yeo. **56**/12; *Richard, of Coundon, yeo. **110**; *Robert, of Witton **103**: **93**/3; draper **92**/24: App. 368; late of Durham, yeo. **55**/8,9; Samuel, of Shincliffe, yeo. **68**/19: **69**/34; Thomas **48**/5: of Hole Row, yeo. **76**/6,18,19: Margaret, wife of 76/18; William, of Towdy Pots, yeo. 65/17; of Wolsingham, yeo. 72/8: 73/16: 92/11: 93/22

Horncliffe, Northd 28/1

Hornby, co. Richmond, N. Yorks. 22*: 12/1,5

Horne, Anthony 93/10; John, of Wolsingham, yeo., alehouse keeper 92/14; Ralph, of Wolsingham, yeo. 29/16

Horner, John, yeo. 91/14,48

Hornesbye, Andrew, late of Milton, yeo. 47/7,8

Horsley, Henry, of Stockley, yeo. 30*: 61/8; Jane, widow 92/24; Robert, lab. 106/28; Thomas, of Old Elvet, gen. App. 361: Jane, wife of App. 362

Hospital of St John Baptist [Barnard Castle] 29/20

Houghall [Durham] 106/10

Houghton, manor of 69/30

Houghton-le-Side 50/12: 105/10

Houghton-le-Spring 32/3: 43/1: 84/18: 92/24,25: 93/5,6,25: 95/7: 106/18; halmote at 69/13; parish of 90/9: 107/17: bridges in 93/35; poor of 92/20: 99/13: rector of 84/18

Howdenshire, Yorks. 8*

Howe, Ralph, late of Carterthorne, yeo. 98/24,25; 99/9; Thomas, yeo. 99/8: 100/26: Margaret, wife of 98/24,25

Howson, William, late of Shotton, yeo. 68/7

Hubbock(e), George, late of Greatham, yeo. 55/7; Robert, of Haydon Bridge, yeo. 26*: 31/1,3; William, of Durham, yeo. 89/17,24

Hucknold, Oswald 47/2: of South Shields, yeo. 47/14: 95/2: Mary, wife of 47/14; Tobias, constable, yeo. 95/2

Hudd, Edmund, yeo. 65/10 (and see Hode)

Hudlei, Robert 26/5

Hudson, Edward, yeo. 47/2; John 103/12; late of Lumley, husbandman 29/1: late of Woodstonehouse, yeo. 29/7; Thomas, 103/11: gen. 95/4,5,8

Hudspeth, Christopher, late of Durham, yeo. 75/28; Edward, tanner 25/7; Thomas, late of Darlington, yeo. 77/20; Toby, yeo. 75/28,29

Hueworth, Robert, yeo. 41/3 (and see Heworth)

Hugh(e), Patrick 84/17; William 106/7

Hugison, Henry, late of Barnard Castle, yeo. 97/4 (cf. Hewitson)

Hulam 98/20; East 98/3

Hull, Elizabeth, widow 95/11; Henry 98/11: yeo. 105/22; Mark, of Esp Green, yeo. 69/17: carpenter App. 303: Elizabeth, wife of App. 304; William, of Hurbuck, yeo. 92/24: Agnes, wife of 92/24

Huller Bush [Barnard Castle] 82/16

Humble (Hommell), Anthony, of Daniel, yeo. 36/2: 88/10; Arthur, yeo. 31/1,3: 88/10; George, yeo. 36/2: late of Daniel, yeo. 99/25,26; John, of Crawcrook, yeo. 99/25; late of Whickham, lab. 77/17: 88/10; Richard, of Daniel, yeo. 99/26,27; Robert, yeo. 36/2; Thomas 80/1: 88/10: 104/8: yeo. 69/9

Humfrey, John, sp. bailiff 77/11: of Bishopton 93/33

Hunnam, — 66/9

Hunstanworth 68/3: 77/17: 91/55: 95/11

Hunt, Richard, dean of Durham 34*: 102: 102/1,2,12,14,33: 103: 103/18–23: 104/15: 105/11,14: 107/7: 108/12: 110: 110/1,4,5,23,30: 343*

*Hunter, Alexander, lab. 65/20,21; Anthony 47/20; James, late of Durham, fuller 91/33; *John, of Medomsley, yeo. 94; Richard 91/41; Robert, churchwarden, yeo. 47/19; lab./yeo. 92/24: App. 218: wife of 92/24; Roland, of Medomsley, yeo. 47/20; *Thomas, yeo. 84; 47/20: Katherine, wife of 47/20; William, yeo. 85/14 (and see Huntour)

Huntergroome, Thomas, of Lamesley, yeo. 91/14,48

Huntley, James, late of Bishopton, lab. 69/6; Ralph, junior, yeo. 98/11; Thomas, of Carham, yeo. 26/1

Huntour, David, lab., Scot 26/1

Hunwick 39/10: 105,109

Hurbuck 92/24

Hurst, see Hirst

Hurwood Loning, parish of Whickham 91/14

Hurworth-on-Tees 38: 64/3: 75/3: 88/19: 92/24: 97; 110/13; App. 209; West 91/51; parish of 100/17: parishioners of 105/11

*Ja(c)kson, Alice, wife of William 58/17; Arthur, of Holmside lane, lab. 72/9,10; Arundel, late of Whiteley, husbandman 3/7,8; Barbara, spinster App. 255; Bartholomew, yeo. 104/5: 105/18; Brian, yeo. 77/13; Charles, of Baldersdale, yeo. 85/3; Christopher, late of Broom House, yeo. 63/20; Edward, yeo. 26/1; Elizabeth, spinster 102/16–18: late of Richmond, widow 107/14; Frances, spinster 95/11; Francis, 100/28: yeo. 85/3; George 47/10: 98/17: bailiff 47/5: lab. 51/1; of Elstob, yeo. 102/15: 103/20; Henry 102/18: junior, yeo. 95/6: late of Woodifield, yeo. 95/6; *John 13: of Elstob, yeo. 39: gen. 42; *of Embleton, yeo. 107: *of Billy Row, yeo. 108; *of Middridge, yeo. 109; yeo. 31/5; yeo. 92/24: Agnes, wife of 92/24; of Billingside, yeo., Agnes wife of App. 313; Laurence, yeo. 102/15: 103/20; Margaret, of Newbiggin, spinster App. 327; Nathaniel, gen. 64/7: late of Darlington, yeo. 87/4: 88/26; Ralph, of Darlington, draper 102/15: 103/20; of Elstob, husbandman 29/5; of Gilesgate, glover 93/14,15; Richard, of Hamsterley 47/40: late of Hutton, yeo. 56/1; of Sunderland, fisher 31/6; Robert, yeo. 26/1; Thomas 29/17: yeo. 50/16: yeo. 95/11: App. 259: wife of 95/11; Toby/Talbott, of Shotton, yeo, 85/3; William, lab. 102/16–18: yeo. 50/17,18: 51/1,2: 52/4; junior, late of Broom House, yeo. 75/24,26: yeo. 78/8; late of East Boldon, yeo. 91/56; yeo., Isabel wife of App. 166
James, **William**, STP, dean of **Durham** 10*,27*,31*,32*,34*: 38,41, 42,44: 44/2: 45–52,54–56: 56/8: 57–63: 63/9,14,23,24: 64,68/A: 68/18: 68A/1–7: 69/1,32,34: 70,71: 71/11,12: 72/A: 72A/1,2: 73: 73/14–21: 74: 76/ 12–16,19,20: 77: 77/22: 80: 80/4: 83: 83/13,15: 86: 86/8,12,13: 87: 87/31, 32: 88: 88/21,26,27,29,30: 89,90: 90A/1: 91: 91/1,16,22,34,36,37,46, 48–65: 92: 92/4,5,22–24,26: 93: 93/2, 3,5,6,26–28,35,37,38: 94: 94/9–11:

95/10,11: 96: 96/12,13,15–17: 97: 98/23: 99/29: 100/7,11,27: 344*
Jarrow 95/11; bridge rates at 98/7; manor of 98/7; parish of 96/4: bridges in 93/35
Jarrowclyff 29/4
Jarvies, Ralph, collector 91/15,16
Jeekell, John, yeo. 87/11
Jefferson, Anthony, lab. 51/2; Miles, churchwarden 68/16,17; *Richard, yeo. 83,84; Robert, yeo. 32/2; Thomas, of *Bowram house*, yeo. 101/11,12; William, of Whitburn, lab. 51/2
Jenison, Elizabeth, spinster App. 403; John, of Walworth, esq. 69/19: 71/19: Mary wife of App. 401
Jenkenson, Anthony, yeo. 29/5
Jilson, Henry 81/15,18
Joblyn, George 12/3
*Johnson, — , spinster 102/4; — , of Broomyholm, widow 92/24; Anne, spinster 102/4; Anthony 78/6; Christopher, lab. 32/2: late of Crayke, yeo. 102/3; *Cuthbert, of Hetton, yeo. 105; Edward, miller 26/2; Eleanor 100/11; George, gen. 92/24; yeo. App. 154; of Seaton, yeo. 105/14; of Twizell, gen. App. 242: Katherine, wife of App. 243; of West Hall, yeo. 68A/1; Gilbert 8/5; James, lab. 62/16; John 110/15: lab. 47/7,8; of Elvet, weaver, 92/24; of Fulforth, tailor 92/24; sp. bailiff 83/12: late of Newcastle, yeo. 86/7,12; of Stella, gen. 92/24: Dorothy, wife of 92/24; yeo. 26/1: 32/2: late of Whitfield, yeo. 41/3: 43/11; Katherine, of Twizell, widow 92/24; Lancelot, yeo. 47/19; Margaret 91/25: spinster 92/24; App. 245; Mariola 41/3; Michael, of Twizell, gen. 69/21: 88/28: 92/24: App. 244 wife of 92/24; Nicholas 77/16: gen. 92/24; Oswald, bailiff 98/8; Ralph, gen. 92/24; late of Piercebridge, yeo. 77/10; Richard 47/13; Robert, son of George 103/5,6: 105/14; late of Elstob, yeo. 107/6; 11/1: of Seaton Carew, yeo. 102/9; of Sedgefield, yeo. 41/3; Samuel 107/24: late of Sedgefield, yeo. 90/12; Simon, yeo. 59/10: late of Staindrop, yeo. 67/1,3; Thomas,

Unthank [Weardale], gen. 11/23; Alice, widow 27/5; Anthony 62/10: Jane, wife of 62/10; late of Hartlepool, yeo. 56/10; Geoffrey 46/11; Henry, of Ryton/Woodside, yeo. 64/3: 73/3; yeo. 65/10; James, of Ebchester, yeo. 66/8: 74/1; Lionel, of Unthank, yeo. 17/2: William, son of 17/2; Nicholas, yeo. 108/8: 110/23; Percival, yeo. 12/5; Peter, of Unthank, gen. 41/16; *Ralph, of Birtley, yeo. 102,104,110; late of Hylton, yeo. 57/8; of Rogerley, gen. 51/4; *Richard 60: of Pelaw, yeo. 102–104; *Roland, gen. 20,23; Thomas, of Consett, yeo. 29/16: late of Stanhope, yeo. 17/3; William, late of Billingham, yeo. 108/8: 110/23

Madewell, Patrick, chaplain 17/5

Maiden Castle 92/10

Mainsforth 31*: 67/12; 103/2,13–16

Mainsford, Edward, of Shincliffe, yeo. 68/19: 69/34; Hugh, yeo. 55/9; John, yeo. 77/10

Maire, Lancelot 89/15: 90A/3; Margaret, of Hardwick App. 228; Robert, late of Hardwick, gen. 60/10: App. 225: Grace, wife of App. 226

Maison, Gregory, bailiff 58/17

Makenea, Robert, farmer 106/29

Mallam, — , widow 92/24; Bartholomew, Anne wife of App. 176; John, yeo. 99/24: Mary, wife of 92/24; Ralph 22/2; *Thomas 17

Maland, Thomas, late of *Halnth'*, yeo. 91/63

Mallerie, William, esq. 67/6

Maltby(e), Francis 69/5: 107/18; Henry, bailiff 81/1,14,16,17: 82/10: 86/5: 87/32; 69/2: late of Durham, yeo. 77/8: 88/24; Robert, bailiff 12*: 47/15,19,20: 50/16: 52/4: 57/3: 63/3,24: 65/9: 67/21: 68/4: 71/12: 75/13,27: 77/11: 81/1,16: 82/9: 83/12: 96/11: 100/3: late of Gateside, yeo. 98/22; lab. 25/1; William, husbandman 25/1

Maneley, John, yeo. 11/13

Manie, John, late of *Brunckhillhaugh*, yeo. 68/3

Mann, Andrew, yeo. 91/14,48; Henry, yeo. 87/11; James, yeo. 87/11

Manners, Robert, lab./yeo. 92/24:

95/11: Anne, wife of 92/24: 95/11; yeo., Agnes wife of App. 291

Manor House [Lanchester] 91/24: 92/24: 94/9: App. 297,298

March(e), Thomas 88/20; yeo. App. 110: wife of App. 111; William 10/13: of Darlington, yeo. 19/2: of Durham, saddler 110/19

Marckham, George 91/45; Margaret 98/5; William 98/5

Margaret (of Anjou), queen 21*; [Old Margerett], widow App. 330

Marles, Edward, of Hylton, yeo. 38/11

*Marley, Henry, of (?)Harnisha, yeo. 38/13: late of Hylton, yeo. 76/13; James, of Middleton Row, yeo. 64/3: Anne wife of App. 47; John 47/61; Marmaduke, late of Newton, yeo. 91/8: 93/27; *Nicholas, of Pelton, yeo. 94,98,102; Ralph, late of Urpeth, yeo. 98/16,17; Robert, of Stockley 30*: 39/7: yeo. 61/8: 67/13; Stephen, clerk 20/1; Thomas 74/16; Widow, spinster 65/10; *William, yeo. 96; of Whitehill, yeo. 92/24; of Wiserley 3/1; of Wolsingham park, yeo. 29/16 (see also Merley)

Marshell, Andrew, late of Layton, lab. 29/9; George 93/23; late of Bedlington, yeo. 83/12: 85/14: 86/7,12: gen., bailiff 106/28; Henry 59/3; John, husbandman 2/3; Richard, of Denton App. 89: Anne, wife of App. 90; Thomas, late of Satley, yeo. 8/7: 11/21; Widow 46/9; William, late of Billingham, yeo. 58/17: 63/25: Alice, wife of 58/17; of Cockerton, husbandman 2/3; of Elvet, yeo. 30*: 61/2: Jane wife of App. 366; late of West Boldon, yeo. 37/1: 41/12

Martindell, John, of Old Park 38/12

Martocke, William, yeo. 56/7

Marton in Cleveland 19/1: 108/8: 110/23

Martyn(e), Edmund, lab. 29/17; John 47/12: late of Birtley, yeo. 57/8; Lionel, of Durham, yeo. 30*: 50/19: 69/7: farmer 72/12: 88/23; Richard 67/4; Robert 72/11; William, late of Birtley, yeo. 57/8

Marwood 63/2

Merrington, Westerton)

Merrington, Marmaduke, of Murton, yeo. 81/15,18

Metcalfe, Anthony, servant 72/13; Eleanor, spinster, 92/24; John, late of Lynesack, yeo. 59/4: yeo. App 63; late of Southside, yeo. 63/17; Margaret, spinster 92/24; Nicholas, late of Harton, yeo. 107/22; Roger 85/1; Sarah, wife of Ralph 103/18

Mettrik(e), James, yeo. 29/16; Ralph, of Redholme, yeo. 29/16; Richard, of Little Danby, yeo. 29/16; Vincent, yeo. 29/16

Meynell, Robert, esq. 23*,24*: 20–23: serjeant at law, 24–34: custos rotulorum 29/20: 344*

Michesoun, William, late of East Boldon, yeo. 87/9,10

Mickleton, Christopher, antiquary 21*

Middle Blackdene 41/11

Middleham, [Bishop] 3/6; bridges in parish of 93/35; park at 3/6

Middlestone 109/3,4,24,25

Middleton-in-Teesdale 6/2: 11/13,18: 48/1: 59/5: 85/11: 110/15; bridges in parish of 93/35

Middleton [One] Row 64/3: 75/11: 87/12–15: 90/4,5: 104/16–18: 105/20–22: division of 24n.*

Middleton [St] George 65/10: 100/24: App. 41–50

*Middleton, Adam, gen. 50/1,2; *Anthony, gen. 28/8: 33; Cuthbert, of Hetton-le-Hill, gen. 75/22; late of Middleton Row, yeo. 105/21; Edward, late of Ingleton, yeo. 110/27; family 20*; *George 16*: 56: late of Silksworth, gen. 50/1,2: 54/6; late of Killerby, husbandman 47/6; Henry, husbandman 25/1; John, gen. App. 190; of Blackwell, yeo. 36/3; Martin, of St Andrew Auckland 38/10; Ralph, of Seaton, gen. 74/16; Richard, of Tunstall, gen., Mary wife of App. 189; Robert 91/28: 92/24: yeo. App. 148; late of Thorpe Thewles, yeo. 75/1; *Thomas 16*,20*: 11: 9/11: 41,45; *of Durham, gen. 105,109,110; *gen. 61: of Seaton, gen. 103,104,106–109; of Belsay, esq. 76/18; *William 16*: 44; 50/6: husbandman 25/1; 105/12: of

Fulthorpe, yeo. 105/1: 107/25

Middridge 57/10: 59/8: 109; Grange 5: 11/1

Mil(n)burn, Alexander, late of West Brandon, lab. 11/3; Andrew, lab. 10/7,11; Anthony, late of Bors, husbandman 25/8; Edward, yeo. 106/28; Francis, informer 105/18; Gavin, late of Bedlington, gen. 106/29: yeo. 85/14; John, husbandman 25/8; Ralph, of Wolviston, yeo. 47/13; Robert, yeo. 29/16: 33/9: of Beckley, lab. 34/3; late of Bedlington, yeo. 66/9; Rose, widow 106/28; Thomas, of West Brandon, lab. 10/7,11

Mill, Robert, yeo. 85/14

Milles, Edward 99/12,13; George, yeo. 85/14

Millot, Robert, of Cocken, esq. 95/10: wife of 95/10; Thomas 345*

Milne Carr [Isle] 25/1

Milnehouse(s) 17/5: 105,108

Milner, [Stokall], John, late of Stockton, lab./servant 9/5; Robert, late of Monkwearmouth, yeo. 78/1; Vincent, yeo. 92/22; *William 9,10: of Aycliffe, husbandman 7/4,5; late of Darlington, lab. 27/6,8,9

Milton, Cumbd 46/10: 47/7,8

Mitchenson, see Michesoun

Mitforth, Christopher, esq. 98/3

Moderby, *Richard 3,9

Moyser, Ralph, of Ryhope, yeo. 93/25; Toby, gen. 68/19: 69/34

Molet, *Robert 11

Molyneux, Edmund, serjeant at law 23*: 20: 345*

Monk Hesleden 64/12: 86/1: 87/31: App. 231–37: parish of App. 228

Monkton 56/11: 76/2: 82/15

Monkwearmouth 39/3,6: 43/1: 44/2: 52/1: 65/10: 76/7,12: 78/1,9: 79/4: 102/33; bridges in parish of 93/35

Mood(i)e (Moody), John, yeo. 85/14; Richard, yeo. 104/6; William, of Tanfield, yeo. 31/2

Moor House [Durham] 2/2: 92/24: 98/23

Moore, Edward, constable of Gateside 80/5; George 46/7: of Escomb, yeo. 105/12: Jane, wife of 105/12; Henry, of Mordon, gen. 92/24: Eleanor, wife of 92/24; John, late of Flock-

102/10,11: App. 10–12,27–33: stocks at 98/6
Neceham, Thomas, husbandman 31/7
Nedem, Francis, of Newcastle, yeo. 29/16
Neden, John, yeo. 53/2
Neile, Richard, bishop 34*: 99/2: 102/3: 103/18: 104/15: 105: 105/13, 14,24: 106/30: 107/25: 110/1
Nelson, George, late of Marton 108/8: 110/23; Luke, late of Tollesby, yeo. 108/8: 110/23; Richard, yeo. 61/13: 63/28
Nesbitt [Hart] 29*: 43/7: 52/9
Netherton [Northd] 52/3: 71/3,4
Netherwitton, Northd 25*
Netherwood, John 78/3
Nettlesworth 16*: 92/24: 95/11
Nevell, Ralph, of *Milnehouse*, yeo. 17/5
Nevey, Cuthbert 107/11
Neville (Nevyll), Alexander, bishop 20,21*; *Arthur 23,29; Cuthbert, esq. 27/2; Henry, earl of Westmorland 26*: 30: 30/5,6: 345*; John, yeo. 26/1,2; Mabel, of *Denehouses* 64/4; Ralph, earl of Westmorland 20*,25*; nephew of, esq. 20*: 1,3–5,10,11: 345*; *Thomas, 17
New Bridge 91/18
Newbiggin 12/4: 37,38: 95/11: 103, 104: App. 307,327; West 61/3,5; [Northd], road from 107/8; in Norhamshire 65/20,21
Newbottle 40/1,2: 67/11: 69/13,30: 84/18
Newburgh [Tynedale] 1/3: 8/4
Newby, Francis 102/17
Newcastle upon Tyne 16*,25*,25n.*: 1/1: 9/7: 11/24: 20/6: 22/3: 23/7: 25/3: 29/1,10,13: 39/2,17: 59/9: 60/4: 71/13: 86/7,12: 100/25: 102/34; alderman of 28*; Hostmen's Company of 16*; mayor of 28*; sheriff of 28*
Newcombe, Michael 66/11; Robert, of Aycliffe, yeo. 65/10; William, late of Winston, yeo. 89/22
Neweham, John, late of Cockerton, husbandman 7/2,3; William, husbandman 7/2,3
Newfield [St Andrew Auckland] 16/3: 34/5: 91/7,61
Newhouses 108
Newland 6/5: 29/16: 93/16; [Northd]

36/5
Newland, John, butcher, 26/2
Newlandside 6/7
Newrawe 38/14
Newsham, Northd 33/7
Newton 41/9: 91/8: 92/24: 93/27: 97: 108/1,4; bridge 51/8; Little 82/17
Newton Bewley 96/7
Newton Cap 39/10: 72/19,20: 76/20: 94,102
Newton *Garthes* App. 183,293,294
Newton Hansard 75/2,8–10
Newton House 78/12
Newton (Neuton), Adam, dean of Durham, esq. 72/12: 78/8: 93/35; George 88/10; Henry, late of Stocksfield hall, yeo. 57/4; *John, yeo. 37: 62/15; Nicholas 88/10,14, 30; *Robert 8; of Monkwearmouth, husbandman 52/1; Thomas 104/2: yeo. 28/3; William 11/5; of Bradley, gen./yeo. 92/24: 95/11: Barbara, wife of 92/24: 95/11; of Gilesgate, yeo. 72/4; late of Ryton, husbandman 24*: 23/5
Nicholl, Richard, of Durham, merchant 27/1; Robert 73/5; Thomas 76/8: yeo. 89/1,2
Nicholson, Anne 99/5; Anthony, of Wheatbottom 95/6; Cuthbert 25/4; George, late of Gateside, smith 102/ 28,32: 103/19; James, yeo. 92/1,2; John, lab. 51/2: of *Helmeden raw*, yeo. 43/3; late of Winston, yeo. 88/12; *Martin, of Willington, yeo. 108; of West Rainton, yeo. 65/10; Robert, mariner 102/32; Thomas 63/19: yeo. 87/11; of Redmires, tailor 96/3; late of Witton-le-Wear 35*: 110/26; William, late of Bishop Auckland, lab. 75/30
Ni(c)kson (Nixon), Christabel, widow App. 367; Gerard, yeo. 16/2; John [Daudel John], late of Bewcastle, yeo. 60/15
Noble, Matthew 39/2: Margaret, late wife of 39/2; Robert, yeo. 41/3; Thomas, of Bewcastle, lab. 33/3,4,6
Nodder, *William 7
Norham [Northd] 9*,11*; castle at 11*,12*; parish of 105/13
Norhamshire [Northd] 7*,8*,24*: 65/20,21; liberty of 24/2: 26/1:

50/4; Robert 108/8: 110/7,23;
*William 58: juror 56/10: yeo. 66

Partus, George, late of Hart, yeo.
39/9: late of Newton, yeo. 108/1,4;
John, late of Newton, yeo. 108/4;
William, of Blakeston, yeo. 68/19.
69/34: 91/26: 92/24: 9ა/11: Helen,
wife of 95/11; of Wynyard, yeo.
105/1,2: 107/25,26: Eleanor, wife of
105/1; 107/24

Paterson, Gillian, of Middleton George,
spinster 65/10; Robert, of Durham,
barker 11/14 (and see Patti(n)son)

Paton, William, late of Hylton, yeo.
11/17

Patryke, John, lab. 29/17

Patti(n)son (Patteson), Christopher,
late of Whickham, yeo. 93/7; Cuthbert 90/6; Dorothy, spinster 110/14;
Henry, of Middle Merrington, yeo.
56/6; John, coroner 72A/1; of
Claypath, yeo., tavern-keeper 92/13;
of Durham, shoemaker 72/6: 92/16:
93/25; late of Greatham, yeo. 62/7:
Anne, wife of 62/7; late of Stanhope, yeo. 93/39; John, late of West
Auckland, lab. 46/7; Marmaduke, of
Stranton, yeo. 65/10; Oswald, yeo.
65/10; Peter, of Chester, yeo. 42/2;
Robert 7/10; Rowland 58/13;
Thomas, lab., Scot 26/1; William,
constable 88/18; yeo. 107/24: late
of Bishopwearmoth, yeo. 76/14;
late of Darlington, cutler 29/15
(and see Paterson)

Paull, Thomas, churchwarden 19/1

Pawle(r), *German 15*: 23–25,28–30

Paxton, Christopher 41/6; George,
junior, late of Hulam, yeo. 98/20;
Gilbert, of Easington 47/36; *Robert,
of Easington, yeo. 106

Peace in Durham 8*; clerk of 10*,
12*,17*,20*,22*,28*; keepers/justices
of 9*,10*: powers of 21–22*

Peacock(e), Dorothy, of Darlington,
spinster 41/5; *George, yeo. 47;
Richard, miller 98/29: yeo. 95/11:
Elizabeth, wife of 95/11; Robert,
late of Durham, butcher 94/2; late
of Greatham, yeo. 63/18

Peak Field 71/5

Pears, William 92/24: Anne, wife of
92/24

*Pear(e)son, Anthony, late of Hart-
ington, lab. 104/2; Eleanor 87/6;
Elizabeth 41/3; George, constable
63/22; late of Bishop Auckland,
yeo. 82/6; late of Brancepeth, yeo.
81/10; of Durham, cordwainer 76/11:
77/2,22; Henry, late of Gateshead,
lab. 85/10,13; John, yeo. 52/2 :
Jane, wife of 52/2; junior, yeo. 52/2:
Beatrice, wife of 52/2; yeo., wife of
App. 294; of Bradbury, yeo. 28/3,6:
yeo./husbandman 29/2,3; late of
Haydon Bridge, yeo. 34/2,4,6;
*Ralph 58; Richard, yeo. 41/3; of
Barnard Castle, lorimer 62/1,8;
Richard, of Coundon 48/5; late of
Raby castle, yeo. 62/13,17–19;
Robert, yeo. 17: 40; junior, late of
Durham, cordwainer 83/10; lab.
51/2: yeo. 29/1: 55/6; *Roger, of
Gateside 17*: 103: yeo. 109; Rowland, yeo. 52/2; Thomas, challon
weaver 56/4: of Gateside, yeo. 64/3:
65/10: 92/22; mayor of Durham, JP
63/22: of Durham, mercer 55/8,9;
senior, of Durham, mercer 72/11,12;
parish constable 88/20; *William,
yeo. 14*,17*: 91: of Sherburn, yeo.
94,99: of Whitehall, yeo. 98,107,108,
110; 76/7: husbandman 25/1; of
Lynesack, yeo. 65/10: 66/14; yeo.,
servant 55/8

Pearte, Cuthbert, butcher 66/18;
Francis, son of John, of Hedleycough,
butcher 66/18; George, late of West
Blackdene, yeo. 58/1,3; John, of the
Intack 81/5

Pearth, John, yeo. 26/1

Peate, Richard, yeo. 92/1

Pedam's Oak [Edmundbyers] 92/6

Peersye, Richard, yeo. 26/1

Peirce, John, of West Blackdene, yeo.
17/5

Peitpott Rayne [Barnard Castle] 33/2

Pelaw 102–104: 105/3,4

Pelton 47/64: 56/12: 94,98,99,102,
106: 106/2; App. 249,250; Grange
82/14: 84/22

Pemberton, George, late of Stanhope,
yeo. 29/16: late of Wolsingham,
yeo. 33/1; *Michael, gen. 40,61; of
Landieu, yeo. 92/24: Mary, wife of
92/24; Robert 52/4

20,22: 23/5: 25: of Shield Row, gen. 26*: 31/1; yeo. 29/16: junior 29/16; late of Beamish park, yeo. 48/1; junior, late of Shield Row, gen. 33/9; senior, of Shield Row, yeo. 29/16; William, of Shield Row, gen. 33/8,9: 91/19: 92/26: 92/24: Anne, wife of 92/24; of Tynemouth, yeo. 29/16

Potter, Brian, of Hutton Henry, yeo. 103/7: 105/15: collector 105/11; Christopher, of Darlington, yeo. App. 83: wife of App. 84; of Walworth, yeo. App. 405; George, yeo. 92/23; Isabel, of Whessoe 38/27; John 69/23: tailor 92/24: wife of 92/24

Pott(s), Anthony, yeo. 83/12: late of *Carrocke*, yeo. 36/4; Thomas, yeo. 85/14: 95/11: Isabel, wife of 95/11

Powle, Thomas, schoolmaster App. 358

Powleson (Pooleson), John, lab./yeo. 92/24: of Medomsley, App. 284: Mary, wife of 92/24: App. 285

Pratt, *Ralph 16*: 25–30,33,34

Preist, Cuthbert 106/17

Presson, Laurence 44/1

Preston-le-Skerne   28/3,6:   29/1–3: 85/5,18–20: 91/22: 92/24: 95/11: 109/5: 110/21: App. 416

Preston in Amounderness, Lancs. 33*: 96/10

Preston, *Ralph, yeo. 37,56; Thomas, late of St Helen Auckland, gen. 3/10: 4/3

Priorman, Cecily, spinster App. 165; Edward, lab. 21/1; George 107/3: 110/10; John, of Bradbury, yeo. 48/6; Richard, of Sedgefield, yeo. 48/3

Prissyke (Purssyke), Henry, husbandman 30/1; Matthew, husbandman 30/2; Thomas, husbandman 30/1

Procter, Isabel, late of Benfieldside, widow 87/23; John 69/31: Isabel, wife of 69/31; Nicholas, of Great Chilton, lab. 49/1

Proude, William, of Hunstanworth, yeo. 95/11: Agnes, wife of 95/11

Pruddoe, William, late of Bellbank, lab. 36/4

Prudhoe, Northd 11/16: 15/1: 16/1:

18/2: 31/3: 33/5,7; castle 22*,23*, 26*,27*: 12/3

Pudsay, Cuthbert, of Harraton, gen. 50/16; *William, kt 11

Pukers, Henry, yeo. 92/24

*Punshon (Punchdon), Edward 29/19: of Shincliffe, yeo. 93/18; Thomas, yeo. 30/1; *Robert, of Pelton, yeo. 99; *William, gen. 34,36; 69/27: of (West) Herrington, yeo. 78/17: gen. 95/7: 99/12,13; of Chester, yeo. 100/15

Purvent, Patrick, yeo. 81/7

Purveyes, Saunders 47/63

Pycher, John, of Thornley, yeo. 10/2

Pye, *Robert, yeo. 96: of Collierley, yeo. 98,99,102; junior, late of Greenlaw, yeo. 68/4

Pygot, Richard, king's sergeant 20*

Pykstones [Wingate] 19/4

Pynckney, George 50/8

P[...]ers, Atkin, of Urpeth, yeo. 56/12

Quarrell' 81/7

Quarrington 29/11: 68/19: 69/34: 78/15: 110/9; bridge 45/1

Quarry House 30/4

Quo Warranto proceedings 7*

Raby 20*: 12/5: 46/10: 59/10: 63/26: 65/10: 67/9: 72/16: 86/8; castle 50/3: 62/12,13,17; east park 62/17: 63/17

Rackwood Hill App. 103–105

Rackwo(o)d, Anne, spinster App. 105; *John 15*: 1,3,7,10; Robert, of Rackwood Hill, gen. App. 103: Margaret, wife of App. 104

Raffe, John, yeo. 95/11: Margaret, wife of 95/11

Ragby, N. Yorks 102/16–18

Raine, Andrew, late of Thringarth,, yeo. 39/12; Michael, of Shipley, yeo. 59/10; Nicholas, late of Marwood, yeo. 63/2

Rainton 10/2: 31/5: 85/2: 91/39; East 2/1; West 65/10: 96/10; pits 107/17

Raket(t), John, of West Butsfield, yeo., Janet wife of App. 315; John 15*,16*,20*,21*,22*: 12–18: chancery clerk 15*,346*; *junior 22–26,

Rethern, William 7/1
Reynold, Anthony, of Darlington, yeo. 92/22
Rice, Griffith, late of North Auckland, esq. 34/1
*Richardson (Recheson), *Christopher, of Archdeacon Newton, yeo. 104; late of Sunderland by the sea, yeo. 38/18,23; Christopher, of Weardale, yeo. 17/5; Cuthbert, lab. 25/1; George, barker 11/14; of Hutton Henry, yeo. 91/12; Henry, lab. 25/1: 28/3: late of Barnard Castle, yeo. 33/2; James, late of Gateside, yeo. 63/25,29; Joan, late of Bishopton, lab. 3/3: 4/5; *John 14,15: bailiff of Gateshead 18/5; esq., receiver 10*: 93/14–16,27,37–39: 346*; husband-man 25/1; junior 54/7: servant/lab. 3/1; late of Bishop Auckland, yeo. 67/5: 72/19; late of Darlington, lab. 63/26; late of Staindrop, shoemaker 72/13; *of Tudhoe, yeo. 94,102; of Wiserley, lab. 3/2: 4/4; Lancelot, 47/18: of Kelloe, yeo. 56/10: 62/11,14; Margaret, of Tuddoe, widow 92/24; Michael, of Durham 89/17,23,24; Nathaniel, sp. bailiff 83/12; late of Newcastle, yeo. 86/7,12; Nicholas 55/6: of Eldon, yeo. 38/9: Sitha, wife of 55/6; Oswald 86/4; Richard, barker 11/14; late of Seaton Carew, lab. 38/21,22: yeo. 88/27; *Robert 15,16; of Knitsley, yeo. 56/12; yeo., Margaret wife of App. 161; *Roger 14: yeo. 92/24: App. 25; Roland 6/4; *Thomas, of Hunwick, yeo. 105,109,110; 77/13; husbandman 25/1: yeo. 26/2; late of Newcastle, shipman 9/12; William 55/1; yeo. 29/16; yeo. 63/1; of Ferryhill, hus-bandman 25/1; of Moor House, yeo. 92/24: Helen, wife of 92/24; of Sedgefield, lab. 56/6
Richmond, N. Yorks. 31/7: 66/12: 92/18: 107/14; archdeaconry of 21*; county of 12/5
Richmond, *Christopher 48,49,52, 60: yeo. 66
Rickabie, *Henry, yeo. 37; Matthew, yeo. 87/1; Robert, of East Boldon, yeo. 26/2,3; William, of Stainton-le-

Street, husbandman 26/3
Rickless [Ryton] 99/25
Ricknall Grange [Aycliffe] 110/31
Riddell, Thomas, esq. 10*: 57: 57/3: 59,60,63,65,66,68/A–70: 85/10: 92/24: kt 106: 106/24,29–31: 107,108: 108/11,12: 109,110: 110/1,21,23,30: 346*: esq., Elizabeth, wife of 92/24; William 10*
Riddlehamhope [Hunstanworth] 81/13: 82/11; South 68/3
Riddyng House [Rogerley] 65/4
Riding 62/9,15,16: 83/2; [Northd] 81/13
Ridle(y), Christopher, late of Coast-ley, gen. 61/12: 63/27; Edward [Henhed], of *Dryburnhalgh* 18/1; Hugh, of *Aldshelis*, yeo. 18/1; John, late of Shotley Bridge, yeo. 98/2; John, of Walltown [Tynedale], gen. 11/22; Nicholas, of Walltown 18/1; Nicholas, of Willimontswick [Hex-ham] 17/4; Ranulph, of Yearhaugh, yeo. 18/1; Thomas, yeo. 11/22: of *Tiphaldwater*, son of Nicholas, yeo. 18/1; William, servant 17/4; late of Hawkhope, gen. 36/4: 60/15; of Staindrop, yeo. App. 109
Ripon, W. Yorks. 63/5
Rippon, *Humphrey, of Aislaby, yeo. 42; Martin, late of Satley, yeo. 101/10; William 85/6: husbandman 30/2
Rising of the North, see Earls' Rebellion
Robertes, Richard, yeo. 50/4; Thomas, late of Bishop Auckland, yeo. 59/6: 64/1
*Robinson, Agnes, of Shadforth, widow 92/24: widow 92/24; Alice, widow 92/24; Alison, widow App. 56; *Anthony, of Hawthorn, yeo. 98; Bartholomew, yeo. 107/24; *Bernard, of Herrington, yeo. 106; Christopher, yeo. 52/2; 108/10: of Brancepeth, lab. 97/15; Cuthbert, husbandman 25/1; late of Windle-stone, yeo. 88/29: 91/6: Elizabeth, wife of 91/6; *Edward 48,51; 96/5: late of Kimblesworth, yeo. 95/9: 96/13; late of Newcastle, yeo. 29/10; Eleanor, of Eppleton, spins-ter 68A/2: App. 180; Elizabeth, late of Darlington, widow 103/4; George, late of Bishop Auckland, yeo. 71/17:

Runtheweit, Thomas 33/2
Ruthall, Thomas, bishop 21*,22*
Rutherford, see Rotherforth
Rutter (Rottour), Alan, late of Middleton-in-Teesdale, yeo. 11/18; Christopher, yeo. 6/2; John, bailiff 86/6; lab. 83/3,4,7: 84/3: 85/16: 89/5; yeo. 95/11: Margaret, wife of 95/11; of New Elvet, pewterer App. 369; Roger, of Middleton, yeo. 6/2; William, yeo. 6/2: 11/13; husbandman 28/2
Ryhope 65/10: 93/2S: 97/10
Ryton 24*: 23/5: 29/18: 31/3: 41/17: 46/4: 64/3: 73/3: 75/15: 84/14: 89/27: 91/64: 99/14,23,25–28: 103/11; Woodside 39/13: 57/7: 99/28: close at 36/2: 73/3; division of 24n.*; parish of 99/2S
R[...],, Thomas, late of Little Chilton, gen. 60/9

Sadberge 30/1: 31/7: 52/5: 95/11; 104: App. 57–65; county of 22*: 6/2; wapentake of 8*,11*
Sadler, Philip, servant 71/2
St Andrew Auckland 34/S: 38/3,7,10: 44/1: 99/20; parish of 90/1,2: 93/3: 105/12: 109/6: 110/22: bridges in 93/3S; church way to 39/10 (see also South Auckland)
St Giles [Durham], parish of 93/14: 98/23: bridges in 93/3S
St Helen Auckland 2: 3/10: 4/3: 24/4: 47/4: 57/4: 59/1,2,7: 78/13: 85/9: 93/37,40: 98/13,14: App. 99,100; parish of 98/24: 99/8,9: 100/26: 101/11,12: bridges in 93/3S: 95/10: constables of 59/1
St John's Chapel, Weardale, Stanhope 41/11,15
St Margaret [Durham], parish of 89/13: 90/7,14: 100/22: App. 336–39
St Nicholas [Durham], parish of 63/22: 98/26: 110/18: constable of 88/20: poor of 92/13,16
St Paul's, London, deanery of 21*
Saire, Mary, spinster App. 140
Salkeld, Thomas, gen. 63/23
Salthaugh Grange, E. Yorks. 56/1
Saltwellside [Gateshead] 23/7: 26/2:

92/24: 100/8
Salvin (Salvayn), Anne, of Butterwick, widow 92/24: App. 22: William, son of gen. 92/24; family 27*; Gerard, esq. 24,27–30,34: 106/20: 346–7*; Roberta, of Thornton, widow 92/24
*Sam(p)son, *Edward 17; John 50/3; Leonard, yeo. 105/2; *Richard, of Pelaw, yeo. 102; Thomas, of Pelaw, yeo. 105/3,4
Sanderson, Christopher 48/7; Cuthbert, of Darlington, yeo. 101/13; Henry, of Brancepeth, esq. 68/6,8,9, 13,15: 69/11,12; of Brancepeth, gen. 97/15: Mary, wife of 97/15: Jane, daughter of 97/15; Jasper, roughmason 48/4; Robert 88/10
Satley 8/7: 11/21: 101/9,10
Sa(u)nders, Christopher, constable 62/9: yeo. 26/1; of Lamesley, yeo. 91/14,48; Cuthbert, yeo. 65/10; Edward, JCP, kt 24*: 25,29: 347*; yeo. 64/3: 65/10; John, lab. 50/17,18; of Lumley, lab. 29/19; yeo. 91/14,48; Leonard, late of Intack, lab. 81/4; Robert, late of Lamesley, yeo. 91/49; William 49/4: yeo. 65/10; of Eighton, yeo. 91/14,48
Saure, John, yeo. 63/10
Savage, William 103/9
Saweter (Sawyerde), John, of Bitchburn, yeo. 3/7,8: 6/3,4: 10/1; Thomas, of Durham, chaplain 2/6
Sawghell, Michael, late of Hylton, gen. 76/12
Sayer, Francis, late of Darlington, yeo. 61/13: 63/28; Peter, yeo. 64/3; *Samuel, of Mordon, gen. 107
Scathlock, Alice, widow App. 24; Robert, butcher 76/11; late of Durham, yeo. 104/8; Thomas, yeo. 28/3: husbandman 29/3; William 39/8
School Aycliffe 97,103
Scott, Anthony, late of Gateside, yeo. 61/13: 63/28: 65/10; George, senior, of Medomsley, yeo. 29/16: junior, yeo. 29/16; John, of Bishop Auckland, cooper 41/1
Scottish borders 7*
Scrafton, William 62/3,4
Scremerston [Norham] 24*,25n.*:

yeo. 65/10; Robert, yeo. 85/1; William, juror 67/2

Shawes 92/24

Shawfeild, John, of Choppington, gen. 42/1

Sheiffeild, George, gen. 105/9

Sheile, Nicholas, of Windyside, yeo. 58/1,4; Ralph 62/7

Sheleydale 56/11

Sheppard, see Shipperd

Sheraton 39

Sheraton, Robert, of Stockton, yeo. 31/5

Sherburn [Durham] 14*: 3/2: 4/4: 38/6: 61/11: 83/10: 94: 99; division of 24n.*; highway at 100/20; Hospital 86/3: 93/35: master and brethren of 94/1: 100/21; township of 93/35

Sheriff's tourn 14*

Sherwood, Christopher, late of *Grens...* 61/13: late of Brancepeth, yeo. 63/28; Edward, of Aldin Grange, yeo. 8/5; John, clerk 9/12

Shield Row 13*,16*,26*,27*,33*: 29/16: 33/7-9: 91/19: 92/24,26

Shields, South 17*,32*: 43/2: 45/2: 47/2,14,32,34: 71/1,6: 75/13: 89/14: 95/2: 104/3: 105/5,17: 106/16,21,22; courthouse at 71/6; mill 99/22; stocks at 95/2

Shieldshaugh [South Shields] 71/1,6

Shildon 42/3: 55/6: 89/3

Shincliffe 30*: 39/2,17: 50/19: 60/11, 12: 68/19: 69/34: 72/11,12: 93/18; bridge 93/35; mill at 39/2

Shipley 59/10: 77/6

Shipley, Thomas, yeo. 81/7

Shipleyburn [Bedburn] 51/4

Shipperd, John, constable 91/11: 93/28; late of Wolviston, yeo. 101/2,3: Mary, wife of 101/3; Thomas 84/12; William, yeo. 101/3

*Shipperson (Shepardson), *John, of Witton, yeo. 38,42,43,45; *of Wearmouth, yeo. 94: 60/13: 76/14: 96: 97/10; *William, of Wearmouth, yeo. 12*: 107; late of Sunderland, yeo. 77/13

Shirwenthousez 18/2

Short, Edward, late of Burn Hall, yeo. 100/1,5,6; John, husbandman 25/1; Matthew, late of Elvet, fuller 93/4;

Richard, yeo. 106/1; Thomas, yeo. 106/1

Shortrede, Richard, lab. 6/8; Robert, lab. 6/8; Roland, lab. 6/8; Thomas, yeo., wife of App. 167; William, lab. 6/8

Shotley Bridge 43/4: 47/49,50: 53/3: 87/27: 98/2; alehouse keeper at 26*

Shotton 63/17: 67/9: 68/7: 85/3: 110; [Northd] 61/12: 63/27

Shotton, Robert, husbandman 2/1; William, of East Rainton, husbandman 2/1: senior, yeo. 10/2

*Shotwell, *Robert 27,28,30,32; *Thomas 49: yeo. 91

Sideburne House, Brancepeth 89/6,16

Sig(ge)swicke, Christopher, of Wackerfield, yeo. 75/25; Henry, late of Whorlton, miller 88/1; John, yeo., bailiff 91/6; late of Thorpe Thewles, yeo. 74/15; Ralph 91/6: of Bellasis, yeo. 45/1; Richard, yeo. 32/2; Robert, late of Darlington, yeo. 95/3: Elizabeth, wife of 95/3; William 104/9: of Hedworth, yeo. 56/6

Siggesworth, John 75/1: 81/8: 82/21; William, late of Redworth, yeo. 61/3,5

Sigston, N. Yorks. see Kirby Sigston

Silksworth 25*,30*: 7/7: 8/6: 28/2: 32/3: 50/1,2: 54/6: 65/10; heiress of 20*

Silvertopp (Sivelltopp), Alice, of Chester 91/43; George 91/43; John, lab. 26/2; of Lamesley, husbandman 11/2; Marion, wife of 11/2; Thomas, late of Chester-le-Street, yeo. 77/10

Simms, John, of Elton, gen. 92/24: Jane, wife of 92/24

Simpson, Agnes, wife of John 77/8; Cuthbert, late of Burtree House, yeo. 97/2; of Ebchester 47/53; David, yeo. 51/2; Edward 47/20: 77/4: yeo. 91/7,61; Eleanor, spinster 95/11: App. 137; Gabriel, late of Blackwell, lab. 36/3; George, bailiff 69/9,26, 27,29; late of Birkby, yeo. 102/7; of *Law* 47/48: yeo. 56/12: 91/17: Isabel, wife of 91/17; yeo. 63/2: of Staindrop, yeo. 64/11; late of Woodham/Longnewton, yeo. 89/15:

Newcastle upon Tyne, yeo. 91/65; late of Sedgefield, lab. 41/4; junior, late of Waldridge, yeo. 57/8; Simon, late of Thorpe Thewles, yeo. 40/4; Thomas 9/5: yeo. 10/2; yeo. 16/1; of Newcastle, baker 1/1; mason 92/24; yeo. 65/10: late of Staindrop, yeo. 67/9; **William, esq.** 98/2: 99/2,13,26,27: 102: 102/3,12–14,33: 103: 103/18,19: 104: 104/7,15: 105: 105/3,5,14,16,24: 106: 106/24,28–30: 107: 107/24–26: 108: 108/11,12: 109: 109/5: 110: 110/1,4,5,21,23,30: 347*: esq., attorney-general 34*: 106/1,2, 28,29: 107/24: 108/9,10,12: 110/20, 23; *of Whitehall 6,26,31: of Esh, esq. 25/1; 9/2; bishop's bailiff 2/4: 58/17: 68/19: 69/34; lab. 26/2; 82/12: yeo. 40/1: 99/25,28;

Smith [Braybath], James, late of Goswick, yeo. 61/13

Smithson, Anthony, late of Fulthorpe, yeo. 96/20; Ralph, late of Wolviston, yeo. 91/8: 93/27

Smurthwayt, Christopher, of Durham, miller 30/4; Roger, late of Pixley Hill, yeo. 72/21

Smyrke, John, of Hutton, yeo. 10/2

Snagg, George 63/14

Sna(i)th(e), Cuthbert, of Witton-le-Wear 96/3; *John, of Witton Gilbert, yeo. 38,42,43,45,47: constable 107/2; William 75/24,26: of Burn Hall 93/4

Snawball, John, of Medomsley, yeo. 31/5; Thomas 62/16: yeo. 63/16; late of Durham/Crossgate, tanner 67/15: 76/10: 91/39

Snawdon, Anthony, late of Layton, yeo./lab. 74/6,9,11,12; John, late of St Helen Auckland, yeo. 85/9; Humphrey, of Mawsfield, yeo. App. 308: Jane, wife of App. 309; Ralph, lab. 51/2; Richard, yeo. 10/13

Snotterton [Staindrop] 107/12

Snow (Snawe), John, yeo. 92/22; Lionel 32/4

Snowclose [Stanhope] 32/5

Snowhope Close [Eastgate] 72/8: 73/16

Snows Green [Benfieldside] 87/24

Sober, Jane, widow, 92/22; William 79/1

Sockburn App. 34,35: parish of 95/11

Softley 97/11

Softley, Thomas, late of Gateside, yeo. 110/5

Somerside, *Leonard, of Chester, yeo. 17*: 104,106,107,109

Somerson, John 35/1

Som(m)er, George, late of Durham, yeo. 81/4; John, late of Bishop Auckland, yeo., alehouse keeper 89/20

Sonkey, Simon, bailiff 85/1: yeo. 77/15; Thomas, late of Durham, yeo. 106/7; William, bailiff 77/15

Soter, Thomas 103/3,4

Sotheron Closes App. 220

Sotheron (Sothorn), Alexander, of Hedley Hall, yeo. 29/16; Christopher, of Hebburn, yeo. 95/11: 100/28; Elizabeth 38/26; Hugh, of Darlington, yeo. 25/4; John, of Ravensworth, yeo. 29/16; Ralph, yeo. 65/10; Richard, late of Ravensworth, yeo. 83/2: 91/13; junior, yeo. 107/5; Robert, of Lofthouse Lintz, husbandman 9/11; Stephen 68/5; Thomas, lab. 26/2: of Ravensworth, yeo. 29/16

Soulby (Sowlebye), John, yeo., Dorothy wife of App. 341; Nicholas, of Winlaton, yeo. 99/14,23

Soulkeld, Nicholas, late of Over Coniscliffe, gen. 63/23

South Church [Auckland] 39/5: 59/2: 84/6,23: 99/20 (see also St Andrew Auckland)

Southfeildes 39/10

Southside 63/17

Southwick 26/2: 51/1,6

Southwick, see Suthwyk

South, Thomas, yeo. 78/11

Sowandburn [Stanhope] 27/5: 28/9: 90/13

Sowerby, John, of Barnard Castle, yeo. 91/34,35: mercer 91/3,4,37; Richard, late of Alwent, yeo. 104/6: 105/16; William, late of Barnard Castle, yeo. 91/35

Spaine, John, bailiff of Chester 43/4; William 73/6

Spark(e), Anthony 107/14; Edward, constable 53/1; *John, yeo. 94: of Tudhoe, yeo. 107; Nicholas, late of Tudhoe, yeo. 98/4,12; Robert, of

Greatham, clerk 31/5
Sparrow(e) (Sparroo), John 62/12,13;
Thomas, yeo. 26/2; William, yeo.
26/2
Spear, George, yeo. 65/10
Speck, Katherine 95/11
Spedling, Magdalen, widow 108/1
Spen 29/16: 61/13: 63/28
Spence, Cuthbert, late of Durham,
joiner 106/3
Spennymoor 48/5
Spicer, see Spyser
Spittal, Northd 61/12: 63/27;
[Tweedmouth, Northd] 80/3
Spittalhaugh, Westd 63/25
Spittle, Elizabeth, widow 106/29;
William, yeo. 85/14
Spoore, Ralph, of Esh, yeo. App. 287:
Margaret, wife of App. 288
Spurleswood (*Spirleswode*) 1/4
Spurner, Richard, yeo., constable of
Elvet 36/1
Spurrett, Marmaduke, of Little Eden,
yeo. 38/24,25
Spyser, William, lab. 21/1
Squire, Marmaduke, yeo. 95/11:
100/8
Stafford, Thomas, yeo. 96/11:
Margaret, wife of 96/11
Staindrop 31*: 11/6: 12/5: 40/4:
59/10: 63/12,26: 64/11: 67/1,3,9:
68/12: 72/13,16,17: 75/14,16:
78/11: 81/2: 89/21,22: 95/11:
98/29: App. 109–11: constable of
67/3; demesne 76/16; road 106/30
Staindrop, see Stayndrop
Stainton-le-Street 26/3: 91/53: 97;
Great 65/10: parish of 107/6; Little
85/9: 96/18
Staithes, N.Yorks. 40/4
Staneban(c)k(e), John, yeo., wife of
52/2; Widow, of Langton 65/10
Stanhope [Weardale] 9*,10*,11*,15*,
22*,23*,25*,30*: 6/7: 9/8: 10/6: 11/10,
13,19,20: 15/1,2: 17: 17/1–3,5: 25/5,6:
26/5: 27/5: 28/9: 29/16: 32/5: 41/16:
51/3,4: 54/7: 58/1: 71/18: 75/4–7,
12,17,24: 81/5,6: 83/3,7: 84/2: 85/15,16:
90/13: 93/39: 104/7,10: 107/8: 110/16:
App. 393; burn, bridges over 93/35;
court leet of 52/8; parish of 41/11,
15: 110/6: bridges in 93/35: church
of 46/1; park at 21*: 6/2,8: 11/9:

67/18: 74/17: 97/11; rectory at 15/2
Staninge, Florence, widow 52/2
Stanley 22/2: 85/6: App. 280–83,396
Stannington, Northd 44/1
Stapilton, Nicholas, yeo. 17/2; Roger,
of Bewcastle, yeo. 17/2; William
12/2: yeo. 19/1
Star Chamber 58/17
Starre, Mary 52/9
Starricke, William, late of Ovingham,
yeo. 50/15
Startforth, *Brian, yeo. 40; John 75/27
Staward, Christopher, late of Lead-
gate, yeo. 91/64
Stayndrop, Peter, of Heighington,
chaplain 10/3; *William 9,18
Steel House [Brancepeth] 95/6
Steel(e), Christopher 47/11; lab. 51/1;
Edward, yeo. 92/1,2; Richard, yeo.
92/1,2; Robert, late of Tudhoe, yeo.
98/12; William, late of Greatham,
lab. 53/1
Stella 92/24: App. 340,341
Stelling, *John 24,28; Robert, late of
Middleton-in-Teesdale, yeo. 59/5
*Stephenson (Stevenson), *Anthony,
of Neasham, yeo. 38; Christopher,
yeo. 11/6; George 106/12; late of
Durham, butcher 22/2; Humphrey,
late of Bishop Auckland, yeo. 92/3;
*John, gen. 84,92: of Byerside, gen.
107; 103/8; of Moor House,
husbandman 2/2: yeo. 16/3: lab.
26/2; Ralph, husbandman/yeo. 2/2:
11/6; Robert, 91/40; lab. 26/2: of
Bishopwearmouth, yeo. 91/15; of
Cleadon, lab. 51/1; late of Hylton,
yeo. 107/11,12: Anne, wife of
107/11,12; Thomas, of Durham,
butcher 2/2; late of Neasham, yeo.
102/10; Widow 99/18; William 94/8;
of Evenwood, husbandman/yeo.
2/2: 11/6; of Knitsley, husbandman
92/24: Frances, wife of 92/24; late
of *Romondby lonyng*, husbandman
3/7,8: 10/1
Stillington [Redmarshall] 95/11: 108:
App. 53: township of 93/35
Stobbert, Cuthbert 77/20; Samson
103/9
Stobbes, Christopher, yeo. 29/16; John,
forester 52/8: of *Streteyate*, yeo.
92/20; Robert, of Pokerley, lab.

58/15; William 69/14,16: collector 38/13: of Westgate, yeo. 51/3: 71/16
Stobbilee 13*,14*: 68/2: 106,108; East 89/29
Stockdaile, George, gen. 92/24: of Girsby, yeo. App. 36; Robert, late of Darlington, yeo. 61/4
Stockden, *Henry, yeo. 40
Stockley 30*: 6/6: 39/7: 56/6: 61/8: 67/13: App. 163
Stocks 98/6: at Gilesgate 93/14: at Neasham 98/6: at Norton 96/9: at South Shields 95/2
Stocksfield hall, Northd 57/4
Stockton 28n.*,30*: 9/5: 31/5: 48/8,9: 52/10: 60/2: 72/3: 73/18: 77/10: 82/17,22; 104/15: 110/30; division of 24n.*; highway 93/36; road from 96/12; ward 8*,13*,14*,16*: 47/13; 103/9
Stockton, George 107/24
Stockwelhewgh 93/6
Stoddart, — , of Brancepeth, widow 95/11; Edward, late of Darlington, cordwainer 82/18; John, yeo. 52/2: Katherine, wife of John 52/2; late of Bolam, yeo. 29/1; Robert 91/23: 94/10: yeo. 92/24; William, of Sherburn 38/6
Stoddry [Dinsdale] App. 75
Stodhoe [Dinsdale] 24/3: 25/2: 26/4; manor of 24*
Stoker, Anthony, late of Durham, litster 67/20; Edward, of Chester, yeo., constable 79/3
Stokhall, Henry, of Newburgh, husbandman 1/3; John [Godelad], husbandman 1/3
Stonecroft, Northd 36/4: 60/15
Stonyford 92/24
Storey (Storie), — , of Whickham, yeo. 56/12; Eleanor, widow App. 79; Francis, of Morton, Mary wife of App. 38; George, late of Durham, yeo. 90/6; Giles 24/2; Hugh, of Great Usworth, yeo. 65/10; Jane, late of Durham, spinster 69/7; *John, gen. 80; lab. 92/24: Elizabeth, wife of 92/24; 47/71: yeo. 65/10; of Gateshead, butcher 100/25; of Low Friarside, yeo., wife of App. 277; senior, yeo. 36/4: late of Rosedean, junior, yeo. 36/4; Matthew,

late of Garretlee, yeo. 36/4; Richard, late of Durham, litster 77/10: of Gilesgate, yeo. 64/3
Storke, William, late of Bishop Auckland, yeo. 77/10
Stotfield 92/4; burn [Stanhope] 52/8: 59/9
Stotfold [Elwick] 75/3: 82/20
Stotie, Edward, late of Chester, yeo. 69/27
Stott, *Thomas, yeo. 96: of Bitchburn, yeo. 98; 85/7: of Framwellgate, yeo. 93/34
Stowle, Thomas, yeo. 75/21
Strangwish(e), Guy, yeo. 38/15–17; Thomas, yeo. 95/11
Stranton 13*: 29/17: 65/10: 67/8: 71/14
Street Gate [Lamesley] 92/20
Stroderyaite [Winlaton] 27*: 33/5
Stuard, Thomas, yeo. 65/10
Styford, Northd 68/3
Suddick, Robert, late of Croxdale, yeo. 88/23: 95/11: Elizabeth, wife of 95/11; of *Sotheron Closes*, yeo., Elizabeth wife of App. 220; William, yeo. 56/9
Sumesgrave [Benfieldside] 69/31
Summer, see Som(m)er
Summerhouse [Gainford] 12/5: App. 129,130: township of 75/25
Sunderland Bridge [Croxdale] 16/3: App. 219; [Durham] 2/5: 6/6: 31/6: 51/8: 100/5: 106/19,20; in Weardale [Stanhope] 83/3,4,7: 84/2,3: 85/15,16
Sunderland by the Sea 7/8: 38/18,23: 77/13: 78/1: 92/22: 93/1: 95/7: 96/11: 97/10: 105/7: 106/23: 107/20
Sunniside 67/22
*Surtees (Suerties), Bertram, of Chester, yeo. 69/9; Christopher 41/5: late of Durham, mercer 82/25: yeo. 12/3; Marmaduke 56/8; *Ralph, yeo. 40,41,51,58,60,66; of Ravensworth, gen. 75/27: 93/12; *Robert, yeo. 61: 12/3: 69/29; *Thomas 11: gen. 110/11; William 47/58: late of Whickham, yeo. 108/9
Suthwyk, John, of Silksworth, yeo. 8/6
Sutton [Sotheron], Cuthbert, yeo. App. 357
Swa(i)nston, Anne, of Gainford, widow 92/24; George, constable 64/6; late of Norton, yeo. 106/27; late of

Teasdale (Teysdell), Richard, late of Slaley, yeo. 81/13; Robert, of Richmond, yeo. 31/7; Thomas, sp. bailiff 96/11; William, of Whickham, lab. 22/4: yeo. 65/10

Tebson, *William 2,10,11

Tedcastle, Thomas, yeo. 103/15,16

Tees, river 7*,8*,33*: 41/13,14: 60/2: 63/2,10–12: 75/14,16: 76/16: 88/1–5: 97/3–5,9: 103/10: 104/15: 105/23; bridges over 93/35

Teesdale forest 29/12

Telfurth*, Edward 24

Tempest, Elizabeth, widow 41/7; John, of Lambton, gen. App. 252: Margery, wife of App. 253; gen. App. 375; Nicholas, gen. 92/24; of Stella, kt, Isabel wife of App. 340; *Robert 11; esq. 23*: 20: 20/7: 24,26–28,30,31: 348*; Roland 19/6; Thomas 21*,23*: 16,17: 348*; William, of Jarrow, gen. 95/11; alehouse keeper 81/2: yeo. 78/11

Tenaunt, *Robert 14,15: bailiff of Durham 12/5: 18/3

Teneswood (Tenesworth), Walter, of Wolsingham, yeo. 92/12; William, of Wolsingham, yeo. 87/19

Tewer (Teuer), *Nicholas, of Heighington, yeo. 97,99; Robert, of Heighington, yeo. 92/24: Jane, wife of 92/24: App. 164; William, late of Chester, yeo. 107/3

Thakerley, George, yeo. 27/7–9

Thew, Thomas 26/1

Thickley 77/15,16; East/Old 38: 63/1: 104/4; West 25/12

Thimbleby 72/8: 73/16: 74/15; Hill 90/13

Thinford 58/18

Thirkeld, Robert, late of Richmond, gen. 66/12

Thirwall, George, late of Prudhoe, yeo. 11/16

Thomas, prior of Durham 19/5; prior of Hexham 13/1

Thomlyngson, *Anthony 25: gen. 29/10

Thompson (Tomson), Anthony, bailiff 47/5; Christopher, yeo. 52/2: Margaret, wife of 52/2; Cuthbert, yeo. 65/10; Edward 66/16; Eleanor, widow App. 122; Elizabeth, of

Escomb, widow 91/5: 92/23; late of Townsteadhowse, spinster 93/21; Gabriel, gen. 92/24; George, yeo. 97/10: of Trimdon, yeo. 91/51; of Wolsingham, yeo. 99/3: Margaret wife of App. 96; Henry, of Haggerston, yeo. 49/2; of Monkwearmouth, yeo. 39/6: Christian, wife of 39/6; John 11/24: 12/2: yeo. 76/14; yeo. 92/1,21; yeo. App. 345; late of Ford [Northd], lab. 9/1,2; of Haggerston, yeo. 49/2: 55/3; of Sedgefield, lab. 56/6; late of Swinhope Burn 11/9; late of West Boldon 87/9; [Jenkyn], barker/yeo. 19/1; Lionel, yeo. 29/16: yeo. 92/23; Margery, spinster 95/11; Matthew, constable 60/4; Michael 91/13; collector 65/17: of Brandon walls, yeo. 72/14,15; Nicholas, late of Ryhope, yeo. 97/10; late of Ushaw, lab. 47/17; Percival, of Houghton, yeo. 95/7: late of Newsham, yeo. 33/7; Peter 47/13; Ralph, yeo. 26/1; yeo. 53/2: of Gateside, yeo. 93/26; Richard, yeo. 97/10: late of Hylton, yeo. 77/10; Robert, lab. 50/17: yeo. 56/7: of Bradbury, yeo. 28/3; late of East Boldon, yeo. 91/57; late of Gateshead, lab. 85/10,13; Thomas, informer 100/13,14: 101/9–13; junior, yeo. 49/2: lab. 51/2: yeo. 56/7; late of Haggerston, yeo. 55/3; late of Morpeth, yeo. 86/4; William, yeo. 92/21,24; yeo. 97/10: of Bishopwearmouth, yeo. 98/29; of Crawcrook 88/10,14,30: yeo. 89/26: 90A/1; 12/3: late of Escomb, yeo. 56/9; of Netherton, yeo. 71/4; yeo. 77/10; late of Newfeild, yeo. 91/7,61; late of Sunderland, blacksmith 77/13

Thoraby, Thomas, late of Durham, yeo. 65/1,22: 104/13: Elizabeth, wife of 65/22

Thornborough, Northd 36/4: 41/8: 60/15

Thornborough, John, bp of Bristol 68/19: 69/34

Thornele, Cuthbert, of Darlington, gen. App. 76

Thorngate in Barnard Castle 29/20

tanner 102/23; weaver 64/11; yeo.
64/11; Richard 88/10: 91/23: lab.
99/25; Robert, late of Staithes, yeo.
40/4; Thomas 88/10: late of Aldin
Grange, yeo. 87/30; bishop's bailiff
7/6; *William 7; 91/4,37: late of
Staindrop, yeo. 67/1
Wall, Brian, late of St Helen Auckland, yeo. 78/13; of Wheatbottom,
yeo. 100/4; Edward, of Horsley, yeo.
17/5; of Ryton, yeo. 73/3; Elizabeth, spinster App. 100; James, of
Escomb 47/41; Jane, of St Helen
Auckland, spinster App. 99; John
43/3: yeo., Jane wife of App. 82;
Katherine, spinster App. 237; Ralph,
yeo. 93/24; Roger, master of House
of Correction 18*; yeo. 29/16;
Thomas, junior, late of Peak Field,
yeo. 71/5
Waller, Richard, yeo. 92/24: 94/10
Wallers [Walles], William, yeo. 55/4
Walles (Wallys), Eleazor, of Durham
82/17; Henry, of Knaresdale, gen.
15/2; John 89/14; Robert, of South
Shields, yeo., constable 104/3: 105/5,
17; Thomas, of East Boldon, lab.
26/3; yeo. 28/1
Wallington, Northd 82/11
Walltown, Northd 11/22: 18/1
Walshe, Agnes, widow 34/1; John,
husbandman 26/2,3; Matthew 34/1;
Robert, lab. 26/2; William, lab. 25/1:
28/3 (and see Welsh)
*Walton, Agnes, of Whitehouse, widow
App. 305; *Arthur, of Lanchester,
yeo. 102,103; George 110/8; Henry,
yeo. 26/2; Hugh 47/15: 82/9; *James
36,52; *John 58; parkkeeper 78/8;
late of Durham, draper 82/25;
Nicholas 58/7; Peter, cordwainer
50/4
Walworth 1/6: 25/4: 69/19: 71/19:
App. 401–05; division of moor 242n.*
Wandisforth, Francis, esq. 24/4
Wandlasse, *Edward, gen. 91
*Ward(e), Cuthbert 92/6: yeo. 29/16:
late of Waskerley, yeo. 33/9; Edward,
sp. bailiff 89/22; James, yeo. 78/11;
*John, of Consett 8,9,23,83; of Chop-
well, gen. 28*: 38/15; *of Hurworth,
yeo. 97: 104/9; Peter, junior, of Chopwell, 28*: gen. 38/16,17; Richard

21*: 6/8; yeo. 32/2; *Robert, of Trimdon, gen. 98: 92/24: Barbara, wife
of 92/24: App. 191; of Darlington,
yeo. 32/2; *William 12,16,19
Wardell, Christine [Katherine], wife
of George 103/2,13,14,16; *George,
of West Morton, yeo. 110; infant
103/13,15; senior, of Mainsforth,
yeo. 103/2,13; Thomas, late of
Heworth, yeo. 96/4,5
Warden [Law] 7/1
Warden, William, of Bruntoft, yeo.
38/5
Wardley 30*: 81/1,16; lane, Heworth
50/18
Wark [on Tweed], Northd 24*: 26/1;
castle 25n.*
Warkworth, Northd 12/2
Warmouth, Thomas, late of Billing-
ham, lab. 46/11
Warrewyk*, Thomas 6
Warroint house, Little Eden App. 187
Warwicke, Robert 78/14
Wascer [Wascall], George, yeo. 91/13
Washington 31*: 26/2: 67/6: 105/8
Waskerley 33/9
Waster, Richard, yeo. 65/10; Robert
110/4: Margaret, wife of 110/4
Wastering, Thomas, of Barnard Castle,
yeo. 88/4
Waterhouses 10/11: 61/10,11: 92/24:
App. 157,158
Wath Cote, N. Riding, Yorks. 32/2
Wating, Elizabeth, widow App. 30;
John, of Neasham, yeo. App. 29;
Richard, lab. 92/24: yeo. 64/3;
William, of Neasham, yeo. App. 27:
Jane, wife of App. 28
Watkyns, Walter, of North Bailey,
yeo. 78/10
Watkynson, William, of Durham 11/7
*Watson, Adam 78/1; of Holehouse,
yeo. 17/5; of Ireshopeburn, yeo.
17/5; Agnes, widow 66/3–5: 68/5;
Ann, late of Brotherlee, spinster
64/9: widow 67/17; Christopher,
late of Whickham 84/13; Cuthbert
50/14; Edmund, late of Nunstain-
ton, husbandman 29/3; Edward, of
Nunstainton, yeo. 28/3,6: 29/2; late
of Staindrop, yeo. 59/10; Elizabeth,
widow 65/10; George, yeo. 95/11:
Anne, wife of 95/11; of Bishop

Westgate [Stanhope] 51/3: 71/16
Westminster 58/17: 82/9: 83/12: 86/5: 87/32: courts at 11*: 40/1
Westmorland, earl of 20*: 1,30: 30/5,6
Westoe 38/26: 39/11: 65/10: 76/2
Westwo(o)d, James, husbandman 7/4,5; John, lab. 6/7,8; bailiff 58/1; Peter 58/6
Westyeate, Northd 66/11
We(a)therell, Gerard, yeo. 39/6; Giles, late of Stockton, yeo. 110/30; Janet, of Bolam, spinster App. 389; John 92/24: spinster App. 80: wife of App. 81; late of Middleton Row, yeo. 75/11; Thomas, late of Middleton Row, yeo. 87/13; William, of Girsby, yeo. 95/11: Eleanor, wife of 95/11
Wetwang, E. Yorks. 56/1
Whally, Edmund 104/14; Gavin, late of Darlington, haberdasher 104/14
Whamsley lane 89/13
Whaplowe, John, late of Wolsingham, lab. 6/1
Wharey, John, yeo. 65/10
Wharham, Robert, of Farrington, yeo. 10/8
Wharton, *Christopher 36: 40/1: gen. 54; Gilbert, gen. 63/1; Philip 102/15: 103/20; Roger 59/7; William 62/1: late of Barnard Castle, yeo. 91/35
Wheatbottom 95/6: 100/4
Wheatley (*Wetlawe*) 10/2; Hill 13*,16*: 42: 97/14: 100/12; heiress of 20*
Wheatley (Wheitley), Agnes, spinster 92/24; Anthony 65/6: late of Bishop Auckland, yeo. 85/4; Christopher, of Wolsingham, yeo. 98/29; George, of Ravensworth, yeo. 75/27: 91/13; John 102/22: of *Urhill*, lab. 58/15; servant 19/6: of Wolsingham, yeo. 87/17; Margaret, spinster 92/24; Martin 74/7: yeo. 91/13; Mary 91/25; Ralph 98/24: late of Bishop Auckland, yeo. 99/8–10: 100/26; Richard, of Darlington, yeo. 71/2; Thomas, collector 91/17; William, late of Chester-le-Street, yeo. 75/19
Whelden, *William, senior 6: 11/14: yeo. 106/1
Whelpdale, John, of Plenmellor, lab. 8/4; *William, senior 11

Whelpden, Christopher, of Wolsingham, yeo. 92/8,9; Henry, of Kyo Lawes, yeo. 29/16; *Robert 14; Roland, of Shield Row, yeo. 29/16
Whelwright, Thomas, gunner 29/16
Whessoe 4/2: 6/1: 38/27: 41/17
Whickham 17*: 20/6: 22/4: 23/6: 29/16: 50/15: 52/4: 53/5: 56/4,5,11, 12: 57/1: 63/21: 64/2: 65/10: 67/2: 68/1,11: 73/3,9,10,19,20: 75/15: 77/11,17: 81/14,17: 83/6: 84/5,7,8, 13,15,24: 89/25: 91/39,48,61: 92/22: 93/7: 95/11: 99/7: 102/21: 105/6: 106/4: 107/5: 108/9,12; church of 84/13; parish of 91/7,14: 98/29; 102/24: bridges in 93/35
Whinhouse [Aycliffe] 98/19
Whitburn 30*: 9/12:26/2: 47/26,44,77: 50/18: 51/2: 52/6: 54/5: 65/10–16: 77/10: 78/4: 79/5,6: 107/23: App. 292; fines in 65/11,12
White Hurworth [Trimdon] 93/8,33
*White, Anthony 66/12: 105/3: late of Shildon, yeo. 55/6; Edward, yeo. 16/3; George, yeo. 23/4; Henry, yeo. 26/1; Isabel 91/25: spinster 92/24; John, lab. 55/6: Anne, wife of 55/6; of Blackwell 47/59: of Brancepeth, whitesmith 56/6; of Great Stainton, yeo. 65/10; Miles, late of Durham, lab. 82/26; Nicholas, late of Gateside, yeo. 57/3; Oswald, yeo. 85/14; Richard, of Kelloe, yeo. 56/10: Jane, wife of 56/10; of Newfield, yeo. 6/6; of Seaton, yeo. 103/5: 105/14; late of Streatlam, yeo. 57/6; of Thornley, yeo. App. 204; *Robert, of Redheugh, gen. 39,43,80; sp. bailiff 96/11; late of Auckland Deanery, lab. 99/20; late of Eldon, yeo. 38/1–4,7–11; yeo. 63/1: of Monkwearmouth, yeo. 65/10: 76/7; of Newfield, yeo. 16/3; *Roland 13; Thomas, yeo. 85/14; William 8/3: junior, yeo. 41/3: senior, yeo. 41/3
Whitehall 6: 20/7: 98,107: App. 251
Whitehead (Whitheid), Quintin, yeo. 60/15; *Thomas 30
Whitehill Hall 91/29: 92/24: App. 346–50
Whitehouse [Durham] 24/3: 25/2: 26/4: 100/6: App. 305

DATE DUE
